Mike Holt's Illustrated Guide

UNDERSTANDING
FUNDAMENTAL
NEC® REQUIREMENTS

Extracted from Understanding the National Electrical Code® Volume 1

Mike Holt Enterprises
MikeHolt.com • 888.632.2633

BASED ON THE
2023 NEC®

NOTICE TO THE READER

The text and commentary in this book is the author's interpretation of the 2023 Edition of NFPA 70®, *National Electrical Code®*. It shall not be considered an endorsement of or the official position of the NFPA® or any of its committees, nor relied upon as a formal interpretation of the meaning or intent of any specific provision or provisions of the 2023 edition of NFPA 70, *National Electrical Code*.

The publisher does not warrant or guarantee any of the products described herein or perform any independent analysis in connection with any of the product information contained herein. The publisher does not assume, and expressly disclaims, any obligation to obtain and include information other than that provided to it by the manufacturer.

The reader is expressly warned to consider and adopt all safety precautions and applicable federal, state, and local laws and regulations. By following the instructions contained herein, the reader willingly assumes all risks in connection with such instructions.

Mike Holt Enterprises disclaims liability for any personal injury, property or other damages of any nature whatsoever, whether special, indirect, consequential or compensatory, directly or indirectly resulting from the use of this material. The reader is responsible for relying on his or her personal independent judgment in determining safety and appropriate actions in all circumstances.

The publisher makes no representation or warranties of any kind, including but not limited to, the warranties of fitness for particular purpose or merchantability, nor are any such representations implied with respect to the material set forth herein, and the publisher takes no responsibility with respect to such material. The publisher shall not be liable for any special, consequential, or exemplary damages resulting, in whole or part, from the reader's use of, or reliance upon, this material.

Mike Holt's Illustrated Guide to Understanding Fundamental NEC® Requirements, based on the 2023 NEC®

Second Printing: January 2024
Author: Mike Holt
Technical Illustrator: Mike Culbreath
Cover Design: Bryan Burch
Layout Design and Typesetting: Cathleen Kwas
COPYRIGHT © 2023 Charles Michael Holt
ISBN 978-1-950431-70-0

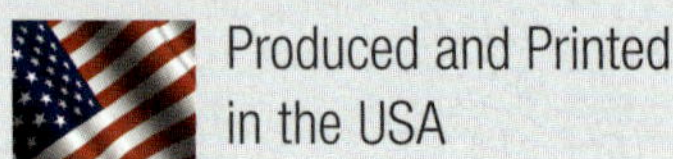

Produced and Printed in the USA

This logo is a registered trademark of Mike Holt Enterprises, Inc.

NEC®, NFPA 70®, NFPA 70E® and *National Electrical Code®* are registered trademarks of the National Fire Protection Association.

Are you an Instructor?

You can request a review copy of this or other Mike Holt Publications:

888.632.2633 • Training@MikeHolt.com

Download a sample PDF of all our publications by visiting MikeHolt.com/Instructors

I dedicate this book to the
Lord Jesus Christ, *my mentor and teacher.*
Proverbs 16:3

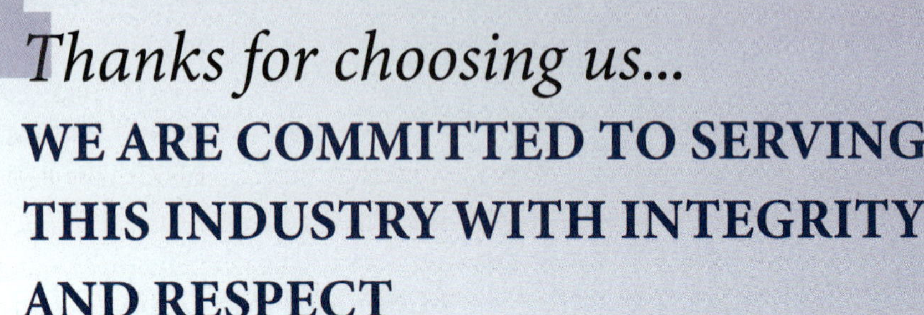

> *Thanks for choosing us...*
> ## WE ARE COMMITTED TO SERVING THIS INDUSTRY WITH INTEGRITY AND RESPECT

Since 1975, we have worked hard to develop products that get results, and to help individuals in their pursuit of success in this exciting industry.

From the very beginning we have been committed to the idea that customers come first. Everyone on my team will do everything they possibly can to help you succeed. I want you to know that we value you and are honored that you have chosen us to be your partner in training.

You are the future of this industry and we know that it is you who will make the difference in the years to come. My goal is to share with you everything that I know and to encourage you to pursue your education on a continuous basis. I hope that not only will you learn theory, *Code*, calculations, or how to pass an exam, but that in the process, you will become the expert in the field and the person others know to trust.

To put it simply, we genuinely care about your success and will do everything that we can to help you take your skills to the next level!

We are happy to partner with you on your educational journey.

God bless and much success,

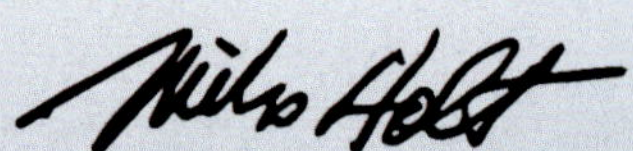

TABLE OF CONTENTS

CHAPTER 3—WIRING METHODS AND MATERIALS

ABOUT THIS TEXTBOOK

Welcome to *Mike Holt's Illustrated Guide to Fundamental NEC®
Requirements, based on the 2023 NEC*. This textbook is intended
to provide you with an introduction to the Code rules you'll need in
order to be an effective electrician. The majority of installations share
a common set of Code rules and this textbook will introduce you to
many of those. This content was carefully selected to help you be
more effective on the job and to get you ready to take your learning
to the next level.

If you are using this book as part of an apprenticeship program, it will
provide you with the knowledge necessary to quickly climb the ladder
at work, because you will develop an understanding of the theories
and the mechanics behind the *National Electrical Code®* rules. As a
newer electrician, we understand you might be on the job working
from the start. Most likely, that work involves the mechanical aspects
of electrical installation, so you'll need some practical knowledge of
the *Code*. To help you, this material will introduce things like, how
many wires can fit in a box, the ampacity of a certain size conductor,
or how big a raceway needs to be for the conductors you're going
to install. These topics will be introduced in a basic format to make
them easy to learn. We'll come back in later books to build on what
you learn in this material to prepare you for your licensing exam.

We hope you enjoy studying one of the most exciting trades in the
industry. Be safe!

The Scope of This Textbook

This textbook covers those installation requirements that we consider
to be important and is based on the following conditions:

1. Power Systems and Voltage. All power-supply systems are
assumed to be one of the following nominal voltages or "voltage
class", unless identified otherwise:

- ▸ 2-wire, single-phase, 120V
- ▸ 3-wire, single-phase, 120/240V
- ▸ 4-wire, three-phase, 120/240V Delta High-Leg
- ▸ 4-wire, three-phase, 208YY120V or 480Y/277V Wye

2. Electrical Calculations. Unless the question or example specifies three-phase, they're based on a single-phase power supply. In
addition, all amperage calculations are rounded to the nearest whole
number in accordance with Section 220.5(B).

3. Conductor Material/Insulation. The conductor material and insulation are copper THWN-2, unless otherwise indicated.

4. Conductor Sizing.

Circuits Rated 100A or Less. Conductors are sized to the 60°C column
of Table 310.16 [110.14(C)(1)(a)(2)]. Where equipment is listed and
identified for use with conductors having at least a 75°C temperature rating, the conductors can be sized to the 75°C column of Table
310.16 [110.14(C)(1)(a)(3)].

Circuits Rated Over 100A. Conductors are sized to the 75°C column
of Table 310.16 [110.14(C)(1)(b)(2)].

5. Overcurrent Protective Device. The term "overcurrent protective device" refers to a molded-case circuit breaker, unless specified
otherwise. Where a fuse is specified, it's a single-element type fuse,
also known as a "onetime fuse," unless the text specifies otherwise.

How to Use This Textbook

This textbook is to be used along with the *NEC* and not as a replacement for it. Be sure to have a copy of the 2023 *National Electrical Code*
handy. You will notice that we have paraphrased a great deal of the
wording, and some of the article and section titles appear different
than those in the actual *Code* book. We believe doing so makes it
easier to understand the content of the rule, so keep that in mind
when comparing this textbook to the *NEC*.

Always compare what is being explained in this textbook to what the
Code book says. This textbook follows the *Code* format, but it does
not cover every requirement. For example, it does not include every
article, section, subsection, exception, or Informational Note. So, do

not be concerned if you see that the textbook contains Exception 1 and Exception 3, but not Exception 2.

Cross-References. Many *NEC* rules refer to requirements located in other sections of the *Code*. This textbook does the same with the intention of helping you develop a better understanding of how the *NEC* rules relate to one another. These cross-references are indicated by *Code* section numbers in brackets, an example of which is "[90.4]."

Informational Notes. Informational Notes contained in the *NEC* will be identified in this textbook as "Note."

Exceptions. Exceptions contained in this textbook will be identified as "Ex" and not spelled out.

As you read through this textbook, allow yourself enough time to review the text along with the outstanding graphics and examples to give yourself the opportunity for a deeper understanding of the *Code*. The articles and rules in this textbook are extracted from *Mike Holt's Understanding the National Electrical Code Volume 1, based on the 2023 NEC*, and are those rules considered relevant and necessary for Level 1 students.

If you want additional information that is not covered in this textbook, consider getting a copy of *Mike Holt's Understanding the National Electrical Code, Volume 1, based on the 2023 NEC*. Visit MikeHolt.com/Code.

Technical Questions

As you progress through this textbook, you might find that you don't understand every explanation, example, calculation, or comment. Don't become frustrated, and don't get down on yourself. Remember, this is the *National Electrical Code*, and sometimes the best attempt to explain a concept isn't enough to make it perfectly clear. Get with others who are knowledgeable about the *NEC* to discuss any topics you find difficult to understand. If you're still confused, visit MikeHolt.com/Forum, and post your question on our free Code Forum. The forum is a moderated community of electrical professionals.

Textbook Errors and Corrections

We're committed to providing you the finest product with the fewest errors and take great care to ensure our textbooks are correct. But we're realistic and know that errors might be found after printing. If you believe that there's an error of any kind (typographical, grammatical, technical, etc.) in this textbook or in the Answer Key, please visit MikeHolt.com/ Corrections and complete the online Textbook Correction Form.

Answer Keys

Digital answer keys are provided for all your purchases of Mike Holt textbooks, and can be found in your online account at Mike Holt Enterprises. Go to MikeHolt.com/MyAccount and log in to your account, or create one if you haven't already. If you are a student using this book in your classes, contact your instructor for access to the answer key.

Key Features

The layout and design of this textbook incorporate special features and symbols designed to help you navigate easily through the material, and to enhance your understanding.

According to Article 100

Throughout the textbook, Mike references definitions that are easily identified by colored text "**According to Article 100,**" at the start of the paragraph.

According to Article 100, "Listed" equipment or materials included in a list published by an organization acceptable to the authority having jurisdiction. The listing organization must periodically inspect the production of listed equipment or material to ensure it meets appropriate designated standards and suitable for a specified purpose.

Full-Color, Detailed Educational Graphics

Industry-leading graphics help you visualize the sometimes complex language of the *Code*, and illustrate the rule in real-world application(s). This is a great aid to reinforce learning.

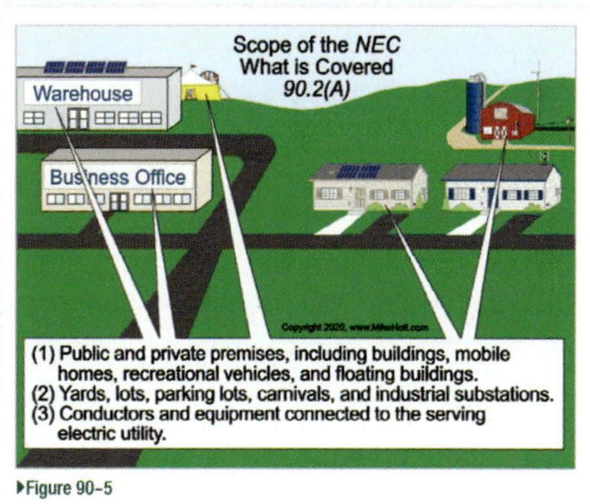

▶Figure 90–5

Author's Comments

These comments provide additional information to help you understand the context.

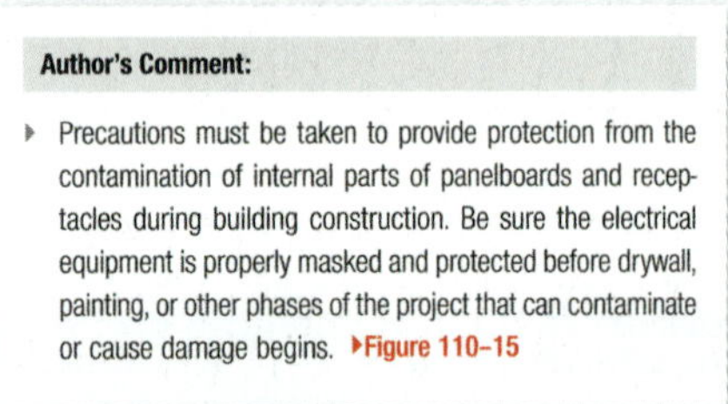

Code Subsections Highlighted

Each first level subsection of each *Code* rule is highlighted in yellow to help you navigate through the text.

Formulas

$$P = I \times E$$

Formulas are easily identifiable in green text on a gray bar.

Modular Color Coded Page Layout

Chapters are color coded and modular to make it easy to navigate through each section of the textbook. As you can see by the Table of Contents, each Chapter has a unique color.

Examples

These practical application questions and answers are contained in framed yellow boxes.

If you see an ellipsis (• • •) at the bottom of the example, it is continued on the following page.

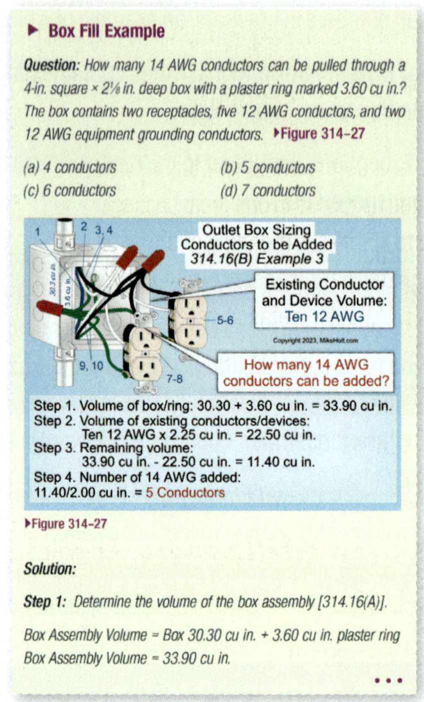

Caution, Danger, and Warning Icons

These icons highlight areas of concern.

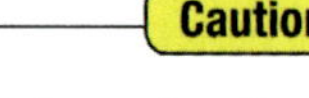

CAUTION: An explanation of possible damage to property or equipment.

WARNING: An explanation of possible severe property damage or personal injury.

DANGER: An explanation of possible severe injury or death.

ADDITIONAL PRODUCTS TO HELP YOU LEARN

Understanding the *National Electrical Code*, based on the 2023 *NEC*, Volume 1 and 2 Textbooks

This product is a combination of Mike's best-selling illustrated textbooks in one great package. Mike's ability to clarify the meaning of the *Code* with his straightforward, concise writing style, along with his full-color detailed instructional graphics, is the reason that these books continue to grow in popularity.

PACKAGE INCLUDES:

Understanding the *National Electrical Code*—Volume 1 Textbook

Understanding the *National Electrical Code*—Volume 2 Textbook

Digital answer keys

Product Code: [23UND12]

To order, visit MikeHolt.com/Code

Understanding Electrical Theory, for *NEC* Applications, Video Program

Whether you're a first-year apprentice still struggling to understand the difference between a volt or ampere, or a veteran journeyman trying to sharpen your troubleshooting skills, this product has something for you. Once you know the principles behind how electricity works, you will be ready to correctly apply the rules in the *National Electrical Code* to the work you do every day.

This video program will take you on a journey that begins with the physics behind how electricity works all the way through topics and concepts that are relevant to everyone working in the electrical industry.

PROGRAM INCLUDES:

Understanding Electrical Theory for *NEC* Applications Textbook
  ▸ *Electrical Theory videos*

Digital answer keys

Plus! A digital version of the textbook

Product Code: [THLIBMM]

To order, visit MikeHolt.com/Theory

Understanding the *NEC* Complete Video Library

Do you want a comprehensive understanding of the *Code*? Then you need Mike's best-selling Understanding the *NEC* Complete Video Library. This program has helped thousands of electricians learn the *Code* because of its easy-to-use format. Mike guides students through the most utilized rules and breaks them down in a complete and thorough way. The full-color instructional graphics in the textbooks help students visualize and understand the concepts being taught; the videos provide additional reinforcement with Mike and the panel discussing each article, its meaning and its application in the real world. When you need to know the *Code*, this program is the best tool you can use to start building your knowledge—there's no other product quite like it.

PROGRAM INCLUDES:

Understanding the *National Electrical Code*, Volume 1 Textbook
- *Understanding the National Electrical Code Volume 1 videos*

Understanding the *National Electrical Code*, Volume 2 Textbook
- *Understanding the National Electrical Code Volume 2 videos*

Bonding and Grounding Textbook
- *Bonding and Grounding videos*

Fundamental *NEC* Calculations Textbook
- *Fundamental NEC Calculations videos*

Understanding the *National Electrical Code* Workbook (Articles 90-480)

Digital answer keys

Plus! A digital version of each textbook

Product Code: [23UNDLIBMM]

2023 *Code* Books and Tabs

The easiest way to use your copy of the *NEC* correctly is to tab it for quick reference. Mike's best-selling tabs make organizing your *Code* book easy. Please note that if you're using it for an exam, you'll need to confirm with your testing authority that a tabbed *Code* book is allowed into the exam room.

PRODUCT INCLUDES:

NFPA Softbound *Code* Book

Mike Holt's *NEC* Tabs

Product Code: [23NECB]

To order, visit MikeHolt.com/Code

HOW TO USE THE *NATIONAL ELECTRICAL CODE*

The original *NEC* document was developed in 1897 as a result of the united efforts of various insurance, electrical, architectural, and other cooperative interests. The National Fire Protection Association (NFPA) has sponsored the *National Electrical Code* since 1911.

The purpose of the *Code* is the practical safeguarding of persons and property from hazards arising from the use of electricity. It isn't intended as a design specification or an instruction manual for untrained persons. It is, in fact, a standard that contains the minimum requirements for an electrical installation that's essentially free from hazard. Learning to understand and use the *Code* is critical to you working safely; whether you're training to become an electrician, or are already an electrician, electrical contractor, inspector, engineer, designer, or instructor.

The *NEC* was written for qualified persons; those who understand electrical terms, theory, safety procedures, and electrical trade practices. Learning to use the *Code* is a lengthy process and can be frustrating if you don't approach it the right way. First, you'll need to understand electrical theory and if you don't have theory as a background when you get into the *NEC*, you're going to struggle. Take one step back if necessary and learn electrical theory. You must also understand the concepts and terms in the *Code* and know grammar and punctuation in order to understand the complex structure of the rules and their intended purpose(s). The *NEC* is written in a formal outline which many of us haven't seen or used since high school or college so it's important for you to pay particular attention to this format. Our goal for the next few pages is to give you some guidelines and suggestions on using your *Code* book to help you understand that standard, and assist you in what you're trying to accomplish and, ultimately, your personal success as an electrical professional!

Language Considerations for the *NEC*

Terms and Concepts

The *NEC* contains many technical terms, and it's crucial for *Code* users to understand their meanings and applications. If you don't understand a term used in a rule, it will be impossible to properly apply the *NEC* requirement. Article 100 defines those that are used generally in two or more articles throughout the *Code*; for example, the term "Dwelling Unit" is found in many articles. If you don't know the *NEC* definition for a "dwelling unit" you can't properly identify its *Code* requirements. Another example worth mentioning is the term "Outlet." For many people it has always meant a receptacle—not so in the *NEC*!

Article 100 contains the definitions of terms used throughout the *Code*. Where a definition is unique to a specific article, the article number is indicated at the end of the definition in parenthesis (xxx). For example, the definition of "Pool" is specific to Article 680 and ends with (680) because it applies ONLY to that article. Definitions of standard terms, such as volt, voltage drop, ampere, impedance, and resistance are not contained in Article 100. If the *NEC* does not define a term, then a dictionary or building code acceptable to the authority having jurisdiction should be consulted.

Small Words, Grammar, and Punctuation

Technical words aren't the only ones that require close attention. Even simple words can make a big difference to the application of a rule. Is there a comma? Does it use "or," "and," "other than," "greater than," or "smaller than"? The word "or" can imply alternate choices for wiring methods. A word like "or" gives us choices while the word "and" can mean an additional requirement must be met.

An example of the important role small words play in the *NEC* is found in 110.26(C)(2), where it says equipment containing overcurrent, switching, "or" control devices that are 1,200A or more "and" over 6 ft wide require a means of egress at each end of the working space. In this section, the word "or" clarifies that equipment containing any of the three types of devices listed must follow this rule. The word "and" clarifies that 110.26(C)(2) only applies if the equipment is both 1,200A or more and over 6 ft wide.

Grammar and punctuation play an important role in establishing the meaning of a rule. The location of a comma can dramatically change the requirement of a rule such as in 250.28(A), where it says a main bonding jumper shall be a wire, bus, screw, or similar suitable conductor. If the comma between "bus" and "screw" was removed, only a "bus screw" could be used. That comma makes a big change in the requirements of the rule.

Slang Terms or Technical Jargon

Trade-related professionals in different areas of the country often use local "slang" terms that aren't shared by all. This can make it difficult to communicate if it isn't clear what the meaning of those slang terms are. Use the proper terms by finding out what their definitions and applications are before you use them. For example, the term "pigtail" is often used to describe the short piece of conductor used to connect a device to a splice, but a "pigtail" is also used for a rubberized light socket with pre-terminated conductors. Although the term is the same, the meaning is very different and could cause confusion. The words "splice" and "tap" are examples of terms often interchanged in the field but are two entirely different things! The uniformity and consistency of the terminology used in the *Code*, makes it so everyone says and means the same thing regardless of geographical location.

NEC Style and Layout

It's important to understand the structure and writing style of the *Code* if you want to use it effectively. The *National Electrical Code* is organized using twelve major components.

1. Table of Contents
2. Chapters—Chapters 1 through 9 (major categories)
3. Articles—Chapter subdivisions that cover specific subjects
4. Parts—Divisions used to organize article subject matter
5. Sections—Divisions used to further organize article subject matter
6. Tables and Figures—Represent the mandatory requirements of a rule
7. Exceptions—Alternatives to the main *Code* rule
8. Informational Notes—Explanatory material for a specific rule (not a requirement)
9. Tables—Applicable as referenced in the *NEC*
10. Annexes—Additional explanatory information such as tables and references (not a requirement)
11. Index
12. Changes to the *Code* from the previous edition

1. Table of Contents. The Table of Contents displays the layout of the chapters, articles, and parts as well as the page numbers. It's an excellent resource and should be referred to periodically to observe the interrelationship of the various *NEC* components. When attempting to locate the rules for a specific situation, knowledgeable *Code* users often go first to the Table of Contents to quickly find the specific *NEC* rule that applies.

2. Chapters. There are nine chapters, each of which is divided into articles. The articles fall into one of four groupings: General Requirements (Chapters 1 through 4), Specific Requirements (Chapters 5 through 7), Communications Systems (Chapter 8), and Tables (Chapter 9).

> Chapter 1—General
> Chapter 2—Wiring and Protection
> Chapter 3—Wiring Methods and Materials
> Chapter 4—Equipment for General Use
> Chapter 5—Special Occupancies
> Chapter 6—Special Equipment
> Chapter 7—Special Conditions
> Chapter 8—Communications Systems (Telephone, Data, Satellite, Cable TV, and Broadband)
> Chapter 9—Tables–Conductor and Raceway Specifications

3. Articles. The *NEC* contains approximately 160 articles, each of which covers a specific subject. It begins with Article 90, the introduction to the *Code* which contains the purpose of the *NEC*, what is covered and isn't covered, along with how the *Code* is arranged. It also gives information on enforcement, how mandatory and permissive rules are written, and how explanatory material is included. Article 90 also includes information on formal interpretations, examination of equipment for safety, wiring planning, and information about formatting units of measurement. Here are some other examples of articles you'll find in the *NEC*:

> Article 110—General Requirements for Electrical Installations
> Article 250—Grounding and Bonding
> Article 300—General Requirements for Wiring Methods and Materials
> Article 430—Motors, Motor Circuits, and Motor Controllers
> Article 500—Hazardous (Classified) Locations
> Article 680—Swimming Pools, Fountains, and Similar Installations
> Article 725—Class 2 and Class 3 Power-Limited Circuits
> Article 800—General Requirements for Communications Systems

4. Parts. Larger articles are subdivided into parts. Because the parts of a *Code* article aren't included in the section numbers, we tend to forget to what "part" an *NEC* rule is relating. For example, Table 110.34(A) contains working space clearances for electrical equipment. If we aren't careful, we might think this table applies to all electrical installations, but Table 110.34(A) is in Part III, which only contains requirements for "Over 1,000 Volts, Nominal" installations. The rules for working clearances for electrical equipment for systems 1,000V, nominal, or less are contained in Table 110.26(A)(1), which is in Part II—1,000 Volts, Nominal, or Less.

5. Sections. Each *NEC* rule is called a "*Code* Section." A *Code* section may be broken down into subdivisions; first level subdivision will be in parentheses like (A), (B),..., the next will be second level subdivisions in parentheses like (1), (2),..., and third level subdivisions in lowercase letters such as (a), (b), and so on.

For example, the rule requiring all receptacles in a dwelling unit bathroom to be GFCI protected is contained in Section 210.8(A)(1) which is in Chapter 2, Article 210, Section 8, first level subdivision (A), and second level subdivision (1).

Note: According to the *NEC Style Manual*, first and second level subdivisions are required to have titles. A title for a third level subdivision is permitted but not required.

Many in the industry incorrectly use the term "Article" when referring to a *Code* section. For example, they say "Article 210.8," when they should say "Section 210.8." Section numbers in this textbook are shown without the word "Section," unless they're at the beginning of a sentence. For example, Section 210.8(A) is shown as simply 210.8(A).

6. Tables and Figures. Many *NEC* requirements are contained within tables, which are lists of *Code* rules placed in a systematic arrangement. The titles of the tables are extremely important; you must read them carefully in order to understand the contents, applications, and limitations of each one. Notes are often provided in or below a table; be sure to read them as well since they're also part of the requirement. For example, Note 1 for Table 300.5(A) explains how to measure the cover when burying cables and raceways and Note 5 explains what to do if solid rock is encountered.

7. Exceptions. Exceptions are *NEC* requirements or permissions that provide an alternative method to a specific rule. There are two types of exceptions—mandatory and permissive. When a rule has several exceptions, those exceptions with mandatory requirements are listed before the permissive exceptions.

Mandatory Exceptions. A mandatory exception uses the words "shall" or "shall not." The word "shall" in an exception means that if you're using the exception, you're required to do it in a specific way. The phrase "shall not" means it isn't permitted.

Permissive Exceptions. A permissive exception uses words such as "shall be permitted," which means it's acceptable (but not mandatory) to do it in this way.

8. Informational Notes. An Informational Note contains explanatory material intended to clarify a rule or give assistance, but it isn't a *Code* requirement.

9. Tables. Chapter 9 consists of tables applicable as referenced in the *NEC*. They're used to calculate raceway sizing, conductor fill, the radius of raceway bends, and conductor voltage drop.

10. Informative Annexes. Annexes aren't a part of the *Code* requirements and are included for informational purposes only.

Annex A. Product Safety Standards
Annex B. Application Information for Ampacity Calculation
Annex C. Conduit, Tubing, and Cable Tray Fill Tables for Conductors and Fixture Wires of the Same Size
Annex D. Examples
Annex E. Types of Construction
Annex F. Availability and Reliability for Critical Operations Power Systems (COPS), and Development and Implementation of Functional Performance Tests (FPTs) for Critical Operations Power Systems
Annex G. Supervisory Control and Data Acquisition (SCADA)
Annex H. Administration and Enforcement
Annex I. Recommended Tightening Torque Tables from UL Standard 486A-486B
Annex J. ADA Standards for Accessible Design
Annex K. Use of Medical Electrical Equipment in Dwellings and Residential Board-and-Care Occupancies

11. Index. The Index at the back of the *NEC* is helpful in locating a specific rule using pertinent keywords to assist in your search.

12. Changes to the *Code*. Changes in the *NEC* are indicated as follows:

▸ Rules that were changed since the previous edition are identified by shading the revised text.

▸ New rules aren't shaded like a change, instead they have a shaded "N" in the margin to the left of the section number.

▸ Relocated rules are treated like new rules with a shaded "N" in the left margin by the section number.

▶ Deleted rules are indicated by a bullet symbol " • " located in the left margin where the rule was in the previous edition. Unlike older editions the bullet symbol is only used where one or more complete paragraphs have been deleted.

▶ A "Δ" represents partial text deletions and or figure/table revisions somewhere in the text. There's no specific indication of which word, group of words, or a sentence was deleted.

How to Locate a Specific Requirement

How to go about finding what you're looking for in the *Code* book depends, to some degree, on your experience with the *NEC*. Experts typically know the requirements so well that they just go to the correct rule. Very experienced people might only need the Table of Contents to locate the requirement for which they're looking. On the other hand, average users should use all the tools at their disposal, including the Table of Contents, the Index, and the search feature on electronic versions of the *Code* book.

Let's work through a simple example: What *NEC* rule specifies the maximum number of disconnects permitted for a service?

Using the Table of Contents. If you're an experienced *Code* user, you might use the Table of Contents. You'll know Article 230 applies to "Services," and because this article is so large, it's divided up into multiple parts (eight parts to be exact). With this knowledge, you can quickly go to the Table of Contents and see it lists the Service Equipment Disconnecting Means requirements in Part VI.

Author's Comment:

▶ The number "70" precedes all page numbers in this standard because the *NEC* is NFPA Standard Number 70.

Using the Index. If you use the Index (which lists subjects in alphabetical order) to look up the term "service disconnect," you'll see there's no listing. If you try "disconnecting means," then "services," you'll find that the Index indicates the rule is in Article 230, Part VI. Because the *NEC* doesn't give a page number in the Index, you'll need to use the Table of Contents to find it, or flip through the *Code* book to Article 230, then continue to flip through pages until you find Part VI.

Many people complain that the *NEC* only confuses them by taking them in circles. Once you gain experience in using the *Code* and deepen your understanding of words, terms, principles, and practices, you'll find it much easier to understand and use than you originally thought.

With enough exposure in the use of the *NEC*, you'll discover that some words and terms are often specific to certain articles. The word "solar" for example will immediately send experienced *Code* book users to Article 690—Solar Photovoltaic (PV) Systems. The word "marina" suggests what you seek might be in Article 555. There are times when a main article will send you to a specific requirement in another one in which compliance is required in which case it will say (for example), "in accordance with 230.xx." Don't think of these situations as a "circle," but rather a map directing you to exactly where you need to be.

Customizing Your *Code* Book

One way to increase your comfort level with your *Code* book is to customize it to meet your needs. You can do this by highlighting and underlining important *NEC* requirements. Preprinted adhesive tabs are also an excellent aid to quickly find important articles and sections that are regularly referenced. However, understand that if you're using your *Code* book to prepare to take an exam, some exam centers don't allow markings of any type. For more information about tabs for your *Code* book, visit MikeHolt.com/Tabs.

Highlighting. As you read through or find answers to your questions, be sure you highlight those requirements in the *NEC* that are the most important or relevant to you. Use one color, like yellow, for general interest and a different one for important requirements you want to find quickly. Be sure to highlight terms in the Index and the Table of Contents as you use them.

Underlining. Underline or circle key words and phrases in the *Code* with a red or blue pen (not a lead pencil) using a short ruler or other straightedge to keep lines straight and neat. This is a very handy way to make important requirements stand out. A short ruler or other straightedge also comes in handy for locating the correct information in a table.

Interpretations

Industry professionals often enjoy the challenge of discussing, and at times debating, the *Code* requirements. These types of discussions are important to the process of better understanding the *NEC* requirements and applications. However, if you decide you're going to participate in one of these discussions, don't spout out what you think without having the actual *Code* book in your hand. The professional way of discussing a requirement is by referring to a specific section rather than talking in vague generalities. This will help everyone involved clearly understand the point and become better educated. In fact, you may become so well educated about the *NEC* that you might even decide to participate in the change process and help to make it even better!

Become Involved in the *NEC* Process

The actual process of changing the *Code* takes about two years and involves hundreds of individuals trying to make the *NEC* as current and accurate as possible. As you advance in your studies and understanding of the *Code*, you might begin to find it very interesting, enjoy it more, and realize that you can also be a part of the process. Rather than sitting back and allowing others to take the lead, you can participate by making proposals and being a part of its development. For the 2023 cycle, there were over 4,000 Public Inputs and 1,956 Public Comments. This resulted in several new articles and a wide array of revised rules to keep the *NEC* up to date with new technologies and pave the way to a safer and more efficient electrical future.

Here's how the process works:

STEP 1—Public Input Stage

Public Input. The revision cycle begins with the acceptance of Public Input (PI) which is the public notice asking for anyone interested to submit input on an existing standard or a committee-approved new draft standard. Following the closing date, the committee conducts a First Draft Meeting to respond to all Public Inputs.

First Draft Meeting. At the First Draft (FD) Meeting, the Technical Committee considers and provides a response to all Public Input. The Technical Committee may use the input to develop First Revisions to the standard. The First Draft documents consist of the initial meeting consensus of the committee by simple majority. However, the final position of the Technical Committee must be established by a ballot which follows.

Committee Ballot on First Draft. The First Draft developed at the First Draft Meeting is balloted. In order to appear in the First Draft, a revision must be approved by at least two-thirds of the Technical Committee.

First Draft Report Posted. First revisions which pass ballot are ultimately compiled and published as the First Draft Report on the document's NFPA web page. This report serves as documentation for the Input Stage and is published for review and comment. The public may review the First Draft Report to determine whether to submit Public Comments on the First Draft.

STEP 2—Public Comment Stage

Public Comment. Once the First Draft Report becomes available, there's a Public Comment period during which anyone can submit a Public Comment on the First Draft. After the Public Comment closing date, the Technical Committee conducts/holds their Second Draft Meeting.

Second Draft Meeting. After the Public Comment closing date, if Public Comments are received or the committee has additional proposed revisions, a Second Draft Meeting is held. At the Second Draft Meeting, the Technical Committee reviews the First Draft and may make additional revisions to the draft Standard. All Public Comments are considered, and the Technical Committee provides an action and response to each Public Comment. These actions result in the Second Draft.

Committee Ballot on Second Draft. The Second Revisions developed at the Second Draft Meeting are balloted. To appear in the Second Draft, a revision must be approved by at least two-thirds of the Technical Committee.

Second Draft Report Posted. Second Revisions which pass ballot are ultimately compiled and published as the Second Draft Report on the document's NFPA website. This report serves as documentation of the Comment Stage and is published for public review.

Once published, the public can review the Second Draft Report to decide whether to submit a Notice of Intent to Make a Motion (NITMAM) for further consideration.

STEP 3—NFPA Technical Meeting (Tech Session)

Following completion of the Public Input and Public Comment stages, there's further opportunity for debate and discussion of issues through the NFPA Technical Meeting that takes place at the NFPA Conference & Expo®. These motions are attempts to change the resulting final Standard from the committee's recommendations published as the Second Draft.

STEP 4—Council Appeals and Issuance of Standard

Issuance of Standards. When the Standards Council convenes to issue an NFPA standard, it also hears any related appeals. Appeals are an important part of assuring that all NFPA rules have been followed and that due process and fairness have continued throughout the standards development process. The Standards Council considers appeals based on the written record and by conducting live hearings during which all interested parties can participate. Appeals are decided on the entire record of the process, as well as all submissions and statements presented.

After deciding all appeals related to a standard, the Standards Council, if appropriate, proceeds to issue the Standard as an official NFPA Standard. The decision of the Standards Council is final subject only to limited review by the NFPA Board of Directors. The new NFPA standard becomes effective twenty days following the Standards Council's action of issuance.

Temporary Interim Amendment—(TIA)

Sometimes, a change to the *NEC* is of an emergency nature. Perhaps an editing mistake was made that can affect an electrical installation to the extent it may create a hazard. Maybe an occurrence in the field created a condition that needs to be addressed immediately and can't wait for the normal *Code* cycle and next edition of the standard. When these circumstances warrant it, a TIA or "Temporary Interim Amendment" can be submitted for consideration.

The NFPA defines a TIA as, "tentative because it has not been processed through the entire standards-making procedures. It is interim because it is effective only between editions of the standard. A TIA automatically becomes a Public Input of the proponent for the next edition of the standard; as such, it then is subject to all of the procedures of the standards-making process."

Author's Comment:

▶ Proposals, comments, and TIAs can be submitted for consideration online at the NFPA website, www.nfpa.org. From the homepage, look for "Codes & Standards," then find "Standards Development," and click on "How the Process Works." If you'd like to see something changed in the *Code*, you're encouraged to participate in the process.

INTRODUCTION TO THE *NATIONAL ELECTRICAL CODE*

Introduction to Article 90—Introduction to the *National Electrical Code*

Article 90 describes the purpose of the *NEC*, when it applies, when it does not, who enforces the *Code*, and the arrangement of the different chapters. Although the information is valuable, this article contains no actual requirements. It only serves to provide the reader with the scope of the *National Electrical Code*.

This article stands alone outside of the chapter structure of the rest of the *Code* and has no parts because it contains no requirements. Take the time to become familiar with all nine sections of Article 90 before you begin your journey through the *NEC*. Doing so will help you better understand when and how to apply the *Code*.

90.1 Scope

Article 90 covers the use, application, arrangement, and enforcement of this *Code*. It also covers how mandatory, permissive, and nonmandatory text is expressed and provides guidance on the examination of equipment, planning wiring, and specifies the use and expression of measurements.

90.2 Use and Application of the *NEC*

(A) Purpose of the *NEC*.

Protect People and Property. The purpose of the *National Electrical Code* is to ensure electrical systems are installed in a manner that protects people and property by minimizing the risks associated with the use of electricity. ▶Figure 90–1

NEC Not a Specification or Instruction Manual. The *NEC* is not a design specification standard, nor is it an instruction manual for the untrained. ▶Figure 90–2

▶Figure 90–1

Author's Comment:

▶ The *Code* is intended to be used by those who are skilled and knowledgeable in electrical theory, electrical systems, building and electrical construction, and the installation and operation of electrical equipment.

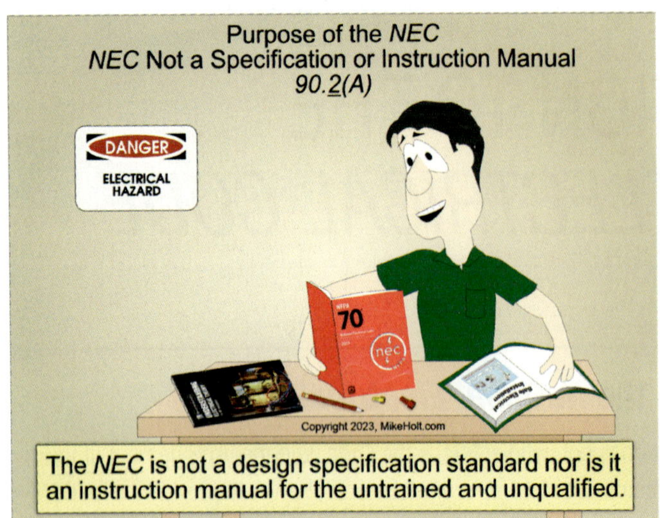

▶Figure 90–2

(B) Essentially Safe Installation.

Considered Safe. The *NEC* contains the requirements considered necessary for safety.

Essentially Free from Hazards. Installations complying with the *Code* and properly maintained are considered essentially free from electrical hazards. ▶Figure 90–3

▶Figure 90–3

NEC Rules not Intended. The requirements contained in the *NEC* are not intended to ensure an electrical installation will be efficient, convenient, adequate for good service, or suitable for future expansion.
▶Figure 90–4

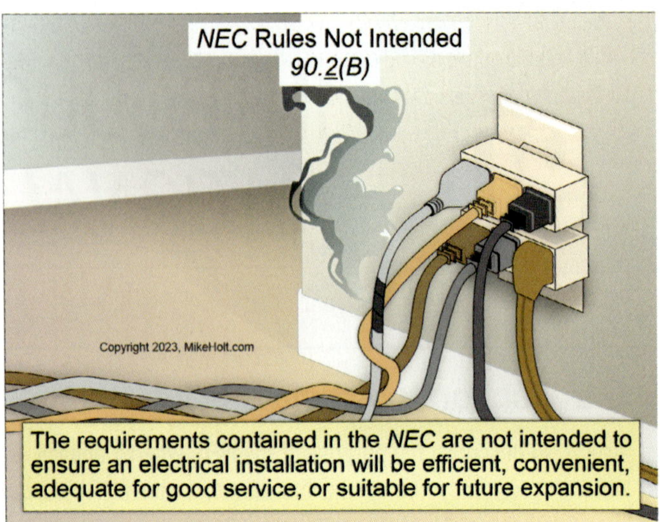

▶Figure 90–4

Note: Hazards often occur because the initial wiring did not provide for increases in the use of electricity resulting in wiring systems becoming overloaded. ▶Figure 90–5

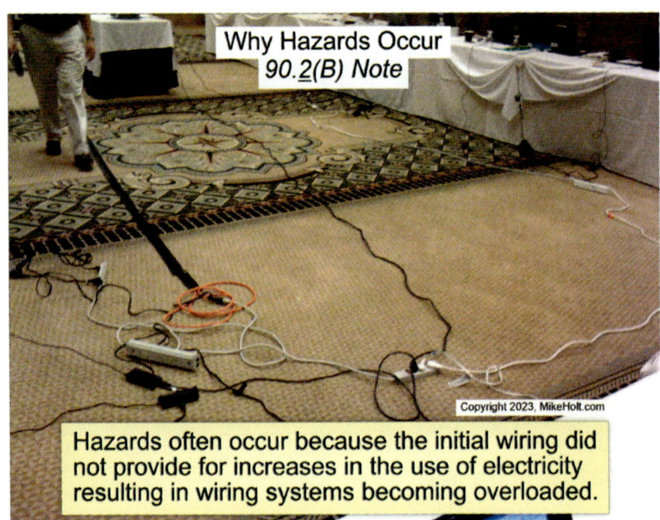

▶Figure 90–5

Author's Comment:

▶ The *NEC* does not require electrical systems to be designed or installed to accommodate future loads. However, consideration should be given not only to ensuring electrical safety (*Code* compliance), but also that the electrical system meets the customers' needs—both for today and in the coming years.

(C) Installations Covered by the *NEC*. The *Code* covers the installation and removal of electrical conductors, equipment, and raceways. It also covers limited-energy and communications conductors, equipment, and raceways, plus optical fiber cables for the following: ▶Figure 90–6

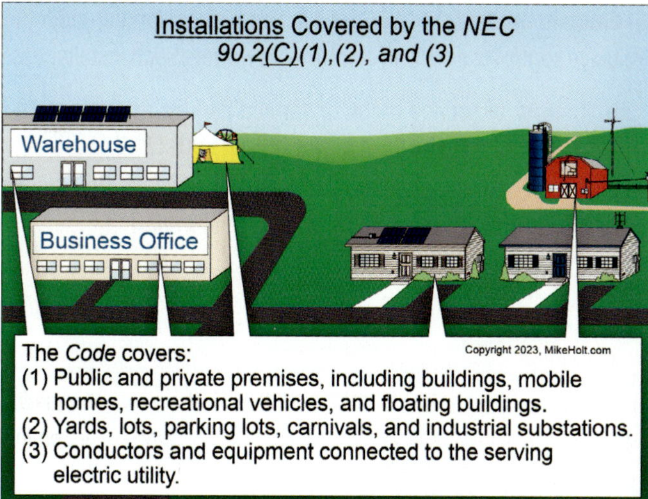

▶Figure 90–6

(1) Public and private premises including buildings, mobile homes, recreational vehicles, and floating buildings.

(2) Yards, lots, parking lots, carnivals, and industrial substations.

(3) Conductors and equipment connected to the serving electric utility.

(4) Installations used by a serving electric utility such as office buildings, warehouses, garages, machine shops, recreational buildings, and other electric utility buildings that are not an integral part of a utility's generating plant, substation, or control center. ▶Figure 90–7

(5) Installations supplying shore power to ships and watercraft in marinas and boatyards, including monitoring of leakage current. ▶Figure 90–8

Author's Comment:

▶ The text in 555.35(B) requires leakage detection equipment to detect leakage current from boats and applies to the load side of the supplying receptacle.

(6) Installations used to export power from vehicles to premises wiring or for bidirectional current flow. ▶Figure 90–9

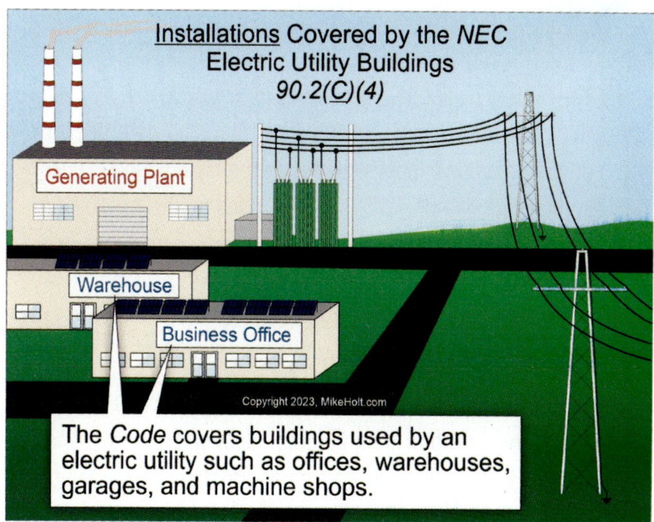

▶Figure 90–7

▶Figure 90–8

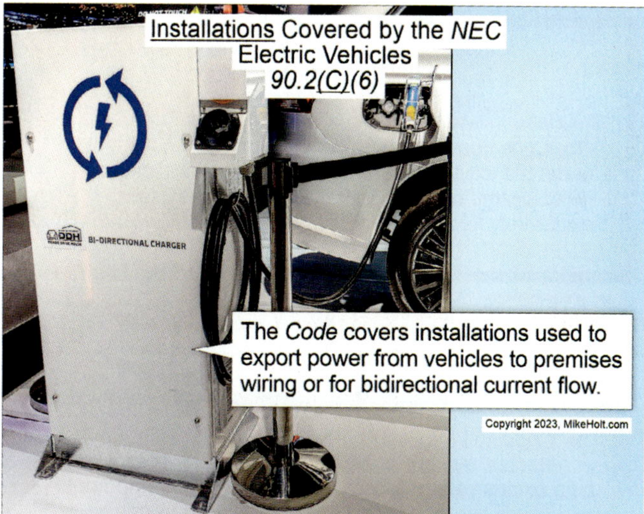

▶Figure 90–9

Author's Comment:

▶ The battery power supply of an electric vehicle can be used "bidirectionally" which means it can be used as a backup or alternate power source to supply premises wiring circuits in the event of a power failure. The rules for this application can be found in Article 625.

(D) Installations Not Covered by the *NEC*. The *Code* does not cover installations of electrical or communications systems for:

(1) Transportation Vehicles. The *NEC* does not cover installations in ships, watercraft (other than floating buildings), aircraft, or automotive vehicles (other than mobile homes and recreational vehicles).

Author's Comment:

▶ An automotive vehicle is any vehicle that may be transported upon a public highway. The wiring of food trucks is not required to comply with the *NEC*, since they are considered automotive vehicles.

(2) Mining Equipment. The *Code* does not cover installations in underground mines or self-propelled mobile surface mining machinery and its attendant electrical trailing cables.

(3) Railways. The *NEC* does not cover installations for railway power, energy storage, and communications wiring.

(4) Communications Utilities. The *Code* does not cover installations of communications equipment under the exclusive control of the communications utility located outdoors or in building spaces used exclusively for these purposes. ▶Figure 90–10

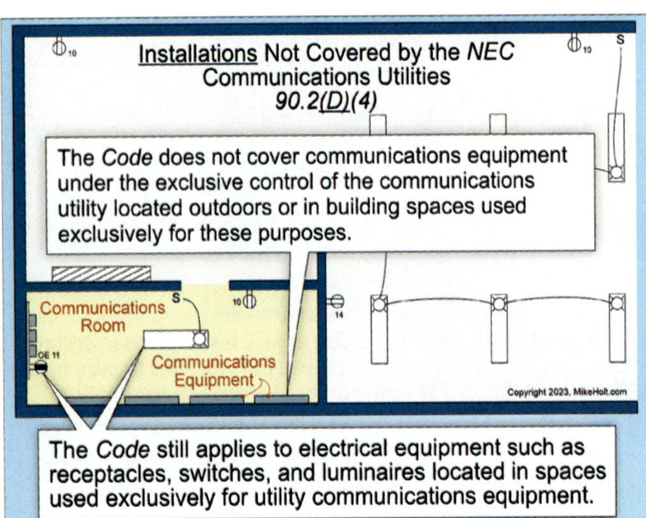

▶Figure 90–10

Author's Comment:

▶ The *Code* still applies to electrical equipment such as receptacles, switches, and luminaires located in spaces used exclusively for utility communications equipment.

(5) Electric Utilities. The *NEC* does not cover installations under the exclusive control of a serving electric utility where such installations:

a. Consist of service drops or service laterals and associated metering. ▶Figure 90–11 and ▶Figure 90–12

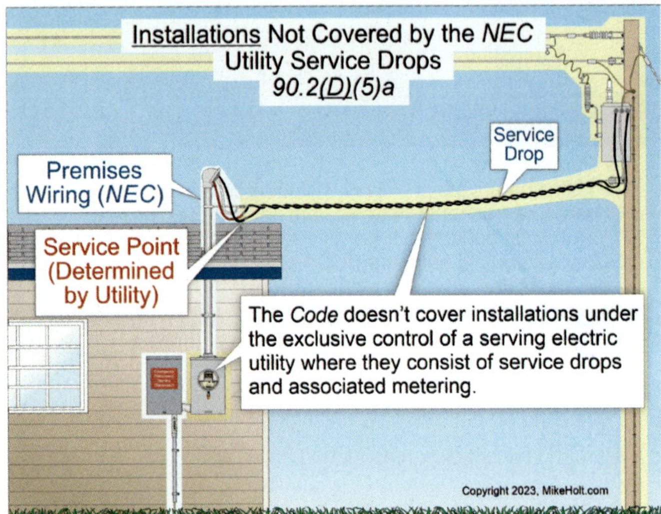

▶Figure 90–11

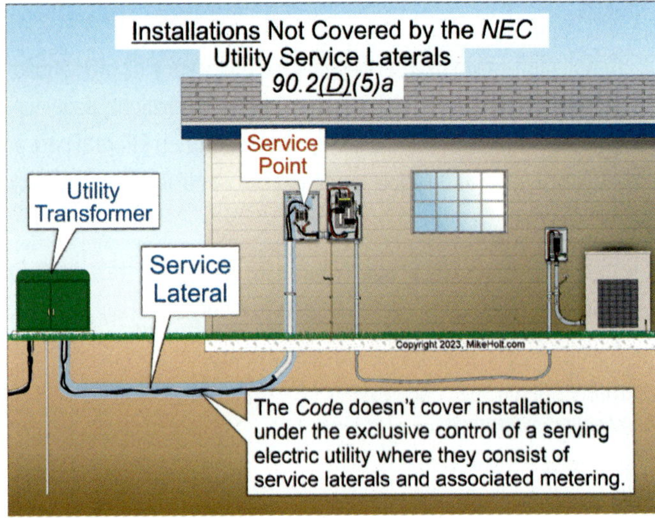

▶Figure 90–12

b. Are on property owned or leased by the utility for the purpose of communications, metering, generation, control, transformation, transmission, energy storage, or distribution of electrical energy. ▶Figure 90–13

▶Figure 90–13

c. Are in legally established easements or rights-of-way. ▶**Figure 90–14**

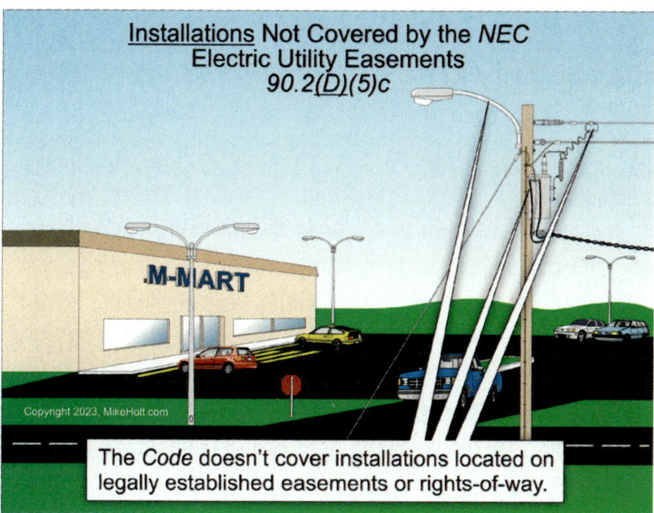

▶Figure 90–14

(E) Relation to International Standards. The requirements of the *NEC* address the fundamental safety principles contained in the International Electrotechnical Commission (IEC) Standard IEC 60364-1, *Low-Voltage Electrical Installations—Part 1: Fundamental Principles, Assessment of General Characteristics, Definitions.*

Note: IEC 60364-1, *Low-Voltage Electrical Installations—Part 1: Fundamental Principles, Assessment of General Characteristics, Definitions, Section 131,* contains fundamental principles of protection for safety that encompass protection against electric shock, thermal effects, overcurrent, fault currents, and overvoltage. All these potential hazards are addressed by the requirements in this *Code.* ▶**Figure 90–15**

▶Figure 90–15

90.3 *Code* Arrangement

General Requirements. The *NEC* consists of an introduction and nine chapters followed by informative annexes. The requirements contained in Chapters 1, 2, 3, and 4 apply generally to all electrical installations. ▶**Figure 90–16**

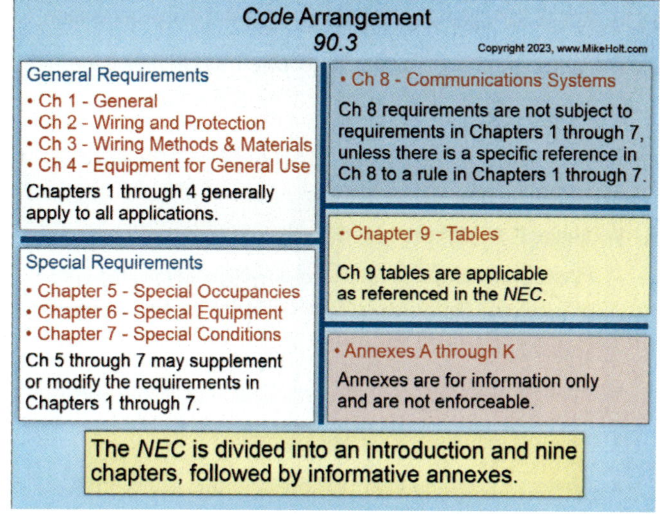

▶Figure 90–16

The requirements contained in Chapters 5, 6, and 7 apply to special occupancies, special equipment, or special conditions, which may supplement or modify the requirements contained in Chapters 1 through 7—but not Chapter 8. Chapter 7 wiring systems covered in this material include:

- Article 722–Cables for Power-Limited Circuits and Optical Fiber
- Article 724–Class 1 Power-Limited Circuits
- Article 725–Class 2 Power-Limited Circuits
- Article 760–Fire Alarm Circuits
- Article 770–Optical Fiber Circuits

Chapter 8 covers communications systems and is not subject to the requirements contained in Chapters 1 through 7, unless specifically referenced in Chapter 8.

Chapter 8 wiring systems covered in this material include:

- Article 800–General Requirements for Communications Systems
- Article 810–Radio and Television Antennas

Chapter 9 consists of tables that apply as referenced in the *NEC*. The tables are used to calculate raceway sizing, conductor fill, the radius of raceway bends, and conductor voltage drop.

Annexes are not part of the requirements of the *Code,* but are included for informational purposes only. There are eleven annexes:

- Annex A. Product Safety Standards
- Annex B. Application Information for Ampacity Calculation
- Annex C. Conduit, Tubing, and Cable Tray Fill Tables for Conductors and Fixture Wires of the Same Size
- Annex D. Examples
- Annex E. Types of Construction
- Annex F. Availability and Reliability for Critical Operations Power Systems (COPS), and Development and Implementation of Functional Performance Tests (FPTs) for Critical Operations Power Systems
- Annex G. Supervisory Control and Data Acquisition (SCADA)
- Annex H. Administration and Enforcement
- Annex I. Recommended Tightening Torque Tables from UL Standard 486A-486B
- Annex J. ADA Standards for Accessible Design
- Annex K. Use of Medical Electrical Equipment in Dwellings and Residential Board-and-Care Occupancies

90.4 *NEC* Enforcement

(A) Suitable for Adoption. The *NEC* is intended to be adopted for mandatory application by governmental bodies that exercise legal jurisdiction over electrical installations. ▶Figure 90–17

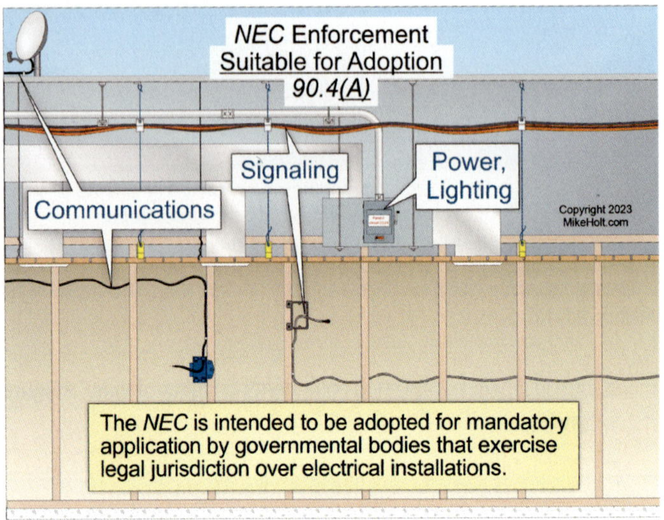

▶Figure 90–17

Author's Comment:

- Once adopted (in part, wholly, or amended), the *National Electrical Code* becomes statutory law for the adopting jurisdiction and is thereby considered a legal document.

(B) AHJ Responsibility. The enforcement of the *NEC* is the responsibility of the "authority having jurisdiction" who is responsible for interpreting *Code* requirements, approving equipment and materials, and granting special permission. ▶Figure 90–18

According to Article 100, "Authority Having Jurisdiction" is defined as the organization, office, or individual responsible for approving equipment, materials, an installation, or a procedure. See 90.4 and 90.7 for more information.

"Approved" is acceptable to the authority having jurisdiction, usually the electrical inspector.

(C) Waiving Requirements and Alternate Methods. By special permission, the authority having jurisdiction may waive *NEC* requirements or approve alternate methods where equivalent safety can be achieved and maintained. ▶Figure 90–19

▶Figure 90–18

▶Figure 90–19

According to Article 100, "Special Permission" is defined as the written consent of the AHJ.

Author's Comment:

▶ According to 90.4(B), the authority having jurisdiction determines the approval of equipment. This means he/she can reject an installation of listed equipment and approve the use of unlisted equipment. Given our highly litigious society, approval of unlisted equipment is becoming increasingly difficult to obtain.

(D) Waiver of Product Requirements. If the *Code* requires products, constructions, or materials that are not yet available at the time the *NEC* is adopted, the authority having jurisdiction can allow products that were acceptable in the previous *Code* that was adopted in the jurisdiction to continue to be used.

Author's Comment:

▶ Typically, the AHJ will approve equipment listed by a product testing organization such as Underwriters Laboratories, Inc. (UL). The *NEC* does not require all equipment to be listed, but many state and local authorities having jurisdictions do. See 90.7, 110.2, and 110.3 and the definitions for "Approved," "Identified," "Labeled," and "Listed" in Article 100

▶ Sometimes it takes years for testing laboratories to establish product standards for new *NEC* product requirements. It takes time before manufacturers can design, manufacture, and distribute those products to the marketplace.

90.5 Mandatory Requirements and Explanatory Material

(A) Mandatory Requirements. The words "shall" or "shall not" indicate a mandatory requirement.

Author's Comment:

▶ For greater ease in reading this material, we will use the word "must" instead of "shall," and "must not" will be used instead of "shall not."

(B) Permissive Requirements. The phrases "shall be permitted" or "shall not be required" indicate the action is permitted, but not required, or there are other options or alternatives permitted.

Author's Comment:

▶ For greater ease in reading, the phrase "shall be permitted" (as used in the *NEC*) has been replaced in this material with "is permitted" or "are permitted."

(C) Explanatory Material. Explanatory material referencing other standards, referencing related sections to an *NEC* rule, or just providing information related to a rule, is included in this *Code* in the form of informational notes or informative annexes. These are not enforceable as *NEC* requirements, unless the standard reference includes a date, the reference is to be considered as the latest edition of the standard.

Author's Comment:

▶ For convenience and ease in reading this material, "Informational Notes" will simply be identified as "Note."

▶ A Note, while not enforceable itself, may reference an enforceable *Code* rule elsewhere in the *NEC*.

▶ Informational Notes are not enforceable, but notes to tables are. Within this material, we will call notes contained in a table "Table Note."

(D) Informative Annexes. Nonmandatory information relative to the use of the *Code* is provided in informative annexes. These annexes are not enforceable as requirements of the *NEC*, but are included for informational purposes only.

90.7 Examination of Equipment for Safety

Product evaluation for *Code* compliance, approval, and safety is typically performed by a qualified electrical testing laboratory (QETL) in accordance with the listing standards.

Except to detect alterations or damage, listed factory-installed internal wiring of equipment does not need to be inspected for *NEC* compliance at the time of installation. ▶Figure 90–20

▶Figure 90–20

Note 1: The requirements contained in Article 300 do not apply to the integral parts of electrical equipment [300.1(B)]. See 110.3 for guidance on safety examinations.

According to Article 100, "Listed" equipment or materials included in a list published by an organization acceptable to the authority having jurisdiction. The listing organization must periodically inspect the production of listed equipment or material to ensure it meets appropriate designated standards and suitable for a specified purpose.

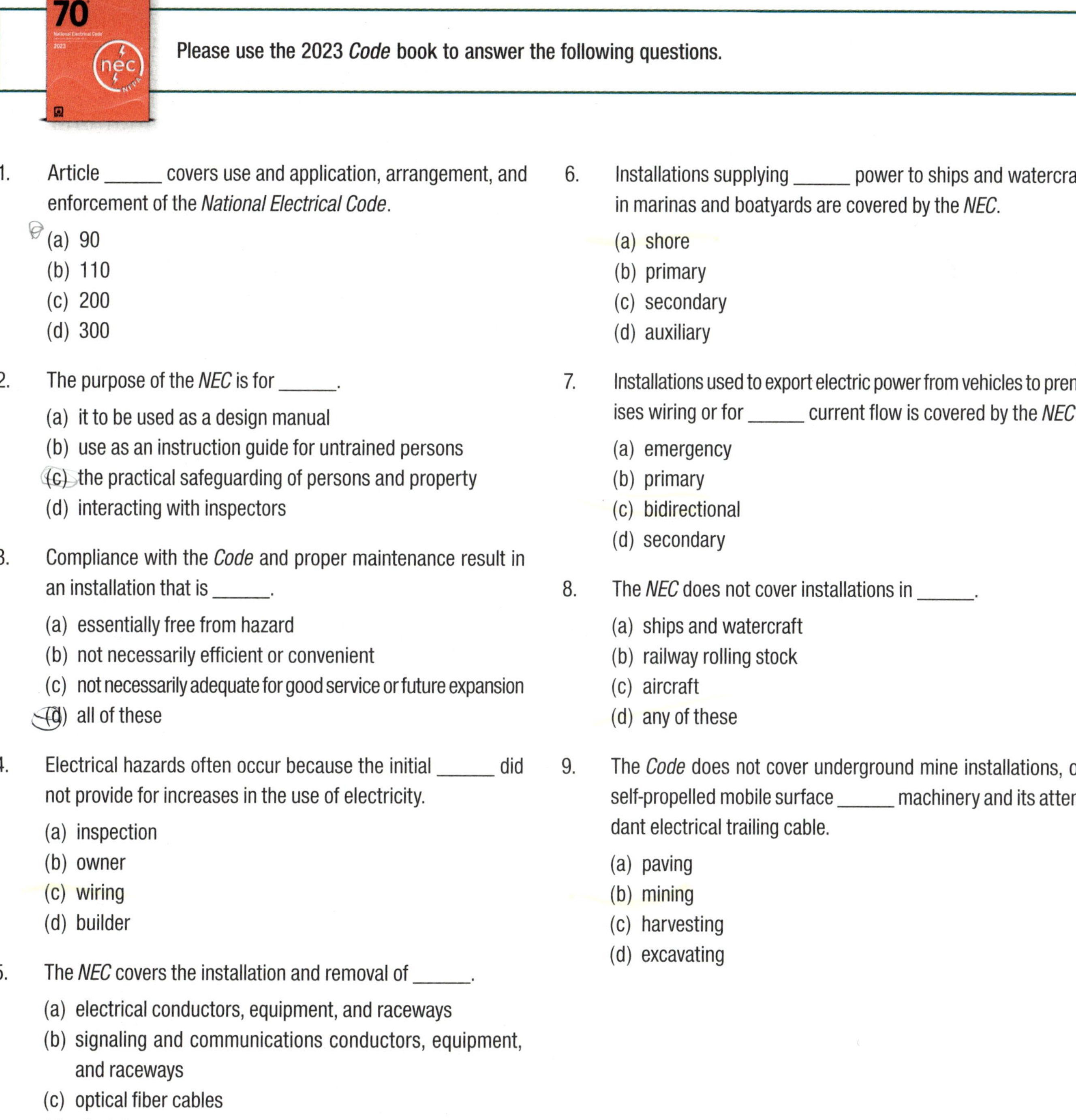

Please use the 2023 *Code* book to answer the following questions.

1. Article ______ covers use and application, arrangement, and enforcement of the *National Electrical Code*.

   (a) 90
   (b) 110
   (c) 200
   (d) 300

2. The purpose of the *NEC* is for ______.

   (a) it to be used as a design manual
   (b) use as an instruction guide for untrained persons
   (c) the practical safeguarding of persons and property
   (d) interacting with inspectors

3. Compliance with the *Code* and proper maintenance result in an installation that is ______.

   (a) essentially free from hazard
   (b) not necessarily efficient or convenient
   (c) not necessarily adequate for good service or future expansion
   (d) all of these

4. Electrical hazards often occur because the initial ______ did not provide for increases in the use of electricity.

   (a) inspection
   (b) owner
   (c) wiring
   (d) builder

5. The *NEC* covers the installation and removal of ______.

   (a) electrical conductors, equipment, and raceways
   (b) signaling and communications conductors, equipment, and raceways
   (c) optical fiber cables
   (d) all of these

6. Installations supplying ______ power to ships and watercraft in marinas and boatyards are covered by the *NEC*.

   (a) shore
   (b) primary
   (c) secondary
   (d) auxiliary

7. Installations used to export electric power from vehicles to premises wiring or for ______ current flow is covered by the *NEC*.

   (a) emergency
   (b) primary
   (c) bidirectional
   (d) secondary

8. The *NEC* does not cover installations in ______.

   (a) ships and watercraft
   (b) railway rolling stock
   (c) aircraft
   (d) any of these

9. The *Code* does not cover underground mine installations, or self-propelled mobile surface ______ machinery and its attendant electrical trailing cable.

   (a) paving
   (b) mining
   (c) harvesting
   (d) excavating

10. Installations of communications equipment under the exclusive control of communications utilities located outdoors or in building spaces used exclusively for such installations _______ covered by the *NEC*.

    (a) are
    (b) are sometimes
    (c) are not
    (d) may be

11. The *Code* does not cover installations under the exclusive control of an electric utility such as _______.

    (a) service drops or service laterals
    (b) electric utility office buildings
    (c) electric utility warehouses
    (d) electric utility garages

12. Chapters 1, 2, 3, and 4 of the *NEC* apply _______.

    (a) generally to all electrical installations
    (b) only to special occupancies and conditions
    (c) only to special equipment and material
    (d) all of these

13. Chapters 5, 6, and 7 of the *NEC* apply to _______ and may supplement or modify the requirements contained in Chapters 1 through 7.

    (a) special occupancies
    (b) special equipment
    (c) special conditions
    (d) all of these

14. Chapter 8 covers _______ systems and is not subject to the requirements of Chapters 1 through 7 unless specifically referenced in Chapter 8.

    (a) communications
    (b) fire alarm
    (c) emergency standby
    (d) sustainable energy

15. Annexes are not part of the requirements of this *Code* but are included for _______ purposes only.

    (a) informational
    (b) reference
    (c) supplemental enforcement
    (d) educational

16. The enforcement of the *NEC* is the responsibility of the authority having jurisdiction, who is responsible for _______.

    (a) making interpretations of rules
    (b) approval of equipment and materials
    (c) granting special permission
    (d) all of these

17. By special permission, the authority having jurisdiction may waive *NEC* requirements or approve alternative methods where equivalent _______ can be achieved and maintained.

    (a) safety
    (b) workmanship
    (c) installations
    (d) job progress

18. If the *Code* requires new products that may not yet be available at the time the *NEC* is adopted, the _______ can allow products that comply with the most recent previous edition of the *Code* adopted by the jurisdiction.

    (a) electrical engineer
    (b) master electrician
    (c) authority having jurisdiction
    (d) none of these

19. In the *NEC*, the word(s) _______ indicate a mandatory requirement.

    (a) shall
    (b) shall not
    (c) shall be permitted
    (d) shall or shall not

20. When the *Code* uses _______, it indicates the actions are allowed but not required.

    (a) shall or shall not
    (b) shall not be permitted
    (c) shall be permitted
    (d) none of these

21. Explanatory material, such as references to other standards, references to related sections of this *Code*, or information related to a *Code* rule, is included in this *Code* in the form of _______.

    (a) informational notes
    (b) footnotes
    (c) table notes
    (d) italicized text

22. Nonmandatory information relative to the use of the *NEC* is provided in informative annexes and are _______.

    (a) included for information purposes only
    (b) not enforceable requirements of the *Code*
    (c) enforceable as a requirement of the *Code*
    (d) included for information purposes only and are not enforceable requirements of the *Code*

23. Except to detect alterations or damage, qualified electrical testing laboratory listed factory-installed _______ wiring of equipment does not need to be inspected for *NEC* compliance at the time of installation.

    (a) external
    (b) associated
    (c) internal
    (d) all of these

GENERAL RULES

Introduction to Chapter 1—General Rules

Chapter 1 of the *NEC* is divided into two articles. The first contains the definitions of important terms used throughout the *Code*, and the second provides the general requirements for all electrical installations. The definitions and rules in this chapter apply to all electrical installations covered by the *NEC*.

Chapter 1 is often overlooked because the rules are very broad and do not clearly apply to specific situations. Be sure you understand the rules, concepts, definitions, and requirements in Chapter 1 as doing so will make a difficult rule(s) much easier to apply. Chapter 1 articles covered by this material are:

▶ **Article 110—General Requirements for Electrical Installations.** This article covers the general requirements for the examination and approval, installation and use, and access to spaces around electrical equipment.

GENERAL REQUIREMENTS FOR ELECTRICAL INSTALLATIONS

Introduction to Article 110—General Requirements for Electrical Installations

Article 110 is the first article in the *NEC* that contains requirements as opposed to overall scope information or definitions. It contains the general rules that apply to all installations and, as such, is the foundation of the *Code*. Topics covered in our material for Article 110 include:

- How equipment is approved
- How to determine when or where equipment can be used
- How to arrange equipment so it is safe to operate and maintain for the end user
- How to identify the characteristics of the systems being installed so future alterations, service, or maintenance can be completed safely

This article is divided into five parts. The first two cover systems under 1000V, nominal and are the only parts of this article covered in this material. As you begin your journey to understanding the *NEC*, remember that many other *Code* rules were written with the understanding that you will come to Article 110 to determine the general requirements. Set yourself up for success by taking the time to read and understand each of these rules.

Part I. General Requirements

110.1 Scope

Article 110 covers the general requirements for the examination, approval, installation, use, and access to spaces around electrical equipment. ▶Figure 110–1

Author's Comment:

- Requirements for people with disabilities include things like mounting heights for switches, receptacles and the requirements for the distance that objects (such as wall sconces) protrude from a wall.

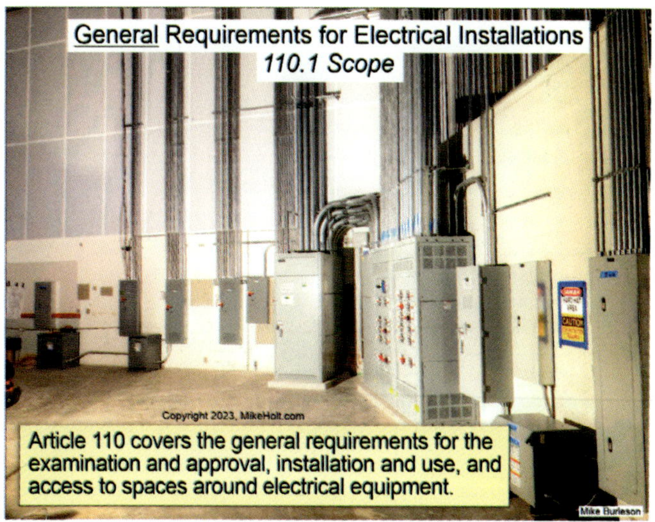

▶Figure 110–1

Note: For information regarding ADA accessibility design, see Annex J.

110.2 Approval of Conductors and Equipment

The authority having jurisdiction must approve all electrical conductors and equipment. ▶Figure 110–2

▶Figure 110–2

According to Article 100, "Approved" means acceptable to the authority having jurisdiction (AHJ), usually the electrical inspector. Product listing does not mean the product is approved, but it can be a basis for approval. ▶Figure 110–3

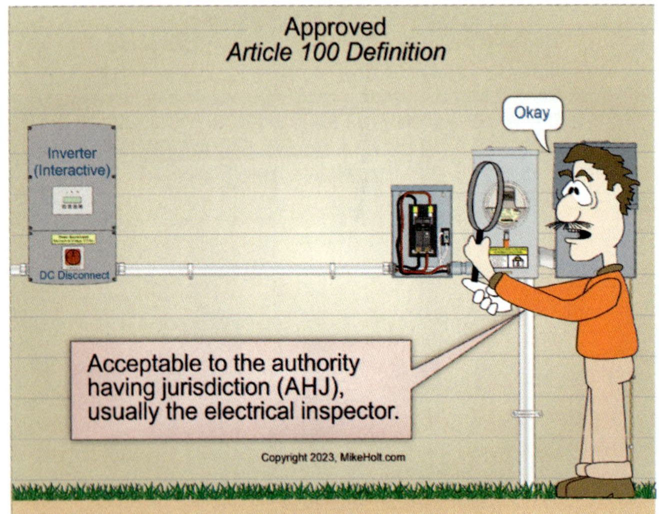

▶Figure 110–3

According to Article 100, "Authority Having Jurisdiction (AHJ)" refers the organization, office, or individual responsible for approving equipment, materials, or an installation. See 90.4 and 90.7 for more information. ▶Figure 110–4

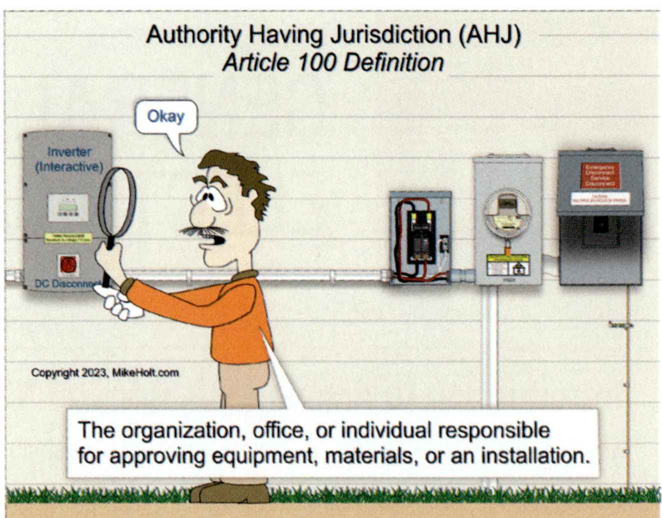

▶Figure 110–4

110.3 Use of Equipment

(B) Installation and Use. Equipment that is listed, labeled, or identified must be installed in accordance with manufacturer's instructions. ▶Figure 110–5

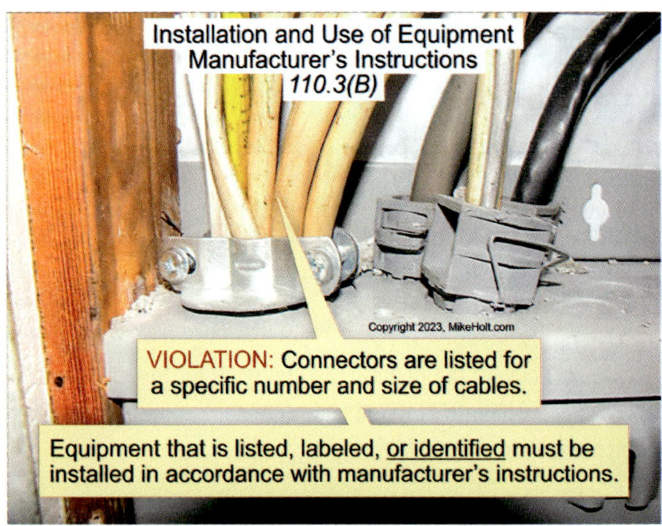

▶Figure 110–5

According to Article 100, "Labeled" mean equipment or materials that have a label, symbol, or other identifying mark in the form of a sticker, decal, printed label, or with the identifying mark molded or stamped into the product by a recognized testing laboratory acceptable to the authority having jurisdiction. ▶Figure 110–6

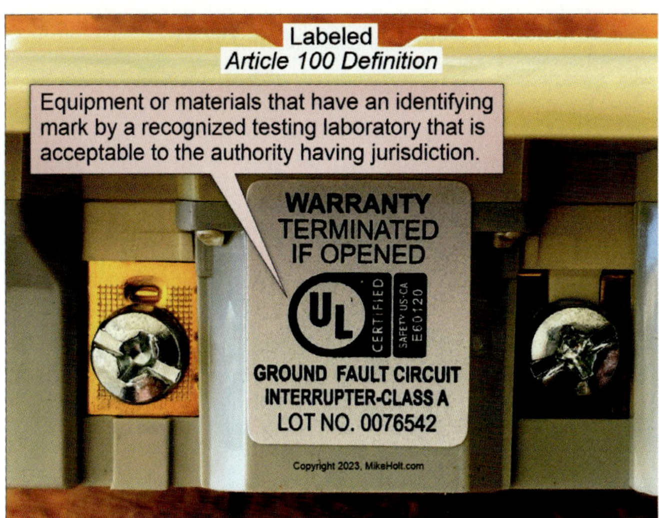

▶Figure 110–6

Note: The installation instructions can be provided in the form of printed material, quick response (QR) code, or the address on the Internet where users can download the required instructions. ▶Figure 110–7

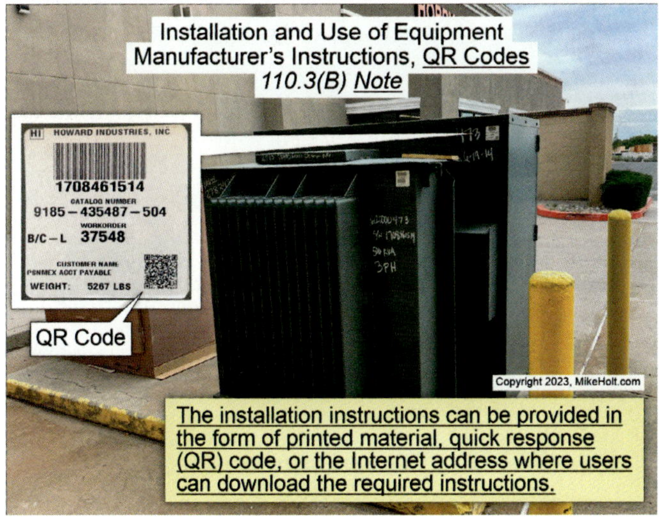

▶Figure 110–7

Author's Comment:

▶ Many electricians simply throw away installation instructions, but that excuse is now becoming less valid since manufacturers are starting to use QR codes on electrical equipment, so the instructions are always readily available.

Conductors must be copper, aluminum, or copper-clad aluminum unless otherwise provided in this *Code*. If the conductor material is not specified in a rule, the sizes given in the *NEC* are based on a copper conductor. ▶Figure 110–8

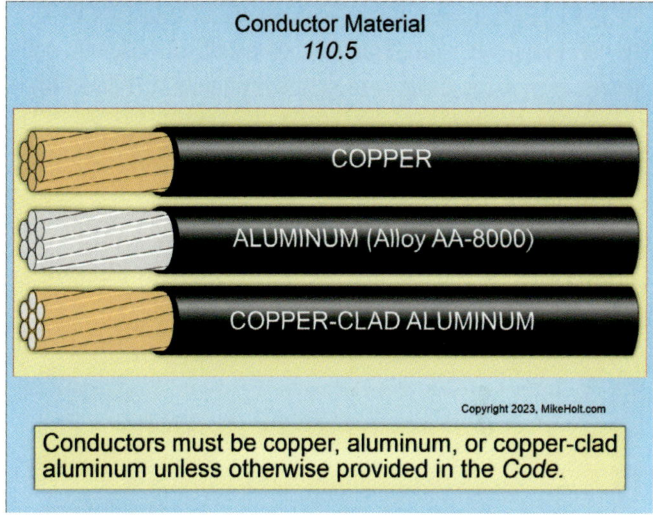

▶Figure 110–8

Conductor sizes are expressed in American Wire Gauge (AWG) or circular mils (cmil). ▶Figure 110–9

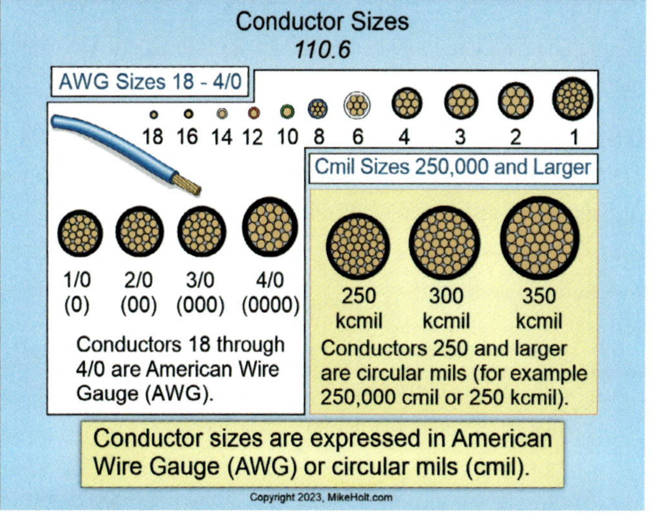

▶Figure 110–9

Author's Comment:

▸ Chapter 9, Table 8 gives the circular mil area of AWG conductors.

110.8 Suitable Wiring Methods

The only wiring methods permitted to be installed in buildings, occupancies, or premises are those recognized by the *NEC*. ▸Figure 110–10

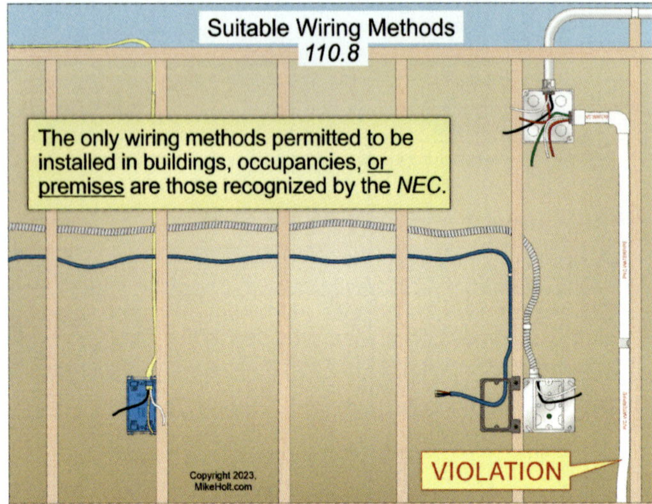

▸Figure 110–10

110.12 Mechanical Execution of Work

Electrical equipment must be installed in a professional and skillful manner. ▸Figure 110–11

Note: For information on accepted industry practices, see ANSI/NECA 1, *Standard for Good Workmanship in Electrical Construction*, and other ANSI-approved installation standards. ▸Figure 110–12

Author's Comment:

▸ This rule is perhaps one of the most subjective of the entire *Code,* and its application is still ultimately a judgment call made by the authority having jurisdiction.

(A) Unused Openings. Unused openings (other than those used for mounting equipment or the operation of equipment), must be closed by fittings that provide protection substantially equivalent to the wall of the equipment. Unused openings that are intended for mounting the equipment are not required to be closed. ▸Figure 110–13

▸Figure 110–11

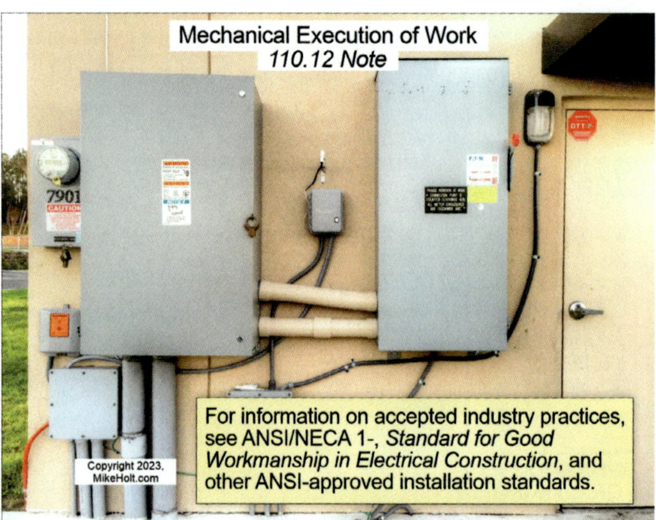

▸Figure 110–12

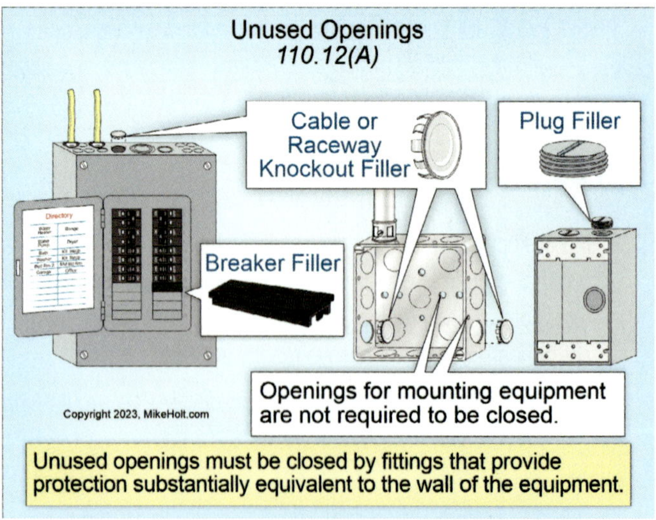

▸Figure 110–13

(B) Integrity of Electrical Equipment. Internal parts of electrical equipment must not be damaged or contaminated by foreign material such as paint, plaster, cleaners, and so forth. ▶Figure 110–14

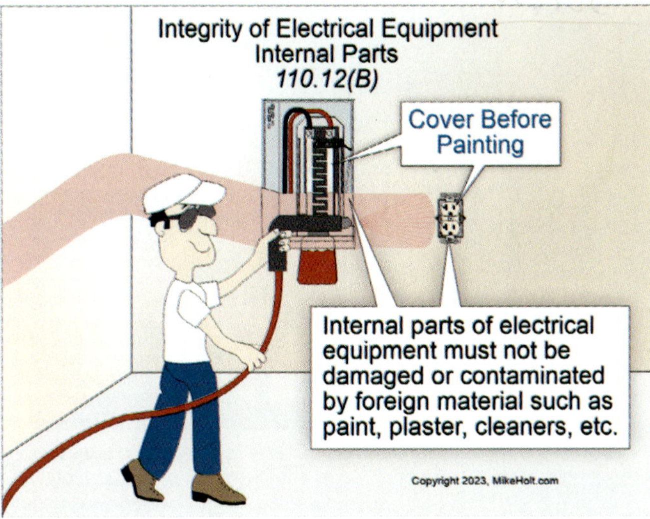

▶Figure 110–14

Author's Comment:

▸ Precautions must be taken to provide protection from the contamination of internal parts of panelboards and receptacles during building construction. Be sure the electrical equipment is properly masked and protected before drywall, painting, or other phases of the project that can contaminate or cause damage begins. ▶Figure 110–15

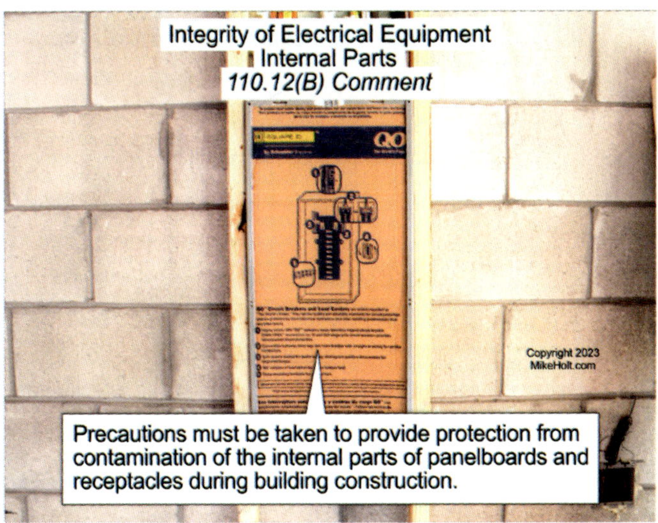

▶Figure 110–15

Electrical equipment containing damaged parts (such as items broken, bent, or cut), or those that have been deteriorated by corrosion, chemical action, or overheating are not permitted to be installed. ▶Figure 110–16

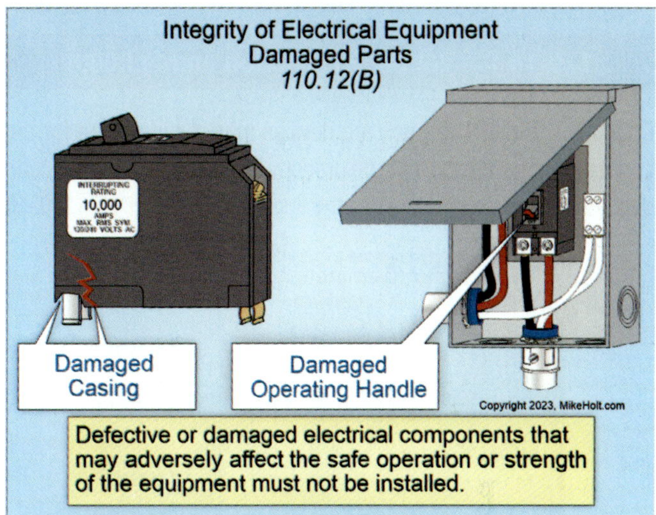

▶Figure 110–16

Author's Comment:

▸ Damaged parts include cracked insulators, arc shields not in place, overheated fuse clips, and damaged or missing switch handles or circuit-breaker handles.

110.13 Mounting and Cooling of Equipment

(A) Mounting. Electrical equipment must be firmly secured to the surface on which it is mounted. ▶Figure 110–17

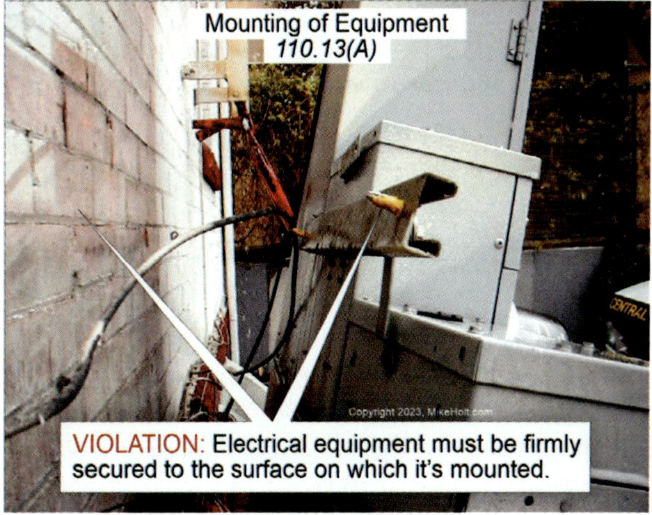

▶Figure 110–17

(B) Cooling. Electrical equipment that depends on heat dissipation must be installed in air-conditioned spaces, or if equipped with a ventilating opening, must maintain proper clearance to dissipate rising warm air.

110.14 Conductor Termination and Splicing

Conductor terminal and splicing devices must be identified for the conductor material and must be properly installed and used in accordance with the manufacturer's instructions [110.3(B)]. ▶Figure 110–18

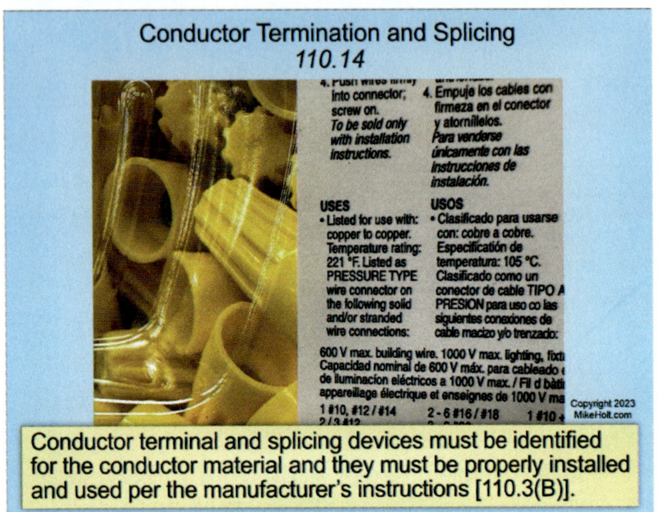

Conductor terminal and splicing devices must be identified for the conductor material and they must be properly installed and used per the manufacturer's instructions [110.3(B)].

▶Figure 110–18

Conductors of dissimilar materials are not permitted in a terminal or splicing device where contact occurs between dissimilar conductors—unless identified for the purpose and conditions of use. ▶Figure 110–19

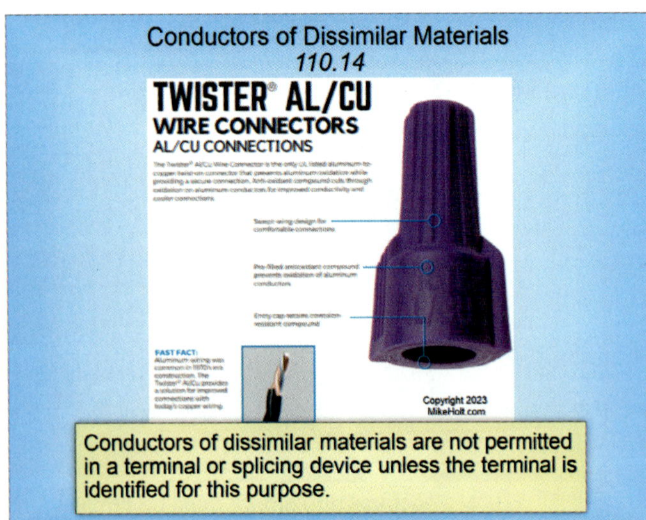

Conductors of dissimilar materials are not permitted in a terminal or splicing device unless the terminal is identified for this purpose.

▶Figure 110–19

According to Article 100, "Identified" means recognized as suitable for a specific purpose, function, use, environment, or application. ▶Figure 110–20

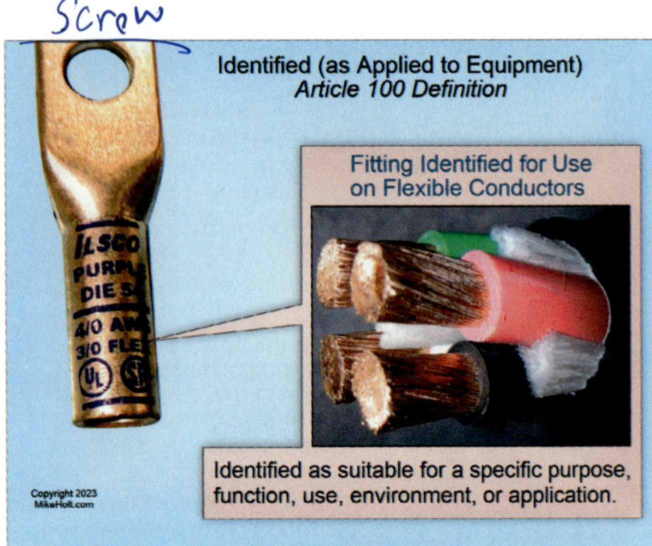

▶Figure 110–20

Author's Comment:

▸ Conductor terminals suitable for aluminum wire only will be marked "AL." Those acceptable for copper wire will be marked "CU." Terminals suitable for copper, copper-clad-aluminum, and aluminum conductors will be marked "CU-AL" or "AL-CU." For 6 AWG and smaller, the markings can be printed on the container or on an information sheet inside the container. A "7" or "75" indicates a 75°C rated terminal, and a "9" or "90" indicates a 90°C rated terminal. If a terminal bears no marking, it can be used only with copper conductors. ▶Figure 110–21

▸ Aluminum wire that was installed prior to the 1972 was the same wire used for utility power transmission lines. This aluminum wire had a major problem with oxidation at terminations and it required an antioxidant at terminations. When the antioxidant was not properly applied to the wire termination, fires were common at the termination. Since 1983, the *National Electrical Code* [310.3(B)] has required aluminum wire to be made from an aluminum alloy (AA-8000). This conductor does not require an antioxidant at terminations. ▶Figure 110–22

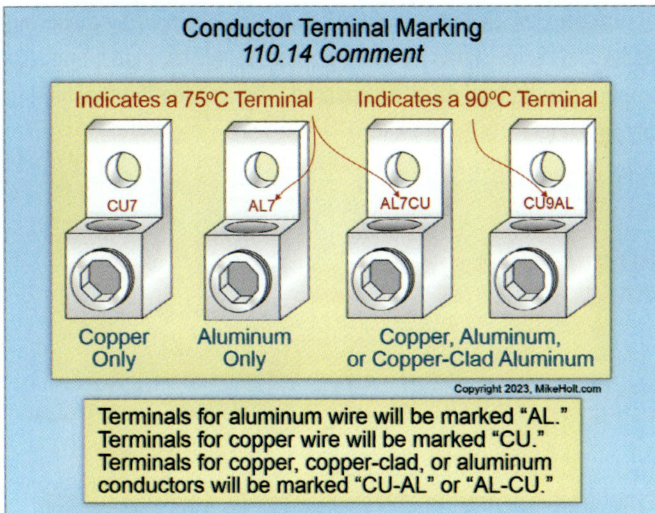

▶Figure 110–21

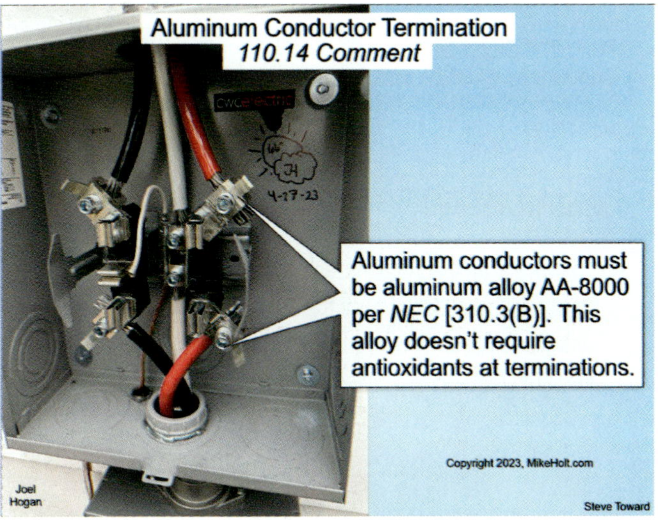

▶Figure 110–22

Connectors and terminals for conductors more finely stranded than Class B and Class C must be identified for the use of finely stranded conductors. ▶Figure 110–23

Author's Comment:

▶ Conductor terminations must comply with the manufacturer's instructions as required by 110.3(B). For example, if the instructions for the device are written, "Suitable for 18-12 AWG Stranded," then only stranded conductors can be used with the terminating device. If they are written, "Suitable for 18-12 AWG Solid," then only solid conductors are permitted, and if the instructions are written, "Suitable for 18-12 AWG," then either solid or stranded conductors can be used with the terminating device.

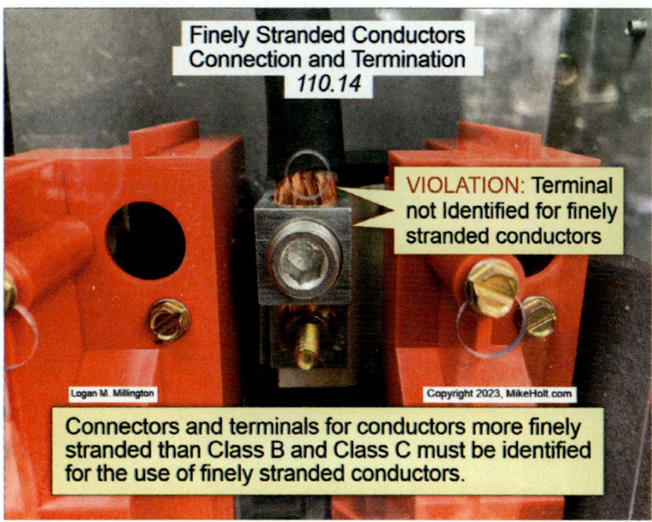

▶Figure 110–23

▶ Few terminations are listed for mixing aluminum and copper conductors, but if they are, that will be marked on the product package or terminal device. The reason copper and aluminum should not be in contact with each other is because corrosion develops between the two different metals due to galvanic action. This results in increased contact resistance at the splicing device, and increased resistance can cause the splice to overheat and result in a fire.

(A) Conductor Terminations. Conductor terminals must ensure a mechanically secure electrical connection by the use of pressure connectors or splicing devices. ▶Figure 110–24

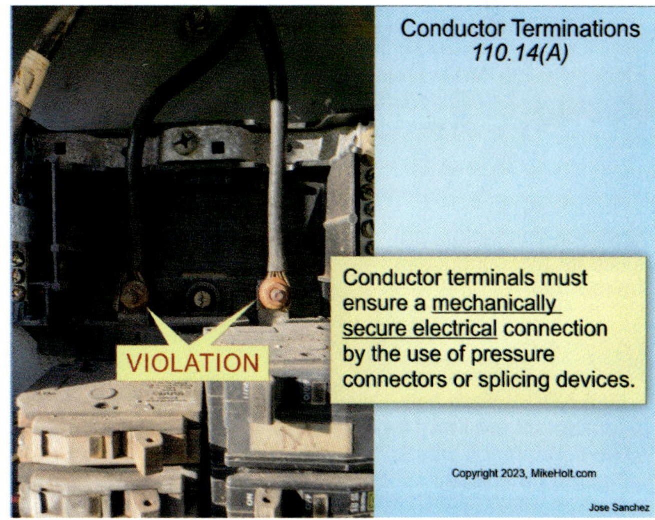

▶Figure 110–24

Terminals are only listed for one conductor, unless marked otherwise. Terminals for more than one conductor must be identified for this purpose, either within the equipment instructions or on the terminal itself. ▶Figure 110–25

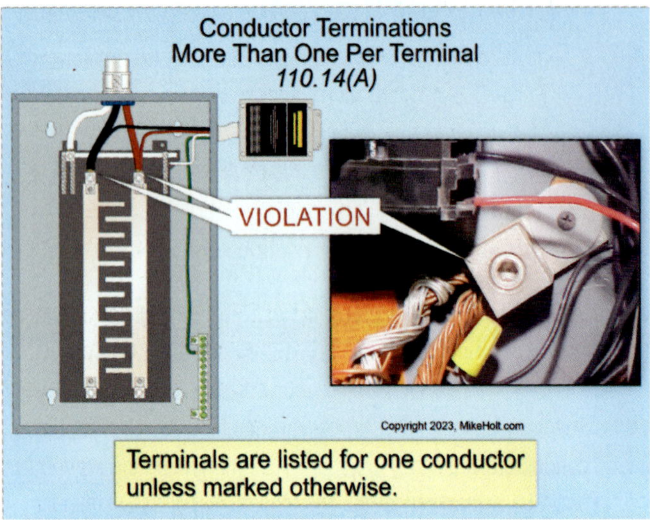

▶Figure 110–25

Author's Comment:

▶ Split-bolt connectors are commonly listed for only two conductors, although some are listed for three. However, it is a common industry practice to terminate as many conductors as possible within a split-bolt connector, even though this violates the *NEC*. ▶Figure 110–26

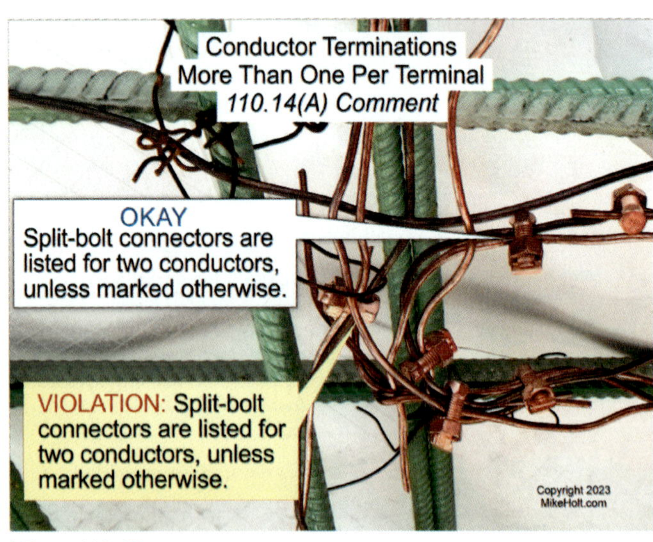

▶Figure 110–26

(B) Conductor Splices. Conductors must be spliced by a splicing device that is identified for the purpose. All splices, joints, and free ends of conductors must be covered with an identified insulating device. ▶Figure 110–27

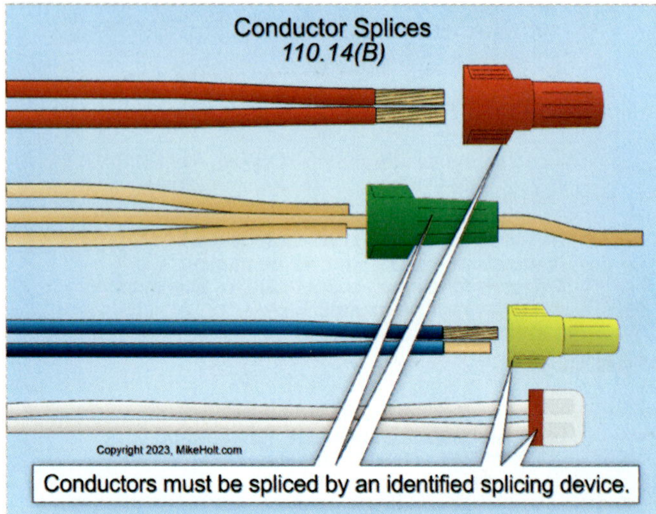

▶Figure 110–27

Author's Comment:

▶ To prevent an electrical hazard, the free ends of conductors must be insulated to prevent the exposed end(s) from touching energized parts. This requirement can be met by using an insulated twist-on or push-on wire connector. ▶Figure 110–28

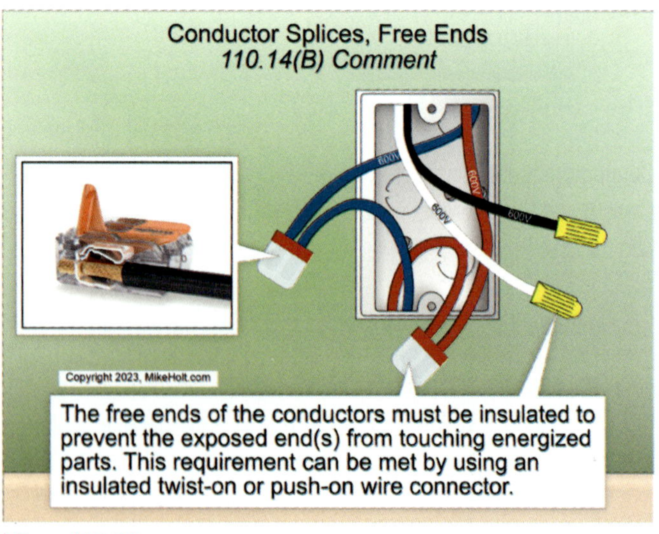

▶Figure 110–28

▸ Pre-twisting conductors before applying twist-on wire connectors has been a very common practice in the field for years. The question (and subsequent debate) has always been, "Is pre-twisting required?" The *NEC* does not require that practice and, in fact, Ideal® made a statement about their Wing-Nut® twist-on connectors which said, "Pre-twisting is acceptable, but not required." Always follow the manufacturer's instructions and there will be no question [110.3(B)]. ▸**Figure 110–29**

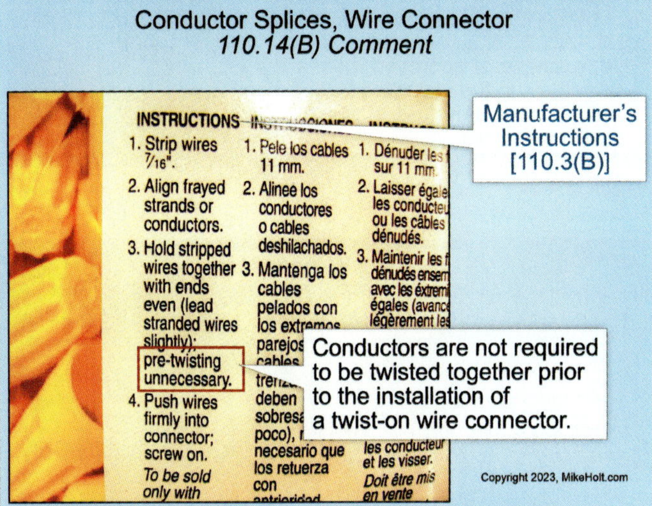

▸Figure 110–29

Single direct burial types UF or USE conductors can be spliced underground with a device listed for direct burial [300.5(E) and 300.15(G)]. ▸Figure 110–30

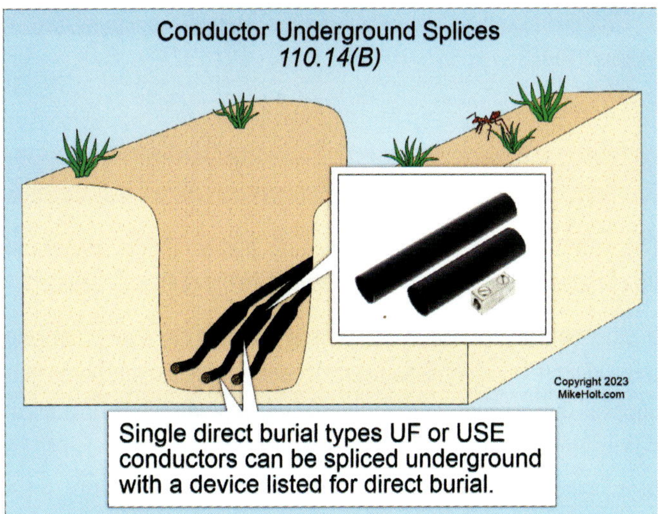

▸Figure 110–30

The individual conductors of multiconductor UF or USE cable can be spliced underground with an underground listed splice kit that encapsulates the conductors and cable jacket.

▸ Electrical connection failures are the cause of many equipment and building fires. Improper terminations, poor workmanship, not following the manufacturer's instructions, and improper torquing can cause poor electrical connections. Improper electrical terminations can damage and melt conductor insulation resulting in short circuits and ground faults.

(D) Torquing of Terminal Connections. Tightening torque values for terminal connections must be as indicated on equipment or instructions. The tool or device used to achieve torque values must be approved by the authority having jurisdiction. ▸Figure 110–31

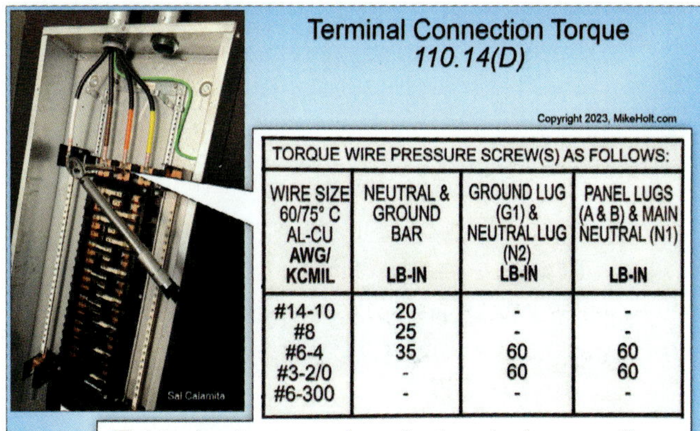

TORQUE WIRE PRESSURE SCREW(S) AS FOLLOWS:

WIRE SIZE 60/75° C AL-CU AWG/ KCMIL	NEUTRAL & GROUND BAR LB-IN	GROUND LUG (G1) & NEUTRAL LUG (N2) LB-IN	PANEL LUGS (A & B) & MAIN NEUTRAL (N1) LB-IN
#14-10	20	-	-
#8	25	-	-
#6-4	35	60	60
#3-2/0	-	60	60
#6-300	-	-	-

Tightening torque values for terminal connections must be as indicated on equipment or installation instructions. An approved means must be used to achieve the indicated torque value.

▸Figure 110–31

▸ Conductors must terminate on device and equipment terminals that have been properly tightened in accordance with the manufacturer's torque specifications included with equipment instructions. Failure to torque terminals properly can result in excessive heating of terminals or splicing devices due to a loose connection. A loose connection can also lead to a glowing arc which increases the heating of the terminal and may ultimately cause a short circuit or ground fault. Any of these can result in a fire or other failure, including an arc flash event. ▸**Figure 110–32** and ▸**Figure 110–33**

▶Figure 110–32

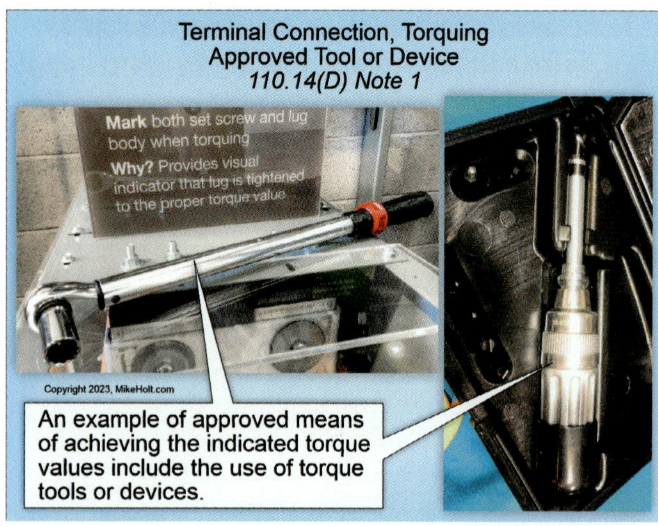

▶Figure 110–34

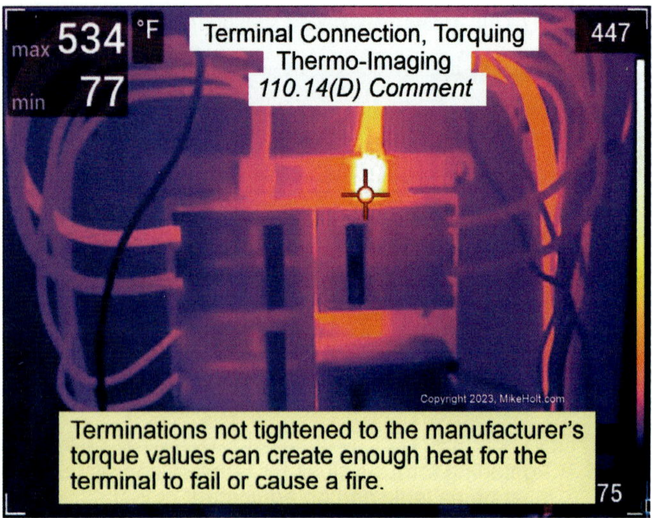

▶Figure 110–33

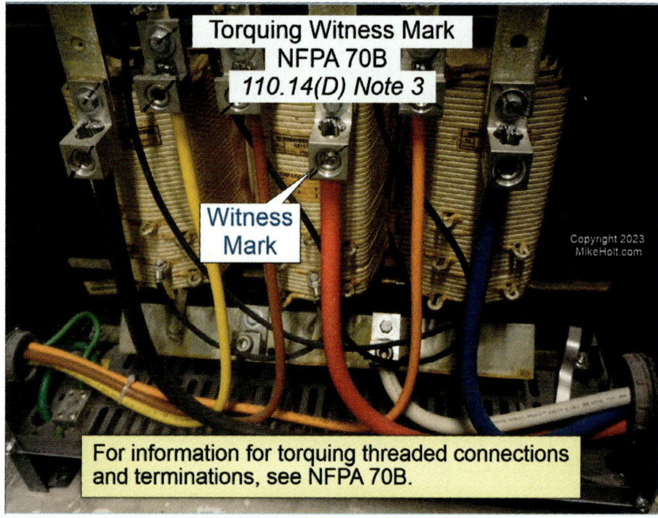

▶Figure 110–35

transformer

Note 1: Examples of approved means of achieving the indicated torque values include the use of torque tools or devices (such as shear bolts or breakaway-style devices) with visual indicators that demonstrate the proper torque has been applied. ▶Figure 110–34

Note 2: In the absence of manufacturer's torque requirements, see Annex I or UL Standard 486A-486B, *Standard for Safety-Wire Connectors,* for torque values. The equipment manufacturer can be contacted if numeric torque values are not indicated on the equipment or the instructions are not available.

Note 3: For information for torquing threaded connections and terminations, see NFPA 70B, *Recommended Practice for Electrical Equipment Maintenance*, Section 8.11. ▶Figure 110–35

110.22 Identification of Disconnecting Means

(A) General. Each disconnect must be legibly marked to indicate its purpose unless located and arranged so the purpose is evident.

In other than one- or two-family dwelling units, the disconnect marking must include the identification and location of the circuit source that supplies the disconnect unless located and arranged so the identification and location of the circuit source is evident. The marking must be of sufficient durability to withstand the environment. ▶Figure 110–36

According to Article 100, "Disconnect" is a device that disconnects the circuit conductors from their power source. ▶Figure 110–37

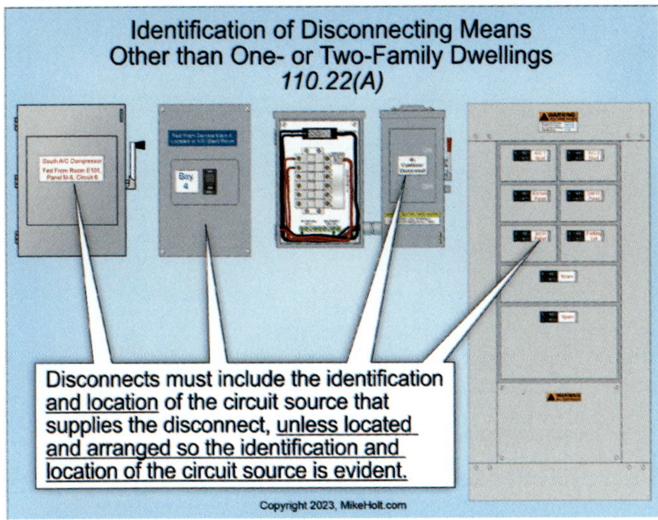

▶Figure 110–36

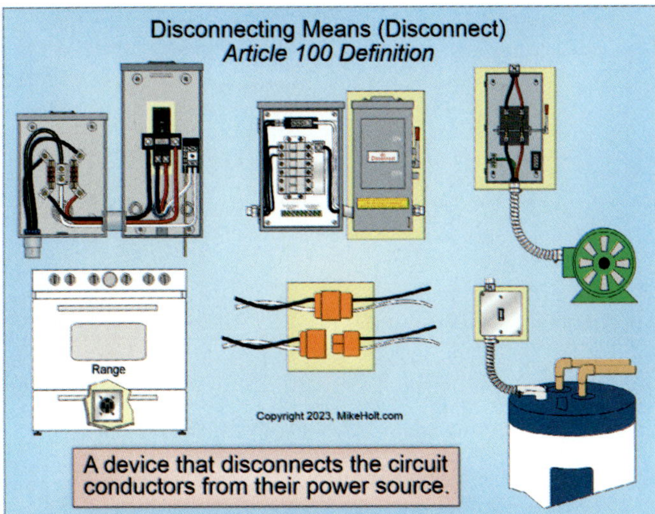

▶Figure 110–37

▶Figure 110–38

▶Figure 110–39

Author's Comment:

▶ See 408.4 for additional requirements for identification markings on circuit directories for switchboards and panelboards.

110.25 Lockable Disconnecting Means

If the *Code* requires a disconnect to be lockable in the open position, the provisions for locking must remain in place whether the lock is installed or not. ▶Figure 110–38 and ▶Figure 110–39

Part II. 1000V, Nominal, or Less

110.26 Spaces Around Electrical Equipment

Working space, access to and egress from working space, must be provided and maintained around equipment to permit safe operation and maintenance of equipment. ▶Figure 110–40

Open equipment doors must not impede access to and egress from the working space. Access or egress to working space is considered impeded if one or more simultaneously opened equipment doors restrict working space access to less than 24 in. wide and 6½ ft high. ▶Figure 110–41

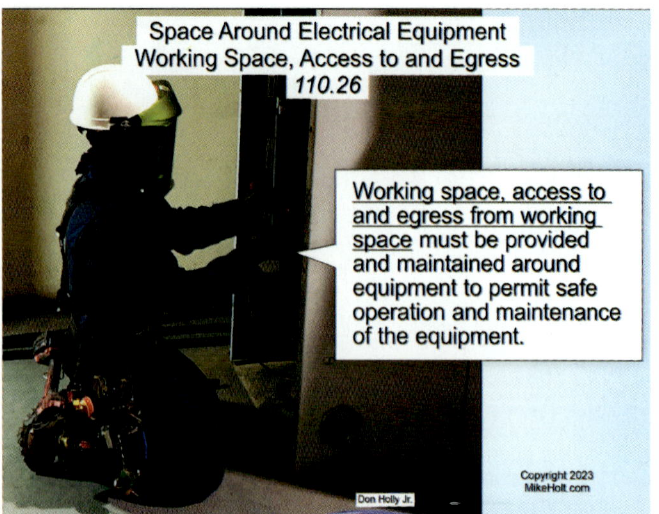

▶Figure 110–40

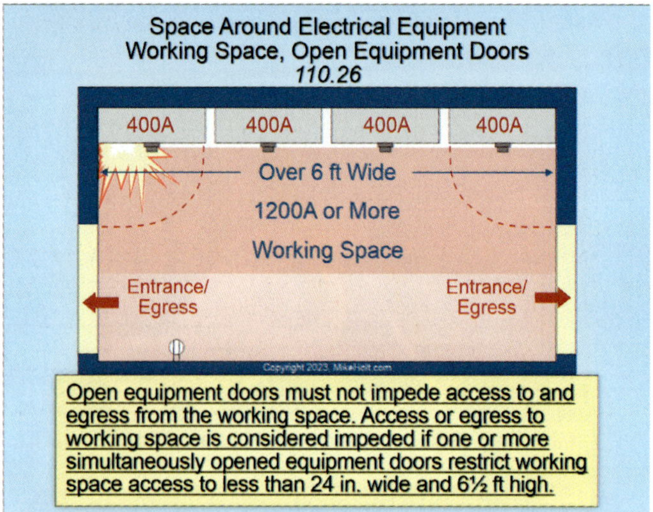

▶Figure 110–41

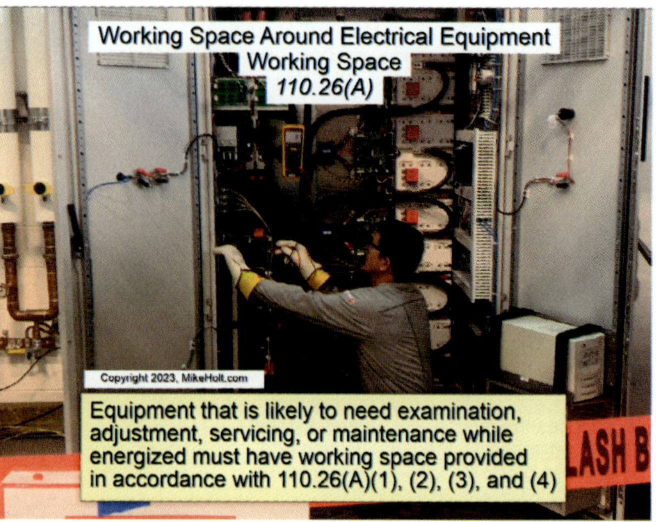

▶Figure 110–42

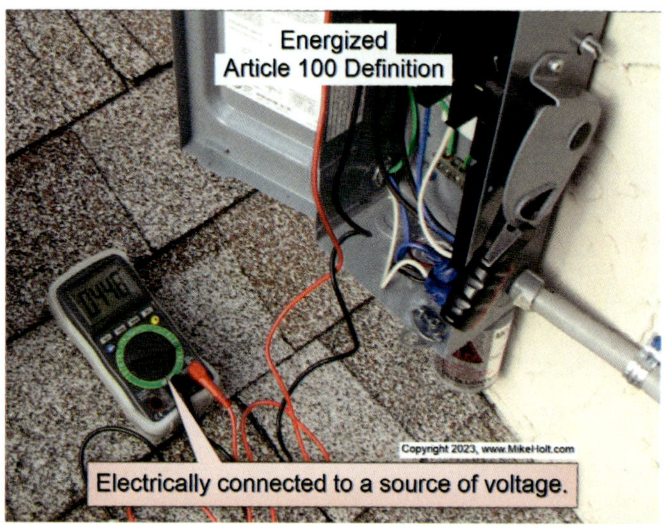

▶Figure 110–43

(A) Working Space. Equipment that is likely to need examination, adjustment, servicing, or maintenance while energized must have working space provided in accordance with 110.26(A)(1), (2), (3), and (4): ▶Figure 110–42

According to Article 100, "Energized" means electrically connected to a source of voltage. ▶Figure 110–43

Author's Comment:

▶ The phrase "while energized" is the root of many debates. As always, check with the authority having jurisdiction to see what equipment he/she believes needs a clear working space.

Note: For guidance in determining the severity of potential exposure, planning safe work practices (including establishing an electrically safe work condition), arc-flash labeling, and selecting personal protective equipment see NFPA 70E, *Standard for Electrical Safety in the Workplace.* ▶Figure 110–44

(1) Depth of Working Space. The depth of working space, which is measured from the enclosure front, cannot be less than the distances contained in Table 110.26(A)(1). These depths are dependent on the voltage-to-ground and three different conditions. ▶Figure 110–45

According to Article 100, "Voltage-to-Ground, Grounded Systems" is the voltage between any phase and neutral conductor. ▶Figure 110–46

Depth of working space must be measured from the enclosure front, not the live parts. ▶Figure 110–47

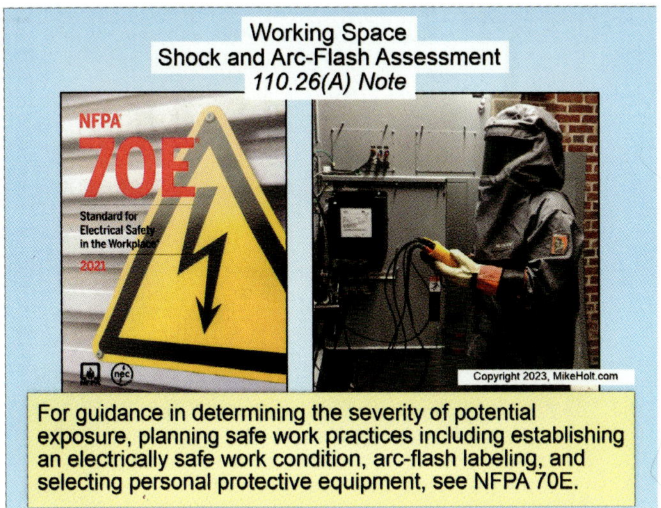

▶Figure 110–44

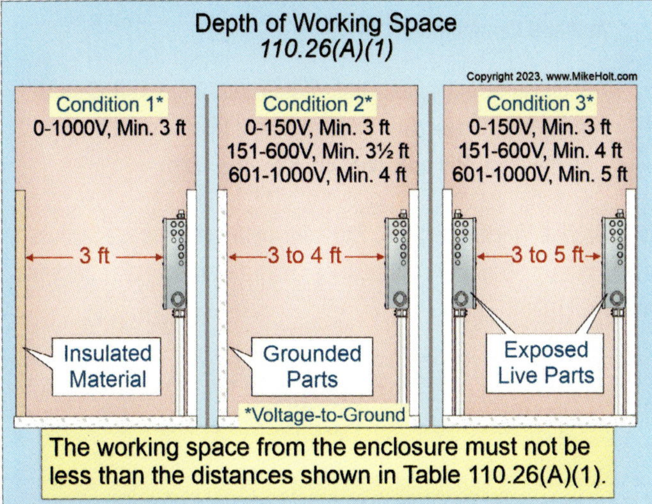

▶Figure 110–45

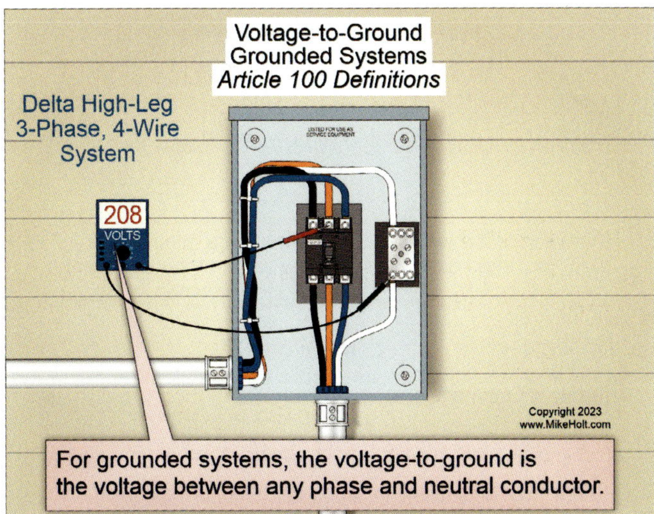

▶Figure 110–46

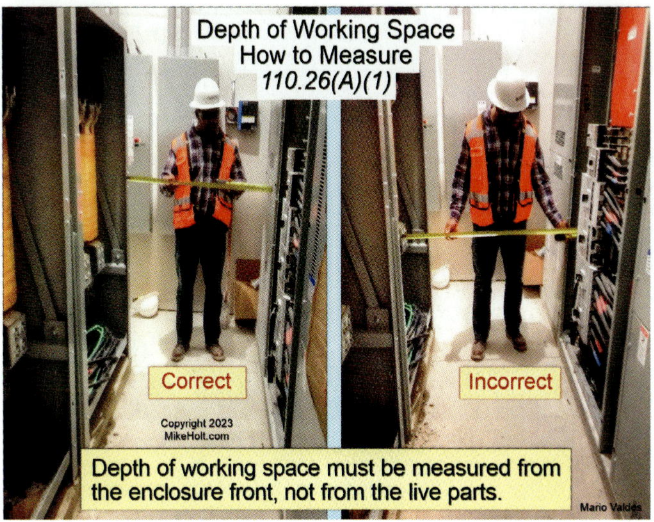

▶Figure 110–47

According to Article 100, "Live Parts" means energized conductive components.

Table 110.26(A)(1) Working Space			
Voltage-to-Ground	Condition 1	Condition 2	Condition 3
0–150V	3 ft	3 ft	3 ft
151–600V	3 ft	3½ft	4 ft
601–1000V	3 ft	4 ft	5 ft

▶Figure 110–48, ▶Figure 110–49, and ▶Figure 110–50

Table Note:

Condition 1: Exposed live parts on one side of the working space and no live or grounded parts (including concrete, brick, or tile walls) on the other side of the working space.

Condition 2: Exposed live parts on one side of the working space and grounded parts on the other. Concrete, brick, tile, and similar surfaces are considered grounded.

Condition 3: Exposed live parts on both sides of the working space.

(a) Rear and Sides of Dead-Front Equipment. Working space is not required at the back or sides of equipment where all connections and renewable, adjustable, or serviceable parts are accessible from the front. ▶Figure 110–51

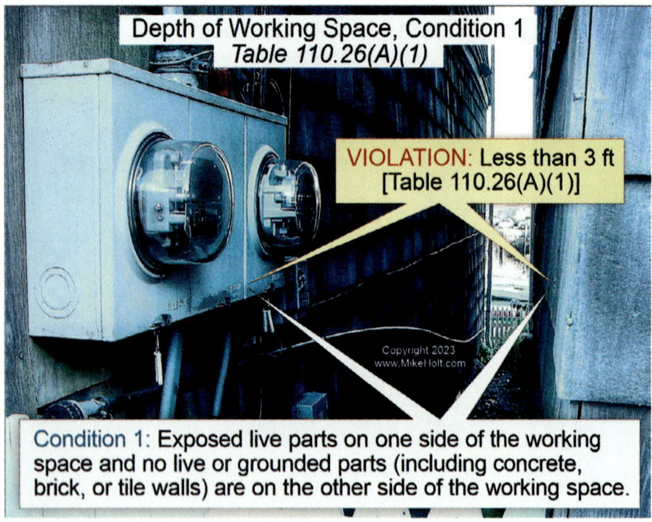

▶Figure 110–48

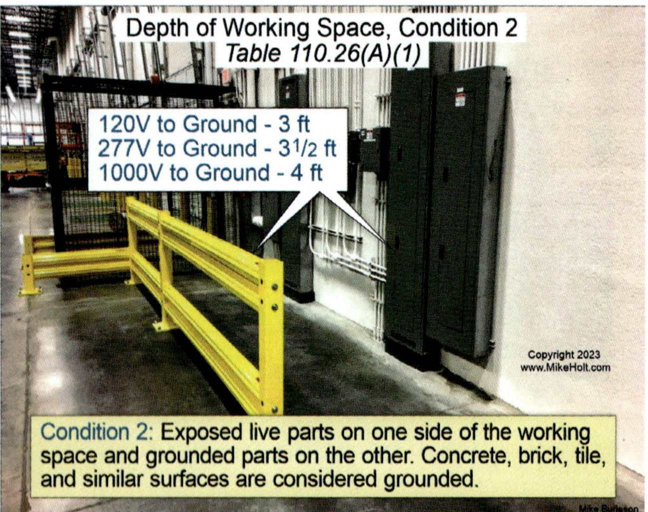

▶Figure 110–49

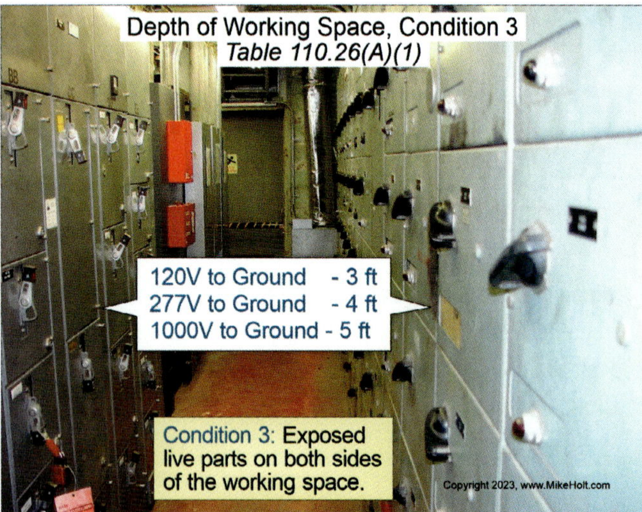

▶Figure 110–50

▶Figure 110–51

▸ Sections of equipment that require rear or side access to make field connections must be marked by the manufacturer on the front of the equipment. See 408.18(C).

(2) Width of Working Space. The width of the working space must be a minimum of 30 in., but in no case less than the width of the equipment.
▶Figure 110–52

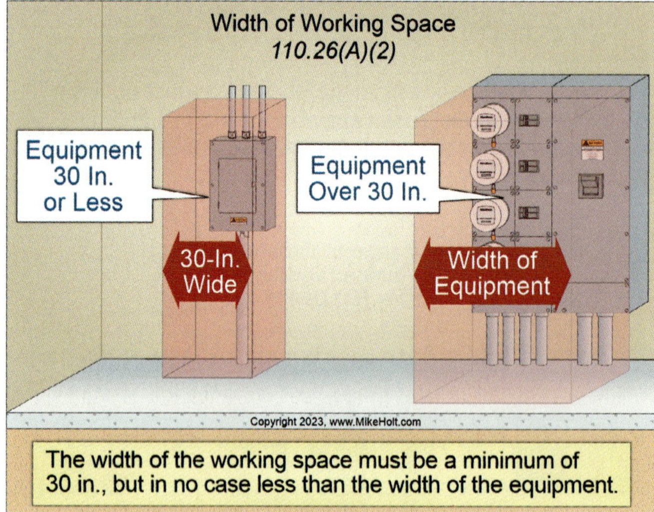

▶Figure 110–52

▸ The width of the working space can be measured from left-to-right, from right-to-left, or simply centered on the equipment. It can overlap the working space for other electrical equipment.
▶Figure 110–53 and ▶Figure 110–54

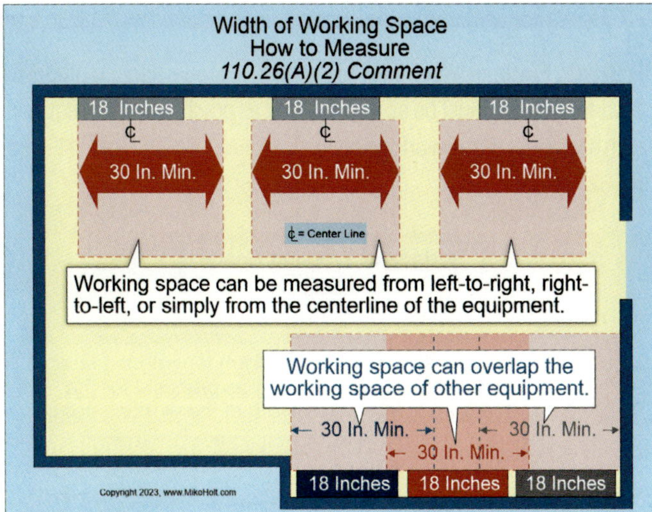

▶Figure 110–53

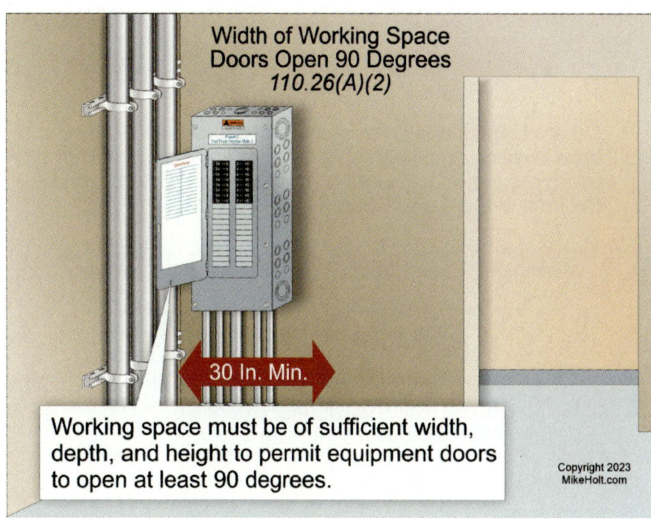

▶Figure 110–55

▶Figure 110–54

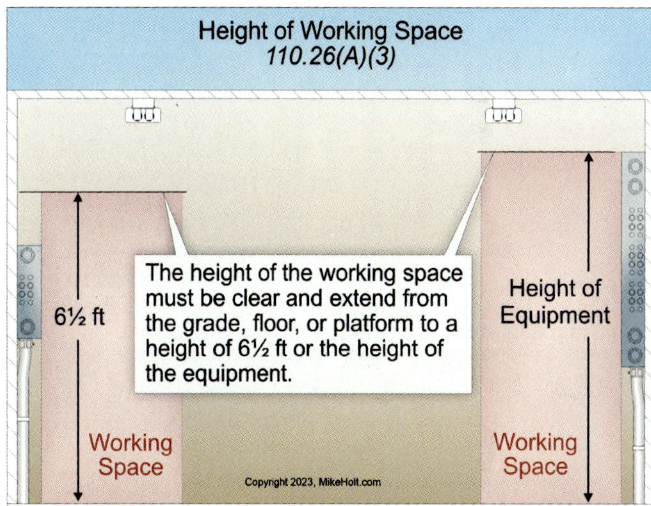

▶Figure 110–56

The working space must be of sufficient width, depth, and height to permit equipment doors to open at least 90 degrees. ▶Figure 110–55

(3) Height of Working Space. The height of the working space must be clear and extend from the grade, floor, or platform to a height of 6½ ft or the height of the equipment, whichever is greater. ▶Figure 110–56

Other equipment such as raceways, cables, wireways, transformers, or support structures (such as concrete pads) are not permitted to extend more than 6 in. into the working space in front of the electrical equipment. ▶Figure 110–57, ▶Figure 110–58, ▶Figure 110–59, and ▶Figure 110–60

Ex 2: The minimum height of working space does not apply to a service disconnect or panelboards rated 200A or less located in an existing dwelling unit.

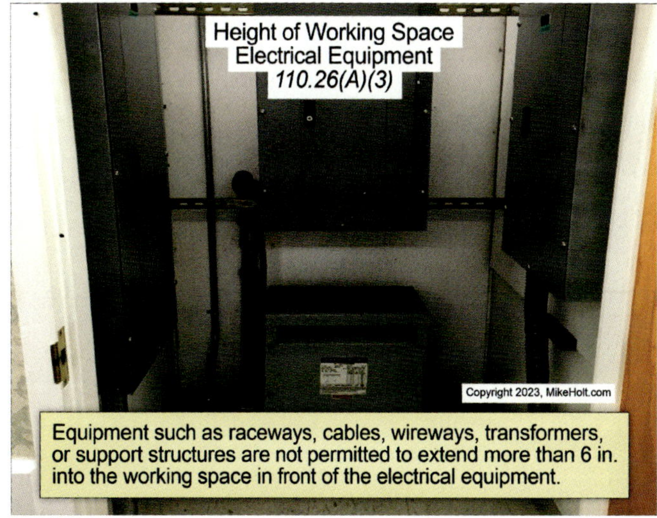

▶Figure 110–57

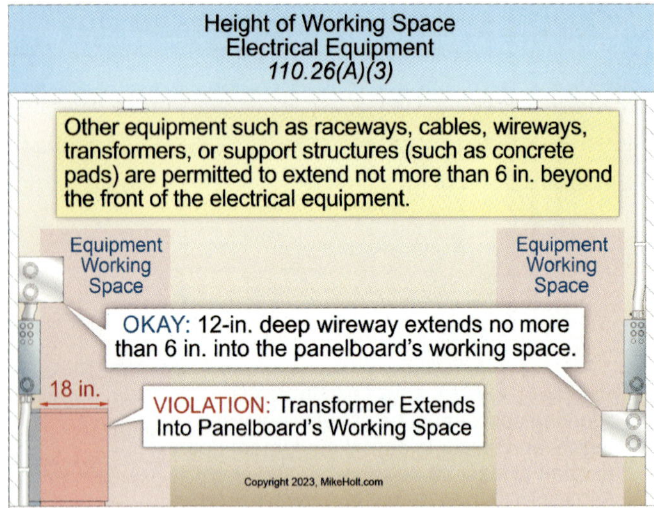

▶Figure 110–58

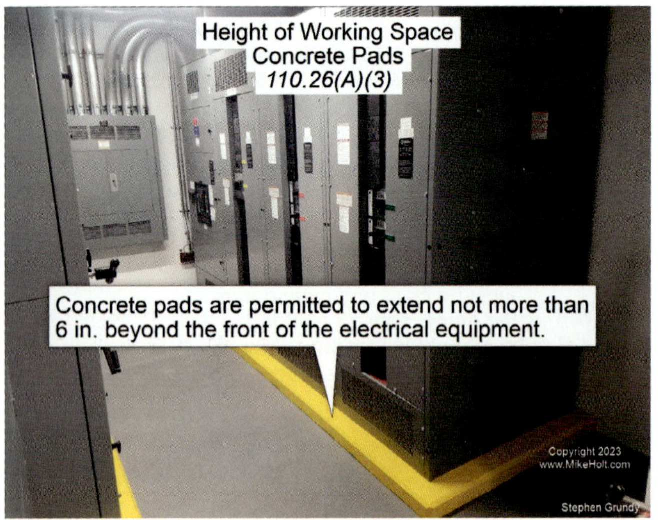

▶Figure 110–59

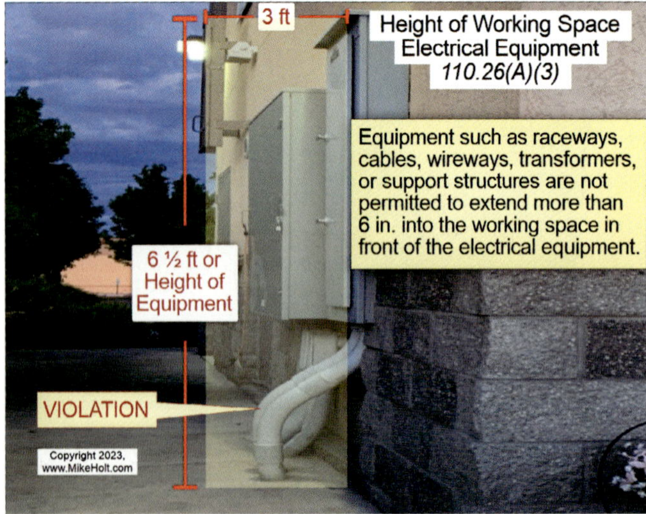

▶Figure 110–60

Ex 3: Meters are permitted to be installed in the required working space.

(6) Grade, Floor, or Working Platform. The grade, floor, or platform for working space must be as level and flat as practical for the required depth and width of the working space. ▶Figure 110–61 and ▶Figure 110–62

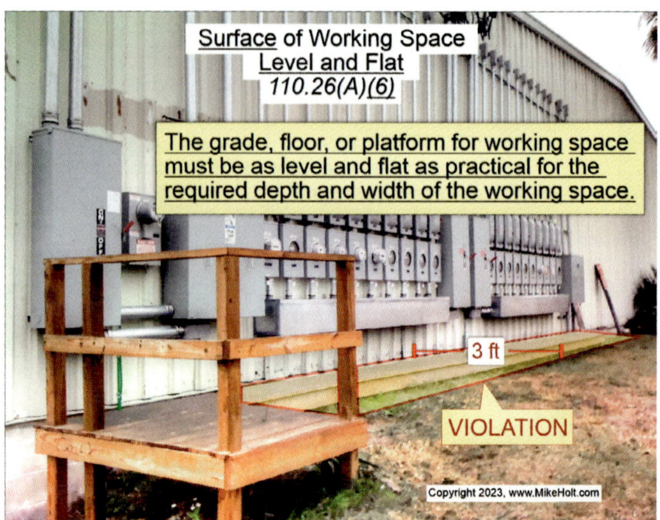

▶Figure 110–61

▶Figure 110–62

(B) Clear Working Space. The working space is not permitted to be used for storage. ▶Figure 110–63 and ▶Figure 110–64

> **Caution**
>
> **CAUTION:** It is very dangerous to service energized parts in the first place, and unacceptable to be subjected to additional dangers by working around bicycles, boxes, crates, appliances, and other impediments.

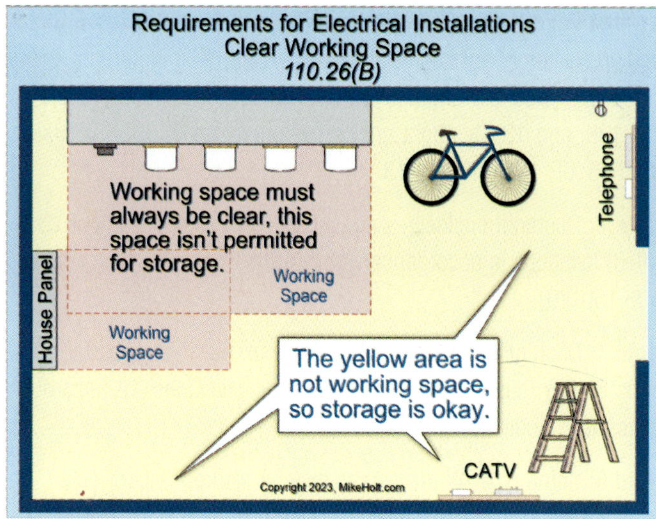

▶Figure 110–63

▶Figure 110–64

When live parts are exposed for inspection or servicing, the working space, if in a passageway or open space, must be suitably guarded.

According to Article 100, "Exposed (to live parts)" means capable of being inadvertently touched or approached nearer than a safe distance by a person. This term applies to parts that are not suitably guarded, isolated, or insulated.

Author's Comment:

▸ When working in a passageway and live parts are exposed for inspection or servicing, the working space should be guarded from use by occupants. In addition, one must be mindful of a fire alarm. If one occurs, many people will need to be evacuated and might congregate while moving through the area.

110.27 Protection Against Physical Damage

(B) Physical Damage. In locations where electrical equipment is likely to be exposed to physical damage, enclosures or guards must be arranged and of such strength as to prevent such damage. ▶Figure 110–65

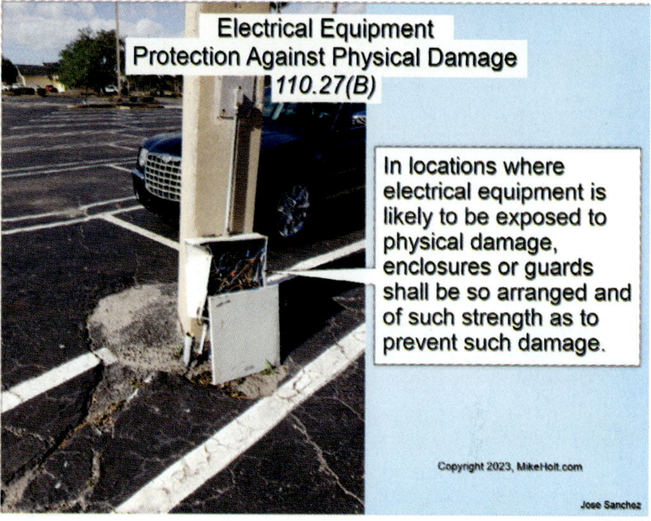

▶Figure 110–65

According to Article 100, "Exposed (as applied to wiring methods)" means on or attached to the surface of a building, or behind panels designed to allow access. ▶Figure 110–66

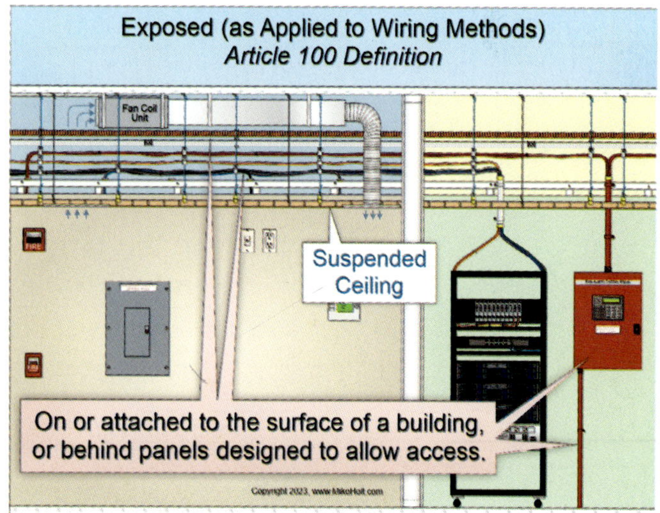

▶Figure 110–66

(C) Warning Signs. Electrical rooms must contain warning signs complying with 110.21(B) forbidding unqualified persons to enter.

110.28 NEMA Enclosure Types

Enclosures must be marked with an enclosure-type number and suitable for the location in accordance with Table 110.28. They are not intended to protect against condensation, icing, corrosion, or contamination that might occur within the enclosure or enters via a raceway or unsealed openings. ▶Figure 110–67

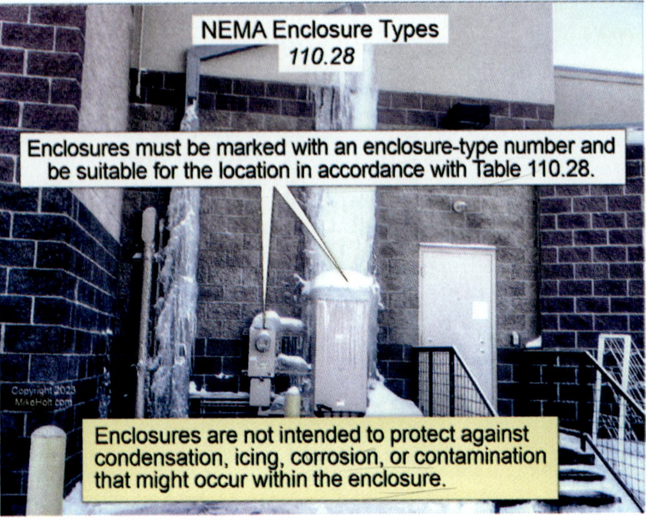

▶Figure 110–67

Note 1: Raintight enclosures include Types 3, 3S, 3SX, 3X, 4, 4X, 6, and 6P. Rainproof enclosures are Types 3R and 3RX. Watertight enclosures are Types 4, 4X, 6, and 6P. Driptight enclosures are Types 2, 5, 12, 12K, and 13. Dusttight enclosures are Types 3, 3S, 3SX, 3X, 4, 4X, 5, 6, 6P, 12, 12K, and 13.

Note 3: Dusttight enclosures are suitable for use in hazardous (classified) locations in accordance with 502.10(B)(4), 503.10(A)(2), and 506.15(C)(9).

Note 4: Dusttight enclosures are suitable for use in unclassified locations and in Class II, Division 2; Class III; and Zone 22 hazardous (classified) locations.

Note 5: Some type 4X enclosures may be marked "indoor only."

REVIEW QUESTIONS

Please use the 2023 *Code* book to answer the following questions.

Article 110—General Requirements for Electrical Installations

1. General requirements for the examination and approval, installation and use, access to and spaces about electrical conductors and equipment; enclosures intended for personnel entry; and tunnel installations are within the scope of ______.

   (a) Article 800
   (b) Article 300
   (c) Article 110
   (d) Annex J

2. The conductors and equipment required or permitted by this *Code* shall be acceptable only if ______.

   (a) labeled
   (b) listed
   (c) approved
   (d) identified

3. Equipment that is ______ or identified for a use shall be installed and used in accordance with any instructions included in the listing, labeling, or identification.

   (a) listed, labeled, or both
   (b) listed
   (c) marked
   (d) suitable

4. If the conductor material is not specified, the sizes given in the *Code* shall apply to ______ conductors.

   (a) aluminum
   (b) copper-clad aluminum
   (c) copper
   (d) all of these

5. Conductor sizes are expressed in American Wire Gauge (AWG) or in ______.

   (a) inches
   (b) circular mils
   (c) square inches
   (d) cubic inches

6. Only wiring methods recognized as ______ are included in this *Code*.

   (a) expensive
   (b) efficient
   (c) suitable
   (d) cost effective

7. Electrical equipment shall be installed ______.

   (a) in a professional and skillful manner
   (b) under the supervision of a licensed person
   (c) completely before being inspected
   (d) all of these

8. Unused openings, other than those intended for the operation of equipment, those intended for mounting purposes, or permitted as part of the design for listed equipment shall be ______.

   (a) filled with cable clamps or connectors only
   (b) taped over with electrical tape
   (c) repaired only by welding or brazing in a metal slug
   (d) closed to afford protection substantially equivalent to the wall of the equipment

9. Internal parts of electrical equipment, including busbars, wiring terminals, insulators, and other surfaces, shall not be damaged or contaminated by foreign materials such as _______, or corrosive residues.

   (a) paint, plaster
   (b) cleaners
   (c) abrasives
   (d) any of these

10. Pressure terminal or pressure splicing connectors and soldering lugs shall be _______ for the material of the conductor and shall be properly installed and used.

    (a) listed
    (b) approved
    (c) identified
    (d) all of these

11. Connectors and terminals for conductors more finely stranded than Class B and Class C, as shown in Chapter 9, Table 10, shall be _______ for the specific conductor class or classes.

    (a) listed
    (b) approved
    (c) identified
    (d) all of these

12. Conductors of dissimilar metals shall not be intermixed in a terminal or splicing connector where physical contact occurs between dissimilar conductors unless the device is _______ for the purpose and conditions of use.

    (a) identified
    (b) listed
    (c) approved
    (d) designed

13. Connection of conductors to terminal parts shall ensure a mechanically secure electrical connection without damaging the conductors and shall be made by means of _______.

    (a) solder lugs
    (b) pressure connectors
    (c) splices to flexible leads
    (d) any of these

14. All _______ shall be covered with an insulation equivalent to that of the conductors or with an identified insulating device.

    (a) splices
    (b) joints
    (c) free ends of conductors
    (d) all of these

15. Tightening torque values for terminal connections shall be as indicated on equipment or in installation instructions provided by the manufacturer. An approved means shall be used to achieve the _______ torque value.

    (a) indicated
    (b) identified
    (c) maximum
    (d) minimum

16. Examples of approved means of achieving the indicated _______ values include torque tools or devices such as shear bolts or breakaway-style devices with visual indicators that demonstrate that the proper torque has been applied.

    (a) pressure
    (b) torque
    (c) tightening
    (d) tension

17. Each disconnecting means shall be legibly marked to indicate its purpose unless located and arranged so _______.

    (a) that it can be locked out and tagged
    (b) it is not readily accessible
    (c) the purpose is evident
    (d) that it operates at less than 300 volts-to-ground

18. If a disconnecting means is required to be lockable open elsewhere in the *NEC*, it shall be capable of being locked in the open position. The provisions for locking shall remain in place with or without _______.

    (a) the power off
    (b) the lock installed
    (c) supervision
    (d) a lock-out tag

19. _____, and access to and egress from working space, shall be provided and maintained about all electrical equipment to permit ready and safe operation and maintenance of such equipment.

    (a) Ventilation
    (b) Unrestricted movement
    (c) Circulation
    (d) Working space

20. Access to or egress from the required working space about electrical equipment is considered impeded if one or more simultaneously opened equipment doors restrict working space access to be less than _____ wide and 6½ ft high.

    (a) 24 in.
    (b) 28 in.
    (c) 30 in.
    (d) 36 in.

21. Working space is required for equipment operating at 1,000V, nominal, or less to ground and likely to require _____ while energized.

    (a) examination
    (b) adjustment
    (c) servicing or maintenance
    (d) all of these

22. NFPA 70E, *Standard for Electrical Safety in the Workplace*, provides guidance, such as determining severity of potential exposure, planning safe work practices including establishing an electrically _____ work condition, arc-flash labeling, and selecting personal protective equipment.

    (a) safe
    (b) efficient
    (c) grounded
    (d) bonded

23. Working space is not required at the back or sides of equipment where all _____ and all renewable, adjustable, or serviceable parts are accessible from the front.

    (a) screws
    (b) connections
    (c) bolts
    (d) doors

24. Working space distances for enclosed live parts shall be measured from the _____ of equipment if the live parts are enclosed.

    (a) enclosure or opening
    (b) front or back
    (c) mounting pad
    (d) footprint

25. The minimum working space on a circuit for equipment operating at 120V to ground, with exposed live parts on one side and no live or grounded parts on the other side of the working space, is _____.

    (a) 1 ft
    (b) 3 ft
    (c) 4 ft
    (d) 6 ft

26. The required working space for access to live parts of equipment operating at 300V to ground, where there are exposed live parts on one side and grounded parts on the other side, is _____.

    (a) 3 ft
    (b) 3½ ft
    (c) 4 ft
    (d) 4½ ft

27. The required working space for access to live parts of equipment operating at 300V to ground, where there are exposed live parts on both sides of the workspace is _____.

    (a) 3 ft
    (b) 3½ ft
    (c) 4 ft
    (d) 4½ ft

28. The width of the working space shall be not be less than _____ wide, or the width of the equipment, whichever is greater.

    (a) 15 in.
    (b) 30 in.
    (c) 40 in.
    (d) 60 in.

29. The minimum height of working spaces shall be clear and extend from the grade, floor, or platform to a height of _______ ft or the height of the equipment, whichever is greater.

    (a) 3 ft
    (b) 6 ft
    (c) 6½ ft
    (d) 7 ft

30. The grade, floor, or platform in the required working space about electrical equipment shall be as level and flat as _______ for the entire required depth and width of the working space.

    (a) practical
    (b) possible
    (c) required
    (d) none of these

31. Working space required by Section 110.26 shall not be used for _______.

    (a) storage
    (b) raceways
    (c) lighting
    (d) accessibility

32. When normally enclosed live parts are exposed for inspection or servicing, the working space, if in a passageway or general open space, shall be suitably _______.

    (a) accessible
    (b) guarded
    (c) open
    (d) enclosed

33. A NEMA Type 1 enclosure is approved for the environmental condition where _______ might be present.

    (a) falling dirt
    (b) falling liquids
    (c) circulating dust
    (d) settling airborne dust

34. Enclosures of switchboards, switchgear, or panelboards that may become ice covered where exposed to sleet may be installed in a _______ enclosure.

    (a) Type 3 or 3R
    (b) Type 3X or RX
    (c) Type 3S or SX
    (d) Type 4 or 4X

35. Enclosure Type 3X for switchboards, switchgear, or panelboards located outdoors are suitable in locations subject to _______.

    (a) rain
    (b) windblown dust
    (c) corrosive agents
    (d) any of these

36. A Type 4X enclosure for switchboards, switchgear, or panelboards located indoors is suitable in locations subject to the environmental condition of _______.

    (a) falling dirt
    (b) falling liquids
    (c) corrosive agents
    (d) any of these

37. The term rainproof is typically used in conjunction with enclosure type(s) _______.

    (a) NEMA 3
    (b) NEMA 3R and 3RX
    (c) NEMA 4
    (d) NEMA 4R and 4RX

WIRING AND PROTECTION

Introduction to Chapter 2—Wiring and Protection

Chapter 2 of the *Code* is divided into eleven articles containing the general rules for wiring and sizing circuits, overcurrent protection of conductors, overvoltage protection of equipment, and bonding and grounding. The rules in this chapter apply to all electrical installations covered by the *NEC*—except as modified in Chapters 5, 6, 7, or specifically referenced in Chapter 8 [90.3].

This chapter can be thought of as the preconstruction phase of a job because it is primarily focused on layout, sizing, and the protection of circuits. Every article in this chapter deals with a different aspect of designing safe wiring for an electrical system. The Chapter 2 articles covered by this material are:

- **Article 200—Use and Identification of Neutral and Grounded-Phase Conductors.** This article has one part containing the requirements for the use and identification of the grounded conductor—which in most cases is the neutral conductor.

- **Article 210—Branch Circuits.** Article 210 is comprised of three parts which contain requirements for the installation, sizing, and protection of branch circuits. General rules are found in Part I and include topics such as conductor sizing, identification, and AFCI and GFCI protection. Parts II and III contain the requirements for branch circuits and required outlets.

- **Article 250—Bonding and Grounding.** Article 250 covers the grounding requirements for providing a path to the Earth to reduce overvoltage from lightning, and the bonding requirements for the low-impedance fault current path necessary to facilitate the operation of overcurrent protective devices in the event of a ground fault.

USE AND IDENTIFICATION OF GROUNDED CONDUCTORS

Introduction to Article 200—Use and Identification of Grounded Conductors

Article 200 contains the requirements for the use and identification of grounded conductors and their terminals. This article has eleven sections covering the requirements for neutral conductors and grounded-phase conductors. Take some time to review electrical theory before you try to attack this article, you must understand how current flow is essential for these rules to make sense. Some topics covered in this material for Article 200 include:

▸ Grounded system connections

▸ Conductor identification

▸ Equipment terminal identification

According to Article 100, "Grounded Conductor" is the circuit conductor that is intentionally connected to the Earth (ground). ▸Figure 200–1

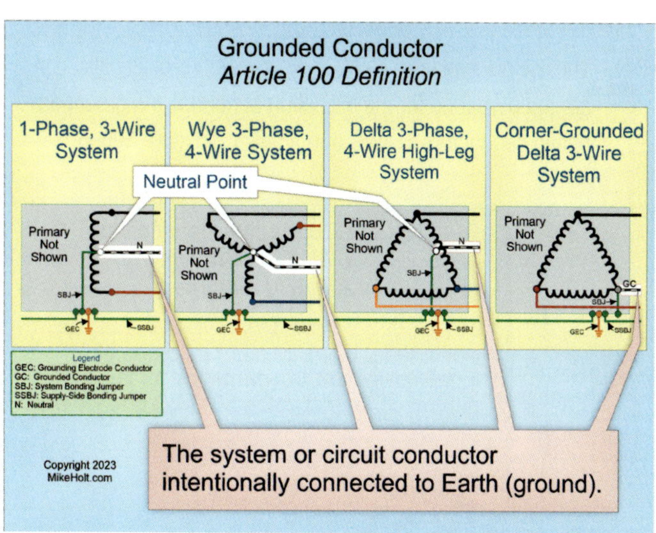

▸Figure 200–1

According to Article 100, "Neutral Conductor" is the conductor connected to the neutral point of a system that is intended to carry current under normal conditions. ▸Figure 200–2

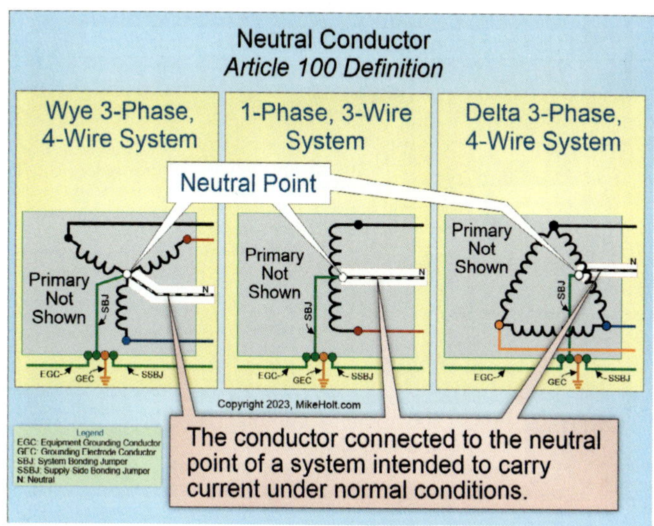

▸Figure 200–2

According to Article 100, "Neutral Point" is the common point of a 4-wire, three-phase, wye-connected system; the midpoint of a 3-wire, single-phase system; or the midpoint of the single-phase portion of a three-phase, delta-connected system. ▸Figure 200–3

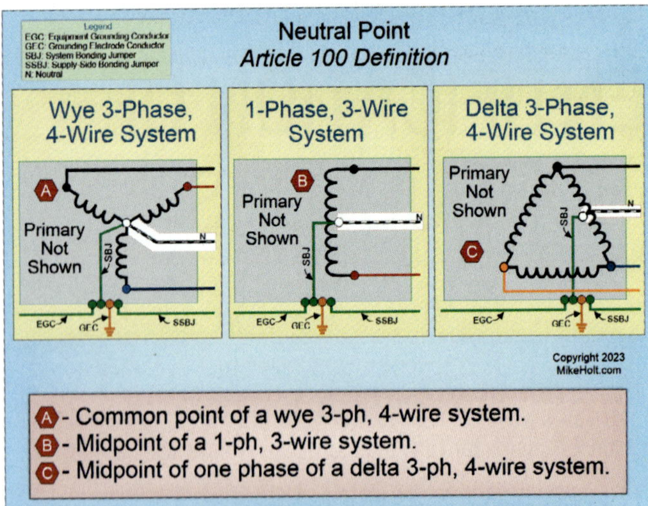

▶Figure 200–3

200.1 Scope

Article 200 contains the requirements for the use and identification of grounded conductors and terminals. ▶Figure 200–4

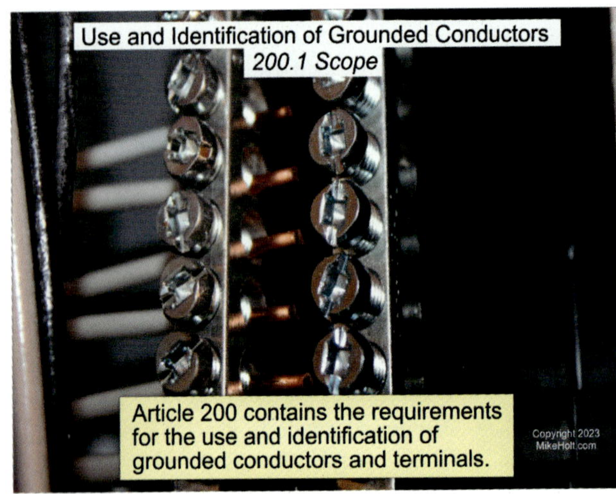

▶Figure 200–4

200.6 Identification of Neutral and Grounded Conductors

(A) 6 AWG or Smaller. The insulation of neutral and grounded-phase conductors 6 AWG and smaller must be identified by any of the following means: ▶Figure 200–5

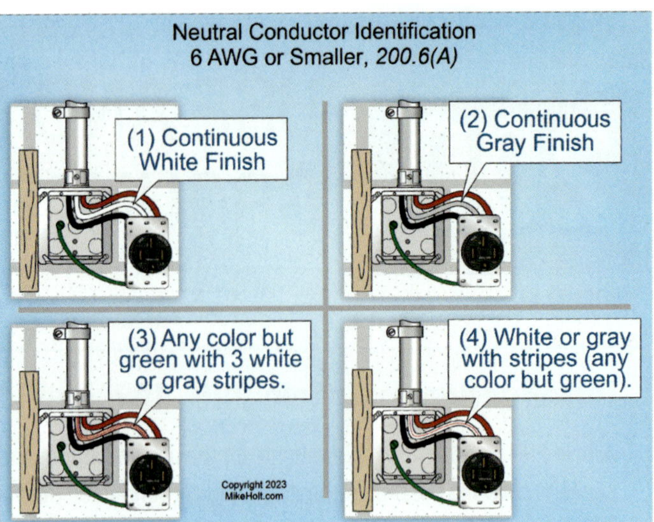

▶Figure 200–5

(1) A continuous white outer finish.

(2) A continuous gray outer finish.

(3) Three continuous white or gray stripes along their entire length on other than green insulated conductor.

(4) An outer covering of a white or gray color with colored tracer threads in the braid identifying the source of manufacture.

> **Author's Comment:**
>
> ▶ The use of white tape, paint, or other methods of identification are not permitted for the insulation of neutral and grounded-phase conductors 6 AWG and smaller. ▶Figure 200–6

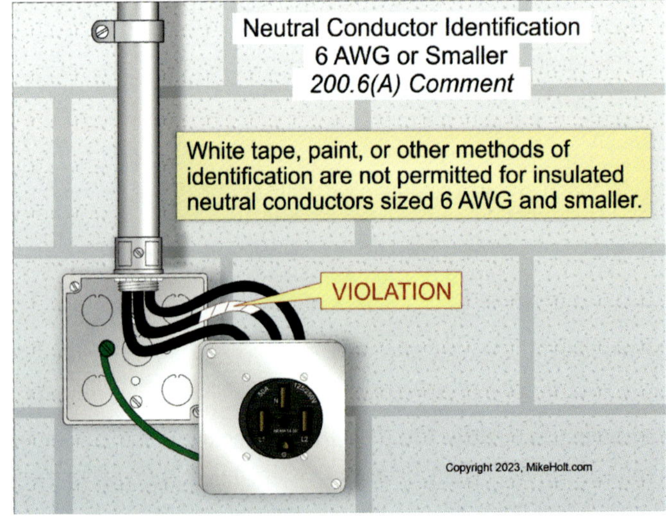

▶Figure 200–6

(B) 4 AWG or Larger. Insulated neutral and grounded-phase conductors 4 AWG or larger must be identified by any of the following means: ▶Figure 200–7

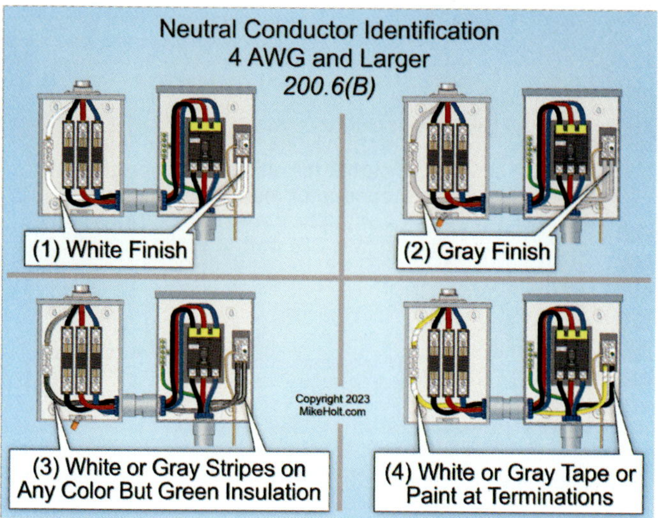

▶Figure 200–7

(1) A continuous white outer finish along the conductor's length.

(2) A continuous gray outer finish along the conductor's length.

(3) Three continuous white or gray stripes along the conductor's entire length on other than green insulation.

(4) The application of identified markings of white or gray at its terminals at the time of installation. The white or gray marking must encircle the conductor insulation.

200.7 Use of White or Gray Color

(A) General. The following insulated conductors can only be used for the neutral or grounded-phase conductor except as permitted in 200.7(C).

(1) A conductor with a continuous white or gray covering.

(2) A conductor with three continuous white or gray stripes.

(3) A marking of a white or gray color at the termination.

(C) Reidentification of Neutral Conductor in Cables. A conductor with white or gray insulation used as a phase conductor is permitted in the following:

(1) Cable Assembly. The white or gray conductor within a cable can be used for the phase conductor if the white conductor is permanently reidentified as a phase conductor by marking tape, painting, or other effective means where the conductor is visible. Identification must encircle the insulation and must be a color other than white, gray, or green. ▶Figure 200–8

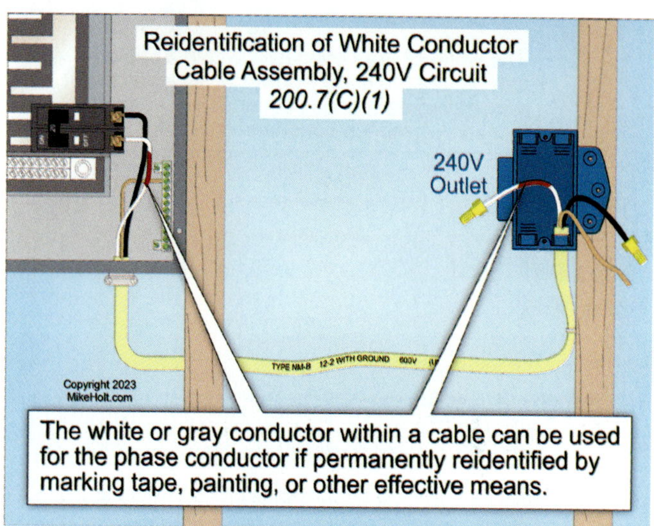

▶Figure 200–8

The white or gray conductor within a cable can be used to supply power to switches if the conductor is reidentified as a phase conductor by marking tape, painting, or other effective means where the conductor is visible. ▶Figure 200–9 and ▶Figure 200–10

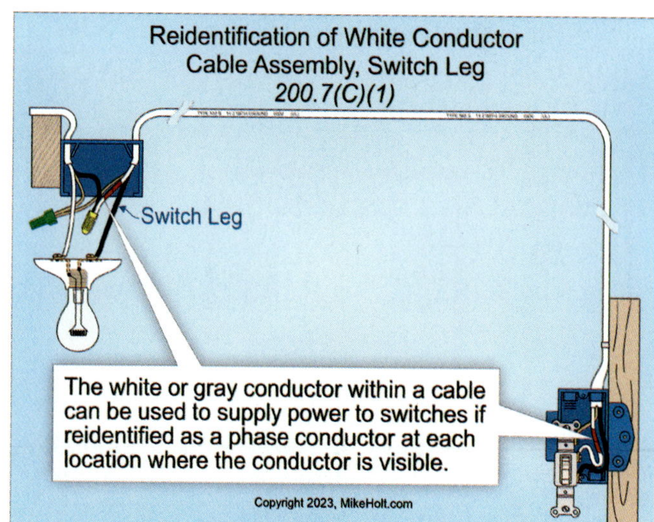

▶Figure 200–9

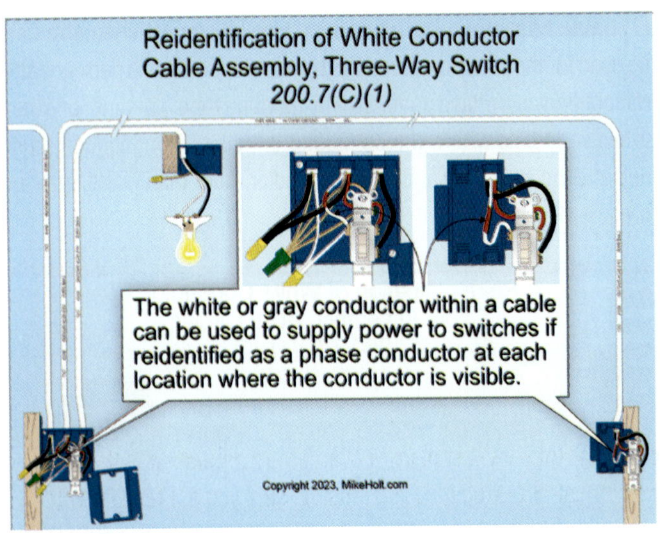

▶Figure 200–10

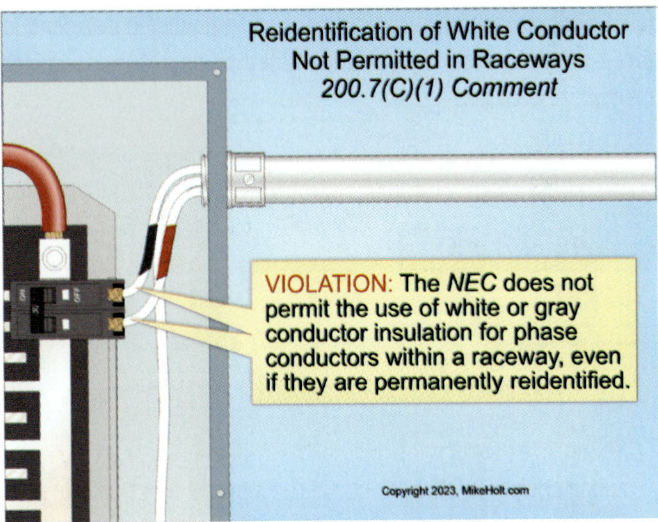

▶Figure 200–11

Author's Comment:

▶ The *NEC* does not permit the use of white or gray conductor insulation for phase conductors within a raceway, even if they are permanently reidentified. ▶Figure 200–11

BRANCH CIRCUITS

Introduction to Article 210—Branch Circuits

This article contains the general requirements for branch circuits which extend from the last point of overcurrent protection to the utilization equipment. Branch circuits account for most circuits run in any electrical installation, so you must be sure you are familiar with these rules. Some topics covered in this material for Article 210 include:

▸ GFCI and AFCI requirements

▸ Branch-circuit ratings

▸ Receptacle and lighting outlet requirements

Part I. General Provisions

210.1 Scope

Article 210 provides the general requirements for branch circuits not over 1000V ac or 1500V dc, such as conductor sizing, overcurrent protection, identification, GFCI and AFCI protection, as well as receptacle outlet and lighting outlet requirements. ▸Figure 210–1

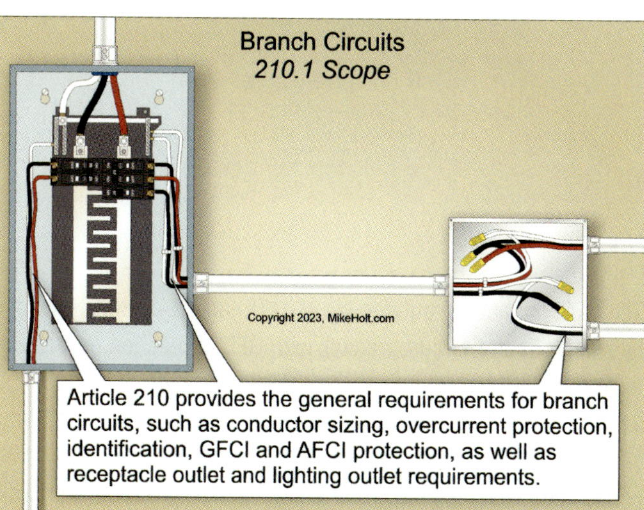

▸Figure 210–1

According to Article 100, "Branch Circuit" consists of the conductors between the final overcurrent protective device and the receptacle outlets, lighting outlets, or other outlets. ▸Figure 210–2

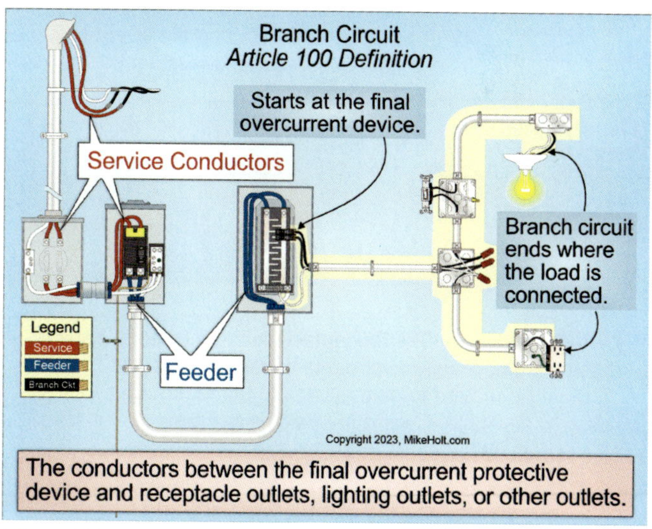

▸Figure 210–2

210.8 GFCI Protection

A GFCI device must provide protection as required in 210.8(A) through (F).
▶Figure 210–3

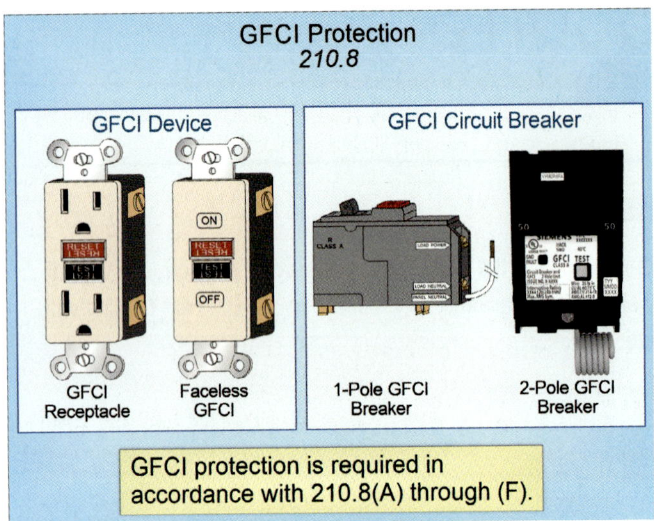

▶Figure 210–3

GFCI protective devices must be in a readily accessible location. ▶Figure 210–4

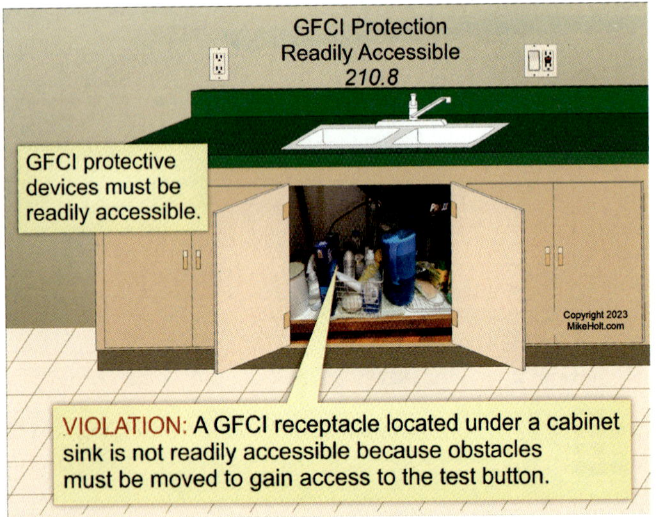

▶Figure 210–4

According to Article 100, "GFCI" is a device intended to protect people by de-energizing a circuit when ground-fault current exceeds the value established for "Class" A device. ▶Figure 210–5

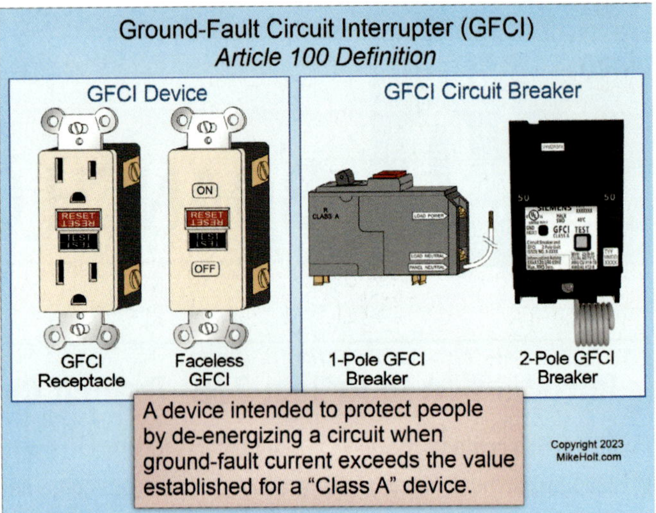

▶Figure 210–5

According to Article 100, "Readily Accessible" means capable of being reached quickly for operation, renewal, or inspection without requiring the use tools (other than keys), climb over or under obstructions, remove obstacles, resort to using portable ladders, and so forth.
▶Figure 210–6 and ▶Figure 210–7

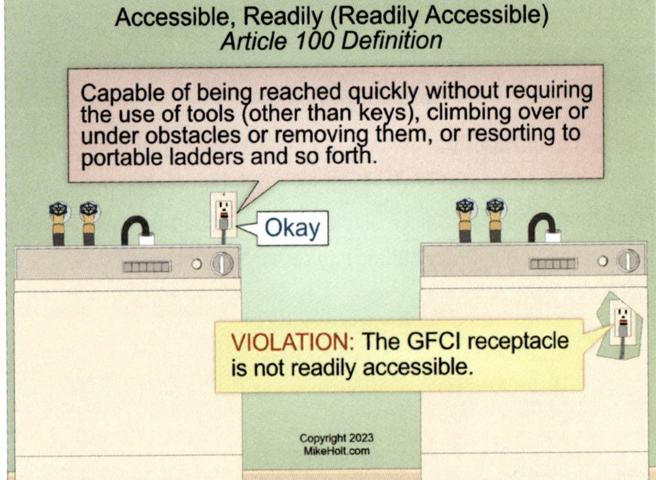

▶Figure 210–6

The GFCI protection required by 210.8(A) and (B) can be provided by using either a circuit breaker with GFCI protection or a receptacle with GFCI protection. For the application of 210.8(A)(8) or (10), 210.8(B)(7), (13), and (15), the distance from the sink or bathtub/shower is measured as the shortest path the power-supply cord connected to the receptacle will follow without piercing a floor, wall, ceiling, or fixed barrier. ▶Figure 210–8

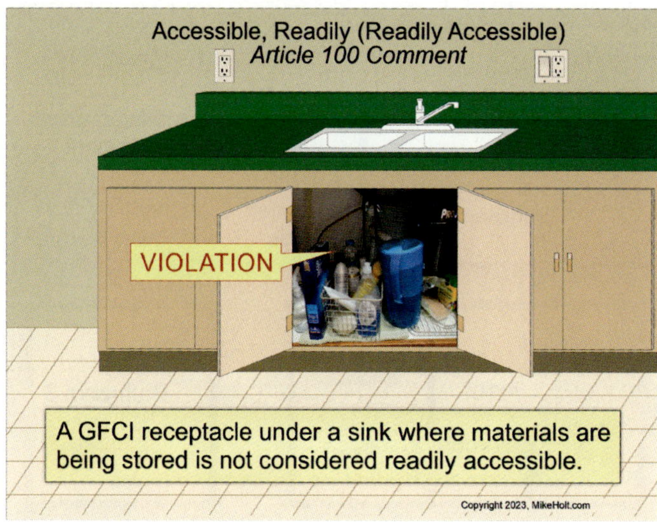

A GFCI receptacle under a sink where materials are being stored is not considered readily accessible.

▶Figure 210–7

For the application of 210.8, the distance is measured as the shortest path the <u>power</u>-supply cord connected to the receptacle will follow without piercing a floor, wall, ceiling, or fixed barrier.

▶Figure 210–8

Author's Comment:

▶ The reference to windows and doors was removed to ensure receptacles within the measured distance as required in 210.8, even if passing through a window or door, are afforded GFCI protection.

▶ The GFCI circuit breaker provides ground-fault protection starting at the breaker, so the entire circuit has ground-fault protection. A GFCI receptacle provides ground-fault protection for whatever is plugged into it and has load-side terminals that provide downstream protection for any other receptacle(s) or device(s) on the circuit. ▶**Figure 210–9**

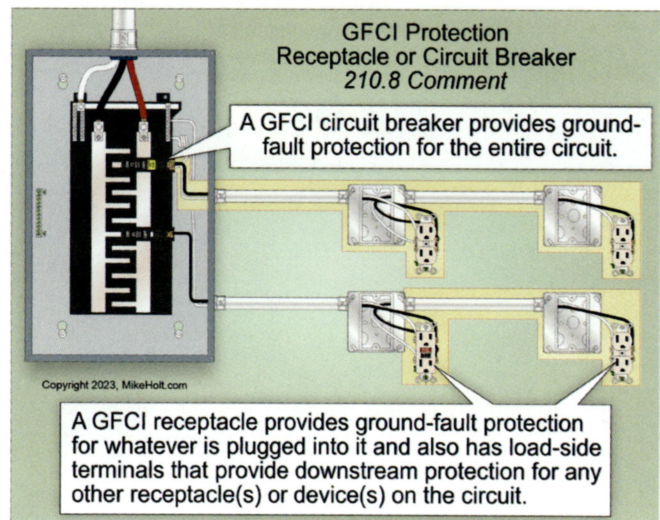

A GFCI receptacle provides ground-fault protection for whatever is plugged into it and also has load-side terminals that provide downstream protection for any other receptacle(s) or device(s) on the circuit.

▶Figure 210–9

(A) Dwelling Units. Receptacles installed in the following dwelling unit locations must be GFCI protected. ▶Figure 210–10

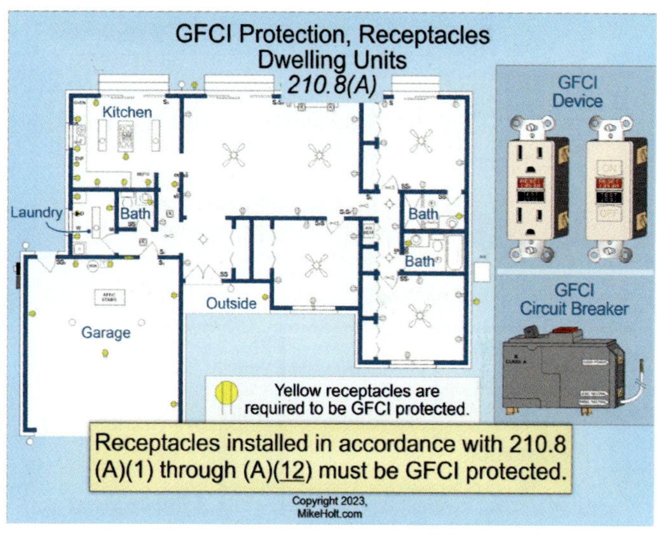

▶Figure 210–10

According to Article 100, "Dwelling Unit" is a single unit that provides independent living facilities with permanent provisions for living, sleeping, cooking, and sanitation. ▶Figure 210–11

▶Figure 210–11

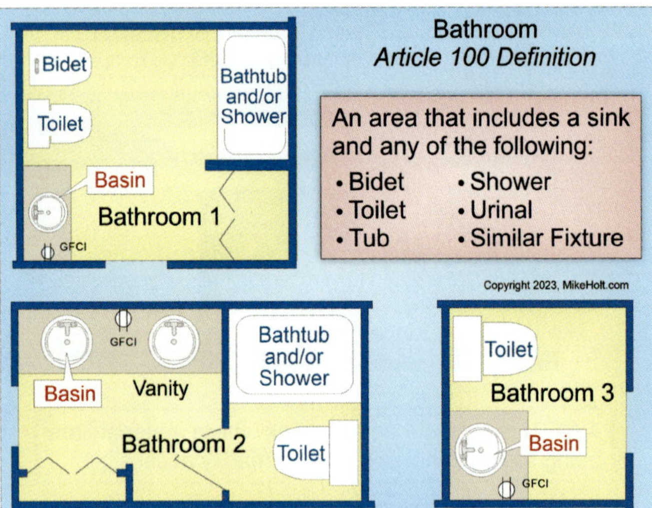

▶Figure 210–13

(1) Bathrooms. GFCI protection is required for receptacles in dwelling unit bathroom areas. ▶Figure 210–12

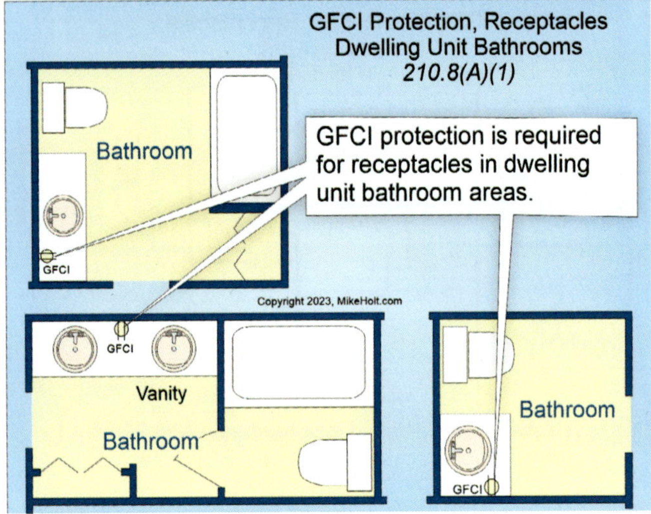

▶Figure 210–12

According to Article 100, "Bathroom Area" is an area that includes a sink (basin) and one or more of the following: toilet, urinal, tub, shower, bidet, or similar plumbing fixture. ▶Figure 210–13

(2) Garages and Accessory Buildings. GFCI protection is required for receptacles in dwelling unit garages and dwelling unit accessory buildings. These buildings are not intended as habitable rooms and limited to storage, work, and other areas of similar use. ▶Figure 210–14

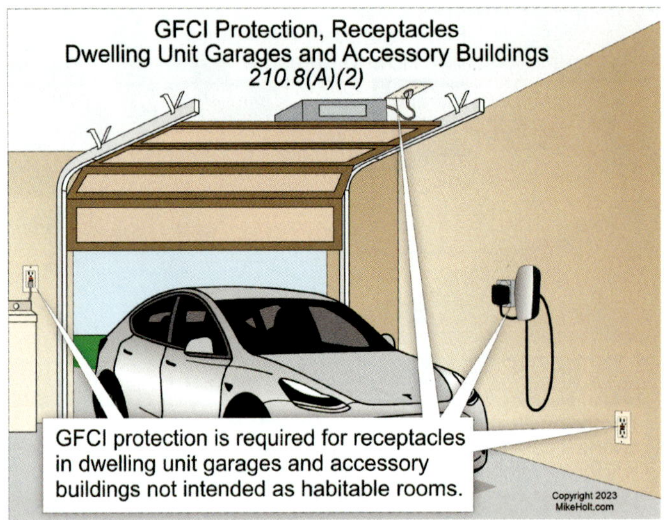

▶Figure 210–14

Author's Comment:

▶ All receptacles installed for the connection of electric vehicle supply equipment must be GFCI protected. ▶Figure 210–15

(3) Outdoors. GFCI protection is required for receptacles located outdoors of a dwelling unit. ▶Figure 210–16

(4) Crawl Spaces. GFCI protection is required for receptacles in dwelling unit crawl spaces at or below grade. ▶Figure 210–17

(5) Basements. GFCI protection is required for receptacles in dwelling unit basements. ▶Figure 210–18

(6) Kitchens. GFCI protection is required for receptacles in dwelling unit kitchens. ▶Figure 210–19

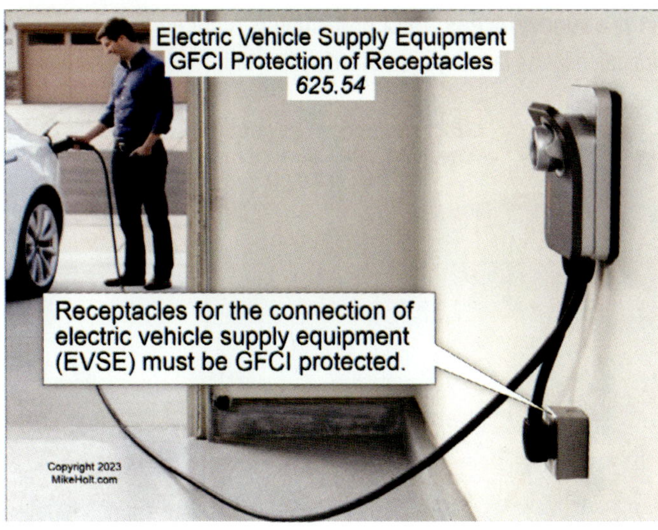

▶Figure 210–15

▶Figure 210–16

▶Figure 210–17

▶Figure 210–18

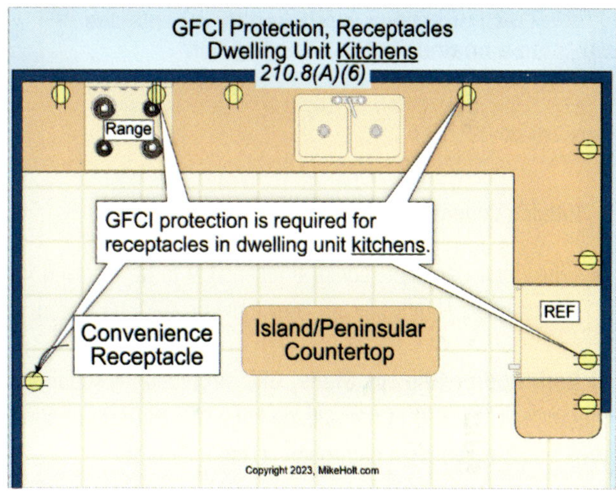

▶Figure 210–19

According to Article 100, "Kitchen" is an area with a sink and permanent provisions for food preparation and cooking.

Author's Comment:

▸ Traditionally this requirement only applied to kitchen countertop receptacles, but now any cord-and-plug-connected appliance in the kitchen such as the range receptacle, refrigerator receptacle, disposal receptacle, and microwave receptacle will require GFCI protection.

(7) Food Preparation Areas. GFCI protection is required for receptacles in areas with sinks with permanent provisions for food preparation, beverage preparation, or cooking.

(8) Sinks. GFCI protection is required for receptacles within 6 ft of the top inside edge of the bowl of a dwelling unit sink.

(9) Boathouses. GFCI protection is required for receptacles in a boathouse for a dwelling unit. ▶Figure 210–20

▶Figure 210–20

Author's Comment:

▶ The *Code* does not require a receptacle to be installed in a boathouse, but if any are, they must be GFCI protected.

(10) Bathtubs or Shower Stalls. GFCI protection is required for receptacles within 6 ft of the outside edge of a bathtub or shower stall not installed within a bathroom. ▶Figure 210–21

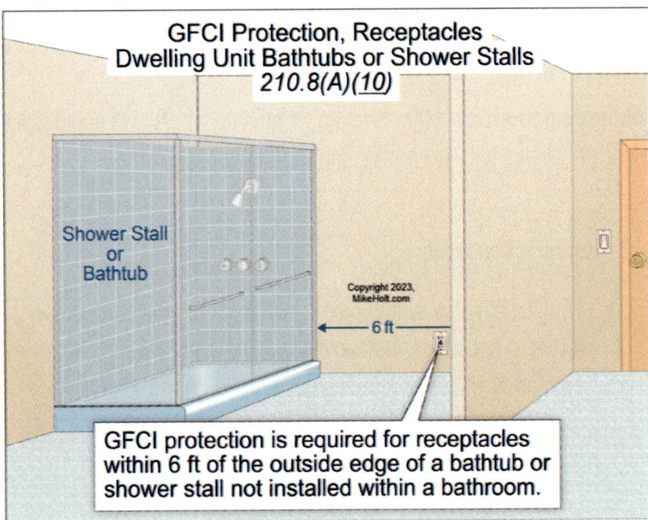

▶Figure 210–21

(11) Laundry Areas. GFCI protection is required for receptacles installed in the laundry area of a dwelling unit. ▶Figure 210–22

▶Figure 210–22

(12) Damp and Wet Locations Indoors. GFCI protection is required for receptacles installed in indoor damp and wet locations.

Ex 1: GFCI protection is not required for a receptacle dedicated to fixed electric snow-melting equipment if the receptacle is not readily accessible and ground-fault protection of equipment (GFPE) is provided as required by 426.28 and 427.22. ▶Figure 210–23

▶Figure 210–23

Ex 2: A receptacle supplying only a permanently installed premises security system is permitted to omit GFCI protection.

Ex 4: GFCI protection is not required for receptacles in dwelling unit bathroom exhaust fans, unless specified by the fan instructions. ▶Figure 210–24

▶Figure 210–24

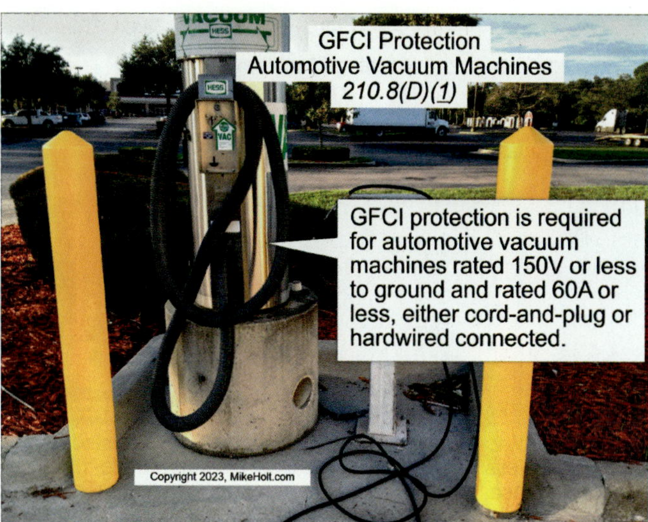

▶Figure 210–25

Author's Comment:

▶ The receptacle for exhaust fans is internal to the exhaust fan. They are not accessible as a convenience cord-and-plug receptacle, therefore GFCI protection is not required.

▶ In accordance with "*UL Guide Information GPWX*," exhaust fans installed in the area directly above the footprint (width and depth of the equipment) of the bathtub or shower must be GFCI protected.

(C) Crawl Space Lighting Outlets. GFCI protection is required for 120V lighting outlets in crawl spaces.

Author's Comment:

▶ A lighting outlet is not required for a dwelling unit crawl space unless the space is used for storage or has equipment requiring servicing [210.70(C)].

(D) Specific Appliance. GFCI protection is required for the following appliances rated 150V or less to ground, rated 60A or less, single- or three-phase, either cord-and-plug or hardwired connected:

(1) Automotive vacuum machines. ▶Figure 210–25

(2) Drinking water coolers and bottle fill stations. ▶Figure 210–26

(3) High-pressure spray washing machines.

(4) Tire inflation machines. ▶Figure 210–27

(5) Vending machines. ▶Figure 210–28

(6) Sump pumps. ▶Figure 210–29

▶Figure 210–26

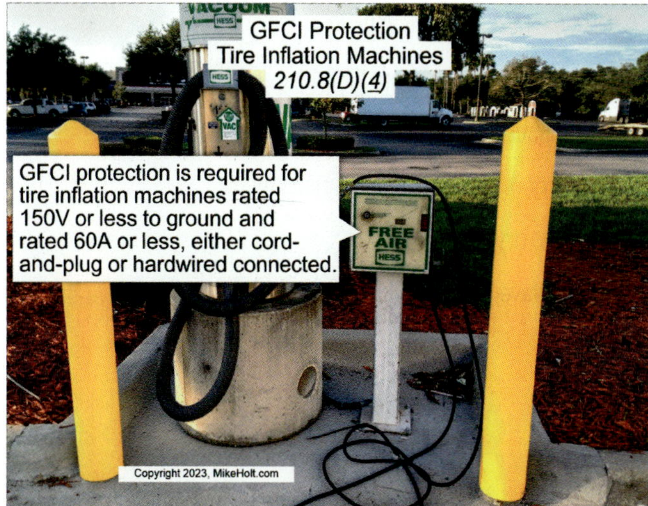

▶Figure 210–27

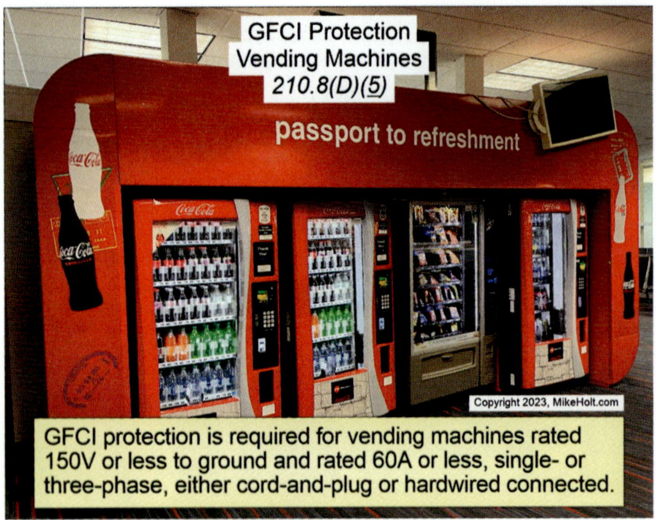

GFCI protection is required for vending machines rated 150V or less to ground and rated 60A or less, single- or three-phase, either cord-and-plug or hardwired connected.

▶Figure 210–28

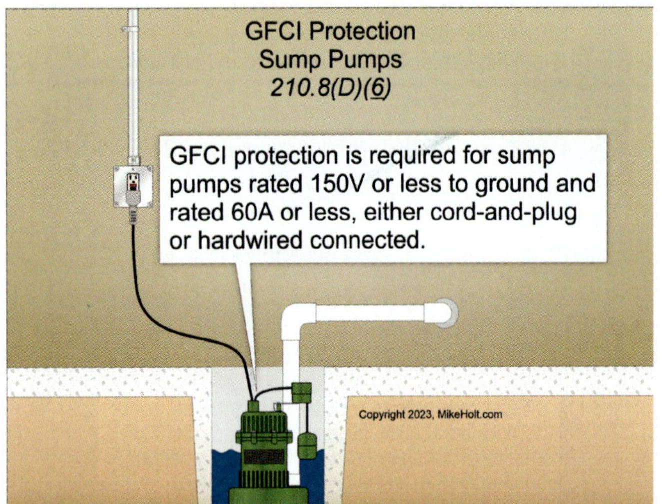

▶Figure 210–29

(7) Dishwashers ▶Figure 210–30

(8) Electric ranges. ▶Figure 210–31

(9) Wall-mounted electric ovens.

(10) Counter-mounted electric cooking units.

(11) Clothes dryers.

(12) Microwave ovens.

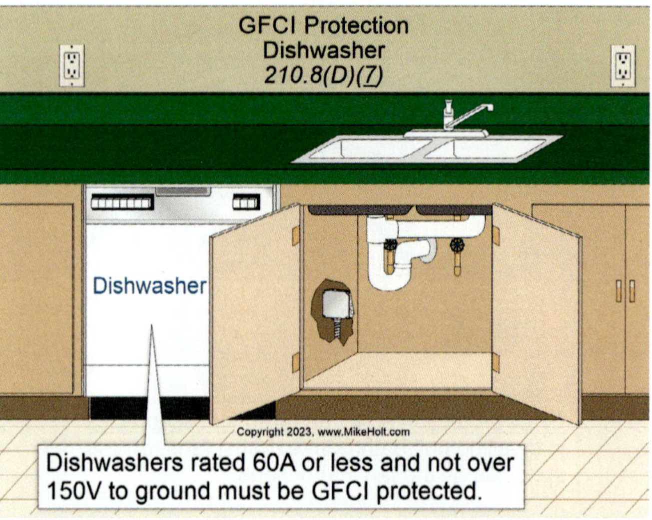

Dishwashers rated 60A or less and not over 150V to ground must be GFCI protected.

▶Figure 210–30

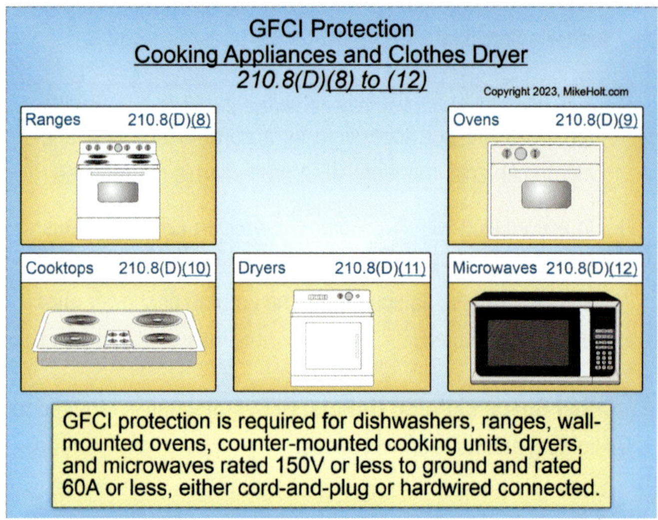

GFCI protection is required for dishwashers, ranges, wall-mounted ovens, counter-mounted cooking units, dryers, and microwaves rated 150V or less to ground and rated 60A or less, either cord-and-plug or hardwired connected.

▶Figure 210–31

Author's Comment:

▶ The appliances in list items 210.8(D)(8) through (12) are commonly installed as hardwired outlets, and the GFCI protection requirements of 210.8(A) and (B) only apply to receptacles. The shock hazards exist whether appliances are hardwired or cord-and-plug connected, and therefore GFCI protection must be provided for the appliance branch circuit or outlet.

(F) Outdoor Dwelling Outlets. GFCI protection is required for all outlets rated 50A or less located outside the following dwelling spaces: ▶Figure 210–32

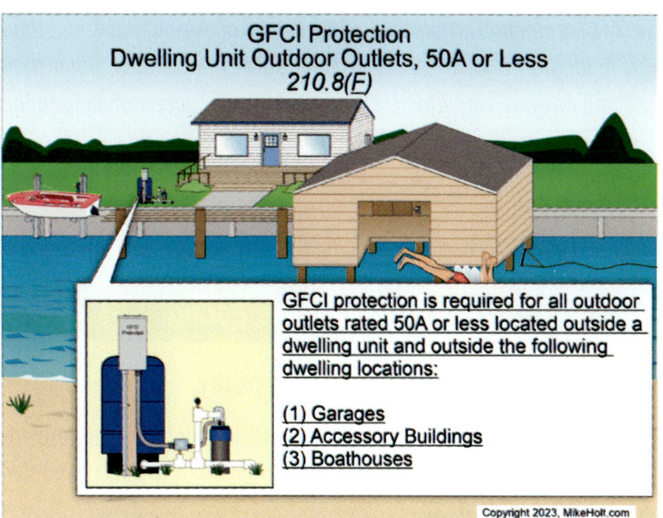

▶Figure 210–32

(1) Garages

(2) Accessory Buildings

(3) Boathouses

According to Article 100, "Outlet" is a point on the wiring system at which current is taken to supply utilization equipment. ▶Figure 210–33

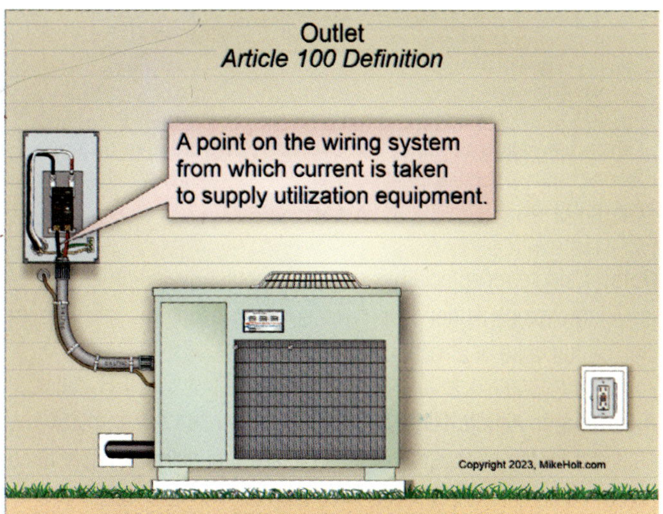

▶Figure 210–33

If equipment connected to any of the above outlets is replaced, the circuit to the outlet must be GFCI protected.

Ex 2: GFCI protection is not required for listed HVAC equipment, such as motor compressors or heat pumps. ▶Figure 210–34

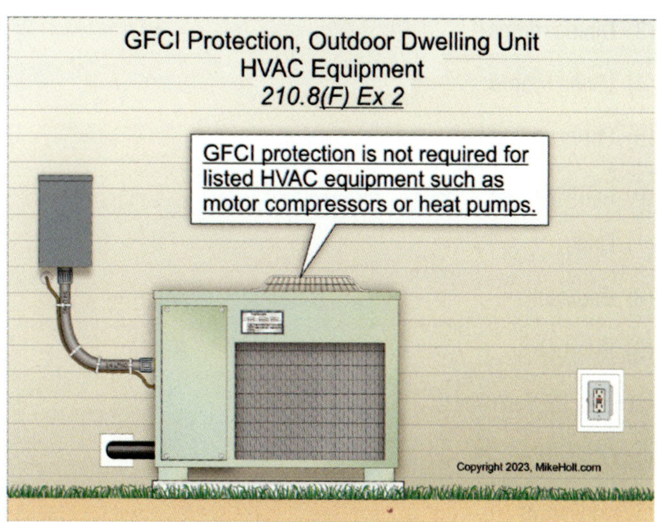

▶Figure 210–34

210.12 Arc-Fault Circuit-Interrupter Protection

AFCI protection is required in accordance with 210.12(B) through (C) and must be in a readily accessible location.

According to Article 100, "Arc-Fault Circuit Interrupter (AFCI)" is a device intended to de-energize the circuit when it detects the current waveform characteristics unique to an arcing fault. ▶Figure 210–35

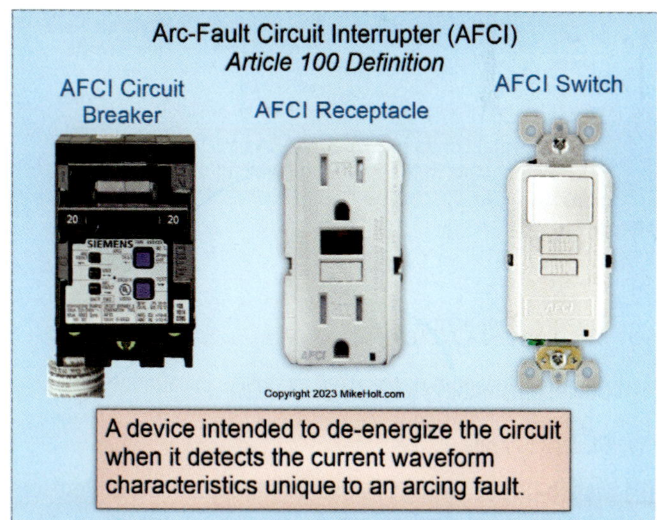

▶Figure 210–35

(B) Dwelling Units. AFCI protection is required for 15A or 20A, 120V branch circuits in the following dwelling unit locations:

(1) Kitchens

(2) Family rooms

(3) Dining rooms

(4) Living rooms

(5) Parlors

(6) Libraries

(7) Dens

(8) Bedrooms

(9) Sunrooms

(10) Recreation rooms

(11) Closets

(12) Hallways

(13) Laundry areas

(14) Similar areas ▶Figure 210–36

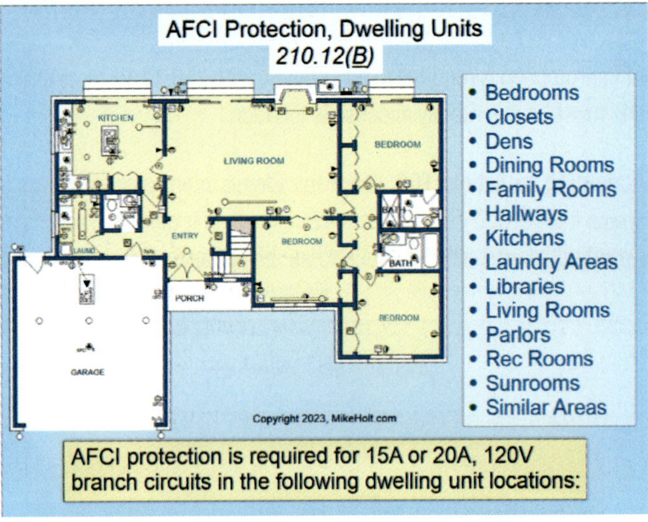

▶Figure 210–36

Author's Comment:

▶ AFCI protection is not required for outlets in bathroom areas, garages, or outside.

(E) Branch-Circuit Wiring Extensions, Modifications, or Replacements.

If 15A or 20A, 120V branch-circuit wiring is extended, modified, or replaced in any of the areas specified in 210.12(B), (C), or (D), the wiring must be AFCI protected by one of the following:

(1) AFCI circuit breaker

(2) AFCI receptacle installed at the first receptacle outlet of the existing branch circuit

Ex: AFCI protection is not required for extension wiring that is less than 6 ft in length (raceway or cable) if no outlets or devices, other than splicing devices, are added. This measurement does not include the conductors inside an enclosure, cabinet, or junction box.

Part II. Branch-Circuit Ratings

210.21 Receptacle Rating

(B) Receptacles—Rating and Load Capacity.

(1) Single Receptacle. A single receptacle must have an ampere rating no less than the rating of the circuit overcurrent protective device. ▶Figure 210–37

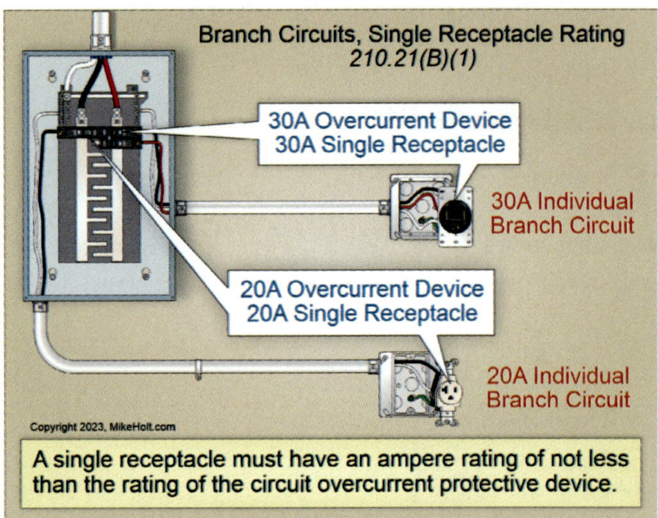

▶Figure 210–37

Note: A single receptacle has only one contact device on its yoke. A duplex receptacle is not a single receptacle since it has two receptacles on the yoke of a receptacle.

According to Article 100, "Receptacle" is a contact device installed at an outlet for the connection of an attachment plug, or for the connection of equipment designed to mate with the contact device.

(2) Total Cord-and-Plug-Connected Load. Where connected to a branch circuit supplying two or more receptacles or outlets, a receptacle is not permitted to supply a total cord-and-plug-connected load in excess of the maximum specified in Table 210.21(B)(2).

Table 210.21(B)(2) Maximum Cord-and-Plug-Connected Load to Receptacle

Circuit Rating (Amperes)	Receptacle Rating (Amperes)	Maximum Load (Amperes)
15 or 20	15	12
20	20	16
30	30	24

(3) Multiple Receptacles. Where multiple receptacles are connected to a branch circuit, their ampere ratings must be in accordance with Table 210.21(B)(3).

Author's Comment:

▸ Table 210.21(B)(3) permits both 15A and 20A receptacles on a 20A multioutlet circuit. ▸Figure 210–38

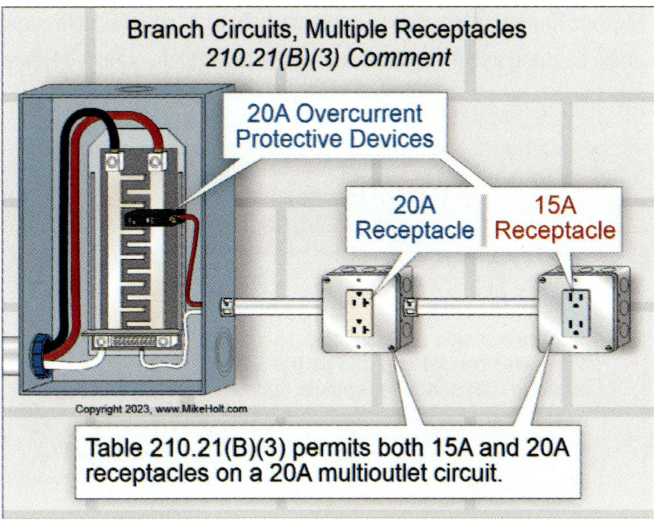

▸Figure 210–38

Table 210.21(B)(3) Receptacle Ratings

Circuit Rating	Receptacle Rating
15A	15A
20A	15A or 20A
30A	30A
40A	50A
50A	50A

Part III. Required Outlets

210.52 Dwelling Unit Receptacle Outlet Requirements

According to Article 100, "Receptacle Outlet" is where receptacles are installed. ▸Figure 210–39

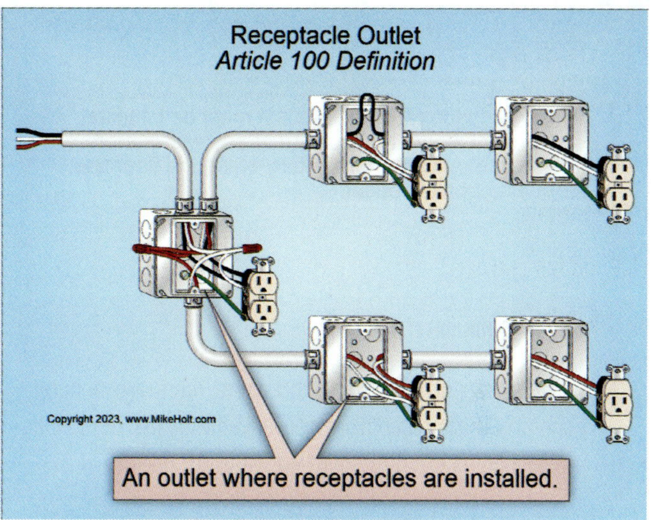

▸Figure 210–39

This section provides the requirements for 15A and 20A, 125V receptacle outlets in dwelling units. Receptacles or receptacle outlets located in the following locations do not count as the required 15A and 20A, 125V receptacle outlets under this section:

(1) Receptacles that are part of a luminaire or appliance.

(2) Receptacles controlled by a listed wall-mounted control device in accordance with 210.70(A)(1) Ex 1.

(3) Receptacle outlets located within cabinets or cupboards.

(4) Receptacle outlets located more than 5½ ft above the floor.

(A) General Requirements for Receptacle Outlets. A receptacle outlet must be installed in the walls for every kitchen, family room, dining room, living room, sunroom, parlor, library, den, bedroom, recreation room, and similar room or area in accordance with 210.52(1), (2), (3), and (4).

(1) Wall Space Receptacle Outlet Spacing. The wall space receptacle outlet must be installed so no point along the floor line of any wall is more than 6 ft, measured horizontally along the floor line, from a receptacle outlet. ▸Figure 210–40

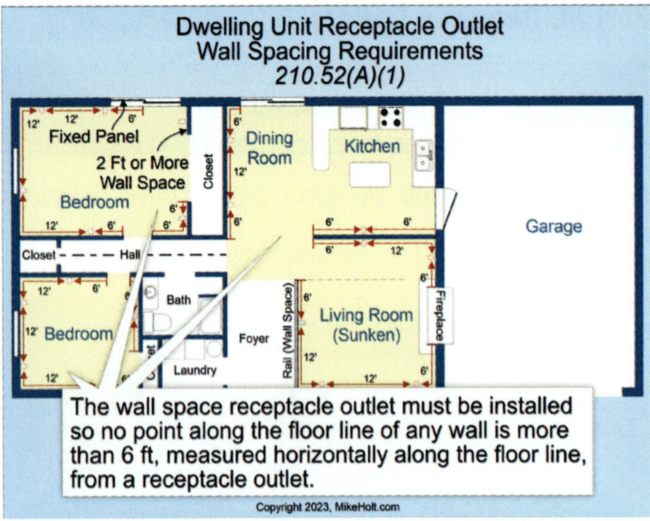

▶Figure 210–40

Author's Comment:

▶ The purpose of this rule is to ensure there are enough general-purpose receptacles conveniently located to reduce the chance an extension cord will be used.

(2) Wall Space Definition. The wall space for receptacle outlet placement includes the following:

(1) Any wall space 2 ft or more in width that is unbroken along the floor line by doorways, fireplaces, stationary appliances, and fixed cabinets without countertops or work surfaces. ▶Figure 210–41 and ▶Figure 210–42

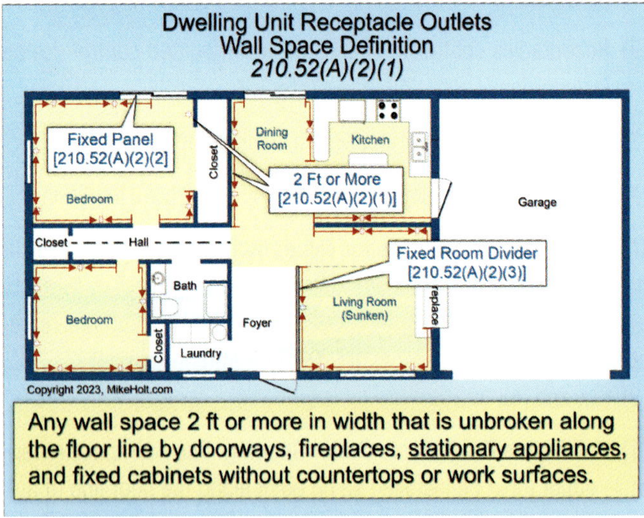

▶Figure 210–41

▶Figure 210–42

(2) The space occupied by fixed panels.

(3) The space occupied by fixed room dividers such as railings.

(3) Floor Receptacles. Floor receptacle outlets within 18 in. of the wall can be counted as the required wall space receptacle outlet. ▶Figure 210–43

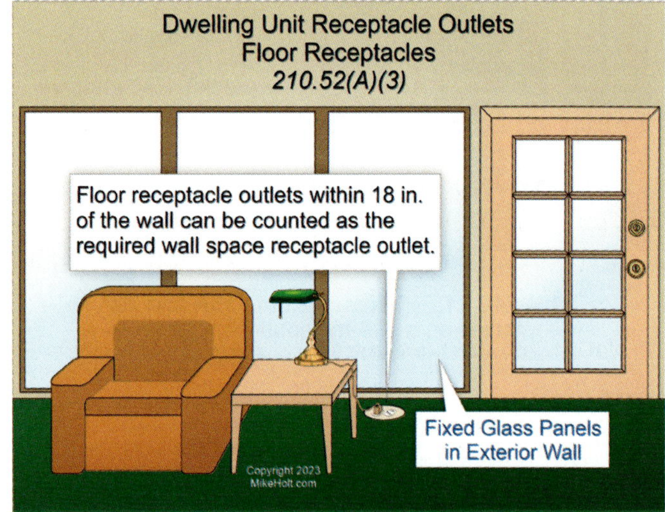

▶Figure 210–43

Author's Comment:

▶ Spaces such as fixed panels in walls [210.52(A)(2)(2)] or fixed room dividers [210.52(A)(2)(3)] may be a railing or be constructed of glass, in which case installing a typical receptacle outlet is impractical. Since these fixed panels or room dividers are still considered a wall space, a floor receptacle within 18 in. can be used for the required receptacle(s).

(4) Countertop Receptacle Outlets. Receptacle outlets installed for countertop surfaces required by 210.52(C) cannot be used to meet the receptacle outlet rules for wall space outlined in 210.52(A).

(B) Small-Appliance Circuit Receptacle Outlets.

(1) Receptacle Outlets. In the kitchen, pantry, breakfast room, and dining room area of a dwelling unit, wall and floor receptacle outlets covered by 210.52(A), countertop outlets covered by 210.52(C), and receptacle outlets for refrigerators must be supplied by two or more 20A, 120V small-appliance branch circuits [210.11(C)(1)]. ▶Figure 210–44

▶Figure 210–44

Ex 2: An individual 15A or larger branch circuit can supply a receptacle outlet for a specific appliance such as a refrigerator in the kitchen, pantry, breakfast room, and dining room area of a dwelling unit. ▶Figure 210–45

(2) Not to Supply Other Outlets. The 20A, 120V small-appliance circuits required by 210.11(C)(1) are not permitted to supply lighting outlets or receptacle outlets outside the kitchen, pantry, breakfast room, or dining room area. ▶Figure 210–46

Ex 2: A receptacle outlet for a gas-fired range, oven, or counter-mounted cooking unit is permitted on the 20A, 120V small-appliance circuit. ▶Figure 210–47

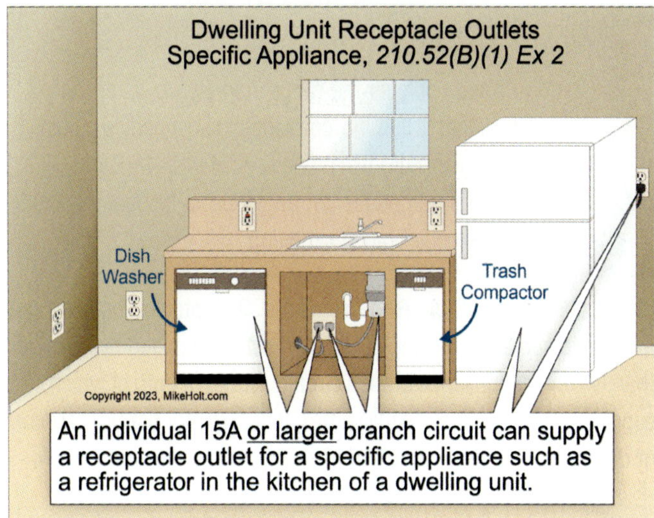

▶Figure 210–45

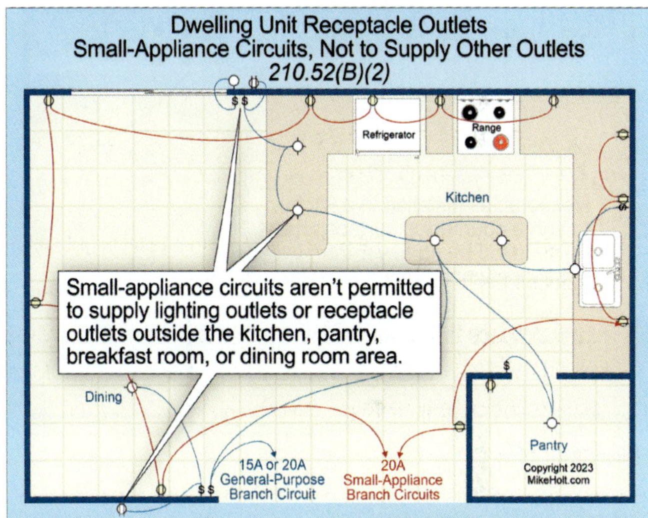

▶Figure 210–46

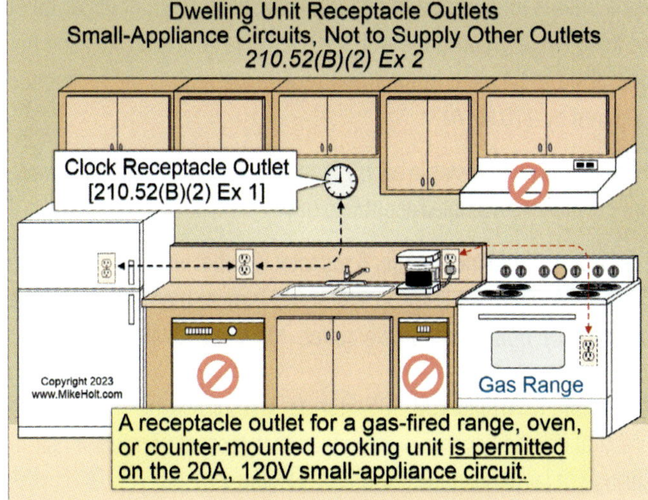

▶Figure 210–47

▸ A range hood (or over-the-range microwave listed as a range hood that is flexible cord-and-plug-connected) must be supplied by an individual branch circuit [422.16(B)(4)(3)]. A hardwired range hood is not permitted to be supplied by the small-appliance branch circuit(s).

(3) Kitchen Receptacle Requirements. Receptacles installed in a kitchen to serve countertop surfaces must be supplied by no fewer than two small-appliance branch circuits, either or both of which can supply receptacle outlets in the same kitchen, pantry, breakfast room, or dining room area as specified in 210.52(B)(1). ▸Figure 210–48

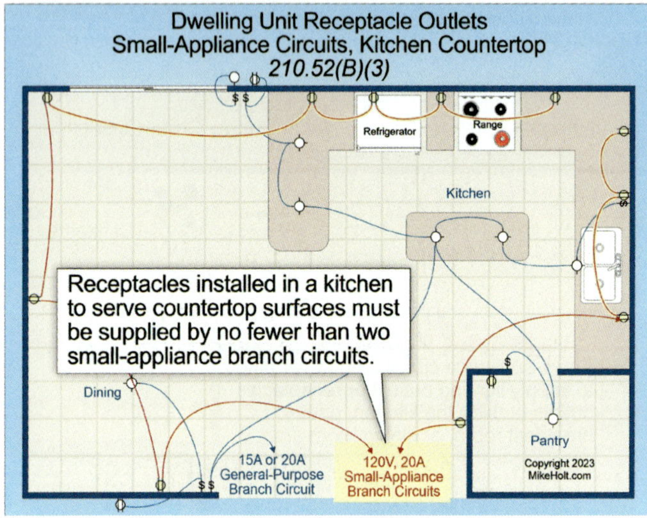

▸Figure 210–48

(C) Countertop Requirements. In kitchens, pantries, breakfast rooms, dining rooms, and similar areas of dwelling units, receptacle outlets for countertop and work surfaces 12 in. or wider must be installed in accordance with 210.52(C)(1) through (C)(3) and not permitted to be used to meet the receptacle outlets for wall space required by 210.52(A).

Two or more receptacles in each 1-ft section of an multioutlet assembly, are considered a single receptacle outlet.

(1) Countertop Wall Spaces. A receptacle outlet must be installed so no point along the countertop wall space is more than 2 ft, measured horizontally, from a receptacle outlet. ▸Figure 210–49

According to Article 100, "Countertop" is a surface intended for food preparation and serving, or a surface that presents a routine risk of spillage of large quantities of water. ▸Figure 210–50

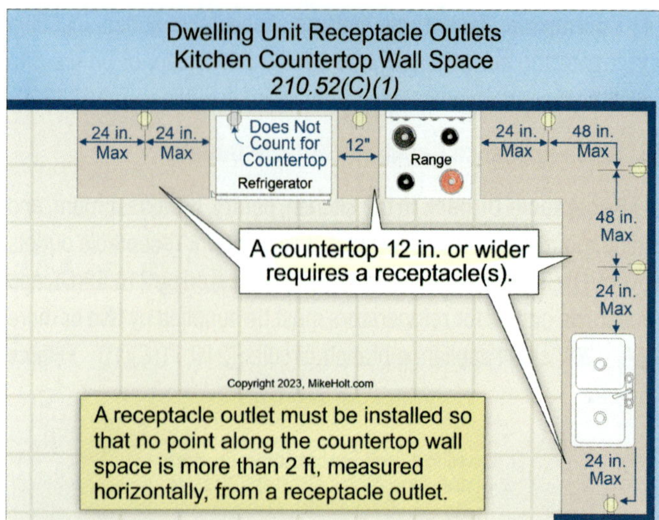

▸Figure 210–49

▸Figure 210–50

Ex 1: A receptacle outlet is not required directly behind a range, counter-mounted cooking unit, or sink in accordance with Figure 210.52(C)(1) in the NEC. ▸Figure 210–51

▸ If the countertop space behind a range or sink is larger than the dimensions noted in Figure 210.52(C)(1) of the *Code* book, then a GFCI-protected receptacle must be installed in that space. This is because (for all practical purposes) if there is enough space for an appliance, it is assumed one will be placed there.

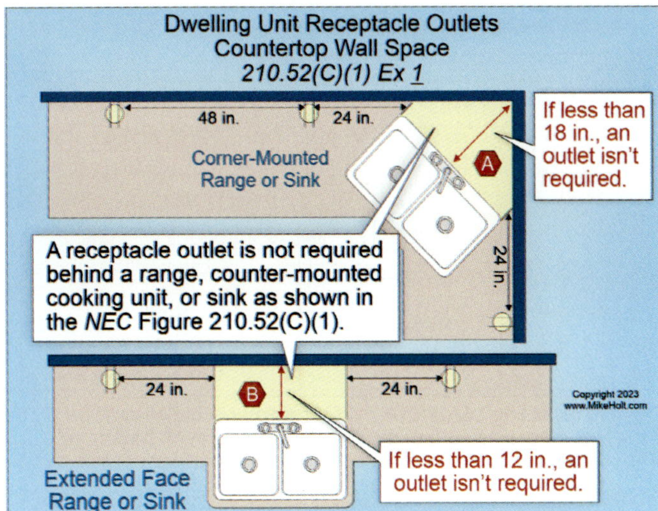

▶Figure 210–51

Ex 2: Where a required receptacle outlet cannot be installed in the wall areas shown in Figure 210.52(C)(1) of the NEC, the required receptacle outlet is permitted to be installed as close as practicable to the countertop area to be served. The total number of receptacle outlets serving the countertop must not be less than the number needed to satisfy 210.52(C)(1). These outlets must be in accordance with 210.52(C)(3).

(2) Island and Peninsular Countertops. If a receptacle outlet is not provided to serve an island or peninsular countertop, provisions must be provided at the island or peninsula for the future addition of a receptacle outlet to serve the island or peninsular countertop. ▶Figure 210–52

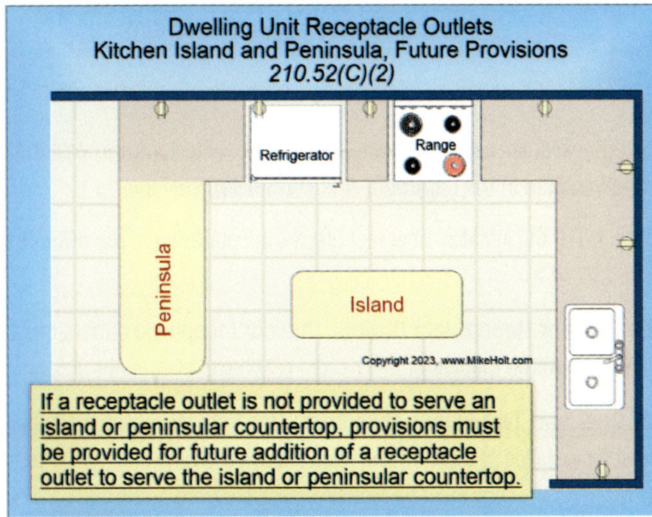

▶Figure 210–52

(3) Countertop Receptacle Location. The required receptacle outlets must be installed in one or more of the following locations:

(1) On or Above Countertops. The required receptacle outlets can be installed on or not more than 20 in. above the countertop. ▶Figure 210–53

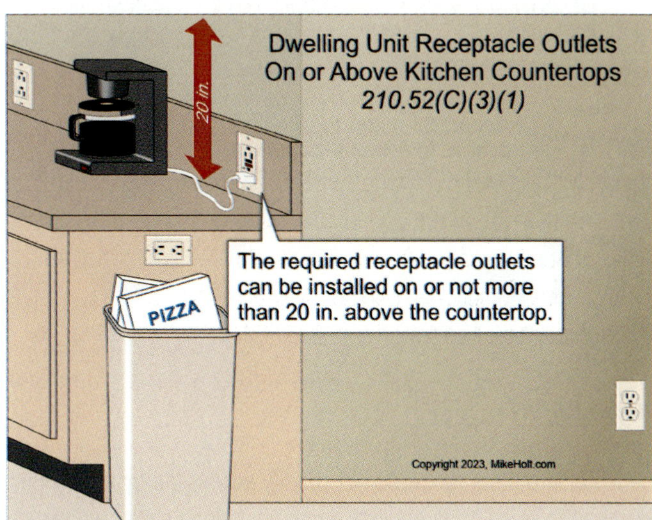

▶Figure 210–53

Author's Comment:

▶ Receptacle outlets installed at islands and peninsulas must be located on or above the countertop or work surface. ▶Figure 210–54

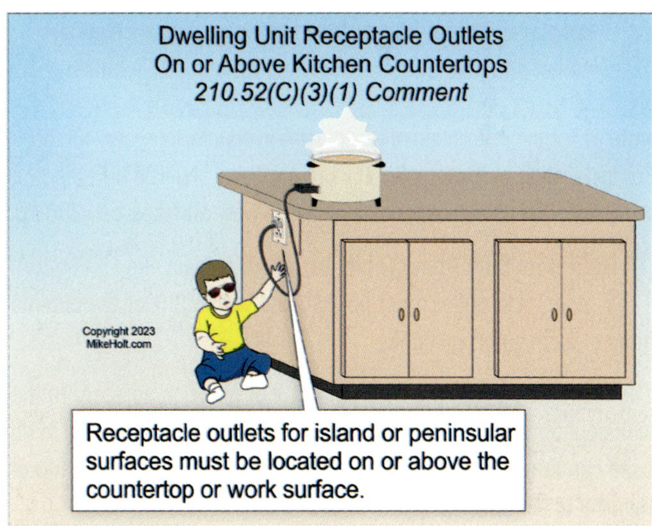

▶Figure 210–54

(2) In Countertops. The required receptacle outlets can be in the countertop with receptacle outlet assemblies listed for use in countertops. ▶Figure 210–55

▶Figure 210–55

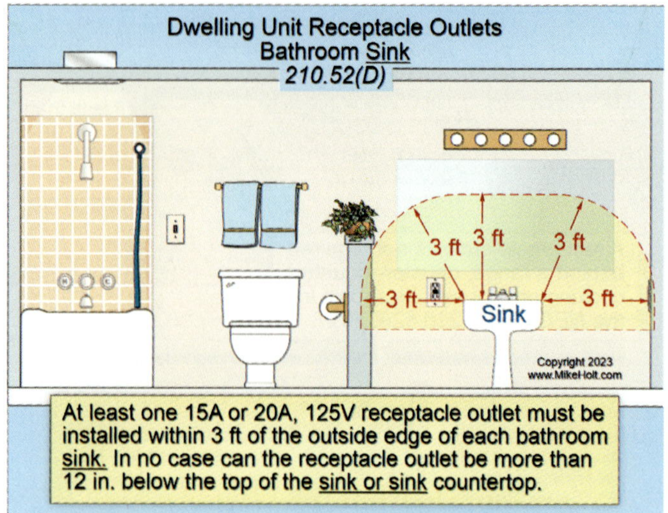

▶Figure 210–56

Receptacle outlets rendered not readily accessible by appliances fastened in place in an appliance garage, behind sinks, ranges, or cooktops [210.52(C)(1) Ex 1], or supplying appliances that occupy assigned spaces, do not count as the required countertop surface receptacle outlets.

Author's Comment:

▶ "Appliance Garage" is an enclosed area on the countertop where an appliance can be stored and hidden from view when not in use. Receptacles installed inside an appliance garage do not count as a required countertop receptacle outlet.

Note 1: For the installation of receptacles in countertops, see 406.5(E). For installation of receptacles in work surfaces, see 406.5(F), and for the installation of multioutlet assemblies in work surfaces, see 380.10.

(D) Bathroom Sink Receptacle Outlet(s). At least one 15A or 20A, 125V receptacle outlet must be installed within 3 ft of the outside edge of each bathroom sink.

The receptacle outlet must be on a wall or partition adjacent to the sink counter surface or on the side or face of the sink cabinet. In no case can the receptacle outlet be more than 12 in. below the top of the sink or sink countertop. ▶Figure 210–56

Author's Comment:

▶ One bathroom receptacle outlet can serve two sinks to meet this requirement if it is within 3 ft of the outside edge of each sink. ▶Figure 210–57

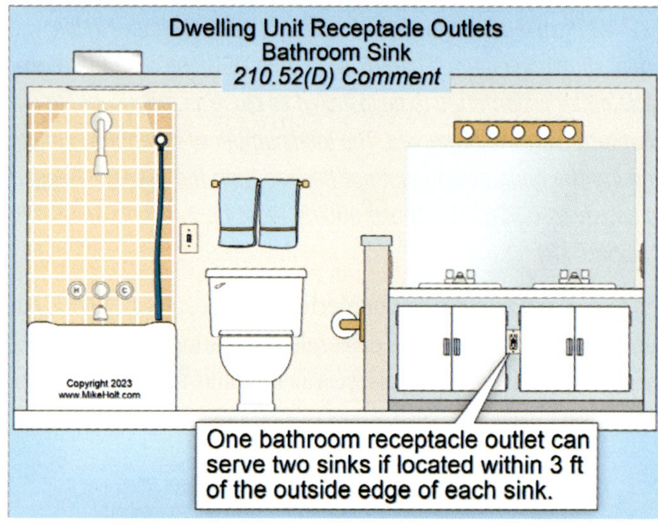

▶Figure 210–57

Receptacle outlet assemblies listed for use in countertops are permitted to be installed in the bathroom sink countertop surface.

Note 1: For the installation of receptacles in countertops, see 406.5(E) and 406.5(G).

(E) Outdoor Receptacle Outlets. Outdoor receptacle outlets must comply with the following:

(1) One- and Two-Family Dwellings. One outdoor receptacle outlet must be installed at the front and back of each dwelling unit (two receptacles in total). They must be readily accessible from grade and cannot be more than 6½ ft above grade. ▶Figure 210–58

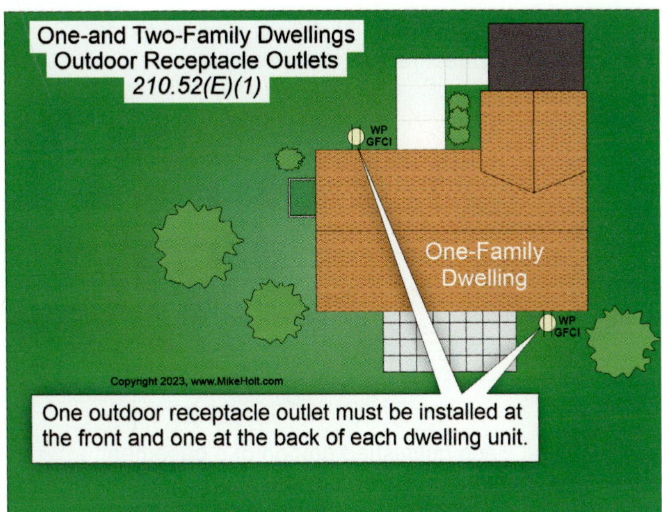

▶Figure 210–58

(2) Multifamily Dwelling. Each dwelling unit of a multifamily dwelling with grade-level entry must have at least one outdoor receptacle outlet, readily accessible from grade, and not more than 6½ ft above grade. ▶Figure 210–59

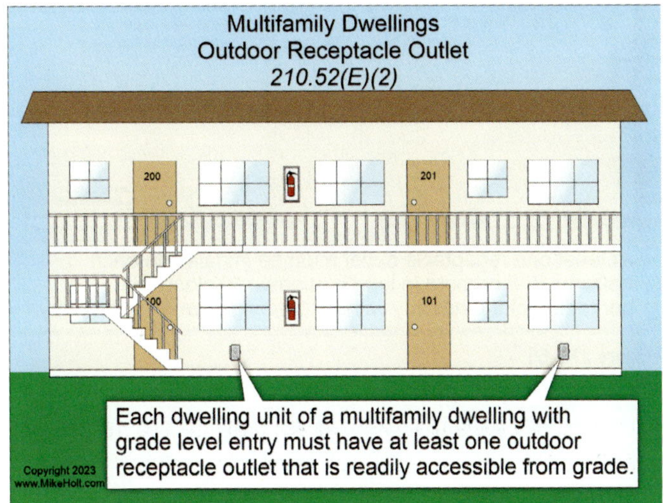

▶Figure 210–59

(3) Balconies, Decks, and Porches. At least one receptacle outlet must be installed not more than 6½ ft above any balcony, deck, or porch surface within 4 in. horizontally of the dwelling unit. ▶Figure 210–60

(F) Laundry Area Receptacle Outlet(s). Each dwelling unit must have one receptacle outlet installed in the area where laundry equipment is intended to be installed. ▶Figure 210–61

Ex 1: A laundry receptacle outlet is not required in a dwelling unit located in a multifamily dwelling building with laundry facilities available to all occupants.

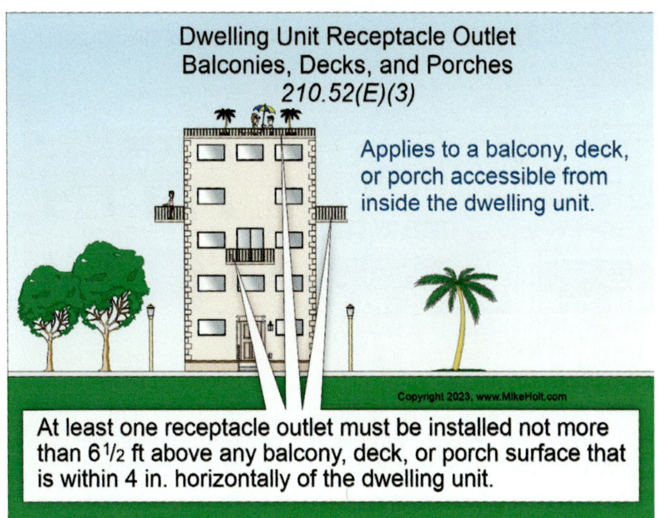

▶Figure 210–60

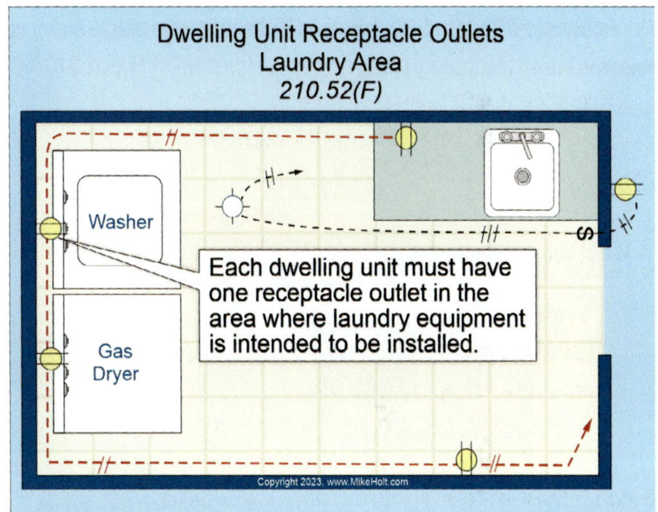

▶Figure 210–61

According to Article 100, "Laundry Area" is designed to contain a laundry tray, washing machine, or clothes dryer regardless of whether laundry equipment is installed.

(G) Garage, Basement, and Accessory Building Receptacle Outlet(s). For one- and two-family dwellings or multifamily dwellings, at least one receptacle outlet must be installed in accordance with 210.52G(1) through (3). Receptacles supplying only a permanently installed premises security system are not considered as meeting these requirements.

(1) Garages. A receptacle outlet is required in each vehicle bay of a garage with electric power and installed no higher than 5 ft 6 in. above the floor. ▶Figure 210–62

Ex: A receptacle outlet is not required in a garage space not attached to an individual dwelling unit of a multifamily dwelling.

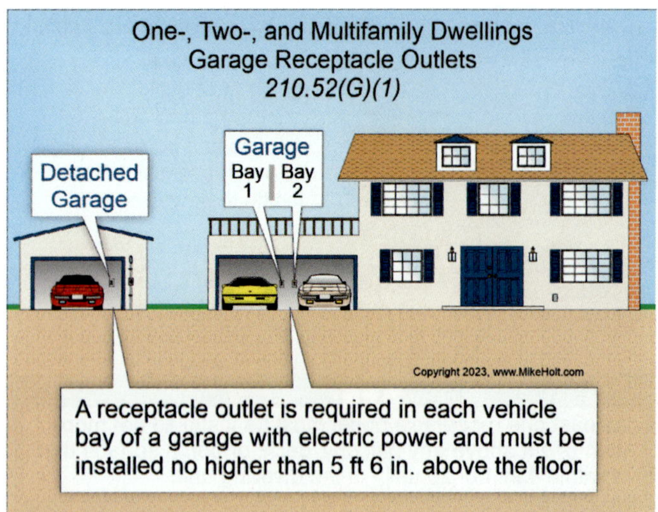

▶Figure 210–62

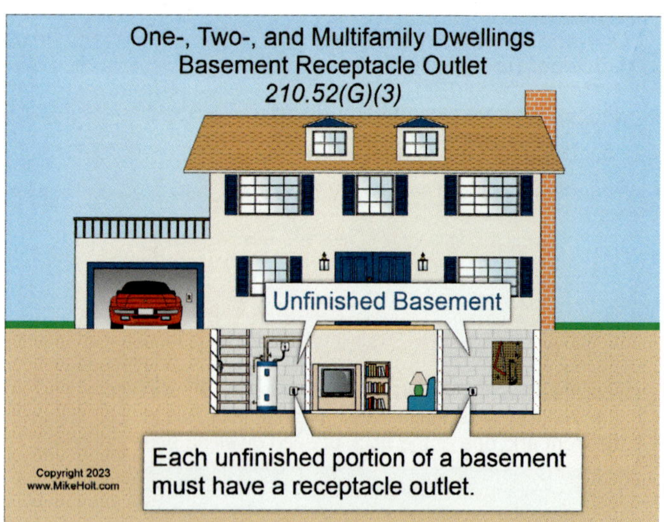

▶Figure 210–64

(2) Accessory Building Receptacle Outlets. A receptacle outlet is required in each accessory building with electric power. ▶Figure 210–63

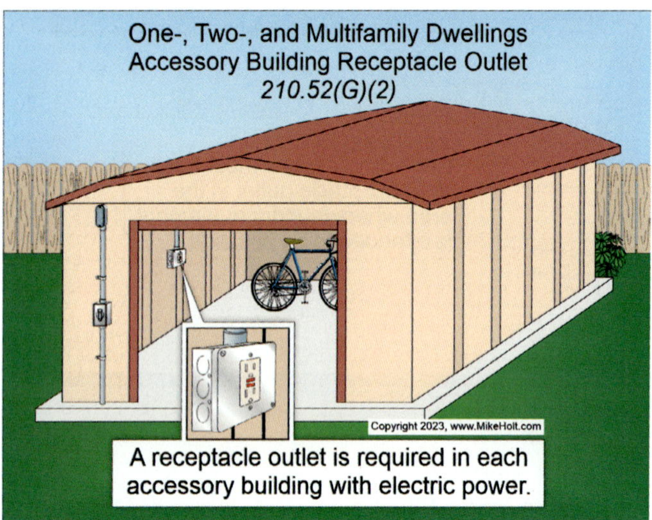

▶Figure 210–63

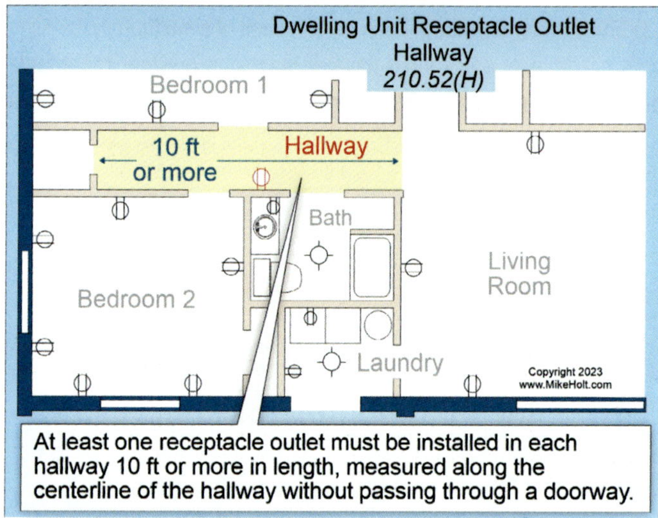

▶Figure 210–65

(3) Basements. Each unfinished portion of a basement must have a receptacle outlet. ▶Figure 210–64

(H) Hallway Receptacle Outlet. At least one receptacle outlet must be installed in each hallway 10 ft or more in length, measured along the centerline of the hallway without passing through a doorway. ▶Figure 210–65

(I) Foyer Receptacle Outlet(s). Foyers having an area greater than 60 sq ft must have a receptacle outlet on any wall space that is 3 ft or more in width and unbroken by doorways, windows next to doors that extend to the floor, and similar openings. ▶Figure 210–66

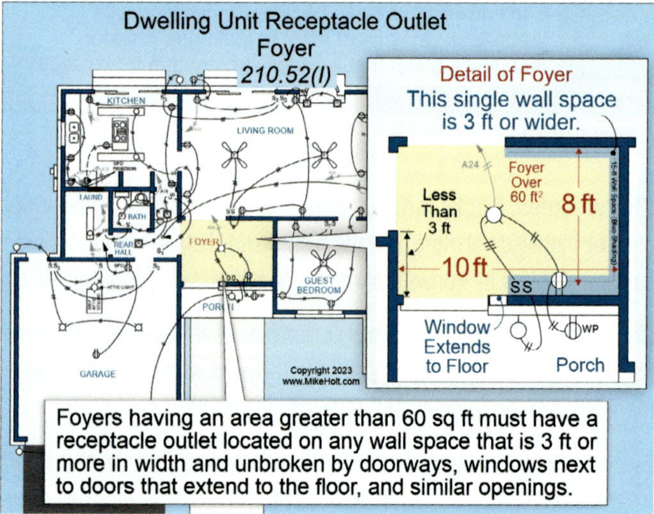

▶Figure 210–66

210.70 Lighting Outlet Requirements

A switch must not rely exclusively on battery power to energize the lighting outlet unless the battery powered switch incorporates a notification means of a low battery level. ▶Figure 210–67

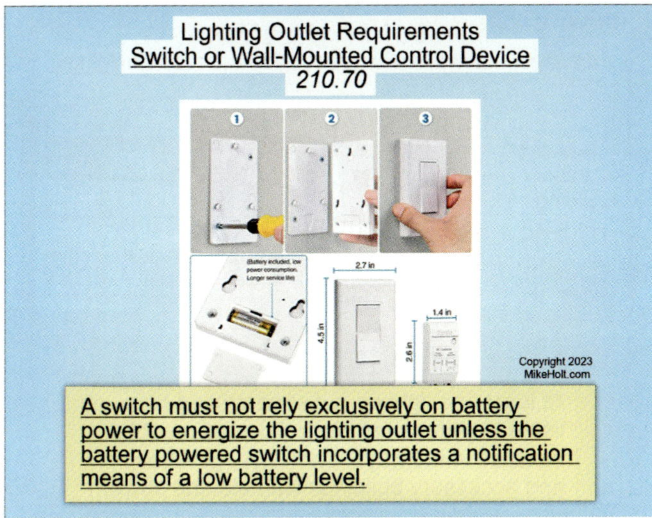

▶Figure 210–67

(A) Dwelling Unit Lighting Outlets. Lighting outlets must be installed in:

(1) Habitable Rooms, Kitchens, Laundry Areas, and Bathrooms. At least one lighting outlet controlled by a listed wall-mounted control device must be installed in every habitable room, kitchen, laundry area, and bathroom area of a dwelling unit. The wall-mounted control device must be on a wall near an entrance to the room. ▶Figure 210–68

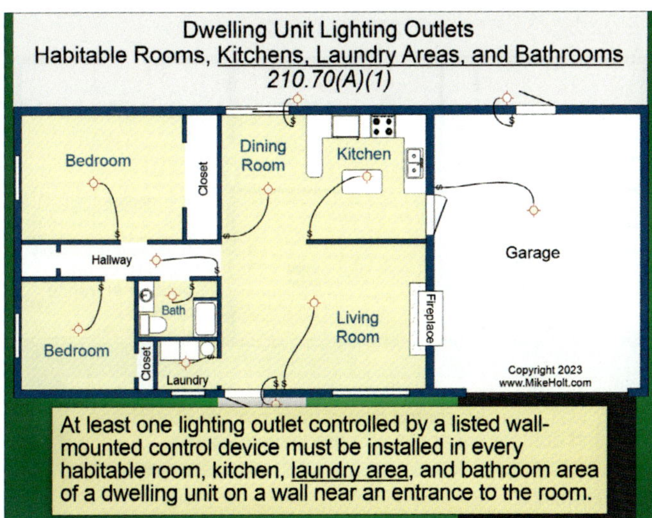

▶Figure 210–68

According to Article 100, "Lighting Outlet" is defined as an outlet for connecting a lampholder or luminaire. ▶Figure 210–69

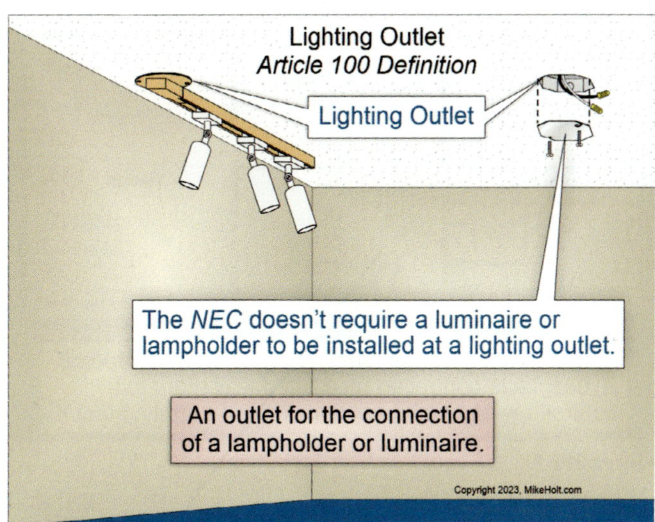

▶Figure 210–69

According to Article 100, "Habitable Room" is defined as a room for living, sleeping, eating, or cooking, excluding bathrooms, toilet rooms, closets, hallways, storage or utility spaces, and similar areas. ▶Figure 210–70

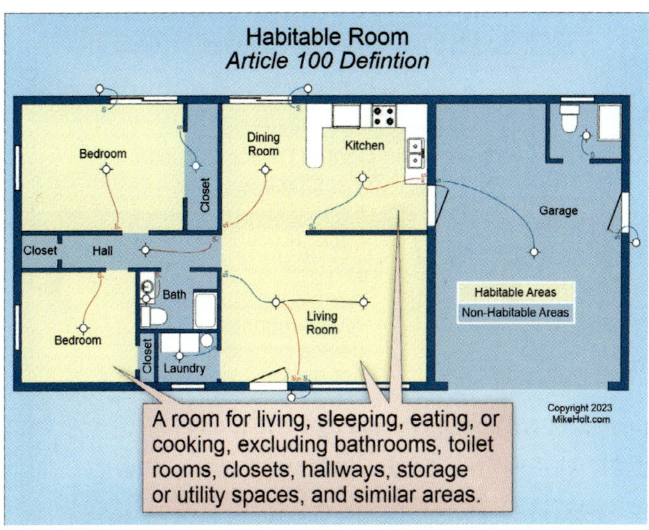

▶Figure 210–70

Ex 1: In other than kitchens, laundry areas, and bathrooms, a receptacle controlled by a listed wall-mounted control device can be used instead of a lighting outlet. ▶Figure 210–71

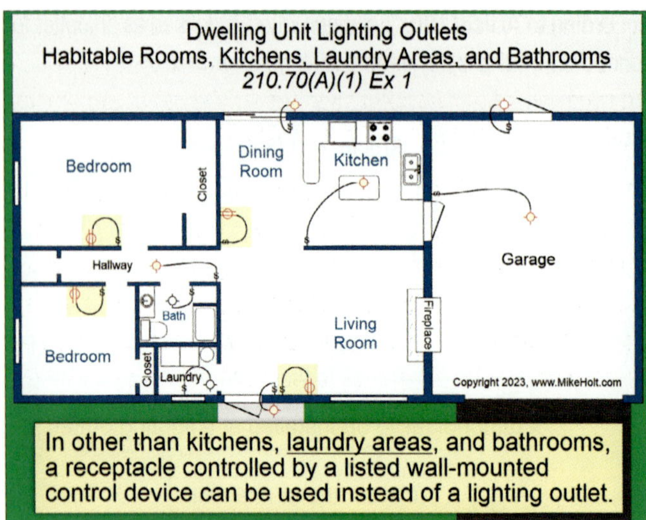

Dwelling Unit Lighting Outlets
Habitable Rooms, Kitchens, Laundry Areas, and Bathrooms
210.70(A)(1) Ex 1

In other than kitchens, laundry areas, and bathrooms, a receptacle controlled by a listed wall-mounted control device can be used instead of a lighting outlet.

▶Figure 210–71

Author's Comment:

▸ The *Code* specifies the location of the lighting outlet, but it does not specify the wall-mounted control device's location. You would naturally not want to install a switch behind a door or other inconvenient location, but the *NEC* does not require you to move the switch to suit the swing of the door. When in doubt as to the best location to place a light switch, consult the job plans or ask the customer. ▶Figure 210–72

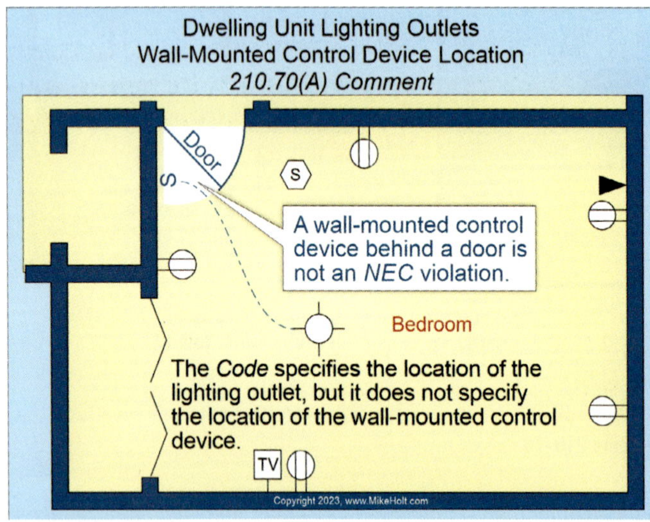

Dwelling Unit Lighting Outlets
Wall-Mounted Control Device Location
210.70(A) Comment

▶Figure 210–72

(2) Additional Locations.

(1) Hallways, Stairways, Garages, and Accessory Buildings. At least one lighting outlet controlled by a listed wall-mounted control device must be installed in hallways, stairways, garages, and accessory buildings with electric power. ▶Figure 210–73

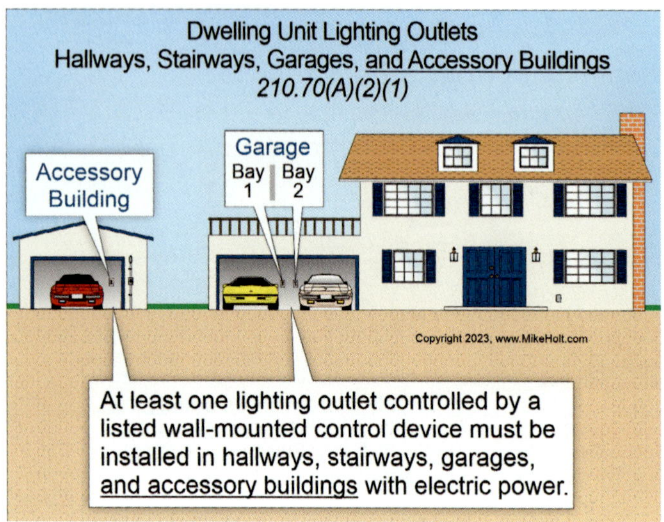

Dwelling Unit Lighting Outlets
Hallways, Stairways, Garages, and Accessory Buildings
210.70(A)(2)(1)

At least one lighting outlet controlled by a listed wall-mounted control device must be installed in hallways, stairways, garages, and accessory buildings with electric power.

▶Figure 210–73

(2) Exterior Entrance. For dwelling units having attached and/or detached garages with electric power, at least one exterior lighting outlet controlled by a listed wall-mounted control device must provide illumination on the exterior side of outdoor entrances with grade-level access. A garage vehicle door is not considered an outdoor entrance or exit. ▶Figure 210–74

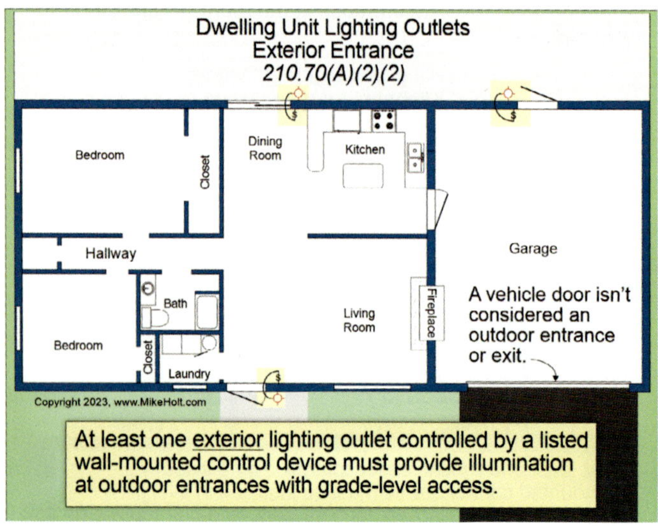

Dwelling Unit Lighting Outlets
Exterior Entrance
210.70(A)(2)(2)

At least one exterior lighting outlet controlled by a listed wall-mounted control device must provide illumination at outdoor entrances with grade-level access.

▶Figure 210–74

Ex to 2: For an outdoor grade-level stairway access to a basement, the lighting outlet that provides illumination on the stairway steps is permitted to be in the basement interior within 5 ft horizontally of the bottommost stairway riser. This lighting outlet is permitted to be controlled by a listed wall-mounted control device or a switch on the luminaire or lampholder.

(3) Stairways. Where a lighting outlet(s) is installed in interior stairways having six risers or more between floor levels, a listed wall-mounted control device for the lighting outlet(s) must be at each floor level and at each landing level that includes a stairway entry to control the lighting outlets. ▶Figure 210–75

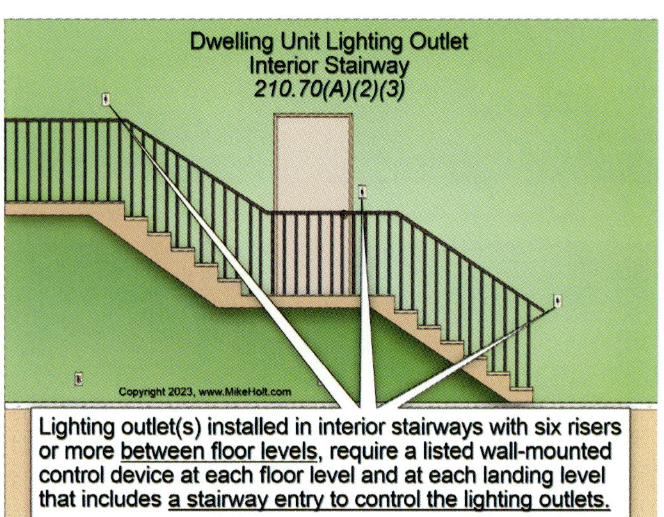

▶Figure 210–75

Ex to (1), (2), and (3): Remote, central, or automatic control of hallway, stairway, and exterior entrance lighting is permitted. ▶Figure 210–76

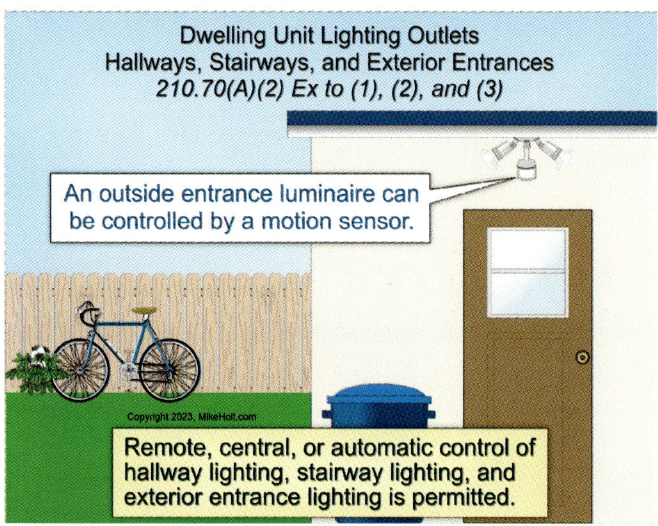

▶Figure 210–76

(4) Dimmer Control. Lighting outlets in stairways [210.70(A)(2)(3)] can be controlled by a listed wall-mounted control device where dimming control can provide a maximum brightness at each control location for the interior stairway illumination.

(C) Storage and Equipment Spaces. At least one lighting outlet that contains a switch (or is controlled by a wall switch) or listed wall-mounted control device must be installed in attics, underfloor spaces, utility rooms, and basements used for storage or containing equipment that requires servicing. The switch or wall-mounted control device must be at the usual point of entrance to these spaces. ▶Figure 210–77

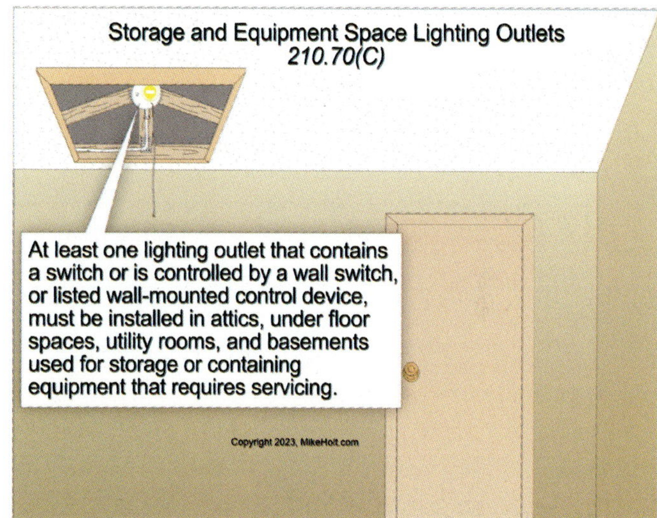

▶Figure 210–77

The lighting outlet must be at the entry to the attic and underfloor space, utility room, or basement. Where a lighting outlet is installed for equipment requiring servicing, it must be installed at or near that equipment.

GROUNDING AND BONDING

Introduction to Article 250—Grounding and Bonding

Article 250 covers the general requirements for bonding and grounding electrical installations. The terminology used in this article has been a source of much confusion over the years so pay careful attention to the definitions pertaining to Article 250. Understanding the difference between bonding and grounding will help you correctly apply the provisions of this article. Because of the massive size and scope of Article 250, Figure 250.1 in the *NEC* is provided as a reference for the locations of the different types of rules. Of the ten parts contained in this article only parts one through seven are covered in this material. Some topics covered in this material include:

▸ Scope

▸ Grounding electrode systems

▸ Grounding electrode types

▸ Grounding electrode installation

▸ Equipment grounding conductors

▸ Equipment grounding conductor connections

Part I. General

250.1 Scope

Article 250 covers the general requirements for grounding and bonding electrical installations. ▸Figure 250–1

Author's Comment:

▸ There are two completely different concepts being covered in this article: "grounding" which is the connection to the Earth, and "bonding" which is connecting conductive metal parts together to ensure electrical conductivity between metal parts. ▸Figure 250–2

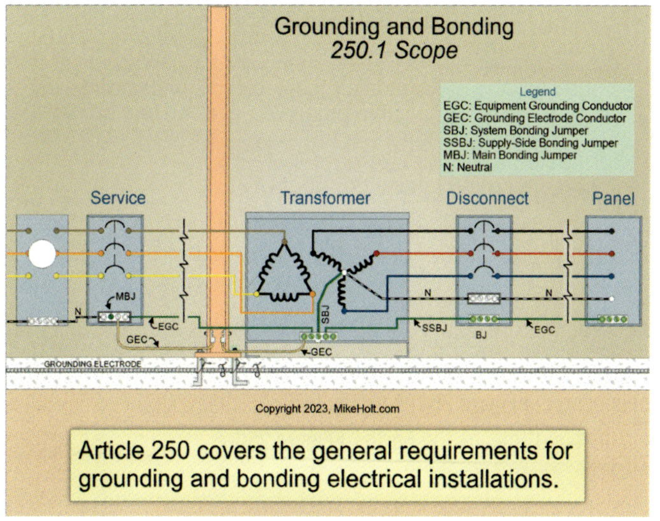

▸Figure 250–1

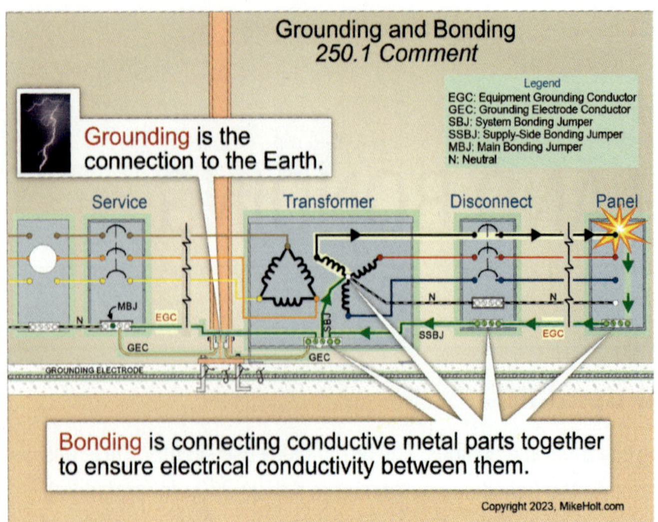

▶Figure 250–2

According to Article 100, "Bonding" means connected to establish electrical continuity and conductivity. ▶Figure 250–3

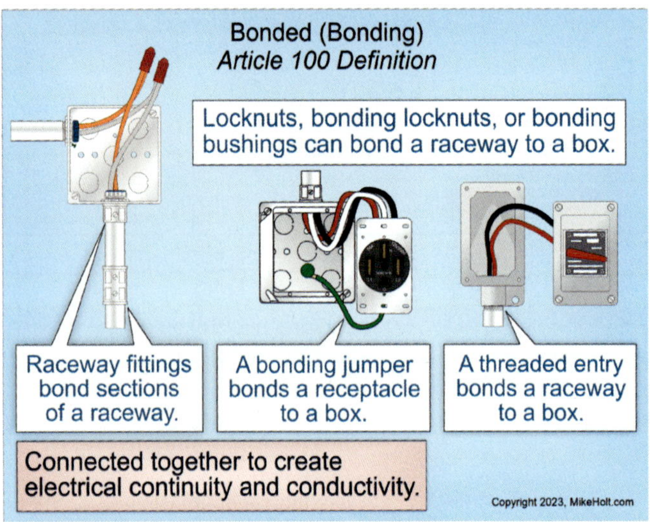

▶Figure 250–3

According to Article 100, "Grounding" means the connection to the Earth (ground) or to a conductive body that extends the ground connection. ▶Figure 250–4

"Ground" means the Earth. ▶Figure 250–5

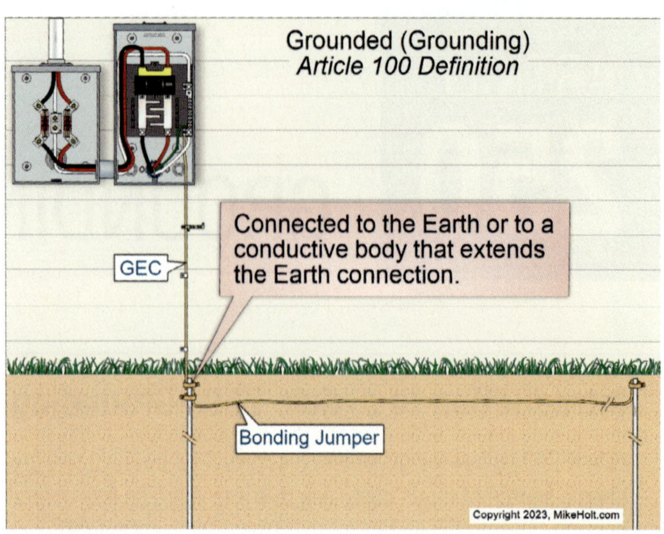

▶Figure 250–4

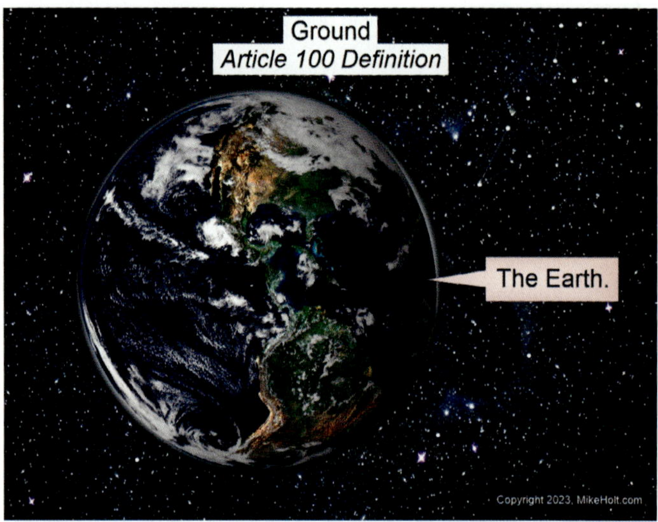

▶Figure 250–5

Part III. Grounding Electrode System and Grounding Electrode Conductor

250.50 Grounding Electrode System

According to Article 100, "Grounding Electrode" is a conducting object used to make a direct electrical connection to the Earth [250.50 through 250.70]. ▶Figure 250–6

A grounding electrode system is comprised of bonding together the grounding electrodes described in 250.52(A)(1) through (A)(8) that are present at a building or structure. ▶Figure 250–7

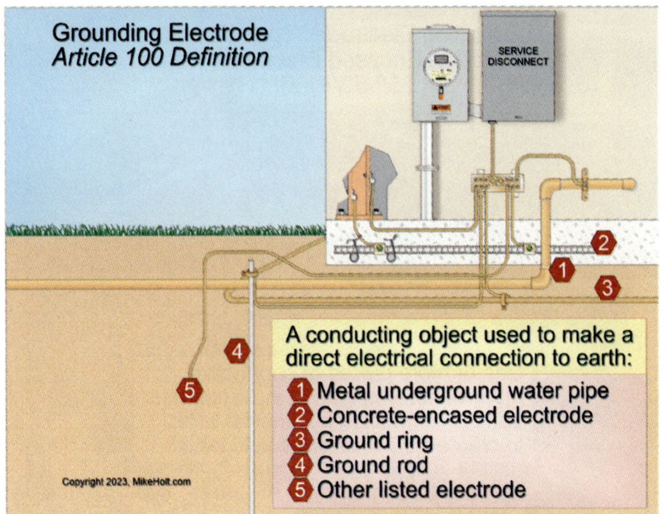

▶Figure 250–6

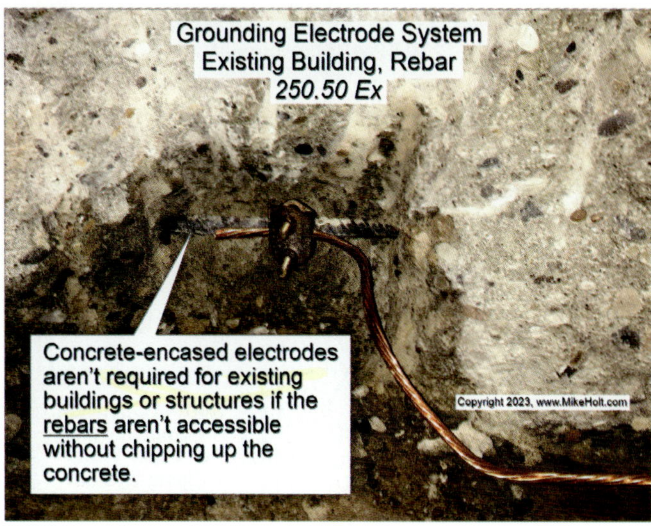

▶Figure 250–8

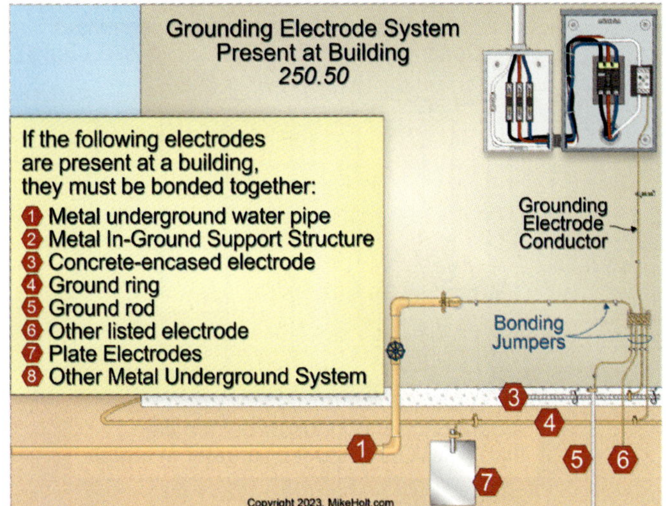

▶Figure 250–7

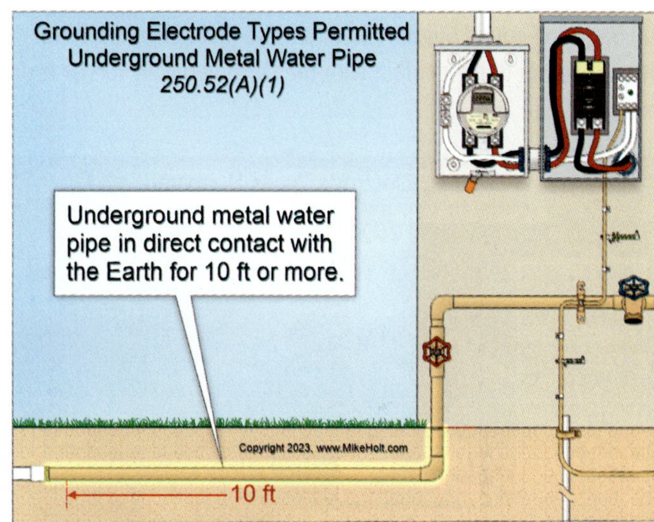

▶Figure 250–9

Ex: Concrete-encased electrodes are not required for existing buildings or structures if the rebar is not accessible without chipping up the concrete. ▶Figure 250–8

250.52 Grounding Electrode Types

(A) Electrodes Permitted.

(1) Underground Metal Water Pipe Electrode. Underground metal water pipe in direct contact with the Earth for 10 ft or more. ▶Figure 250–9

Author's Comment:

▸ Controversy about using metal underground water piping as a grounding electrode has existed since the early 1900s. The water industry believes that neutral current flowing on water piping corrodes the metal. For more information, contact the American Water Works Association about their report, *Effects of Electrical Grounding on Pipe Integrity and Shock Hazard,* Catalog No. 90702, 1.800.926.7337. ▶Figure 250–10

▸ Where there is a common metal underground water piping system, it is possible for the service neutral to be open and not show any symptoms that are typically associated with open service neutrals. This can create a dangerous condition for water workers who open the underground water pipe when it is acting as the service neutral.

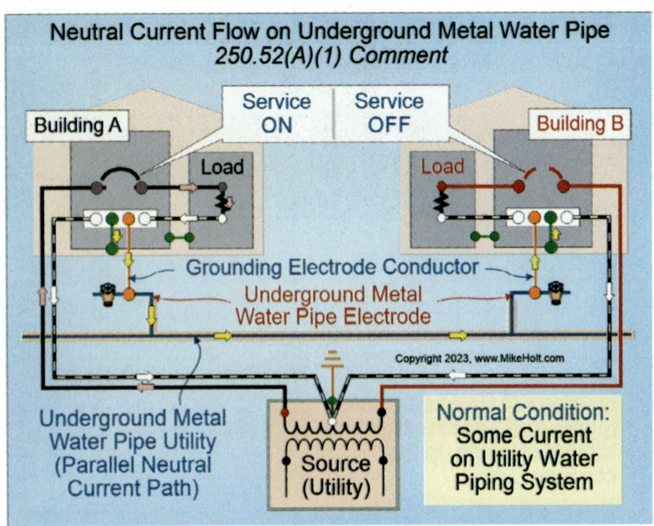

▶Figure 250–10

(2) Metal In-Ground Support Structure(s). Metal in-ground support structure(s) in direct contact with the Earth vertically for 10 ft or more. ▶Figure 250–11

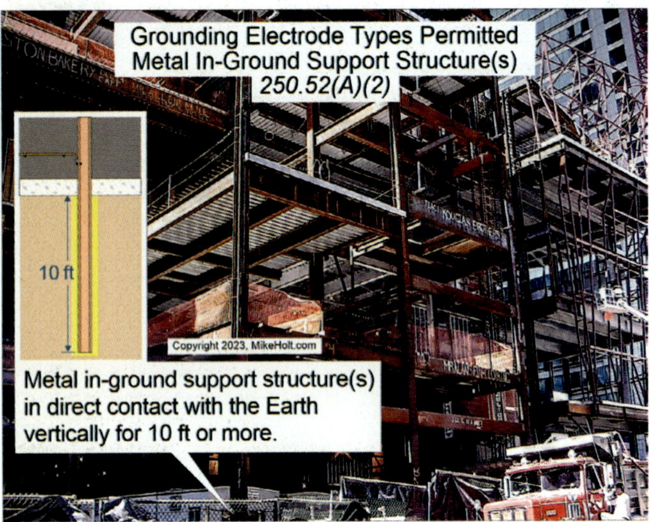

▶Figure 250–11

Note: Metal in-ground support structures include—but are not limited to—pilings, casings, and other structural metal.

(3) Concrete-Encased Electrode. Concrete-encased electrodes must be one of the following:

(1) Rebar. One or more pieces of conductive rebar of not less than ½ in. diameter that are connected by steel tie wires to create a 20 ft or greater length. ▶Figure 250–12

(2) Conductor. A bare copper conductor not smaller than 4 AWG and 20 ft or greater in length. ▶Figure 250–13

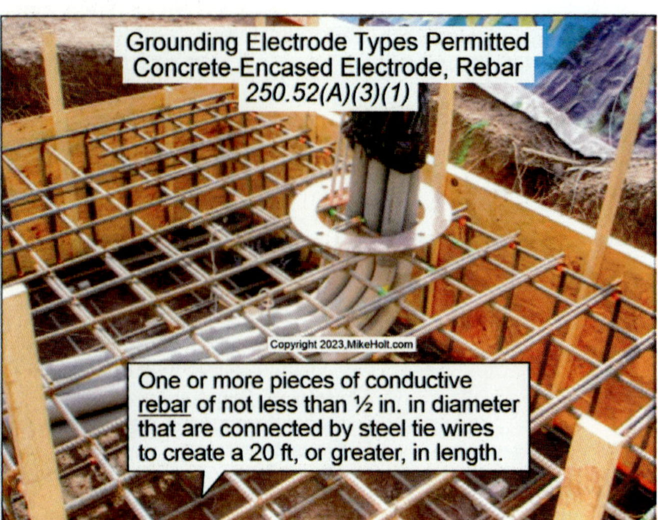

▶Figure 250–12

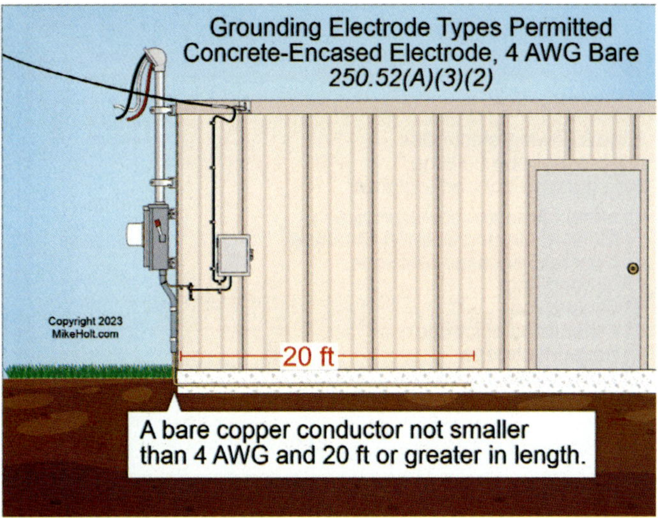

▶Figure 250–13

Rebar or Conductor. The rebar or bare copper conductor used as part of the concrete-encased electrode must be encased by at least 2 in. of concrete that is in direct contact with the Earth. ▶Figure 250–14

The concrete-encased electrode can be horizontal or vertical within a foundation or footing that is in direct contact with the Earth. If multiple concrete-encased electrodes are present at a building, only one is required to serve as a grounding electrode.

Note: Rebar in concrete that is not in direct contact with the Earth because of insulation, vapor barriers, or similar items is not considered to be a concrete-encased electrode. ▶Figure 250–15

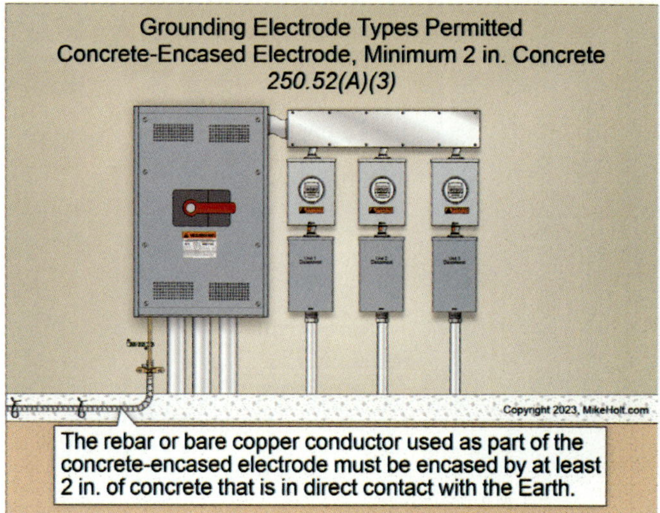

▶Figure 250–14

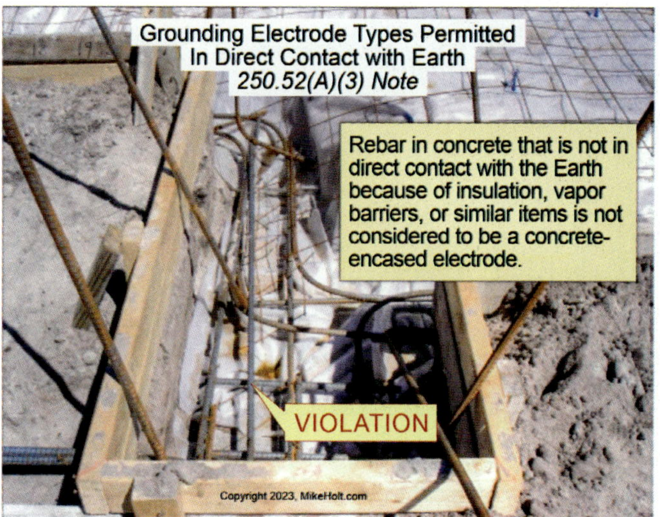

▶Figure 250–15

Author's Comment:

▶ A grounding electrode conductor connected to a concrete-encased grounding electrode is not required to be larger than 4 AWG copper [250.66(B)].

▶ A concrete-encased grounding electrode is also called "Ufer Ground," named after a consultant working for the U.S. Army during World War II. The technique Herbert G. Ufer created was necessary because the site needing grounding had no underground water table and little rainfall. The desert site was a series of bomb storage vaults near Flagstaff, Arizona. This type of grounding electrode generally offers the lowest ground resistance for the cost. In fact, Mr. Ufer's method is so effective that ground rods are not necessary!

(4) Ground Ring. A direct buried bare copper conductor not smaller than 2 AWG encircling a building. ▶Figure 250–16

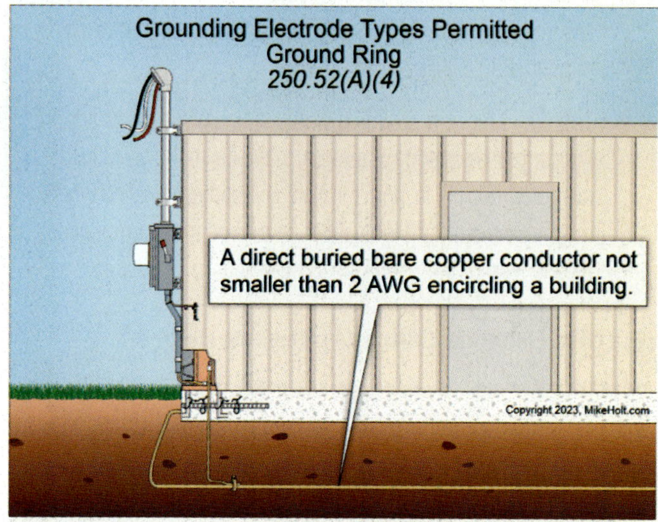

▶Figure 250–16

Author's Comment:

▶ A ground ring encircling a building must not be installed less than 30 in. below the surface of the Earth [250.53(F)].

(5) Ground Rod. Ground rods at least 8 ft in length in contact with the Earth. ▶Figure 250–17

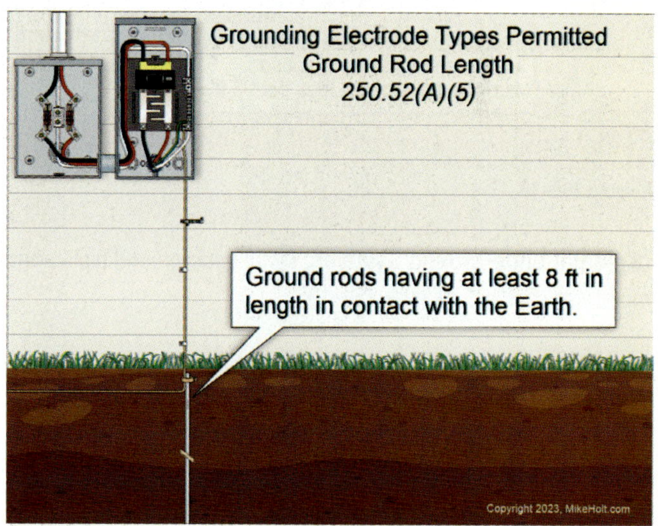

▶Figure 250–17

Author's Comment:

▸ The grounding electrode conductor, if it is the sole connection to the rod(s), is not required to be larger than 6 AWG copper [250.66(A)].

▸ The diameter of a ground rod has an insignificant effect on the contact resistance of a rod(s) to the Earth. However, larger diameter rods (¾ in. and 1 in.) are sometimes installed where mechanical strength is desired, or is needed to compensate for the loss of the electrode's metal due to corrosion.

(6) Listed Electrode. Other listed grounding electrodes.

(7) Plate Electrode. A steel plate of not less than ¼ in. thick with an exposed surface area of not less than 288 sq inches (2 ft). ▸Figure 250–18

▸Figure 250–19

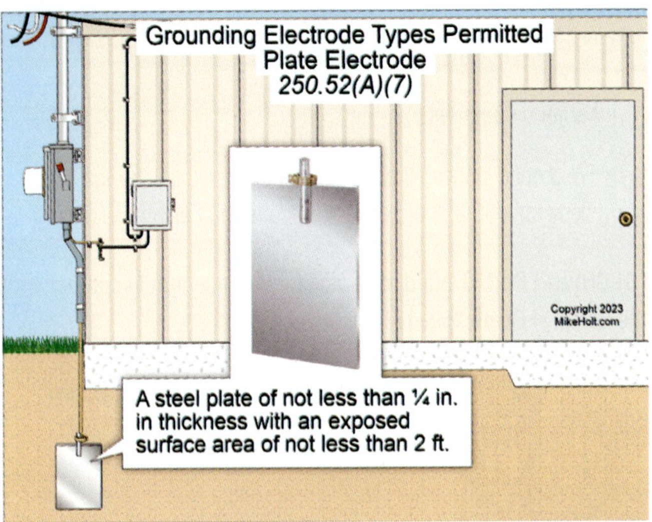

▸Figure 250–18

(8) Metal Underground Systems. Metal underground piping and metal well casings. ▸Figure 250–19

Author's Comment:

▸ The grounding electrode conductor to the metal underground system must be sized in accordance with Table 250.66.

(B) Not Permitted for Use as a Grounding Electrode.

(1) Underground metal gas piping systems are not permitted to be used as a grounding electrode. ▸Figure 250–20

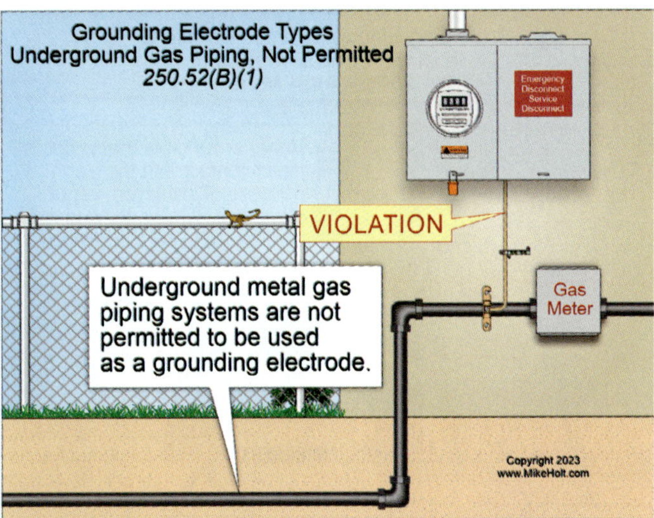

▸Figure 250–20

(2) Aluminum is not permitted to be used as a grounding electrode.

(3) The swimming pool shell structural rebar described in 680.26(B)(1) and (B)(2) is not permitted to be used as a grounding electrode. ▸Figure 250–21

250.53 Grounding Electrode Installation

(A) Ground Rods. Ground rods must be free from nonconductive coatings such as paint or enamel. ▸Figure 250–22

(1) Below Permanent Moisture Level. If practicable, rod, pipe, and plate electrodes must be embedded below the permanent moisture level.

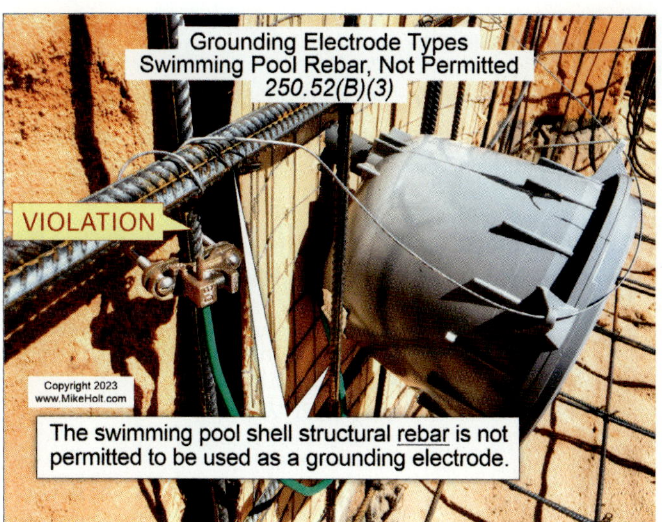

▶Figure 250–21

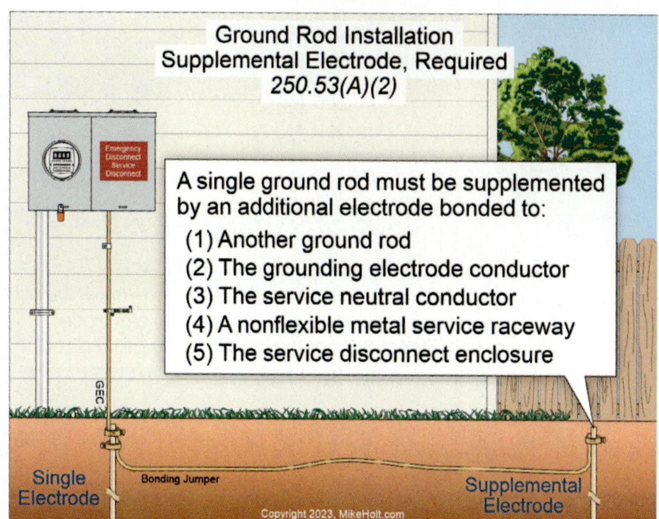

▶Figure 250–23

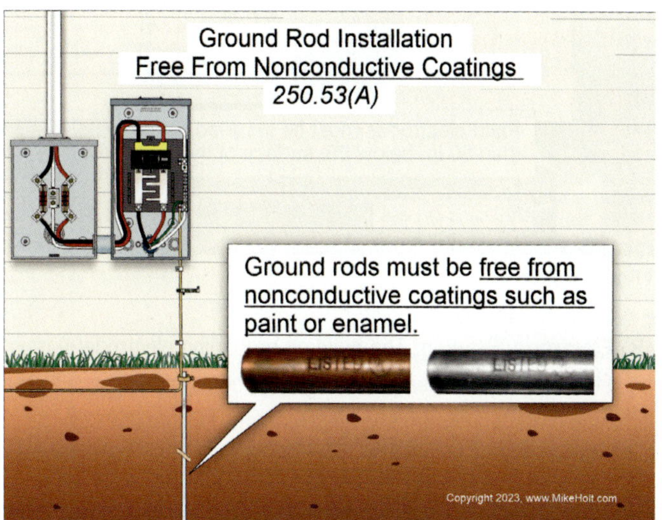

▶Figure 250–22

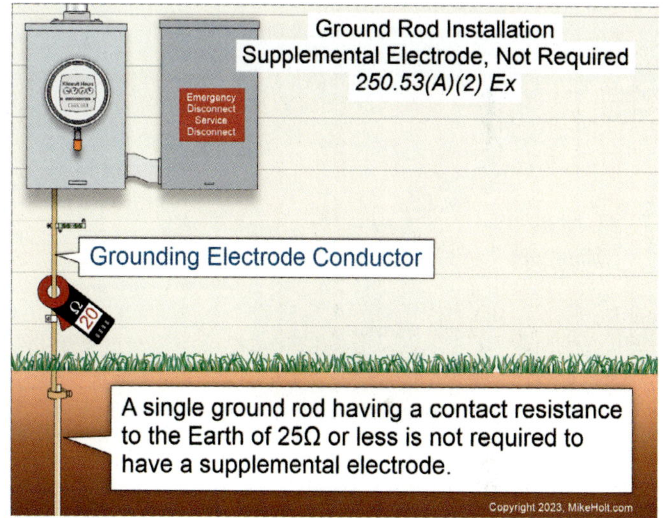

▶Figure 250–24

(2) Supplemental Electrode. A single ground rod must be supplemented by an additional electrode. The supplemental electrode must be bonded to: ▶Figure 250–23

(1) Another ground rod

(2) The grounding electrode conductor

(3) The service neutral conductor

(4) A nonflexible metal service raceway

(5) The service-disconnect enclosure

Ex: A single ground rod having a contact resistance to the Earth of 25Ω or less is not required to have a supplemental electrode. ▶Figure 250–24

(3) Supplemental Ground Rod, Spacing. A ground rod serving as a supplemental electrode must be at least 6 ft apart from the other ground rod. ▶Figure 250–25

(4) Rod Electrodes. Ground rods must be driven to a depth of not less than 8 ft. Where rock bottom is encountered, the ground rod can be driven at an angle not to exceed 45 degrees or be placed in a trench that is at least 30 in. deep. ▶Figure 250–26

The upper end of the ground rod must be flush with or below ground level, unless the grounding electrode conductor attachment is protected against physical damage as specified in 250.10. ▶Figure 250–27

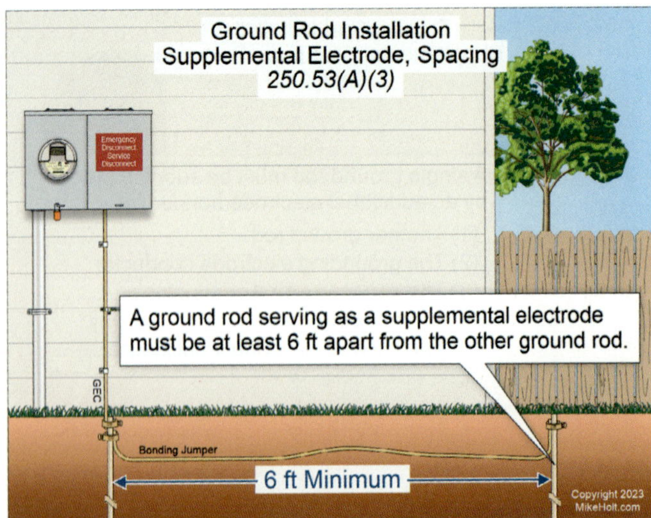

▶Figure 250–25

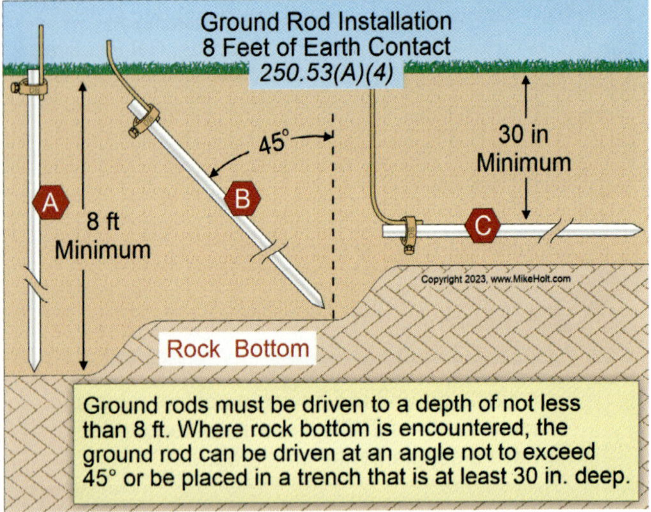

▶Figure 250–26

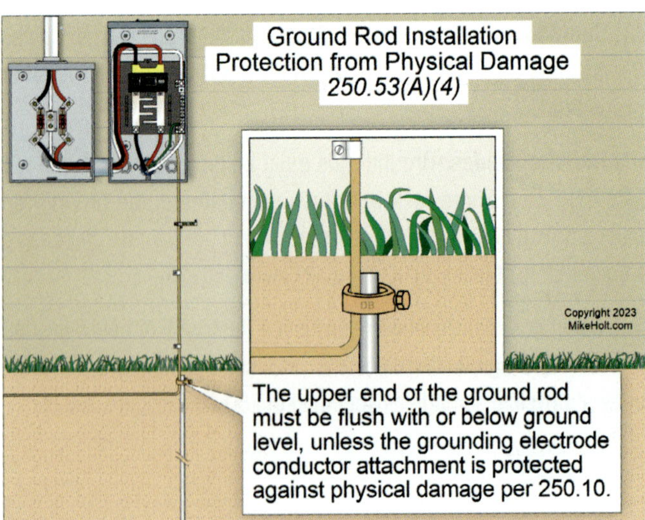

▶Figure 250–27

▸ When the grounding electrode attachment fitting is underground (below ground level), it must be listed for direct soil burial [250.70(A)].

(5) Plate Electrode. Plate electrodes must be installed no less than 30 in. below the surface of the Earth. ▶Figure 250–28

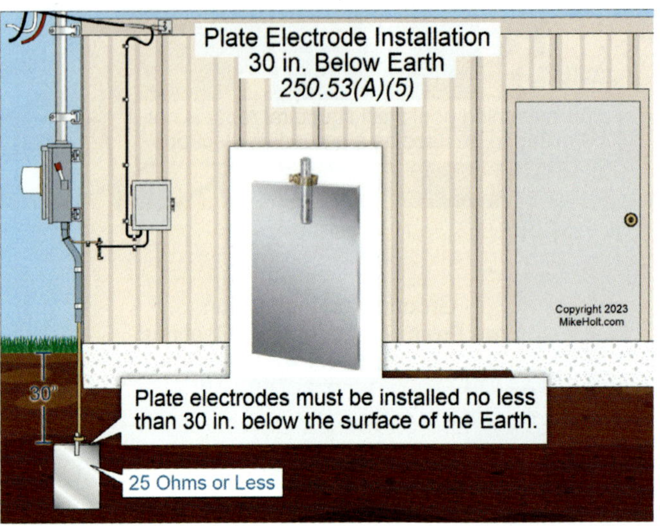

▶Figure 250–28

(B) Electrode Spacing. The building grounding electrode(s) must be at least 6 ft from other grounding electrode systems, such as the lightning protection grounding electrode(s). ▶Figure 250–29

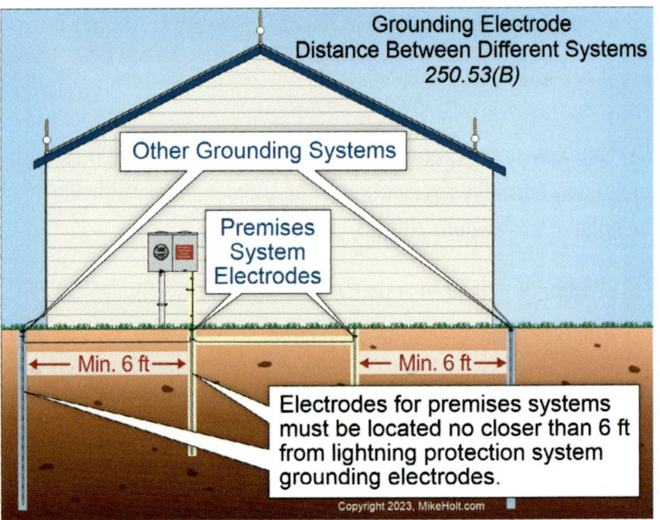

▶Figure 250–29

(C) Grounding Electrode Bonding Jumper. Grounding electrode bonding jumpers must be copper when within 18 in. of the Earth [250.64(A)]. Exposed grounding electrode bonding jumpers must be securely fastened to the surface and protected from physical damage [250.64(B)]. Grounding electrode bonding jumpers installed in metal raceways must be bonded at both ends [250.64(E)]. The bonding jumper to each electrode must be sized in accordance with 250.66. ▶Figure 250–30

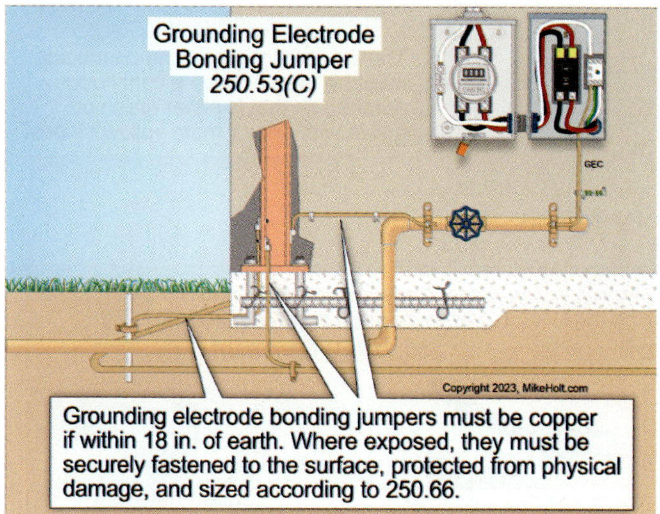

▶Figure 250–30

When the grounding electrode conductor termination is encased in concrete or buried, the termination fittings must be listed for this purpose [250.70(A)].

(D) Underground Metal Water Pipe Electrode.

(1) Continuity. The continuity of interior metal water piping systems must not rely on water meters or filtering devices. ▶Figure 250–31

(2) Water Pipe Supplemental Electrode. When an underground metal water pipe grounding electrode is present, it must be supplemented by any of the following electrodes:

▸ Metal frame of the building electrode [250.52(A)(2)]

▸ Concrete-encased electrode [250.52(A)(3)]

▸ Rod electrode [250.52(A)(5)]

▸ Other type of listed electrode [250.52(A)(6)]

▸ Metal underground piping electrode [250.52(A)(8)]

The grounding electrode conductor for the supplemental electrode must be bonded to any of the following: ▶Figure 250–32

(1) Grounding electrode conductor

(2) Service neutral conductor

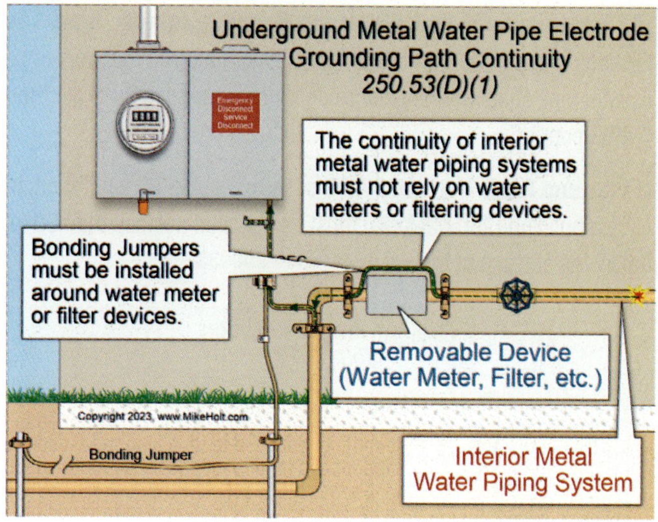

▶Figure 250–31

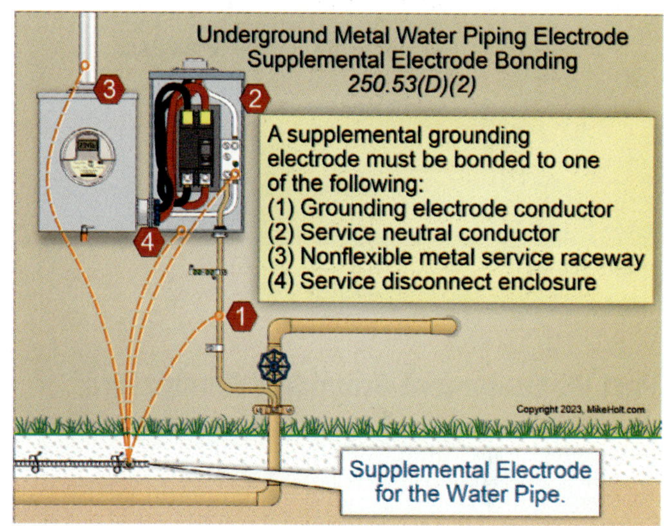

▶Figure 250–32

(3) Nonflexible metal service raceway

(4) Service-disconnect enclosure

Author's Comment:

▸ Because a metal underground waterpipe electrode could be replaced by a plastic water pipe, the supplemental electrode must be installed as if it is the only electrode for the system.

Ex: The supplemental electrode can be bonded to interior metal water piping not more than 5 ft from the point of entrance to the building [250.68(C)(1)].

(E) Supplemental Rod Electrode Bonding Jumper Size. The grounding electrode bonding jumper to a ground rod that serves as a water pipe supplemental electrode is not required to be larger than 6 AWG copper.

(F) Ground Ring. The bare 2 AWG or larger copper conductor encircling a building [250.52(A)(4)] must be installed not less than 30 in. below the surface of the Earth. ▶Figure 250–33

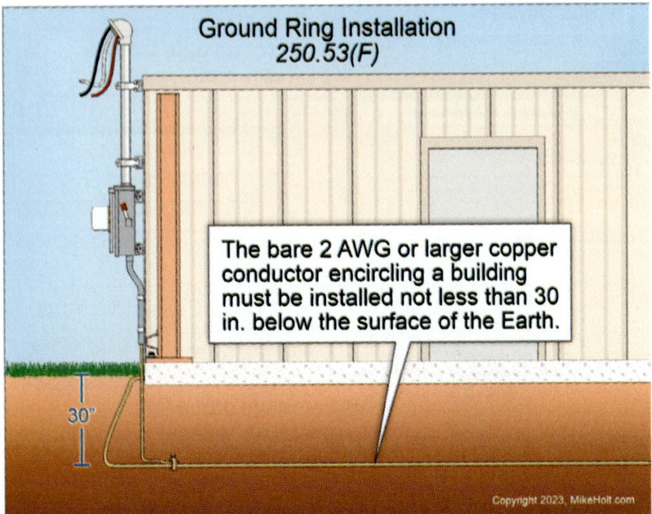

▶Figure 250–33

Part VI. Equipment Grounding Conductors

250.119 Identification of Wire-Type Equipment Grounding Conductors

(A) General. Unless required to be insulated in this *Code*, equipment grounding conductors can be bare or covered.

Conductors 6 AWG and Smaller. Insulated equipment grounding conductors 6 AWG and smaller, must have a continuous outer finish that is either green or green with one or more yellow stripes. ▶Figure 250–34

Conductors with insulation that is green or green with one or more yellow stripes are not permitted to be used as phase or neutral conductors.

> **Author's Comment:**
>
> ▶ The *NEC* does not require the color green to identify the grounding electrode conductor. ▶Figure 250–35

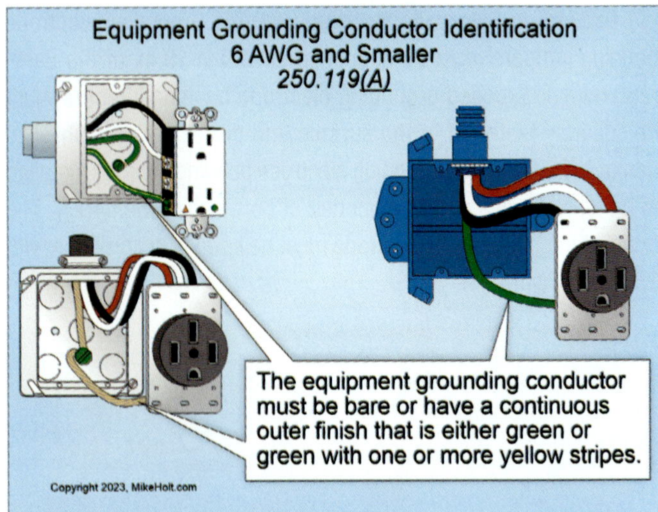

▶Figure 250–34

▶Figure 250–35

(B) Conductors 4 AWG and Larger. Insulated equipment grounding conductors 4 AWG and larger, must comply with 250.119(B)(1) and (B)(2).

(1) Identified Where Accessible. Insulated equipment grounding conductors 4 AWG and larger that do not comply with 250.119(A) must be reidentified with green marking in accordance with 250.119(B)(2) where the conductor is accessible. ▶Figure 250–36

(2) Identification at Terminals. The equipment grounding conductor identification at terminations must comply with one of the following: ▶Figure 250–37

a. Bare by removing the conductor insulation.

b. Coloring the insulation green.

c. Marking the insulation with green tape or green adhesive labels.

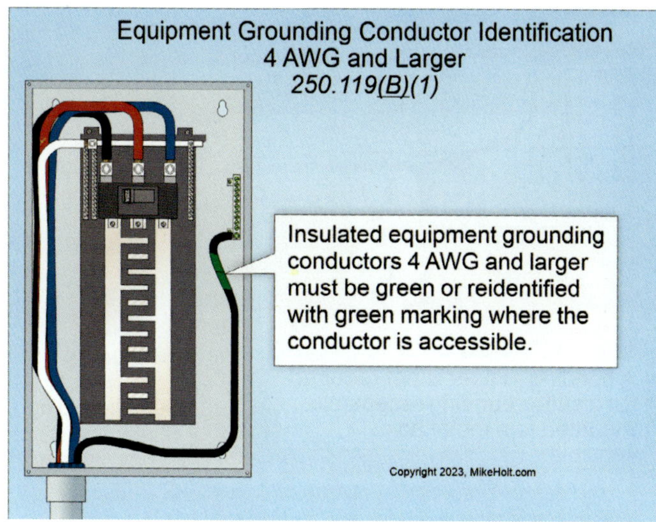

▶Figure 250–36

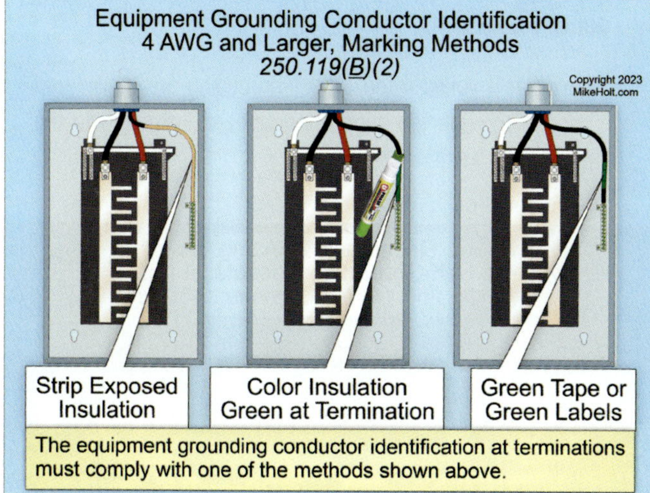

▶Figure 250–37

(C) Multiconductor Cable. One or more insulated conductors, regardless of size in a multiconductor cable, at the time of installation are permitted to be permanently identified as equipment grounding conductors at every point where the conductors are accessible by one of the following means:

(1) Stripping the insulation from the entire exposed length.

(2) Coloring the exposed insulation green.

(3) Marking the exposed insulation with green tape or green adhesive labels and must encircle the conductor.

Part VII. Equipment Grounding Conductor Connections

250.146 Connecting Receptacle Grounding Terminal to an Equipment Grounding Conductor

An equipment bonding conductor is required to connect the grounding terminals of a receptacle to a metal box, except as permitted in 250.146(A) through (D). ▶Figure 250–38

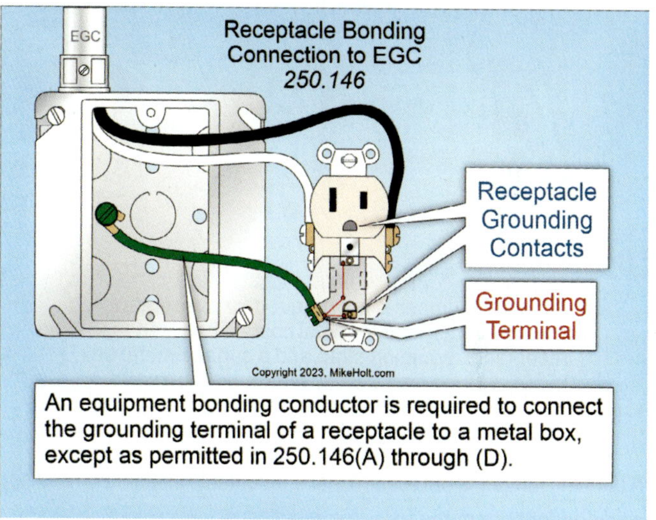

▶Figure 250–38

Author's Comment:

▶ The *NEC* does not restrict the position of the receptacle grounding terminal—it can be up, down, or sideways. *Code* proposals to specify the mounting position of receptacles have always been rejected. ▶Figure 250–39

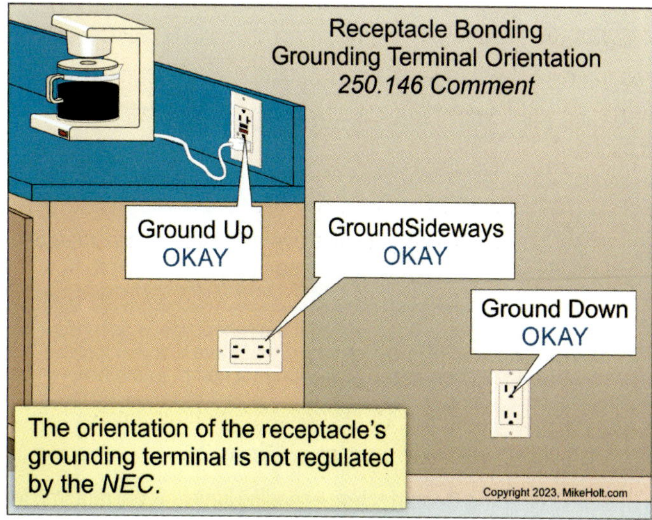

▶Figure 250–39

(A) Surface-Mounted Box. A bonding jumper is not required for a receptacle having direct metal-to-metal contact between the receptacle mounting yoke and a surface metal box. To ensure sufficient metal-to-metal contact, at least one of the insulating retaining washers on the yoke screw must be removed. ▶Figure 250–40

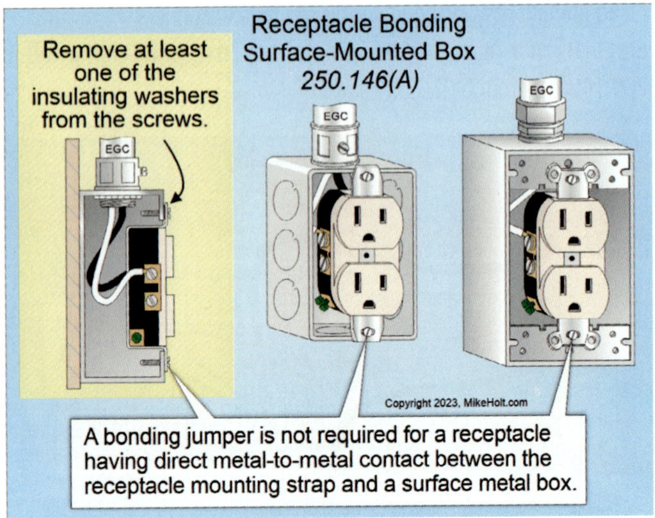

▶Figure 250–40

A bonding jumper is not required for a receptacle installed on a raised cover under both of the following conditions:

(1) The receptacle is attached to the metal cover with at least two fasteners that have a thread locking, or screw or nut locking means.

(2) The cover mounting holes are on a flat non-raised portion of the cover. ▶Figure 250–41

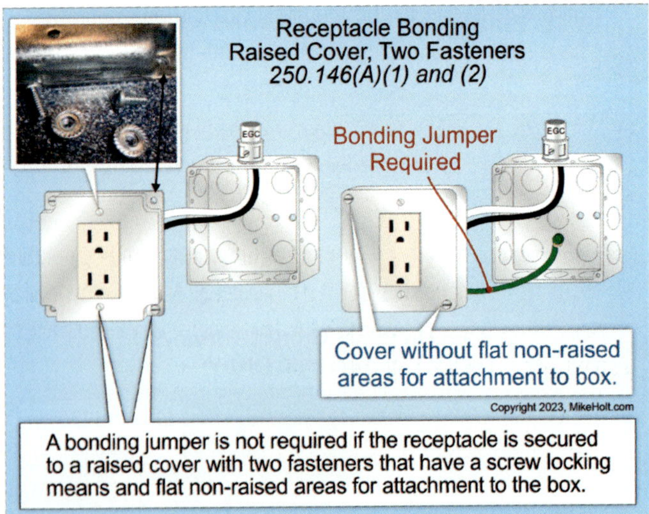

▶Figure 250–41

(B) Self-Grounding Receptacles. A bonding jumper is not required for a self-grounding receptacle mounted to a metal box. ▶Figure 250–42

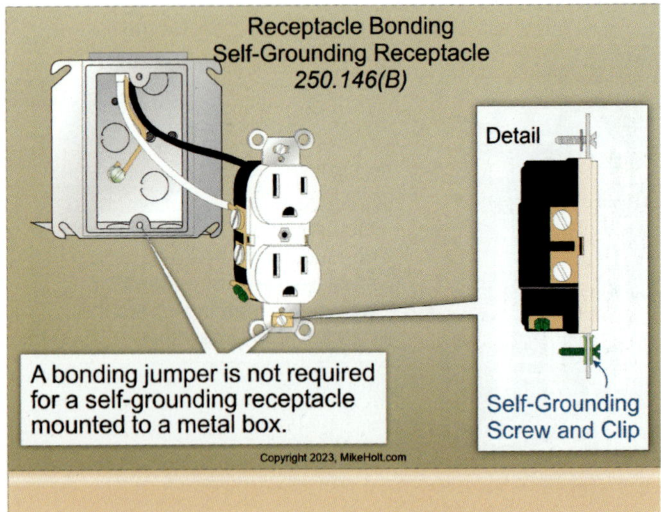

▶Figure 250–42

Author's Comment:

▶ Receptacle yokes listed as self-grounding are considered bonded through the supporting screws connected to the metal box. ▶Figure 250–43

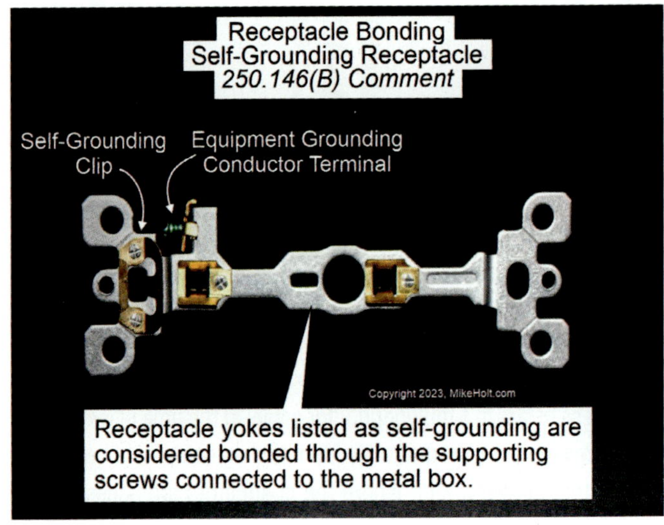

▶Figure 250–43

250.148 Continuity and Attachment of Equipment Grounding Conductors in Boxes

If circuit conductors are spliced or terminate to equipment in a box, the equipment grounding conductor must comply with 250.148(A) through (D).

(A) Connections and Splices. Equipment grounding conductors must be connected together in accordance with 110.14(B) and 250.8. ▶Figure 250–44

▶Figure 250–44

(B) Continuity of Equipment Grounding Conductors. Equipment grounding conductors must be connected in a manner where the disconnection or removal of a receptacle, device, or luminaire will not interrupt its electrical continuity. ▶Figure 250–45

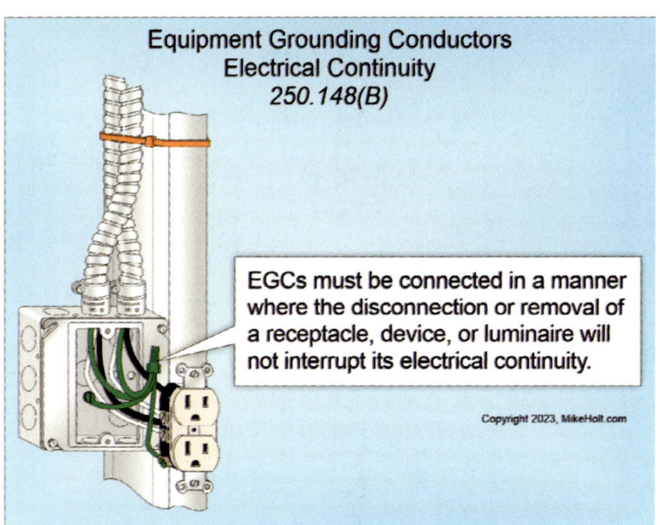

▶Figure 250–45

(C) Metal Boxes. Bonding jumpers and equipment grounding conductors must be connected to the metal box by a device that serves no other purpose. ▶Figure 250–46 and ▶Figure 250–47

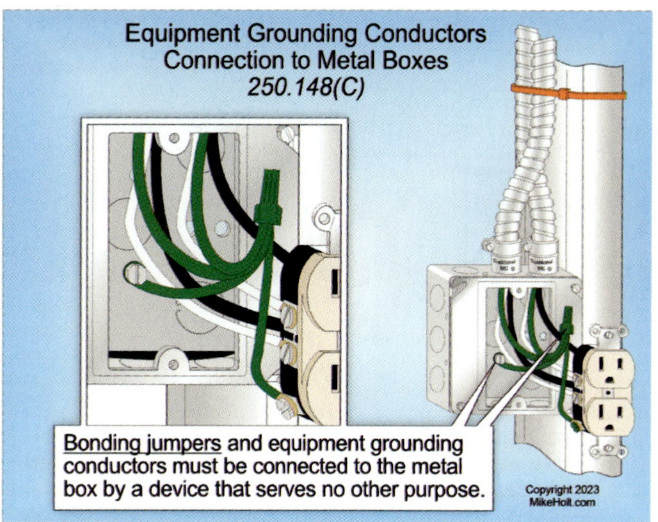

▶Figure 250–46

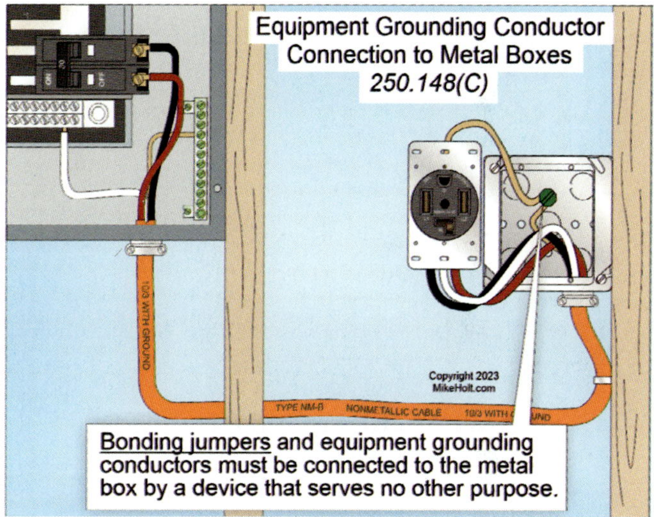

▶Figure 250–47

Ex: The circuit equipment grounding conductor for an isolated ground receptacle [250.146(D)] is not required to be bonded to other equipment grounding conductors or metal box. ▶Figure 250–48

(D) Nonmetallic Boxes. One or more equipment grounding conductors brought into a nonmetallic outlet box shall be arranged to provide a connection to any fitting or device in that box requiring connection to an equipment grounding conductor.

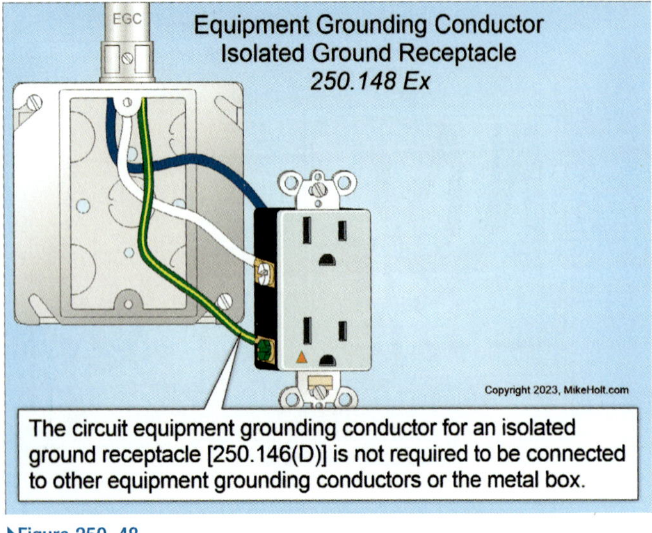

▶Figure 250–48

REVIEW QUESTIONS

Please use the 2023 *Code* book to answer the following questions.

Article 200—Use and Identification of Grounded Conductors

1. Article 200 provides the requirements for ______.

   (a) identification of terminals
   (b) grounded conductors in premises wiring systems
   (c) identification of grounded conductors
   (d) all of these

2. An insulated grounded conductor ______ or smaller shall be identified by a continuous white or gray outer finish, or by three continuous white or gray stripes along its entire length on other than green insulation.

   (a) 8 AWG
   (b) 6 AWG
   (c) 4 AWG
   (d) 3 AWG

3. At the time of installation, grounded conductors ______ or larger can be identified by a distinctive white or gray marking at their terminations.

   (a) 10 AWG
   (b) 8 AWG
   (c) 6 AWG
   (d) 4 AWG

4. A ______ shall be used only for the grounded circuit conductor, unless otherwise permitted in 200.7(B) and (C).

   (a) conductor with continuous white or gray covering
   (b) conductor with three continuous white or gray stripes on other than green insulation
   (c) marking of white or gray color at the termination
   (d) any of these

5. The white conductor within a cable assembly can be used for a(an) ______ conductor where permanently reidentified to indicate its use as an ungrounded conductor at each location where the conductor is visible and accessible.

   (a) grounded
   (b) ungrounded
   (c) equipment grounding
   (d) grounding electrode

Article 210—Branch Circuits

1. Article 210 provides the general requirements for ______ not over 1,000V ac, 1,500V dc, nominal.

   (a) outside branch circuits
   (b) branch circuits
   (c) ungrounded conductors
   (d) feeder calculations

2. A listed Class A GFCI shall provide protection in accordance with 210.8(A) through (F). The GFCI protective device shall be installed in a(an) ______ location.

   (a) circuit breaker type only
   (b) accessible
   (c) readily accessible
   (d) concealed

3. For the purposes of section 210.8, the distance from receptacles shall be measured as the shortest path the power supply cord connected to the receptacle would follow without piercing a ______ or fixed barrier.

   (a) floor
   (b) wall
   (c) ceiling
   (d) any of these

4. All 125V through 250V receptacles that are not readily accessible and supplied by single-phase branch circuits dedicated to electric ______ equipment shall be permitted to be installed in accordance with 426.28 or 427.22, as applicable.

   (a) snow-melting
   (b) deicing
   (c) pipeline and vessel heating
   (d) any of these

5. A receptacle supplying only a permanently installed premises ______ shall be permitted to omit ground-fault circuit-interrupter protection.

   (a) sump pump
   (b) refrigerator
   (c) security system
   (d) well pump

6. Factory-installed receptacles mounted internally to bathroom ______ assemblies shall not require GFCI protection unless required by the installation instructions or listing.

   (a) surface-mounted luminaire
   (b) exhaust fan
   (c) electric baseboard heat
   (d) all of these

7. All 125V through 250V receptacles installed in dwelling unit ______ and supplied by single-phase branch circuits rated 150V or less to ground shall have ground-fault circuit-interrupter protection for personnel.

   (a) hallways
   (b) bedrooms
   (c) closets
   (d) bathrooms

8. GFCI protection shall be provided for all 125V through 250V receptacles installed in dwelling unit ______.

   (a) attics
   (b) garages and accessory buildings
   (c) utility rooms
   (d) dens

9. All 125V through 250V receptacles installed in crawl spaces at or below grade level of dwelling units shall have ______ protection.

   (a) AFCI
   (b) GFCI
   (c) GFPE
   (d) none of these

10. GFCI protection shall be provided for all 125V through 250V ______ in dwelling unit basements.

    (a) receptacles
    (b) switches
    (c) outlets
    (d) disconnects

11. In dwelling unit kitchens, GFCI protection shall be provided for 125V through 250V receptacles ______.

    (a) installed to serve the countertop surfaces
    (b) within 6 ft from the top inside edge of the bowl of the sink
    (c) installed to serve above or below the countertop surfaces
    (d) serving the kitchen

12. In dwelling units, GFCI protection shall be provided for 125V through 250V receptacles installed in areas with sinks and permanent provisions for ______.

    (a) food preparation
    (b) beverage preparation
    (c) cooking
    (d) any of these

13. All 125V through 250V receptacles installed in dwelling unit boathouses shall have ______ protection.

    (a) GFCI
    (b) AFCI
    (c) GFPE
    (d) SPGFCI

14. GFCI protection shall be provided for crawl space lighting outlets not exceeding ______.

    (a) 120V
    (b) 125V
    (c) 240V
    (d) 250V

15. According to Article 210, GFCI protection shall be provided for the branch circuit or outlet supplying ______ rated 150V or less to ground and 60A or less, single- or three-phase.

    (a) sump pumps
    (b) wall-mounted ovens
    (c) clothes dryers
    (d) all of these

16. For dwellings, all outdoor outlets, other than those covered in 210.8(A) Ex 1, and supplied by single-phase branch circuits rated 150V or less to ground, ______, shall be provided with GFCI protection.

    (a) 15A or more
    (b) 20A or less
    (c) 30A or less
    (d) 50A or less

17. For dwellings, all outdoor outlets, other than those covered in 210.8(A) Ex 1, including outlets installed in ______, rated 50A or less, shall be provided with GFCI protection

    (a) garages that have floors located at or below grade level
    (b) accessory buildings
    (c) boathouses
    (d) all of these

18. All 120V, single-phase, 10A, 15A, and 20A branch circuits supplying outlets or devices installed in dwelling unit ______ shall be AFCI protected.

    (a) kitchens
    (b) garages
    (c) bathrooms
    (d) outdoor areas

19. All 120V, single-phase, 10A, 15A, and 20A branch circuits supplying outlets or devices installed in dwelling unit ______ shall be AFCI protected by any of the means described in 210.12(A)(1) through (6).

    (a) kitchens
    (b) family rooms
    (c) dining rooms
    (d) all of these

20. If branch-circuit wiring for any of the areas specified in 210.12(B), (C), or (D) is modified, replaced, or extended, the branch circuit shall be protected by a ______.

    (a) listed outlet branch-circuit type AFCI located at the first receptacle outlet of the existing branch circuit
    (b) listed combination GFPE circuit breaker only
    (c) GFCI circuit breaker
    (d) GFCI at first receptacle in the circuit

21. A single receptacle installed on an individual branch circuit shall have an ampere rating not less than the rating of the ______.

    (a) branch circuit
    (b) device listing
    (c) manufacturer's instructions
    (d) equipment current rating

22. The rating of any one cord-and plug-connected utilization equipment on a 15A, 120V branch circuit shall not exceed ______.

    (a) 12A
    (b) 15A
    (c) 16A
    (d) 20A

23. If a 20A branch circuit supplies multiple receptacles, the receptacles shall have an ampere rating of no less than ______.

    (a) 10A
    (b) 15A
    (c) 20A
    (d) 30A

24. The dwelling unit 15- and 20A receptacle outlets required by the *Code* are in addition to any receptacles that are ______.

    (a) part of a luminaire or appliance
    (b) located within cabinets or cupboards
    (c) located more than 5½ ft above the floor
    (d) any of these

25. A receptacle outlet shall be installed so no point along the floor line of any wall is more than ______, measured horizontally along the floor line, from a receptacle outlet.

    (a) 6 ft
    (b) 8 ft
    (c) 10 ft
    (d) 12 ft

26. In a dwelling unit, any wall space including space measured around corners and unbroken along the floor line by doorways, fireplaces, fixed cabinets, and similar openings shall be considered wall space when the wall space is at least ______ wide.

    (a) 2 ft
    (b) 3 ft
    (c) 4 ft
    (d) 6 ft

27. In dwelling units, when determining the spacing of receptacle outlets, ______ on exterior walls shall not be considered wall space.

    (a) fixed panels
    (b) fixed glass
    (c) sliding panels
    (d) all of these

28. Floor receptacle outlets shall not be counted as part of the required number of receptacle outlets for dwelling unit wall spaces, unless they are located within ______ of the wall.

    (a) 6 in.
    (b) 12 in.
    (c) 18 in.
    (d) 24 in.

29. Receptacles installed for ______ and similar work surfaces as specified in 210.52(C) shall not be considered as the receptacle outlets required by 210.52(A).

    (a) countertops
    (b) tables
    (c) peninsulas
    (d) none of these

30. The two or more small-appliance branch circuits specified in 210.52(B)(1) shall have ______.

    (a) no more than one outlet
    (b) no other outlets
    (c) unlimited outlets
    (d) supply only one appliance

31. Receptacle outlets are required for kitchen countertops and work surfaces that are ______ and wider.

    (a) 12 in.
    (b) 15 in.
    (c) 18 in.
    (d) 24 in.

32. Kitchen wall countertop and work surface space receptacle outlets shall be installed so that no point along the wall line is more than ______ measured horizontally from a receptacle outlet in that space.

    (a) 10 in.
    (b) 12 in.
    (c) 16 in.
    (d) 24 in.

33. If a receptacle outlet is not provided to serve an island or peninsular countertop or work surface, provisions shall be provided at the island or peninsula for the ______ addition of a receptacle outlet to serve the island or peninsular countertop or work surface.

    (a) future
    (b) permanent
    (c) possible
    (d) none of these

34. Kitchen and dining room countertop receptacle outlets in dwelling units shall be installed on or above the countertop or work surface, but not more than ______ above the countertop or work surface.

    (a) 12 in.
    (b) 18 in.
    (c) 20 in.
    (d) 24 in.

35. In dwelling units, the required bathroom receptacle outlet can be installed on the side or face of the sink cabinet if not more than ______ below the top of the sink or sink countertop.

    (a) 12 in.
    (b) 18 in.
    (c) 20 in.
    (d) 24 in.

36. In dwelling unit bathrooms, not less than one 15A or 20A, 125V receptacle outlet shall be installed within _______ of the outside edge of each bathroom basin.

    (a) 2 ft
    (b) 3 ft
    (c) 4 ft
    (d) 5 ft

37. There shall be at least _______ receptacle(s) installed outdoors at a one-family dwelling and each unit of a two-family dwelling unit that is at grade level.

    (a) one
    (b) two
    (c) three
    (d) four

38. At least one receptacle outlet not more than _______ above a balcony, deck, or porch shall be installed at each balcony, deck, or porch that is attached to and accessible from a dwelling unit.

    (a) 2 ft
    (b) 3 ft
    (c) 6½ ft
    (d) 8 ft

39. A laundry receptacle outlet shall not be required in each dwelling unit of a multifamily building if laundry facilities are provided on the _______ for all building occupants.

    (a) premises
    (b) outside
    (c) inside
    (d) roof

40. For one- and two-family dwellings, at least one receptacle outlet shall be installed in each _______.

    (a) separate unfinished portion of a basement
    (b) attached or detached garage with electric power
    (c) accessory building with electric power
    (d) all of these

41. For one- and two-family dwellings, and multifamily dwellings, at least one receptacle outlet shall be installed in each separate _______ of a basement.

    (a) unfinished portion
    (b) hallway
    (c) stairway
    (d) all of these

42. Hallways in dwelling units that are _______ or longer require a receptacle outlet.

    (a) 6 ft
    (b) 8 ft
    (c) 10 ft
    (d) 12 ft

43. Foyers with an area greater than _______ shall have a receptacle located in each wall space 3 ft or more in width unbroken by doorways, windows next to doors that extend to the floor, and similar openings.

    (a) 40 sq ft
    (b) 60 sq ft
    (c) 80 sq ft
    (d) 100 sq ft

44. Required lighting outlet switch or wall-mounted control devices shall not rely exclusively on a _______ unless a means is provided for automatically energizing the lighting outlets upon battery failure.

    (a) battery
    (b) solar cell
    (c) thermocouple
    (d) none of these

45. At least one lighting outlet controlled by a listed _______ shall be installed in every habitable room, kitchen, laundry area, and bathroom of a dwelling unit.

    (a) wall-mounted control device
    (b) switch
    (c) occupancy sensor
    (d) motion detector

46. In rooms other than kitchens, laundry areas, and bathrooms of dwelling units, one or more receptacles controlled by a listed wall-mounted control device shall be permitted in lieu of _______.

    (a) lighting outlets
    (b) luminaires
    (c) the receptacles required by 210.52(B) and (D)
    (d) all of these

47. At least one lighting outlet controlled by a listed wall-mounted control device shall be installed in dwelling unit hallways, stairways, and ______.

    (a) attached garages
    (b) detached garages with electric power
    (c) accessory buildings with electric power
    (d) all of these

48. For dwelling units, attached garages, detached garages with electric power, and accessory buildings with electric power, at least ______ exterior lighting outlet(s) controlled by a listed wall-mounted control device shall be installed to provide illumination on the exterior side of outdoor entrances or exits with grade-level access.

    (a) one
    (b) two
    (c) three
    (d) one or two

49. Where lighting outlets are installed for an interior stairway with ______ risers between floor levels, there shall be a listed wall-mounted control device at each floor level and at each landing level that includes a stairway entry to control the lighting outlets.

    (a) three or more
    (b) four or more
    (c) six or more
    (d) any number of

50. In a dwelling unit, dimmer control of lighting outlets for interior stairways installed in accordance with 210.70(A)(2)(3) shall not be permitted unless the listed control devices can provide dimming control ______ at each control location for the interior stairway illumination.

    (a) for illumination
    (b) for emergency lighting
    (c) to maximum brightness
    (d) for effective lighting

51. At least one lighting outlet ______ shall be located at the point of entry to the attic, underfloor space, utility room, or basement where these spaces are used for storage or contain equipment requiring servicing.

    (a) that is unswitched
    (b) containing or controlled by a switch or listed wall-mounted control device
    (c) that is GFCI protected
    (d) that is shielded from damage

Article 250—Grounding and Bonding

1. General requirements for grounding and bonding of electrical installations and the location of grounding connections are within the scope of ______.

    (a) Article 110
    (b) Article 200
    (c) Article 250
    (d) Article 680

2. Concrete-encased electrodes ______ shall not be required to be part of the grounding electrode system if the rebar is not accessible for use without disturbing the concrete.

    (a) in hazardous (classified) locations
    (b) in health care facilities
    (c) of existing buildings or structures
    (d) in agricultural buildings with equipotential planes

3. In order for a metal underground water pipe to be used as a grounding electrode, it shall be in direct contact with the earth for ______.

    (a) 5 ft
    (b) 10 ft or more
    (c) less than 10 ft
    (d) 20 ft or more

4. One or more metal in-ground support structure(s) in direct contact with the earth vertically for ______ or more, with or without concrete encasement, is permitted to be a grounding electrode in accordance with 250.52.

    (a) 4 ft
    (b) 6 ft
    (c) 8 ft
    (d) 10 ft

5. Rebar in multiple pieces used as a concrete-encased electrode shall be connected together by ______ tie wires or other effective means.

    (a) steel
    (b) plastic
    (c) aluminum
    (d) fiber glass

6. An electrode encased by at least 2 in. of concrete, located horizontally near the bottom or vertically and within that portion of a concrete foundation or footing that is in direct contact with the earth, is permitted as a grounding electrode when it consists of a bare copper conductor not smaller than ______.

    (a) 8 AWG
    (b) 6 AWG
    (c) 4 AWG
    (d) 1/0 AWG

7. If multiple concrete-encased electrodes are present at a building or structure, it shall be permissible to bond only ______ into the grounding electrode system.

    (a) one
    (b) two
    (c) three
    (d) four

8. The minimum length of a 4 AWG concrete-encased electrode is at least ______.

    (a) 10 ft
    (b) 20 ft
    (c) 25 ft
    (d) 50 ft

9. Concrete-encased grounding electrodes that are installed where the concrete is installed with ______ is not considered to be in direct contact with the earth.

    (a) insulation
    (b) vapor barriers
    (c) films
    (d) any of these

10. A ground ring encircling the building or structure can be used as a grounding electrode when the ______.

    (a) ring is in direct contact with the earth
    (b) ring consists of at least 20 ft of bare copper conductor
    (c) bare copper conductor is not smaller than 2 AWG
    (d) all of these

11. Grounding electrodes of the rod type less than ______ in diameter shall be listed.

    (a) ½ in.
    (b) ⅝ in.
    (c) ¾ in.
    (d) 1 in.

12. Rod and pipe grounding electrodes shall not be less than ______ in length.

    (a) 6 ft
    (b) 8 ft
    (c) 10 ft
    (d) 20 ft

13. A buried iron or steel plate used as a grounding electrode shall expose not less than ______ of surface area to exterior soil.

    (a) 2 sq ft
    (b) 4 sq ft
    (c) 9 sq ft
    (d) 10 sq ft

14. Grounding electrodes of bare or electrically conductive coated iron or steel plates shall be at least ______ thick.

    (a) ⅛ in.
    (b) ¼ in.
    (c) ½ in.
    (d) ¾ in.

15. Metal underground systems or structures such as piping systems, underground tanks, and underground metal well casings that are not bonded to a metal ______ are permitted as grounding electrodes.

    (a) gas pipe
    (b) fire-sprinkler pipe
    (c) water pipe
    (d) none of these

16. ______ shall not be used as a grounding electrode(s).

    (a) Metal underground gas piping systems
    (b) Aluminum
    (c) Swimming pool structures and structural rebar
    (d) all of these

17. ______ electrodes shall be free from nonconductive coatings such as paint or enamel.

    (a) Rod
    (b) Pipe
    (c) Plate
    (d) all of these

18. If practicable, rod, pipe, and plate electrodes shall be embedded ______.

    (a) directly below the electrical meter
    (b) on the north side of the building
    (c) below permanent moisture level
    (d) all of these

19. The grounding electrode conductor to a ground rod that serves as a supplemental electrode for the metal water pipe electrode is not required to be larger than ______ copper wire.

    (a) 8 AWG
    (b) 6 AWG
    (c) 4 AWG
    (d) 3 AWG

20. Where the resistance-to-ground of 25 ohms or less is not achieved for a single rod electrode, ______.

    (a) other means besides electrodes shall be used in order to provide grounding
    (b) the single rod electrode shall be supplemented by one additional electrode
    (c) additional electrodes shall be added until 25 ohms is achieved
    (d) any of these

21. If multiple rod, pipe, or plate electrodes are installed to supplement the water pipe electrode, they shall not be less than ______ apart.

    (a) 3 ft
    (b) 4 ft
    (c) 5 ft
    (d) 6 ft

22. A rod or pipe electrode shall be installed such that at least ______ of length is in contact with the soil.

    (a) 30 in.
    (b) 6 ft
    (c) 8 ft
    (d) 10 ft

23. Where rock bottom is encountered, a rod or pipe electrode shall be driven at an angle not to exceed ______ from the vertical.

    (a) 15 degrees
    (b) 30 degrees
    (c) 45 degrees
    (d) 60 degrees

24. The upper end of the rod electrode shall be ______ ground level unless the aboveground end and the grounding electrode conductor attachment are protected against physical damage as specified in 250.10.

    (a) no more than 1 in. above
    (b) no more than 2 in. above
    (c) no more than 3 in. above
    (d) flush with or below ground level

25. Plate electrodes shall be installed not less than ______ below the surface of the earth.

    (a) 30 in.
    (b) 4 ft
    (c) 5 ft
    (d) 6 ft

26. Where a metal underground water pipe is used as a grounding electrode, the continuity of the grounding path or the bonding connection to interior piping shall not rely on ______ and similar equipment.

    (a) bonding jumpers
    (b) water meters or filtering devices
    (c) grounding clamps
    (d) all of these

27. If the supplemental electrode is a rod, pipe, or plate electrode, that portion of the bonding jumper that is the sole connection to the supplemental grounding electrode is not required to be larger than ______ copper.

    (a) 8 AWG
    (b) 6 AWG
    (c) 4 AWG
    (d) 1 AWG

28. When a ground ring is used as a grounding electrode, it shall be installed at a depth below the earth's surface of not less than ______.

    (a) 18 in.
    (b) 24 in.
    (c) 30 in.
    (d) 8 ft

29. A wire-type equipment grounding conductor can be identified by ______.

    (a) a continuous outer finish that is green
    (b) being bare
    (c) a continuous outer finish that is green with one or more yellow stripes
    (d) any of these

30. An insulated wire-type equipment grounding conductor ______ and larger shall be at the time of installation, if the insulation does not comply with 250.119(A), permanently identified as an equipment grounding conductor at each end and at every point where the conductor is accessible.

    (a) 8 AWG
    (b) 6 AWG
    (c) 4 AWG
    (d) 1/0 AWG

31. One or more insulated conductors in a multiconductor cable, at the time of installation, shall be permitted to be permanently identified as equipment grounding conductors at each end and at every point where the conductors are accessible by coloring the insulation ______.

    (a) green
    (b) grey
    (c) green with a yellow stripe
    (d) white or silver

32. A(An) ______ shall be used to connect the grounding terminal of a grounding-type receptacle to a metal box that is connected to an equipment grounding conductor.

    (a) equipment bonding jumper
    (b) grounded conductor jumper
    (c) equipment bonding jumper or grounded conductor jumper
    (d) equipment bonding jumper and grounded conductor jumper

33. Where the metal box for a receptacle is surface mounted, direct metal-to-metal contact between the device yoke and the box shall be permitted to ground the receptacle to the box if at least ______ of the insulating washers of the receptacle is (are) removed.

    (a) one
    (b) two
    (c) three
    (d) four

34. A listed exposed work cover can be the grounding and bonding means for a surface-mounted metal box when the device is attached to the cover with at least ______ permanent fastener(s) and the exposed work cover mounting holes are located on a non-raised portion of the cover.

    (a) one
    (b) two
    (c) three
    (d) four

35. Receptacle yokes or contact devices designed and ______ as self-grounding can, in conjunction with the supporting screws, establish the equipment bonding between the device yoke and a flush-type box.

    (a) approved
    (b) advertised
    (c) listed
    (d) installed

36. All ______ that are spliced or terminated within the box shall be connected together. Connections and splices shall be made in accordance with 110.14(B) and 250.8 except that insulation shall not be required.

    (a) neutral conductors
    (b) equipment grounding conductors
    (c) phase conductors
    (d) switch-legs

37. The arrangement of grounding connections shall ensure that the disconnection or the removal of a luminaire, receptacle, or other device fed from the box does not interrupt the electrical continuity of the ______ conductor(s) providing an effective ground-fault current path.

    (a) grounded
    (b) ungrounded
    (c) equipment grounding
    (d) all of these

38. For the continuity of equipment grounding conductors and attachment in boxes, a connection used for ______ shall be made between the metal box and the equipment grounding conductor(s).

    (a) bonding
    (b) connections and splices
    (c) extending the length of the circuit
    (d) no other purpose

39. A connection used for no other purpose shall be made between the metal box and the equipment grounding conductor(s). The equipment bonding jumper or equipment grounding conductor shall be sized from Table 250.122 based on the largest _______ conductors in the box.

    (a) overcurrent device protecting circuit
    (b) ungrounded
    (c) grounded
    (d) neutral

40. One or more equipment grounding conductors brought into a nonmetallic outlet box shall be arranged to provide a connection to _______ in that box requiring connection to an equipment grounding conductor.

    (a) any fitting or device
    (b) a ground clip
    (c) a clamp(s)
    (d) the grounded conductor

WIRING METHODS AND MATERIALS

Introduction to Chapter 3—Wiring Methods and Materials

Chapter 3 of the *Code* is divided into fifty-one articles containing the general rules for wiring and sizing circuits, overcurrent protection of conductors, overvoltage protection of equipment, and bonding and grounding. The rules in this chapter apply to all electrical installations covered by the *NEC*—except as modified in Chapters 5, 6, 7, or specifically referenced in Chapter 8 [90.3].

This chapter can be thought of as the rough in phase of a job because it is primarily focused on the wiring methods and materials used to rough out an installation. Every article in this chapter deals with a different method or material used to get wiring from point "A" to point "B" in a system. The Chapter 3 articles covered by this material are:

Wiring Method Articles

▶ **Article 300—General Requirements for Wiring Methods and Materials.** Article 300 contains the general requirements for all wiring methods included in the *Code*, except for Class 2 power-limited, fire alarm and coaxial cables, which are covered in Chapters 7 and 8.

▶ **Article 310—Conductors for General Wiring.** This article contains the general requirements for conductors such as insulation markings, ampacity ratings, and conductor use. There is also a section that addresses single-family dwelling service and feeder conductors exclusively. Article 310 does not apply to conductors that are part of flexible cords, fixture wires, or conductors that are an integral part of equipment [90.7 and 310.1].

▶ **Article 312—Cabinets, Cutout Boxes, and Meter Socket Enclosures.** Article 312 covers the installation and construction specifications for cabinets and meter socket enclosures.

▶ **Article 314—Outlet, Device, Pull, and Junction Boxes; Conduit Bodies; Fittings; and Handhole Enclosures.** Installation requirements for outlet boxes, pull and junction boxes, as well as conduit bodies and handhole enclosures are contained in this article.

Cable Articles

Articles 320 through 340 address specific types of cables. If you take the time to become familiar with the various types of cables, you will be able to:

  ▶ Understand what is available for doing the work.

  ▶ Recognize cable types having special *NEC* requirements.

  ▶ Avoid buying cable you cannot install due to *Code* requirements you cannot meet with that wiring method.

. . .

Here is a brief overview of the cable articles covered in this material:

▶ **Article 320—Armored Cable (Type AC).** Armored cable is an assembly of insulated conductors, 14 AWG through 1 AWG, individually wrapped with waxed paper. The conductors are contained within a flexible metal (steel or aluminum) spiral sheath that interlocks at the edges. Armored cable looks like flexible metal conduit. Many electricians call this metal cable "BX®."

▶ **Article 330—Metal-Clad Cable (Type MC).** Metal-clad cable encloses insulated conductors in a metal sheath of corrugated, smooth copper or aluminum tubing, or spiral interlocked steel or aluminum. The physical characteristics of Type MC cable make it a versatile wiring method permitted in almost any location and for almost any application. The most used Type MC cable is the interlocking kind, which looks like armored cable or flexible metal conduit.

▶ **Article 334—Nonmetallic-Sheathed Cable (Type NM).** Nonmetallic-sheathed cable is commonly referred to by its trade name "Romex®." It encloses two, three, or four insulated conductors, 14 AWG through 2 AWG, within a nonmetallic outer jacket. Because this cable is manufactured in this manner, it contains a separate (usually bare) equipment grounding conductor. Nonmetallic-sheathed cable is commonly used for residential wiring applications but may sometimes be permitted for use in commercial occupancies.

▶ **Article 336—Power and Control Tray Cable (Type TC).** Power and control tray cable is flexible, inexpensive, and easily installed. It provides very limited physical protection for the conductors, so the installation restrictions are rigorous. Its low cost and relative ease of installation make it a common wiring method for industrial applications.

▶ **Article 338—Service-Entrance Cable (Types SE and USE).** Service-entrance and underground service-entrance cables can be a single conductor or a multiconductor assembly within an overall nonmetallic outer jacket or covering. These cables are most often used for services not over 1000V but are also permitted for feeders and branch circuits. When used as a service conductor(s) or a service-entrance conductor(s), pre-manufactured Type "SE" cable assemblies will typically contain two insulated phase conductors and a bare neutral conductor. When permitted for use as a feeder or branch circuit, Type SE cable is usually designated as Type "SER" and will contain the same three conductors as Type SE but a fourth conductor (which is insulated) will be added to serve as the neutral conductor.

▶ **Article 340—Underground Feeder and Branch-Circuit Cable (Type UF).** Underground feeder cable is a moisture-, fungus-, and corrosion-resistant cable suitable for direct burial in the Earth and is available in sizes 14 AWG through 4/0 AWG [340.104]. Multiconductor UF cable is covered in molded plastic that surrounds the insulated conductors.

Raceway Articles

Articles 342 through 390 address specific types of raceways. Refer to Article 100 for the definition of a raceway. If you take the time to become familiar with the various types of raceways, you will be able to:

▶ Understand what is available for doing the work.

▶ Recognize raceway types having special *Code* requirements.

▶ Avoid buying a raceway you cannot install due to *NEC* requirements you cannot meet with that wiring method.

Here is a brief overview of the raceway articles included in this material:

▶ **Article 342—Intermediate Metal Conduit (IMC).** Intermediate metal conduit is a circular metal raceway with the same outside diameter as rigid metal conduit. The wall thickness of this type of conduit is less than that of rigid metal conduit, so it has a larger interior cross-sectional area for holding conductors. Intermediate metal conduit is lighter and less expensive than rigid metal conduit and is approved by the *Code* for use in the same applications as rigid metal conduit. This type of conduit also uses a different steel alloy, which makes it stronger than rigid metal conduit, even though the walls are thinner.

▶ **Article 344—Rigid Metal Conduit (RMC).** Rigid metal conduit is like intermediate metal conduit, except the wall thickness is larger, so it has a smaller interior cross-sectional area. This type of conduit is heavier than intermediate metal conduit and is permitted for use in the same applications as intermediate metal conduit (IMC).

▶ **Article 348—Flexible Metal Conduit (FMC).** Flexible metal conduit is a raceway of circular cross section made of a helically wound, interlocked metal strip of either steel or aluminum. It is commonly called "Greenfield" (after its inventor) or "Flex."

▶ **Article 350—Liquidtight Flexible Metal Conduit (LFMC).** Liquidtight flexible metal conduit is a raceway of circular cross section with an outer liquidtight, nonmetallic, sunlight-resistant jacket over an inner flexible metal core, with associated couplings, connectors, and fittings. It is listed for the installation of electrical conductors. This type of conduit is commonly called "Sealtite®" or simply "liquidtight." Liquidtight flexible metal conduit is similar in construction to flexible metal conduit, but it has an outer thermoplastic covering.

▶ **Article 352—Rigid Polyvinyl Chloride Conduit (PVC).** Rigid polyvinyl chloride conduit is a nonmetallic raceway of circular cross section with integral or associated couplings, connectors, and fittings. It is listed for the installation of electrical conductors.

▶ **Article 356—Liquidtight Flexible Nonmetallic Conduit (LFNC).** Liquidtight flexible nonmetallic conduit (commonly referred to as "Carflex®") is a raceway of circular cross section with an outer liquidtight, nonmetallic, sunlight-resistant jacket over an inner flexible core, with associated couplings, connectors, and fittings.

▶ **Article 358—Electrical Metallic Tubing (EMT).** Electrical metallic tubing is a nonthreaded thinwall raceway of circular cross section designed for the physical protection and routing of conductors and cables. Compared to rigid metal conduit and intermediate metal conduit, electrical metallic tubing is relatively easy to bend, cut, and ream. EMT is not threaded, so all connectors and couplings are of the threadless type. It is available in a range of colors, such as red and blue.

▶ **Article 362—Electrical Nonmetallic Tubing (ENT).** Electrical nonmetallic tubing is a pliable, corrugated, circular raceway made of PVC. It is often referred to as "Smurf Pipe" or "Smurf Tube," because it was only available in blue when it was first available. The nickname is a reference to the children's cartoon characters "The Smurfs." It is now available in many other colors.

▶ **Article 376—Metal Wireways.** A metal wireway is a sheet metal trough with hinged or removable covers making the electrical conductors and cables housed and protected inside accessible. Metal wireways must be installed as complete and contiguous systems.

▶ **Article 380—Multioutlet Assemblies.** A multioutlet assembly is a surface, flush, or freestanding raceway designed to hold conductors and receptacles. It is assembled in the field or at the factory.

▶ **Article 386—Surface Metal Raceways.** A surface metal raceway is a metal raceway intended to be mounted to a surface with associated accessories, in which conductors are placed after the raceway has been installed as a complete system.

Cable Trays

▶ **Article 392—Cable Trays.** A cable tray system is a unit or assembly of units or sections with associated fittings forming a structural system used to securely fasten or support cables and raceways. A cable tray is not a raceway. It is a support system for raceways, cables, and enclosures.

Notice as you read through the various wiring methods that the *NEC* attempts to use similar section numbering for similar topics from one article to the next. It uses the same digits after the decimal point in the section numbers for the same topic. This makes it easier to locate the specific requirements of a particular article. For example, the rules for securing and supporting can be found in the section ending with ".30" of each article.

GENERAL REQUIREMENTS FOR WIRING METHODS AND MATERIALS

Introduction to Article 300—General Requirements for Wiring Methods and Materials

Article 300 contains the general requirements for all installed wiring methods included in the *NEC*. Because the *Code* is an installation standard this article does not apply where these wiring methods are integral parts of electrical equipment.

Because Article 300 contains the general requirements for wiring methods and materials, you must have a solid understanding of these rules to correctly and safely install the wiring methods included in Chapter 3. Some topics covered in this material include:

- ▸ Conductors
- ▸ Terminations
- ▸ Burial Depth
- ▸ Electrical and mechanical continuity of raceways and cables
- ▸ Securing and supporting
- ▸ Length of free conductors

Part I. General Requirements

300.1 Scope

(A) All Wiring Installations. Article 300 contains the general requirements for wiring methods and materials for power and lighting. ▸Figure 300–1

Author's Comment:

- ▸ The requirements contained in Article 300 do not apply to Class 2 power-limited circuits, fire alarm circuits, optical fiber cables, or coaxial cable, unless they are specifically reference in the appropriate article.

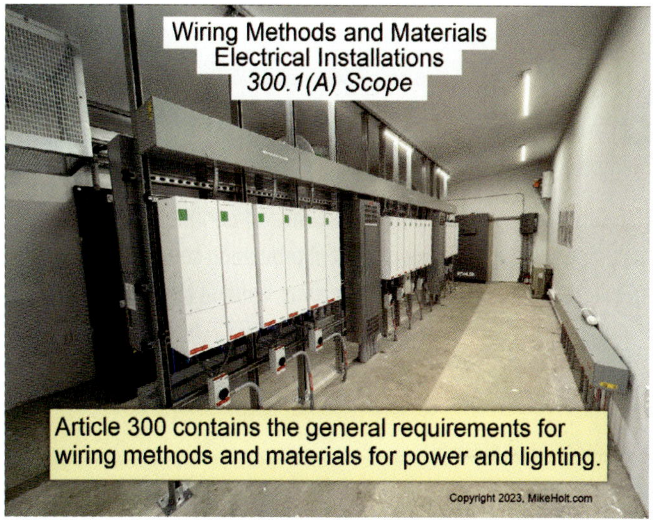

▸Figure 300–1

(B) Integral Parts of Equipment. The requirements contained in Article 300 do not apply to the integral parts of electrical equipment. ▶Figure 300–2

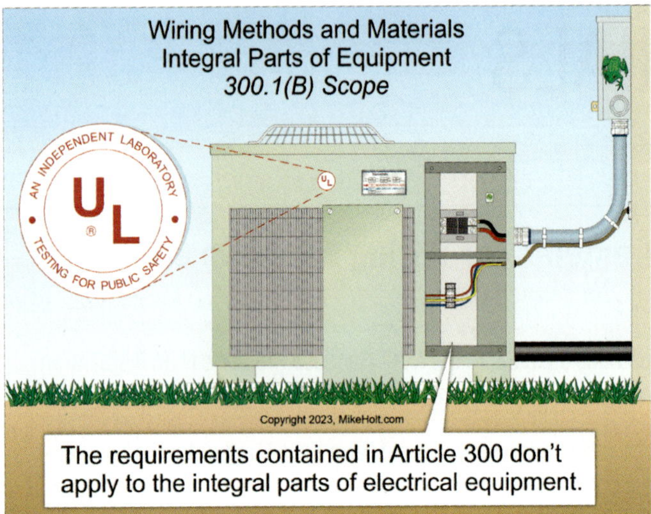

▶Figure 300–2

Author's Comment:

▶ Integral wiring of equipment is covered by various product standards and not the *NEC*. It is the intent of this *Code* that the factory-installed internal wiring of equipment processed by a qualified testing laboratory does not need to be inspected [90.7].

300.3 Conductors

(A) Conductors. Conductors must be installed in a Chapter 3 wiring method, such as raceways, cables, or cable trays. ▶Figure 300–3

(B) Conductors Grouped Together. All conductors of a circuit, including the neutral and equipment grounding conductors, must be installed together in the same raceway, conduit body, cable, trench, or cable tray except as permitted by 300.3(B)(1) through (4). ▶Figure 300–4

Author's Comment:

▶ The equipment grounding conductor must be grouped together with the circuit conductors to provide a low impedance path during a short-circuit or ground-fault event. ▶Figure 300–5

▶Figure 300–3

▶Figure 300–4

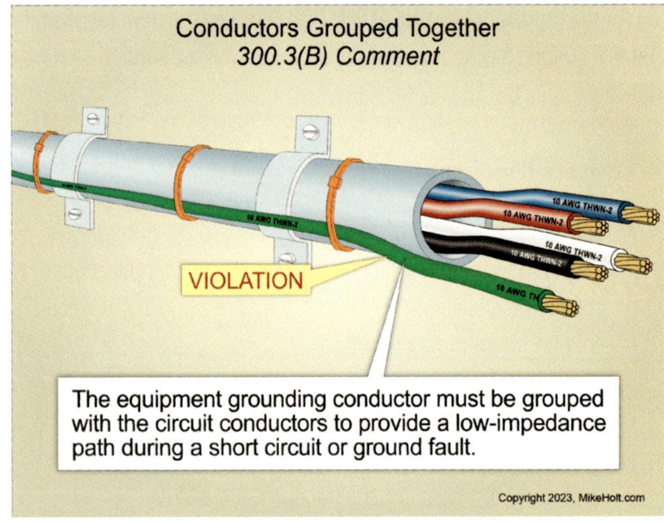

▶Figure 300–5

(1) Paralleled Installations. All conductors of a parallel set must be installed within the same raceway, cable, or cable tray in accordance with 310.10(G). ▶Figure 300–6

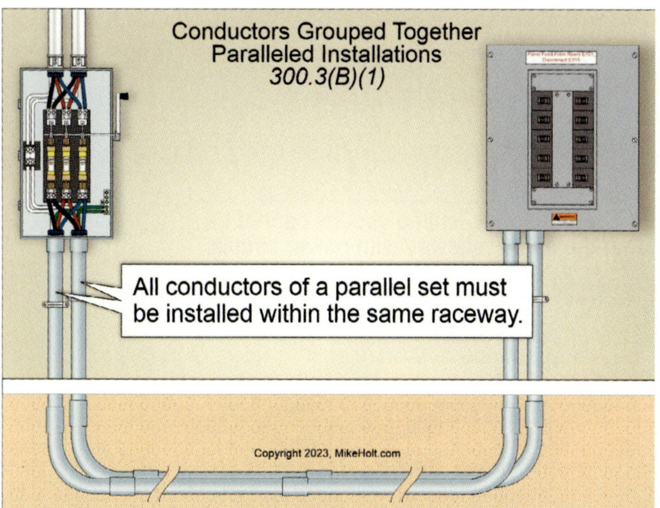

▶Figure 300–6

Connections, taps, or extensions made from paralleled conductors must connect to all conductors of the paralleled set.

Author's Comment:

▶ Grouping all phase, neutral, and equipment grounding and bonding conductors of the circuit helps minimize the inductive heating of the surrounding steel raceways and enclosures for alternating-current circuits. See 300.20(A). ▶Figure 300–7

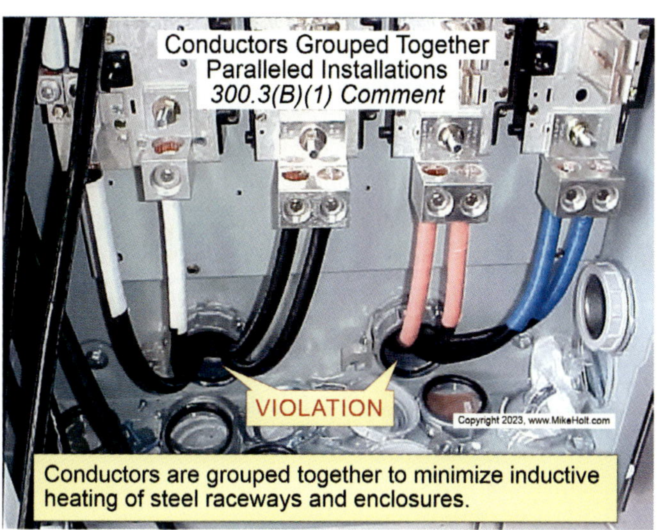

▶Figure 300–7

Ex: Isolated parallel phase and neutral conductors can be installed in individual underground nonmetallic raceways (Phase A in raceway 1, Phase B in raceway 2, and so forth) as permitted by 300.5(I) Ex 2, if the installation complies with 300.20(B). ▶Figure 300–8

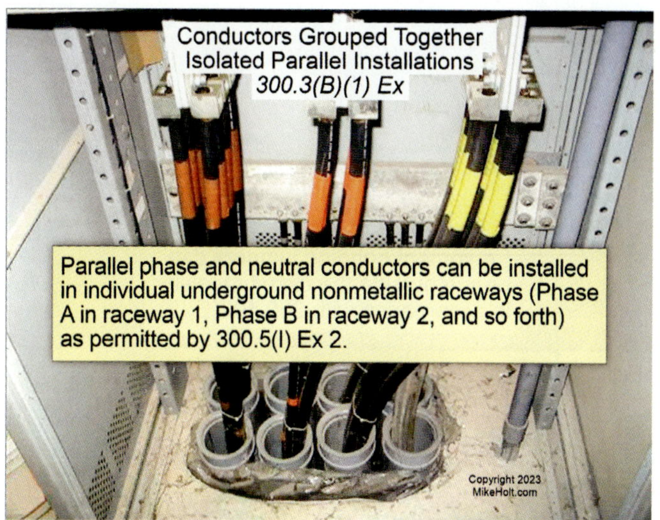

▶Figure 300–8

(2) Bonding Jumpers Outside the Raceway. Equipment bonding jumpers for dc circuits can be run separately from the circuit conductors in accordance with 250.134(2) Ex 2. ▶Figure 300–9

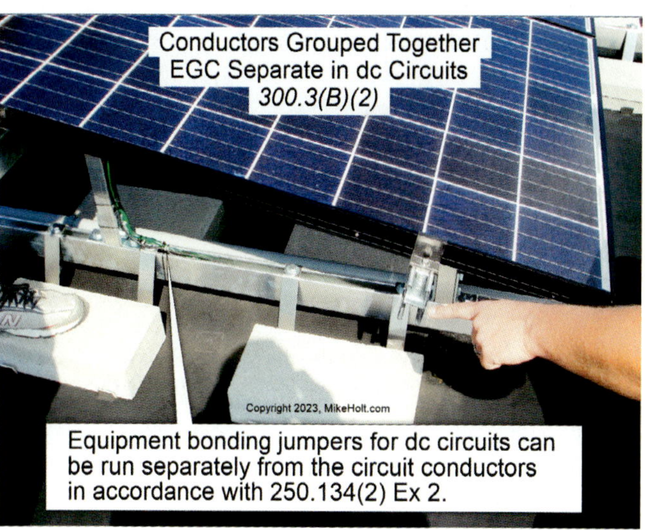

▶Figure 300–9

Equipment bonding jumpers can be run outside the circuit raceway in accordance with 250.102(E)(2). ▶Figure 300–10

▶Figure 300–10

(C) Mixing Conductors of Different Voltage Systems.

(1) Voltage Insulation Rating. Power conductors can occupy the same raceway, cable, or enclosure if all conductors have an insulation voltage rating not less than the maximum circuit voltage. ▶Figure 300–11

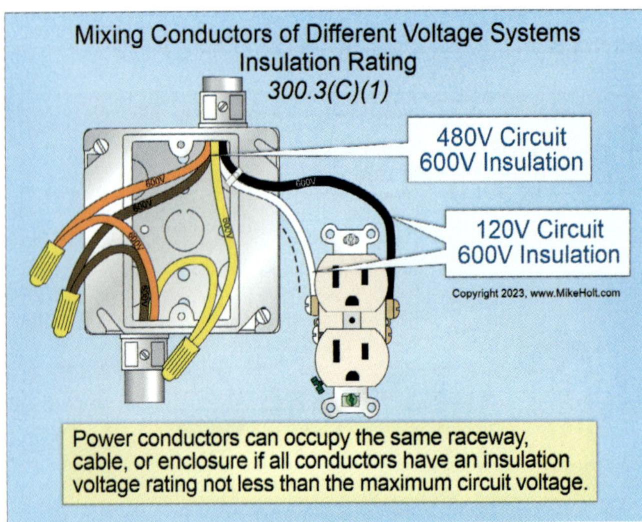

▶Figure 300–11

Author's Comment:

▶ The maximum circuit voltage in the raceway is what determines the minimum voltage rating for the insulation of the conductors—not the maximum insulation voltage of the conductors in the raceway. For example, a 120/240V circuit installed in a raceway with 600V insulated conductors must have all conductors with a minimum insulation voltage rating of 240V not 600V.

Note 1: Class 2 power-limited circuits must be separated from power circuits in raceways, so the higher-voltage conductors do not accidentally energize the Class 2 power-limited circuits [725.136(A)]. ▶Figure 300–12

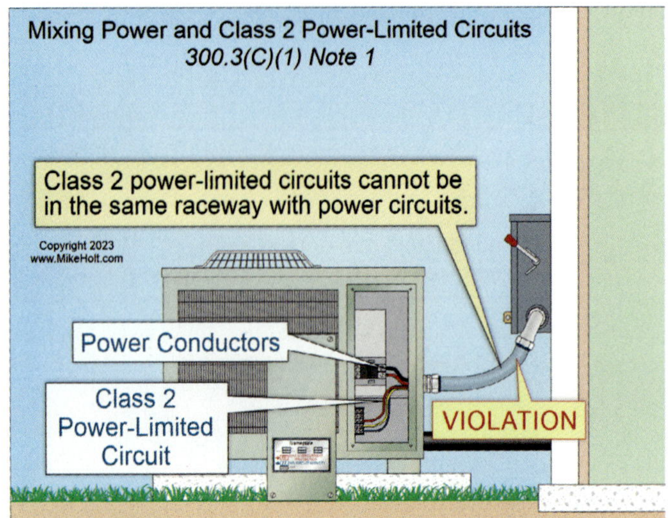

▶Figure 300–12

300.4 Protection Against Physical Damage

Where subject to physical damage, conductors, raceways, and cables must be protected in accordance with 300.4(A) through (H).

(A) Cables and Raceways Through Wood Members.

Author's Comment:

▶ When the following wiring methods are installed through wood members, they must comply with 300.4(A)(1) or (2).

- ▶ Armored Cable, Article 320
- ▶ Electrical Nonmetallic Tubing, Article 362
- ▶ Flexible Metal Conduit, Article 348
- ▶ Liquidtight Flexible Metal Conduit, Article 350
- ▶ Liquidtight Flexible Nonmetallic Conduit, Article 356
- ▶ Metal-Clad Cable, Article 330
- ▶ Nonmetallic-Sheathed Cable, Article 334
- ▶ Service-Entrance Cable, Article 338
- ▶ Underground Feeder and Branch-Circuit Cable, Article 340

(1) Bored Holes in Wood Members. Holes through wood framing members for cables or raceways must be not less than 1¼ in. from the edge of the wood member. If the edge of a drilled hole in a wood framing member is less than 1¼ in. from the edge of the framing member, a steel plate ¹⁄₁₆ in. thick of sufficient length and width must be installed to protect the wiring method from screws and nails. ▶Figure 300–13

▶Figure 300–13

Ex 1: A steel plate is not required to protect rigid metal conduit, intermediate metal conduit, PVC conduit, reinforced thermosetting resin conduit (RTRC), or electrical metallic tubing.

(2) Notches in Wood Members. If notching of wood framing members for cables and raceways is permitted by the building code, a ¹⁄₁₆ in. thick steel plate of sufficient length and width must be installed to protect the wiring method laid in those wood notches from penetration by screws and nails. ▶Figure 300–14

Ex 1: A steel plate is not required to protect rigid metal conduit, intermediate metal conduit, PVC conduit, or electrical metallic tubing.

Caution

⚠ **CAUTION:** Many wood and metal framing members (especially joists and beams) have specific drilling and/or notching instructions meant to maintain structural integrity. Building code requirements limit the diameter of the hole to ⅓ the depth of the joist framing member. Notching is limited to ¼ the depth of joist framing members in accordance with the IBC 2308, *International Building Code* and IRC 5208, *International Residential Code*.

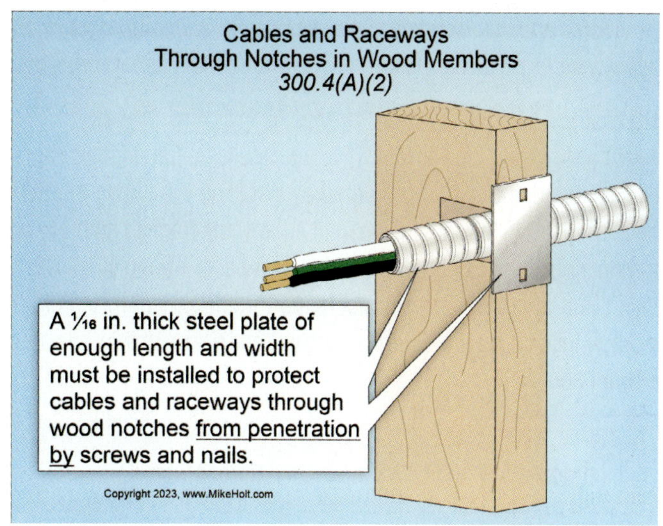

▶Figure 300–14

(B) Nonmetallic-Sheathed Cable and Electrical Nonmetallic Tubing Through Metal Framing Members.

(1) Type NM Cable, Metal Framing Members. If Type NM cable passes through factory or field-made openings in metal framing members, the cable must be protected by listed bushings or grommets that cover all metal edges. The protection fitting must be securely fastened in the opening before the installation of the cable. ▶Figure 300–15

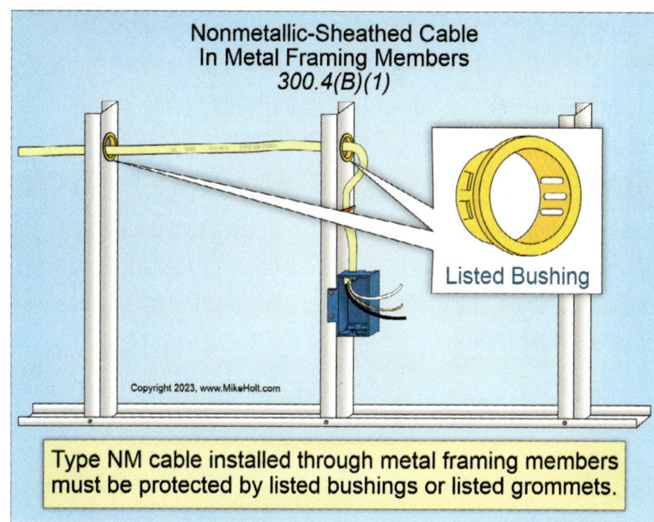

▶Figure 300–15

(2) Type NM Cable and Electrical Nonmetallic Tubing. If nails or screws are likely to penetrate Type NM cable or electrical nonmetallic tubing, a steel sleeve, steel plate, or steel clip not less than ¹⁄₁₆ in. thick must be installed to protect the cable or tubing.

Ex: A listed and marked steel plate less than ¹/₁₆ in. thick that provides equal or better protection against nail or screw penetration is permitted.

(D) Cables and Raceways Parallel to Framing Members and Furring Strips. Cables or raceways run parallel to framing members or furring strips must be protected by installing the wiring method not less than 1¼ in. from the nearest edge of the framing member or furring strip. If the edge of the framing member or furring strip is less than 1¼ in. away, a ¹/₁₆ in. thick steel plate of sufficient length and width must be installed to protect the wiring method from screws and nails. ▶Figure 300–16

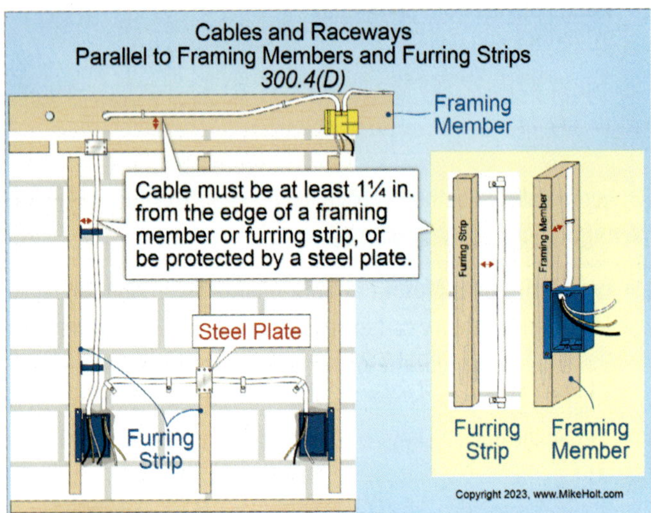

▶Figure 300–16

Ex 1: Protection is not required for rigid metal conduit, intermediate metal conduit, PVC conduit, or electrical metallic tubing.

(E) Wiring Under Metal-Corrugated Roof Decking. Cables, raceways, and boxes under metal-corrugated sheet roof decking are not permitted to be within 1½ in. of the roof decking, measured from the lowest surface of the roof decking to the top of the cable, raceway, or box. ▶Figure 300–17

Author's Comment:

▶ A similar requirement applies to luminaires installed in or under roof decking [410.10(F)].

Note: Raceways or cables installed under metal roof decking might be penetrated by screws or other mechanical devices designed to "hold down" the waterproof membrane or roof insulating material.

Ex 1: Spacing from roof decking does not apply to rigid metal conduit and intermediate metal conduit with listed steel or malleable iron fittings and boxes.

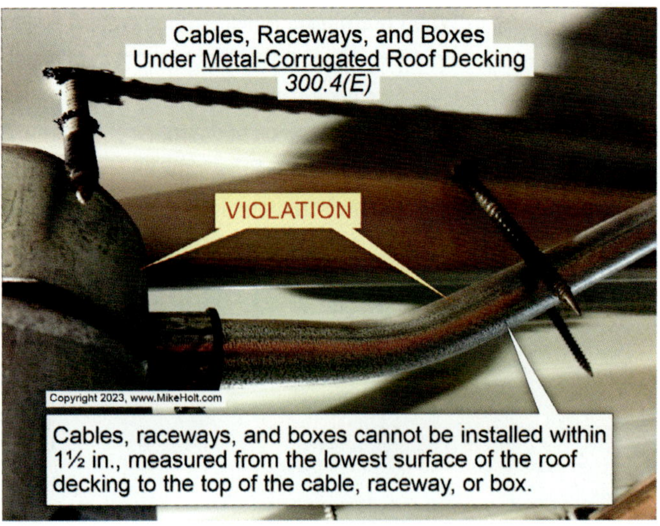

▶Figure 300–17

Ex 2: The 1½ in. spacing is not required where metal-corrugated sheet roof decking is covered with a minimum of 2 in. of concrete, measured from the top of the corrugated roofing.

(G) Raceway Termination Fittings. Raceways containing insulated circuit conductors 4 AWG and larger that enter a cabinet, box, enclosure, or raceway must be protected prior to the installation of the conductors as follows:

(1) An identified raceway fitting providing a smoothly rounded insulating surface ▶Figure 300–18

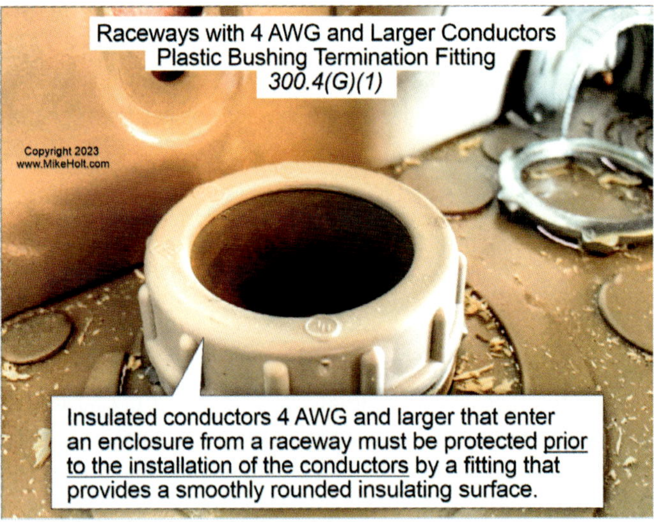

▶Figure 300–18

(2) A listed metal raceway fitting with smoothly rounded edges ▶Figure 300–19

Conduit bushings constructed of metal can be used to secure a fitting or raceway.

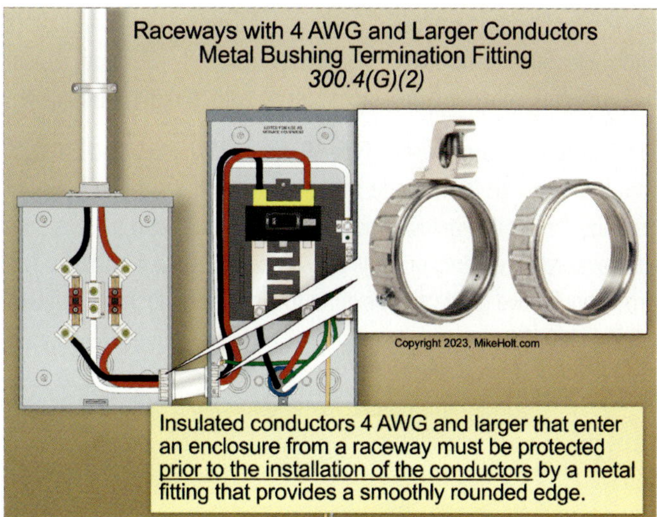

▶Figure 300–19

▶Figure 300–21

(H) Structural Joints. A listed expansion/deflection fitting, or other means approved by the authority having jurisdiction, must be used where a raceway crosses a structural joint intended for expansion, contraction, or deflection.

300.5 Underground Installations

(A) Minimum Burial Cover Requirements. When cables or raceways are installed underground, they must have a minimum burial cover in accordance with Table 300.5(A). ▶Figure 300–20

Table 300.5(A) Minimum Cover Requirements in Inches

Location	Column 1 Buried Cables	Column 2 RMC or IMC	Column 3 EMT or Nonmetallic Raceways
Under Building	0	0	0
Dwelling Unit	24/12*	6	18
Dwelling Unit Driveway	18/12*	6	18/12*
Under Roadway	24	24	24
Other Locations	24	6	18

Residential branch circuits rated 120V or less with GFCI protection and maximum protection of 20A.

See the table in the NEC for full details.

Note 1 to Table 300.5: "Cover" is measured as the shortest distance from the top of the underground cable or raceway to the top surface of finished grade. ▶Figure 300–22

Note 6 to Table 300.5: Directly buried electrical metallic tubing (EMT) must comply with 358.10.

Minimum Underground Cover Depth — Table 300.5(A)

	Column 1 UF or USE Cables or Conductors	Column 2 RMC or IMC	Column 3 EMT or Nonmetallic Raceways	Column 4 Residential 15A & 20A GFCI 120V Branch Ckts
Dwelling Unit Driveway and Parking Area	18 in.	18 in.	18 in.	12 in.
Under Roadway Driveway Parking Lot	24 in.	24 in.	24 in.	24 in.
Other Locations	24 in.	6 in.	18 in.	12 in.

Copyright 2023 www.MikeHolt.com

▶Figure 300–20

Author's Comment:

▶ There are no burial cover requirements for raceways underneath a building. ▶Figure 300–21

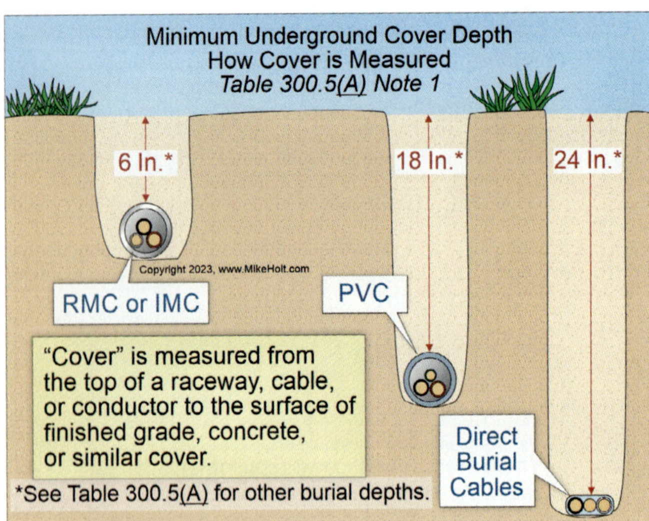

▶Figure 300–22

(B) Wet Locations. Cables and insulated conductors installed in raceways and enclosures underground must be listed as suitable for a wet location in accordance with 310.10(C). ▶Figure 300–23

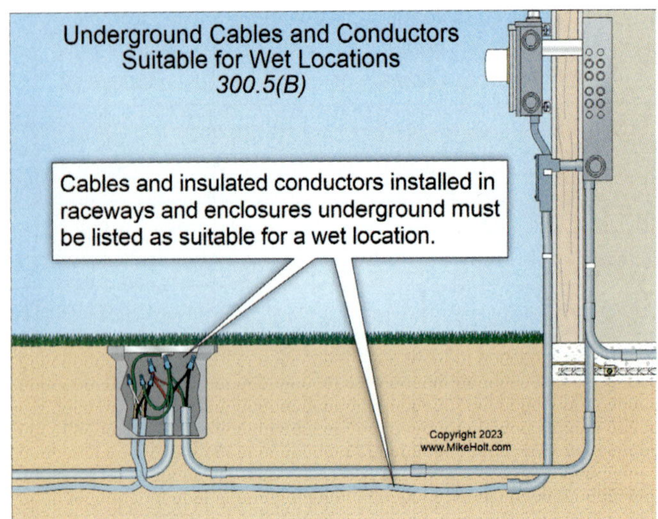

▶Figure 300–23

According to Article 100, "Wet Location" includes installations underground, in concrete slabs in direct contact with the Earth, locations subject to saturation with water, and unprotected locations exposed to weather. See 300.9 for raceways in wet locations above ground.

(C) Cables and Conductors Under Buildings. Cables and conductors installed under a building must be installed within a raceway that extends past the outside walls of the building.

Ex 2: Type MC cable listed for direct burial or concrete encasement is permitted under a building without installation within a raceway [330.10(A)(5) and 330.10(A)(11)].

(D) Protecting Underground Cables and Conductors. Conductors and cables such as Types MC, UF, and USE installed underground must be protected from damage in accordance with 300.5(1) through (4).

(1) Emerging from Grade. Type UF and USE cables and conductors that emerge from grade must be protected against physical damage. Protection below grade is required to extend no less than the cover requirements of Table 300.5 and not more than 18 in. The protection above grade must extend to a height of not less than 8 ft. ▶Figure 300–24

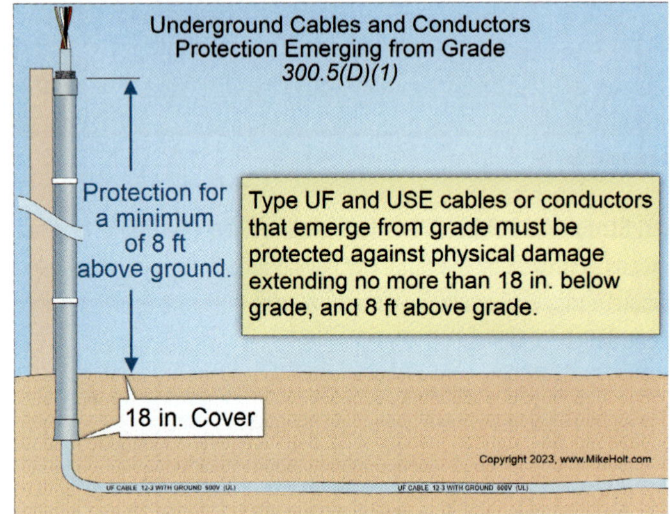

▶Figure 300–24

> **Author's Comment:**
>
> ▸ Where a raceway is subject to physical damage, the conductors must be installed in EMT, RMC, IMC, RTRC-XW, or Schedule 80 PVC conduit [300.5(D)(4)].

(2) Conductors Entering Buildings. Underground conductors and cables that enter a building must be protected to the point of entrance.

(3) Underground Service Conductors. Underground service-entrance conductors (USE) must have their location identified by a warning ribbon placed in the trench at least 12 in. above the underground conductors. ▶Figure 300–25

> **Author's Comment:**
>
> ▸ The *NEC* does not require a warning ribbon for conductors under the exclusive control of the utility [90.2(D)(5)].
>
> ▸ The requirements for a warning ribbon do not apply to underground service conductors that are installed in a raceway or encased in concrete

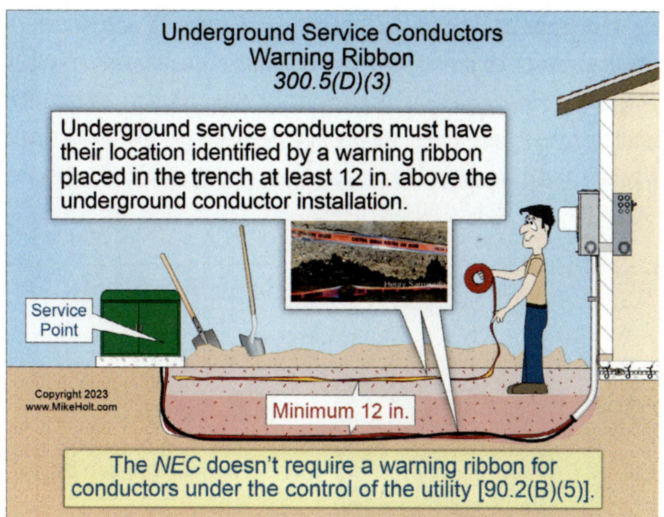

▶Figure 300–25

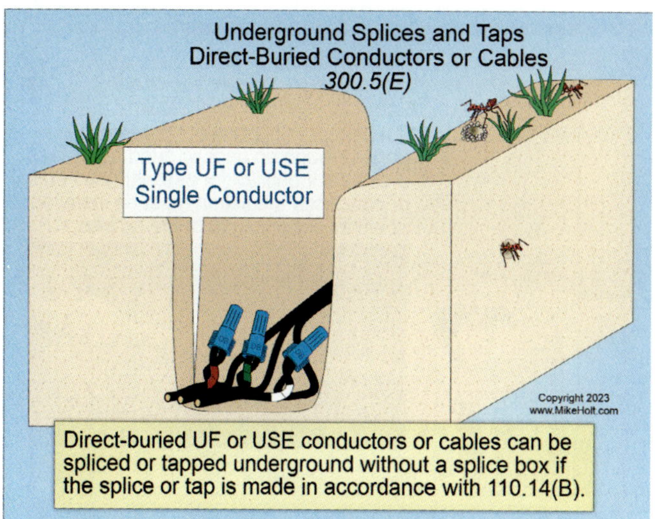

▶Figure 300–27

(4) Raceway Damage. Where an underground raceway emerging from grade is subject to physical damage, the conductors must be installed in EMT, RMC, IMC, RTRC-XW, or Schedule 80 PVC conduit. ▶Figure 300–26

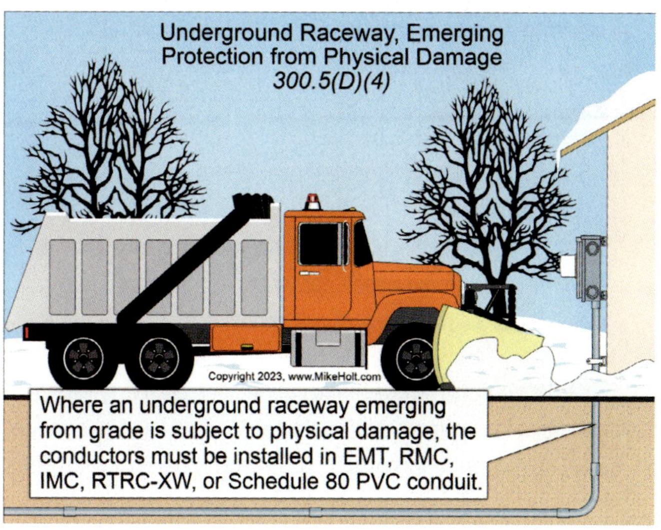

▶Figure 300–26

(E) Underground Splices and Taps. Direct-buried UF or USE conductors or cables can be spliced or tapped underground without a splice box [300.15(G)], if the splice or tap is made in accordance with 110.14(B). ▶Figure 300–27

(F) Backfill. Backfill material for underground wiring must not damage underground raceways, cables, or conductors. ▶Figure 300–28

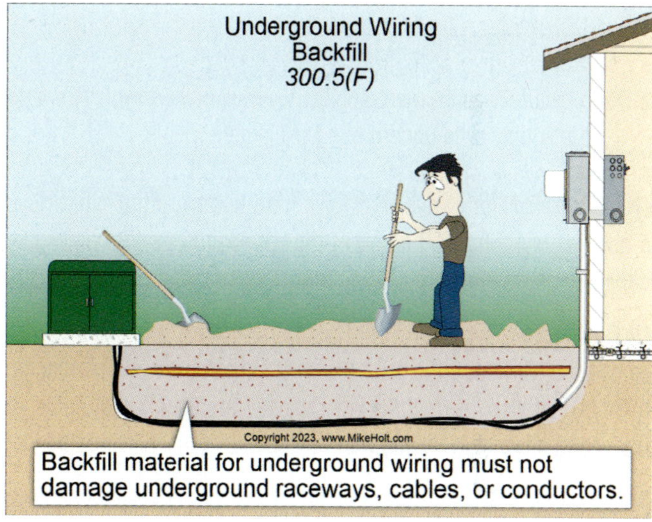

▶Figure 300–28

Author's Comment:

▶ Large rocks, chunks of concrete, steel rods, mesh, and other sharp-edged objects are not permitted to be used for backfilling material because they can damage the underground conductors, cables, or raceways.

(G) Raceway Seals. If moisture might contact energized live parts through an underground raceway, a seal identified for use with the cable or conductor insulation must be installed at either or both ends of the raceway [225.27 and 230.8]. ▶Figure 300–29

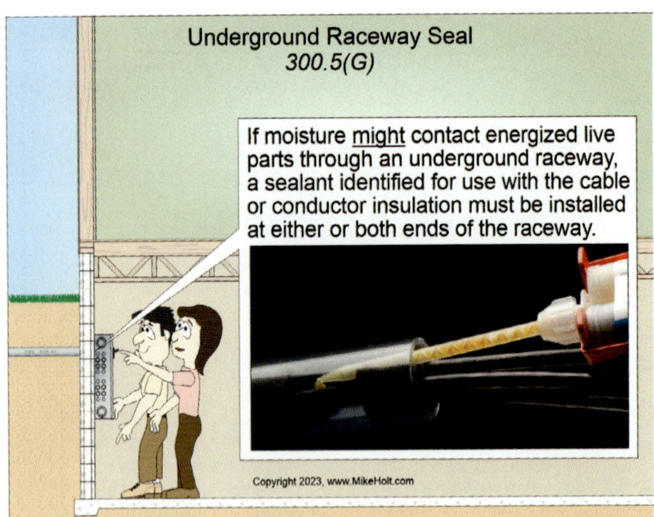

▶Figure 300–29

Author's Comment:

▶ Moisture is a common problem for equipment downhill from the supply or in underground equipment rooms.

(H) Bushing. Raceways that terminate underground must have a bushing or fitting at the end of the raceway to protect emerging cables or conductors.

(I) Conductors Grouped Together. Underground conductors of the same circuit (including the neutral and equipment grounding conductor) must be installed inside the same raceway, multiconductor cable, or near each other in the same trench. See 300.3(B). ▶Figure 300–30

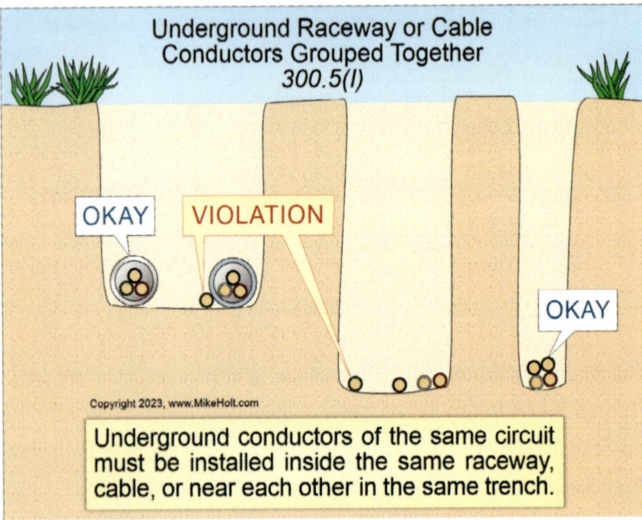

▶Figure 300–30

Ex 2: Underground parallel conductors can have the conductors of each phase or neutral installed in separate nonmetallic raceways where inductive heating at raceway terminations is reduced by using aluminum locknuts and cutting a slot between the individual holes through which the conductors pass as required by 300.20(B). ▶Figure 300–31

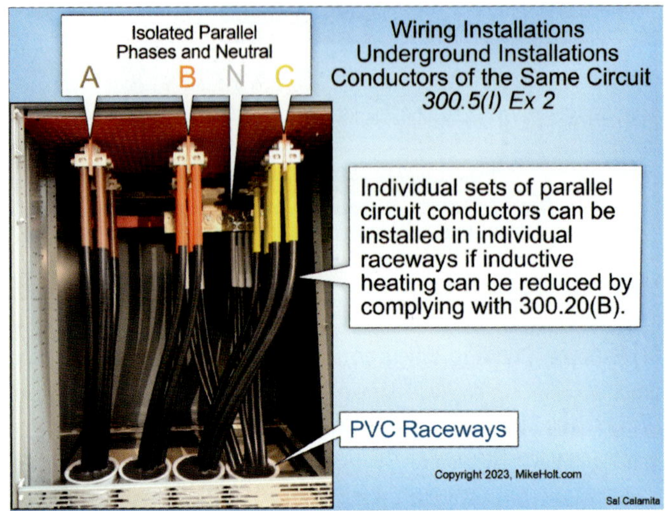

▶Figure 300–31

Author's Comment:

▶ Separating phase and neutral conductors in individual PVC conduits makes it easier to terminate larger parallel installations, but it also results in elevated electromagnetic fields (EMF). Keeping the phase and neutral conductors close to each other helps reduce circuit impedance.

(J) Earth Movement. Direct-buried conductors, cables, or raceways that are subject to movement by settlement or frost must be arranged to prevent damage to conductors or equipment connected to the wiring.

300.6 Protection Against Corrosion

Raceways, cable trays, cable armor, boxes, cable sheathing, cabinets, enclosures, elbows, couplings, fittings, supports, and support hardware must be suitable for the environment.

(A) Steel Equipment. Steel raceways, cables, cable trays, cabinets, enclosures, fittings, and support hardware must be protected against corrosion by a coating of approved corrosion-resistant material. ▶Figure 300–32

▶Figure 300–32

Author's Comment:

▶ In accordance with "*UL Guide Information DYIX,*" supplementary corrosion protection is required when a steel raceway transitions from concrete encasement to the soil. ▶Figure 300–33

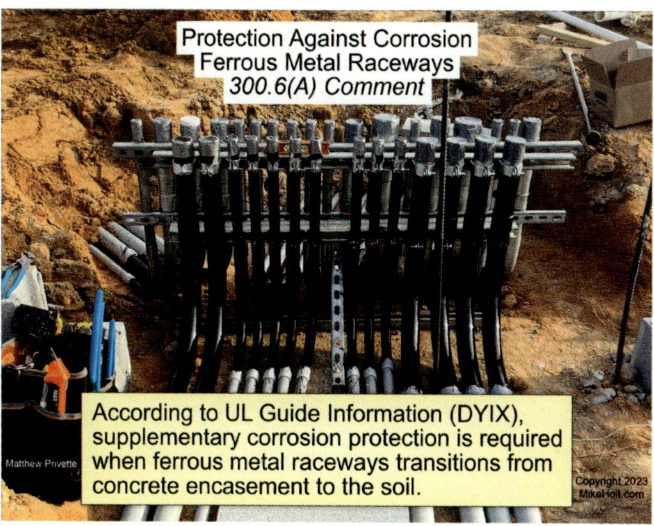

▶Figure 300–33

Where corrosion protection is required and IMC or RMC is threaded in the field, the threads must be coated with an approved electrically conductive, corrosion-resistant compound.

300.7 Raceways Exposed to Different Temperatures

(A) Sealing. If a raceway is subjected to different temperatures and where condensation is known to be a problem, the raceway must be filled with a material approved by the authority having jurisdiction that will prevent the circulation of warm air to a colder section of the raceway. Sealants must be identified for use with cable insulation, conductor insulation, a bare conductor, a shield, or other components.
▶Figure 300–34 and ▶Figure 300–35

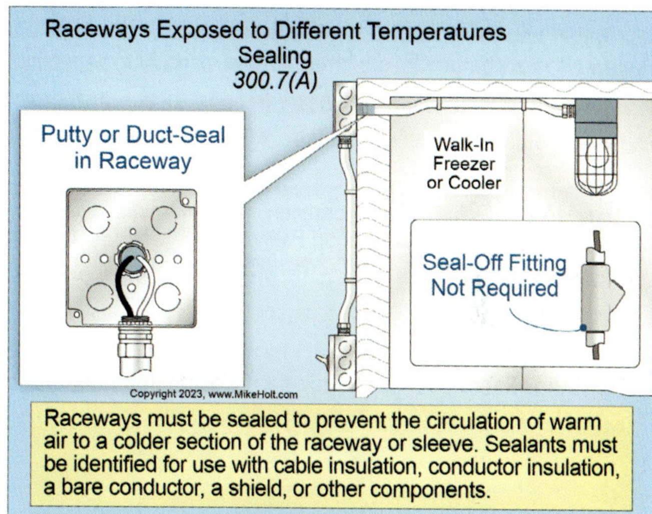

▶Figure 300–34

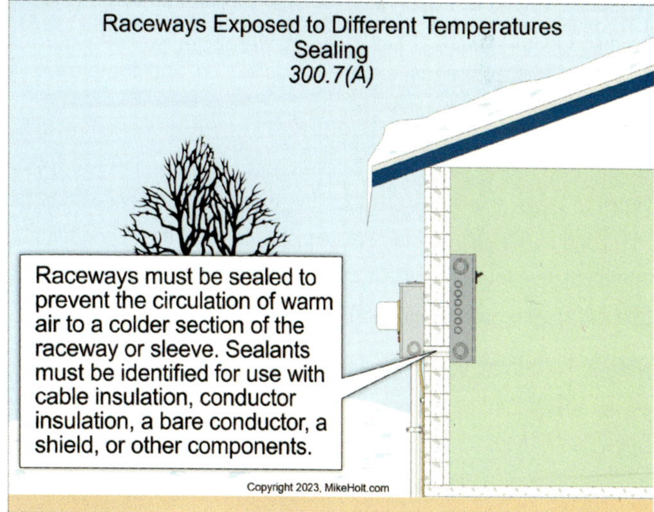

▶Figure 300–35

Author's Comment:

▸ One common product used for this is electrical duct seal and it is so identified. There are other identified products such as Polywater's FST Duct Sealant. Typical expanding foams used to seal buildings are not identified for this application.

According to Article 100, "Identified" means marked suitable for the purpose by the manufacturer, and recognized as suitable for a specific purpose, function, use, environment, or application.

(B) Expansion, Expansion-Deflection, and Deflection Fittings. Raceways must be provided with expansion, expansion-deflection, or deflection fittings where necessary to compensate for thermal expansion, deflection, and contraction. ▸Figure 300–36

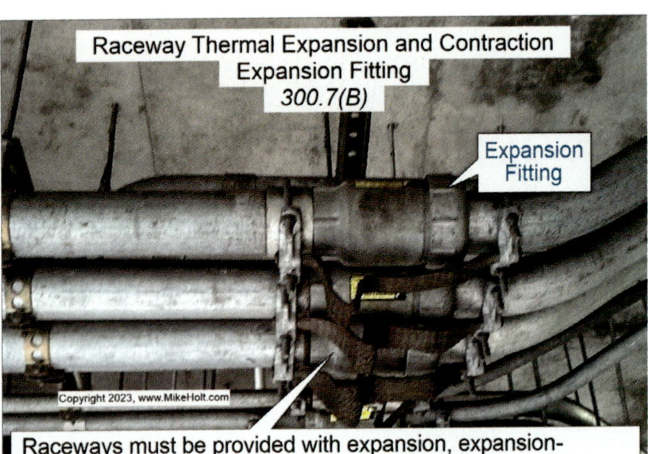

▸Figure 300–36

Note 1: Table 352.44(A) provides the expansion characteristics for PVC conduit. The expansion characteristics for rigid metal conduit and intermediate metal is determined by multiplying the values from Table 352.44(A) by 0.20. ▸Figure 300–37

Note.2: For information on expansion and expansion-deflection fittings, see NEMA FB 2.40, *Installation Guidelines for Expansion and Expansion/Deflection Fittings.*

300.9 Raceways in Wet Locations Above Grade

The interior of raceways installed in wet locations above ground is considered a wet location. Insulated conductors and cables installed in raceways in above ground wet locations must be listed for use in wet locations in accordance with 310.10(C). ▸Figure 300–38

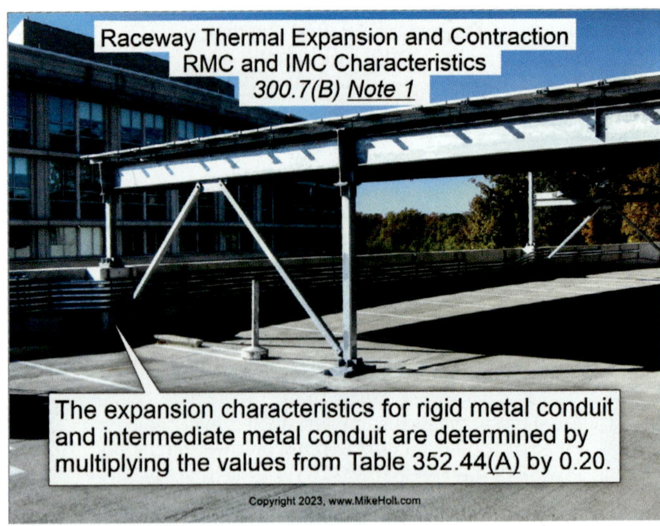

▸Figure 300–37

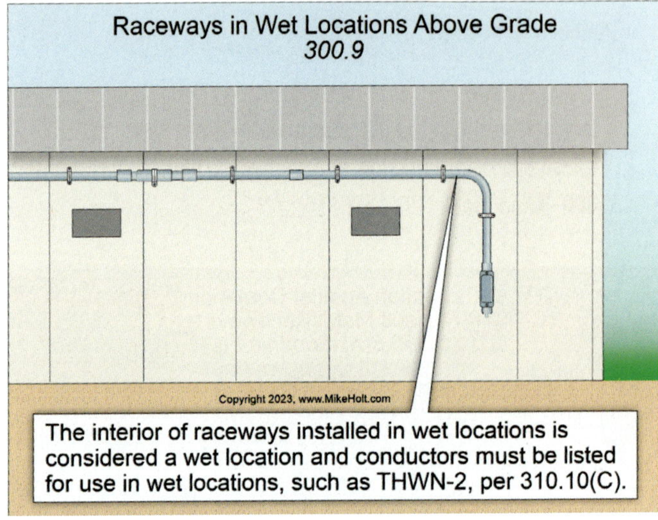

▸Figure 300–38

Author's Comment:

▸ In addition to 310.10(C), Table 310.4(A)(1) can be used to find other insulation types permitted in wet locations.

According to Article 100, "Wet Location" means installations underground or in concrete slabs in contact with the Earth, and locations subject to water spray or exposed to weather.

300.10 Electrical Continuity

Metal raceways, cable armor, and metal enclosures must be metallically joined together to provide electrical continuity [250.4(A)(3)]. ▸Figure 300–39

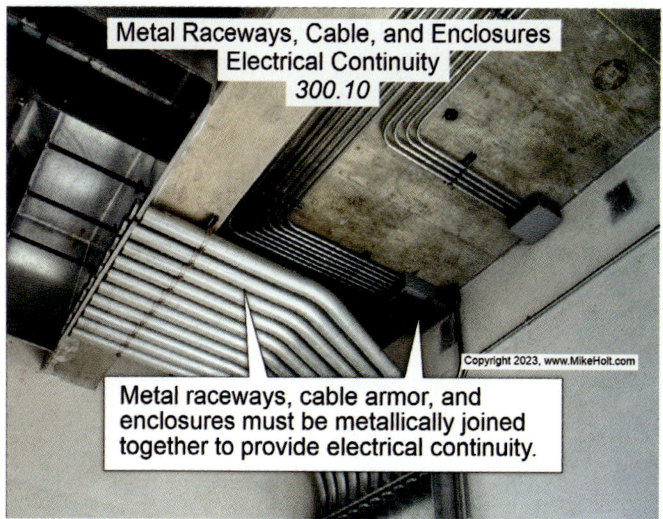

▶Figure 300–39

Author's Comment:

▶ The purpose of electrical continuity between metal parts is to establish the effective ground-fault current path necessary to open the circuit overcurrent protective device in the event of a ground fault [250.4(A)(5)]. ▶**Figure 300–40**

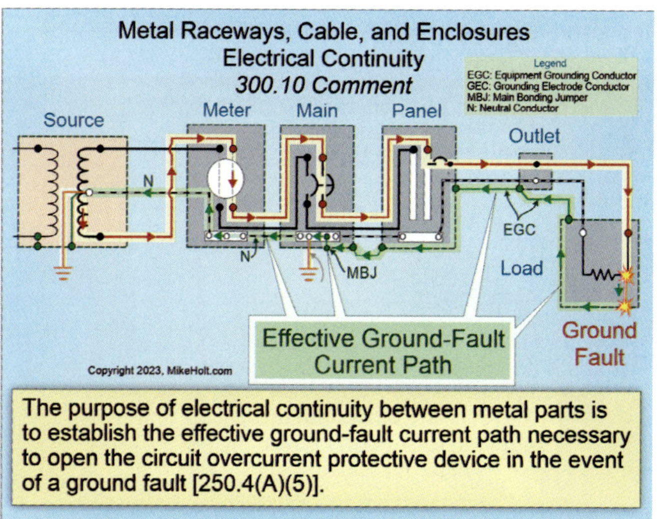

▶Figure 300–40

Ex 1: Short lengths of metal raceways used for the support or protection of cables are not required to be electrically continuous or connected to the circuit equipment grounding conductor [250.86 Ex 2 and 300.12 Ex 1]. ▶**Figure 300–41**

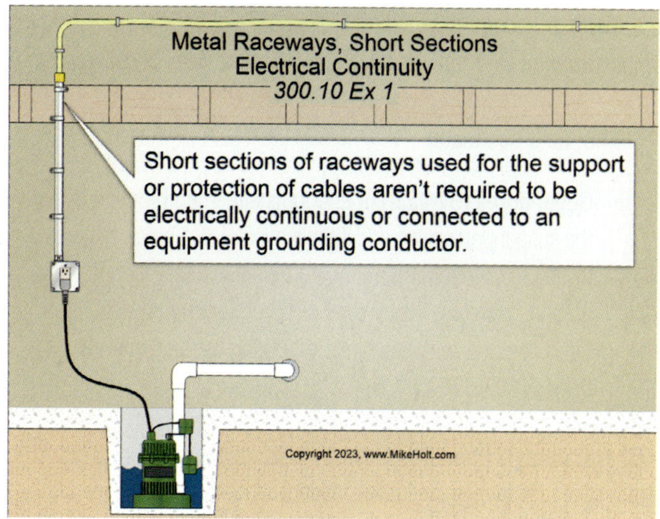

▶Figure 300–41

300.11 Securing and Supporting

(A) Secured in Place. Raceways, cable assemblies, and enclosures must be securely fastened in place.

(B) Wiring Systems Installed Above Suspended Ceilings. Ceiling-support wires or the ceiling grid are not permitted to support raceways or cables. Independent support wires secured at both ends can be used to support raceways or cables. ▶**Figure 300–42**

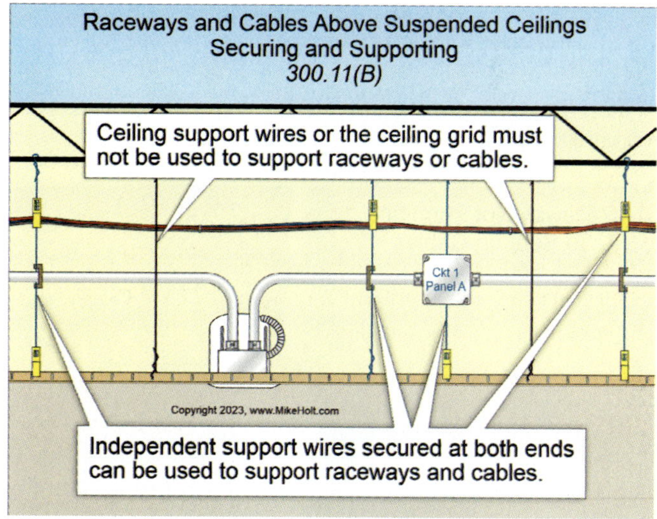

▶Figure 300–42

(1) Fire-Rated Assemblies. Electrical wiring within the cavity of a fire-rated ceiling assembly must be supported by independent support wires attached to the ceiling assembly. The independent support wires must be distinguishable from the suspended-ceiling support wires by color, tagging, or other effective means.

Ex: Electrical wiring can be supported by ceiling-support wires if installed in accordance with the ceiling system manufacturer's instructions.

Author's Comment:

▸ Outlet boxes [314.23(D)] and luminaires can be secured to the suspended-ceiling grid if the luminaire is securely fastened to the ceiling-framing members by mechanical means such as bolts, screws, rivets, clips or other securing means identified for use with the type of ceiling-framing member(s) used [410.36(B)].

(C) Raceways Used for Support. Raceways are not permitted to support raceways or cables, except as follows: ▸Figure 300–43 and ▸Figure 300–44

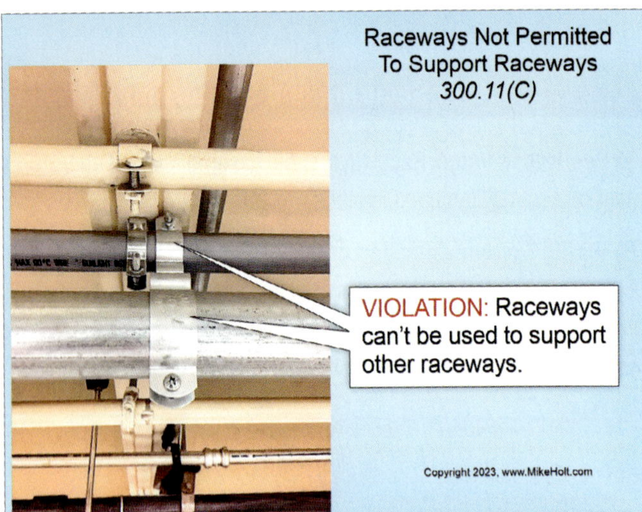

▸Figure 300–43

▸Figure 300–44

(2) Class 2 Power-Limited Cables. Class 2 power-limited cables can be supported by the raceway that supplies power to the equipment controlled by the Class 2 power-limited cable. ▸Figure 300–45

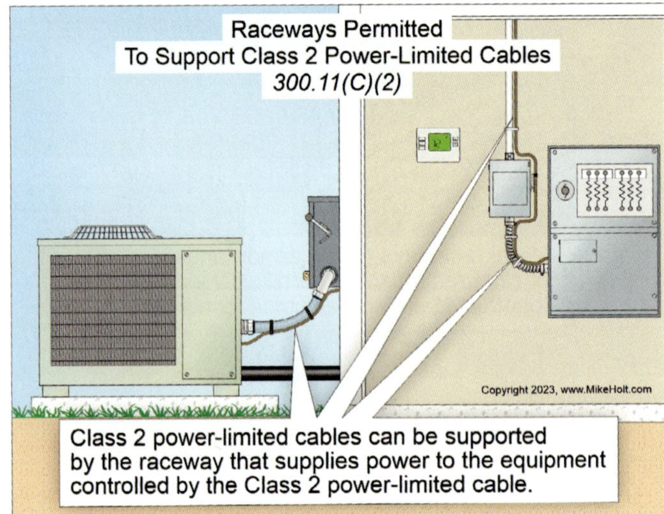

▸Figure 300–45

(3) Boxes. Raceways are permitted to support boxes in accordance with 314.23.

(D) Cables Not Used as Means of Support. Cables are not permitted to support raceways or cables. ▸Figure 300–46

▸Figure 300–46

300.12 Mechanical Continuity

Raceways and cable sheaths must be mechanically continuous between boxes, cabinets, conduit bodies, fittings, or other enclosures. ▸Figure 300–47 and ▸Figure 300–48

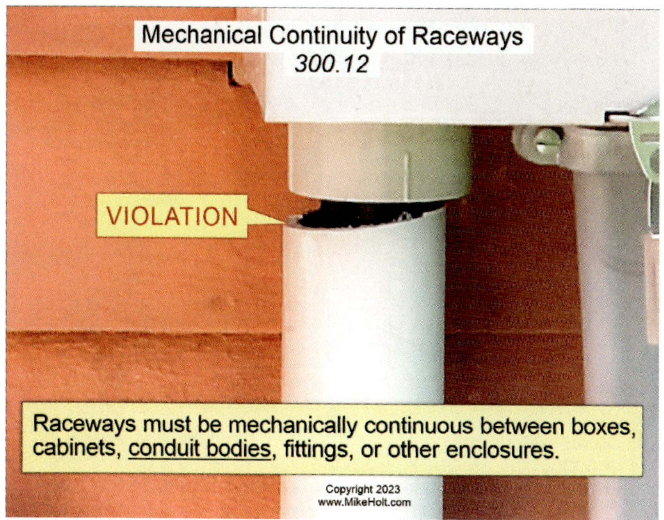

▶Figure 300–47

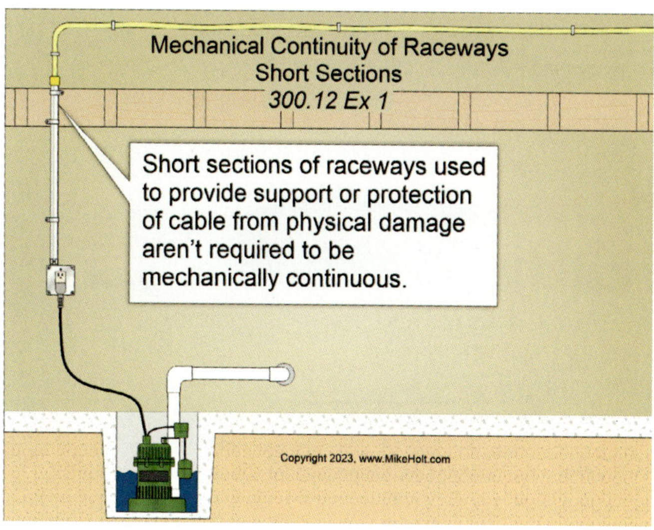

▶Figure 300–49

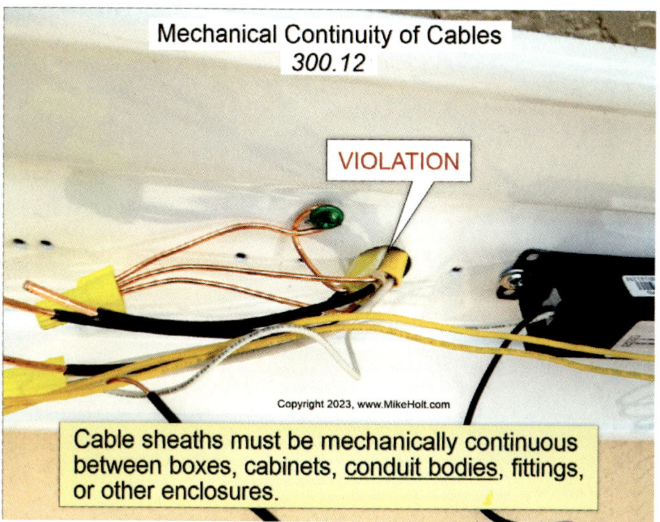

▶Figure 300–48

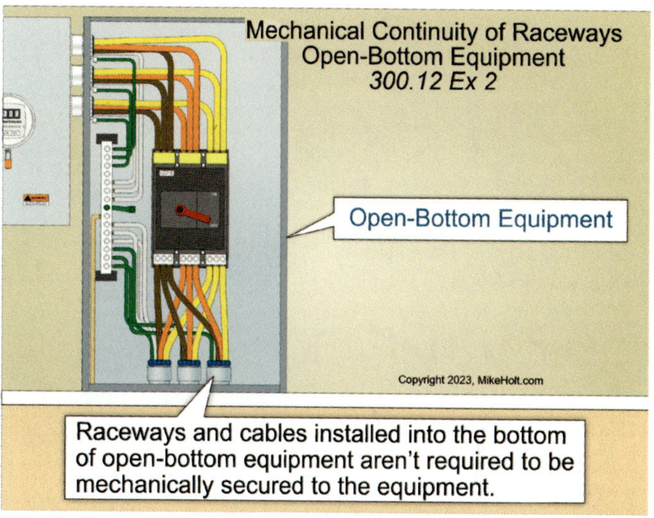

▶Figure 300–50

Ex 1: Short sections of raceways used to provide support or protection of cables from physical damage aren't required to be mechanically continuous [250.86 Ex 2 and 300.10 Ex 1]. ▶Figure 300–49

Ex 2: Raceways and cables installed into the bottom of open-bottom equipment such as switchboards, motor control centers, floor- or pad-mounted transformers aren't required to be mechanically secured to the equipment. ▶Figure 300–50

300.13 Mechanical and Electrical Continuity of Conductors—Splices and Pigtails

(A) Conductor Splices. Conductor splices and taps must be made inside enclosures in accordance with 300.15. Splices are not permitted in raceways, except as permitted for wireways in accordance with 376.56. ▶Figure 300–51

300.14 Conductor Length at Boxes

At least 6 in. of spliced or unspliced conductor, measured from the point in the box where the conductors enter the enclosure, must be provided for conductor splices or terminations. ▶Figure 300–52

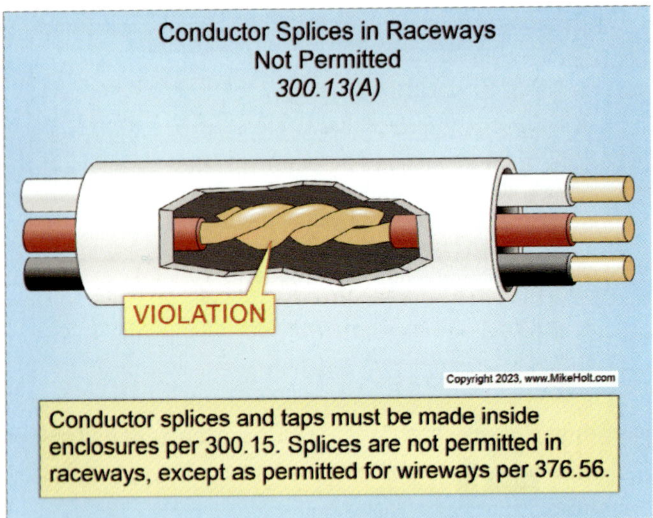

Conductor splices and taps must be made inside enclosures per 300.15. Splices are not permitted in raceways, except as permitted for wireways per 376.56.

▶Figure 300–51

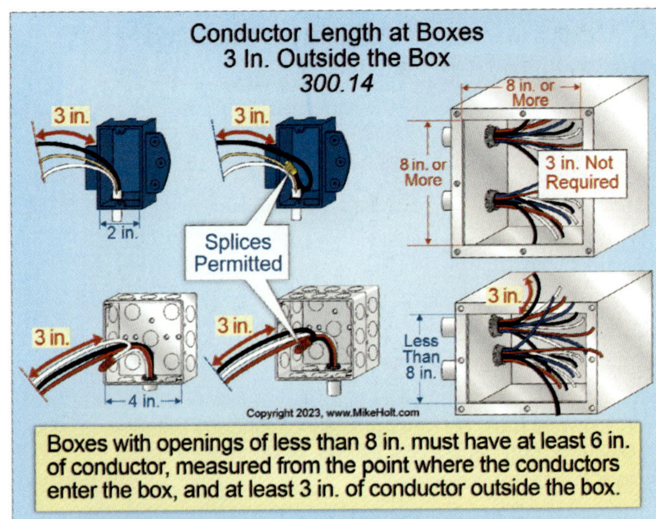

Boxes with openings of less than 8 in. must have at least 6 in. of conductor, measured from the point where the conductors enter the box, and at least 3 in. of conductor outside the box.

▶Figure 300–53

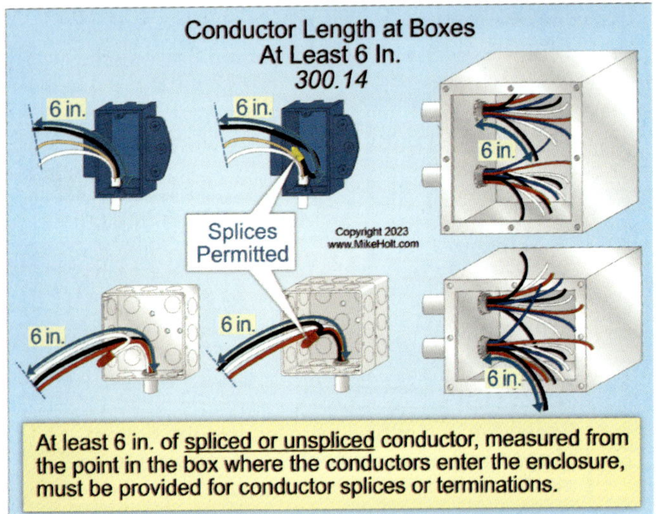

At least 6 in. of spliced or unspliced conductor, measured from the point in the box where the conductors enter the enclosure, must be provided for conductor splices or terminations.

▶Figure 300–52

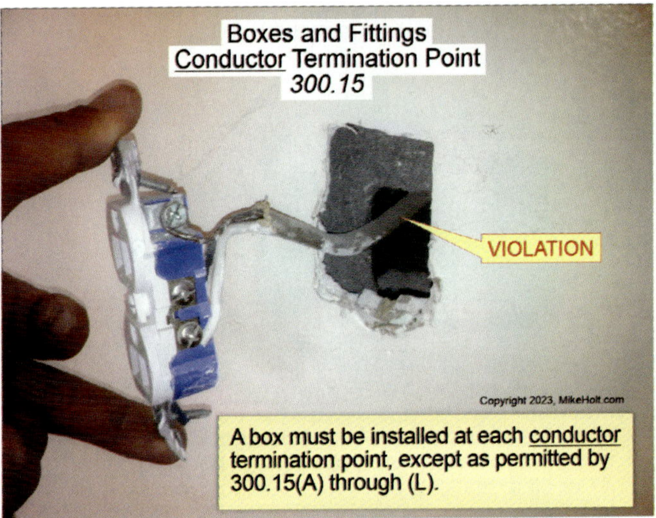

A box must be installed at each conductor termination point, except as permitted by 300.15(A) through (L).

▶Figure 300–54

Boxes with openings less than 8 in. at any dimension must have at least 6 in. of conductor, measured from the point where the conductors enter the box, and at least 3 in. of conductor outside the box. ▶Figure 300–53

300.15 Boxes or Fittings, Splices and Terminations

A box must be installed at each conductor splice point or conductor termination point, except as permitted by 300.15(A) through (L): ▶Figure 300–54 and ▶Figure 300–55

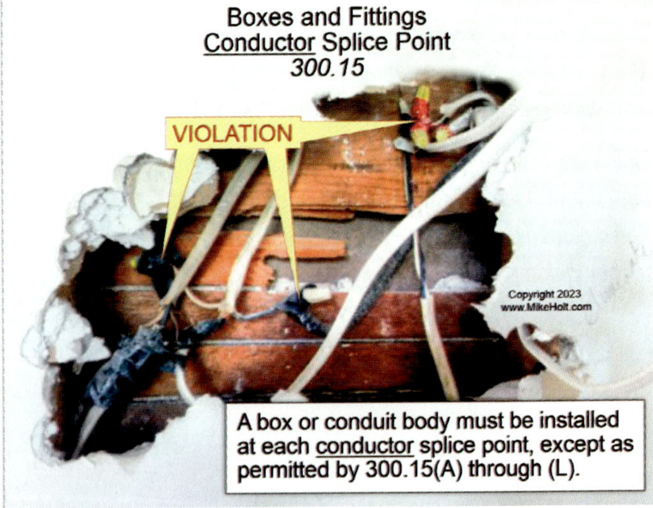

A box or conduit body must be installed at each conductor splice point, except as permitted by 300.15(A) through (L).

▶Figure 300–55

▸ Boxes are not required for: ▸**Figure 300–56**

  ▸ Class 2 Power-Limited Circuits, 725.3
  ▸ Coaxial Cable, 800.3
  ▸ Optical Fiber Cable, 770.3

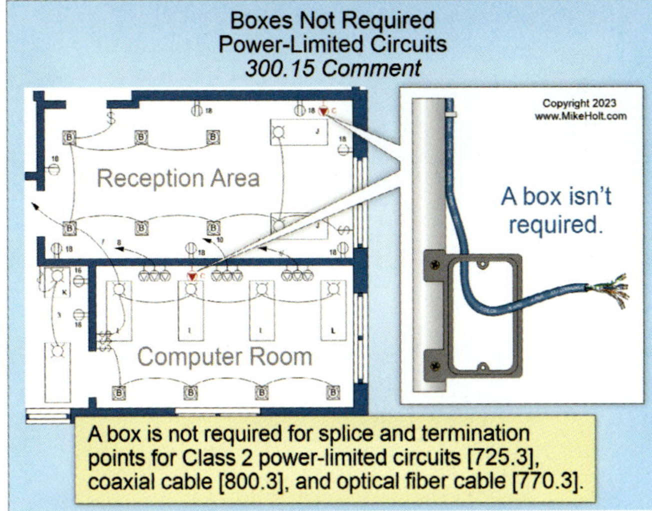

▸Figure 300–56

Fittings and connectors must only be used with the specific wiring methods for which they are designed and listed. ▸**Figure 300–57**

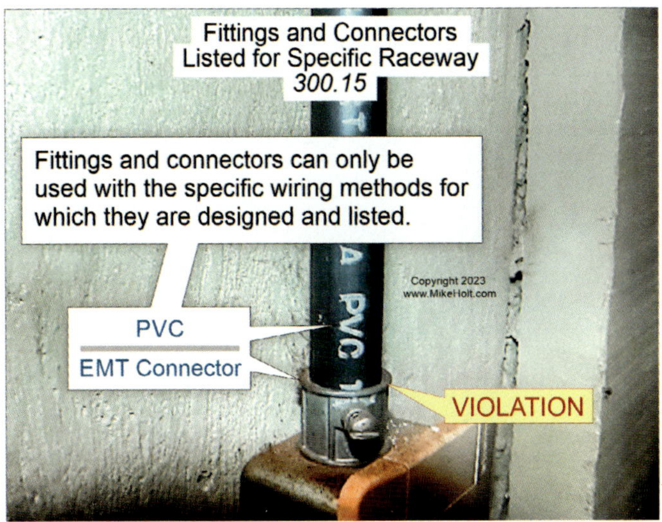

▸Figure 300–57

▸ Type NM cable connectors are not permitted to be used with Type AC cable. Electrical metallic tubing fittings are not permitted to be used with rigid metal conduit or intermediate metal conduit unless listed for the purpose.

▸ PVC conduit couplings and connectors are permitted to be installed with electrical nonmetallic tubing if the proper glue is used in accordance with the manufacturer's instructions [110.3(B)]. See 362.48.

(A) Wiring Methods with Interior Access. A box is not required for wiring methods with removable covers such as wireways, multioutlet assemblies, and surface raceways.

(G) Underground Conductor and Cable Splices. A box is not required where a splice is made underground if Type UF or USE conductors are spliced with a splicing device listed for direct burial. ▸**Figure 300–58**

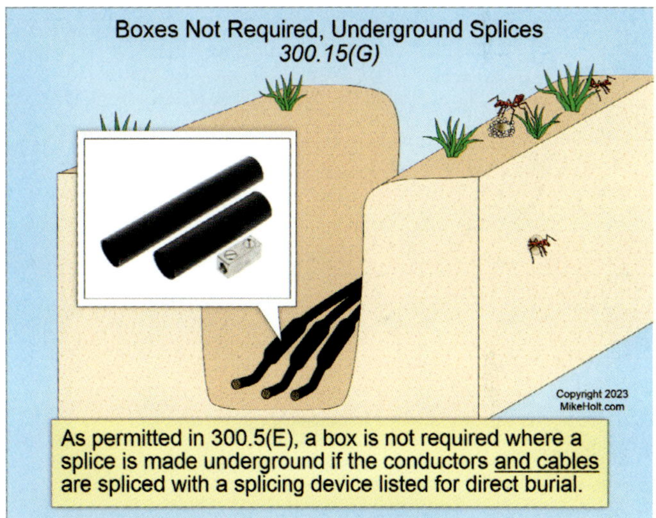

▸Figure 300–58

▸ The only conductors permitted to be direct buried are Type UF [340.10(1)] and Type USE [338.10(B)(4)(b)(2)].

CONDUCTORS FOR GENERAL WIRING

Introduction to Article 310—Conductors for General Wiring

This article contains the general requirements for conductors such as their insulation markings, ampacity ratings, and conditions of use. It does not apply to conductors that are part of flexible cords, fixture wires, or to those that are an integral part of equipment [90.7 and 300.1(B)]. Some topics covered in this material include:

- Conductor size and material
- Insulation types
- Conductor identification and marking
- Conductor ampacity

Article 310 consists of three parts:

- Part I. General
- Part II. Construction Specifications
- Part III. Installation

Part I. General

310.1 Scope

Article 310 contains the general requirements, insulation markings, ampacity, and conditions of use for conductors rated up to 2000V. ▶Figure 310–1

Note: For flexible cords and cables, see Article 400. For fixture wires, see Article 402.

310.3 Conductors, Minimum Size and Material

(A) Minimum Size Conductors. The minimum sizes of conductors are 14 AWG copper or 12 AWG aluminum or copper-clad aluminum, except as permitted elsewhere in this *Code*.

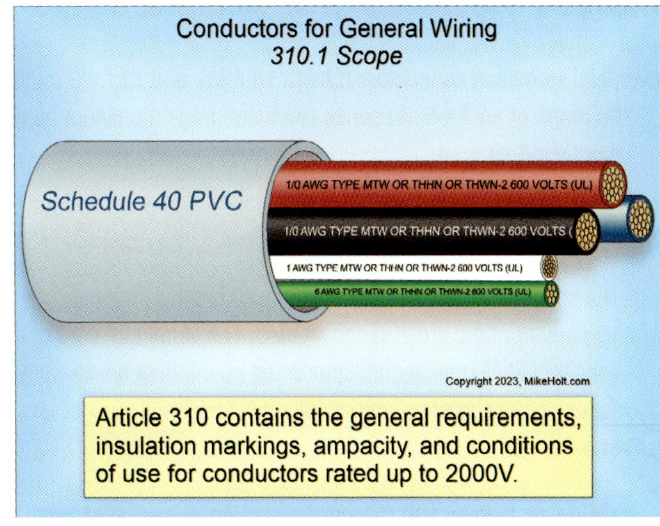

▶Figure 310–1

Author's Comment:

▸ There is a misconception that 12 AWG copper is the smallest conductor permitted for commercial or industrial facilities. Although it is not true based on *NEC* rules, it might be a job specification or local code requirement.

▸ Conductors smaller than 14 AWG are permitted to be installed for Class 1 power-limited circuits [724.43], fixture wire [402.6], and motor control circuits [Table 430.72(B)].

(B) Conductor Material. Conductors must be copper, aluminum, or copper-clad aluminum. Aluminum and copper-clad aluminum conductors must comply with the following: ▸Figure 310–2

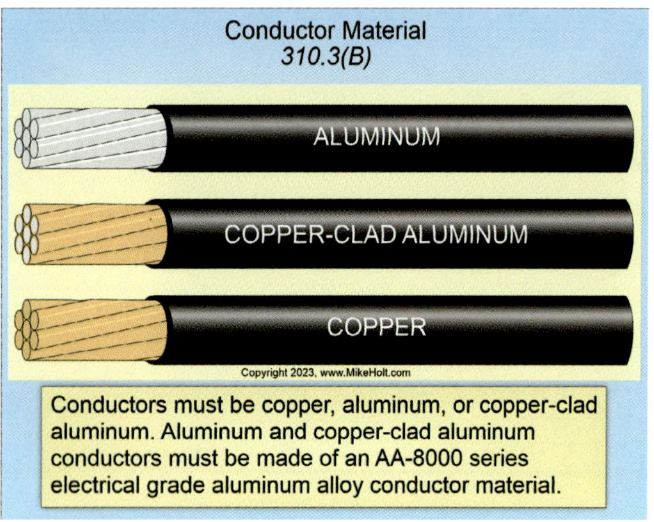

▸Figure 310–2

(1) Solid aluminum conductors 8 AWG, 10 AWG, and 12 AWG must be made of an AA-8000 series electrical grade aluminum alloy conductor material.

(2) Stranded aluminum conductors must be made of an AA-8000 series electrical grade aluminum alloy conductor material.

(3) The copper of a copper-clad aluminum conductor only makes up 10 percent of the cross-sectional area. The aluminum core of a copper-clad aluminum conductor must be made of an AA-8000 series electrical grade aluminum alloy conductor material. ▸Figure 310–3

According to Article 100, "Copper-Clad Aluminum Conductor" is drawn from a copper-clad aluminum rod, with the copper metallurgically bonded to an aluminum core. ▸Figure 310–4

▸Figure 310–3

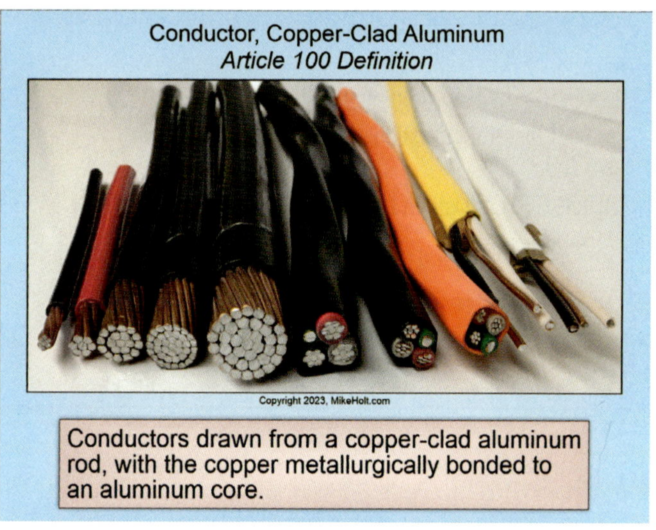

▸Figure 310–4

(4) Copper-clad aluminum conductor material must be listed.

(C) Stranded Conductors. Conductors 8 AWG and larger installed in a raceway must be stranded, unless specifically permitted or required elsewhere in this *Code* to be solid. ▸Figure 310–5

Author's Comment:

▸ According to 250.120(C), exposed equipment grounding conductors 8 AWG and smaller for direct-current circuits [250.134(2) Ex 2], such as those required by 690.45 for solar PV systems, are permitted to be run separately from the circuit conductors. Where an 8 AWG or smaller exposed equipment grounding conductor is subject to physical damage, it must be installed in a raceway or cable.

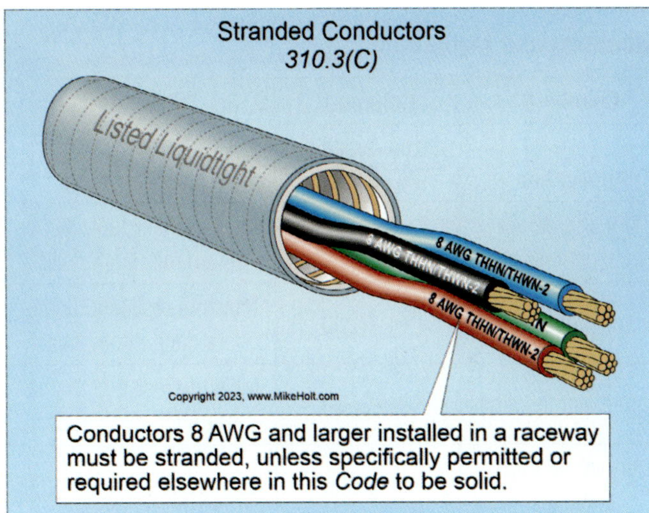

▶Figure 310–5

- A grounding electrode conductor is an example of where an 8 AWG and larger solid conductor can be installed in a raceway when it is required to be protected from physical damage [250.64(B)].

(D) Insulated. Conductors must be insulated, unless specifically permitted to be bare. ▶Figure 310–6

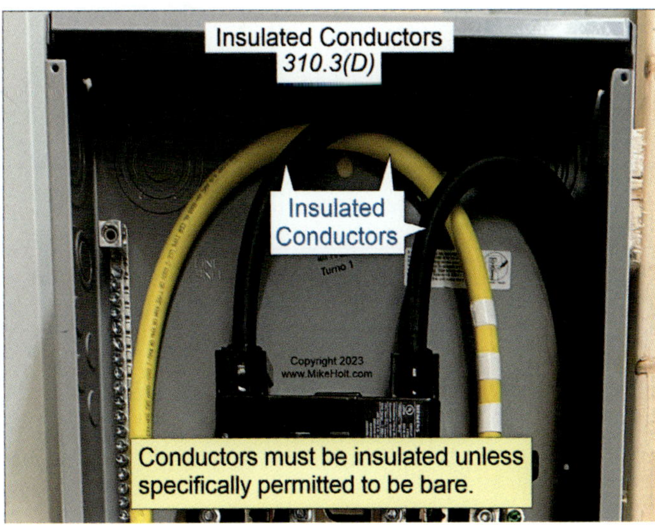

▶Figure 310–6

Part II. Construction Specifications

310.4 Conductor Construction and Application

Table 310.4(1) provides information on conductor insulation properties such as letter type, maximum operating temperature, application, insulation, and outer cover properties. ▶Figure 310–7

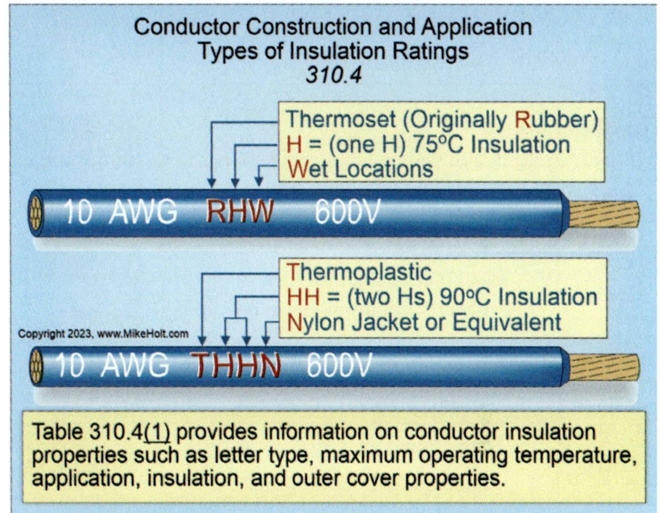

▶Figure 310–7

Author's Comment:

- The following explains the lettering on conductor insulation [Table 310.4(1)]:

    - No H   60°C insulation rating
    - H   75°C insulation rating
    - HH   90°C insulation rating permitted in dry locations
    - -2   90°C insulation rating permitted in wet locations
    - N   Nylon outer cover
    - T   Thermoplastic insulation
    - U   Underground
    - W   Permitted in wet or damp locations
    - X   Thermoset insulation
    - R   Rubber insulation

Table 310.4(1) Conductor Applications and Insulations

Type Letter	Column 2 Insulation	Column 3 Max. Operating Temperature	Column 4 Application	Column 5 Sizes Available AWG or kcmil	Column 6 Outer Covering
RHH	Flame-retardant thermoset	90°C	Dry and damp locations	14–2000	Moisture-resistant, flame-retardant, nonmetallic
RHW	Flame-retardant, moisture-resistant thermoset	75°C	Dry and wet locations	14–2000	Moisture-resistant, flame-retardant, nonmetallic
RHW-2	Flame-retardant, moisture-resistant thermoset	90°C	Dry and wet locations	14–2000	Moisture-resistant, flame-retardant, nonmetallic
THHN	Flame-retardant, heat-resistant thermoplastic	90°C	Dry and damp locations	14–1000	Nylon jacket or equivalent
THHW	Flame-retardant, moisture- and heat-resistant thermoplastic	75°C 90°C	Dry and wet locations	14–1000	None
THW	Flame-retardant, moisture- and heat-resistant thermoplastic	75°C	Dry, damp, and wet locations	14–2000	None
THW-2	Flame-retardant, moisture- and heat-resistant thermoplastic	90°C	Dry, damp, and wet locations	14–1000	None
THWN	Flame-retardant, moisture- and heat-resistant thermoplastic	75°C	Dry, damp, and wet locations	14–1000	Nylon jacket or equivalent
THWN-2	Flame-retardant, moisture- and heat-resistant thermoplastic	90°C	Dry, damp, and wet locations	14–1000	Nylon jacket or equivalent
TW	Flame-retardant, moisture-resistant thermoplastic	60°C	Dry, damp, and wet locations	14–2000	None
USE	Heat- and moisture-resistant	75°C	See Article 338	14–2000	Moisture-resistant nonmetallic
USE-2	Heat- and moisture-resistant	90°C	See Article 338	14–2000	Moisture-resistant nonmetallic

Author's Comment:

▸ It is common to see conductors with a multiple insulation rating, such as THHN/THWN. This type of conductor can be used in a dry location at the THHN 90°C ampacity. If it is used in a wet location, you must adhere to the THWN ampacity rating of the 75°C column of Table 310.16 for THWN insulation types. ▸**Figure 310–8**

▸ When a "–2" is at the end of an insulation type (such as THWN-2), the conductor has a maximum operating temperature of 90°C and is suitable to be installed in a dry or wet location. ▸**Figure 310–9**

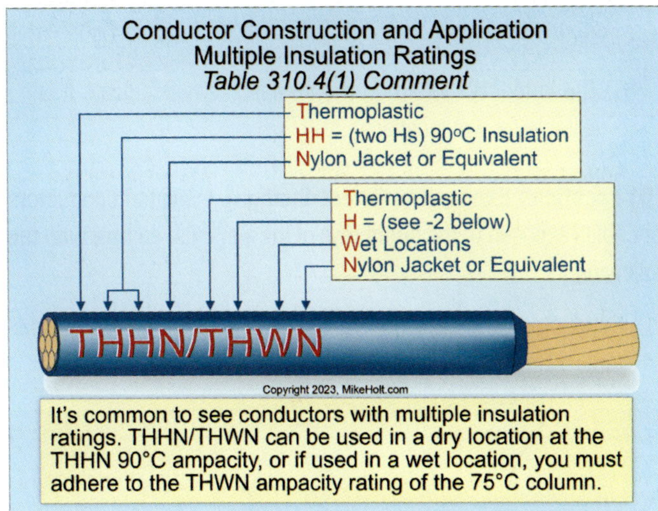

▶Figure 310–8

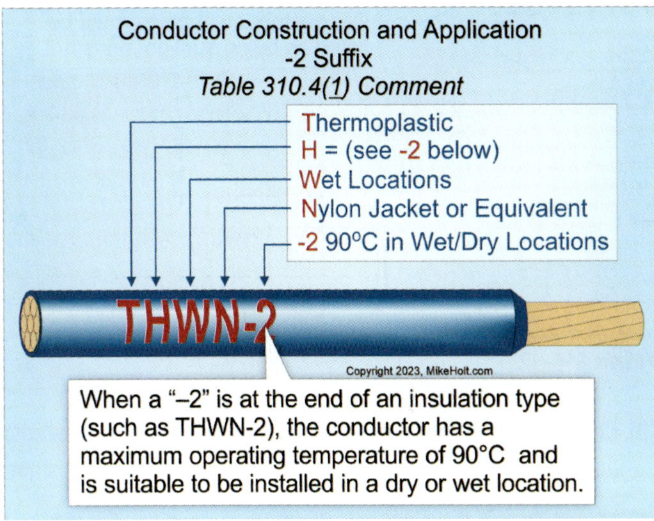

▶Figure 310–9

▶ Table 310.4(1) Conductor Insulation Example

Question: Which of the following describe(s) Type THHN insulation?

(a) Thermoplastic insulation.

(b) Suitable for dry or damp locations.

(c) A maximum operating temperature of 90°C.

(d) all of these

Answer: *(d) all of these*

310.6 Conductor Identification

(A) Neutral Conductor. Insulated neutral conductors must be identified white or gray in accordance with 200.6.

(B) Equipment Grounding Conductor. Insulated equipment grounding conductors must be identified green or green with yellow stripe in accordance with 250.119.

(C) Identification of Phase Conductors. Phase conductor insulation can be any color but white [200.7] or green [250.119]. ▶Figure 310–10

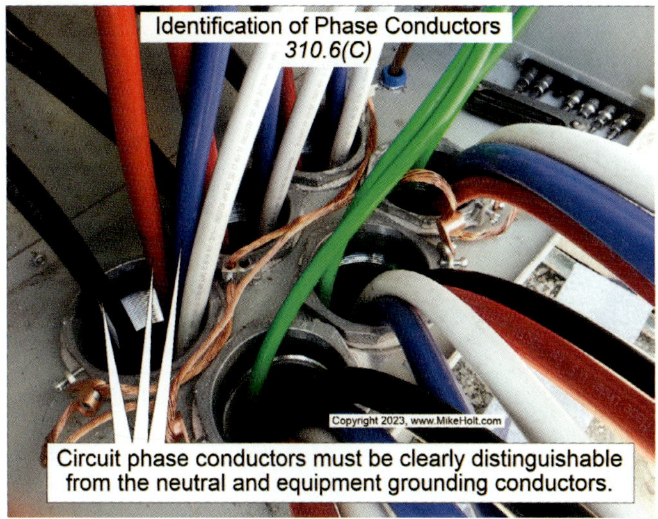

▶Figure 310–10

Where premises wiring is supplied from more than one nominal voltage system, branch-circuit phase conductors must be identified in accordance with 210.5(C), and feeders must be identified in accordance with 215.12(C).

Ex: Conductor identification is permitted in accordance with 200.7.

Author's Comment:

▶ Although the *NEC* does not require a specific color code for phase conductors, electricians often use the following color system: ▶Figure 310–11

  ▸ 120/240V, single-phase—black, red, and white
  ▸ 120/208V, three-phase—black, red, blue, and white
  ▸ 120/240V, three-phase—(high-leg) black, orange, blue, and white
  ▸ 277/480V, three-phase—brown, orange, yellow, and gray; or, brown, purple, yellow, and gray

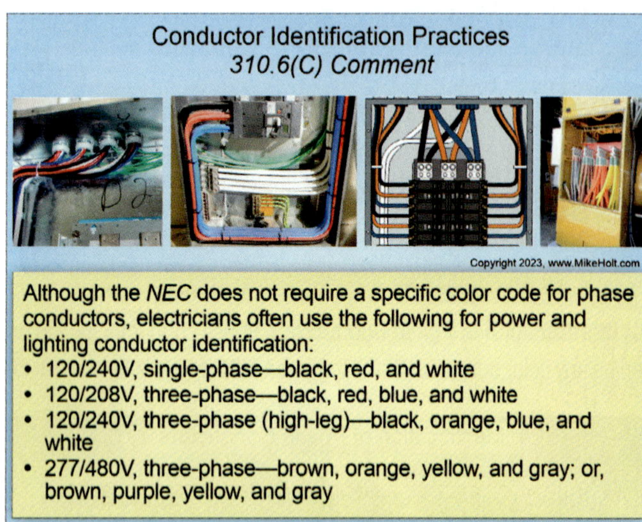

Conductor Identification Practices
310.6(C) Comment

Copyright 2023, www.MikeHolt.com

Although the *NEC* does not require a specific color code for phase conductors, electricians often use the following for power and lighting conductor identification:
- 120/240V, single-phase—black, red, and white
- 120/208V, three-phase—black, red, blue, and white
- 120/240V, three-phase (high-leg)—black, orange, blue, and white
- 277/480V, three-phase—brown, orange, yellow, and gray; or, brown, purple, yellow, and gray

▶Figure 310–11

Part III. Installation

310.10 Uses Permitted

Conductors described in Table 310.4(1) are permitted for use in any of the wiring methods covered in Chapter 3.

(A) Dry Locations. Insulated conductors used in dry locations can be any of the types identified in Table 310.4.

(B) Dry and Damp Locations. Insulated conductors typically used in dry and damp locations include THHN, THHW, THWN, THWN-2, and XHHW.

(C) Wet Locations. Insulated conductors typically used in wet locations include THHW, THWN, THWN-2, XHHW, XHHW-2, XHHN, XHWN, and XHWN-2. Cables must be moisture impervious and listed for wet locations.

▸ The letter "W" found on the insulation types indicate it is suitable for wet locations.

(D) Locations Exposed to Direct Sunlight. Insulated conductors or cables exposed to the direct rays of the sun must comply with the following:

(1) Conductors and cables must be listed as being sunlight resistant. ▶Figure 310–12

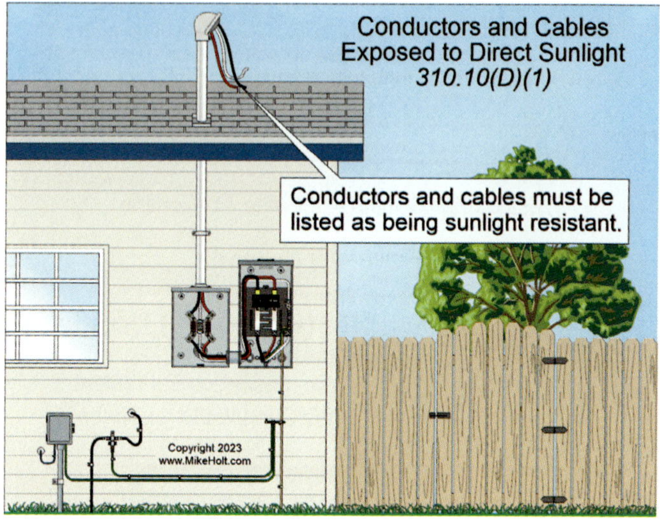

▶Figure 310–12

(2) Conductors and cables must be covered with insulating material (such as tape or sleeving) that is listed as being sunlight resistant.

(E) Direct Burial Conductors. Conductors used for direct burial applications must be of a type identified for such use.

CABINETS, CUTOUT BOXES, AND METER SOCKET ENCLOSURES

Introduction to Article 312—Cabinets, Cutout Boxes, and Meter Socket Enclosures

Article 312 covers the installation and construction specifications for cabinets for panelboards, cutout boxes for disconnects, and meter socket enclosures. Notice that these rules cover the cabinets and enclosures that contain electrical equipment such as panel boards—not the equipment itself. Some topics covered in this material include:

▸ Damp and wet locations

▸ Repairing noncombustible surfaces

▸ Cable terminations

Part I. General

312.1 Scope

Article 312 covers the installation and construction specifications for cabinets for panelboards, cutout boxes for disconnects, and meter socket enclosures. ▸Figure 312–1

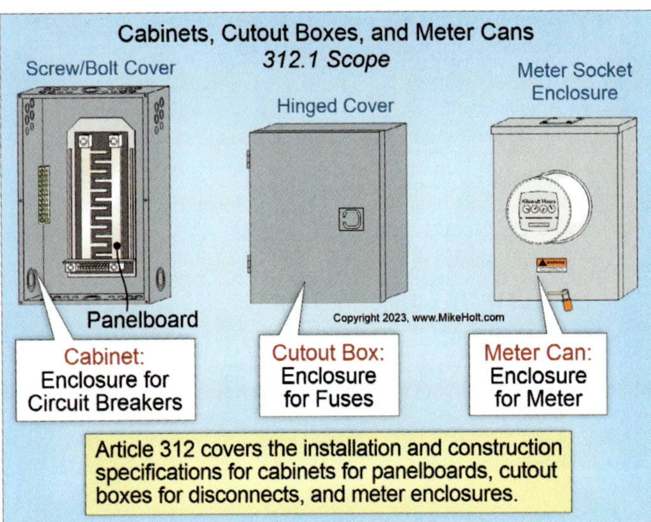

▸Figure 312–1

According to Article 100, "Cabinet" is a surface- or flush-mounted enclosure provided with a frame in which a door can be hung. ▸Figure 312–2

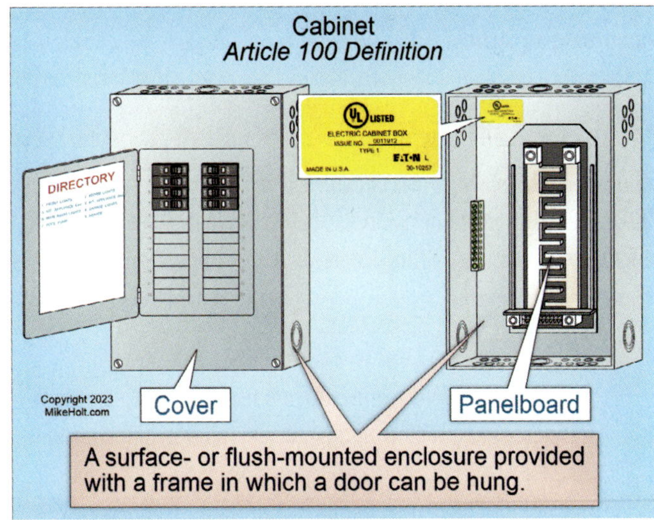

▸Figure 312–2

According to Article 100, "Cutout Box" is an enclosure designed for surface mounting that has swinging doors or covers secured directly to and telescoping with the walls of the enclosure. ▶Figure 312–3

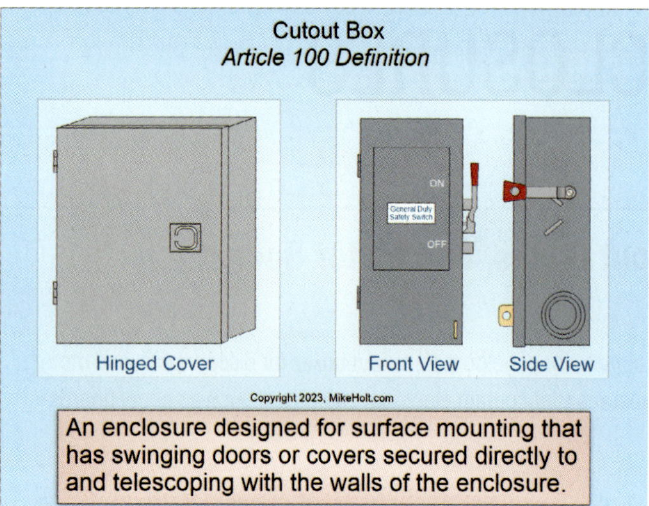

▶Figure 312–3

312.2 Damp or Wet Locations

Weatherproof. Cabinets for panelboards, cutout boxes for disconnects, and meter socket enclosures installed in damp or wet locations must be weatherproof.

According to Article 100, "Weatherproof" means constructed or protected so exposure to the weather will not interfere with successful operation [Article 100].

Above Live Parts. Raceways or cables in wet locations entering above the level of live parts of cabinets, cutout boxes, and meter socket enclosures must use a fitting listed for wet locations. ▶Figure 312–4

Author's Comment:

▶ In accordance with *"UL Guide Information DWTT,"* sealing locknuts are permitted on the outside or inside of the enclosure for RMC, IMC, or inside the enclosure for connectors if marked for this use on the fitting carton.

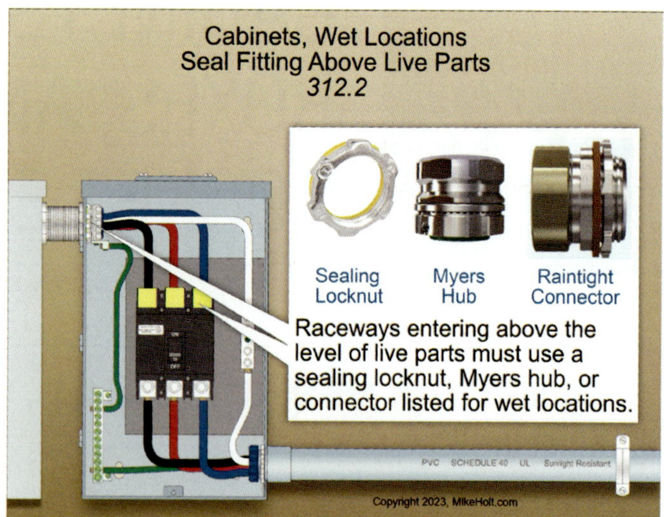

▶Figure 312–4

312.3 Position in Walls

Cabinets for panelboards installed in walls of noncombustible material must be installed so the front edge of the cabinet is set back no more than ¼ in. from the finished surface. In walls constructed of wood or other combustible material, cabinets for panelboards must be flush with the finished surface or project outward. ▶Figure 312–5

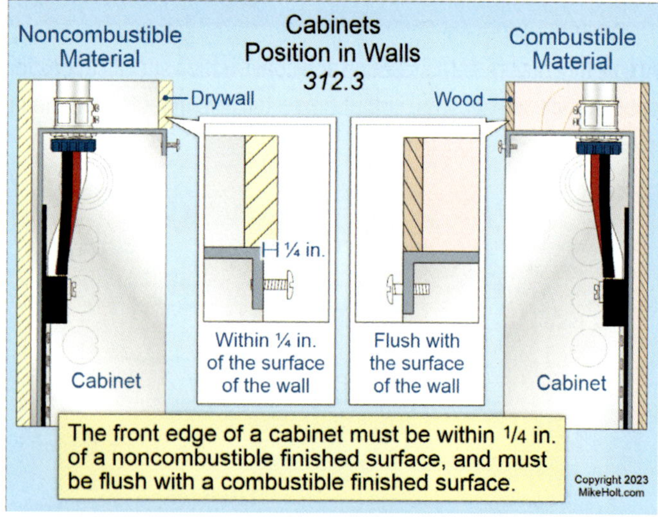

▶Figure 312–5

312.4 Repairing Gaps in Noncombustible Surfaces

Recessed cabinets for panelboards and cutout boxes in noncombustible surfaces (plaster, drywall, or plasterboard) must not have a gap of more than ⅛ in. around any edge of the cabinet. ▶Figure 312–6

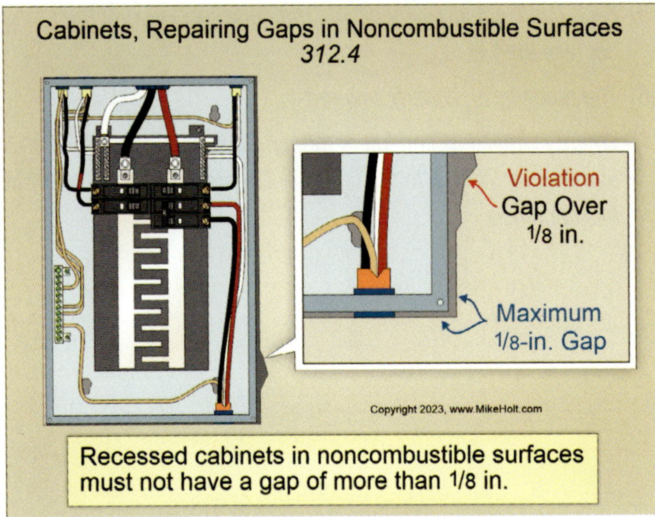

▶Figure 312–6

312.5 Cable Termination to Enclosures

(C) Cable Termination. Cables must be secured to the cabinet, cutout box, or meter socket enclosure with fittings listed for the cable type. See 300.12 and 300.15. ▶Figure 312–7 and ▶Figure 312–8

▶Figure 312–7

▶Figure 312–8

Author's Comment:

▶ In accordance with "*UL Guide Information PXJV,*" type NM cable clamps or cable connectors are only suitable for a single NM cable unless that clamp or connector is identified for more than one cable. Some Type NM cable clamps are listed for two or more Type NM cables within a single fitting. ▶Figure 312–9

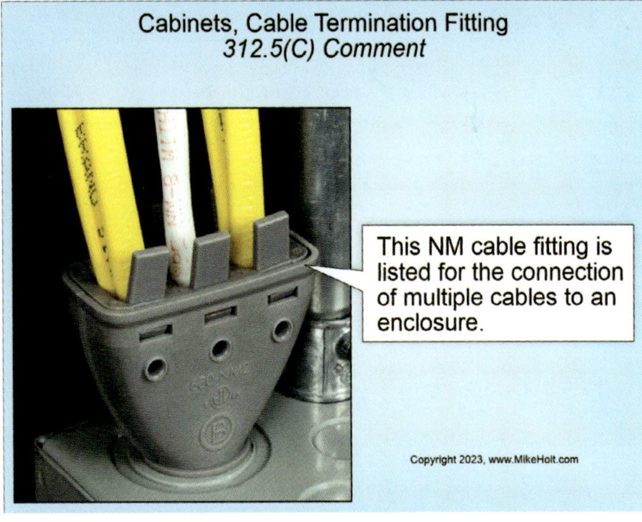

▶Figure 312–9

Ex 1: Nonmetallic-sheathed cables are not required to be secured to the cabinet, cutout box, and meter socket enclosure if the cables enter the top of a surface-mounted enclosure through a nonflexible raceway not less than 18 in. or more than 10 ft long, if all the following conditions are met: ▶Figure 312–10

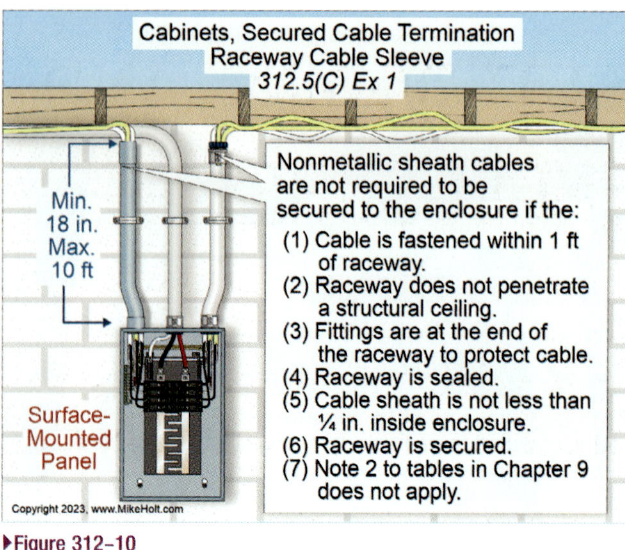

▶Figure 312–10

(1) Each cable is fastened within 12 in. of the raceway.

(2) The raceway does not penetrate a structural ceiling.

(3) Fittings are provided on the raceway to protect the cables from abrasion.

(4) The raceway is sealed.

(5) Each cable sheath extends into the enclosure beyond the fitting not less than ¼ in.

(6) The raceway is properly secured.

(7) Where installed as conduit or tubing, Chapter 9, Table 1 Notes 5 and 9 apply. Note 2 to the tables in Chapter 9 does not apply to this condition.

BOXES, CONDUIT BODIES, AND HANDHOLE ENCLOSURES

Introduction to Article 314—Boxes, Conduit Bodies, and Handhole Enclosures

This article contains the installation requirements for outlet and device boxes, pull and junction boxes, conduit bodies, and handhole enclosures. Some topics covered in this material include:

- Nonmetallic, and metal boxes
- Number of conductors in a box or conduit body
- Conductor and cables entering boxes
- Surface- and flush-mounted installations
- Repairing noncombustible surfaces around boxes
- Accessibility
- Handhole enclosures

Part I. General

314.1 Scope

Article 314 contains the installation requirements for outlet boxes, pull and junction boxes, conduit bodies, and handhole enclosures. This article also includes installation requirements for fittings used to connect raceways and cables to boxes or conduit bodies. ▶Figure 314–1

314.3 Nonmetallic Boxes

Nonmetallic boxes can only be used with nonmetallic cables and raceways.

Ex 1: Metal raceways and metal cables entering nonmetallic boxes must be bonded to the circuit equipment grounding conductor. ▶Figure 314–2

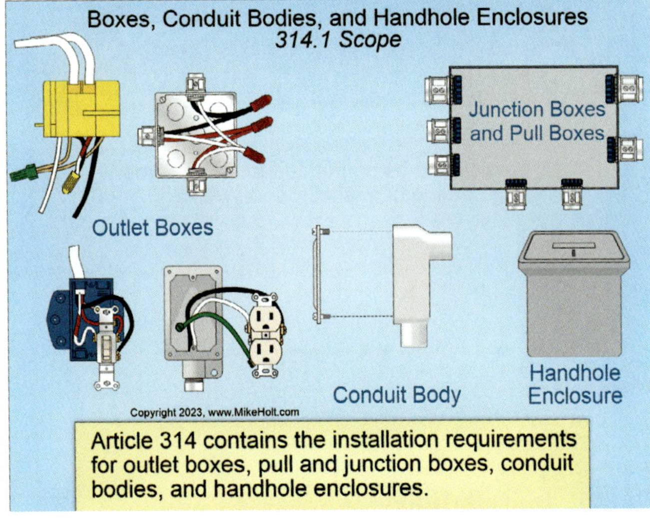

▶Figure 314–1

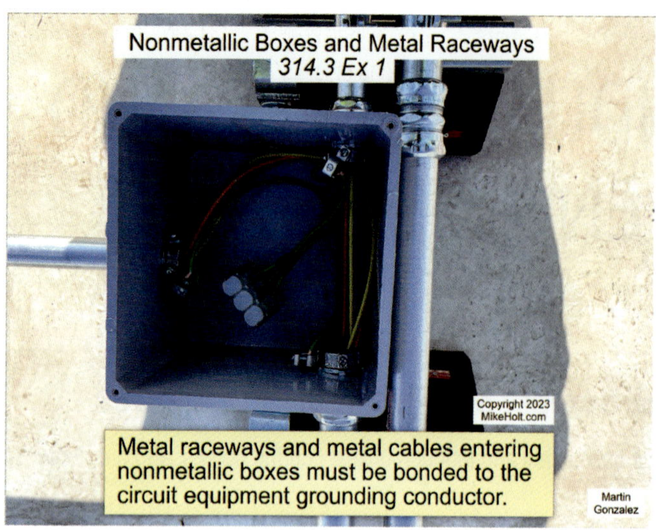

Metal raceways and metal cables entering nonmetallic boxes must be bonded to the circuit equipment grounding conductor.

▶Figure 314–2

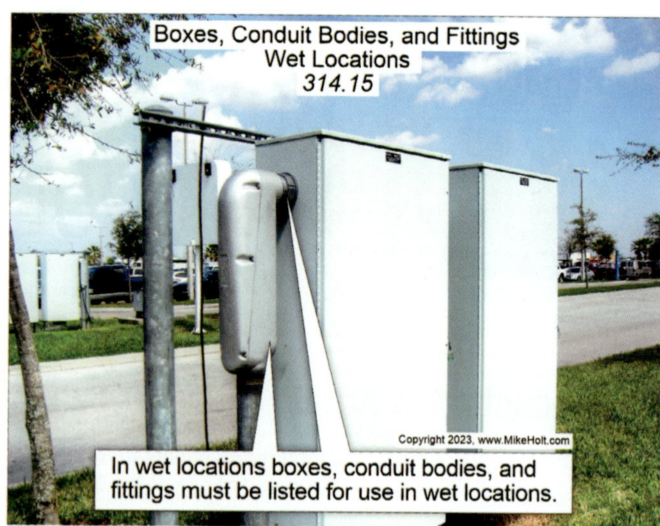

In wet locations boxes, conduit bodies, and fittings must be listed for use in wet locations.

▶Figure 314–4

314.4 Metal Boxes

Metal boxes must be connected to the equipment grounding conductor in accordance with 250.148(C). ▶Figure 314–3

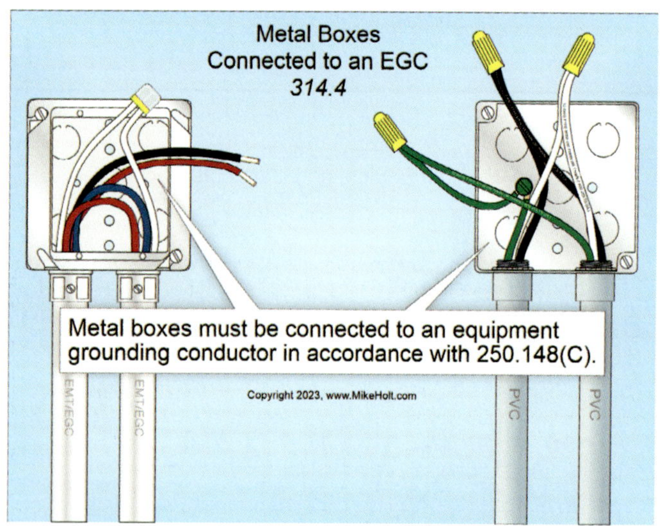

▶Figure 314–3

In wet locations boxes, conduit bodies, and fittings must be listed for use in wet locations

▶Figure 314–5

314.16 Outlet Box Sizing

Boxes containing 6 AWG and smaller conductors must be sized in an approved manner to provide sufficient free space for all conductors. In no case can the volume of the box, as calculated in 314.16(A), be less than the volume requirement as calculated in 314.16(B). ▶Figure 314–6

Part II. Installation

314.15 Wet Locations

In wet locations boxes, conduit bodies, and raceway and cable connectors must be listed for use in wet locations. ▶Figure 314–4 and ▶Figure 314–5

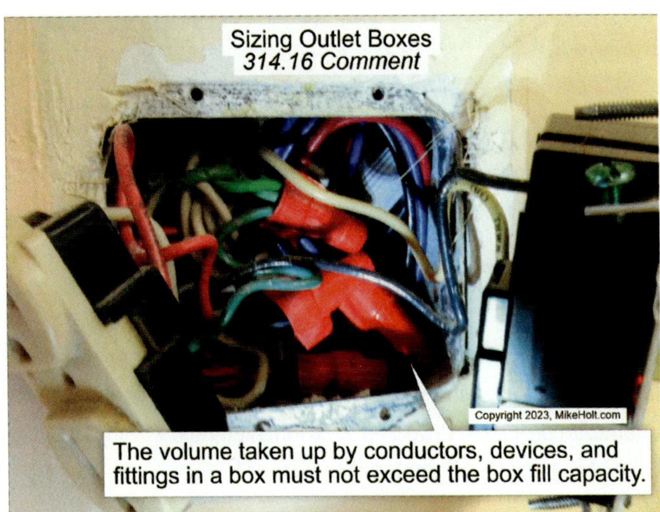

▶Figure 314–6

Author's Comment:

▸ The requirements for sizing boxes and conduit bodies containing conductors 4 AWG and larger are in 314.28, and those for sizing handhole enclosures are contained in 314.30(A). An outlet box is generally used for the attachment of devices and luminaires and has a specific amount of space (volume) for conductors, devices, and fittings. The volume taken up by conductors, devices, and fittings in a box must not exceed the box fill capacity.

Boxes and conduit bodies enclosing conductors 4 AWG or larger must also comply with the provisions of 314.28.

(A) Box Volume. The volume of a box is the total volume of its assembled parts including plaster rings, raised covers, and extension rings. The total volume includes only those parts marked with their volumes in cubic inches listed in Table 314.16(A). ▶Figure 314–7

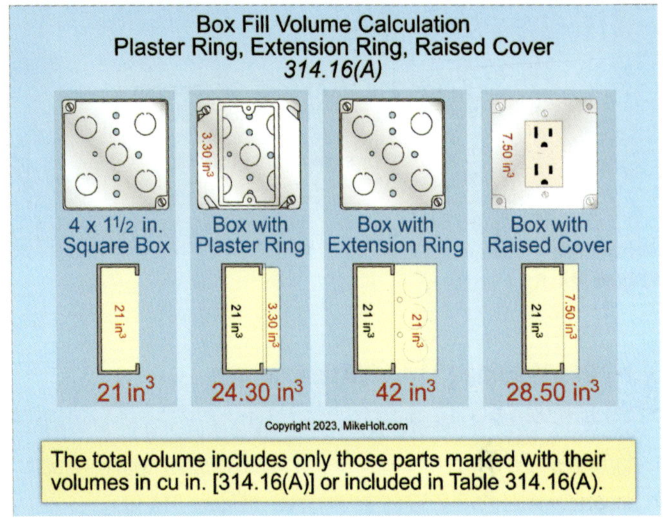

▶Figure 314–7

Table 314.16(A) Metal Boxes*								
Box Trade Size		Minimum Volume	Maximum Number of Conductors (arranged by AWG size)					
in.	Box Shape	in³	18	16	14	12	10	8
(4 × 1¼)	round/octagonal	12.50	8	7	6	5	5	4
(4 × 1½)	round/octagonal	15.50	10	8	7	6	6	5
(4 × 2⅛)	round/octagonal	21.50	14	12	10	9	8	7
(4 × 1¼)	square	18.00	12	10	9	8	7	6
(4 × 1½)	square	21.00	14	12	10	9	8	7
(4 × 2⅛)	square	30.30	20	17	15	13	12	10
(4¹¹⁄₁₆ × 1¼)	square	25.50	17	14	12	11	10	8
(4¹¹⁄₁₆ × 1½)	square	29.50	19	16	14	13	11	9
(4¹¹⁄₁₆ × 2⅛)	square	42.00	28	24	21	18	16	14

*Table 314.16(A) does not consider switches, receptacles, luminaire studs, luminaire hickeys, cable clamps, or equipment grounding conductors. ▶Figure 314–8

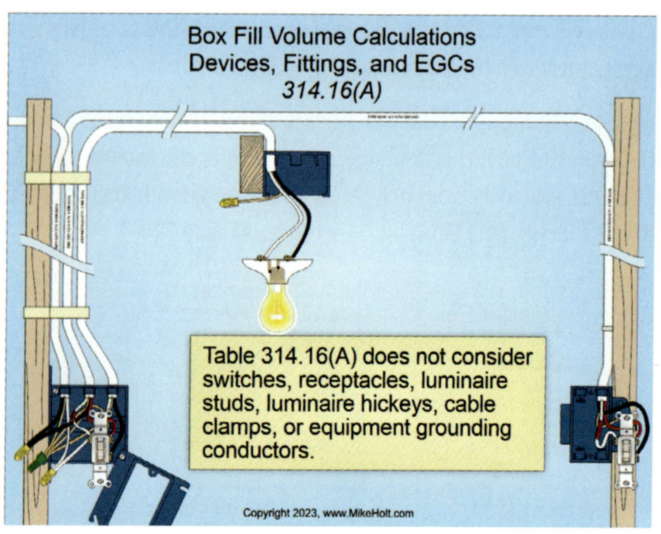

▶Figure 314–8

▶ Box Volume [314.16(A)], Example

Question: *What is the total box volume for a 4 in. × 4 in. × 1½ in. outlet box and a 4 in. × 4 in. × 1½ in. extension box with a domed cover marked with a 7.50 cu in. volume?* ▶Figure 314–9

(a) 44.50 cu in.   (b) 46.50 cu in.   (c) 47.50 cu in.   (d) 49.50 cu in.

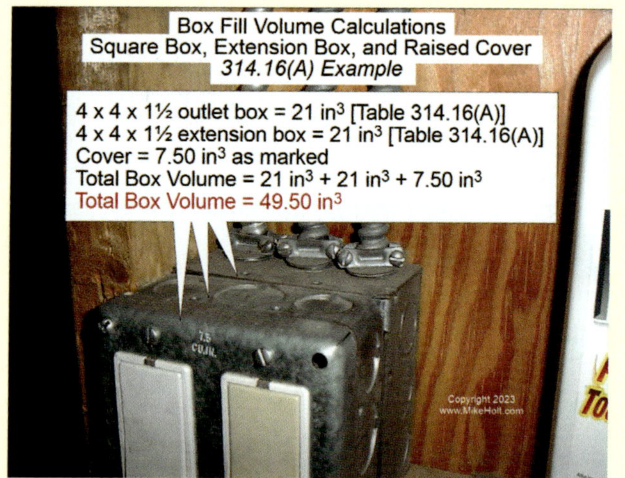

▶Figure 314–9

Solution:

Volume of a 4 in. × 4 in. × 1½ in. Outlet Box = 21 cu in. [Table 314.16(A)].

Volume of a 4 in. × 4 in. × 1½ in. Extension box = 21 cu in. [Table 314.16(A)].

Cover Volume = 7.50 cu in. as marked

Total Box Volume = 21 cu in. + 21 cu in. + 7.50 cu in.
Total Box Volume = 49.50 cu in.

Note: *Do not calculate the actual volume of a box contained in Table 314.16(A) since the table volume is based on the inside dimensions of the box, not the outside dimensions.*

Answer: *(d) 49.50 cu in.*

Where a box is provided with barriers, the volume is apportioned to each of the resulting spaces. Each barrier, if not marked with its volume, is considered to take up ½ cu in. if metal and 1 cu in. if nonmetallic. ▶Figure 314–10 and ▶Figure 314–11

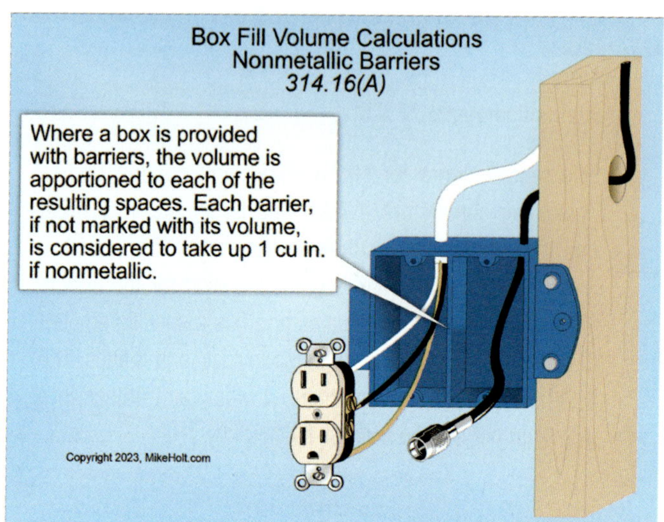

▶Figure 314–10

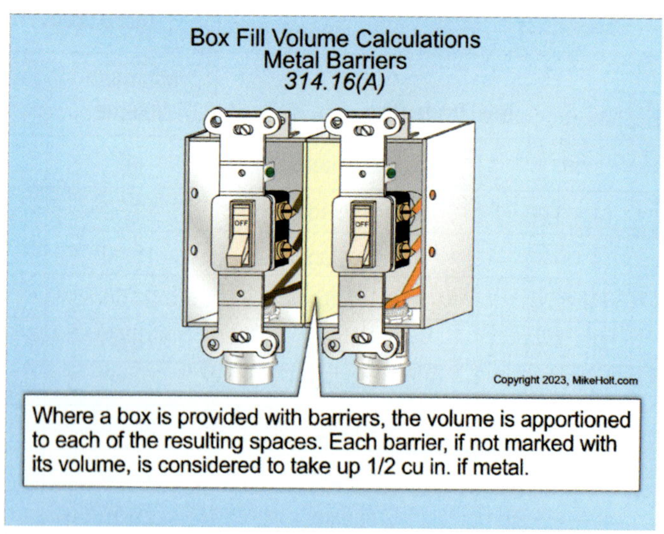

▶Figure 314–11

Author's Comment:

▶ When all the conductors in an outlet box are the same size (insulation does not matter), Table 314.16(A) can be used to determine the number of conductors permitted in the outlet box, or to determine the required outlet box size for the given number of conductors.

▶ If the outlet box contains switches, receptacles, luminaire studs, luminaire hickeys, cable clamps, or equipment grounding conductors, then allowance must be made for these items which are not reflected in Table 314.16(A).

▶ Table 314.16(A) Example

Question: Which 4-in. square outlet box is the smallest permitted for three 12 AWG, THW conductors and six 12 AWG, THHN conductors?

(a) 4 in. × 1¼ in. square   *(b) 4 in. × 1½ in. square*

(c) 4 in. × 2⅛ in. square   *(d) 4 in. × 2⅛ in. with extension*

Answer: (b) 4 in. × 1½ in. square

---

(1) Standard Boxes. Metal boxes not marked with their volume must use the volume from Table 314.16(A).

(2) Nonmetallic Boxes. The volume for nonmetallic boxes must be legibly marked by the manufacturer.

(B) Box Fill Calculations. The calculated conductor volumes determined by 314.16(B)(1) through (B)(6) are added together using Table 314.16(B)(1) to determine the total volume of the conductors, devices, and fittings.

Raceway and cable fittings, including locknuts and bushings, are not counted for box fill calculations. ▶Figure 314–12

Each space within a box with a barrier must be calculated separately. ▶Figure 314–13

(1) Conductor Volume. Each conductor that originates outside the box and terminates or is spliced inside the box counts as a single conductor volume as shown in Table 314.16(B)(1). ▶Figure 314–14

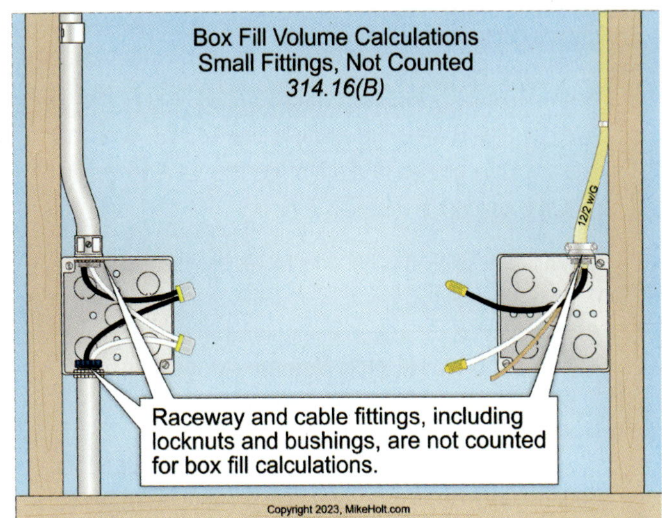

▶Figure 314–12

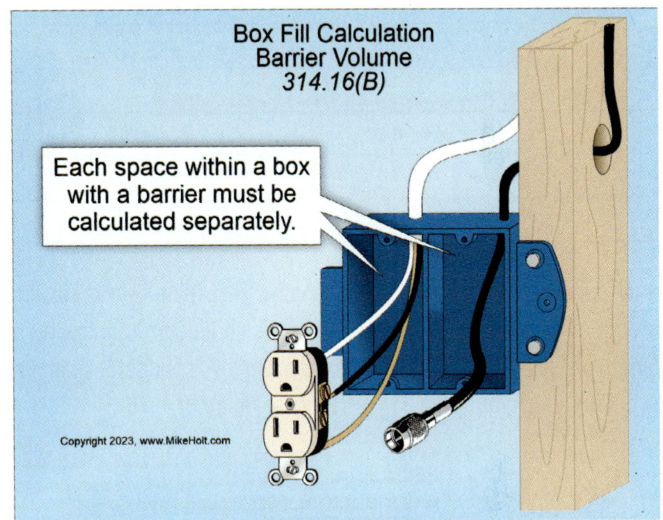

▶Figure 314–13

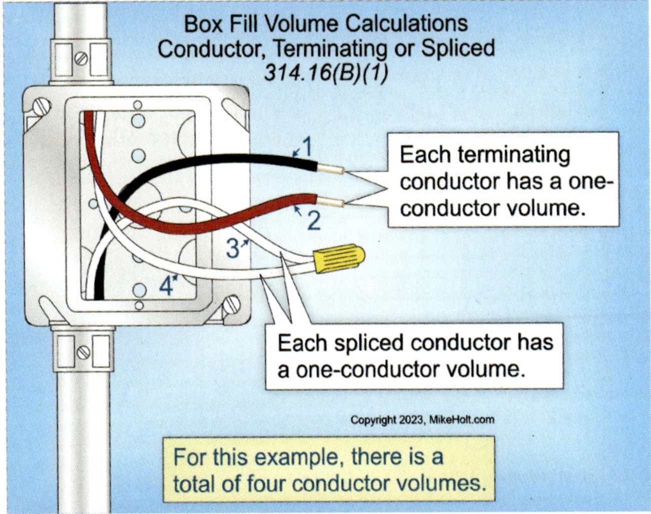

▶Figure 314–14

Author's Comment:

▸ Table 314.6(B)(1) lists the conductor cu in. volumes for 18 AWG through 6 AWG. For example, one 14 AWG conductor has a volume of 2 cu in. If a box has four 14 AWG conductors, the conductor volume is 8 cu in.

▸ Conductor insulation is not a factor for box fill calculations.

Table 314.16(B)(1) Volume Allowance Required per Conductor	
Conductor AWG Size	Free Space Required for Each Conductor (cu in.)
18	1.50
16	1.75
14	2.00
12	2.25
10	2.50
8	3.00
6	5.00

Each conductor loop having a total length of less than 12 in. is considered a single conductor volume, and each conductor loop having a length of not less than 12 in. is considered as two conductor volumes in accordance with Table 314.16(B)(1). ▸Figure 314–15

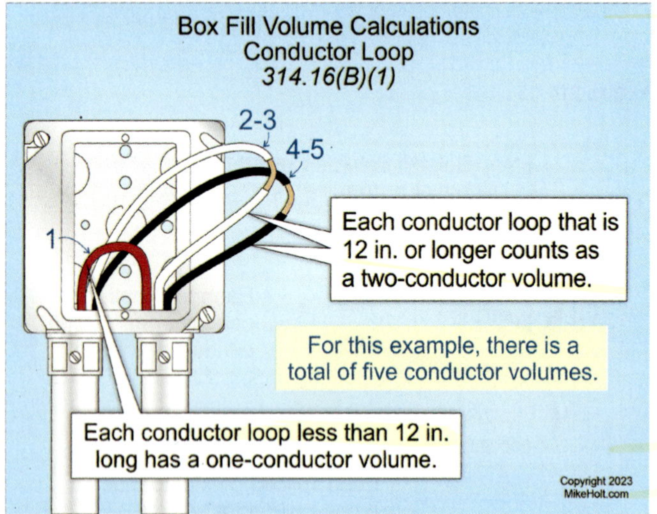

▸Figure 314–15

Author's Comment:

▸ At least 6 in. of conductor, measured from the point in the box where the conductor enters the enclosure, must be available at each point for conductor splices or terminations. ▸Figure 314–16

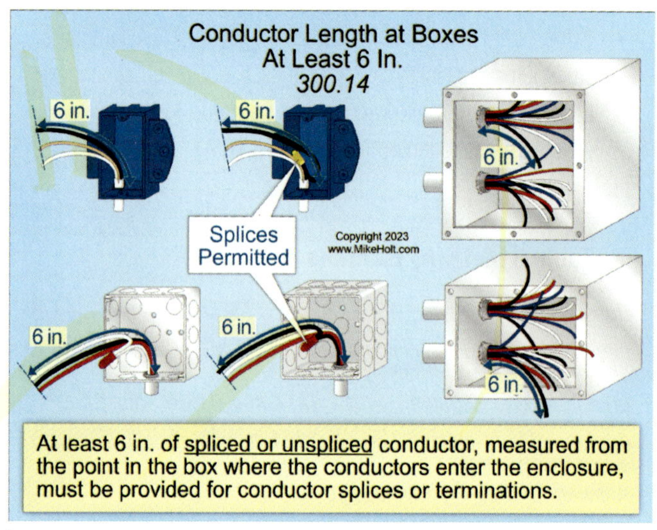

▸Figure 314–16

▸ Boxes having openings of less than 8 in. in any dimension must have at least 6 in. of conductor, measured from the point where the conductor enters the box, and at least 3 in. of conductor outside the box. ▸Figure 314–17

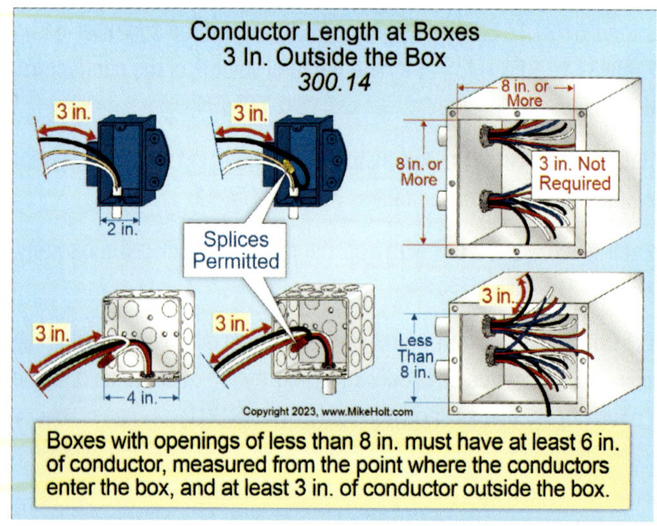

▸Figure 314–17

Conductors that originate and terminate within the box, such as pigtails and bonding jumpers, are not counted as a conductor volume. ▸Figure 314–18

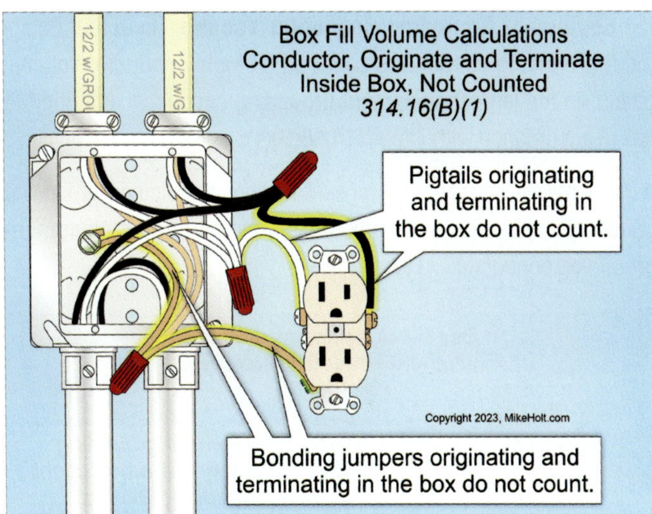

▶Figure 314–18

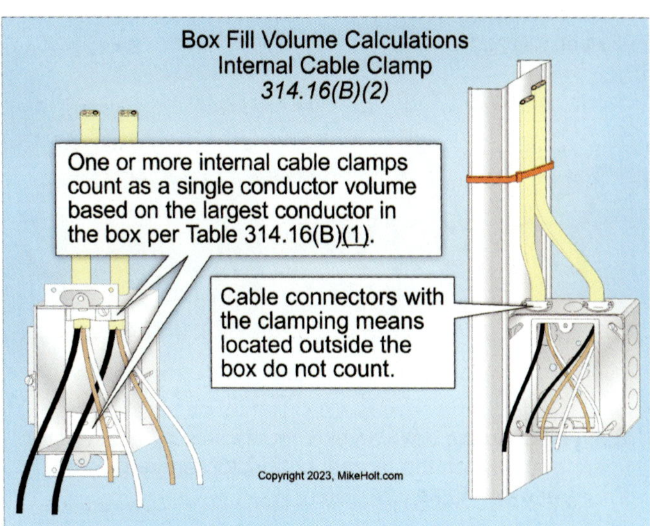

▶Figure 314–20

Ex: Equipment grounding conductors, circuit conductors, and not more than four fixture wires smaller than 14 AWG are not counted as a conductor volume if they enter the box from a domed luminaire or similar canopy, such as a ceiling paddle fan canopy. ▶Figure 314–19

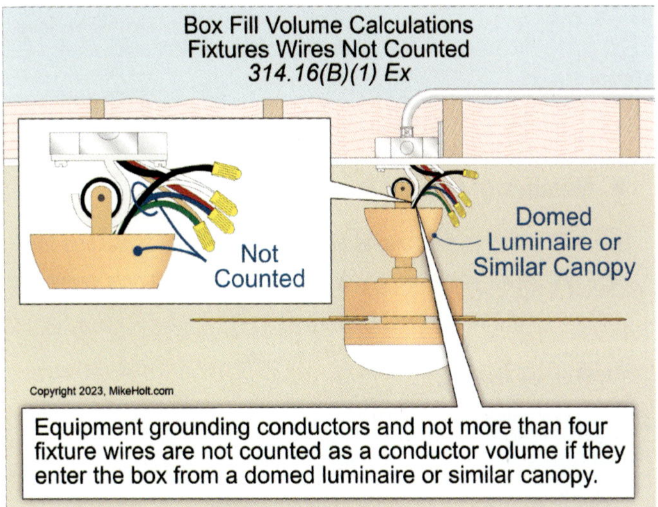

▶Figure 314–19

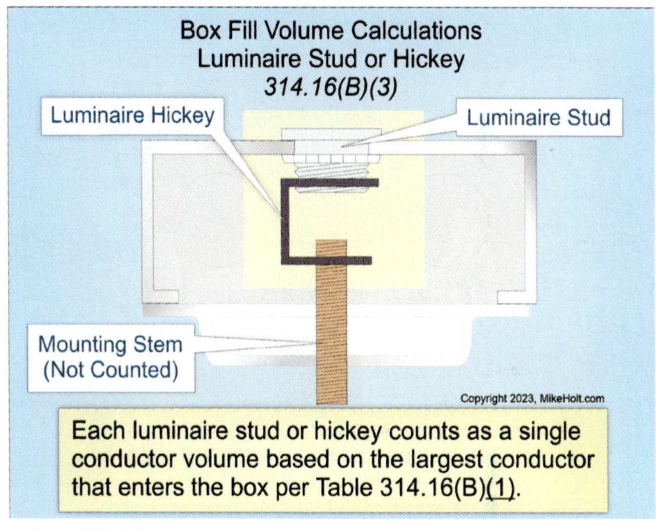

▶Figure 314–21

(2) Cable Clamp Volume. Cable clamps that are part of the outlet box are counted as a single conductor volume based on the largest conductor in the box in accordance with Table 314.16(B)(1). ▶Figure 314–20

(3) Support Fitting Volume. Each luminaire stud or luminaire hickey counts as a single conductor volume based on the largest conductor that enters the box in accordance with Table 314.16(B)(1). ▶Figure 314–21

(4) Device Yoke Volume. Each single-gang device yoke counts as two conductor volumes based on the largest conductor that terminates on the device in accordance with Table 314.16(B)(1). ▶Figure 314–22

Author's Comment:

▶ A device yoke is the mounting structure for a receptacle, switch, switch with pilot light, switch/receptacle, and so forth. ▶Figure 314–23

Each device yoke wider than 2 in. counts as a two-conductor volume for each gang required for mounting, based on the largest conductor that terminates on the device in accordance with Table 314.16(B)(1). ▶Figure 314–24

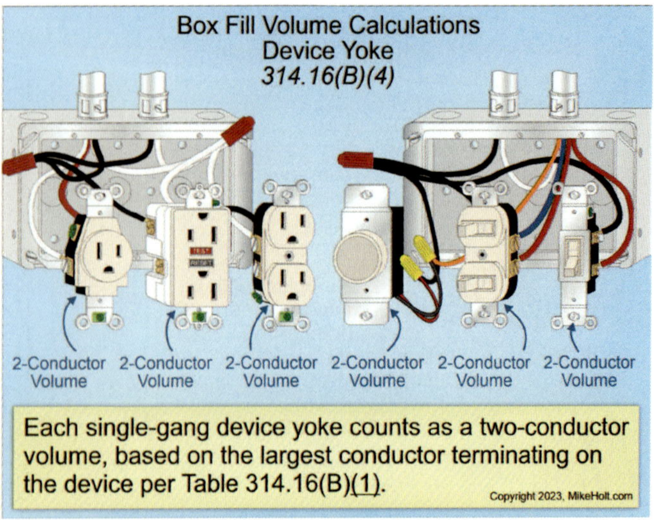

▶Figure 314–22

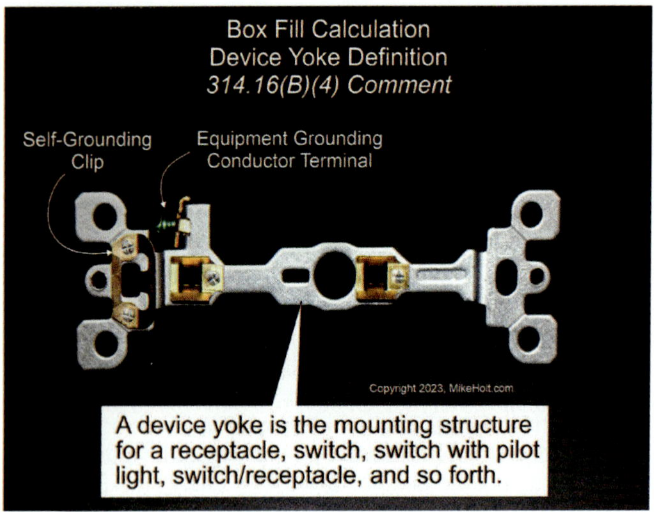

▶Figure 314–23

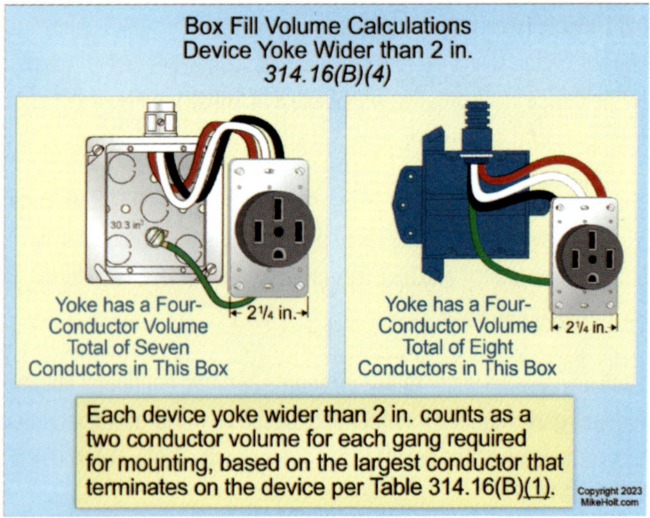

▶Figure 314–24

(5) Equipment Grounding Conductor Volume. Up to four equipment grounding conductors count as a single conductor volume, based on the largest equipment grounding conductor entering the box in accordance with Table 314.16(B)(1).

A ¼ volume allowance applies for each additional equipment grounding conductor that enters the box, based on the largest equipment grounding conductor. ▶Figure 314–25

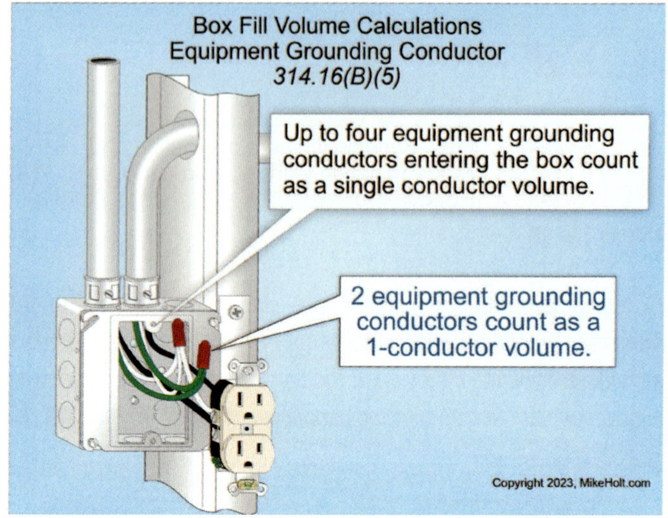

▶Figure 314–25

▶ Number of Conductors Example

Question: *What is the volume fill for a 4-gang box containing four 14/2 NM cables and one 14/3 NM cable, three single-pole switches, and one three-way switch?* ▶Figure 314–26

(a) 35.50 cu in.   (b) 37.50 cu in.   (c) 39.50 cu in. (d) 40.50 cu in.

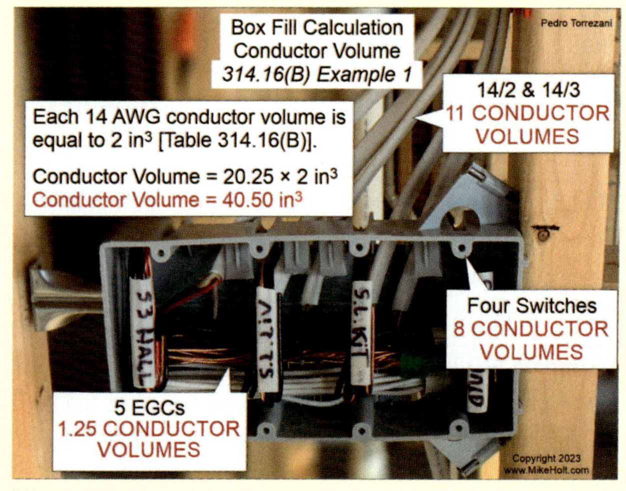

▶Figure 314–26

Solution:

Four 14/2 NM Cables	8–14 AWG conductor volumes
One 14/3 NM Cable	3–14 AWG conductor volumes
Five EGCs	1.25–14 AWG conductor volumes
Four Switches	+ 8–14 AWG conductor volumes
Total	20.25–14 AWG conductor volumes

Each 14 AWG conductor volume is equal to 2 cu in. [Table 312.6(B)(1)].

20.25 conductor volumes × 2 cu in. = 40.50 cu in.

Answer: (d) 40.50 cu in.

▶ Box Fill Example

Question: How many 14 AWG conductors can be pulled through a 4-in. square × 2⅛ in. deep box with a plaster ring marked 3.60 cu in.? The box contains two receptacles, five 12 AWG conductors, and two 12 AWG equipment grounding conductors. ▶Figure 314–27

(a) 4 conductors	(b) 5 conductors
(c) 6 conductors	(d) 7 conductors

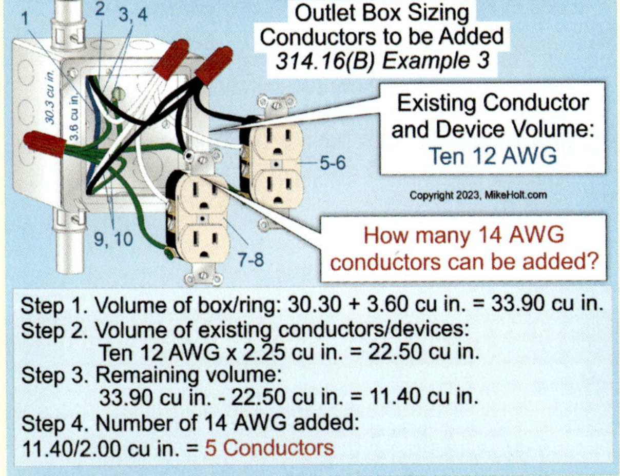

▶Figure 314–27

Solution:

Step 1: Determine the volume of the box assembly [314.16(A)].

Box Assembly Volume = Box 30.30 cu in. + 3.60 cu in. plaster ring
Box Assembly Volume = 33.90 cu in.

Step 2: Determine the volume of the devices and conductors in the box.

Two–receptacles	4–12 AWG
Five–12 AWG conductors	5–12 AWG
Two–12 AWG equipment grounding conductors	1–12 AWG
	10–12 AWG

Total Device Volume and Conductors = Ten–12 AWG × 2.25 cu in.
Total Device Volume and Conductors = 22.50 cu in.

Step 3: Determine the remaining volume permitted for the 14 AWG conductors (volume of the box minus the volume of the conductors).

Remaining Volume = 33.90 cu in. – 22.50 cu in.
Remaining Volume = 11.40 cu in.

Step 4: Determine the number of 14 AWG conductors (at 2.00 cu in. each) permitted in the remaining volume of 11.40 cu in.:

14 AWG = 2.00 cu in. each [Table 312.6(B)(1)]
11.40 cu in./2.00 cu in. = 5 conductors

Five 14 AWG conductors can be pulled through.

Answer: (b) 5 conductors

(C) Conduit Bodies.

(1) General. The maximum number of conductors permitted shall be the maximum number permitted by Table 1 of Chapter 9 for the conduit or tubing to which it is attached.

(2) With Splices, Taps, or Devices. Only those conduit bodies that are durably and legibly marked by the manufacturer with their volume shall be permitted to contain splices, taps, or devices. The maximum number of conductors shall be calculated in accordance with 314.16(B).

314.17 Cables That Enter Boxes

(B) Boxes. The installation of cables in boxes must comply with the following:

(2) Cables Entering Through Cable Clamps. Where cable assemblies (Type NM or UF) are used, the sheath must extend not less than ¼ in. inside the box and beyond the end of any cable clamp. ▶Figure 314–28

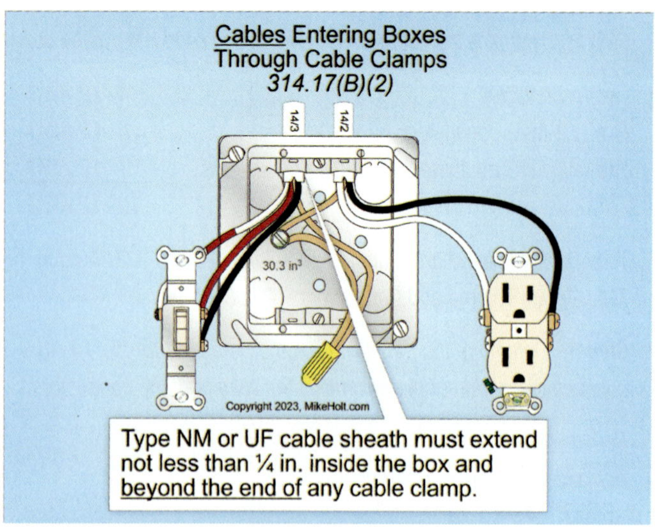

▶Figure 314–28

Author's Comment:

▸ Two Type NM cables can terminate in a single cable clamp if it is listed for this purpose.

314.20 Flush-Mounted Boxes

Noncombustible Walls and Ceilings. Installation within walls or ceilings finished with a noncombustible material must have the front edge of the box, plaster ring, extension ring, or listed extender set back no more than ¼ in. from the finished surface. ▶Figure 314–29

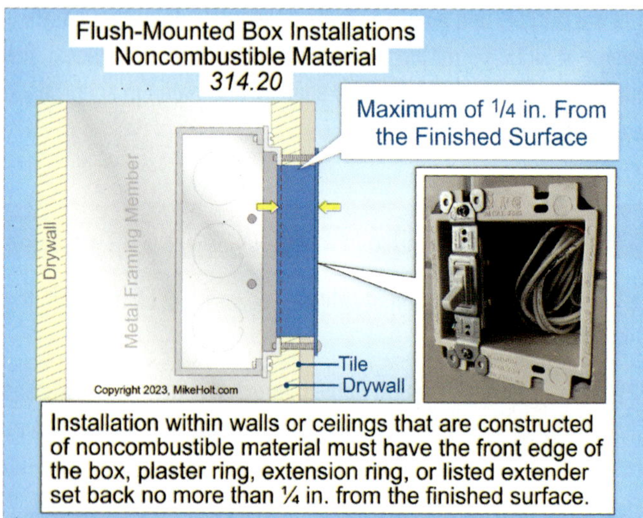

▶Figure 314–29

Combustible Walls and Ceilings. Installation within walls or ceilings constructed of wood or other combustible material must have the front edge of the box, plaster ring, extension ring, or listed extender extend to, or project out from, the finished surface. ▶Figure 314–30

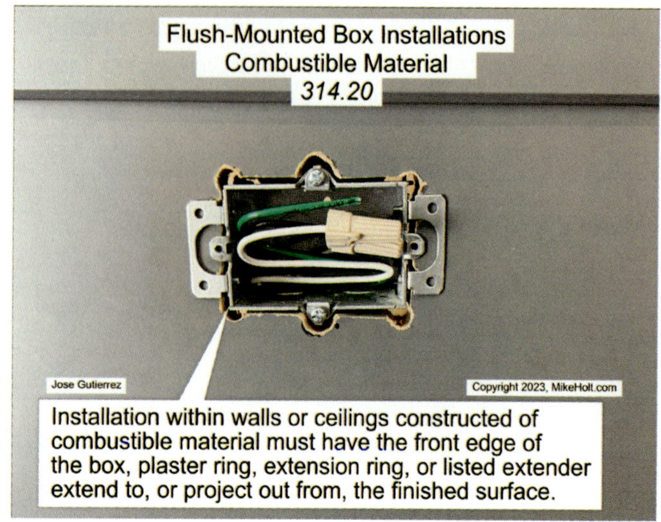

▶Figure 314–30

Author's Comment:

▸ Plaster rings and extension rings are available in a variety of depths to meet the above requirements.

▸ Final finished surfaces such as backsplashes and tile may need the use of listed extenders to meet the requirements of this section.

314.21 Repairing Noncombustible Surfaces

Gaps around boxes that are recessed in noncombustible surfaces (such as plaster, drywall, or plasterboard) must be repaired so there will be no gap greater than ⅛ in. at the edge of the box. ▶Figure 314–31

Author's Comment:

▸ Other examples of noncombustible surfaces include ceramic wall tile, ceramic or marble floor tile, brick, cinder block, and other types of masonry or stone. All these examples are subject to the requirements of 314.20 and 314.21.

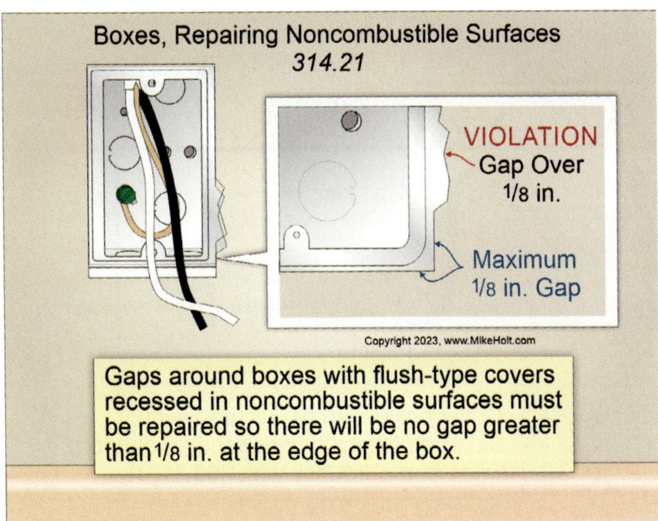

▶Figure 314–31

314.23 Securing Boxes

(A) Securing Boxes to Surface. Boxes secured to a building or other surface must be rigidly and securely fastened in place. ▶Figure 314–32

▶Figure 314–32

(B) Securing Boxes to Structural Member. A box can be secured to a structural member or from grade using a metal or wood brace.

(2) Braces. Boxes can be secured to a metal, plastic, or wood brace.

Metal Braces. Boxes can be secured to metal braces that has protection against corrosion. ▶Figure 314–33

▶Figure 314–33

Wood Brace. Boxes can be secured to wood braces not less than a nominal 1 in. × 2 in. ▶Figure 314–34

▶Figure 314–34

(C) Securing Boxes to Finished Surface. Boxes can be secured to a finished surface (drywall, plaster walls, or ceilings) by clamps or fittings identified for the purpose. ▶Figure 314–35

(D) Securing Boxes to Suspended-Ceiling. Outlet boxes can be secured to supporting elements of a suspended ceiling by any of the following methods:

(1) Ceiling Framing Members. An outlet box can be secured to suspended-ceiling framing members by bolts, screws, rivets, clips, or other means identified for the suspended-ceiling framing member(s). ▶Figure 314–36

▶Figure 314–35

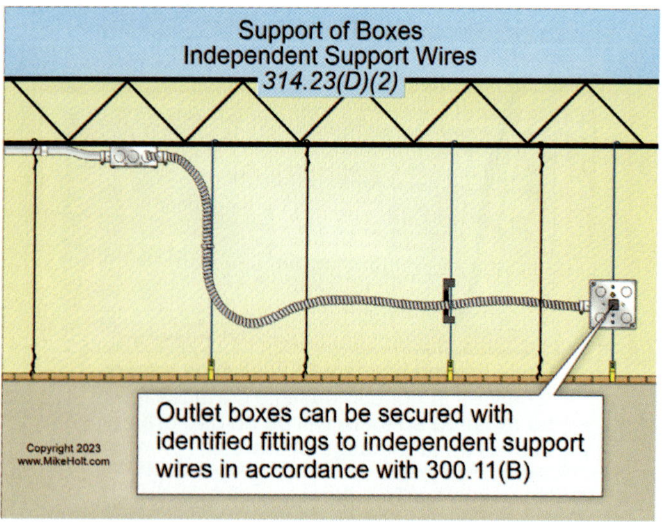

▶Figure 314–37

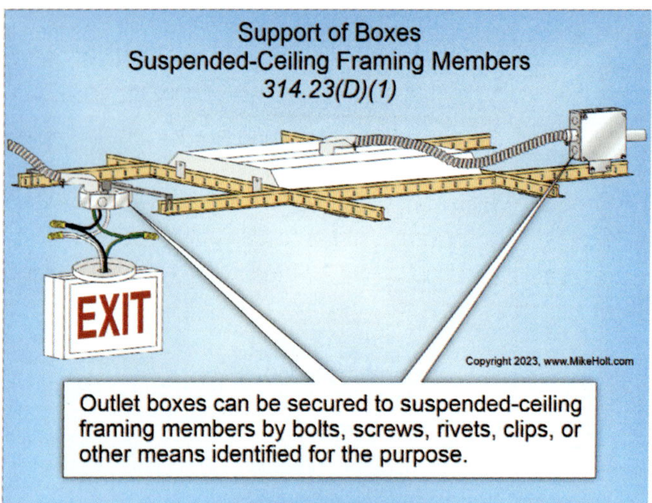

▶Figure 314–36

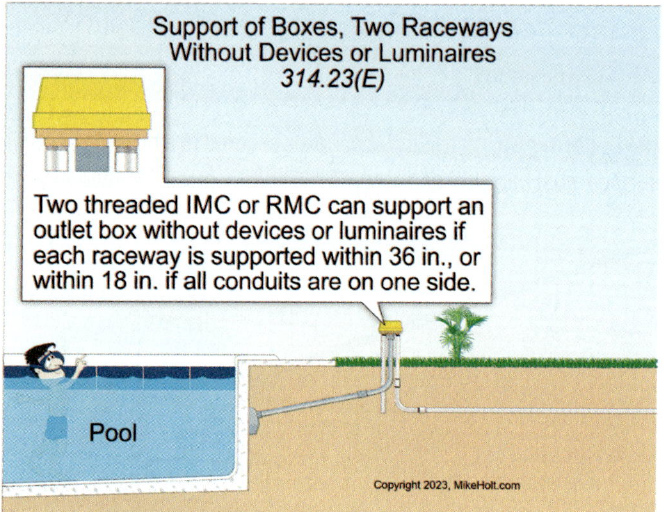

▶Figure 314–38

(2) Independent Support Wires. Outlet boxes can be secured with identified fittings to independent support wires in accordance with 300.11(B). ▶Figure 314–37

(E) Securing Boxes without Devices or Luminaires with Threaded Raceway. Two intermediate metal or rigid metal conduits, threaded wrenchtight into the enclosure, can be used to secure an outlet box that does not contain a device or luminaire if each raceway is supported within 36 in. of the box or within 18 in. of the box if all conduit entries are on the same side of the box. ▶Figure 314–38

Ex: The following wiring methods are permitted to support a conduit body with only one conduit entry, provided the size of the conduit body is not larger than the largest size of the conduit or tubing: ▶Figure 314–39

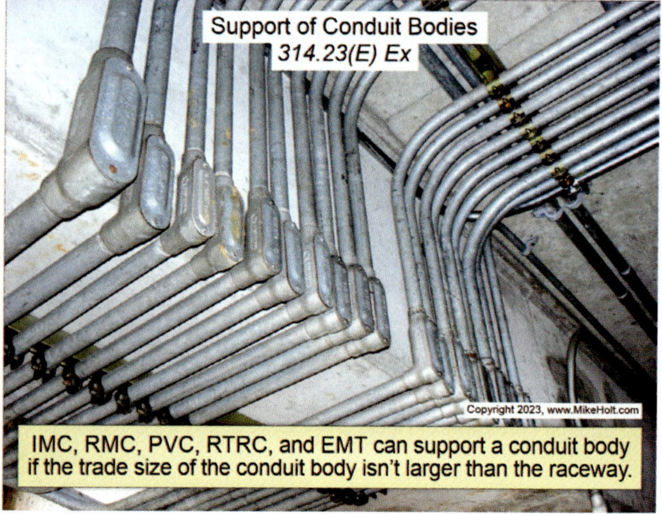

▶Figure 314–39

(1) *Intermediate metal conduit*

(2) *Rigid metal conduit*

(3) *Rigid polyvinyl chloride conduit*

(4) *Reinforced thermosetting resin conduit*

(5) *Electrical metallic tubing*

(F) Securing Boxes with Devices or Luminaires with Threaded Raceway. Two intermediate metal or rigid metal conduits, threaded wrenchtight into the enclosure, can be used to secure an outlet box containing devices or luminaires if each raceway is supported within 18 in. of the box. ▶Figure 314–40, ▶Figure 314–41, and ▶Figure 314–42

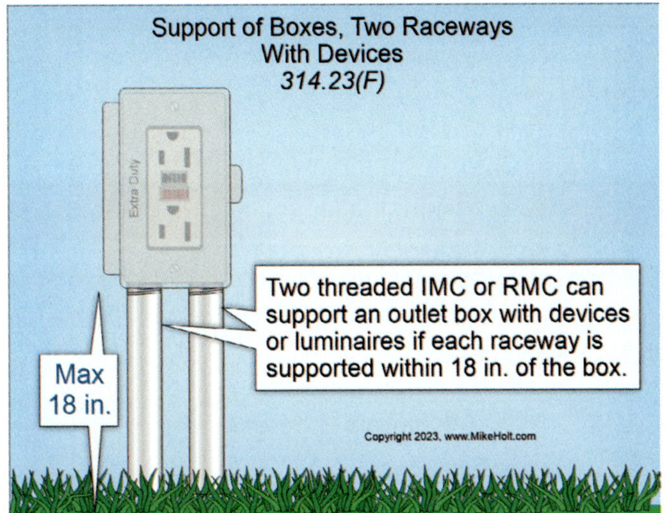

▶Figure 314–40

▶Figure 314–41

▶Figure 314–42

(G) Boxes in Concrete or Masonry. Boxes that are identified as suitably protected from corrosion can be embedded in concrete or masonry.

(H) Pendant Boxes.

(1) Flexible Cord. Boxes containing a hub are permitted to use a listed cord grip attachment fitting marked for use with a threaded hub to support a box from a flexible cord [400.10(A)(1) and 400.14]. ▶Figure 314–43

▶Figure 314–43

314.29 Wiring to be Accessible

Boxes, conduit bodies, and handhole enclosures must be installed so that wiring and devices contained within them can be rendered accessible in accordance with 314.29(A) and (B).

(A) In Buildings. Boxes and conduit bodies must be installed so the wiring and devices contained within the boxes and conduit bodies are accessible. ▸Figure 314–44

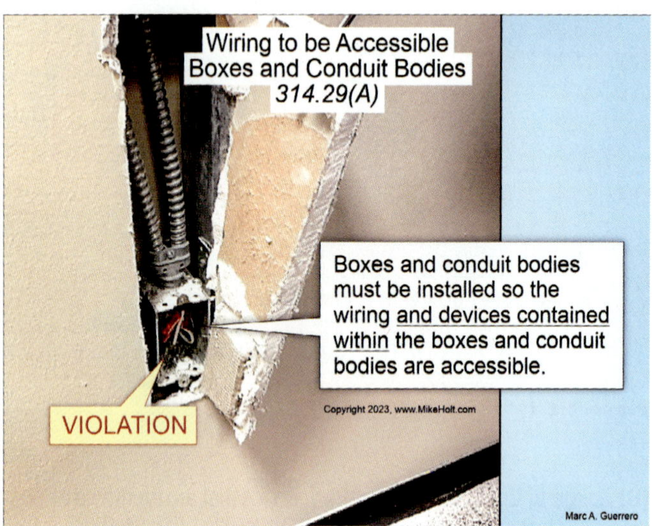

▸Figure 314–44

According to Article 100, "Accessible (as applied to wiring methods)" means capable of being removed or exposed without damaging the building structure or finish or not permanently closed in or blocked by the building structure, other electrical equipment, other building systems (piping, ducts, drains, or other mechanical systems), or the building finish. ▸Figure 314–45

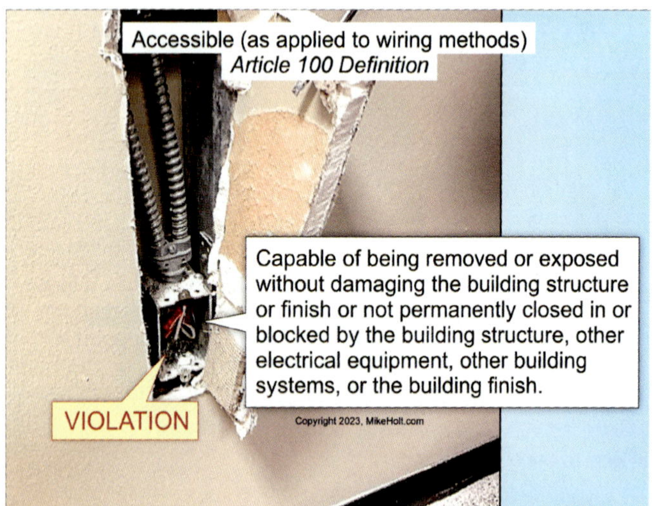

▸Figure 314–45

(B) Handhole Enclosures. Handhole enclosures must be installed so that the wiring within is accessible without excavating sidewalks, paving, earth, or other substances used to establish the finished grade. ▸Figure 314–46

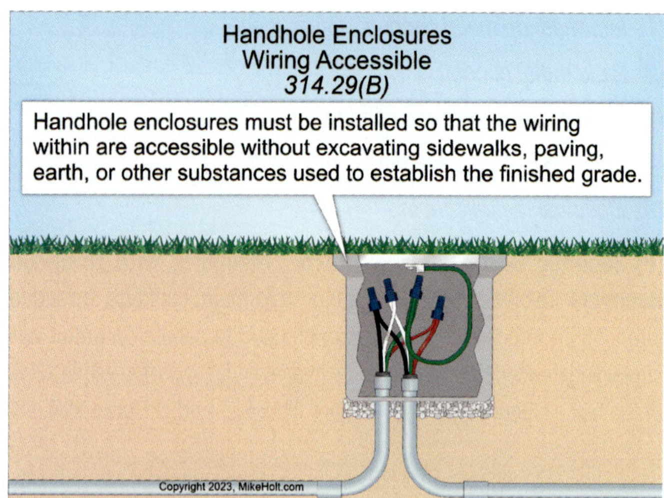

▸Figure 314–46

314.30 Handhole Enclosures

Handhole enclosures must be identified for underground use and be designed and installed to withstand all loads likely to be imposed on them. ▸Figure 314–47

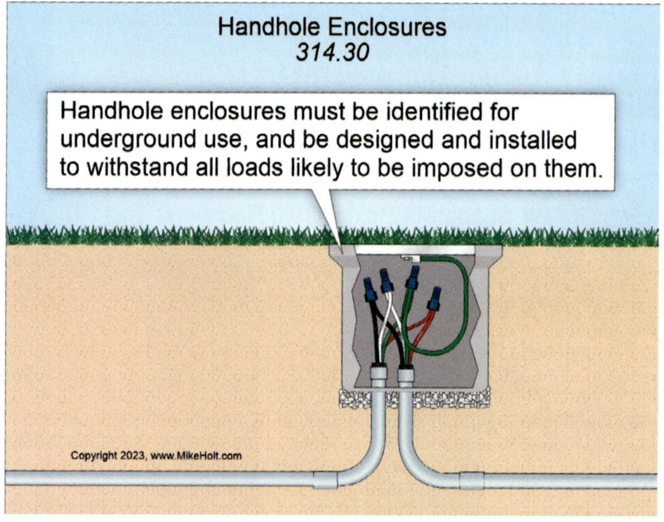

▸Figure 314–47

According to Article 100, "Handhole Enclosure" is an underground enclosure with an open or closed bottom that is sized to allow personnel to reach into but not enter the enclosure. ▸Figure 314–48

(B) Wiring Entries. Underground raceways and cables entering a handhole are not required to be mechanically connected to the handhole. ▸Figure 314–49

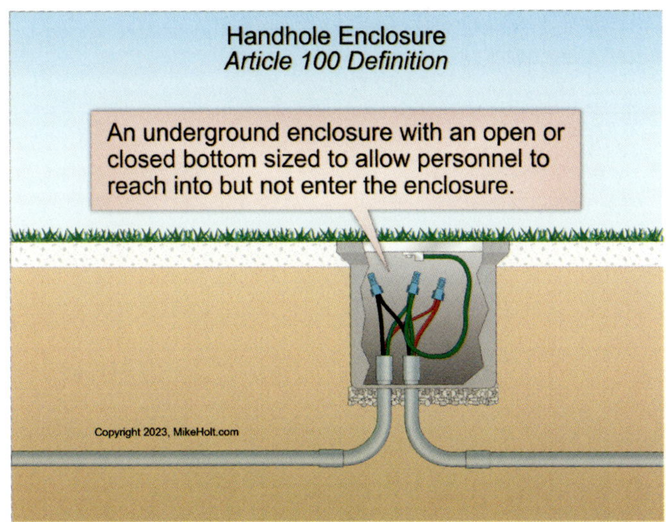

▶Figure 314–48

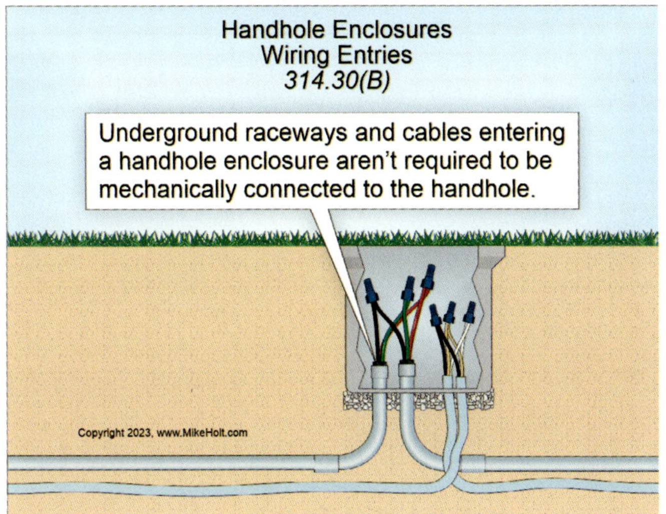

▶Figure 314–49

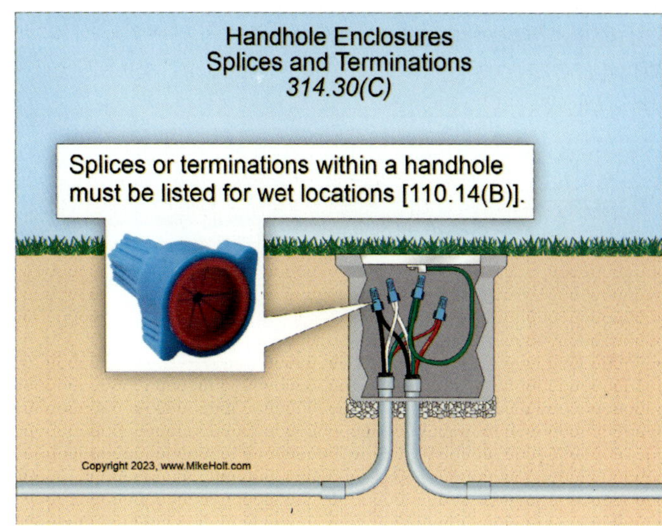

▶Figure 314–50

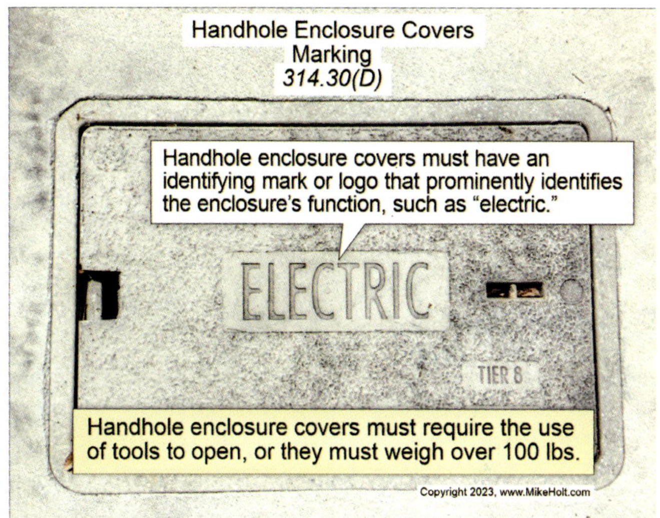

▶Figure 314–51

(C) Enclosure Wiring. Splices or terminations within a handhole must be listed for wet locations [110.14(B)]. ▶Figure 314–50

(D) Covers. Handhole covers must have an identifying mark or logo that prominently identifies the function of the handhole, such as "electric." Handhole covers must require the use of tools to open, or they must weigh over 100 lb. ▶Figure 314–51

Metal covers and exposed conductive surfaces of handhole enclosures must be connected to the circuit equipment conductor in accordance with 250.96(A). ▶Figure 314–52

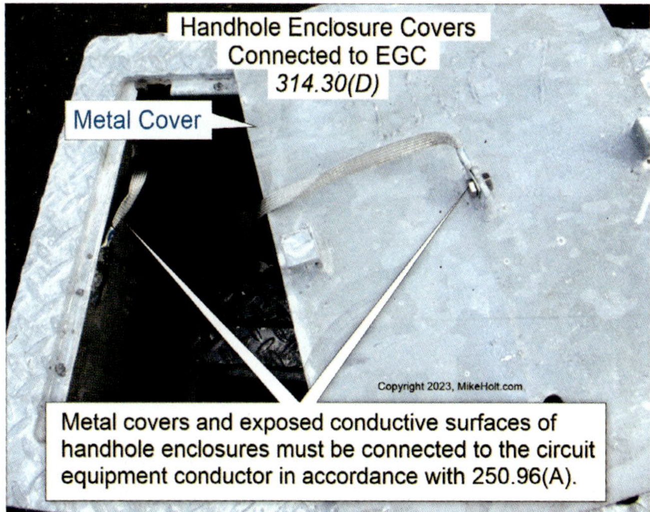

▶Figure 314–52

ARMORED CABLE (TYPE AC)

Introduction to Article 320—Armored Cable (Type AC)

Article 320 covers the use, installation, and construction specifications of armored cable (Type AC). AC cable is an assembly of up to four phase conductors and one neutral insulated conductor, sizes 14 AWG through 1 AWG, individually wrapped in a moisture-resistant, fire-retardant paper contained within a flexible spiral metal sheath. Some topics covered in this material include:

▸ Uses permitted

▸ Uses not permitted

▸ Installation in accessible roof spaces

▸ Securing and supporting

According to Article 100, "Type AC" is a fabricated assembly of conductors in a flexible interlocked metallic armor with an internal bonding strip in intimate contact with the armor for its entire length. ▸Figure 320–1

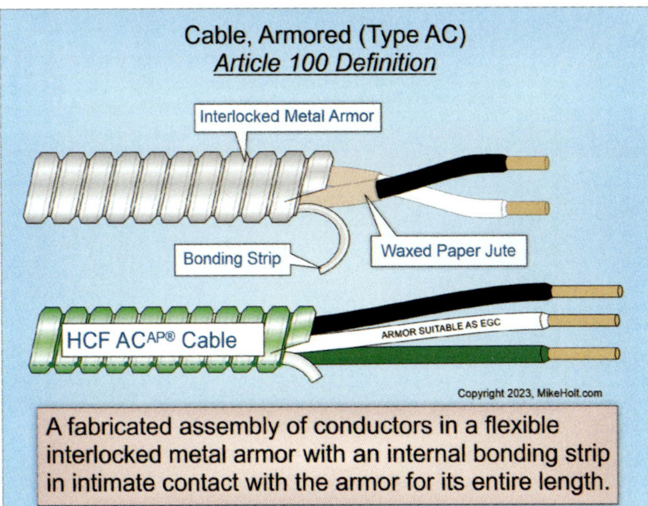

▸Figure 320–1

Part I. General

320.1 Scope

This article covers the use, installation, and construction specifications of armored cable, Type AC. ▸Figure 320–2

Part II. Installation

320.10 Uses Permitted

Type AC cable can be used or installed as follows:

(1) For feeders and branch circuits in both exposed and concealed installations.

(2) In cable trays.

(3) In dry locations.

(4) Embedded in plaster in dry locations.

(5) In air voids of block walls where not exposed to excessive moisture or dampness.

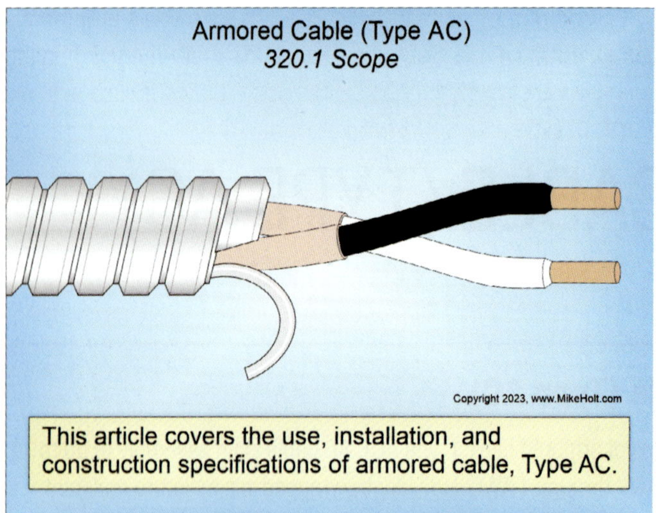

▶Figure 320–2

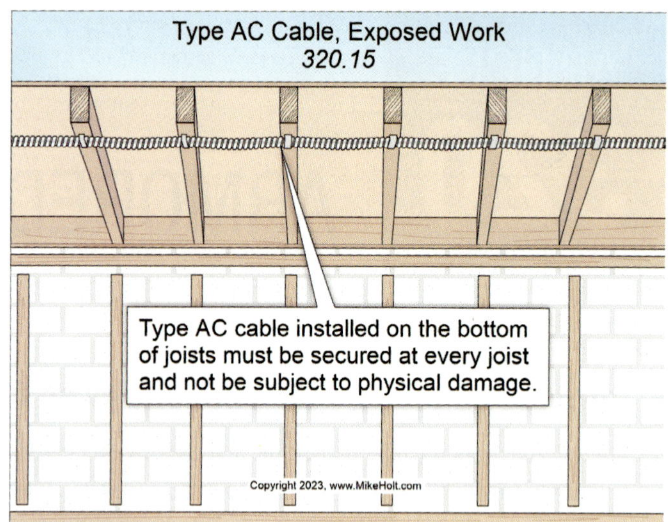

▶Figure 320–3

Note: The "Uses Permitted" is not an all-inclusive list, which indicates other suitable uses are permitted if approved by the authority having jurisdiction.

Author's Comment:

▶ Type AC cable can also be installed in a plenum space in accordance with 300.22(C)(1).

320.12 Uses Not Permitted

Type AC cable is not permitted to be installed:

(1) Where subject to physical damage.

(2) In damp or wet locations.

(3) In air voids of block or tile walls where such walls are exposed or subject to excessive moisture or dampness.

(4) Where exposed to corrosive conditions.

(5) Embedded in plaster finish or concrete in wet or damp locations.

320.15 Exposed Work

Exposed Type AC cable, except as provided in 300.11(B), must closely follow the surface of the building finish or running boards. If installed on the bottom of floor or ceiling joists, it must be secured at every joist and must not be subject to physical damage. ▶Figure 320–3

320.23 In Roof Spaces

(A) Cables Run Across the Top of Framing Members. Type AC cable in roof spaces within 6 ft of the nearest edge of the scuttle hole entrance run across the top of framing members must be protected by guard strips that are at least as high as the cable. ▶Figure 320–4

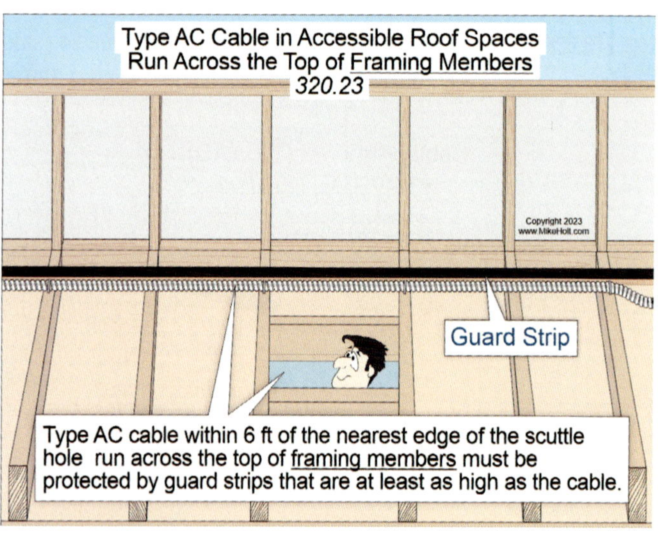

▶Figure 320–4

320.30 Securing and Supporting

(A) General. Type AC cable must be supported and secured by staples, cable ties listed and identified for securing and supporting, straps, hangers, similar fittings, or other approved means designed and installed so the cable is not damaged. ▶Figure 320–5

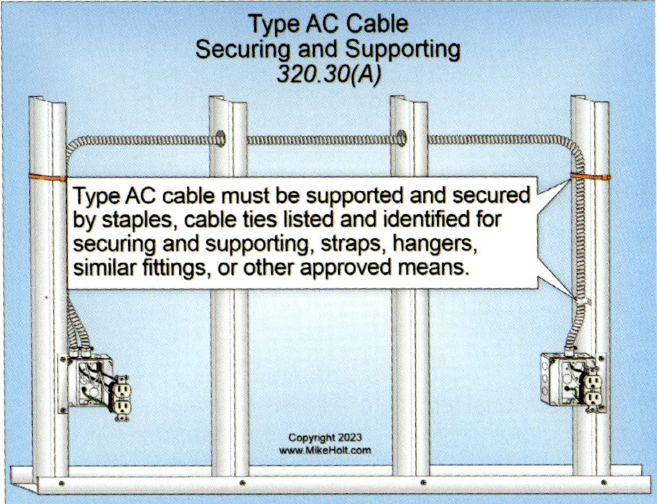

▶Figure 320–5

Type AC cable fittings are permitted as a means of cable support.

(B) Securing. Type AC cable must be secured within 12 in. of every outlet box, junction box, cabinet, or fitting and at intervals not exceeding 4½ ft. ▶Figure 320–6

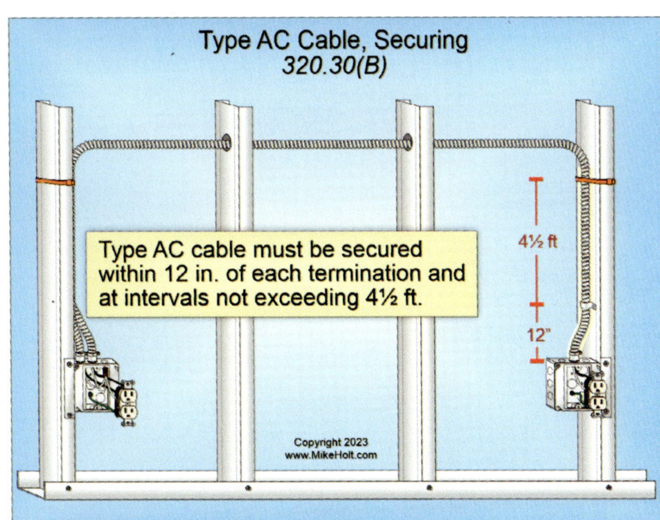

▶Figure 320–6

(C) Supporting. Type AC cable must be supported at intervals not exceeding 4½ ft. Cables installed horizontally through framing members are considered supported and secured if such support does not exceed 4½-ft intervals. ▶Figure 320–7

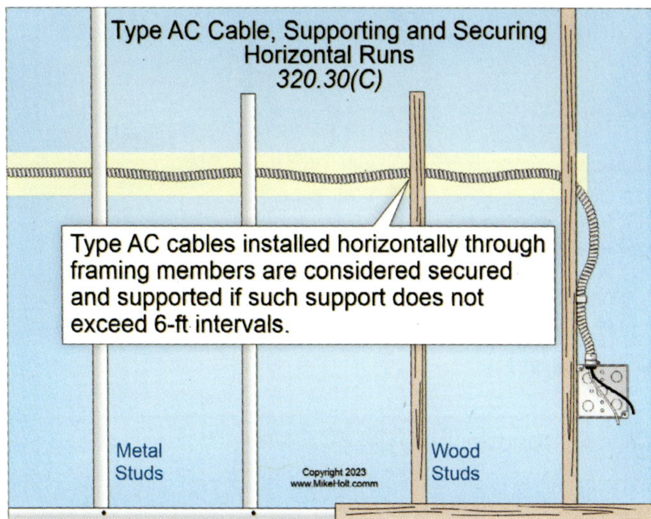

▶Figure 320–7

(D) Unsupported and Unsecured Cables.

(1) Type AC cable can be unsupported and unsecured where fished through concealed spaces.

(2) Type AC cable can be unsupported and unsecured where not more than 2 ft long at terminals and where flexibility is necessary.

(3) Type AC cable can be unsupported and unsecured where not more than 6 ft long from the last point of cable support or Type AC cable fitting to the point of connection to a luminaire within an accessible ceiling. ▶Figure 320–8

320.40 Boxes and Fittings

Unless the design of the termination fitting provides protection, an insulating anti-short bushing (sometimes called a "redhead") must be installed at all Type AC cable terminations. The termination fitting must permit the visual inspection of the anti-short bushing once the cable has been installed. ▶Figure 320–9

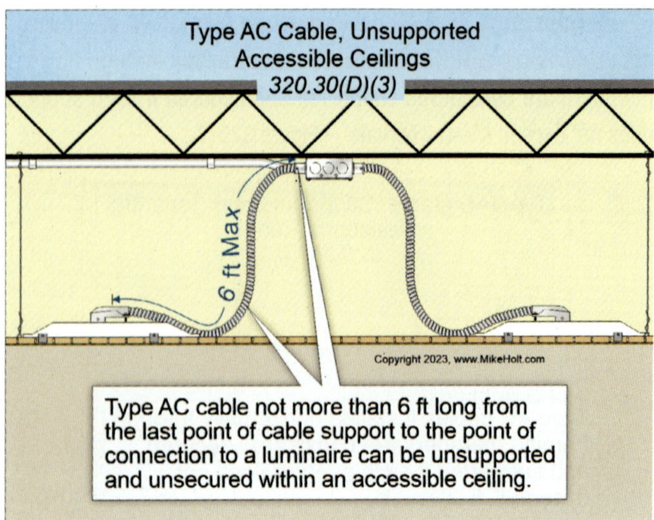

▶Figure 320–8

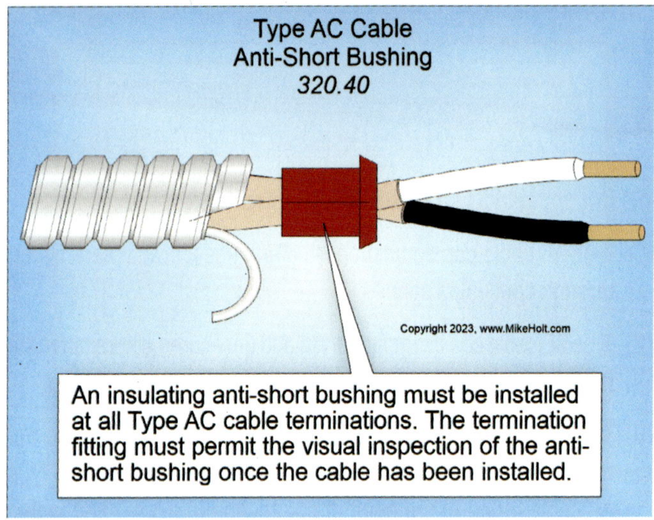

▶Figure 320–9

▸ To protect the conductors from abrasion, Type AC cable must terminate in boxes or fittings specifically listed for Type AC cable [300.15]. ▶Figure 320–10

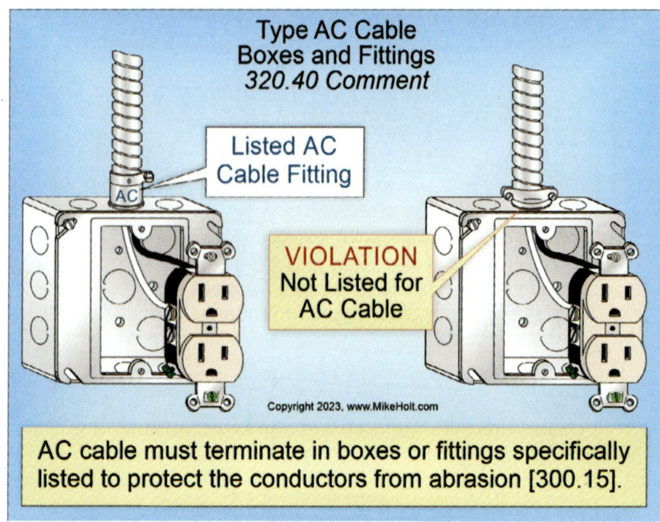

▶Figure 320–10

▸ The internal aluminum bonding strip within the cable serves no electrical purpose once it is outside the cable and can be cut off, but many electricians use it to secure the anti-short bushing to the cable. See 320.108.

METAL-CLAD CABLE (TYPE MC)

Introduction to Article 330—Metal-Clad Cable (Type MC)

This article covers the use, installation, and construction specifications of metal-clad cable (Type MC). Type MC cable is an assembly of any number of insulated conductors, 18 AWG through 2000 kcmil, with an overall polypropylene wrap enclosed in a metal sheath of either corrugated or smooth copper or aluminum tubing, or in spiral interlocked steel or aluminum. Some topics covered in this material include:

- ▶ Uses permitted
- ▶ Uses not permitted
- ▶ Installation in accessible roof spaces
- ▶ Securing and supporting

According to Article 100, "Type MC" is a factory assembly of one or more insulated circuit conductors, with or without optical fiber members, enclosed in an armor of interlocking metal tape, or a smooth or corrugated metallic sheath. ▶Figure 330–1

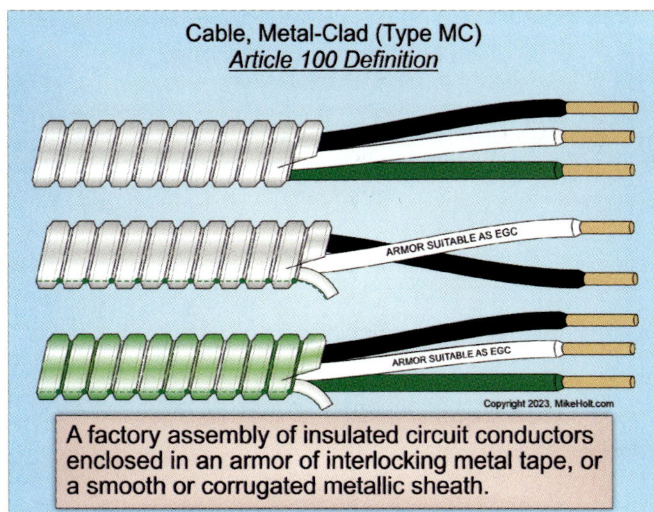

▶Figure 330–1

Part I. General

330.1 Scope

Article 330 covers the use, installation, and construction specifications of metal-clad cable, Type MC. ▶Figure 330–2

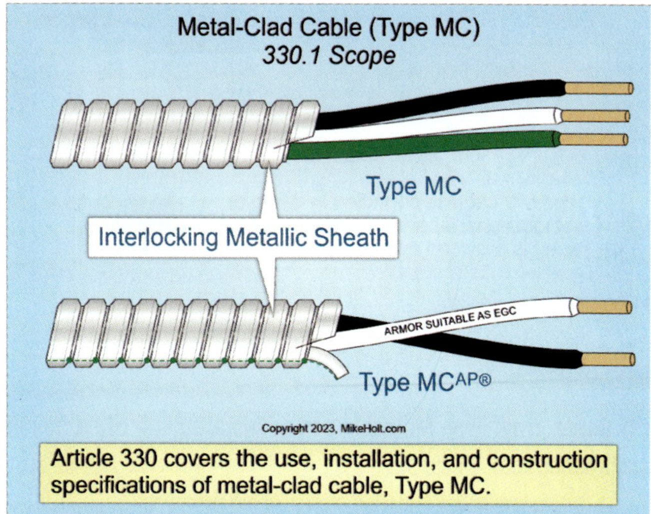

▶Figure 330–2

Part II. Installation

330.10 Uses Permitted

(A) General Uses. Type MC cable can be used:

(1) For branch circuits, feeders, and services.

(2) For power, lighting, and power-limited circuits.

(3) For indoor or outdoor locations.

(4) Exposed or concealed.

(5) To be directly buried (if identified for the purpose).

(6) In a cable tray (if identified for the purpose).

(7) In a raceway.

(8) As aerial cable on a messenger.

(9) In hazardous (classified) locations as permitted in 501.10(B)(5), 502.10(B)(4), and 503.10(A)(1).

(10) Embedded in plaster in dry locations.

(11) In damp or wet locations, where a corrosion-resistant jacket is provided over the metallic sheath. ▶Figure 330–3

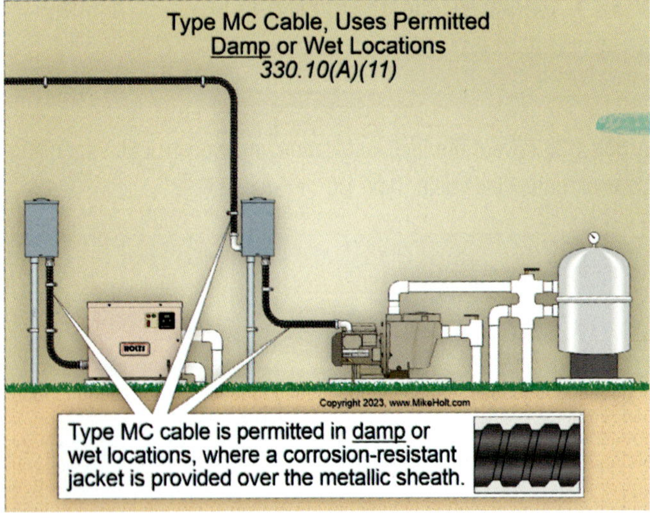

▶Figure 330–3

(B) Specific Uses.

(1) Cable Tray. Type MC cable can be installed in a cable tray in accordance with Article 392.

(2) Direct Buried. Direct-buried cables must be protected in accordance with 300.5.

(3) Installed as Service-Entrance Cable. Type MC cable is permitted to be used as service-entrance cable when installed in accordance with 230.43.

(4) Installed Outside Buildings. Type MC cable installed outside buildings must comply with 225.10, 396.10, and 396.12.

330.12 Uses Not Permitted

Type MC cable is not permitted to be used where:

(1) Subject to physical damage.

(2) Exposed to the destructive corrosive conditions in a. or b., unless the metallic sheath or armor is resistant to the conditions, or is protected by material resistant to the conditions:

    a. Direct burial in the Earth or embedded in concrete unless identified for the application.

    b. Exposed to cinder fills, strong chlorides, caustic alkalis, or vapors of chlorine or hydrochloric acids.

330.15 Exposed Work

Exposed runs of Type MC cable, except as provided in 300.11(B), must closely follow the surface of the building finish or running boards. Type MC cable installed on the bottom of floor or ceiling joists must be secured at every joist and not be subject to physical damage. ▶Figure 330–4

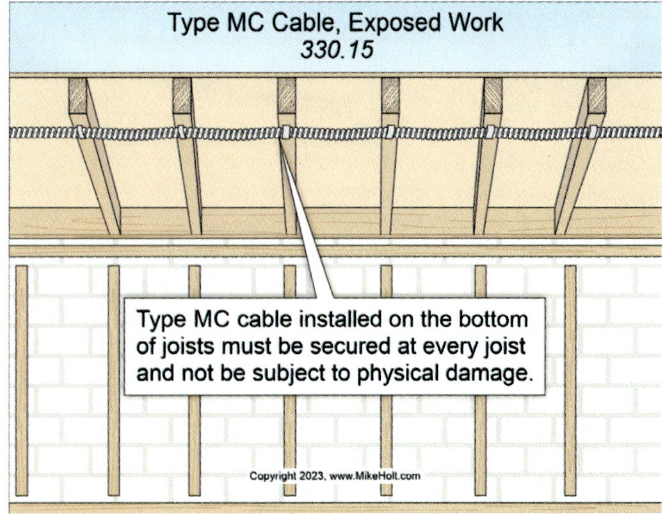

▶Figure 330–4

330.23 In Roof Spaces

Type MC cable in roof spaces within 6 ft of the nearest edge of the scuttle hole run across the top of framing members must be protected by guard strips that are at least as high as the cable in accordance with 320.23. ▶Figure 330–5

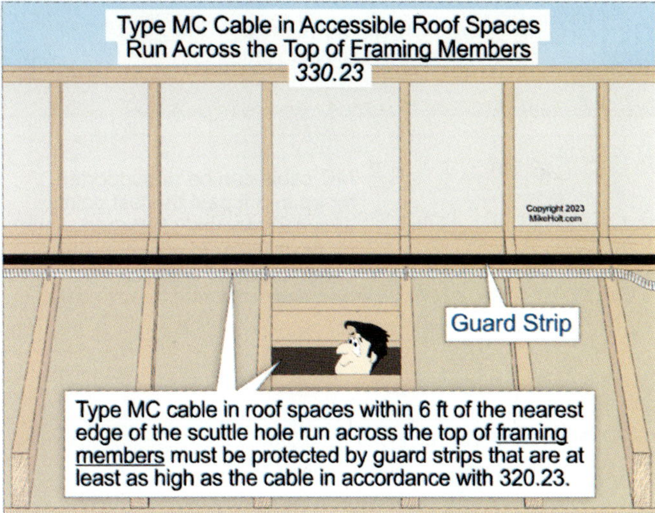

▶Figure 330–5

330.30 Securing and Supporting

(A) General. Type MC cable must be supported and secured by staples, cable ties listed and identified for securing and supporting, straps, hangers, similar fittings, or other approved means designed and installed so the cable is not damaged. ▶Figure 330–6

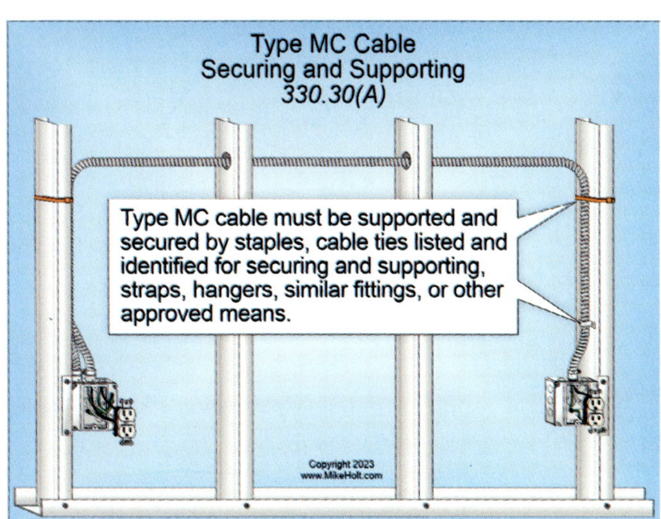

▶Figure 330–6

Type MC cable fittings are permitted as a means of cable support.

(B) Securing. Type MC cable with four or fewer conductors sized no larger than 10 AWG must be secured within 12 in. of every outlet box, junction box, cabinet, or fitting and at intervals not exceeding 6 ft. ▶Figure 330–7

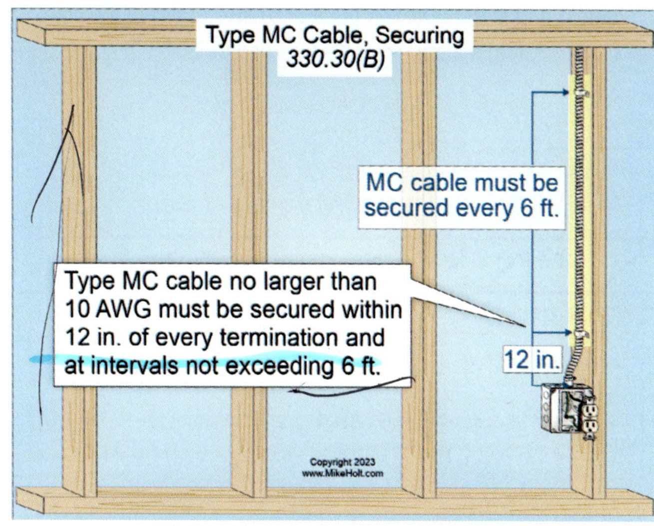

▶Figure 330–7

(C) Supporting. Type MC cable must be supported at intervals not exceeding 6 ft. Cables installed horizontally through framing members are considered secured and supported if such support does not exceed 6-ft intervals. ▶Figure 330–8

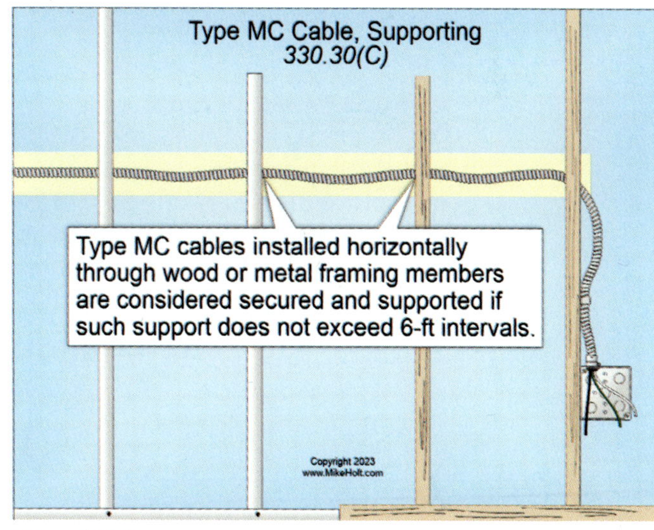

▶Figure 330–8

(D) Unsupported and Unsecured Cables.

(1) Type MC cable can be unsupported and unsecured where fished through concealed spaces in a finished building and support is impractical.

(2) Type MC cable can be unsupported and unsecured where not more than 6 ft long from the last point of cable support to the point of connection to a luminaire within an accessible ceiling. ▶Figure 330–9

(3) Type MC cable can be unsupported and unsecured where not more than 3 ft from the last point where it is securely fastened to provide flexibility for equipment that requires movement after installation, or to connect equipment where flexibility is necessary to minimize the transmission of vibration from the equipment. ▶Figure 330–10

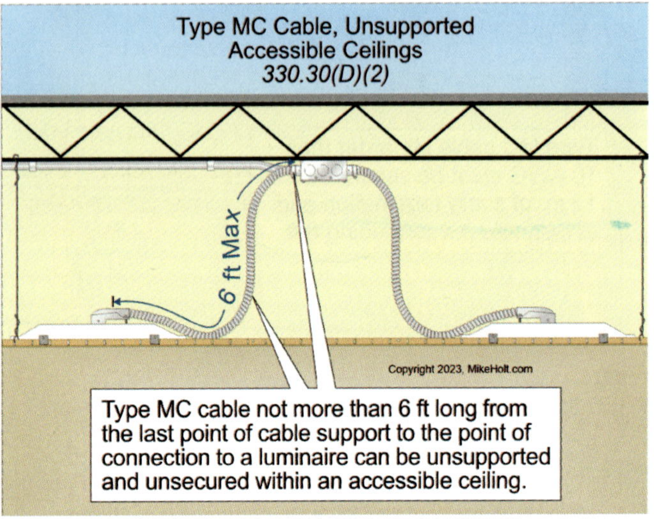

▶Figure 330–9

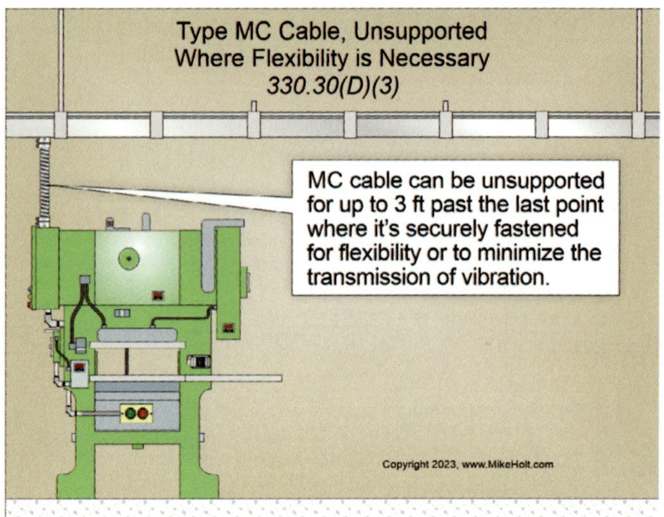

▶Figure 330–10

NONMETALLIC-SHEATHED CABLE (TYPE NM)

Introduction to Article 334—Nonmetallic-Sheathed Cable (Type NM)

Article 334 covers the use, installation, and construction specifications of nonmetallic-sheathed cable (Type NM). Type NM cable is an assembly of insulated conductors and an insulated or bare equipment grounding conductor, 14 AWG through 2 AWG, with an overall nonmetallic flame-retardant sheath. This type of cable provides limited physical protection for the conductors inside the sheath, so its uses are limited by the building construction type. Its low cost and relative ease of installation makes it a common wiring method for residential and light commercial applications. Some topics covered in this material include:

▸ Uses permitted

▸ Uses not permitted

▸ Exposed work

▸ Installation in accessible roof spaces

▸ Securing and supporting

According to Article 100, "Type NM" is a wiring method that encloses two or more insulated conductors within an outer nonmetallic jacket. ▸Figure 334–1

Author's Comment:

▸ It is the generally accepted practice in the electrical industry to call Type NM cable "Romex®," a registered trademark of the Southwire Company.

Part I. General

334.1 Scope

Article 334 covers the use, installation, and construction specifications of nonmetallic-sheathed cable, Type NM. ▸Figure 334–2

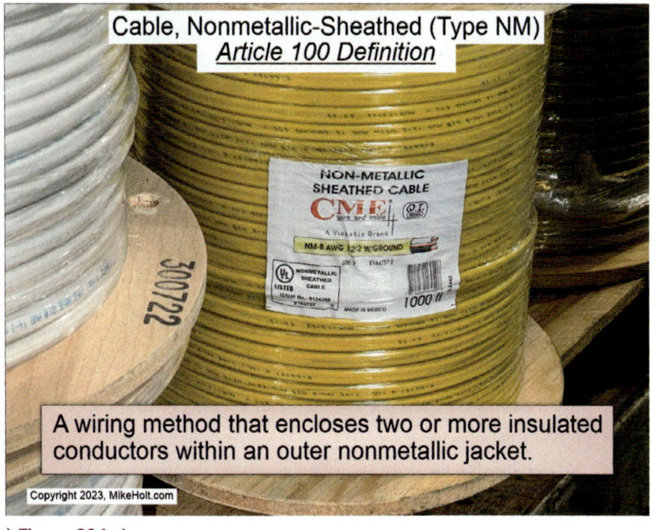

▸Figure 334–1

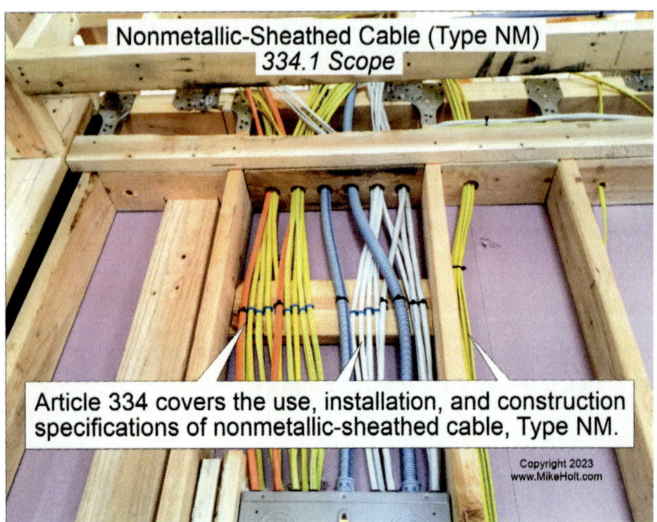

▶Figure 334–2

Part II. Installation

334.10 Type NM Cable, Uses Permitted

Type NM cables is permitted in:

(1) One-family and two-family dwellings and their garages and storage buildings. ▶Figure 334–3

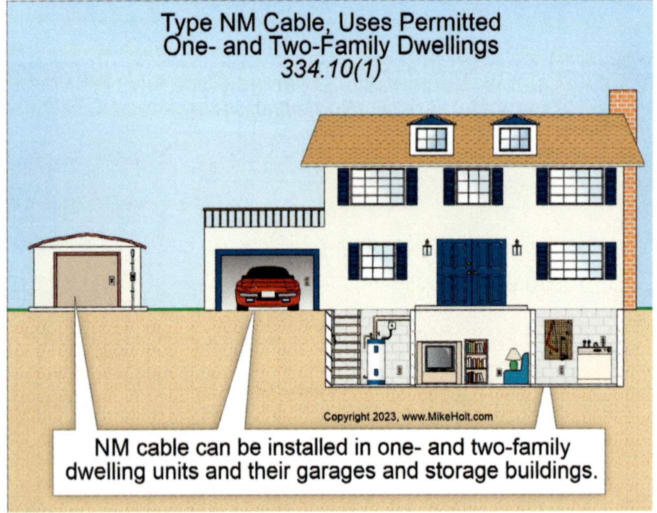

▶Figure 334–3

(2) Multifamily dwellings and their detached garages in buildings of Types III, IV, and V construction. ▶Figure 334–4

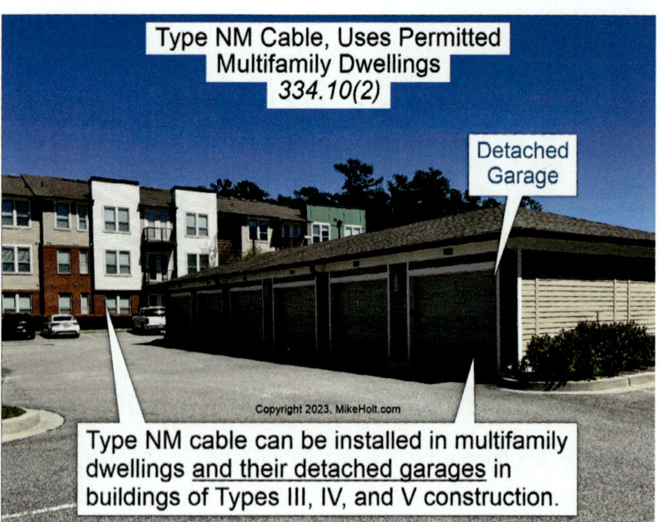

▶Figure 334–4

(3) Other buildings of Types III, IV, and V construction where the cable must be concealed within walls, floors, or ceilings that provide a thermal barrier of material with at least a 15-minute finish rating as identified in listings of fire-rated assemblies. ▶Figure 334–5

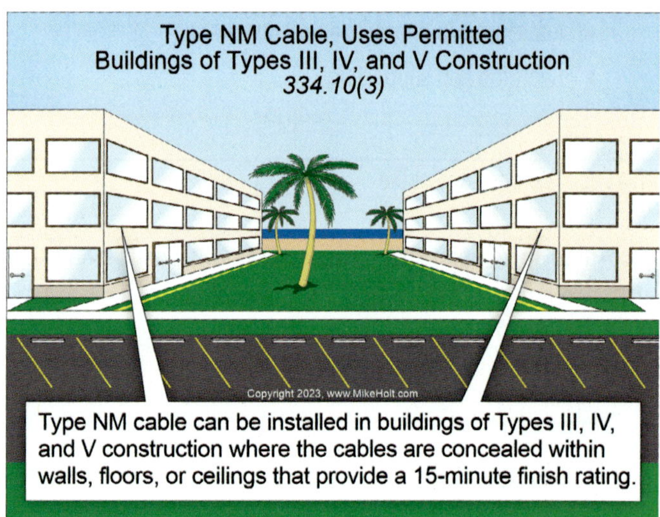

▶Figure 334–5

Note 1: For additional information on building code construction types, see NFPA 220, *Standard on Types of Building Construction*.

Note 2: See Annex E of the *NEC* for the determination of building types and the limits of the number of stories permitted for each type.

334.12 Uses Not Permitted

(A) Locations. Type NM cable is not permitted:

(1) In any dwelling or structure not specifically permitted in 334.10(1), (2), (3), and (5).

(2) Exposed within a dropped or suspended ceiling in other than dwelling units. ▶Figure 334–6

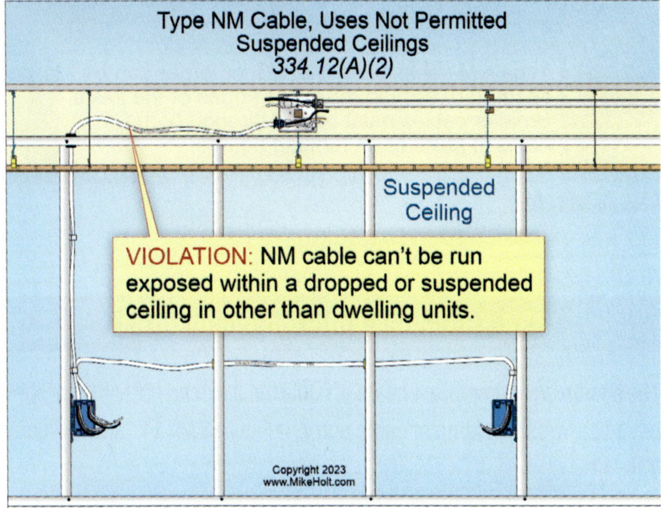

▶Figure 334–6

(3) As service-entrance cable.

(4) In commercial garages having hazardous (classified) locations, as defined in 511.3.

(5) In theaters and similar locations, except where permitted in 518.4(B).

(6) In motion picture studios.

(7) In storage battery rooms.

(8) In hoistways, or on elevators or escalators.

(9) Embedded in poured cement, concrete, or aggregate.

(10) In any hazardous (classified) location, except where permitted by other sections in this *Code*.

(B) Conditions. Type NM cable is not permitted to be used under the following conditions or in the following locations:

(1) If exposed to corrosive fumes or vapors.

(2) If embedded in masonry, concrete, adobe, fill, or plaster.

(3) In a shallow chase in masonry, concrete, or adobe and covered with plaster, adobe, or similar finish.

(4) In wet or damp locations. ▶Figure 334–7

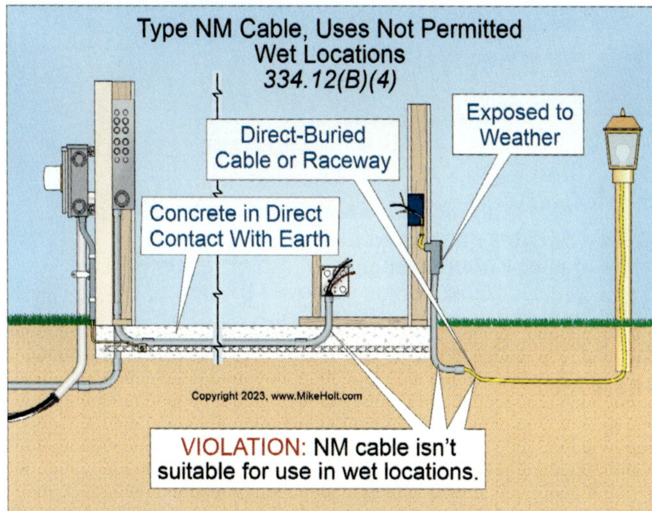

▶Figure 334–7

Author's Comment:

▸ Raceways above the vapor barrier in ground floor slabs are not located in a wet location because the concrete is not in direct contact with the Earth [Article 100].

334.15 Exposed Work

Except as provided in 300.11(B), exposed Type NM cable can be installed as follows:

(A) Surface of the Building. Exposed Type NM cable must closely follow the surface of the building.

(B) Protected from Physical Damage. Nonmetallic-sheathed cable must be protected from physical damage by a raceway (Schedule 80 PVC, RMC, IMC, or EMT), guard strips, or other means approved by the authority having jurisdiction. ▶Figure 334–8

Where Type NM cable is installed in a raceway, a bushing or adapter that provides protection from abrasion at the point of cable entry is required. ▶Figure 334–9

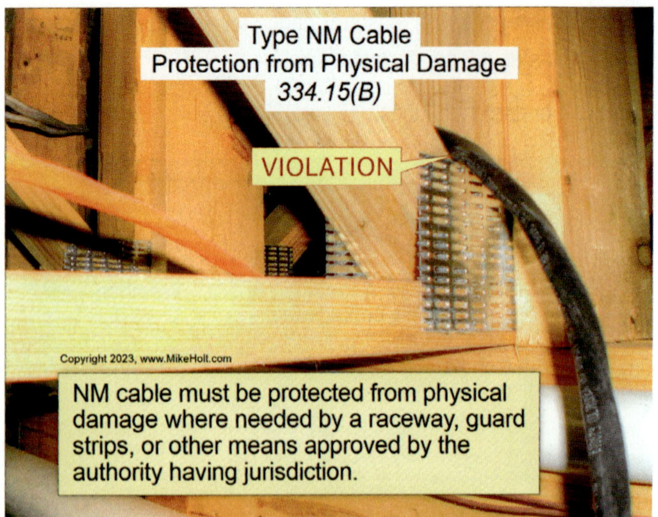

▶Figure 334–8

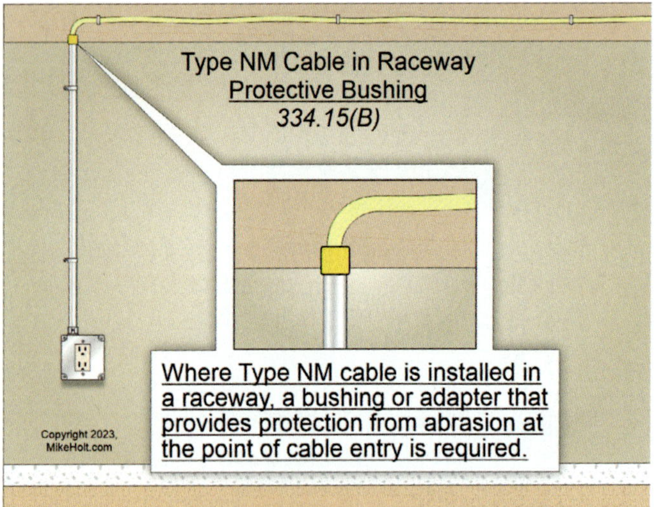

▶Figure 334–9

(C) In Unfinished Basements and Crawl Spaces. If Type NM cable is installed at angles with joists in unfinished basements and crawl spaces, cables containing conductors not smaller than two 6 AWG, or three 8 AWG, can be secured directly to the lower edges of the joists. Smaller cables must be installed through bored holes in joists or on running boards. ▶Figure 334–10

Type NM cable installed on a wall of an unfinished basement or crawl space subject to physical damage must be protected in accordance with 300.4, or be installed within a raceway with a nonmetallic bushing or adapter that provides protection from abrasion at the point where the cable enters the raceway. The cable must be secured within 12 in. of the point where it enters the raceway.

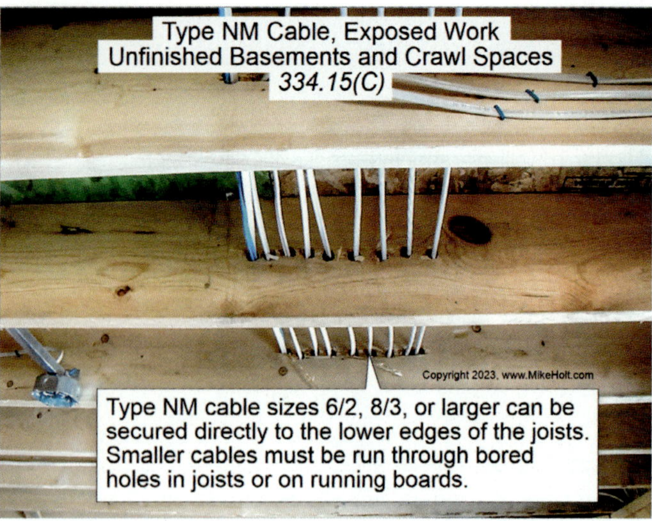

▶Figure 334–10

334.19 Cables Entering Enclosures

The sheath on nonmetallic-sheathed cable must extend no less than ¼ in. beyond any cable clamp or cable entry. ▶Figure 334–11 and ▶Figure 334–12

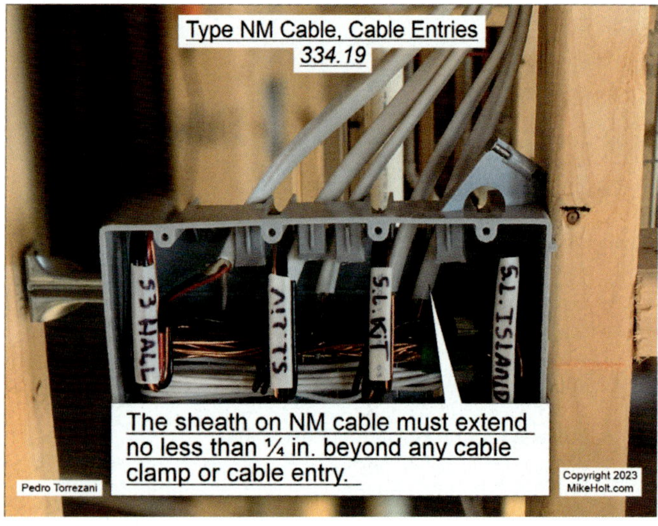

▶Figure 334–11

334.23 Accessible Roof Spaces

Type NM cable in roof spaces within 6 ft of the nearest edge of the scuttle hole run across the top of framing members must be protected by guard strips that are at least as high as the cable in accordance with 320.23. ▶Figure 334–13

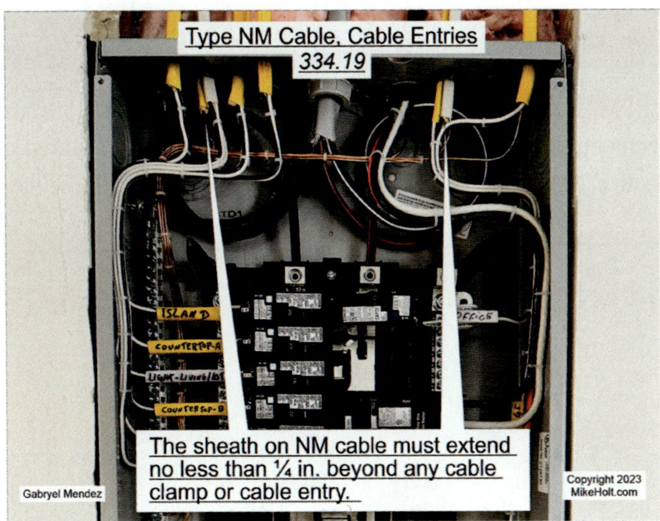

▶Figure 334–12

▶Figure 334–14

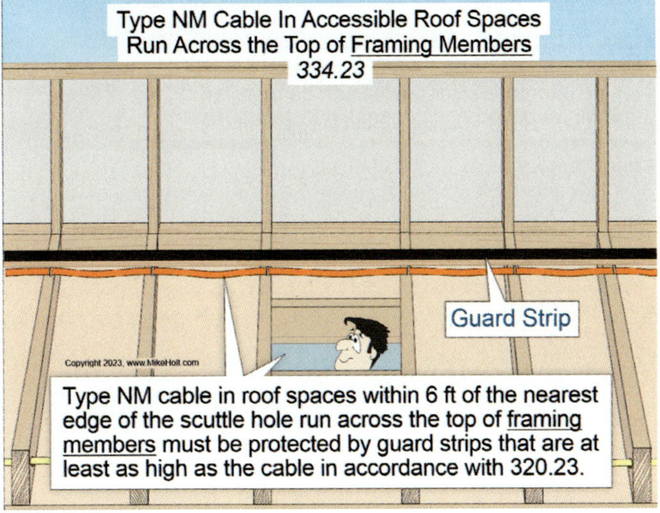

▶Figure 334–13

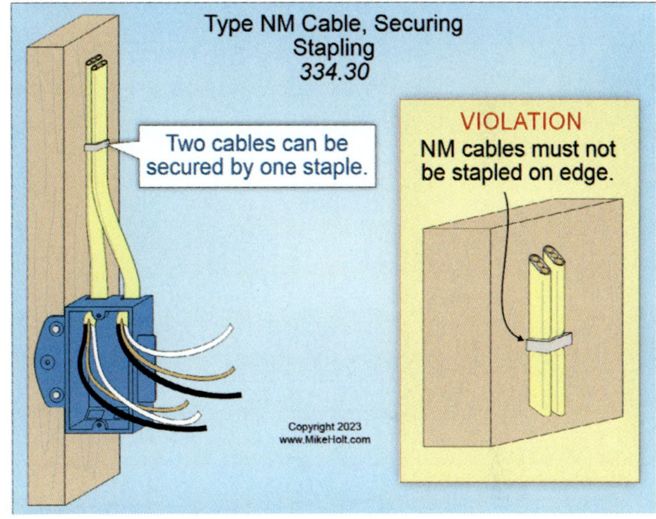

▶Figure 334–15

334.30 Securing and Supporting

Type NM cable must be supported and secured by staples or straps, cable ties (listed and identified for securing and supporting), hangers or similar fittings at intervals not exceeding 4½ ft and within 12 in. of every cable entry termination into boxes, cabinets, or fittings. ▶Figure 334–14

Two-wire (flat) Type NM cable is not permitted to be stapled on edge. ▶Figure 334–15

(A) Horizontal Runs. Type NM cable installed horizontally in bored or punched holes in wood or metal framing members, or notches in wooden members, is considered secured and supported if the distance between supports does not exceed 4½ ft, and the cable is secured within 1 ft of termination. ▶Figure 334–16

(B) Unsupported. Type NM cable can be unsupported in the following situations:

(1) Where the cable is fished between access points through concealed spaces in finished buildings, and support is impractical.

(2) Not more than 4½ ft of unsupported cable is permitted from the last point of support within an accessible ceiling for the connection of luminaires or equipment in a dwelling unit.

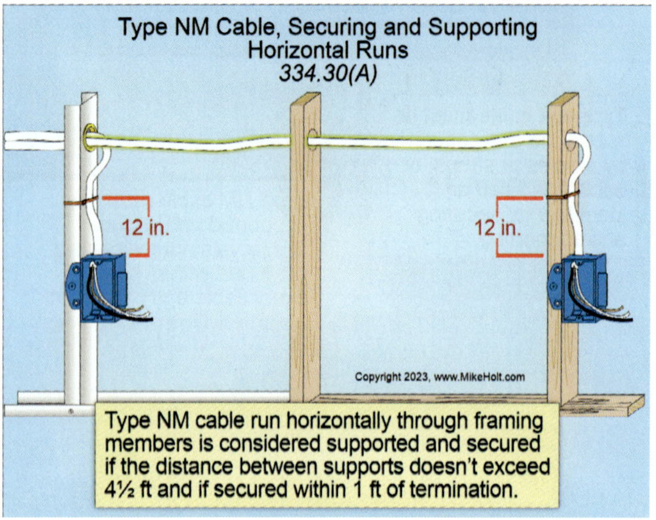

▶Figure 334–16

334.40 Boxes and Fittings

(B) NM Cable Interconnector Devices. A listed for use without a box nonmetallic-sheathed cable interconnector device can be installed in both exposed and concealed installations. ▶Figure 334–17

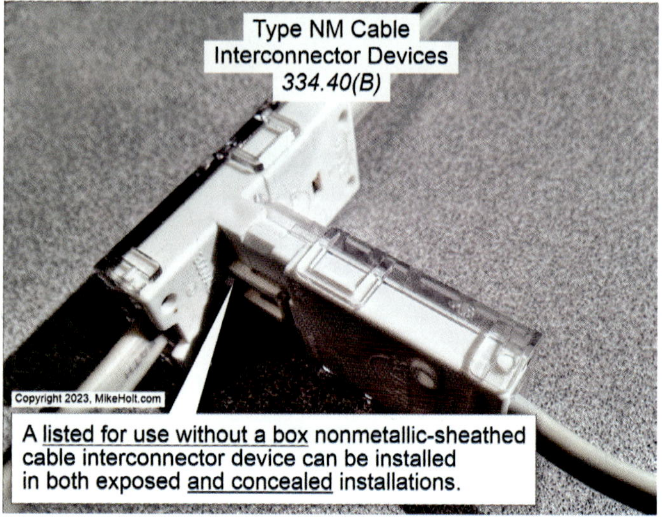

▶Figure 334–17

POWER AND CONTROL TRAY CABLE (TYPE TC)

Introduction to Article 336—Power and Control Tray Cable (Type TC)

This article covers the use and installation of power and control tray cable (Type TC). Type TC cable is flexible, inexpensive, and easily installed making it an attractive wiring method for industrial applications and for generators. Some topics covered in this material include:

▸ Uses permitted

▸ Uses not permitted

According to Article 100, "Power and Control Tray (Type TC)" is a factory assembly of two or more insulated conductors (with or without associated bare or covered equipment grounding conductors) under a nonmetallic jacket. ▸Figure 336–1

Part I. General

336.1 Scope

This article covers the use and installation of power and control tray cable (Type TC). ▸Figure 336–2

Part II. Installation

336.10 Uses Permitted

Type TC cable is permitted to be used:

(1) For power, lighting, and power-limited circuits.

(2) In cable trays including those with mechanically discontinuous segments up to 1 ft.

(3) In raceways.

(4) In outdoor locations supported by a messenger wire.

(5) For Class 1 power-limited circuits in accordance with Article 724.

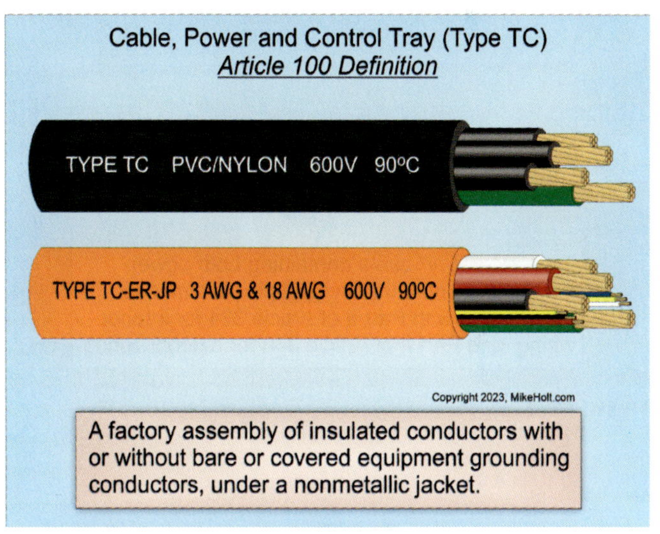

▸Figure 336–1

(7) Between a cable tray and equipment if it complies with 336.10(7)(a) through (f).

(8) In wet locations where the cable is resistant to moisture and corrosive agents.

(9) Type TC-ER-JP cable containing both power conductors and control circuits must be installed in accordance with Part II of Article 334 for interior wiring and Part II of Article 340 for exterior wiring. ▸Figure 336–3

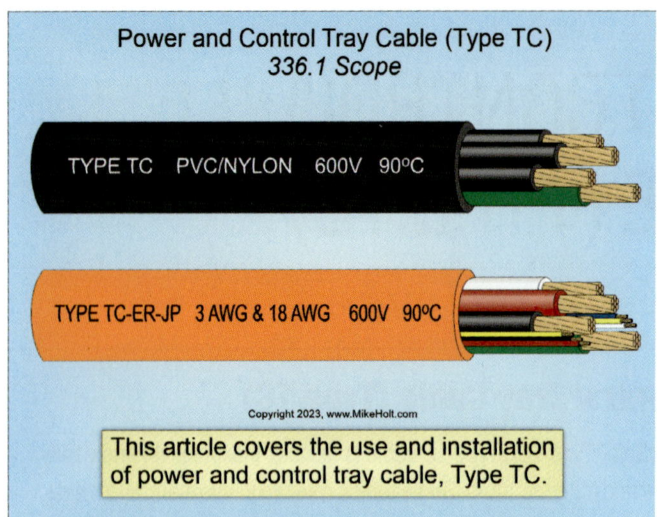

▶Figure 336–2

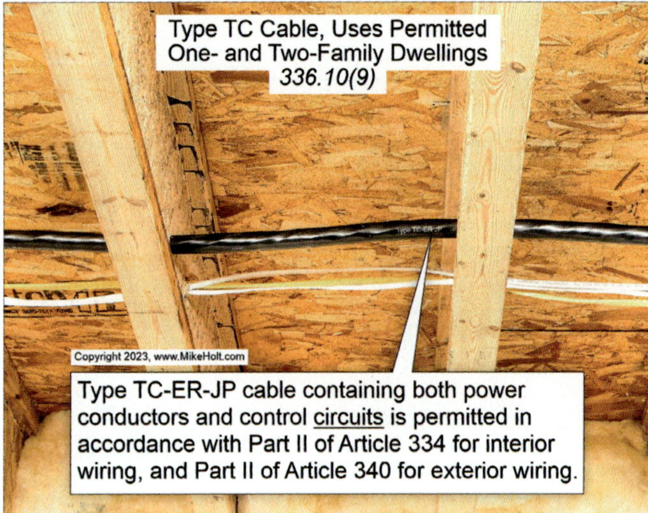

▶Figure 336–3

Author's Comment:

▶ In accordance with *"UL Guide Information QPOR,"* for Type TC-ER-JP cable, the "ER" marking identifies it as suitable for exposed runs and the suffix "-JP" identifies it as being suitable for pulling through wood framing members.

▶ It is important to note that this permitted use only applies if the Type TC cable contains both power and control conductors. It is not a blanket permission to use this cable for dwelling unit branch circuits and feeders.

Ex: Where Type TC cable is used to connect a generator and its associated equipment, the cable ampacity limitations of 334.80 and 340.80 do not apply.

(10) Direct buried where identified for direct burial.

(11) In hazardous (classified) locations as permitted in this *Code*.

(12) For service-entrance conductors where identified for such use and marked "Type TC-ER."

336.12 Uses Not Permitted

Type TC cables are not permitted:

(1) Where exposed to physical damage.

(2) Outside a raceway or cable tray system, except as permitted in 336.10(4), (7), (9), and (10).

(3) Exposed to the direct rays of the sun, unless identified as sunlight resistant.

SERVICE-ENTRANCE CABLE (TYPES SE AND USE)

Introduction to Article 338—Service-Entrance Cable (Types SE and USE)

Article 338 covers the use, installation, and construction specifications of service-entrance cable (Types SE and USE). These cables can be a single conductor or a multiconductor assembly in sizes 14 AWG and larger for copper, and 12 AWG and larger for aluminum or copper-clad aluminum, within an overall nonmetallic outer jacket or covering. Some topics covered in this material include:

- ▶ Uses permitted
- ▶ Uses not permitted

According to Article 100, "Service-Entrance Cable (Types SE and USE)" cable is a single or multiconductor cable with an overall covering. ▶Figure 338–1

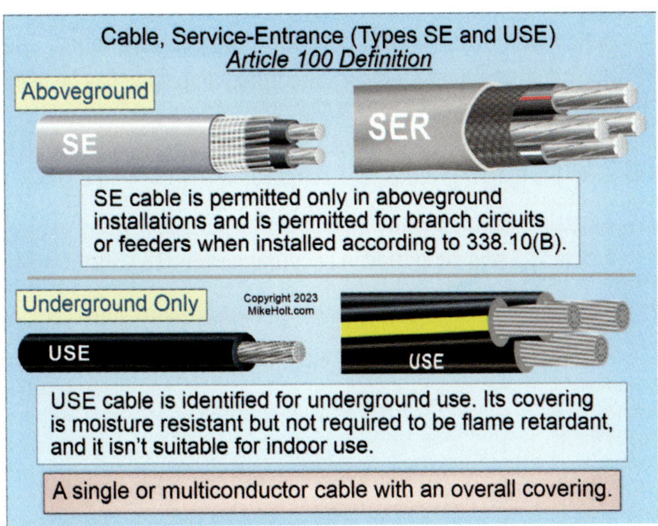

▶Figure 338–1

Part I. General

338.1 Scope

Article 338 covers the use, installation, and construction specifications of service-entrance cable (Types SE and USE). ▶Figure 338–2

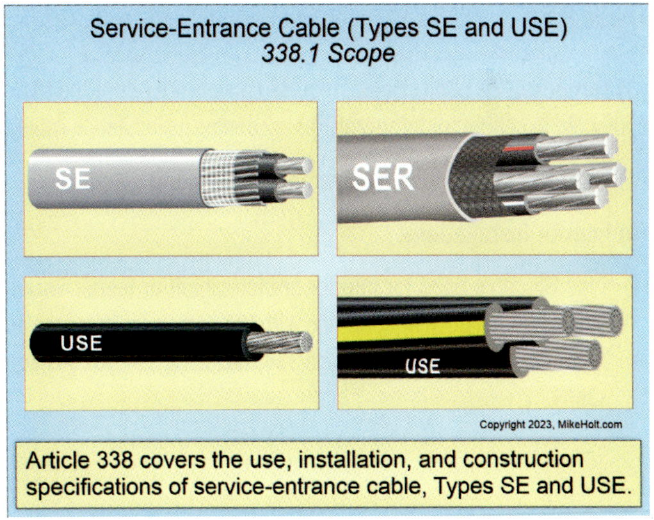

▶Figure 338–2

Part II. Installation

338.10 Uses Permitted

(A) Service-Entrance Conductors. Types SE and USE cables can be used as service-entrance conductors in accordance with Article 230.

(B) Branch Circuits or Feeders.

(2) Uninsulated Conductors. Type SE cable is permitted for branch circuits and feeders where the neutral conductor is insulated, and the uninsulated conductor is only used for equipment grounding. ▶Figure 338–3

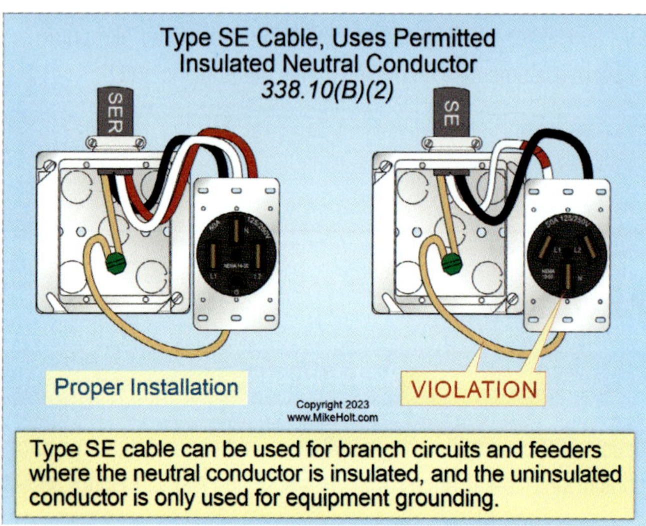

▶Figure 338–3

(3) Temperature Limitations. Type SE cable is not permitted to be subjected to conductor temperatures exceeding its insulation rating.

(4) Installation Methods for Branch Circuits and Feeders.

(a) Interior Installations.

(1) Type SE cable used for interior branch circuit or feeder wiring must be installed in accordance with the same requirements as Type NM cable in Part II of Article 334, excluding 334.80. ▶Figure 338–4

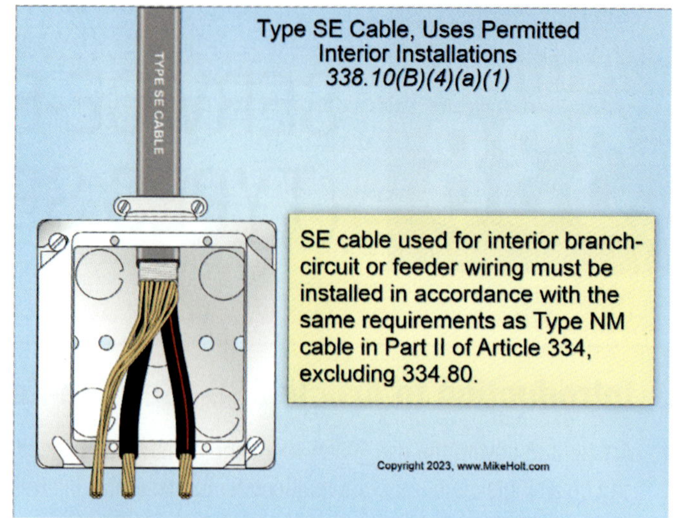

▶Figure 338–4

(2) Where more than two Type SE cables containing two or more current-carrying conductors in each cable are bundled in contact with thermal insulation, caulking, or sealing foam, the ampacity of each conductor must be adjusted in accordance with Table 310.15(C)(1).

(3) The ampacity of Type SE cable conductors 10 AWG and smaller, where installed in contact with thermal insulation or for conductor ampacity correction and/or adjustment, must be sized in accordance with 60°C (140°F) conductor temperature rating. The maximum conductor temperature rating ampacity may be used for adjustment and/or correction.

(b) Exterior Installations.

(1) Type USE cable must be installed in accordance with Part I of Article 225 and supported in accordance with 334.30.

(2) Where Type USE cable is run underground, the cable must comply with Part II of Article 340.

Author's Comment:

▶ In accordance with "*UL 44 Standard for Thermoset-Insulated Wires and Cables*," when Type USE-2 is used in multiple ratings, such as RHH and RHW-2, it is taken as a single insulated conductor. The voltage rating on the USE-2 rating is 600V whereas the typical RHH/RHW-2 is rated at 1000V.

338.12 Uses Not Permitted

(A) Service-Entrance Cable. Type SE cable is not permitted under the following conditions or locations:

(1) Where subject to physical damage.

(2) Underground with or without a raceway.

(B) Underground Service-Entrance Cable. Type USE cable is not permitted:

(1) For interior wiring.

(2) Above ground, except where protected against physical damage in accordance with 300.5(D).

330 MC

CLAD

UNDERGROUND FEEDER AND BRANCH-CIRCUIT CABLE (TYPE UF)

Introduction to Article 340—Underground Feeder and Branch-Circuit Cable (Type UF)

This article covers the use, installation, and construction specifications of underground feeder and branch-circuit cable (Type UF). Type UF cable is an assembly of conductors in sizes 14 AWG through 4/0 AWG [340.104] covered in a moisture-, fungus-, and corrosion-resistant sheath suitable for direct burial in the Earth. The sheath of multiconductor Type UF cable is a molded plastic that encases the insulated conductors. It can be difficult to strip off the sheath without damaging the conductor insulation or cutting yourself, so be careful. Some topics covered in this material include:

▸ Uses permitted

▸ Uses not permitted

According to Article 100, "Underground Feeder Cable (Type UF)" is a factory assembly of insulated conductors with an integral or an overall covering of nonmetallic material suitable for direct burial in the Earth. ▸Figure 340–1

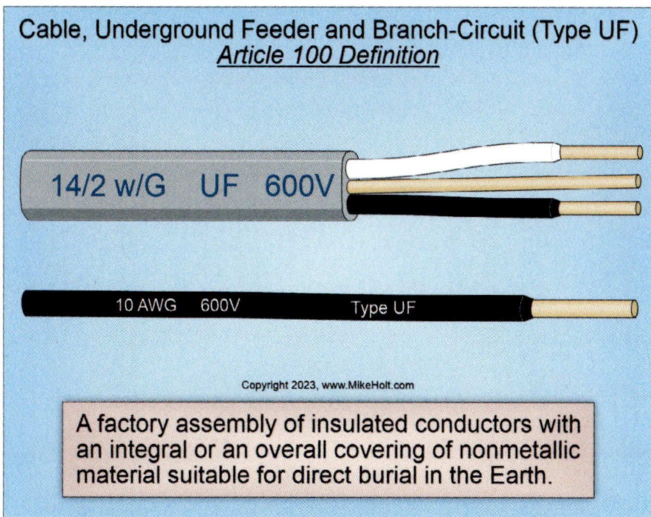

▸Figure 340–1

Part I. General

340.1 Scope

Article 340 covers the use, installation, and construction specifications of underground feeder and branch-circuit cable, Type UF. ▸Figure 340–2

Part II. Installation

340.10 Uses Permitted

Type UF cable is permitted:

(1) Underground in accordance with 300.5.

(2) As a single conductor in a trench or raceway with circuit conductors.

(3) For wiring in wet, dry, or corrosive locations.

(4) Where installed as nonmetallic-sheathed cable, the installation must comply with Parts II and III of Article 334, except for 334.12(B).

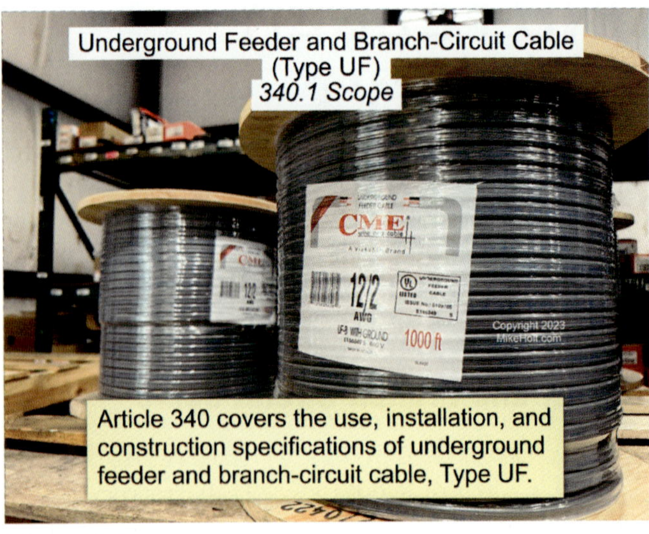

▶Figure 340–2

340.12 Uses Not Permitted

Type UF cable is not permitted to be used:

(1) As service-entrance cable [230.43].

(2) In commercial garages [Article 511].

(3) In theaters [520.5].

(4) In motion picture studios [530.11].

(5) In storage battery rooms [Article 480].

(6) In hoistways [Article 620].

(7) In hazardous (classified) locations, except as specifically permitted by other articles in this *Code*.

(8) Embedded in concrete.

(9) Exposed to direct sunlight unless identified.

Note: The sunlight-resistant marking on the outer jacket does not apply to the individual conductors.

(10) Where subject to physical damage. ▶Figure 340–3

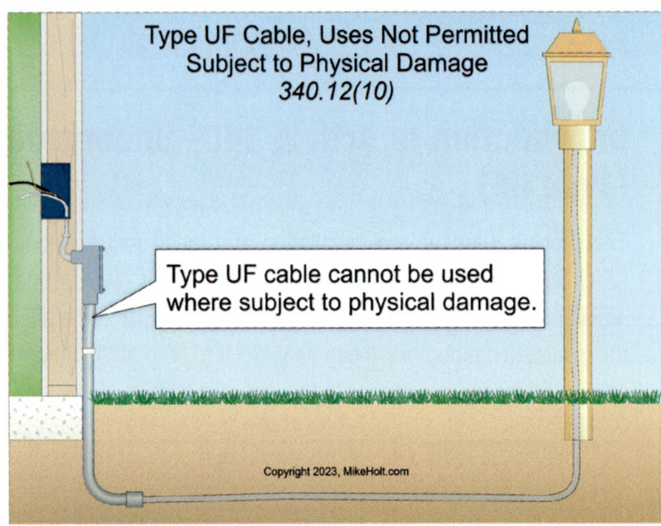

▶Figure 340–3

(11) As overhead cable, except where installed as messenger-supported wiring in accordance with Part II of Article 396.

Author's Comment:

▶ UF cable is not permitted in ducts or plenum spaces [300.22(C)(1)], or in patient care spaces of health care facilities [517.13].

ARTICLE 342
INTERMEDIATE METAL CONDUIT (IMC)

Introduction to Article 342—Intermediate Metal Conduit (IMC)

Article 342 covers the use, installation, and construction specifications of intermediate metal conduit (IMC) and associated fittings. IMC is a circular metal raceway that can be threaded and is available in trade sizes from ½ to 6. It has the same outside diameter as rigid metal conduit (RMC) [Article 344] but is made of a stronger metal which allows a thinner wall, making it lighter and providing a larger interior cross-sectional area for holding conductors. Some topics covered in this material include:

- Uses permitted
- Dissimilar Metals
- Bending, reaming, and threading
- Securing and supporting
- Bushings

According to Article 100, "IMC" is a steel raceway of circular cross section that can be threaded with integral or associated couplings, listed for the installation of electrical conductors. ▶Figure 342–1

▶Figure 342–1

Author's Comment:

- The type of steel from which intermediate metal conduit is manufactured, the process by which it is made, and the corrosion protection applied are all equal (or superior) to that of rigid metal conduit.

Part I. General

342.1 Scope

Article 342 covers the use, installation, and construction specifications of intermediate metal conduit (IMC) and associated fittings. ▶Figure 342–2

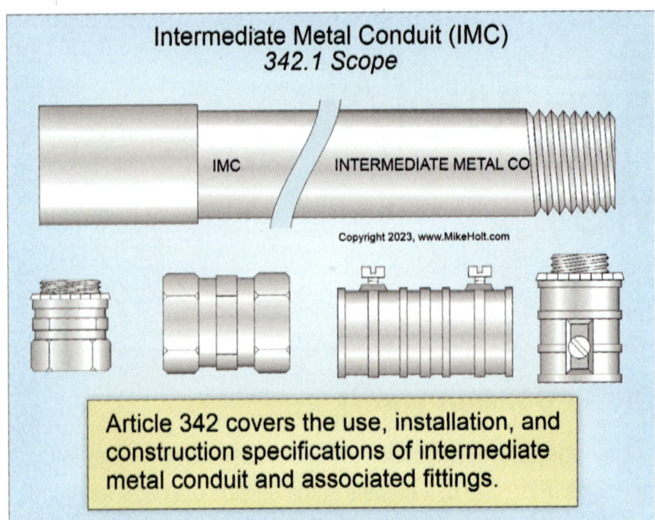

▶Figure 342–2

Part II. Installation

342.10 Uses Permitted

(A) Atmospheric Conditions and Occupancies. IMC is permitted in all atmospheric conditions and occupancies.

(B) Corrosive Environments. IMC, elbows, couplings, and fittings can be installed in concrete, in direct contact with the Earth, in direct burial applications, or in areas subject to severe corrosive influences if provided with supplementary corrosion protection approved for the condition.

Note: See 300.6 for protection against corrosion.

Author's Comment:

▶ In accordance with "*UL Guide Information DYIX*," supplementary corrosion protection is required when IMC and associated fittings are buried in soil having a resistivity less than 2000Ω. In addition, supplementary corrosion protection is required at the point where IMC transitions from concrete encasement to the soil.

(E) Severe Physical Damage. IMC is permitted where subject to severe physical damage.

342.14 Dissimilar Metals

Where practical, contact of IMC with dissimilar metals should be avoided to prevent the deterioration of the metal because of galvanic action. Aluminum and stainless steel fittings and enclosures are permitted to be used with galvanized steel Type IMC where not subject to severe corrosive influences.

342.24 Bends

(A) How Made. Raceway bends are not permitted to be made in any manner that will damage the raceway or significantly change its internal diameter (no kinks).

Author's Comment:

▶ This is not a problem if you use a bender in accordance with the manufacturer's instructions.

(B) Degrees of Bends in One Run. To reduce the stress and friction on conductor insulation, the total degree of bends (including offsets) between pull points is not permitted to exceed 360 degrees. ▶Figure 342–3 and ▶Figure 342–4

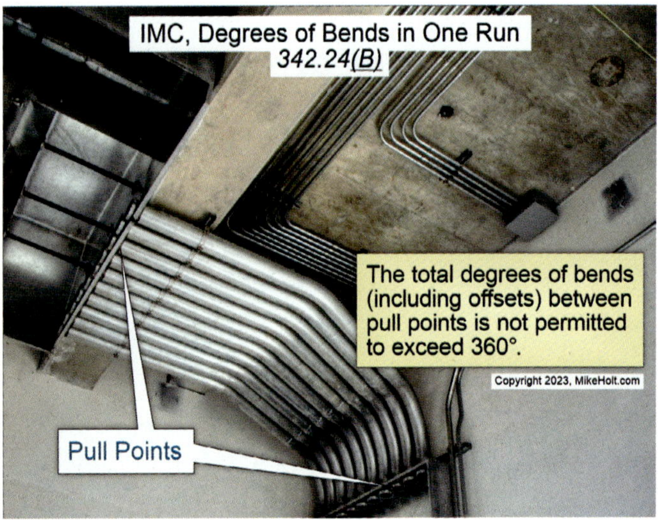

▶Figure 342–3

Author's Comment:

▶ There is no maximum distance between pull boxes because this is a design issue rather than a safety issue.

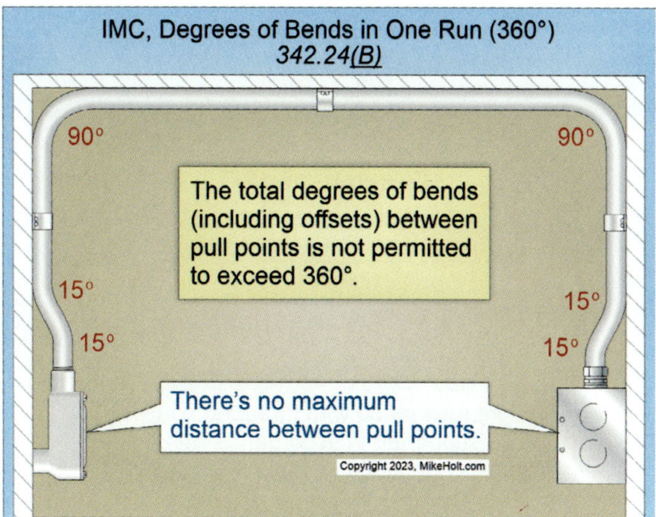

▶Figure 342–4

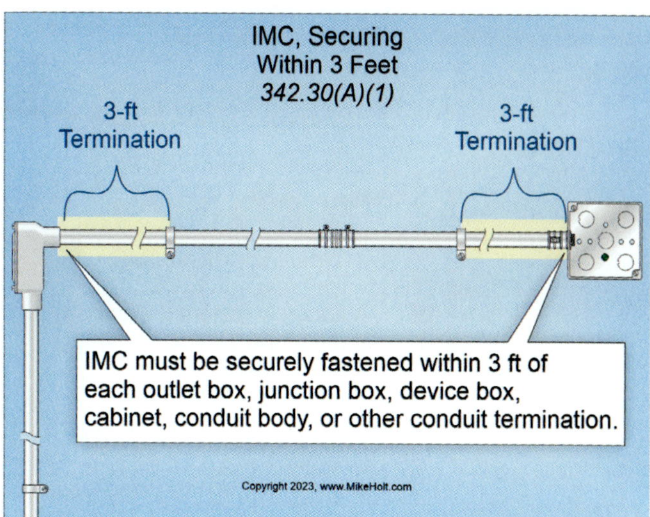

▶Figure 342–5

342.28 Reaming

When the raceway is cut in the field, reaming is required to remove the rough edges.

Author's Comment:

▶ It is a commonly accepted practice to ream small raceways with a screwdriver or the backside of pliers. However, when the raceway is cut with a three-wheel-pipe cutter, a reaming tool is required to remove the sharp edge or burr of the indented raceway. When conduits are threaded in the field, the threads must be coated with an electrically conductive, corrosion-resistant compound approved by the authority having jurisdiction in accordance with 300.6(A).

342.30 Securing and Supporting

IMC must be securely fastened in place and supported in accordance with 342.30(A) and (B).

(A) Securely Fastened. IMC must be secured in accordance with any of the following:

(1) Fastened within 3 ft of each outlet box, junction box, device box, cabinet, conduit body, or other conduit termination. ▶Figure 342–5

Author's Comment:

▶ Fastening is required within 3 ft of terminations—not within 3 ft of each coupling.

(2) When structural members do not permit the raceway to be secured within 3 ft of a box or termination fitting, the raceway must be secured within 5 ft of the termination. ▶Figure 342–6

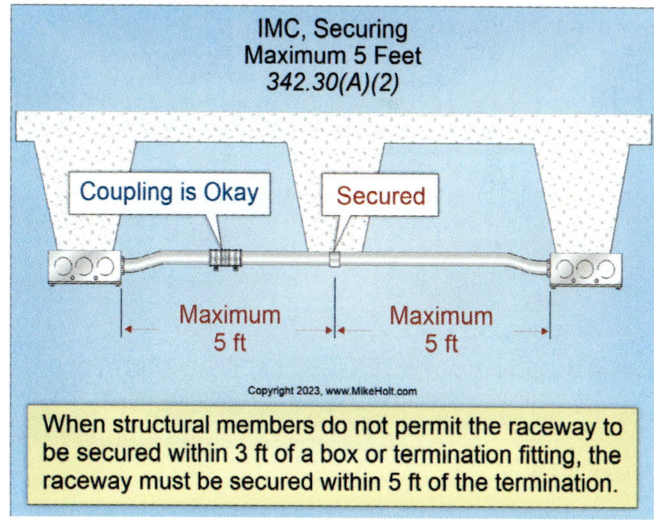

▶Figure 342–6

(3) Where approved, IMC is not required to be securely fastened within 3 ft of the service head for an above-the-roof termination of a mast. ▶Figure 342–7

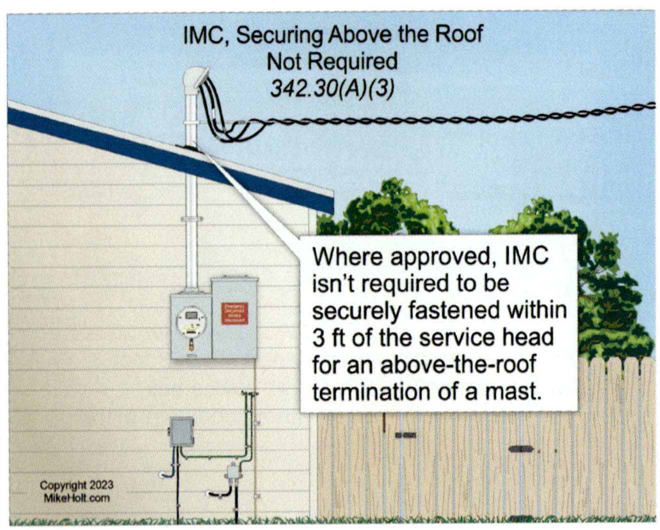

▶Figure 342–7

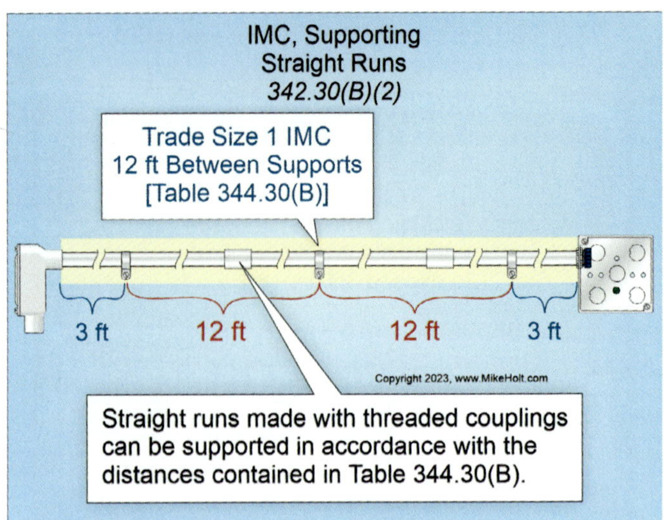

▶Figure 342–9

(B) Supports.

(1) General. IMC must be supported at intervals not exceeding 10 ft.

(2) Straight Runs. Straight horizontal runs made with threaded couplings can be supported in accordance with the distances contained in Table 344.30(B). ▶Figure 342–8 and ▶Figure 342–9

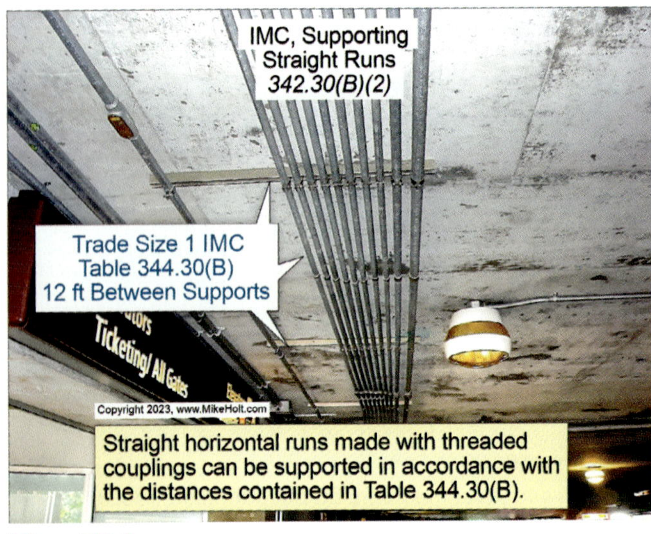

▶Figure 342–8

Table 344.30(B) Supports for Rigid Metal Conduit	
Trade Size	**Support Spacing**
½–¾	10 ft
1	12 ft
1¼–1½	14 ft
2–2½	16 ft
3 and larger	20 ft

(3) Vertical Risers. Exposed vertical risers of IMC for fixed equipment can be supported at intervals not exceeding 20 ft if the conduit is made up with threaded couplings, firmly supported, securely fastened at the top and bottom of the riser, and if no other means of support is available. ▶Figure 342–10

(4) Horizontal Runs. IMC installed horizontally through framing members is considered supported and secured if such support does not exceed 10-ft intervals, and the conduit is secured within 3 ft of termination.

> **Author's Comment:**
>
> ▸ IMC must be provided with expansion fittings where necessary to compensate for thermal expansion and contraction [300.7(B)]. The expansion characteristics for metal raceways are determined by multiplying the values from Table 352.44 by 0.20. Those for aluminum raceways are determined by multiplying the values from Table 352.44 by 0.40 [300.7(B) Note].

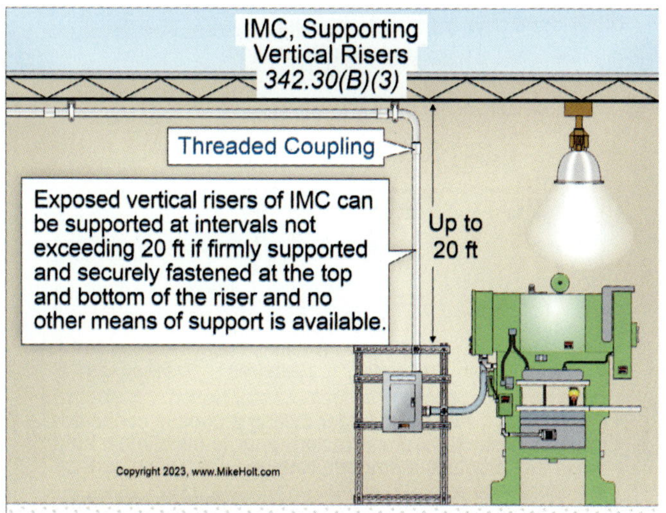

▶Figure 342–10

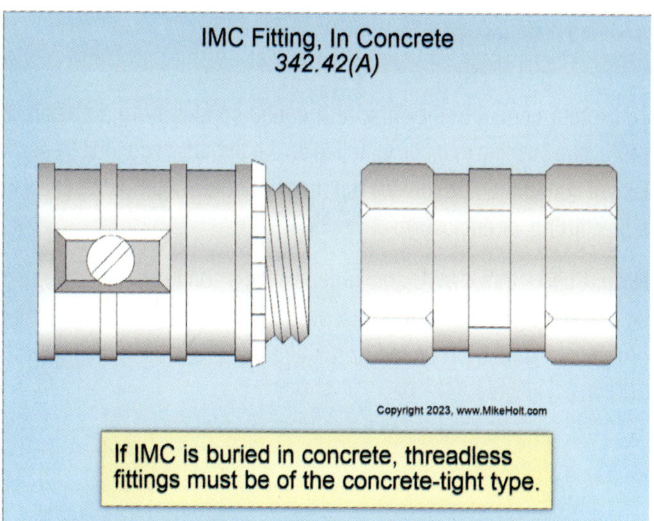

▶Figure 342–11

342.42 Couplings and Connectors

(A) Installation.

Effective Ground-Fault Path. Threadless couplings and connectors must be made up tight to maintain an effective ground-fault current path to safely conduct fault current in accordance with 250.4(A)(5), 250.96(A), and 300.10.

Author's Comment:

▶ Loose locknuts have been found to nearly disintegrate before a fault was cleared because loose termination fittings increase the impedance of the ground-fault current path.

Concrete Buried. If buried in concrete, threadless fittings must be of the concrete-tight type. ▶Figure 342–11

Wet Locations. Fittings installed in wet locations must be listed for use in wet locations to prevent moisture or water from entering or accumulating within the enclosure as required by 314.15. ▶Figure 342–12

(B) Running Threads. Running threads are not permitted for the connection of couplings, but they are permitted at other locations. ▶Figure 342–13

▶Figure 342–12

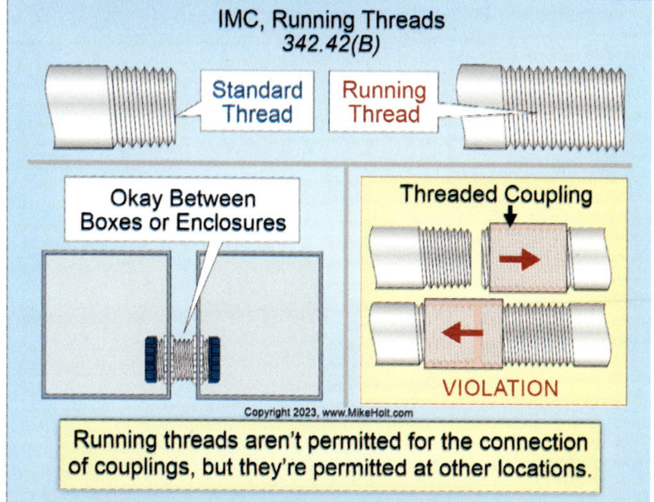

▶Figure 342–13

342.46 Bushings

To protect conductors exiting a threaded conduit from abrasion, a protective bushing must be installed on the threads of conduit (regardless of conductor size) unless the raceway enters a threaded entry in a box, fitting, or enclosure.

Note: Conductors 4 AWG and larger exiting a conduit connector must be protected from abrasion prior to the installation by a fitting that provides a smooth, rounded, insulating surface in accordance with 300.4(G). ▶Figure 342–14

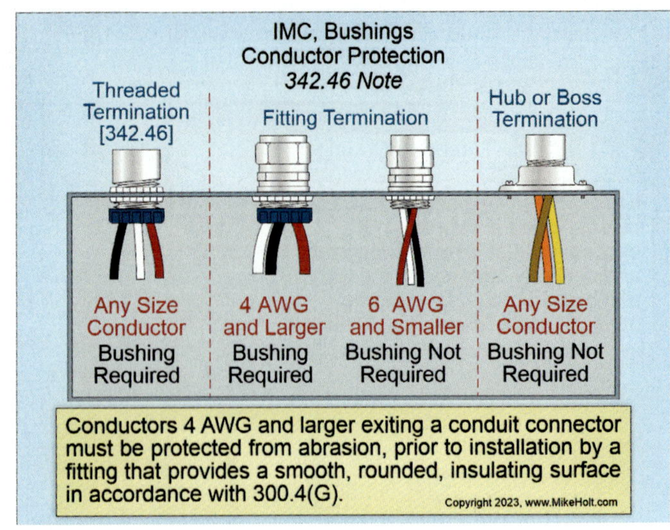

▶Figure 342–14

RIGID METAL CONDUIT (RMC)

Introduction to Article 344—Rigid Metal Conduit (RMC)

This article covers the use, installation, and construction specifications of rigid metal conduit (RMC) and associated fittings. RMC, commonly called "rigid," has long been the standard raceway used to protect conductors from physical damage and from difficult environments. This type of conduit is available in trade sizes up to 6, can be threaded, and has the same outside diameter as intermediate metal conduit but has a thicker wall. It can be made of a variety of metals including steel, aluminum, red brass, and stainless steel. Some topics covered in this material include:

▸ Uses permitted

▸ Dissimilar metals

▸ Bending, reaming, and threading

▸ Securing and supporting

▸ Bushings

According to Article 100, "Rigid Metal Conduit (RMC)" is a listed metal raceway of circular cross section with integral or associated couplings listed for the installation of electrical conductors. ▸Figure 344–1

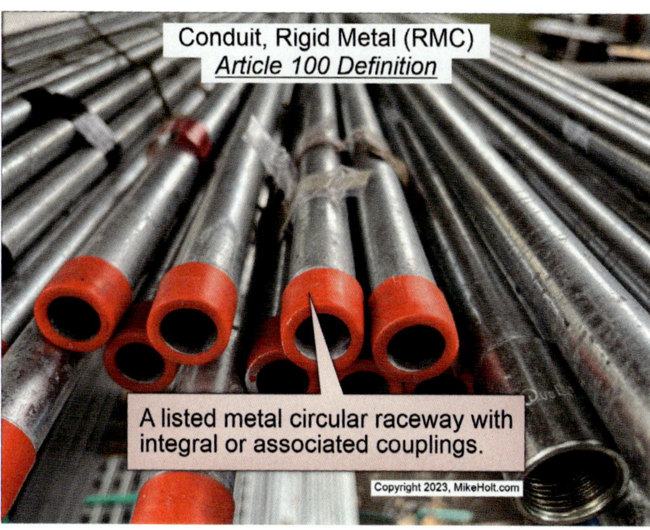

▸Figure 344–1

Part I. General

344.1 Scope

Article 344 covers the use, installation, and construction specifications of rigid metal conduit (RMC) and associated fittings. ▸Figure 344–2

Part II. Installation

344.10 Uses Permitted

(A) Atmospheric Conditions and Occupancies.

(1) RMC is permitted in all atmospheric conditions and occupancies.

(B) Corrosive Environments.

(1) RMC fittings, elbows, and couplings can be installed in concrete, in direct contact with the Earth, in direct burial applications, or in areas subject to severe corrosive influences if approved for the condition.

▶Figure 344–2

(D) Wet Locations. Support fittings (such as screws, straps, and so forth) installed in a wet location must be made of corrosion-resistant material or protected by corrosion-resistant coatings.

Note: See 300.6 for protection against corrosion.

Author's Comment:

▸ In accordance with "*UL Guide Information DYIX,*" supplementary corrosion protection is required when RMC and associated fittings are buried in soil having a resistivity less than 2000Ω. In addition, supplementary corrosion protection is required at the point where RMC transitions from concrete encasement to the soil.

(E) Severe Physical Damage. RMC is permitted where subject to severe physical damage.

344.14 Dissimilar Metals

If practical, contact of RMC with dissimilar metals should be avoided to prevent the deterioration of the metal because of galvanic action. Aluminum and stainless steel fittings and enclosures are permitted to be used with galvanized steel rigid metal conduit where not subject to severe corrosive influences.

344.22 Number of Conductors

The number of conductors in RMC is not permitted to exceed the percentage fill specified in Chapter 9, Table 1. Raceways must be large enough to permit the installation and removal of conductors without damaging the conductors' insulation.

Cables are permitted to be installed in RMC where such use is not prohibited by the respective cable articles. The number of cables must not exceed the percentage fill specified in Chapter 9, Table 1.

Author's Comment:

▸ See 300.17 for examples of how to size raceways when conductors are not all the same size.

344.24 Bends

(A) How Made. Raceway bends are not permitted to be made in any manner that will damage the raceway or significantly change its internal diameter (no kinks). The radius of the curve of any field bend to the centerline of the conduit is not permitted to be less than indicated in Chapter 9, Table 2.

Author's Comment:

▸ This is not a problem if you use a bender in accordance with the manufacturer's instructions.

(B) Degrees of Bends in One Run. To reduce stress and friction on conductor insulation, the total degrees of bends (including offsets) between pull points is not permitted to exceed 360 degrees. ▶Figure 344–3

Author's Comment:

▸ There is no maximum distance between pull boxes because this is a design issue, not a safety issue.

344.28 Reaming and Threading

When the raceway is cut in the field, reaming is required to remove the rough edges.

▶Figure 344–3

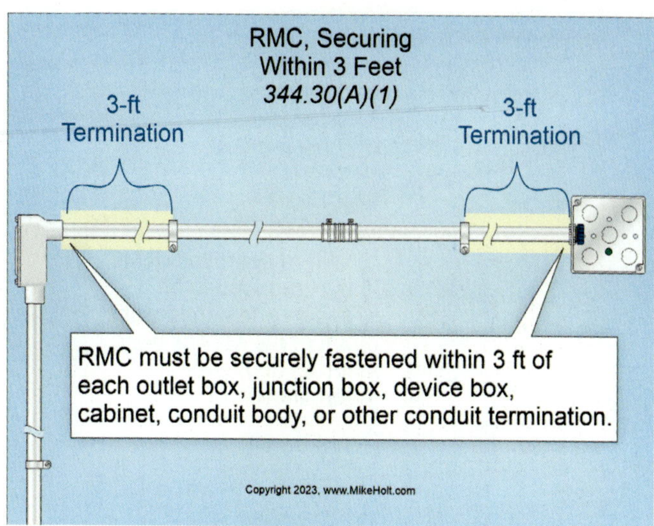

▶Figure 344–4

Author's Comment:

▸ It is a commonly accepted practice to ream small raceways with a screwdriver or the backside of pliers. However, when the raceway is cut with a three-wheel pipe cutter, a reaming tool is required to remove the sharp edge of the indented raceway. When conduit is threaded in the field, the threads must be coated with an electrically conductive, corrosion-resistant compound approved by the authority having jurisdiction in accordance with 300.6(A).

PVC-coated RMC must be threaded in accordance with manufacturer's instructions to prevent damage to the exterior coating.

344.30 Securing and Supporting

RMC must be securely fastened in place and supported in accordance with 344.30(A) and (B).

(A) Securely Fastened. RMC must be secured in accordance with any of the following:

(1) Fastened within 3 ft of each outlet box, junction box, device box, cabinet, conduit body, or other conduit termination. ▶Figure 344–4

Author's Comment:

▸ Fastening is required within 3 ft of terminations—not within 3 ft of each coupling.

(2) When structural members do not permit the raceway to be secured within 3 ft of a box or termination fitting, the raceway must be secured within 5 ft of the termination. ▶Figure 344–5

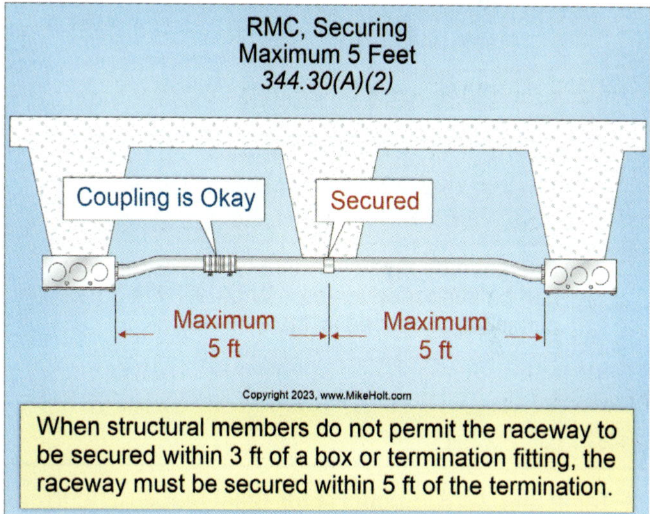

▶Figure 344–5

(3) Where approved, RMC is not required to be securely fastened within 3 ft of the service head for an above-the-roof termination of a mast. ▶Figure 344–6

(B) Supports.

(1) General. RMC must be supported at intervals not exceeding 10 ft.

(2) Straight Runs. Straight runs made with threaded couplings can be supported in accordance with the distances contained in Table 344.30(B). ▶Figure 344–7

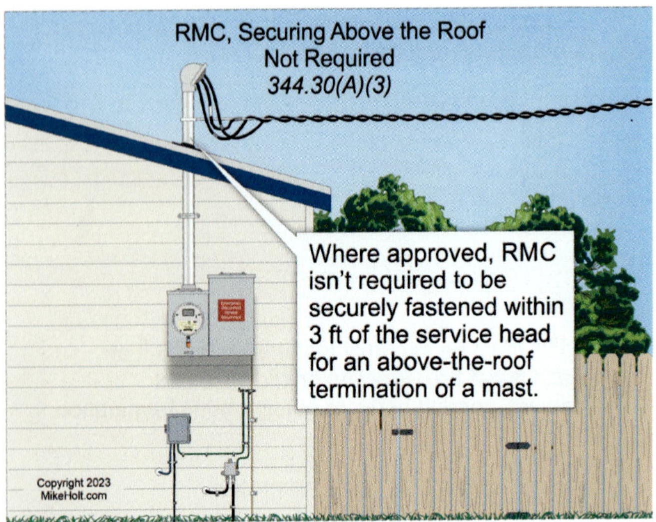

▶Figure 344–6

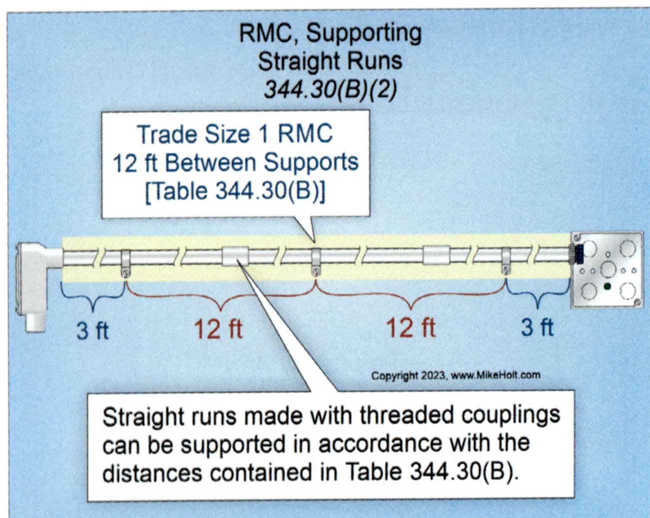

▶Figure 344–7

Table 344.30(B) Supports for Rigid Metal Conduit

Trade Size	Support Spacing
½–¾	10 ft
1	12 ft
1¼–1½	14 ft
2–2½	16 ft
3 and larger	20 ft

(3) Vertical Risers. Exposed vertical risers for fixed equipment can be supported at intervals not exceeding 20 ft if the conduit is made up with threaded couplings, firmly supported, securely fastened at the top and bottom of the riser, and if no other means of support is available. ▶Figure 344–8

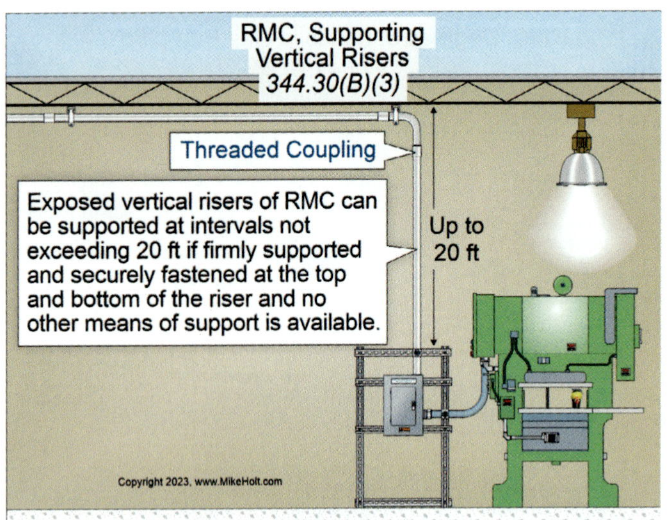

▶Figure 344–8

(4) Horizontal Runs. Conduits installed horizontally through framing members are considered supported and secured if such support does not exceed 10-ft intervals, and the conduit is secured within 3 ft of termination.

> **Author's Comment:**
>
> ▸ RMC must be provided with expansion fittings where necessary to compensate for thermal expansion and contraction [300.7(B)]. The expansion characteristics for metal raceways are determined by multiplying the values from Table 352.44 by 0.20. Those for aluminum raceways are determined by multiplying the values from Table 352.44 by 0.40 [300.7(B) Note].

344.42 Couplings and Connectors

(A) Installation. Threadless couplings and connectors must be made up tight to maintain an effective ground-fault current path to safely conduct fault current in accordance with 250.4(A)(5), 250.96(A), and 300.10.

> **Author's Comment:**
>
> ▸ Loose locknuts have been found to burn away before a fault was cleared because loose connections increase the impedance of the ground-fault current path.

Buried in Concrete. If buried in concrete, threadless fittings must be of the concrete-tight type. ▶Figure 344–9

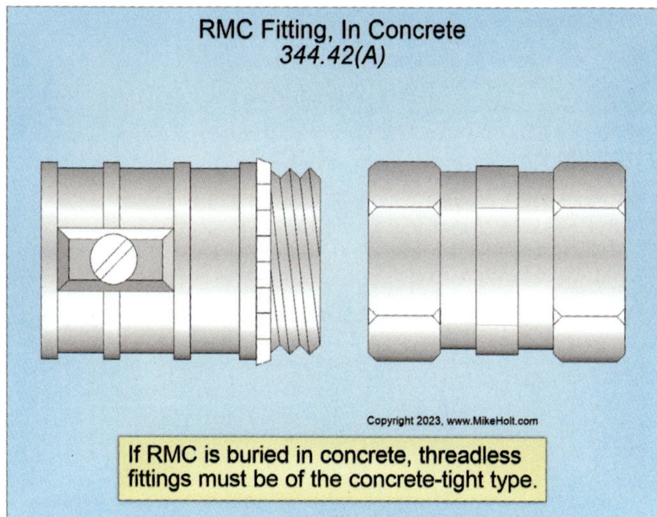

▶Figure 344–9

Wet Locations. If installed in wet locations, fittings must be listed for use in wet locations and prevent moisture or water from entering or accumulating within the enclosure in accordance with 314.15.

(B) Running Threads. Running threads are not permitted for the connection of couplings, but they are permitted at other locations.
▶Figure 344–10

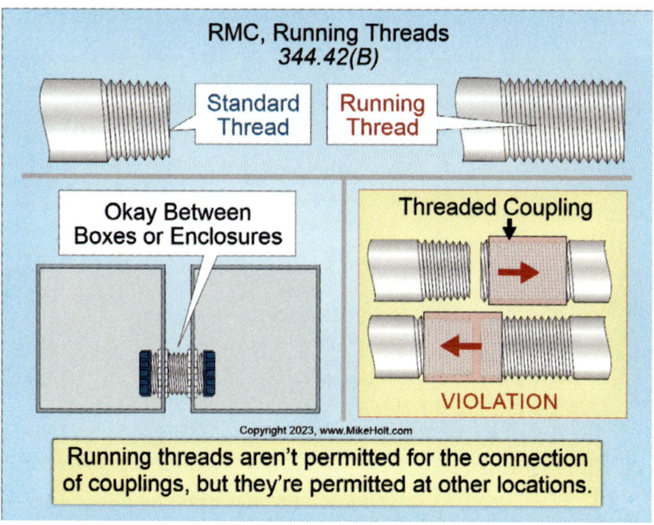

▶Figure 344–10

To protect conductors exiting a threaded conduit from abrasion, a bushing must be installed on the threads of conduit (regardless of conductor size) unless the raceway enters a threaded entry in a box, fitting, or enclosure.

Author's Comment:

▸ In accordance with "*UL 514B Standard for Conduit, Tubing, and Cable Fittings*" section 5.4.1.1, a conduit fitting must be provided with a positive end stop for the conduit and a smooth rounded throat to protect against abrasion of insulation on conductors entering the conduit.

Note: Conductors 4 AWG and larger exiting a conduit connector must be protected from abrasion, prior to the installation by a fitting that provides a smooth, rounded, insulating surface in accordance with 300.4(G).
▶Figure 344–11

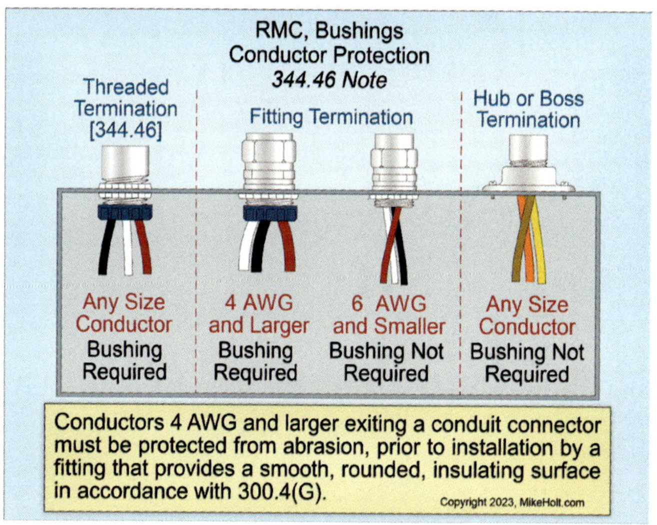

▶Figure 344–11

FLEXIBLE METAL CONDUIT (FMC)

Introduction to Article 348—Flexible Metal Conduit (FMC)

Article 348 covers the use, installation, and construction specifications for flexible metal conduit (FMC) and associated fittings. FMC, commonly called "flex" or sometimes "Greenfield" (after its inventor), is a raceway made a spiral interlocked steel or aluminum strip. It is primarily used where flexibility is necessary or where equipment moves, shakes, or vibrates. Some topics covered in this material include:

- ▸ Uses permitted
- ▸ Uses not permitted
- ▸ Size
- ▸ Bending and trimming
- ▸ Securing and supporting
- ▸ Couplings and connectors

According to Article 100, "Flexible Metal Conduit (FMC)" is a raceway of circular cross section made of a helically wound, formed, interlocked metal strip, and listed for the installation of electrical conductors. ▸Figure 348–1

Part I. General

348.1 Scope

Article 348 covers the use, installation, and construction specifications for flexible metal conduit (FMC) and associated fittings. ▸Figure 348–2

Part II. Installation

348.10 Uses Permitted

FMC is permitted to be installed exposed or concealed.

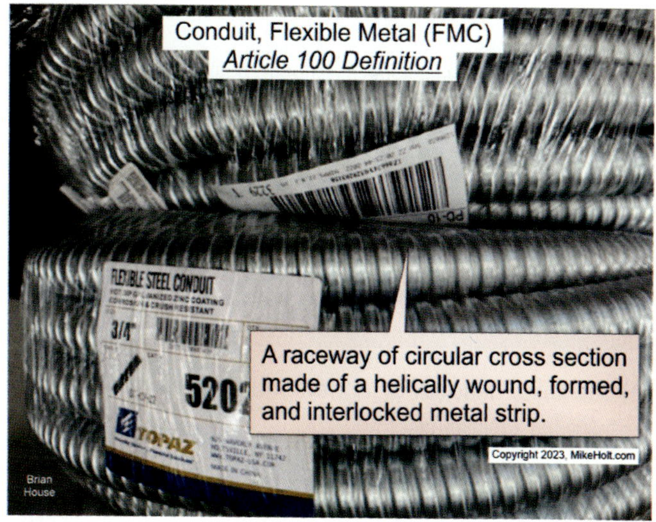

▸Figure 348–1

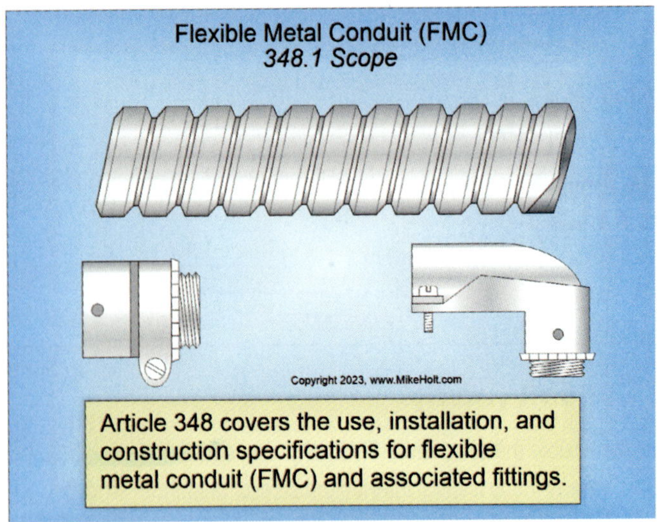

▶Figure 348–2

▶Figure 348–3

348.12 Uses Not Permitted

FMC is not permitted:

(1) In wet locations.

(2) In hoistways, other than as permitted in 620.21(A)(1).

(3) In storage battery rooms.

(4) In any hazardous (classified) location, except as permitted by 501.10(B).

(5) Exposed to material having a deteriorating effect on the installed conductors.

(6) Underground or embedded in poured concrete. ▶Figure 348–3

(7) Where subject to physical damage.

348.20 Trade Size

(A) Minimum. Trade size ½. However, trade size ⅜ is permitted for the following applications

(1) For enclosing the leads of motors.

(2) Not exceeding 6 ft in length for any of the following: ▶Figure 348–4

   a. For utilization equipment.

   b. As part of a listed assembly.

   c. For luminaire tap connections in accordance with 410.117(C).

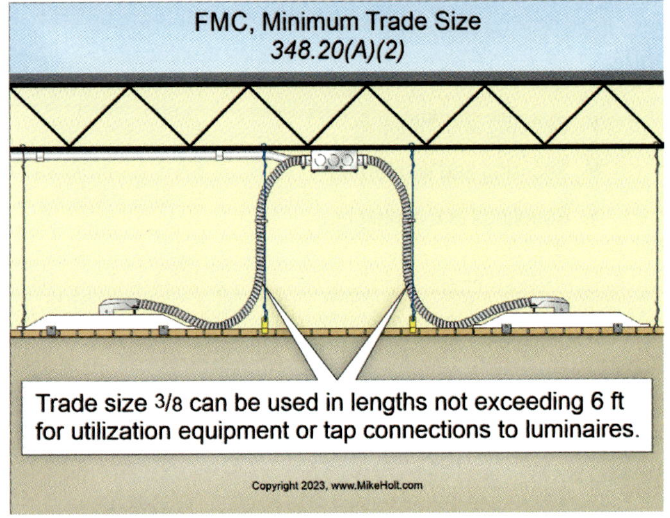

▶Figure 348–4

(5) As part of a listed assembly used to interconnect luminaires per 410.137(C).

(B) Maximum. Trade size 4.

348.24 Bends

(A) How Made. Bends must be made so the conduit will not be damaged, and its internal diameter will not be effectively reduced. The radius of the curve of the inner edge of any field bend is not permitted to be less than shown in Chapter 9, Table 2, using the column "Other Bends."

Author's Comment:

▶ A ½ FMC has a bending radius of 4 in. from the curve of the inner edge [Chapter 9 Table 2]. If the bending radius is exceeded, the conduit will be compromised and a new section will be required to be installed.

(B) Degrees of Bends in One Run. To reduce the stress and friction on conductor insulation, the total degrees of bends (including offsets) between pull points is not permitted to exceed 360 degrees.

348.28 Trimming

The cut ends of FMC must be trimmed to remove the rough edges, but is not necessary if fittings are threaded into the convolutions.

348.30 Securing and Supporting

(A) Securely Fastened. FMC must be securely fastened by a means approved by the authority having jurisdiction within 1 ft of termination, and it must be secured and supported at intervals not exceeding 4½ ft. ▶Figure 348–5

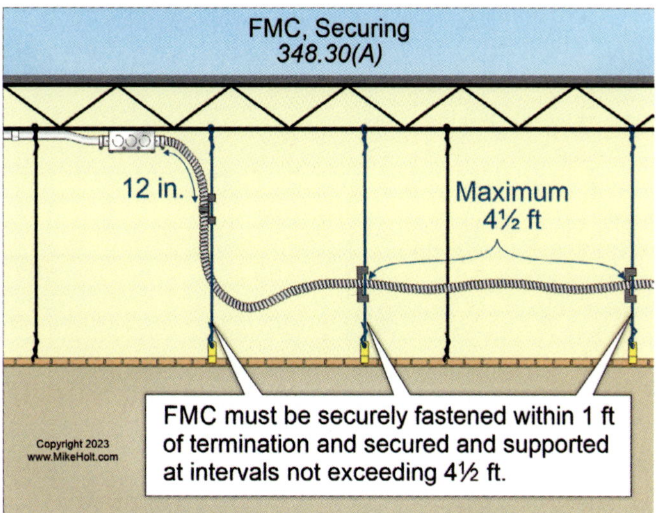

▶Figure 348–5

Where cable ties are used to secure and support Type FMC, they must be listed and identified for securing and supporting.

Ex 1: FMC is not required to be securely fastened or supported where fished between access points through concealed spaces and supporting is impractical.

Ex 2: If flexibility is necessary after installation, unsecured lengths from the last point of securement are not permitted to exceed: ▶Figure 348–6

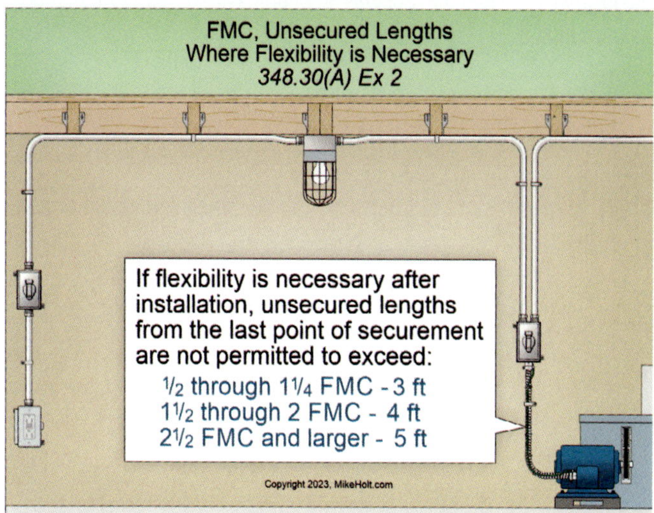

▶Figure 348–6

(1) 3 ft for trade sizes ½ through 1¼

(2) 4 ft for trade sizes 1½ through 2

(3) 5 ft for trade sizes 2½ and larger

Ex 4: FMC can be unsecured within an accessible ceiling for lengths not exceeding 6 ft from the last point of securement. Listed FMC fittings are considered a means of securement and support. ▶Figure 348–7

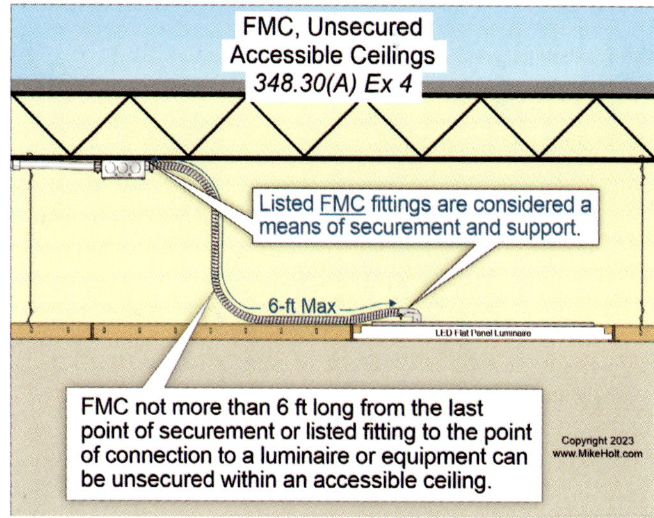

▶Figure 348–7

(B) Horizontal Runs. FMC installed horizontally through framing members is considered supported and secured if such support does not exceed 4½ ft and the raceway is secured within 1 ft of terminations.

▶Figure 348–8

348.42 Couplings and Connectors

Angle connectors are not permitted to be concealed inside drywall or concrete.

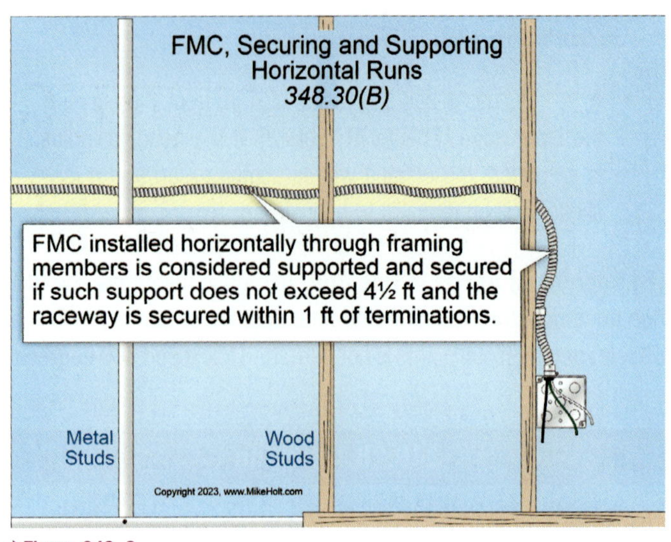

▶Figure 348–8

LIQUIDTIGHT FLEXIBLE METAL CONDUIT (LFMC)

Introduction to Article 350—Liquidtight Flexible Metal Conduit (LFMC)

This article covers the use, installation, and construction specifications of liquidtight flexible metal conduit (LFMC) and associated fittings. LFMC, with its associated connectors and fittings, is a flexible raceway commonly available in trade size ½ and larger. It is used for connections to equipment that vibrates or must be occasionally moved. LFMC is commonly called "Sealtight®" or "liquidtight." It is similar in use and construction to flexible metal conduit but has an outer liquidtight thermoplastic covering that provides protection from liquids and some corrosive effects. Some topics covered in this material include:

- Uses permitted
- Uses not permitted
- Size
- Bending and trimming
- Securing and supporting

According to Article 100, "Liquidtight Flexible Metal Conduit (LFMC)" is a raceway of circular cross section, having an outer liquidtight, nonmetallic, sunlight-resistant jacket over an inner flexible metal core, with associated connectors and fittings, listed for the installation of electrical conductors. ▶Figure 350–1

▶Figure 350–1

Part I. General

350.1 Scope

Article 350 covers the use, installation, and construction specifications of liquidtight flexible metal conduit (LFMC) and associated fittings. ▶Figure 350–2

Part II. Installation

350.10 Uses Permitted

Listed LFMC is permitted, either exposed or concealed, at any of the following locations:

(1) If flexibility is required.

(2) In hazardous (classified) locations in accordance with Chapter 5.

(3) For direct burial if listed and marked for this purpose. ▶Figure 350–3

▶Figure 350–2

▶Figure 350–3

350.12 Uses Not Permitted

LFMC must not be used where subject to physical damage. ▶Figure 350–4

350.20 Trade Size

(A) Minimum. LFMC smaller than trade size ½ is not permitted to be used.

Ex: LFMC can be smaller than trade size ½ if installed in accordance with 348.20(A).

▶Figure 350–4

(B) Maximum. LFMC larger than trade size 4 is not permitted to be used.

350.24 Bends

(A) How Made. Bends must be made so the conduit will not be damaged, and the internal diameter will not be effectively reduced.

(B) Degrees of Bends in One Run. To reduce the stress and friction on conductor insulation, the total degrees of bends (including offsets) between pull points is not permitted to exceed 360 degrees. ▶Figure 350–5

▶Figure 350–5

350.28 Trimming

Cut ends of LFMC must be trimmed both inside and outside the raceway to remove rough edges.

350.30 Securing and Supporting

LFMC must be securely fastened in place and supported in accordance with 350.30(A) and (B).

(A) Securely Fastened. LFMC must be securely fastened by a means approved by the authority having jurisdiction within 1 ft of termination. They must be secured and supported at intervals not exceeding 4½ ft. ▶Figure 350–6

▶Figure 350–6

Where cable ties are used for securing LFMC, they must be listed and identified for securement and support.

Ex 1: LFMC is not required to be securely fastened or supported where fished between access points through concealed spaces and supporting is impractical.

Ex 2: If flexibility is necessary after installation, unsecured lengths from the last point of securement are not permitted to exceed: ▶Figure 350–7

(1) 3 ft for trade sizes ½ through 1¼

(2) 4 ft for trade sizes 1½ through 2

(3) 5 ft for trade sizes 2½ and larger

Ex 4: LFMC can be unsecured within an accessible ceiling for lengths not exceeding 6 ft from the last point of securement. ▶Figure 350–8

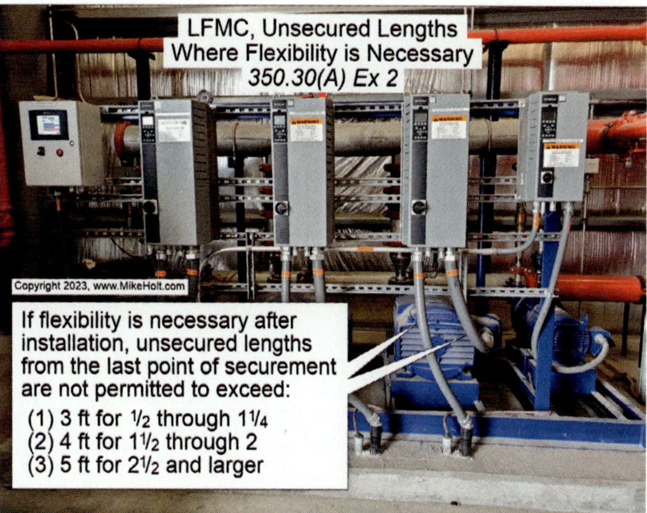

▶Figure 350–7

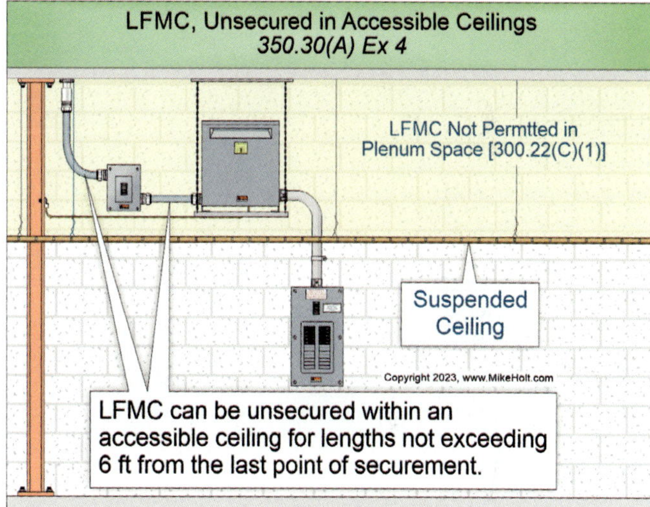

▶Figure 350–8

LFMC fittings are permitted as a means of securement and support.

Author's Comment:

▶ This last sentence following the four exceptions means that the use of LFMC fittings as the means of securing and supporting only applies to installations made using one of the four exceptions. It should not be interpreted as permission to use these fittings to secure and support LFMC in all applications.

(B) Horizontal Runs. LFMC installed horizontally through framing members is considered supported and secured if such support does not exceed 4½ ft, and the raceway is secured within 1 ft of termination.

RIGID POLYVINYL CHLORIDE CONDUIT (PVC)

Introduction to Article 352—Rigid Polyvinyl Chloride Conduit (PVC)

Article 352 covers the use, installation, and construction specifications of polyvinyl chloride conduit (PVC) and associated fittings. PVC is a rigid nonmetallic conduit that is available in trade sizes ½ to 6. Two wall thicknesses ("schedules") are available. Schedule 40 PVC is used in most applications that are not subject to physical damage. Schedule 80 PVC, which has the same outside diameter but a thicker wall, is used where resistance to physical damage is required. This type of conduit is inexpensive, lightweight, and easily installed. It is permitted in concrete, corrosive areas, underground, and in wet locations. Some topics covered in this material include:

- ▸ Uses permitted
- ▸ Uses not permitted
- ▸ Bending and trimming
- ▸ Securing and supporting
- ▸ Expansion fittings
- ▸ Bushings

According to Article 100, "Polyvinyl Chloride Conduit (PVC)" is a rigid nonmetallic raceway of circular cross section with integral or associated couplings, connectors, and fittings listed for the installation of electrical conductors. ▸Figure 352–1

Part I. General

352.1 Scope

Article 352 covers the use, installation, and construction specifications of polyvinyl chloride conduit (PVC) and associated fittings. ▸Figure 352–2

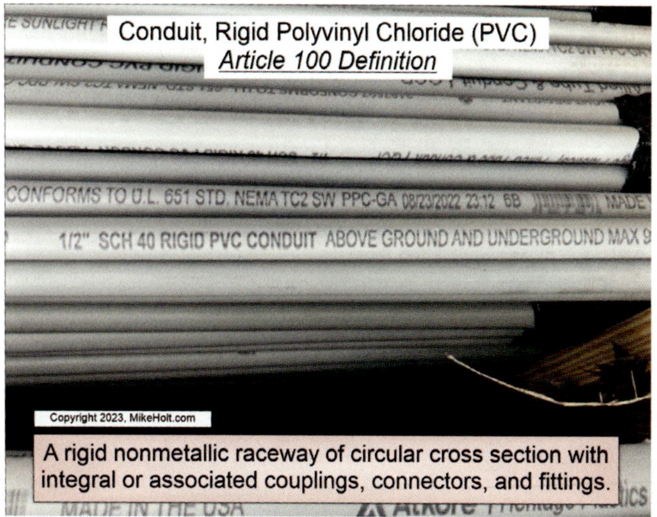

▸Figure 352–1

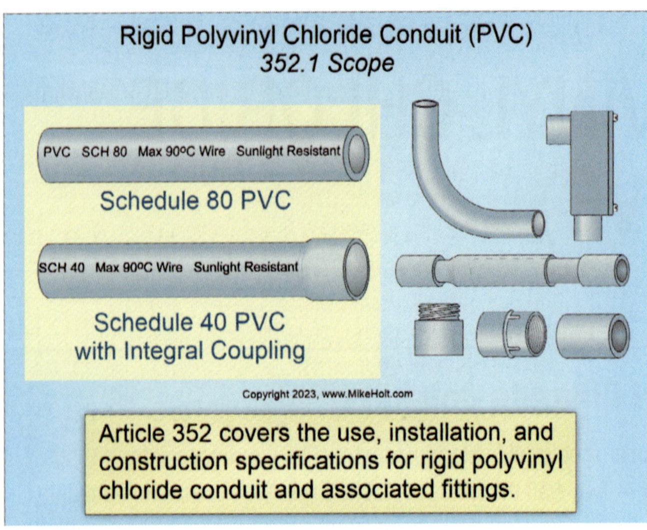

▶Figure 352–2

Part II. Installation

352.10 Uses Permitted

PVC conduit is permitted in the following applications:

Note: In extreme cold, PVC conduit can become brittle and is more susceptible to physical damage.

(A) Concealed. PVC conduit is permitted to be concealed within walls, floors, or ceilings.

(B) Encased in Concrete. PVC conduit is permitted to be encased in concrete. ▶Figure 352–3

▶Figure 352–3

(C) Corrosive Influences. PVC conduit is permitted in areas subject to severe corrosion for which the material is specifically approved by the authority having jurisdiction.

(E) Wet Locations. PVC conduit is permitted in wet locations such as dairies, laundries, canneries, car washes, and other areas frequently washed. It is also permitted in outdoor locations. Support fittings (such as straps, screws, and bolts) must be made of corrosion-resistant materials or protected with a corrosion-resistant coating in accordance with 300.6(A).

(F) Dry and Damp Locations. PVC conduit is permitted in dry and damp locations except where limited in 352.12.

(G) Exposed. Schedule 40 PVC conduit is permitted to be installed in exposed locations where the raceway is not subject to physical damage. ▶Figure 352–4

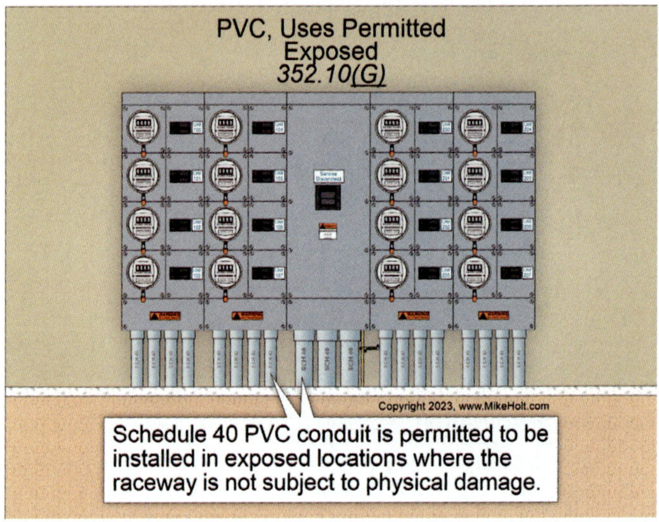

▶Figure 352–4

(H) Underground. PVC conduit is permitted to be direct buried and underground encased in concrete.

(K) Physical Damage. Where subject to physical damage, Schedule 80 PVC and associated fitting must be used. ▶Figure 352–5

Note: All listed PVC conduit fittings are suitable for connection to both Schedule 40 and Schedule 80 PVC conduit.

▶Figure 352–5

352.12 Uses Not Permitted

PVC conduit is not permitted in the following environments:

(A) Hazardous (Classified) Locations. PVC conduit is not permitted to be used in hazardous (classified) locations except as permitted by 501.10(A)(1)(1) Ex, 501.10(B)(1)(6), 502.10(B)(7), 503.10(A)(1), 504.20, 514.8 Ex 2, and 515.8(A).

(B) Support of Luminaires. PVC conduit is not permitted to be used for the support of luminaires or other equipment.

(C) Physical Damage. PVC conduit is not permitted to be used where subject to physical damage unless installed in Schedule 80 PVC [352.10(K)]. ▶Figure 352–6

▶Figure 352–6

Author's Comment:

▸ Schedule 40 PVC conduit is not identified for use where subject to physical damage, but Schedule 80 PVC conduit is [352.10(K)].

(D) Ambient Temperature. PVC conduit is not permitted to be installed if the ambient temperature exceeds 50°C (122°F).

Author's Comment:

▸ PVC conduit and fittings are not permitted to be installed in environmental air spaces (plenums) [300.22(C)].

352.24 Bends

(A) How Made. Raceway bends are not permitted to be made in any manner that will damage the raceway or significantly change its internal diameter (no kinks).

Author's Comment:

▸ PVC can be bent by hand, with a heat gun, or a heat box. Just make sure you do not damage the PVC.

(B) Degrees of Bends in One Run. To reduce the stress and friction on conductor insulation, the total degrees of bends (including offsets) between pull points is not permitted to exceed 360 degrees. ▶Figure 352–7

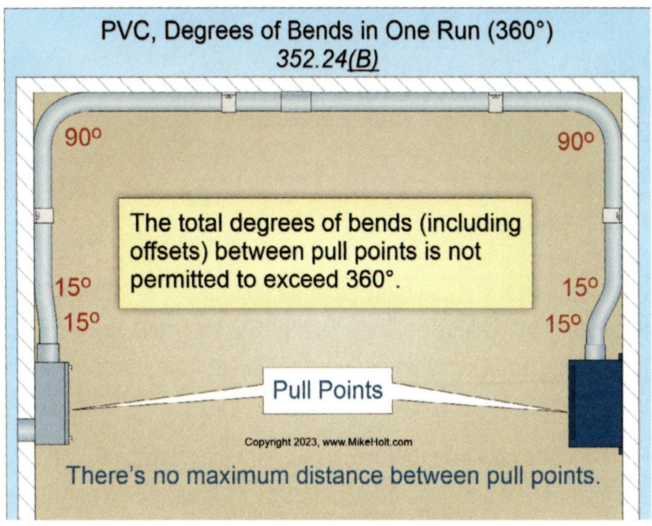

▶Figure 352–7

352.28 Trimming

The cut ends of PVC conduit must be trimmed (inside and out) to remove the burrs and rough edges.

Author's Comment:

▸ Trimming PVC conduit is very easy since most of the burrs will rub off with your fingers, and a knife will smooth the rough edges.

352.30 Securing and Supporting

PVC conduit must be fastened and supported in accordance with 352.30(A) and (B) so movement from thermal expansion and contraction is permitted.

(A) Securely Fastened. PVC conduit must be secured within 3 ft of every box, cabinet, or termination fitting (such as a conduit body). ▸Figure 352–8

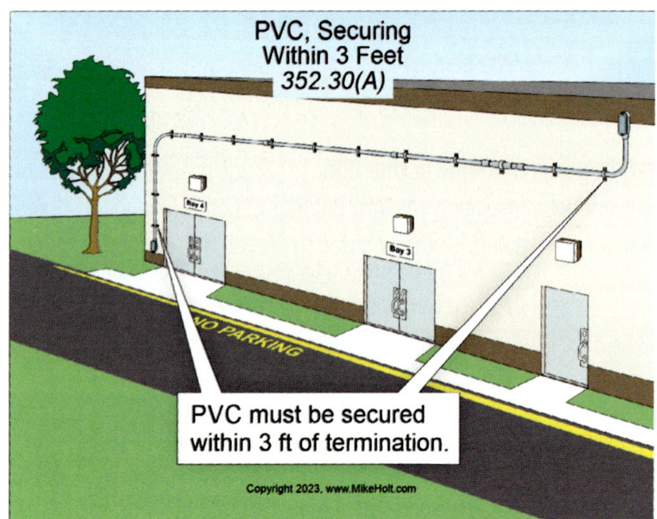

▸Figure 352–8

(B) Supports. PVC conduit must be supported at intervals not exceeding the values in Table 352.30(B). The raceway must be fastened in a manner that permits movement from thermal expansion or contraction. ▸Figure 352–9

PVC conduit installed horizontally through framing members is considered supported and secured if such support does not exceed Table 352.30(B) requirements, and the raceway is secured within 3 ft of termination.

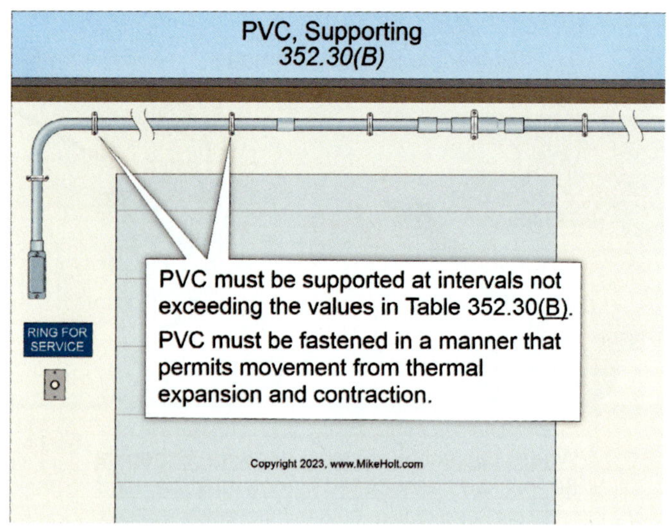

▸Figure 352–9

Table 352.30(B) Support of Rigid PVC	
Trade Size	Support Spacing
½–1	3 ft
1¼–2	5 ft
2½–3	6 ft
3½–5	7 ft
6	8 ft

352.44 Expansion Fittings

(A) Thermal Expansion and Contraction. If PVC conduit is installed in a straight run between securely mounted items such as boxes, cabinets, elbows, or other conduit terminations, expansion fittings must be provided if the expansion or contraction length change in Table 352.44(A) is expected to be ¼ in. or greater. ▸Figure 352–10

Author's Comment:

▸ When determining the number and setting of expansion fittings, you must read the manufacturer's documentation. For example, instructions for Carlon® expansion fittings for PVC conduit say that when it has sunlight exposure, 30°F must be added to the high ambient temperature.

(B) Earth Movement. When necessary to compensate for earth settling or movement (including frost heave), expansion fittings above ground must be installed.

Note: See 300.5(J).

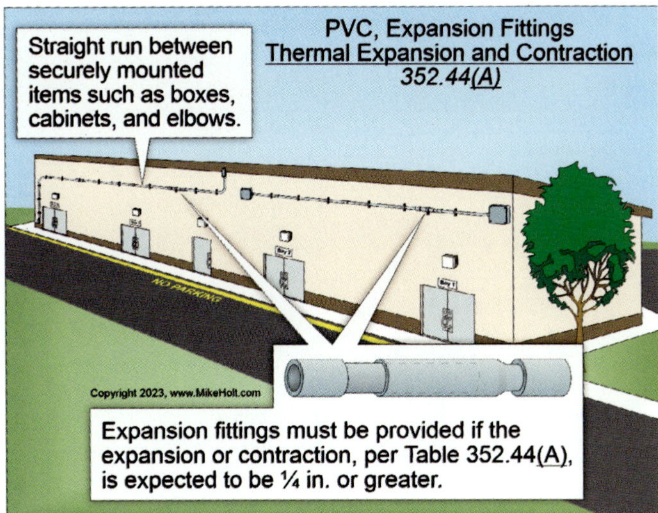

▶Figure 352–10

Table 352.44(A) Expansion Characteristics of PVC Rigid Nonmetallic Conduit Coefficient of Thermal Expansion

Temperature Change (°C)	Length of Change of PVC Conduit (mm/m)	Temperature Change (°F)	Length Change of PVC Conduit (in./100 ft)
5	0.30	5	0.20
10	0.61	10	0.41
15	0.91	15	0.61
20	1.22	20	0.81
25	1.52	25	1.01
30	1.83	30	1.22
35	2.13	35	1.42
40	2.43	40	1.62
45	2.74	45	1.83
50	3.04	50	2.03
55	3.35	55	2.23
60	3.65	60	2.43
65	3.95	65	2.64
70	4.26	70	2.84
75	4.56	75	3.04
80	4.87	80	3.24
85	5.17	85	3.45
90	5.48	90	3.65
95	5.78	95	3.85
100	6.08	100	4.06

352.46 Bushings

A protective bushing or adapter shall be provided to protect the wire from abrasion unless the box, fitting, or enclosure design provides equivalent protection. ▶Figure 352–11

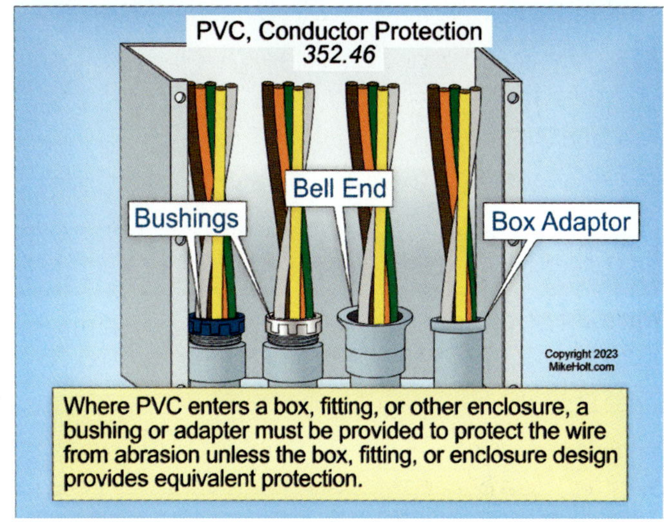

▶Figure 352–11

Author's Comment:

▶ In accordance with "*UL 651 Standard for Schedule 40 and 80 PVC Conduit and Fittings*" section 5.1.2, the inner and outer surfaces of a fitting are not permitted to be subject to peeling, scaling, or flaking and must be smooth and free from blisters, cracks, or other defects. The fitting must have a smooth, rounded inlet hole to afford protection to the conductors. In the case of a molded product, excess flashing must be removed from the mold line of all interior surfaces so there are no sharp edges or obstructions to the passage of wiring or mating products in the intended use of the product.

Note: Conductors 4 AWG and larger that enter an enclosure must be protected from abrasion (during and after installation) by a fitting that provides a smooth, rounded insulating surface (such as an insulating bushing), unless the design of the box, fitting, or enclosure provides equivalent protection in accordance with 300.4(G). ▶Figure 352–12

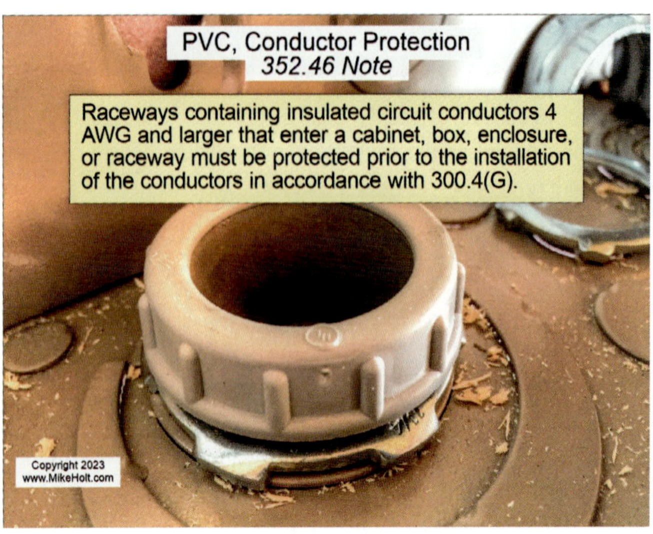

▶Figure 352–12

LIQUIDTIGHT FLEXIBLE NONMETALLIC CONDUIT (LFNC)

Introduction to Article 356—Liquidtight Flexible Nonmetallic Conduit (LFNC)

This article covers the use, installation, and construction specifications of liquidtight flexible nonmetallic conduit (LFNC) and associated fittings. LFNC has an inner flexible core with an outer liquidtight, nonmetallic, sunlight-resistant jacket. It is available in trade sizes ½ to 4 and is sometimes referred to as "Carflex®." Some topics covered in this material include:

- Uses permitted
- Uses not permitted
- Bending and trimming
- Securing and supporting

According to Article 100, "Liquidtight flexible nonmetallic conduit (LFNC)" is a raceway of circular cross section with an outer liquidtight, nonmetallic, sunlight-resistant jacket over a flexible inner core, with associated couplings, connectors, and fittings, listed for the installation of electrical conductors. ▸Figure 356–1

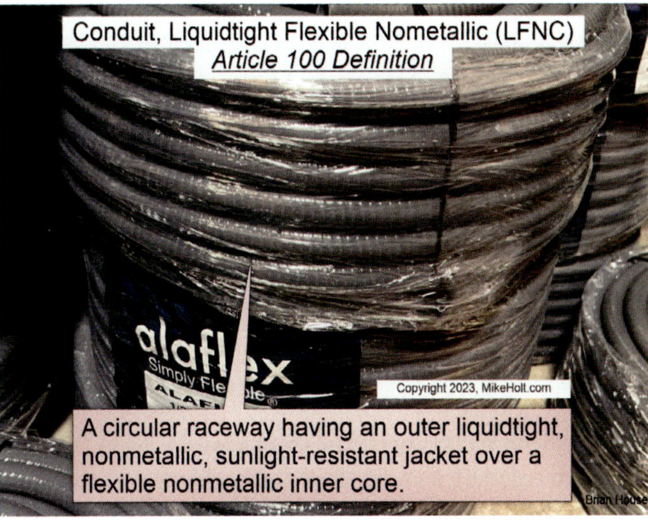

▸Figure 356–1

Part I. General

356.1 Scope

Article 356 covers the use, installation, and construction specifications of liquidtight flexible nonmetallic conduit (LFNC) and associated fittings. ▸Figure 356–2

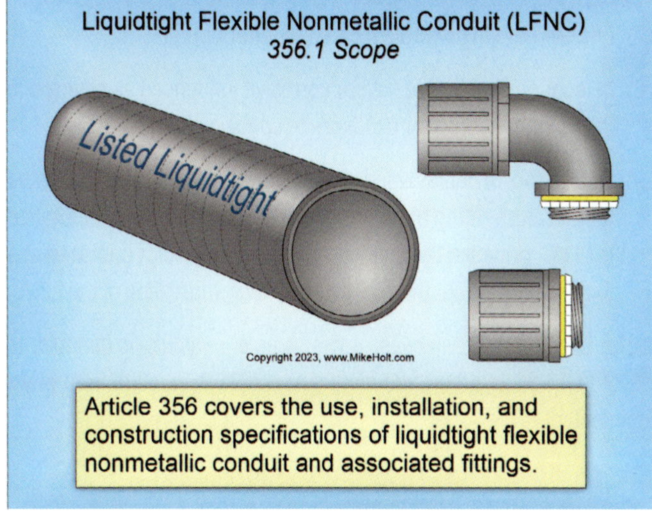

▸Figure 356–2

Part II. Installation

356.10 Uses Permitted

Listed LFNC is permitted (either exposed or concealed) at any of the following purposes and locations:

(1) If flexibility is required.

(2) If protection from liquids, vapors, machine oils, or solids is required.

(3) Outdoors, if listed and marked for this purpose.

(4) Directly buried in the Earth if listed and marked for this purpose. ▶Figure 356–3

▶Figure 356–3

(5) Installed in lengths over 6 ft if secured in accordance with 356.30.

(7) Encasement in concrete if listed for direct burial.

(8) In locations subject to severe corrosive influences as covered in 300.6 where listed for exposure to specific chemicals.

(9) Conductors or cables rated at a temperature higher than the listed temperature rating of LFNC conduit are permitted to be installed in LFNC, provided the conductors or cables are not operated at a temperature higher than the listed temperature rating of the LFNC.

Note: Extreme cold can cause some types of nonmetallic conduits to become brittle and therefore more susceptible to damage from physical contact.

356.12 Uses Not Permitted

LFNC is not permitted:

(1) Where subject to physical damage.

(2) If the ambient temperature and/or conductor temperature exceeds its listing.

(3) Longer than 6 ft, except if approved by the authority having jurisdiction as essential for a required degree of flexibility.

(4) In any hazardous (classified) location except as permitted by 501.10(B)(2), 502.10(A)(2) and (B)(2), and 504.20.

356.24 Bends

(A) How Made. Raceway bends are not permitted to be made in any manner that will damage the raceway or significantly change its internal diameter (no kinks).

(B) Degrees of Bends in One Run. To reduce the stress and friction on conductor insulation, the total degrees of bends (including offsets) between pull points is not permitted to exceed 360 degrees.

356.30 Securing and Supporting

LFNC must be securely fastened and supported in accordance with any of the following:

(1) The conduit must be securely fastened at intervals not exceeding 3 ft and within 1 ft of termination when installed in lengths longer than 6 ft. ▶Figure 356–4

Where cable ties are to be used to secure and support LFNC, they must be listed for the application, securing, and supporting.

(2) Securing or supporting is not required if LFNC is fished or installed in lengths not exceeding 3 ft at terminals if flexibility is required.

(3) Runs of LFNC installed horizontally through framing members are considered supported and secured if such support does not exceed 3 ft, and the raceway is secured within 1 ft of termination.

(4) Securing or supporting LFNC is not required if installed in lengths not exceeding 6 ft from the last point where the raceway is securely fastened for connections within an accessible ceiling to a luminaire(s) or other equipment. For the purposes of this allowance, listed fittings are considered support. ▶Figure 356–5

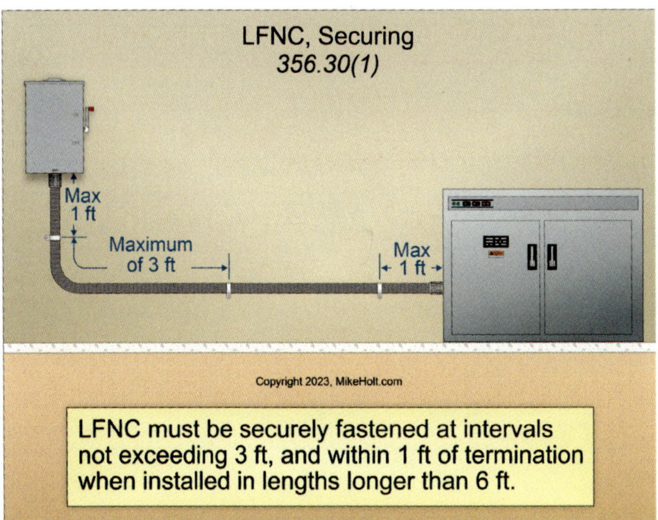

▶Figure 356–4

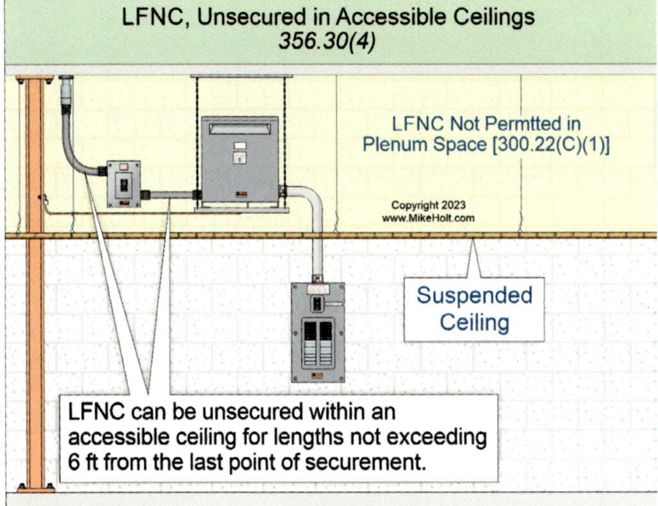

▶Figure 356–5

356.42 Fittings

Only fittings that are listed for use with LFNC can be used [300.15]. Angle fittings cannot be installed where concealed. Straight LFNC fittings are permitted for direct burial or encasement in concrete. ▶Figure 356–6

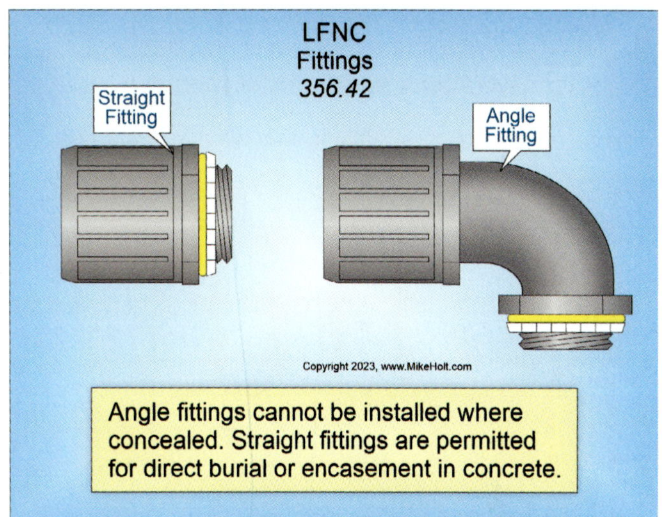

▶Figure 356–6

ELECTRICAL METALLIC TUBING (EMT)

Introduction to Article 358—Electrical Metallic Tubing (EMT)

Article 358 covers the use, installation, and construction specifications of electrical metallic tubing (EMT) and associated fittings. EMT is a lightweight metal tubing that is easy to bend, cut, and ream but it cannot be threaded. It is the most common raceway used in commercial and industrial installations. Some topics covered in this material include:

▶ Uses permitted

▶ Uses not permitted

▶ Bending, reaming, and threading

▶ Securing and supporting

According to Article 100, "Electrical Metallic Tubing (EMT)" is an unthreaded thinwall circular metallic raceway used for the installation of electrical conductors. When joined together with listed fittings and enclosures as a complete system, it is a reliable wiring method providing both physical protection for conductors as well an effective ground-fault current path. ▶Figure 358–1

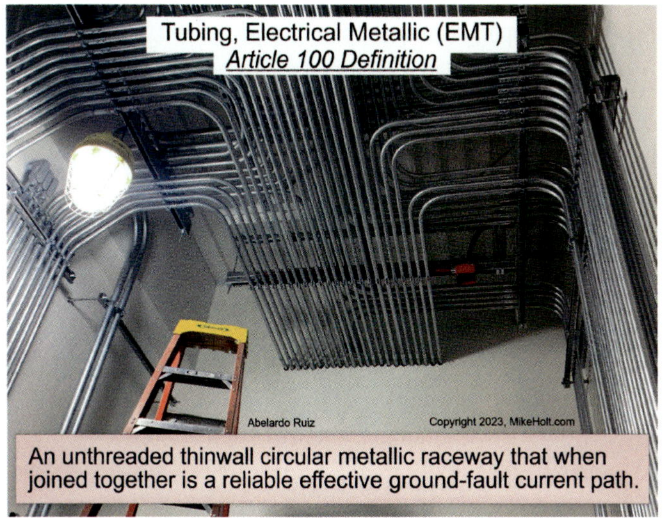

An unthreaded thinwall circular metallic raceway that when joined together is a reliable effective ground-fault current path.

▶Figure 358–1

Part I. General

358.1 Scope

Article 358 covers the use, installation, and construction specifications of electrical metallic tubing (EMT) and associated fittings. ▶Figure 358–2

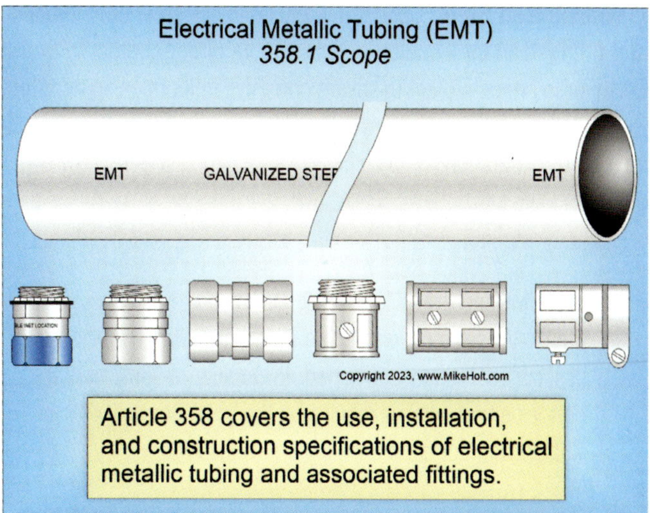

▶Figure 358–2

Part II. Installation

358.10 Uses Permitted

(A) Exposed and Concealed. EMT is permitted to be used exposed and concealed for the following applications:

(1) In concrete and in direct contact with the Earth with fittings identified for direct burial.

(2) In dry, damp, or wet locations. ▶Figure 358–3

(3) In any hazardous (classified) location as permitted by other articles in this *Code*.

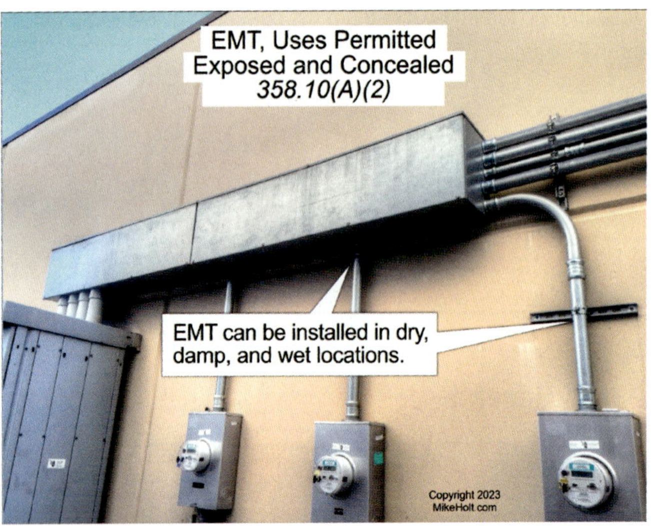

▶Figure 358–3

(B) Corrosive Environments.

(1) Galvanized Steel. Galvanized and stainless steel EMT, elbows, and fittings can be installed in concrete, in direct contact with the Earth, or in areas subject to severe corrosive influences. In addition, they must be protected by corrosion protection and approved as suitable for the condition.

> **Author's Comment:**
>
> ▶ In accordance with *"UL Guide Information FJMX,"* supplementary corrosion protection is required when EMT and associated fittings are buried. In addition, supplementary corrosion protection is required at the point where EMT transitions from concrete encasement to the soil.

(D) Wet Locations. Support fittings (such as screws, straps, and so forth) installed in a wet location must be made of corrosion-resistant material.

Note: See 300.6 for protection against corrosion.

> **Author's Comment:**
>
> ▶ If installed in wet locations, fittings for EMT must be listed for use in wet locations and prevent moisture or water from entering or accumulating within the enclosure in accordance with 314.15 [358.42].

358.12 Uses Not Permitted

EMT is not permitted to be used under the following conditions:

(1) Where subject to severe physical damage. ▶Figure 358–4

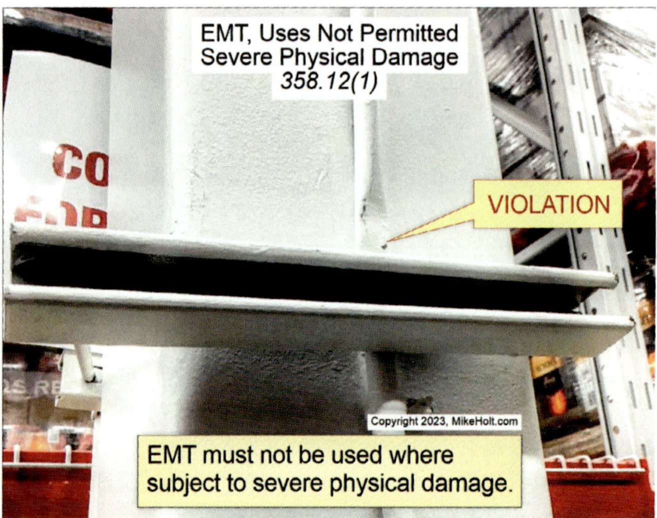

▶Figure 358–4

(2) For the support of luminaires or other equipment. ▶Figure 358–5

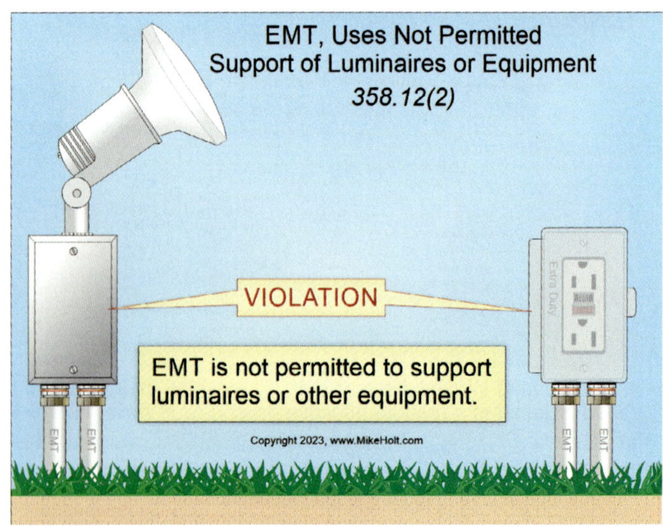

▶Figure 358–5

358.24 Bends

(A) How Made. Raceway bends are not permitted to be made in any manner that will damage the raceway or significantly change its internal diameter (no kinks).

Author's Comment:

▸ This is generally not a problem because typical EMT benders are made to comply with this requirement.

(B) Degrees of Bends in One Run. To reduce the stress and friction on conductor insulation, the total degrees of bends in the tubing (including offsets) between pull points cannot exceed 360 degrees. ▸Figure 358–6

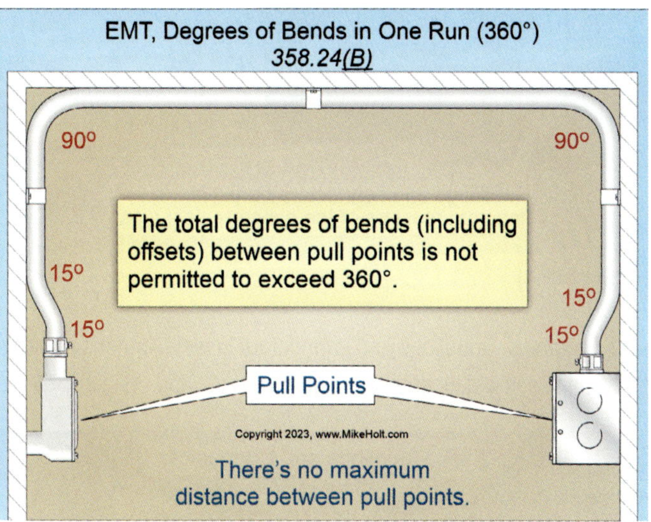

▸Figure 358–6

Author's Comment:

▸ There is no maximum distance between pull boxes because this is a design issue, not a safety issue.

358.28 Reaming

(A) Reaming. Reaming to remove the burrs and rough edges is required when the raceway is cut. ▸Figure 358–7

Author's Comment:

▸ It is considered an accepted practice to ream small raceways with a screwdriver or lineman's pliers.

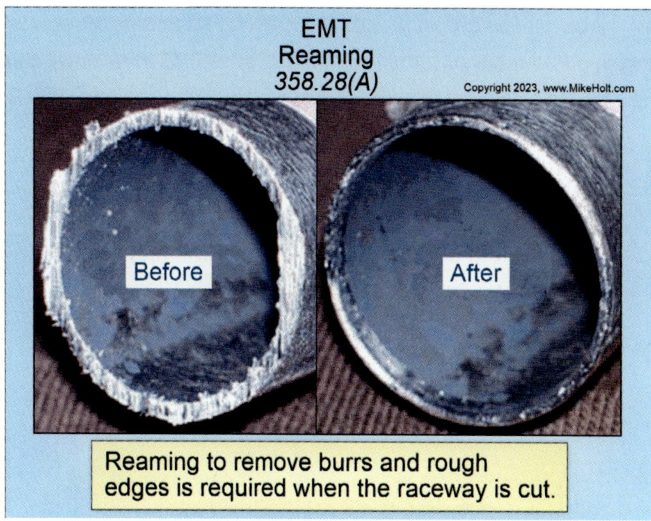

▸Figure 358–7

358.30 Securing and Supporting

(A) Securely Fastened. EMT must be securely fastened in place and supported in accordance with the following: ▸Figure 358–8

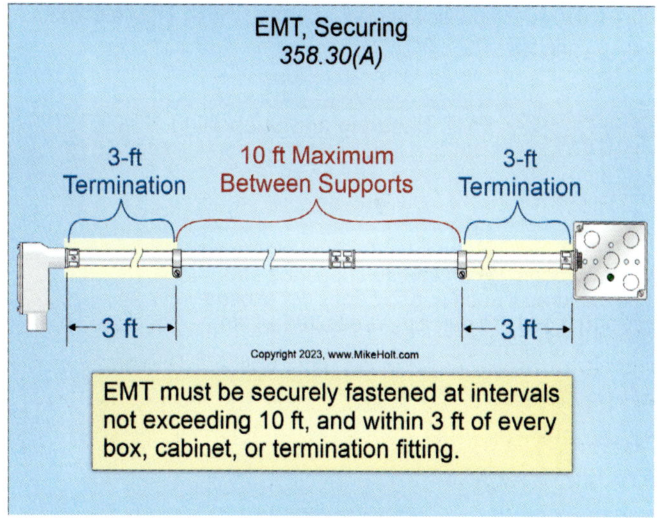

▸Figure 358–8

(1) EMT must be securely fastened at intervals not exceeding 10 ft.

(2) The tubing must be securely fastened within 3 ft of every box, cabinet, or termination fitting.

Author's Comment:

▸ Fastening is required within 3 ft of termination, not within 3 ft of a coupling.

Ex 1: When structural members do not permit the raceway to be secured within 3 ft of a box or termination fitting, an unbroken raceway can be secured within 5 ft of a box or termination fitting. ▶Figure 358–9

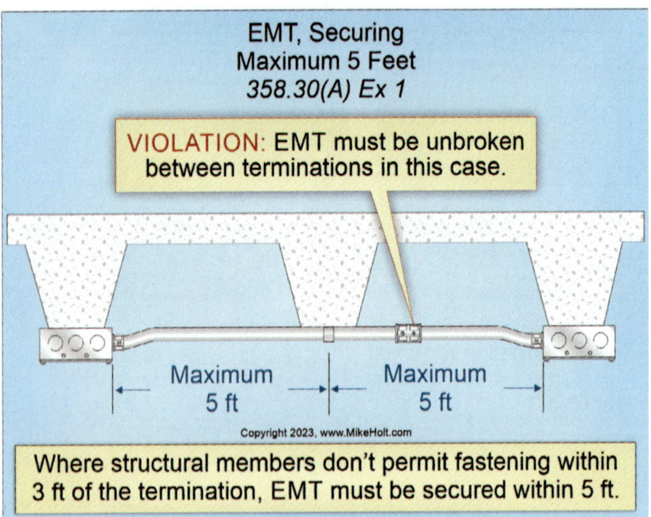

▶Figure 358–9

(B) Horizontal Runs. EMT installed horizontally through framing members is considered supported and secured if such support does not exceed 10 ft, and the raceway is secured within 3 ft of termination. ▶Figure 358–10

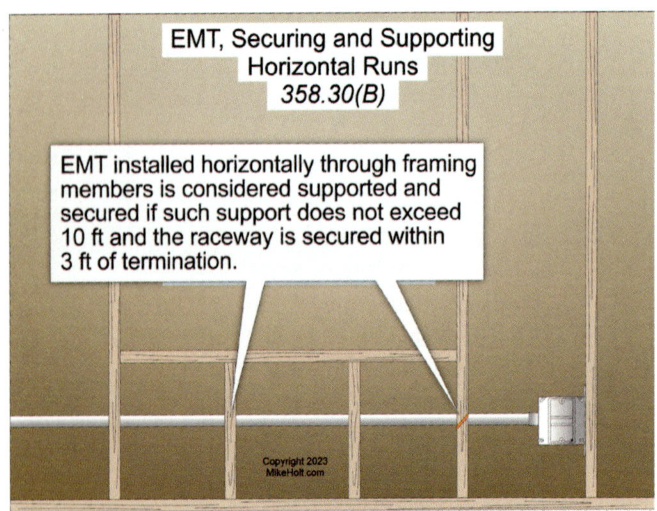

▶Figure 358–10

Couplings and connectors must be made up tight to maintain an effective ground-fault current path to safely conduct fault current in accordance with 250.4(A)(5), 250.96(A), and 300.10.

Buried in Concrete. Couplings and connectors buried in concrete must be of the concrete-tight type. ▶Figure 358–11

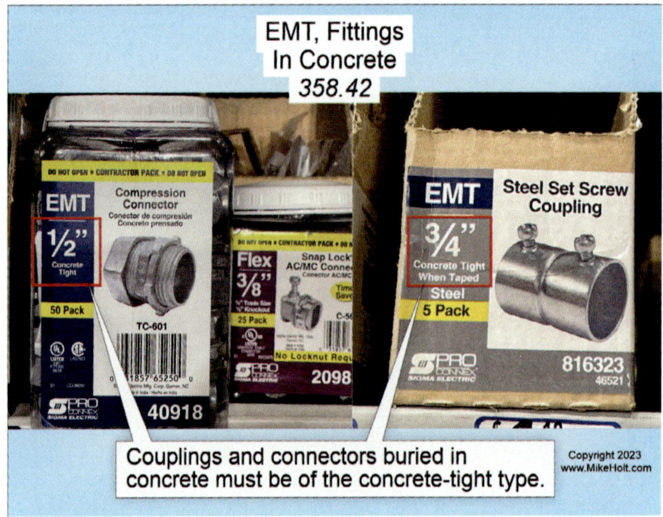

▶Figure 358–11

Wet Locations. Couplings and connectors in wet locations must be listed for use in wet locations. ▶Figure 358–12 and ▶Figure 358–13

▶Figure 358–12

▶Figure 358–13

Author's Comment:

▸ In accordance with "*UL Guide Information DWTT,*" some EMT fittings are marked on the carton as "concrete-tight when taped" and can be used in concrete.

ARTICLE 362

ELECTRICAL NONMETALLIC TUBING (ENT)

Introduction to Article 362—Electrical Nonmetallic Tubing (ENT)

This article covers the use, installation, and construction specifications of electrical nonmetallic tubing (ENT) and associated fittings. ENT is a nonmzetallic, pliable, corrugated, circular raceway. It is often referred to as "Smurf Pipe" or "Smurf Tube" after the cartoon characters by the same name because it was only available in blue when it was first available, but now comes in additional colors. This type of tubing is fragile and is not sunlight resistant, so it has limited uses. Some topics covered in this material include:

- ▸ Uses permitted
- ▸ Uses not permitted
- ▸ Bending and trimming
- ▸ Securing and supporting
- ▸ Bushings

According to Article 100, "Electrical Nonmetallic Tubing (ENT)" is a pliable, corrugated, circular raceway of circular cross section with integral or associated couplings, connectors, and fittings that are listed for the installation of electrical conductors. It is composed of a material that is resistant to moisture and chemical atmospheres, and it is also flame retardant. ▸Figure 362–1

Part I. General

362.1 Scope

Article 362 covers the use, installation, and construction specifications of electrical nonmetallic tubing (ENT) and associated fittings. ▸Figure 362–2

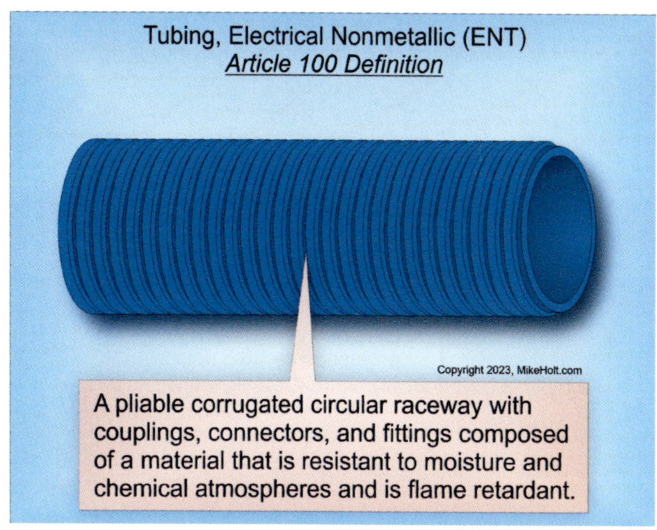

▸Figure 362–1

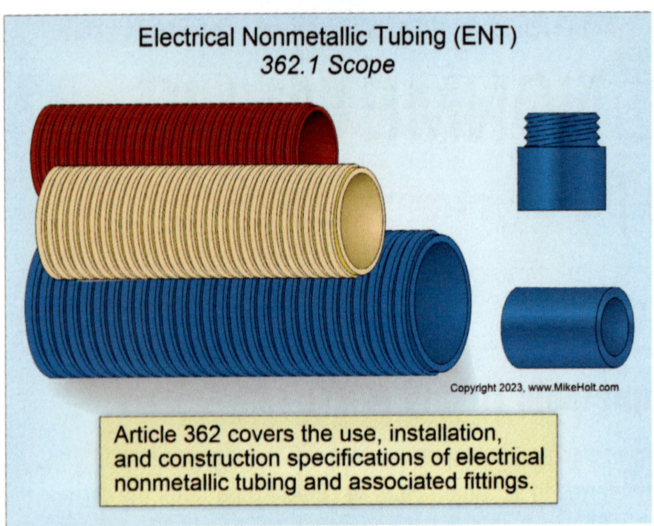

▶Figure 362–2

Part II. Installation

362.10 Uses Permitted

Electrical nonmetallic tubing is permitted as follows:

(1) In buildings not exceeding three floors. ▶Figure 362–3

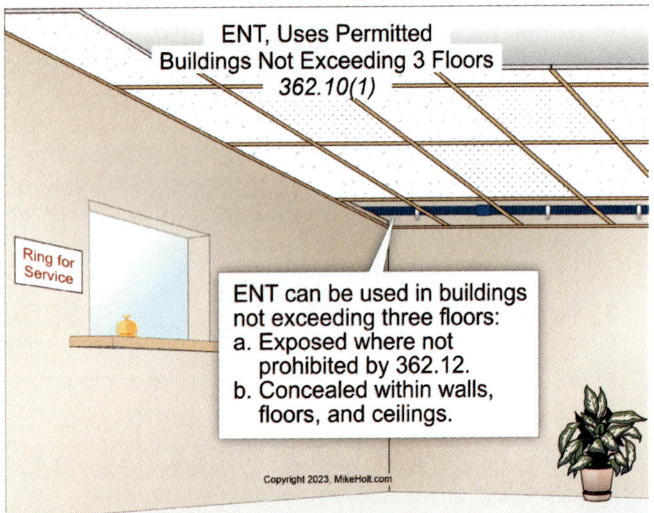

▶Figure 362–3

   a. Exposed, where not prohibited by 362.12.

   b. Concealed within walls, floors, and ceilings.

(2) In buildings exceeding three floors, where installed concealed within combustible or noncombustible walls, floors, or ceilings that provide a thermal barrier having a 15-minute finish rating, as identified in listings of fire-rated assemblies. ▶Figure 362–4

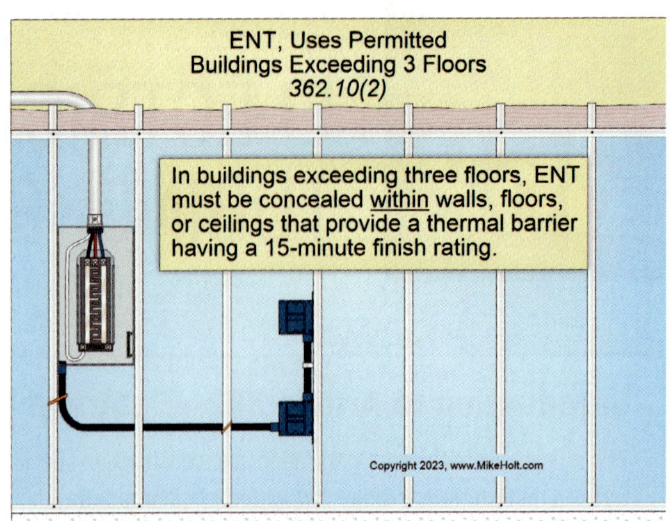

▶Figure 362–4

Ex to (2): If an approved automatic fire protective system is installed on all floors, electrical nonmetallic tubing is permitted exposed or concealed in buildings of any height. ▶Figure 362–5

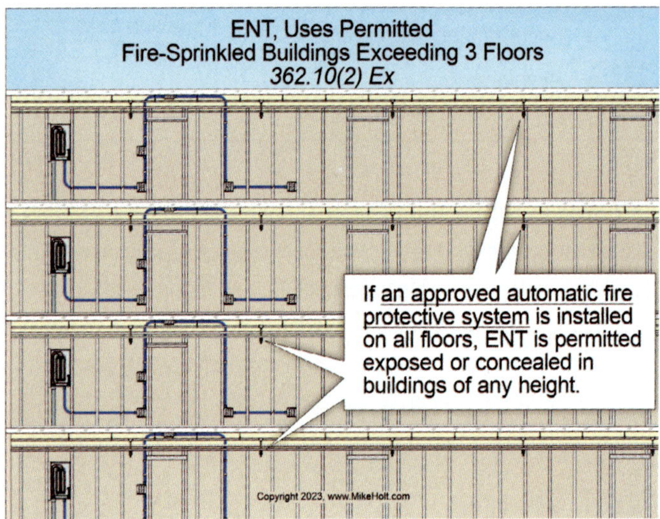

▶Figure 362–5

Author's Comment:

▶ ENT is not permitted above a suspended ceiling used as a plenum space [300.22(C)].

(3) In severe corrosive and chemical locations [300.6] when identified for this use.

(4) In dry and damp concealed locations if not prohibited by 362.12.

(5) Above a suspended ceiling if the suspended ceiling provides a thermal barrier having a 15-minute finish rating, as identified in listings of fire-rated assemblies. ▶Figure 362–6

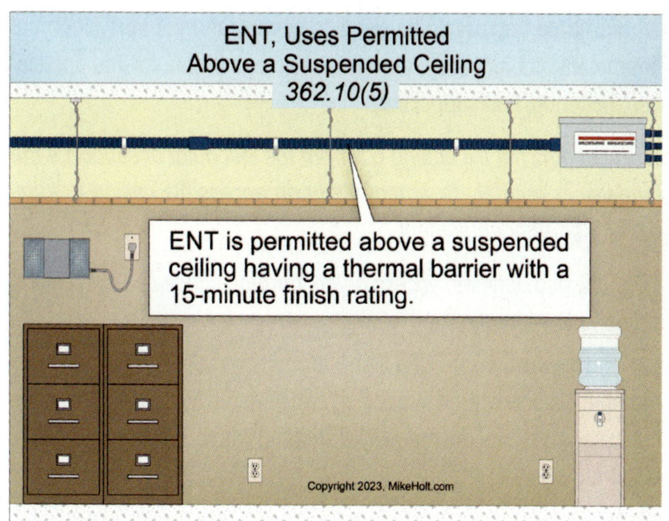

▶Figure 362–6

Ex to (5): If an approved automatic fire protective system is installed on all floors, ENT is permitted above a suspended ceiling that does not have a 15-minute finish rated thermal barrier. ▶Figure 362–7

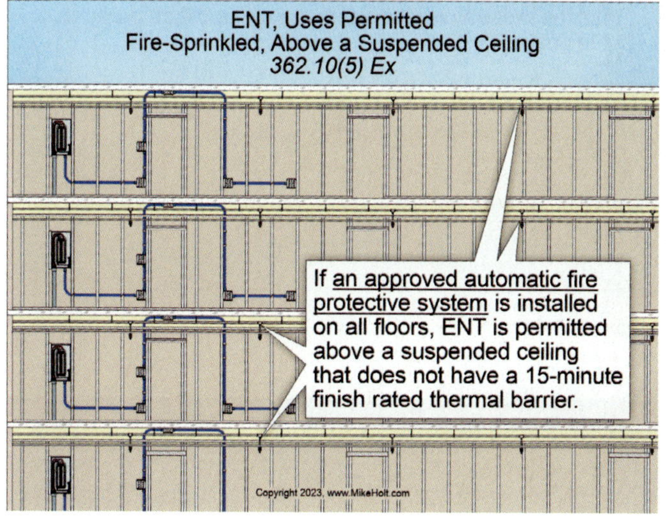

▶Figure 362–7

(6) Encased in poured concrete floors, ceilings, walls, and slabs.

(7) Embedded in a concrete slab provided fittings identified for the purpose are used.

(8) In wet locations or in a concrete slab on or below grade with fittings listed for the purpose.

362.12 Uses Not Permitted

ENT is not permitted to be used in the following applications:

(1) In any hazardous (classified) location, except as permitted by 504.20 and 505.15(A).

(2) For the support of luminaires or equipment. See 314.23.

(3) If the ambient temperature exceeds 50°C (122°F).

(4) For direct burial in the Earth.

> **Author's Comment:**
>
> ▸ Electrical nonmetallic tubing is permitted to be encased in concrete [362.10(6)].

(5) Exposed in buildings over three floors, except as permitted by 362.10(1), 362.10(5) Ex, and 362.10(8).

(6) In assembly occupancies or theaters, except as permitted by 518.4 and 520.5.

(7) Exposed to the direct rays of the sun. ▶Figure 362–8

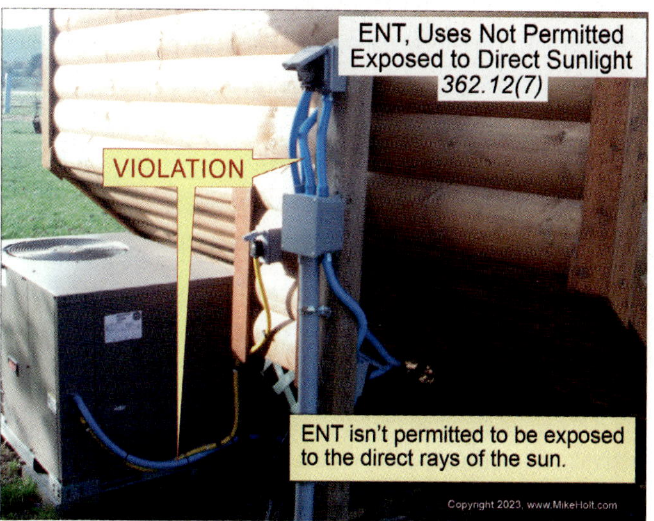

▶Figure 362–8

> **Author's Comment:**
>
> ▸ Exposing electrical nonmetallic tubing to direct sunlight for an extended time may result in the product becoming brittle, unless it is listed to resist the effects of ultraviolet (UV) radiation.

(8) Where subject to physical damage.

> **Author's Comment:**
>
> ▸ Electrical nonmetallic tubing is prohibited in ducts, plenum spaces [300.22(C)], and patient care space circuits in health care facilities [517.13(A)].

362.24 Bends

(A) How Made. Raceway bends are not permitted to be made in any manner that will damage the raceway or significantly change its internal diameter (no kinks).

(B) Degrees of Bends in One Run. To reduce the stress and friction on conductor insulation, the total degrees of bends in the tubing (including offsets) between pull points cannot exceed 360 degrees.

362.28 Trimming

The cut ends of electrical nonmetallic tubing must be trimmed (inside and out) to remove the burrs and rough edges.

Author's Comment:

▸ Trimming electrical nonmetallic tubing is very easy since most of the burrs will rub off with your fingers, and a knife will smooth the rough edges.

362.30 Securing and Supporting

ENT must be securely fastened in place by an approved means and supported in accordance with 362.30(A) and (B).

(A) Securely Fastened. ENT must be secured within 3 ft of every box, cabinet, or termination fitting (such as a conduit body) and at intervals not exceeding 3 ft. ▸Figure 362–9

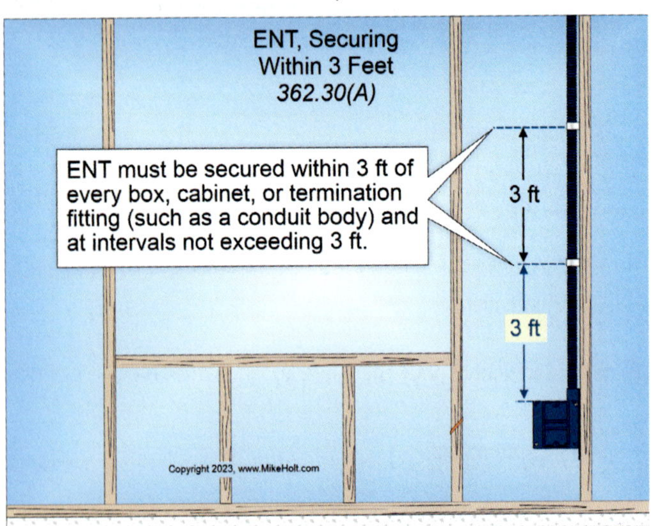

▸Figure 362–9

Where cable ties are to be used to secure and support electrical nonmetallic tubing, they must be listed as suitable for the application, securing, and supporting.

Ex 2: Lengths not exceeding 6 ft from the last point of support if the raceway is securely fastened within an accessible ceiling to luminaire(s) or other equipment.

Ex 3: If fished between access points through concealed spaces and securing is impractical.

(B) Horizontal Runs. ENT installed horizontally through framing members is considered supported and secured if such support does not exceed 3 ft, and the raceway is secured within 3 ft of terminations. ▸Figure 362–10

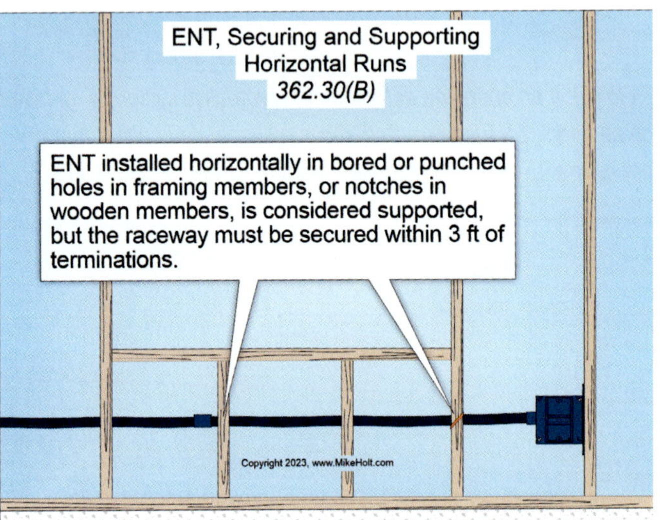

▸Figure 362–10

362.46 Bushings

Where ENT enters a box, fitting, or other enclosure, a bushing or adapter must be provided to protect the wire from abrasion, unless the box fitting or enclosure design provides equivalent protection.

Note: Conductors 4 AWG and larger that enter an enclosure must be protected from abrasion (during and after installation) by a fitting that provides a smooth, rounded insulating surface (such as an insulating bushing), unless the design of the box, fitting, or enclosure provides equivalent protection in accordance with 300.4(G).

METAL WIREWAYS

Introduction to Article 376—Metal Wireways

Article 376 covers the use, installation, and construction specifications of metal wireways and associated fittings. Metal wireways are commonly used where access to conductors inside a raceway is required to make terminations, splices, or taps to several devices at a single location. They are often incorrectly called "auxiliary gutters" or "gutters" in the field. Wireways and auxiliary gutters are similar in design but a wireway is a raceway [Article 100] while an auxiliary gutter [Article 366] is not—it is a supplemental enclosure for wiring. Some topics covered in this material include:

- ▶ Uses permitted
- ▶ Uses not permitted
- ▶ Securing and supporting
- ▶ Splices, taps, and power distribution blocks

According to Article 100, "Metal Wireway" is a sheet metal trough with hinged or removable covers for housing and protecting electrical conductors and cable, and in which conductors are placed after the raceway has been installed. ▶Figure 376–1

▶Figure 376–1

Part I. General

376.1 Scope

Article 376 covers the use, installation, and construction specifications of metal wireways and associated fittings. ▶Figure 376–2

Part II. Installation

376.10 Uses Permitted

Wireways are permitted to be used in the following manners:

(1) Exposed.

(2) In any hazardous (classified) location as permitted by other articles in the *Code*.

(3) In wet locations where listed for the purpose. ▶Figure 376–3

Understanding Fundamental 2023 NEC Requirements | MikeHolt.com | **205**

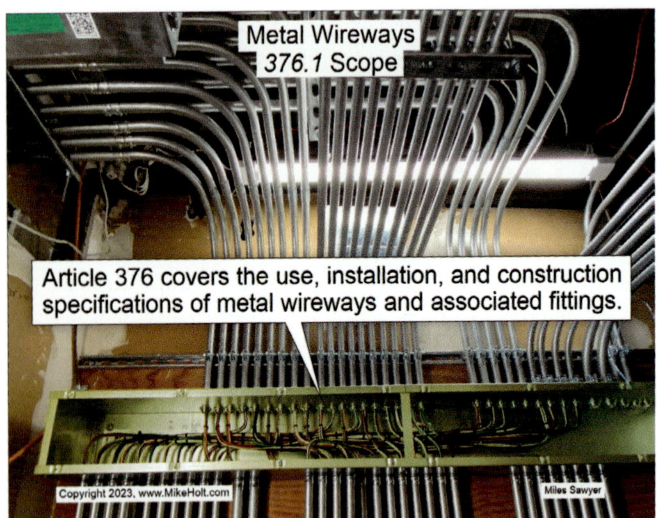

▶Figure 376–2

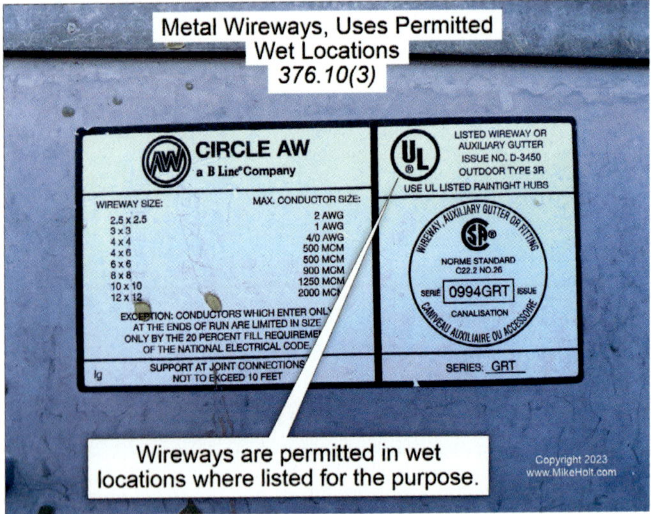

▶Figure 376–3

Author's Comment:

▶ Wireways are not required to be listed in damp or dry locations.

(4) Unbroken through walls, partitions, and floors.

376.12 Uses Not Permitted

Wireways are not permitted to be used:

(1) Where subject to severe physical damage.

(2) Where subject to severe corrosive environments.

376.30 Supports

Wireways must be supported in accordance with 376.30(A) and (B).

(A) Horizontal Support. If installed horizontally, metal wireways must be supported at each end and at intervals not exceeding 5 ft. The distance between supports must not exceed 10 ft. ▶Figure 376–4

▶Figure 376–4

(B) Vertical Support. If installed vertically, metal wireways must be securely supported at intervals not exceeding 15 ft and with no more than one joint between supports. ▶Figure 376–5

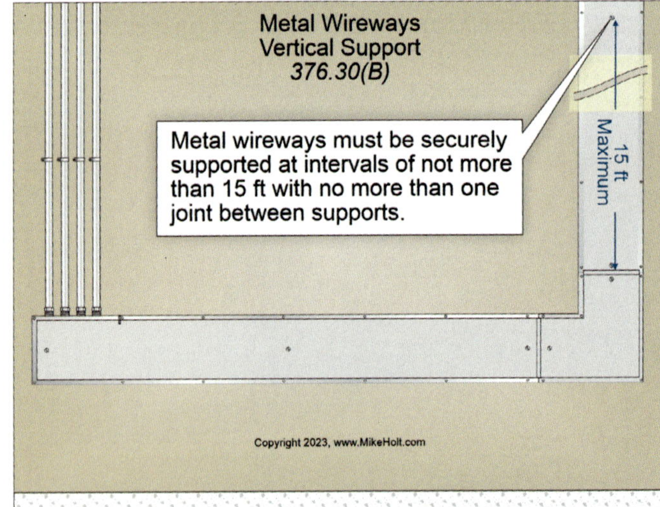

▶Figure 376–5

376.56 Splices, Taps, and Power Distribution Blocks

(A) Splices and Taps. Splices and taps in metal wireways must be accessible and not permitted to fill the wireway to more than 75 percent of the wireway's cross-sectional area. ▶Figure 376–6

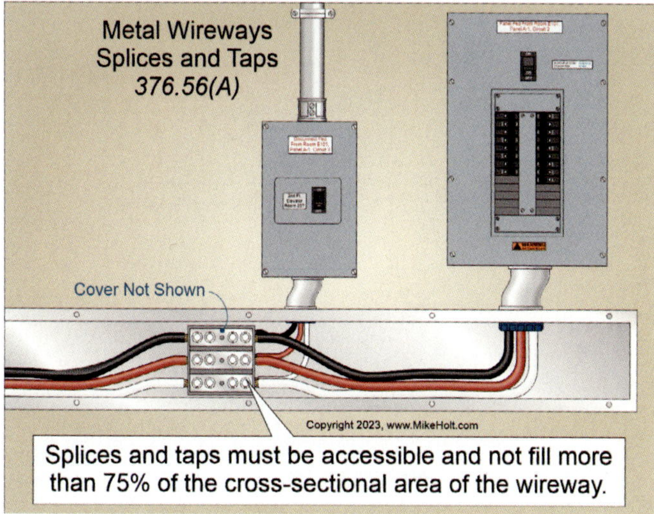

▶Figure 376–6

(B) Power Distribution Blocks.

(1) Installation. Power distribution blocks installed in wireways must be listed. If installed on the supply side of the service disconnect, they must be marked "SUITABLE FOR USE ON THE LINE SIDE OF SERVICE EQUIPMENT" or equivalent. ▶Figure 376–7

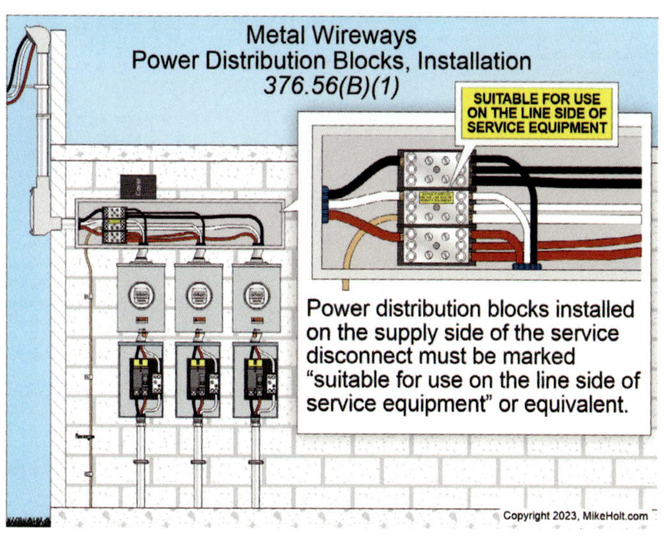

▶Figure 376–7

(2) Size of Enclosure. In addition to the wiring space requirements [376.56(A)], the power distribution block must be installed in a metal wireway not smaller than specified in the instructions for the power distribution block.

(3) Wire-Bending Space. Wire-bending space at the terminals of power distribution blocks must comply with 312.6(B).

(4) Live Parts. Power distribution blocks are not permitted to have uninsulated exposed live parts in the metal wireway after installation, whether the wireway cover is installed or not. ▶Figure 376–8

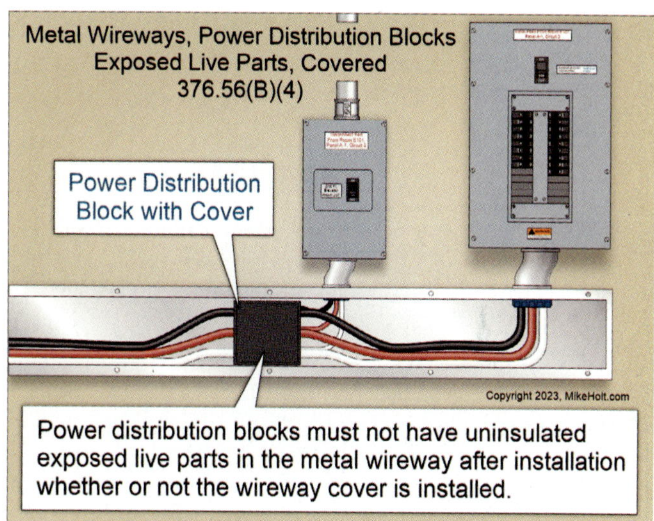

▶Figure 376–8

(5) Conductors. Conductors must be installed so the terminals of the power distribution block are not obstructed. ▶Figure 376–9

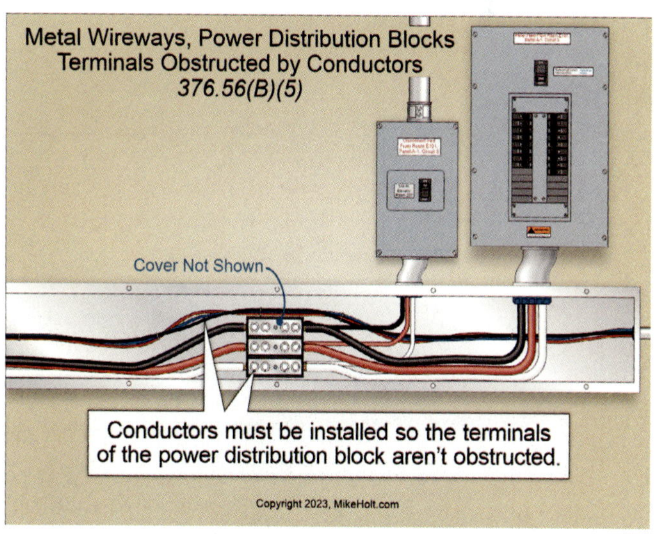

▶Figure 376–9

MULTIOUTLET ASSEMBLIES

Introduction to Article 380—Multioutlet Assemblies

This article covers the use and installation requirements for multioutlet assemblies. A multioutlet assembly is a surface, flush, or free-standing raceway designed to hold conductors and receptacles. It can be assembled in the field or at the factory and is not required to be listed. Some topics covered in this material include:

▸ Uses permitted

▸ Uses not permitted

According to Article 100, "Multioutlet Assembly" is a surface, flush, or freestanding assembly containing receptacles. ▸Figure 380–1

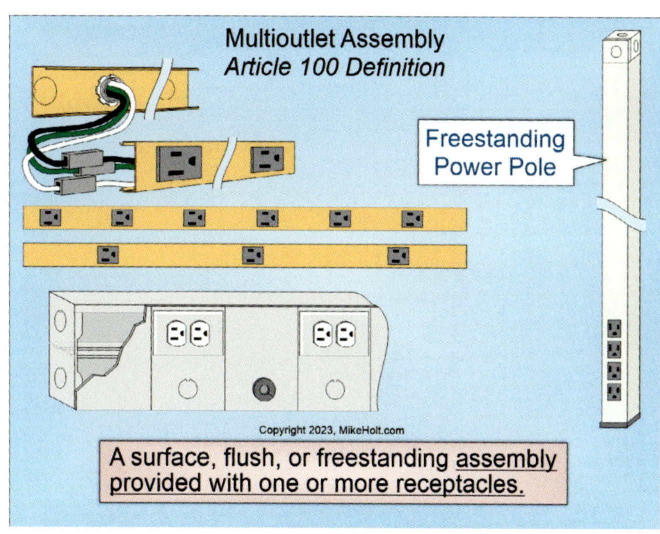

▸Figure 380–1

Author's Comment:

▸ Portable assemblies such as power strips are relocatable power taps—not multioutlet assemblies. ▸Figure 380–2

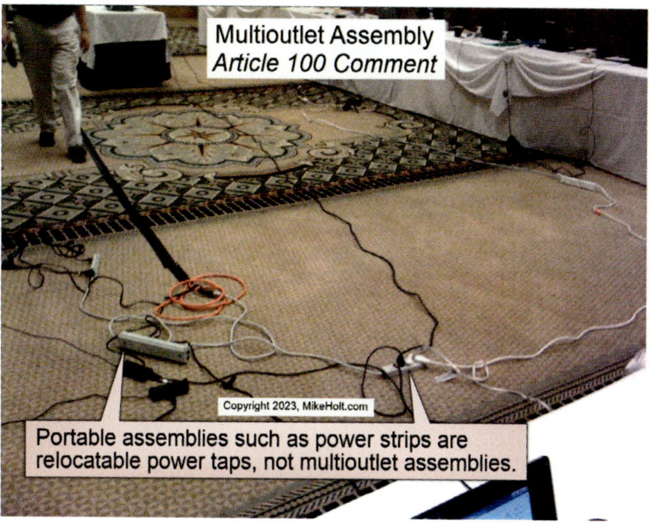

▸Figure 380–2

Part I. General

380.1 Scope

Article 380 covers the use and installation requirements for multioutlet assemblies. ▸Figure 380–3

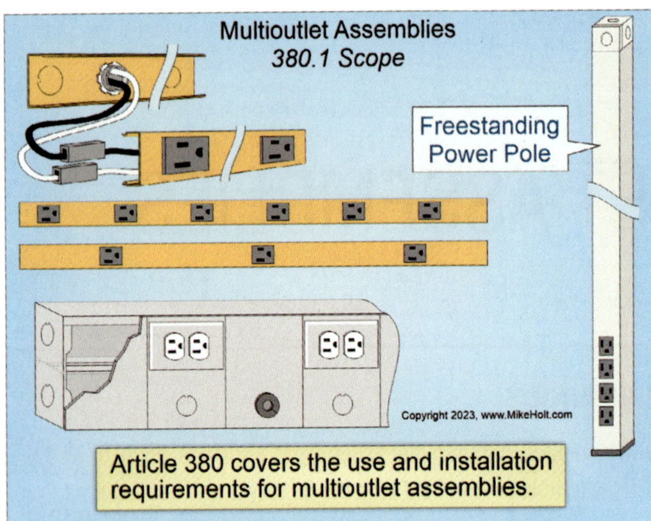

▶Figure 380–3

Part II. Installation

380.10 Uses Permitted

Multioutlet assemblies are only permitted in dry locations.

380.12 Uses Not Permitted

A multioutlet assembly must not be installed as follows:

(1) Concealed.

(2) Where subject to severe physical damage.

(3) If the voltage is 300V or more between conductors, unless the metal has a thickness of not less than 0.04 in.

(4) Where subject to corrosive vapors.

(5) In hoistways.

(6) In any hazardous (classified) location except as permitted elsewhere in this *Code*.

(7) Where cord-and-plug-connected.

380.76 Through Partitions

Metal multioutlet assemblies can pass through a dry partition provided no receptacle is concealed in the wall, and the cover of the exposed portion of the system can be removed.

SURFACE METAL RACEWAYS

Introduction to Article 386—Surface Metal Raceways

Article 386 covers the use, installation, and construction specifications of surface metal raceways and associated fittings. Surface metal raceways are often used where exposed traditional raceway systems are not aesthetically pleasing and raceway concealment is not economically feasible. They come in several colors and shapes and may be referred to as "Wiremold®" in the field. Some topics covered in this material include:

▸ Uses permitted

▸ Uses not permitted

▸ Securing and supporting

According to Article 100, "Surface Metal Raceway" is a raceway with associated fittings in which conductors are placed after the raceway has been installed as a complete system. ▸Figure 386–1

Part I. General

386.1 Scope

Article 386 covers the use, installation, and construction specifications of surface metal raceways and associated fittings. ▸Figure 386–2

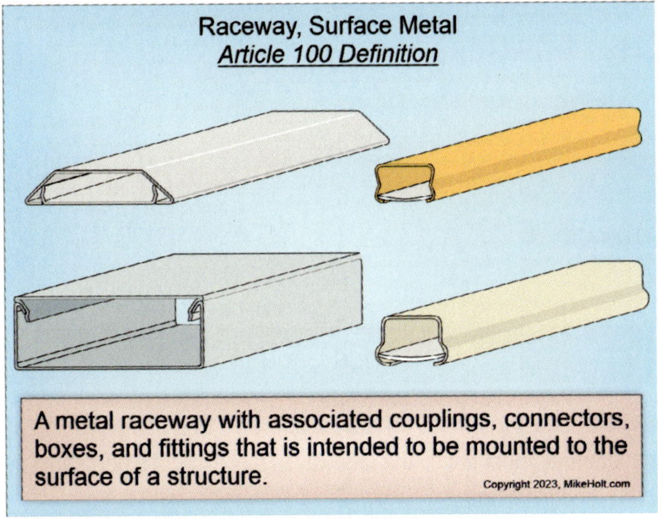

▸Figure 386–1

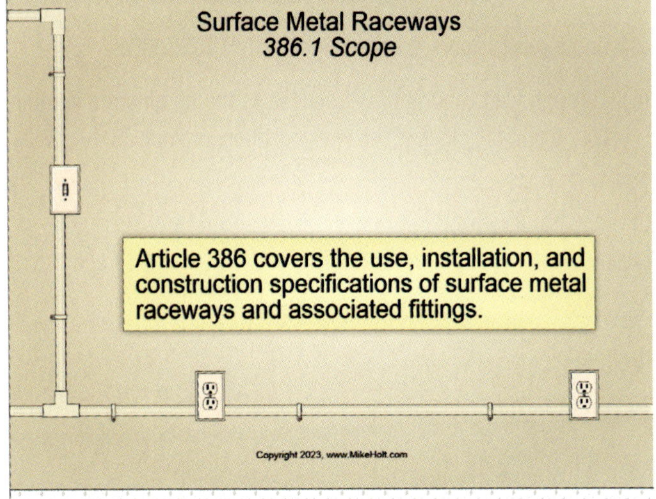

▸Figure 386–2

Author's Comment:

▸ Surface metal raceways are available in different shapes and sizes and can be mounted on walls, ceilings, or floors.

Part II. Installation

386.10 Uses Permitted

Surface metal raceways are permitted to be used:

(1) In dry locations. ▸Figure 386–3

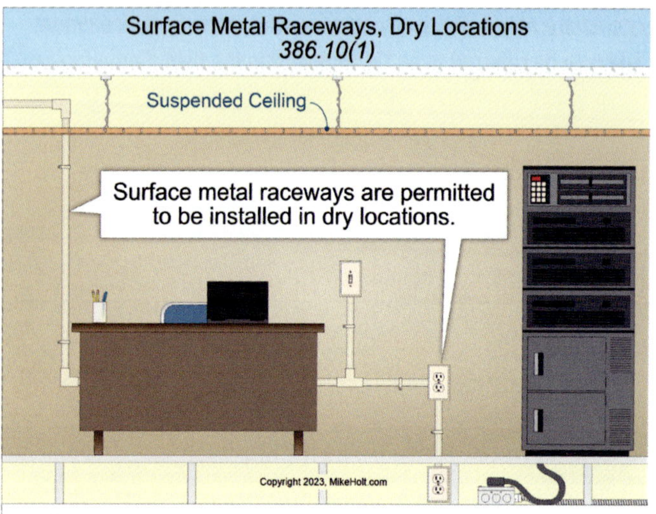

▸Figure 386–3

(2) In Class I, Division 2 locations in accordance with 501.10(B)(3).

(3) Under raised floors in accordance with 645.5(E)(2).

(4) Through walls and floors, if access to the conductors is maintained on both sides of the wall, partition, or floor.

386.12 Uses Not Permitted

Surface metal raceways are not permitted to be used:

(1) Where subject to severe physical damage unless approved by the authority having jurisdiction.

(2) If the voltage is 300V or more between conductors unless the metal has a thickness of not less than 0.04 in.

(3) Where subject to corrosive vapors.

(4) In hoistways.

(5) If concealed, except as permitted in 386.10.

386.30 Securing and Supporting

Surface metal raceways and fittings must be supported in accordance with the manufacturer's instructions. ▸Figure 386–4

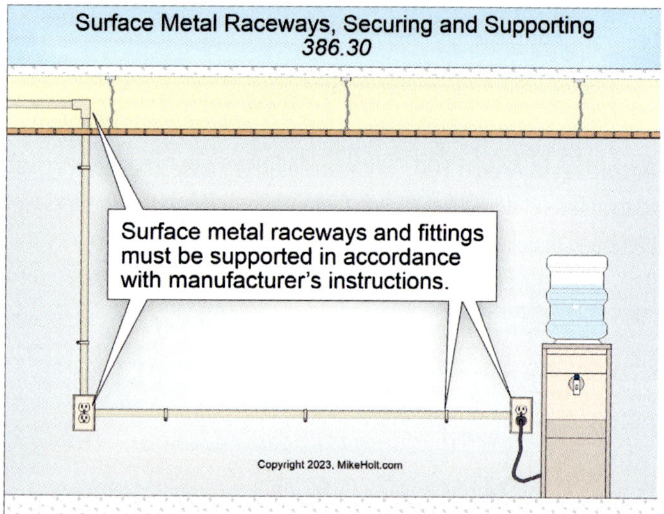

▸Figure 386–4

386.56 Splices and Taps

Splices and taps must be accessible and they, along with any conductors, must not fill the raceway to more than 75 percent of its cross-sectional area.

CABLE TRAYS

Introduction to Article 392—Cable Trays

This article covers cable tray systems including ladder, ventilated trough, ventilated channel, solid bottom, and other similar structures. A cable tray system is a unit or an assembly of units or sections with associated fittings forming a structural system used to securely fasten or support cables and raceways. Some topics covered in this material include:

- ▶ Uses permitted
- ▶ Uses not permitted
- ▶ Cable tray installation
- ▶ Conductor installation
- ▶ Securing and supporting

According to Article 100, "Cable Tray System" is a unit, assembly of units, or sections with associated fittings forming a rigid structural system used to securely fasten or support cables and raceways. ▶Figure 392–1

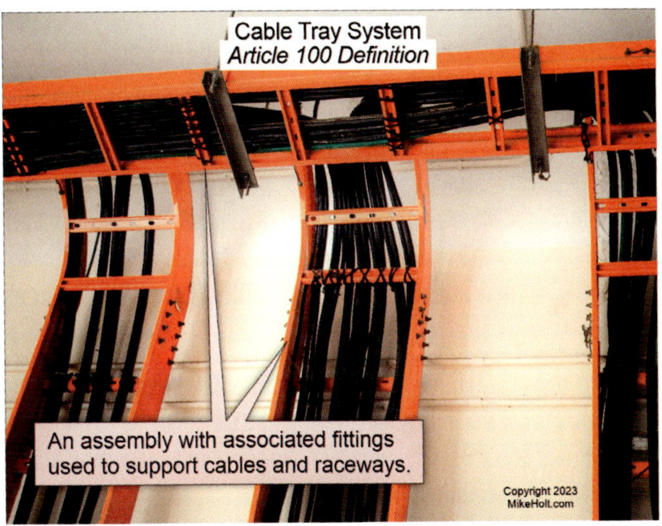

▶Figure 392–1

Part I. General

392.1 Scope

Article 392 covers cable tray systems, ladder, ventilated trough, ventilated channel, solid bottom, and other similar structures. ▶Figure 392–2

Part II. Installation

392.10 Uses Permitted

Cable trays can be used as a support system for wiring methods containing branch circuits, feeders, service conductors, and Chapters 7 and 8 wiring methods. ▶Figure 392–3

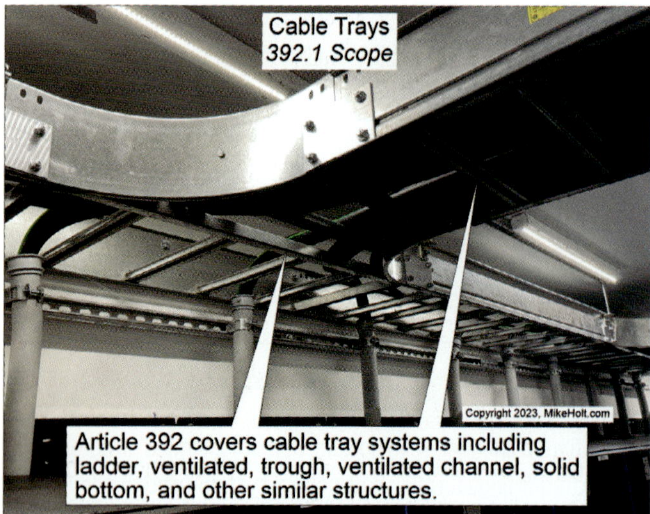

▶Figure 392–2

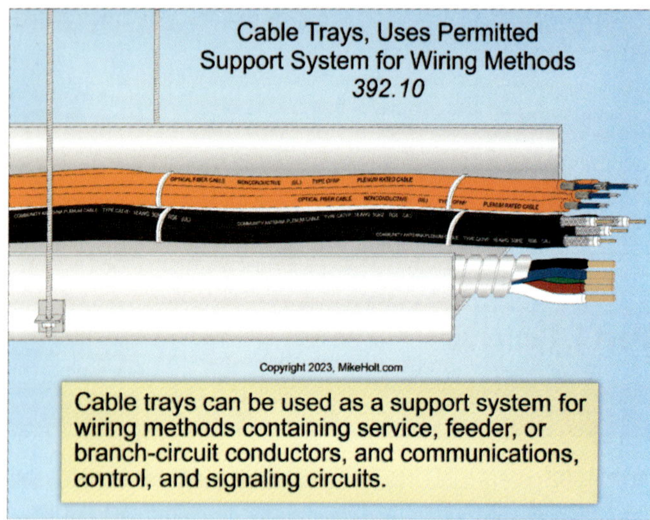

▶Figure 392–3

392.12 Uses Not Permitted

Cable tray systems are not permitted in hoistways or where subject to severe physical damage.

392.18 Cable Tray Installations

(A) Complete System. Cable trays must be installed as a complete system, except that mechanically discontinuous segments between cable tray runs (or between cable tray runs and equipment) are permitted. The system must provide for the support of the cables and raceways in accordance with their corresponding articles. ▶Figure 392–4

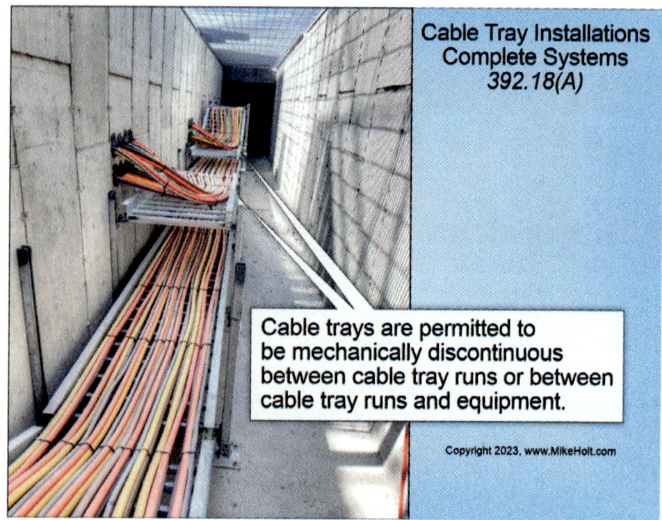

▶Figure 392–4

A bonding jumper, sized in accordance with 250.102 and installed in accordance with 250.96, must bond the sections of metal cable tray, or the cable tray and raceway or equipment.

(B) Completed Before Installation. Each run of cable tray must be completed before the installation of cables or conductors.

(D) Through Partitions and Walls. Cable trays can extend through partitions and walls, or vertically through platforms and floors, if the installation is made in accordance with the firestopping requirements of 300.21.

(E) Exposed and Accessible. Cable trays must be exposed and accessible, except as permitted by 392.18(D).

(F) Adequate Access. Sufficient space must be provided and maintained about cable trays to permit adequate access for installing and maintaining the cables.

(G) Raceways, Cables, and Boxes Supported from Cable Trays. In industrial facilities where conditions of maintenance and supervision ensure only qualified persons will service the installation, cable tray systems can support raceways, cables, boxes, and conduit bodies. ▶Figure 392–5

For raceways terminating at a cable tray, a listed cable tray clamp or adapter must be used to securely fasten the raceway to the cable tray system. The raceway must be supported and secured in accordance with the appropriate raceway article.

Raceways or cables running parallel to a cable tray system can be attached to the bottom or side of the cable tray system. The raceway or cable must be fastened and supported in accordance with the appropriate raceway or cable article.

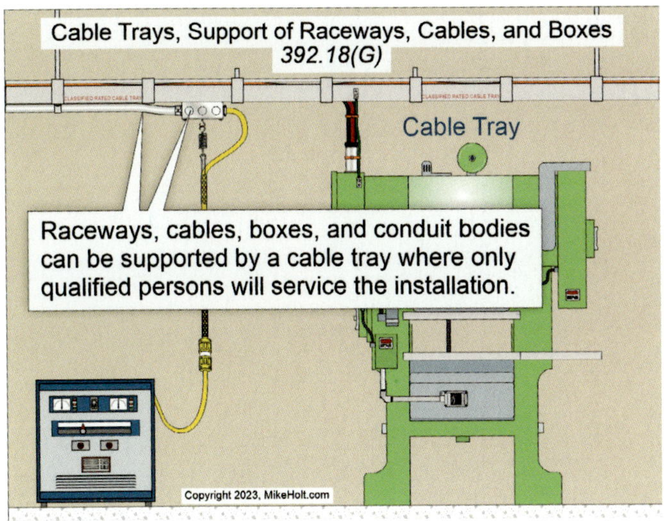

▶Figure 392–5

Boxes and conduit bodies attached to the bottom or side of a cable tray system must be fastened and supported in accordance with 314.23.

(H) Marking. Cable trays containing conductors operating at over 600V must have a permanent, legible warning notice carrying the wording, "DANGER—HIGH VOLTAGE—KEEP AWAY" placed in a readily visible position on all cable trays, with the spacing of warning notices not to exceed 10 ft. The danger marking(s) or labels must comply with 110.21(B).

392.30 Securing and Supporting

(A) Cable Trays. Cable trays must be supported in accordance with the manufacturers' instructions.

(B) Cables and Conductors. Cables and conductors must be secured to and supported by the cable tray system in accordance with the following:

(4) Cable ties must be listed and identified for the application and for securement and support.

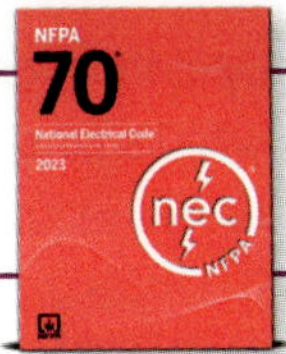

Please use the 2023 *Code* book to answer the following questions.

Article 300—General Requirements for Wiring Methods and Materials

1. The requirements of Article 300 are not intended to apply to the conductors that form an _______ part of equipment or listed utilization equipment.

   (a) exterior
   (b) integral
   (c) interior
   (d) none of these

2. All conductors of the same circuit, including the grounded and equipment grounding conductors and bonding conductors shall be contained within the same _______, unless otherwise permitted elsewhere in the *Code*.

   (a) raceway
   (b) conduit body
   (c) trench
   (d) all of these

3. The requirement to run all paralleled circuit conductors within the same _______ applies separately to each portion of the paralleled installation.

   (a) raceway or auxiliary gutter
   (b) cable tray or trench
   (c) cable or cord
   (d) all of these

4. Conductors installed in nonmetallic raceways run underground shall be permitted to be arranged as isolated _______ installations. The raceways shall be installed in close proximity, and the conductors shall comply with 300.20(B).

   (a) neutral
   (b) grounded conductor
   (c) phase
   (d) all of these

5. Conductors for ac and dc circuits under 1,000V ac and 1,500V dc, can occupy the same _______ provided that all conductors have an insulation rating equal to the maximum voltage applied to any conductor.

   (a) equipment wiring enclosure
   (b) cable
   (c) raceway
   (d) any of these

6. Where a cable or raceway-type wiring method is installed through bored holes in joists, rafters, or wood members, the holes shall be bored so that the edge of the hole is _______ the edges of the wood member.

   (a) not less than 1¼ in. from
   (b) immediately adjacent to
   (c) not less than ¹⁄₁₆ in. from
   (d) 90° away from

7. Cables laid in wood notches require protection against nails or screws by using a steel plate at least ______ thick, installed before the building finish is applied.

    (a) ¹⁄₁₆ in.
    (b) ⅛ in.
    (c) ¼ in.
    (d) ½ in.

8. A ¹⁄₁₆-in. steel plate for ______ is not required for protection when installed in wood notches.

    (a) UF cable
    (b) NM cable
    (c) MC cable
    (d) intermediate metal conduit

9. Where NM cables pass through cut or drilled slots or holes in metal members, the cable shall be protected by ______ which are installed in the opening prior to the installation of the cable and which securely cover all metal edges.

    (a) anti-short devices
    (b) sleeves
    (c) plates
    (d) listed bushings or grommets

10. Where nails or screws are likely to penetrate nonmetallic-sheathed cable or ENT installed through metal framing members, a steel sleeve, steel plate, or steel clip not less than ______ in thickness shall be used to protect the cable or tubing.

    (a) ¹⁄₁₆ in.
    (b) ⅛ in.
    (c) ½ in.
    (d) ¾ in.

11. Where cables and nonmetallic raceways are installed parallel to framing members, the nearest outside surface of the cable or raceway shall be ______ the nearest edge of the framing member where nails or screws are likely to penetrate.

    (a) not less than 1¼ in. from
    (b) immediately adjacent to
    (c) not less than ¹⁄₁₆ in. from
    (d) 90 degrees away from

12. A cable, raceway, or box installed under metal-corrugated sheet roof decking shall be supported so the top of the cable, raceway, or box is not less than ______ from the lowest surface of the roof decking to the top of the cable, raceway, or box.

    (a) ½ in.
    (b) 1 in.
    (c) 1½ in.
    (d) 2 in.

13. When installed under metal-corrugated sheet roof decking, ______ and intermediate metal conduit, with listed steel or malleable iron fittings and boxes, shall not be required to comply with 300.4(E).

    (a) rigid metal conduit
    (b) electrical metallic tubing
    (c) Schedule 80 PVC
    (d) all of these

14. Where electrical equipment is installed under metal-corrugated sheet roof decking, the 1½-in. spacing is not required where metal-corrugated sheet roof decking is covered with a concrete slab with a minimum thickness of ______, measured from the top of the corrugated roofing.

    (a) ½ in.
    (b) 1 in.
    (c) 1½ in.
    (d) 2 in.

15. Conduit bushings installed to protect insulated conductors ______ or larger contained within raceways that are constructed wholly of insulating material, shall not be used to secure a fitting or raceway.

    (a) 4 AWG
    (b) 6 AWG
    (c) 8 AWG
    (d) 10 AWG

16. Where raceways contain 4 AWG or larger insulated circuit conductors and these conductors enter a cabinet, a box, an enclosure, or a raceway the conductors shall be protected from abrasion during and after installation by an identified fitting providing a smoothly rounded ______ surface.

    (a) fiberglass
    (b) plastic
    (c) insulating
    (d) gray

17. Where raceways contain 4 AWG or larger insulated circuit conductors and these conductors enter a cabinet, a box, an enclosure, or a raceway the conductors shall be protected from abrasion during and after installation by ______.

    (a) an identified fitting that provides a smooth rounded insulating surface
    (b) a listed metal fitting that has smooth rounded edges
    (c) threaded hubs that provide a smooth rounded or flared entry
    (d) any of these

18. A listed expansion/deflection fitting or other approved means shall be used where a raceway crosses a ______ intended for expansion, contraction, or deflection used in buildings, bridges, parking garages, or other structures.

    (a) junction box
    (b) structural joint
    (c) cable tray
    (d) Unistrut® hanger

19. The minimum cover requirement for UF cable that supplies a 120V, 30A circuit is ______.

    (a) 2 in.
    (b) 4 in.
    (c) 6 in.
    (d) 12 in.

20. Electrical metallic tubing that is directly buried under a two-family dwelling driveway shall have at least ______ of cover.

    (a) 6 in.
    (b) 12 in.
    (c) 18 in.
    (d) 24 in.

21. Rigid metal conduit that is directly buried outdoors shall have at least ______ of cover.

    (a) 6 in.
    (b) 12 in.
    (c) 18 in.
    (d) 24 in.

22. When installing PVC underground without concrete cover, there shall be a minimum of ______ of cover.

    (a) 6 in.
    (b) 12 in.
    (c) 18 in.
    (d) 24 in.

23. A PVC raceway covered in 2 in. of concrete is required to have a minimal buried depth of ______.

    (a) 6 in.
    (b) 12 in.
    (c) 18 in.
    (d) 24 in.

24. The minimum cover requirement for UF cable that supplies a 120V, 15A GFCI-protected circuit under a driveway of a one-family dwelling is ______.

    (a) 6 in.
    (b) 12 in.
    (c) 16 in.
    (d) 24 in.

25. For a dwelling location, direct buried cables that are GFCI protected at no more than 20A shall have a cover of ______.

    (a) 6 in.
    (b) 12 in.
    (c) 18 in.
    (d) 24 in.

26. UF cable used with a 24V landscape lighting system can have a minimum cover of ______.

    (a) 6 in.
    (b) 12 in.
    (c) 18 in.
    (d) 24 in.

27. ______ shall be defined as the shortest distance measured between a point on the top surface of direct-buried cable and the top surface of finished grade.

    (a) Notched
    (b) Cover
    (c) Gap
    (d) Spacing

28. The interior of underground raceways shall be considered a ______ location.

    (a) wet
    (b) dry
    (c) damp
    (d) corrosive

29. Underground cable and conductors installed under a building shall be ______.

    (a) in the same trench
    (b) in a raceway
    (c) encased in concrete
    (d) under at least 2 in. of concrete

30. MC Cable ______ for direct burial or concrete encasement shall be permitted under a building without installation in a raceway in accordance with 330.10(A)(5).

    (a) listed
    (b) identified
    (c) tagged
    (d) labeled

31. Where direct-buried conductors and cables emerge from grade, they shall be protected by enclosures or raceways to a point at least ______ above finished grade.

    (a) 3 ft
    (b) 6 ft
    (c) 8 ft
    (d) 10 ft

32. Direct-buried service conductors that are not encased in concrete and that are buried 18 in. or more below grade shall have their location identified by a warning ribbon placed in the trench at least ______ above the underground installation.

    (a) 6 in.
    (b) 10 in.
    (c) 12 in.
    (d) 18 in.

33. ______ conductors or cables can be spliced or tapped without the use of splice boxes when the splice or tap is made in accordance with 110.14(B).

    (a) Direct-buried
    (b) Wet location
    (c) Ungrounded
    (d) Grounded

34. Backfill used for underground wiring shall not damage ______ or prevent adequate compaction of fill or contribute to corrosion.

    (a) raceways
    (b) cables
    (c) conductors
    (d) any of these

35. Conduits or raceways through which moisture might contact live parts shall be ______ at either or both ends.

    (a) crimped
    (b) taped
    (c) bushed
    (d) sealed or plugged

36. A(An) ______, with an integral bushed opening shall be used at the end of a conduit or other raceway that terminates underground where the conductors or cables emerge as a direct burial wiring method.

    (a) splice kit
    (b) connector
    (c) adapter
    (d) bushing or terminal fitting

37. All conductors of the same circuit shall be ______, unless otherwise specifically permitted in the *Code*.

    (a) bonded
    (b) grounded
    (c) the same size
    (d) in the same raceway or cable or be in close proximity in the same trench

38. Direct-buried conductors, cables, or raceways which are subject to movement by settlement or frost shall be arranged to prevent damage to the ______ or to equipment connected to the raceways.

    (a) cable
    (b) raceway
    (c) enclosed conductors
    (d) expansion fitting

39. Raceways, cable trays, cablebus, auxiliary gutters, cable armor, boxes, cable sheathing, cabinets, enclosures (other than surrounding fences and walls), elbows, couplings, fittings, supports, and support hardware shall be of materials suitable for ______.

    (a) corrosive locations
    (b) wet locations
    (c) the environment in which they are to be installed
    (d) damp locations

40. Where corrosion protection is necessary and the conduit is threaded anywhere other than at the factory where the product is listed, the threads shall be coated with a(an) ______ electrically conductive, corrosion-resistant compound.

    (a) marked
    (b) listed
    (c) labeled
    (d) approved

41. Where portions of cable raceways or sleeves are required to be sealed due to different temperatures, sealants shall be identified for use with ______, a bare conductor, a shield, or other components.

    (a) low temperature conditions
    (b) high temperature conditions
    (c) a stranded conductor
    (d) cable insulation or conductor insulation

42. Raceways shall be provided with expansion, expansion-deflection, or deflection fittings where necessary to compensate for thermal expansion, deflection, and ______.

    (a) contraction
    (b) warping
    (c) bending
    (d) cracking

43. Where raceways are installed in wet locations above grade, the interior of these raceways shall be considered a ______ location.

    (a) wet
    (b) dry
    (c) damp
    (d) corrosive

44. Metal raceways, cable armor, and other metal enclosures shall be ______ joined together into a continuous electric conductor so as to provide effective electrical continuity.

    (a) electrically
    (b) permanently
    (c) metallically
    (d) physically

45. Raceways, cable assemblies, boxes, cabinets, and fittings shall be ______ fastened in place.

    (a) securely
    (b) supported and
    (c) approved as
    (d) none of these

46. Where independent support wires of a suspended ceiling assembly are used to support raceways, cable assemblies, or boxes above a ceiling, they shall be secured at ______ end(s).

    (a) one
    (b) both
    (c) the line and load
    (d) at the attachment to the structural member

47. Wiring located within the cavity of a fire-rated floor-ceiling or roof-ceiling assembly shall not be secured to, or supported by, the ceiling assembly, including the ceiling support ______.

    (a) wires
    (b) hangers
    (c) rods
    (d) none of these

48. Raceways may be used as a means of support where the raceway contains power-supply conductors for electrically controlled equipment and is used to ______ Class 2 or Class 3 circuit conductors or cables that are solely for the purpose of connection to the equipment control circuits.

    (a) support
    (b) secure
    (c) strap
    (d) none of these

49. Cable wiring methods shall not be used as a means of support for ______.

    (a) other cables
    (b) raceways
    (c) nonelectrical equipment
    (d) any of these

50. Raceways, cable armors, and cable sheaths shall be ______ between cabinets, boxes, conduit bodies, fittings, or other enclosures or outlets.

    (a) continuous
    (b) protected
    (c) buried
    (d) encased in concrete

51. Mechanical continuity of raceways, cable armors, and cable sheaths as required by 300.12 does not apply to ______.

    (a) MI Cable
    (b) MC Cable
    (c) short sections of raceways used for support or protection of cable assemblies
    (d) any of these

52. Conductors in raceways shall be ______ between outlets, boxes, devices, and so forth.

    (a) continuous
    (b) installed
    (c) copper
    (d) in conduit

53. Where the opening to an outlet, junction, or switch point is less than 8 in. in any dimension, the length of free conductor of each conductor, spliced or unspliced, shall extend at least ______ outside the opening of the enclosure.

    (a) 1 in.
    (b) 3 in.
    (c) 6 in.
    (d) 12 in.

54. Fittings and connectors shall be used only with the specific wiring methods for which they are ______ and listed.

    (a) designed
    (b) identified
    (c) marked
    (d) labeled

55. A box or conduit body shall not be required for splices and taps in ______ conductors and cables as long as the splice is made with a splicing device that is identified for the purpose.

    (a) direct-buried
    (b) exposed
    (c) concealed
    (d) none of these

Article 310—Conductors for General Wiring

1. The minimum size copper conductor permitted for voltage ratings up to 2,000V is ______.

    (a) 14 AWG
    (b) 12 AWG
    (c) 10 AWG
    (d) 8 AWG

2. Solid aluminum conductors of 8 AWG, 10 AWG, and 12 AWG shall be made of an AA-______ series electrical grade aluminum alloy conductor material.

    (a) 1,350
    (b) 2,000
    (c) 6,000
    (d) 8,000

3. Stranded aluminum conductors 8 AWG through 1,000 kcmil marked as ______ shall be made of an AA-8000 series electrical grade aluminum alloy conductor material.

    (a) UF
    (b) NM
    (c) NMC
    (d) SE

4. The ______ core of a copper-clad aluminum conductor shall be made of an AA-8000 series electrical grade aluminum alloy conductor material.

    (a) aluminum
    (b) copper
    (c) steel
    (d) iron

5. Conductors in Article 300 shall be of copper, aluminum, or copper-clad aluminum, unless otherwise specified. Copper-clad aluminum conductor material shall be ______.

    (a) identified for the use
    (b) listed
    (c) indicated as suitable
    (d) approved

6. Where installed in raceways, conductors ______ and larger shall be stranded, unless specifically permitted or required elsewhere in the *NEC*.

    (a) 10 AWG
    (b) 8 AWG
    (c) 6 AWG
    (d) 4 AWG

7. Conductors for general wiring not specifically permitted elsewhere in this *Code* to be covered or bare shall ______.

    (a) not be permitted
    (b) be insulated
    (c) be rated
    (d) be listed

8. Insulated conductors with the letters HH in their designation have a ______ insulation rating in a dry location.

    (a) 60°C
    (b) 75°C
    (c) 90°C
    (d) 110°C

9. Insulated conductors with letter designation of ______, are permitted in a wet location with a maximum operating temperature of 90°C.

    (a) USE
    (b) RHW
    (c) XHWN
    (d) THWN-2

10. Conductors with TW insulation have a temperature rating of ______.

    (a) 60°C
    (b) 75°C
    (c) 90°C
    (d) 110°C

11. The insulation of USE-2 cable is ______ resistant.

    (a) heat
    (b) moisture
    (c) sunlight
    (d) heat and moisture

12. Conductors that are intended for use as ungrounded conductors, whether used as a single conductor or in multiconductor cables, shall be finished to be clearly distinguishable from ______ conductors.

    (a) grounded
    (b) ungrounded
    (c) equipment grounding
    (d) grounded and equipment grounding

13. The conductors described in 310.4 shall be permitted for use in any of the ______ covered in Chapter 3 and as specified in their respective tables or as permitted elsewhere in this *Code*.

    (a) wiring methods
    (b) cables
    (c) conduits
    (d) tubing

14. Insulated conductors and cables used in ______ shall be any of the types identified in this *Code*.

    (a) dry and damp locations
    (b) dry locations
    (c) damp locations
    (d) wet and damp locations

15. Insulated conductors and cables used in ______ shall be Types FEP, FEPB, MTW, PFA, RHH, RHW, RHW-2, SA, THHN, THW, THW-2, THHW, THWN, THWN-2, TW, XHH, XHHW, XHHW-2, XHHN, XHWN, XHWN-2, Z, or ZW.

    (a) dry and damp locations
    (b) dry locations
    (c) damp locations
    (d) wet and damp locations

16. Insulated conductors and cables used in wet locations shall be ______.

    (a) moisture-impervious metal-sheathed
    (b) types MTW, RHW, RHW-2, TW, THW, THW-2, THHW, THWN, THWN-2, XHHW, XHHW-2, XHWN, XHWN-2 or ZW
    (c) of a type listed for use in wet locations
    (d) any of these

Article 312—Cabinets, Cutout Boxes, And Meter Enclosures

1. Article ______ covers the installation and construction specifications of cabinets, cutout boxes, and meter socket enclosures.

    (a) 300
    (b) 310
    (c) 312
    (d) 314

2. Cabinets, cutout boxes, and meter socket enclosures installed in wet locations shall be ______.

    (a) waterproof
    (b) raintight
    (c) weatherproof
    (d) watertight

3. In walls constructed of wood or other ______ material, electrical cabinets shall be flush with the finished surface or project therefrom.

    (a) nonconductive
    (b) porous
    (c) fibrous
    (d) combustible

4. Noncombustible surfaces that are broken or incomplete shall be repaired so there will be no gaps or open spaces greater than ______ at the edge of a cabinet or cutout box employing a flush-type cover.

(a) ⅟₃₂ in.
(b) ⅟₁₆ in.
(c) ⅛ in.
(d) ¼ in.

5. Where cable is used, each cable shall be ______ to the cabinet, cutout box, or meter socket enclosure.

(a) secured
(b) supported
(c) strapped
(d) stapled

6. Nonmetallic-sheathed cables can enter the top of surface-mounted cabinets, cutout boxes, and meter socket enclosures through nonflexible raceways not less than 18 in. and not more than ______ in length if all of the required conditions are met.

(a) 3 ft
(b) 10 ft
(c) 25 ft
(d) 100 ft

Article 314—Boxes, Conduit Bodies, and Handhole Enclosures

1. The installation and use of all boxes and conduit bodies used as outlet, device, junction, or pull boxes, depending on their use, and handhole enclosures, are covered within ______.

(a) Article 110
(b) Article 200
(c) Article 300
(d) Article 314

2. Nonmetallic boxes can be used with ______.

(a) nonmetallic sheaths
(b) nonmetallic raceways
(c) flexible cords
(d) all of these

3. Where internal ______ means are provided between all entries, nonmetallic boxes shall be permitted to be used with metal raceways or metal-armored cables.

(a) grounding
(b) bonding
(c) connecting
(d) splicing

4. Metal boxes shall be ______ in accordance with Article 250.

(a) grounded
(b) bonded
(c) secured
(d) grounded and bonded

5. Boxes, conduit bodies, and fittings installed in wet locations shall be listed for use in ______ locations.

(a) wet
(b) damp
(c) dry
(d) corrosive

6. Boxes and conduit bodies shall be of an approved size to provide free space for all enclosed ______.

(a) conductors
(b) splices
(c) terminations
(d) all of these

7. According to the *NEC*, the volume of a 3 in. × 2 in. × 2 in. device box for conductor fill is ______.

(a) 8 cu in.
(b) 10 cu in.
(c) 12 cu in.
(d) 14 cu in.

8. A metal box sized ______ can accommodate nine 12 AWG conductors.

(a) 4 in. × 4 in. × 1¼ in.
(b) 3¾ in. × 2 in. × 3 in.
(c) 3¾ in. × 2 in. × 3½ in.
(d) none of these

9. The number of 12 THWN-2 conductors permitted in a 4 × 4 × 1½ box is ______.

(a) 7
(b) 9
(c) 11
(d) 13

10. The total volume occupied by one 12/3 NM cable, one 12/2 NM cable, two internal cable clamps, and a single-pole switch is ______.
    - (a) 2.00 cu in.
    - (b) 4.50 cu in.
    - (c) 14.50 cu in.
    - (d) 20.25 cu in.

11. When counting the number of conductors in a box, a conductor running through the box with an unbroken loop or coil not less than twice the minimum length required for free conductors shall be counted as ______ double volume(s) allowance.
    - (a) one
    - (b) two
    - (c) three
    - (d) four

12. Equipment grounding conductor(s), and not more than ______ fixture wire(s) smaller than 14 AWG is(are) permitted to be omitted from the calculations where they enter the box from a domed luminaire or similar canopy and terminate within that box.
    - (a) one
    - (b) two
    - (c) three
    - (d) four

13. Where one or more internal cable clamps are present in the box, a single volume allowance shall be made based on the ______ present in the box.
    - (a) largest conductor
    - (b) smallest conductor
    - (c) average conductor size
    - (d) number of devices

14. Where a luminaire stud or hickey is present in the box, ______ volume allowance shall be made for each type of fitting, based on the largest conductor present in the box.
    - (a) a single
    - (b) a double
    - (c) a ¼
    - (d) no additional

15. For the purposes of determining box fill, each device or utilization equipment in the box which is wider than a single device box counts as two volume allowances for each ______ required for the mounting.
    - (a) in.
    - (b) ft
    - (c) gang
    - (d) box

16. A device or utilization equipment wider than a single 2 in. device box shall have ______ volume allowance provided for each gang required for mounting.
    - (a) a single
    - (b) a double
    - (c) a ¼
    - (d) no additional

17. Where up to four equipment grounding conductors enter a box, ______ volume allowance in accordance with Table 314.16(B) shall be made based on the largest equipment grounding conductor entering the box.
    - (a) a single
    - (b) a double
    - (c) a ¼
    - (d) no additional

18. Conduit bodies that are durably and legibly marked by the manufacturer with their ______ can contain splices, taps, or devices.
    - (a) volume
    - (b) size
    - (c) rating
    - (d) capacity

19. Where cable assemblies with nonmetallic sheaths are used, the sheath shall extend not less than ______ inside the box and beyond any cable clamp.
    - (a) ¼ in.
    - (b) ⅜ in.
    - (c) ½ in.
    - (d) ¾ in.

20. In installations within noncombustible walls or ceilings, the front edge of a box, plaster ring, extension ring, or listed extender employing a flush-type cover, shall be set back not more than ______ from the finished surface.
    (a) ⅛ in.
    (b) ¼ in.
    (c) ⅜ in.
    (d) ½ in.

21. Noncombustible surfaces that are broken or incomplete around boxes employing a flush-type cover shall be repaired so there will be no gaps or open spaces larger than ______ at the edge of the box.
    (a) ¹⁄₁₆ in.
    (b) ⅛ in.
    (c) ¼ in.
    (d) ½ in.

22. An outlet box or enclosure mounted on a building or other surface shall be ______.
    (a) rigidly and securely fastened in place
    (b) supported by cables that protrude from the box
    (c) supported by cable entries from the top and permitted to rest against the supporting surface
    (d) permitted to be supported by the raceway(s) terminating at the box

23. In accordance with Article 314, metal braces used for the support of boxes shall be protected against ______.
    (a) corrosion
    (b) weather
    (c) rain
    (d) snow

24. A wood brace used for supporting a box for structural mounting shall have a cross-section not less than nominal ______.
    (a) 1 in. × 2 in.
    (b) 2 in. × 2 in.
    (c) 2 in. × 3 in.
    (d) 2 in. × 4 in.

25. When mounting an enclosure in a finished surface, the enclosure shall be ______ secured to the surface by clamps, anchors, or fittings identified for the application.
    (a) temporarily
    (b) partially
    (c) never
    (d) rigidly

26. Outlet boxes can be secured to suspended-ceiling framing members by mechanical means such as ______, or by other means identified for use with the suspended-ceiling framing member(s).
    (a) bolts
    (b) screws
    (c) rivets
    (d) any of these

27. Support wire(s) used for enclosure support in suspended ceilings shall be fastened at ______ so as to be taut within the ceiling cavity.
    (a) each end
    (b) each corner
    (c) each ceiling support
    (d) the ceiling grid

28. Enclosures not over 100 cu in. having threaded entries and not containing a device shall be considered to be supported where ______ or more conduits are threaded wrenchtight into the enclosure and each conduit is secured within 3 ft of the enclosure.
    (a) one
    (b) two
    (c) three
    (d) four

29. Two intermediate metal or rigid metal conduits threaded wrenchtight into an enclosure can be used to support an outlet box containing devices or luminaires if each raceway is supported within ______ of the box.
    (a) 12 in.
    (b) 18 in.
    (c) 24 in.
    (d) 36 in.

30. A pendant box shall be supported from a multiconductor cord or cable in an approved manner that protects the conductors against strain. A connection to a box equipped with a hub shall be made with a(an) ______ cord grip attachment fitting marked for use with a threaded hub.
    (a) approved
    (b) listed
    (c) marked
    (d) identified

31. Underground ______ shall be installed so they are accessible without excavating sidewalks, paving, earth, or other substance that is to be used to establish the finished grade.

    (a) boxes and handhole enclosures
    (b) conduit bodies
    (c) handhole enclosures
    (d) none of these

32. Handhole enclosures shall be designed and installed to withstand ______.

    (a) 600 lb of pressure
    (b) 3,000 lb of pressure
    (c) 6,000 lb of pressure
    (d) all loads likely to be imposed on them

33. Underground raceways and cable assemblies entering a handhole enclosure shall extend into the enclosure, but they are not required to be ______.

    (a) bonded
    (b) insulated
    (c) mechanically connected to the enclosure
    (d) electrically connected to the enclosure

34. Conductors, splices, or terminations in a handhole enclosure shall be listed as suitable for ______.

    (a) wet locations
    (b) damp locations
    (c) direct burial in the earth
    (d) exterior use

35. Handhole enclosure covers shall have an identifying mark or logo that prominently identifies the function of the enclosure, such as ______.

    (a) danger
    (b) utility
    (c) high voltage
    (d) electric

36. Handhole enclosure covers shall require the use of tools to open, or they shall weigh over ______.

    (a) 45 lb
    (b) 70 lb
    (c) 100 lb
    (d) 200 lb

Article 320—Armored Cable (Type AC)

1. Article ______ covers the use, installation, and construction specifications for armored cable.

    (a) 300
    (b) 310
    (c) 320
    (d) 334

2. AC cable is permitted in ______.

    (a) wet locations
    (b) corrosive conditions
    (c) damp locations
    (d) cable trays

3. Armored cable shall not be installed ______.

    (a) in damp or wet locations
    (b) where subject to physical damage
    (c) where exposed to corrosive conditions
    (d) all of these

4. Exposed runs of AC cable can be installed on the underside of joists where supported at each joist and located so it is not subject to physical damage.

    (a) physical damage
    (b) severe damage
    (c) minor damage
    (d) any of these

5. Where AC cable is run across the top of a framing member(s) in an attic space not accessible by permanently installed stairs or ladders, guard strip protection shall only be required within ______ of the scuttle hole or attic entrance.

    (a) 3 ft
    (b) 4 ft
    (c) 5 ft
    (d) 6 ft

6. AC cable shall be supported and/or secured by ______.

    (a) staples or straps
    (b) cable ties listed and identified for securement and support
    (c) AC cable fittings
    (d) any of these

7. AC cable fittings shall not be permitted as a means of cable support.

    (a) True
    (b) False

8. AC cable shall be secured at intervals not exceeding 4½ ft and within ______ of every outlet box, cabinet, conduit body, or fitting.

    (a) 6 in.
    (b) 8 in.
    (c) 10 in.
    (d) 12 in.

9. Horizontal runs of AC cable installed in wooden or metal framing members or similar supporting means shall be considered supported and secured where such support does not exceed ______ intervals.

    (a) 2-ft
    (b) 3-ft
    (c) 4½-ft
    (d) 6-ft

10. Armored cable used to connect recessed luminaires or equipment within an accessible ceiling can be unsupported and unsecured for lengths up to ______.

    (a) 2 ft
    (b) 3 ft
    (c) 4½ ft
    (d) 6 ft

Article 330—Metal-Clad Cable (Type MC)

1. Article ______ covers the use, installation, and construction specifications of metal-clad cable, MC.

    (a) 300
    (b) 310
    (c) 320
    (d) 330

2. MC cable shall be permitted for ______.

    (a) branch circuits
    (b) feeders
    (c) services
    (d) any of these

3. MC cable is permitted for use in damp or wet locations where a corrosion-resistant jacket is provided over the metallic covering and ______.

    (a) the metallic covering is impervious to moisture.
    (b) a jacket resistant to moisture is provided under the metal covering.
    (c) the insulated conductors under the metallic covering are listed for use in wet locations.
    (d) any of these

4. MC cable shall not be used ______.

    (a) where subject to physical damage
    (b) direct buried in the earth or embedded in concrete unless identified for direct burial
    (c) exposed to cinder fills, strong chlorides, caustic alkalis, or vapors of chlorine or of hydrochloric acids
    (d) all of these

5. Exposed runs of MC cable, except as provided in 300.11(B), shall closely follow the surface of the ______.

    (a) building finish
    (b) running boards
    (c) underside of joists
    (d) any of these

6. MC cable shall be supported and secured by staples; cable ties ______ for securement and support; straps, hangers, or similar fittings; or other approved means designed and installed so as not to damage the cable.

    (a) listed and identified
    (b) marked or labeled
    (c) installed and approved
    (d) any of these

7. MC cable fittings shall be permitted as a means of cable support.

    (a) True
    (b) False

8. Unless otherwise permitted in the *Code*, MC cable shall be secured at intervals not exceeding ______.

    (a) 3 ft
    (b) 4 ft
    (c) 6 ft
    (d) 8 ft

9. MC cable containing four or fewer conductors, sized no larger than 10 AWG, shall be secured within ______ of every box, cabinet, fitting, or other cable termination.

    (a) 8 in.
    (b) 12 in.
    (c) 18 in.
    (d) 24 in.

10. Unless otherwise permitted in the *Code*, MC cable installed horizontally through wooden or metal framing members is considered secured and supported where such support does not exceed ______ intervals.

    (a) 3-ft
    (b) 4-ft
    (c) 6-ft
    (d) 8-ft

11. MC cable can be unsupported and unsecured where the cable is ______.

    (a) fished between access points through concealed spaces in finished buildings or structures
    (b) not more than 2 ft in length at terminals where flexibility is necessary
    (c) not more than 8 ft from the last point of support within an accessible ceiling
    (d) installed in attic spaces

Article 334—Nonmetallic-Sheathed Cable (Type NM)

1. NM and NMC cables are permitted in ______, except as prohibited in 334.12.

    (a) one- and two-family dwellings and their attached/detached garages and storage buildings
    (b) multifamily dwellings and their detached garages permitted to be of Types III, IV, and V construction
    (c) other structures permitted to be of Types III, IV, and V construction
    (d) any of these

2. NM cable can be installed in multifamily dwellings and their detached garages permitted to be of Type(s) ______ construction.

    (a) III
    (b) IV
    (c) V
    (d) all of these

3. NM cable shall not be permitted to be installed ______ in dropped or suspended ceilings in other than one- and two-family and multifamily dwellings.

    (a) concealed
    (b) exposed
    (c) open
    (d) hidden

4. NM cable shall not be used ______.

    (a) in other than dwelling units
    (b) in the air void of masonry block not subject to excessive moisture
    (c) for exposed work
    (d) embedded in poured cement, concrete, or aggregate

5. NM cable shall closely follow the ______ of the building finish or running boards when run exposed.

    (a) surface
    (b) edges
    (c) corners
    (d) none of these

6. NM cable shall be protected from physical damage by ______.

    (a) EMT
    (b) Schedule 80 PVC conduit
    (c) RMC
    (d) any of these

7. Where conduit or tubing is used for the protection from physical damage of NM cable, it shall be provided with a bushing or adapter that provides protection from abrasion at the point the cable ______ the raceway.

    (a) enters and exits
    (b) leaves and comes into
    (c) begins and ends
    (d) none of these

8. Where NM cable is run at angles with joists in unfinished basements and crawl spaces, it is permissible to secure cables not smaller than ______ conductors directly to the lower edges of the joist.

    (a) three, 6 AWG
    (b) four, 8 AWG
    (c) four, 10 AWG
    (d) two 6 AWG or three 8 AWG

9. NM cable on a wall of an unfinished basement installed in a listed raceway shall have a ______ installed at the point where the cable enters the raceway.

    (a) suitable insulating bushing or adapter
    (b) sealing fitting
    (c) bonding bushing
    (d) junction box

10. The sheath on nonmetallic-sheathed cable shall extend not less than ______ beyond any cable clamp or cable entry.

    (a) ⅛ in.
    (b) ¼ in.
    (c) ⅜ in.
    (d) ½ in.

11. When NM cable is run across the top of a floor joist in an attic without permanent ladders or stairs, guard strips within ______ of the scuttle hole or attic entrance shall protect the cable.

    (a) 3 ft
    (b) 4 ft
    (c) 5 ft
    (d) 6 ft

12. NM cable can be supported and secured by ______.

    (a) staples
    (b) cable ties listed and identified for securement and support
    (c) straps
    (d) any of these

13. Flat NM cables shall not be stapled on edge.

    (a) True
    (b) False

14. Nonmetallic-sheathed cable shall be permitted to be unsupported where the cable is ______.

    (a) fished between access points through concealed spaces in finished buildings or structures
    (b) not more than 6 ft from the last point of cable support to the point of connection to a luminaire within an accessible ceiling in one-, two-, or multifamily dwellings
    (c) between framing members and exterior masonry walls
    (d) where installed in attics

15. A box is not required for NM cable where used with ______.

    (a) self-contained switches
    (b) self-contained receptacles
    (c) listed nonmetallic-sheathed cable interconnector devices
    (d) any of these

Article 336—Power and Control Tray Cable (Type TC)

1. Article ______ covers the use, installation, and construction specifications for power and control tray cable, TC.

    (a) 326
    (b) 330
    (c) 334
    (d) 336

2. TC cable can be used ______.

    (a) for power, lighting, control, and signal circuits
    (b) in cable trays including those with mechanically discontinuous segments up to 1 ft
    (c) for Class 1 control circuits as permitted in Parts II and III of Article 725
    (d) all of these

3. TC-ER-JP cable shall be permitted for ______ in one- and two-family dwelling units.

    (a) branch circuits
    (b) feeders
    (c) branch circuits and feeders
    (d) service conductors

4. Where TC-ER-JP cable is used to connect a generator and associated equipment having terminals rated ______ or higher, the cable shall not be limited in ampacity by 334.80 or 340.80.

    (a) 60°C
    (b) 75°C
    (c) 90°C
    (d) 100°C

5. TC cable shall be permitted to be direct buried, where ______ for such use.

    (a) identified
    (b) approved
    (c) listed
    (d) labeled

6. TC cable shall be permitted for use in hazardous (classified) locations where specifically ______ by other articles in this *Code*.

    (a) required
    (b) permitted
    (c) approved
    (d) identified

7. Which of following statements about power and control tray cable is incorrect?

    (a) It may be used in a raceway.
    (b) It may be used for power, lighting, or control circuits.
    (c) It may be installed where it will be exposed to physical damage.
    (d) It may be used in cable trays in hazardous locations where the conditions of maintenance and supervision ensure that only qualified persons will service the installation.

8. TC cable shall not be used where ______.

    (a) it will be exposed to physical damage
    (b) installed outside of a raceway or cable tray system, unless permitted in 336.10(4), 336.10(7), 336.10(9), and 336.10(10)
    (c) exposed to direct rays of the sun, unless identified as sunlight resistant
    (d) all of these

Article 338—Service-Entrance Cable (Types SE and USE)

1. ______ cable can be used for interior wiring as long as it complies with the installation requirements of Part II of Article 334, excluding 334.80.

    (a) SE
    (b) UF
    (c) MI
    (d) FCC

2. Where more than two SE cables are installed in contact with thermal insulation, caulk, or sealing foam without maintaining spacing between cables, the ampacity of each conductor shall be ______ in accordance with Table 310.15(C)(1).

    (a) increased
    (b) adjusted
    (c) corrected
    (d) multiplied

3. For interior installations of SE cable with ungrounded conductor sizes ______ and smaller, where installed in thermal insulation, the ampacity shall be in accordance with 60°C (140°F) conductor temperature rating.

    (a) 14 AWG
    (b) 12 AWG
    (c) 10 AWG
    (d) 8 AWG

4. USE cable is not permitted for ______ wiring.

    (a) underground
    (b) interior
    (c) aerial
    (d) aboveground installations

Article 340—Underground Feeder and Branch-Circuit Cable (Type UF)

1. Article 340 covers the use, installation, and construction specifications for underground feeder and branch-circuit cable, ______.

    (a) USE
    (b) UF
    (c) UFC
    (d) NMC

2. A permitted wiring method for use in underground installations is ______.

    (a) SE cable
    (b) UF cable
    (c) THHN in PVC conduit
    (d) NM in a raceway

3. UF cable is permitted to be installed as single-conductor cables, when all conductors of the feeder or branch circuit, including the grounded conductor and equipment grounding conductor, if any, are ______.

    (a) run in the same trench
    (b) within a nonmetallic raceway
    (c) within a metallic raceway
    (d) none of these

4. UF cable can be used as service entrance cable.

    (a) True
    (b) False

5. UF cable can be used in commercial garages.

    (a) True
    (b) False

6. UF cable shall not be used in ______.

    (a) motion picture studios
    (b) storage battery rooms
    (c) hoistways
    (d) all of these

7. UF cable shall not be used ______.

    (a) in any hazardous (classified) location except as otherwise permitted in this *Code*
    (b) embedded in poured cement, concrete, or aggregate
    (c) where exposed to direct rays of the sun, unless identified as sunlight resistant
    (d) all of these

8. UF cable shall not be used where subject to physical damage.

    (a) True
    (b) False

Article 342—Intermediate Metal Conduit (IMC)

1. Article ______ covers the use, installation, and construction specifications for intermediate metal conduit (IMC) and associated fittings.

    (a) 342
    (b) 348
    (c) 352
    (d) 356

2. IMC, elbows, couplings, and fittings shall be permitted to be installed in concrete, in direct contact with the earth, in direct burial applications, or in areas subject to severe corrosive influences where protected by corrosion protection ______ for the condition.

    (a) identified
    (b) approved
    (c) listed
    (d) suitable

3. IMC conduit shall be permitted to be installed where subject to ______ physical damage.

    (a) severe
    (b) minor
    (c) minimal
    (d) massive

4. Where practicable, contact of dissimilar metals shall be avoided in an IMC raceway installation to prevent the possibility of ______.

    (a) corrosion
    (b) galvanic action
    (c) short circuits
    (d) ground faults

5. The total degrees of bends in a run of IMC shall not exceed ______ between pull points.

    (a) 120 degrees
    (b) 180 degrees
    (c) 270 degrees
    (d) 360 degrees

6. Where intermediate metal conduit is threaded in the field, a standard cutting die with a taper of ______ per ft shall be used.

    (a) ½ in.
    (b) ¾ in.
    (c) 1 in.
    (d) 1½ in.

7. IMC shall be secured ______.

    (a) by fastening within 3 ft of each outlet box, junction box, device box, cabinet, conduit body, or other conduit termination
    (b) within 5 ft of a box or termination fitting when structural members do not readily permit the raceway to be secured within 3 ft of the termination
    (c) except when the IMC is within 3 ft of the service head for an above-the-roof termination of a mast
    (d) any of these

8. Trade size 1 IMC run straight with threaded couplings shall be supported at intervals not exceeding ______.

    (a) 8 ft
    (b) 10 ft
    (c) 12 ft
    (d) 15 ft

9. Horizontal runs of IMC supported by openings through framing members at intervals not exceeding ______ and securely fastened within 3 ft of terminations shall be permitted.

    (a) 5 ft
    (b) 8 ft
    (c) 10 ft
    (d) 15 ft

10. Threadless couplings approved for use with IMC in wet locations shall be ______.

    (a) rainproof
    (b) listed for wet locations
    (c) moistureproof
    (d) concrete-tight

11. Running threads shall not be used on IMC for connection at
    ______.

    (a) couplings
    (b) terminal adapters
    (c) enclosures
    (d) threadless connectors

12. Where IMC enters a box, fitting, or other enclosure, ______ shall
    be provided to protect the wire from abrasion unless the design
    of the box, fitting, or enclosure affords equivalent protection.

    (a) a bushing
    (b) duct seal
    (c) electrical tape
    (d) seal fittings

Article 344—Rigid Metal Conduit (RMC)

1. Article 344 covers the use, installation, and construction specifications for ______ conduit and associated fittings.

   (a) intermediate metal
   (b) rigid metal
   (c) electrical metallic
   (d) aluminum metal

2. RMC and fittings are permitted to be installed in concrete, in
   direct contact with the earth, in direct burial applications, or
   in areas subject to severe corrosive influences when protected
   by ______ approved for the condition.

   (a) ceramic
   (b) corrosion protection
   (c) backfill
   (d) a natural barrier

3. All supports, bolts, straps, screws, and so forth, associated
   with the installation of RMC in wet locations shall be ______.

   (a) weatherproof
   (b) made of stainless steel
   (c) made of aluminum
   (d) protected against corrosion

4. RMC conduit shall be permitted to be installed where subject
   to ______ physical damage.

   (a) severe
   (b) minor
   (c) minimal
   (d) massive

5. Stainless steel and aluminum fittings and enclosures shall be
   permitted to be used with galvanized steel RMC, and galvanized
   steel fittings and enclosures shall be permitted to be used with
   aluminum RMC where not subject to ______.

   (a) physical damage
   (b) severe corrosive influences
   (c) excessive moisture
   (d) all of these

6. The total degrees of bends in a run of RMC shall not exceed
   ______ between pull points.

   (a) 120 degrees
   (b) 180 degrees
   (c) 270 degrees
   (d) 360 degrees

7. Cut ends of RMC shall be ______ or otherwise finished to
   remove rough edges.

   (a) threaded
   (b) reamed
   (c) painted
   (d) galvanized

8. PVC-coated RMC shall be ______ in accordance with manufacturer's instructions to prevent damage to the exterior coating.

   (a) threaded
   (b) cut
   (c) bent
   (d) none of these

9. RMC shall be securely fastened within ______ of each outlet
   box, junction box, device box, cabinet, conduit body, or other
   conduit termination.

   (a) 3 ft
   (b) 4 ft
   (c) 5 ft
   (d) 6 ft

10. Where framing members do not readily permit fastening, RMC
    may be fastened within ______ of each outlet box, junction box,
    device box, cabinet, conduit body, or other conduit termination.

    (a) 3 ft
    (b) 4 ft
    (c) 5 ft
    (d) 8 ft

11. Where approved, RMC shall not be required to be securely fastened within _______ of the service head for above-the-roof termination of a mast.

    (a) 1 ft
    (b) 2 ft
    (c) 3 ft
    (d) 5 ft

12. Trade size 2 MC run straight with threaded couplings shall be supported at intervals not exceeding _______.

    (a) 10 ft
    (b) 12 ft
    (c) 14 ft
    (d) 16 ft

13. The maximum distance between supports for a vertical installation of trade size 2 RMC is _______.

    (a) 16 ft
    (b) 10 ft
    (c) 20 ft
    (d) 18 ft

14. Horizontal runs of RMC supported by openings through _______ at intervals not exceeding 10 ft and securely fastened within 3 ft of termination points shall be permitted.

    (a) walls
    (b) trusses
    (c) rafters
    (d) framing members

15. Threadless couplings and connectors used with RMC buried in masonry or concrete shall be the _______ type.

    (a) raintight
    (b) wet and damp location
    (c) nonabsorbent
    (d) concrete tight

16. Threadless couplings and connectors used with RMC in wet locations shall be _______.

    (a) listed for wet locations
    (b) listed for damp locations
    (c) nonabsorbent
    (d) weatherproof

17. Running threads shall not be used on RMC for connection at _______.

    (a) boxes
    (b) cabinets
    (c) couplings
    (d) meter sockets

18. Where RMC enters a box, fitting, or other enclosure, _______ shall be provided to protect the wire from abrasion, unless the design of the box, fitting, or enclosure affords equivalent protection.

    (a) a bushing
    (b) duct seal
    (c) electrical tape
    (d) seal fittings

Article 348—Flexible Metal Conduit (FMC)

1. Article 348 covers the use, installation, and construction specifications for flexible metal conduit (FMC) and associated _______.

    (a) fittings
    (b) connections
    (c) terminations
    (d) devices

2. FMC shall be permitted to be used in exposed locations only.

    (a) True
    (b) False

3. FMC shall not be installed _______.

    (a) in wet locations
    (b) embedded in poured concrete
    (c) where subject to physical damage
    (d) all of these

4. Bends in FMC shall be made so that the conduit is not damaged and the internal diameter of the conduit is _______.

    (a) larger than $\frac{3}{8}$ in.
    (b) not effectively reduced
    (c) increased
    (d) larger than 1 in.

5. The total degrees of bends in a run of FMC _______ between pull points.

    (a) shall not be made
    (b) need not be limited (in degrees)
    (c) shall not exceed 360 degrees
    (d) shall not exceed 180 degrees

6. Cut ends of FMC shall be trimmed or otherwise finished to remove rough edges, except where fittings ______.

    (a) are the crimp-on type
    (b) thread into the convolutions
    (c) contain insulated throats
    (d) are listed for grounding

7. Flexible metal conduit shall be supported at intervals not exceeding ______.

    (a) 1 ft
    (b) 3 ft
    (c) 4½ ft
    (d) 6 ft

8. Cable ties used to securely fasten flexible metal conduit shall be ______ for securement and support.

    (a) approved
    (b) labeled
    (c) listed
    (d) listed and identified

9. Flexible metal conduit shall not be required to be ______ where fished between access points through concealed spaces in finished buildings or structures and supporting is impracticable.

    (a) fastened
    (b) strapped
    (c) complete
    (d) secured and supported

10. For flexible metal conduit, if flexibility is necessary after installation, unsecured lengths from the last point the raceway is securely fastened shall not exceed ______.

    (a) 3 ft for trade sizes ½ through 1¼
    (b) 4 ft for trade sizes 1½ through 2
    (c) 5 ft for trade sizes 2½ and larger
    (d) all of these

11. FMC to a luminaire or electrical equipment within an accessible ceiling is permitted to be unsupported for not more than ______ from the last point where the raceway is securely fastened, including securement and support by listed FMC fittings.

    (a) 3 ft
    (b) 5 ft
    (c) 6 ft
    (d) 8 ft

Article 350—Liquidtight Flexible Metal Conduit (LFMC)

1. The use, installation, and construction specifications for liquidtight flexible metal conduit (LFMC) and associated fittings are covered within Article ______.

    (a) 300
    (b) 334
    (c) 350
    (d) 410

2. The use of LFMC shall be permitted for direct burial where listed and ______ for the purpose.

    (a) marked
    (b) identified
    (c) labeled
    (d) approved

3. The minimum size liquid tight flexible metal conduit is ______.

    (a) trade size ⅜
    (b) trade size ½
    (c) trade size ¾
    (d) trade size 1

4. All cut ends of LFMC conduit shall be ______ inside and outside to remove rough edges.

    (a) sanded
    (b) trimmed
    (c) brushed
    (d) any of these

5. Liquidtight flexible metal conduit shall be securely fastened by a means approved by the authority having jurisdiction within ______ of termination.

    (a) 6 in.
    (b) 10 in.
    (c) 12 in.
    (d) 10 ft

6. Where used to securely fasten LFMC, cable ties shall be ______ for securement and support.

    (a) identified
    (b) labeled
    (c) marked
    (d) listed and identified

7. LFMC shall not be required to be secured or supported where fished between access points through _______ spaces in finished buildings or structures and supporting is impractical.

    (a) concealed
    (b) exposed
    (c) hazardous (classified)
    (d) completed

8. For liquidtight flexible metal conduit, if flexibility is necessary after installation, unsecured lengths from the last point the raceway is securely fastened shall not exceed _______.

    (a) 3 ft for trade sizes ½ through 1¼
    (b) 4 ft for trade sizes 1½ through 2
    (c) 5 ft for trade sizes 2½ and larger
    (d) all of these

Article 352—Rigid Polyvinyl Chloride Conduit (PVC)

1. Article 352 covers the use, installation, and construction specifications for _______ and associated fittings.

    (a) ENT
    (b) RMC
    (c) IMC
    (d) PVC

2. Extreme _______ may cause PVC conduit to become brittle, and therefore more susceptible to damage from physical contact.

    (a) sunlight
    (b) corrosive conditions
    (c) heat
    (d) cold

3. PVC conduit shall be permitted to be _______.

    (a) encased in concrete
    (b) used for the support of luminaires
    (c) installed in movie theaters
    (d) none of these

4. PVC conduit is permitted in locations subject to severe corrosive influences and where subject to chemicals for which the materials are specifically _______.

    (a) approved
    (b) identified
    (c) listed
    (d) non-hazardous

5. Schedule 40 PVC conduit shall be permitted for _______ work.

    (a) rough-in
    (b) exposed
    (c) airplane
    (d) automobile

6. Schedule _______ shall be permitted for exposed work where subject to physical damage.

    (a) 20 PVC conduit
    (b) 30 PVC conduit
    (c) 40 PVC conduit
    (d) 80 PVC conduit

7. All _______ PVC conduit fittings are suitable for connection to both Schedule 40 and Schedule 80 PVC conduit.

    (a) listed
    (b) marked
    (c) labeled
    (d) identified

8. PVC conduit shall not be used _______, unless specifically permitted.

    (a) in hazardous (classified) locations
    (b) for the support of luminaires or other equipment
    (c) where subject to physical damage unless it is Schedule 80
    (d) all of these

9. Field bends in PVC conduit shall be made only _______.

    (a) by hand forming the bend
    (b) with identified bending equipment
    (c) with a truck exhaust pipe
    (d) by use of an open flame torch

10. The total degrees of bends in a run of PVC shall not exceed _______ between pull points.

    (a) 120 degrees
    (b) 180 degrees
    (c) 270 degrees
    (d) 360 degrees

11. The _______ ends of PVC conduit shall be trimmed inside and outside to remove the burrs and rough edges.

    (a) cut
    (b) new
    (c) old
    (d) blunt

12. PVC conduit shall be securely fastened within _______ of each box.

    (a) ½ ft
    (b) 1 ft
    (c) 2 ft
    (d) 3 ft

13. PVC conduit trade sizes 1¼ to 2 shall be supported no greater than _______ between supports.

    (a) 3 ft
    (b) 4 ft
    (c) 5 ft
    (d) 6 ft

14. Expansion fittings for PVC conduit shall be provided to compensate for thermal expansion and contraction where the length change, in accordance with Table 352.44(A), is expected to be _______ or greater in a straight run between securely mounted items such as boxes, cabinets, elbows, or other conduit terminations.

    (a) ⅟₁₆ in.
    (b) ⅛ in.
    (c) ¼ in.
    (d) ½ in.

15. Expansion fittings for underground runs of direct buried PVC conduit emerging from the ground shall be provided above grade when required to compensate for _______.

    (a) earth settling
    (b) earth movement
    (c) frost heave
    (d) all of these

16. Where a PVC conduit enters a box, fitting, or other enclosure, a _______ or adapter shall be provided to protect the wire from abrasion unless the box, fitting, or enclosure design provides equivalent protection.

    (a) bushing
    (b) connector
    (c) coupling
    (d) insulator

Article 356—Liquidtight Flexible Nonmetallic Conduit (LFNC)

1. Article _______ covers the use, installation, and construction specifications for liquidtight flexible nonmetallic conduit (LFNC) and associated fittings.

    (a) 300
    (b) 334
    (c) 350
    (d) 356

2. LFNC shall be permitted for _______.

    (a) direct burial where listed and marked for the purpose
    (b) where flexibility is required for installation, operation, or maintenance
    (c) outdoors where listed and marked for this purpose
    (d) all of these

3. LFNC shall be permitted to be used exposed or concealed in locations subject to severe _______ influences or where subject to chemicals for which the materials are specifically approved.

    (a) corrosive
    (b) wet
    (c) dry
    (d) damp

4. Extreme cold can cause some types of liquidtight flexible nonmetallic conduit to become _______ and therefore more susceptible to damage from physical contact.

    (a) stiff
    (b) larger
    (c) weak
    (d) brittle

5. Liquidtight nonmetallic flexible conduit is not permitted to be used _______.

    (a) where subject to physical damage
    (b) where ambient and conductor temperatures exceed its listing
    (c) in lengths greater than 6 ft unless approved
    (d) all of these

6. Bends in LFNC shall be made so that the conduit will not be damaged and the internal diameter of the conduit will not be effectively reduced. Bends can be made _______.

    (a) manually without auxiliary equipment
    (b) with bending equipment identified for the purpose
    (c) with any kind of conduit bending tool that will work
    (d) by the use of an open flame torch

7. The total degrees of bends in a run of LFNC shall not exceed
   _______ between pull points.

   (a) 120 degrees
   (b) 180 degrees
   (c) 270 degrees
   (d) 360 degrees

8. Cable ties used to secure and support LFNC shall be _______
   for the application and for securing and supporting.

   (a) identified
   (b) labeled
   (c) listed
   (d) marked

9. Where LFNC conduit is installed in lengths exceeding _______,
   the conduit shall be securely fastened at intervals not exceeding
   3 ft and within 12 in. on each side of every outlet box, junction
   box, cabinet, or fitting.

   (a) 2 ft
   (b) 3 ft
   (c) 6 ft
   (d) 10 ft

10. Securing or supporting of LFNC is not required where installed
    in lengths not exceeding _______ from the last point where the
    raceway is securely fastened for connections within an acces-
    sible ceiling to a luminaire(s) or other equipment.

    (a) 3 ft
    (b) 6 ft
    (c) 8 ft
    (d) 10 ft

Article 358—Electrical Metallic Tubing (EMT)

1. Article _______ covers the use, installation, and construction
   specifications for electrical metallic tubing (EMT) and associated fittings.

   (a) 334
   (b) 350
   (c) 356
   (d) 358

2. The use of EMT shall be permitted in concrete in direct contact
   with the earth, in direct burial applications with fittings identified
   for direct burial, or in areas subject to severe _______ influences,
   where installed in accordance with 358.10(B).

   (a) corrosive
   (b) weather
   (c) sunlight
   (d) none of these

3. Galvanized steel and stainless steel EMT, elbows, couplings,
   and fittings can be installed in concrete, in direct contact with
   the earth, or in areas subject to severe corrosive influences
   where _______.

   (a) protected by corrosion protection
   (b) made of aluminum
   (c) made of stainless steel
   (d) listed for wet locations

4. When EMT is installed in wet locations, all supports, bolts,
   straps, and screws shall be _______.

   (a) made of aluminum
   (b) protected against corrosion
   (c) made of stainless steel
   (d) of nonmetallic materials only

5. EMT shall not be used where _______.

   (a) subject to severe physical damage or used for the support
       of luminaires or other equipment except conduit bodies no
       larger than the largest trade size of the tubing
   (b) embedded in concrete
   (c) protected from corrosion only by enamel
   (d) installed in wet locations

6. Raceway bends are not permitted to be made in any manner
   that will _______ the raceway.

   (a) damage
   (b) kink
   (c) change the internal diameter of
   (d) damage and change the internal diameter of

7. The total degrees of bends in a run of EMT shall not exceed
   _______ between pull points.

   (a) 120 degrees
   (b) 180 degrees
   (c) 270 degrees
   (d) 360 degrees

8. EMT shall be securely fastened in place at intervals not to exceed ______.

    (a) 4 ft
    (b) 5 ft
    (c) 8 ft
    (d) 10 ft

9. EMT run between termination points shall be securely fastened within ______ of each outlet box, junction box, device box, cabinet, conduit body, or other tubing termination.

    (a) 12 in.
    (b) 18 in.
    (c) 2 ft
    (d) 3 ft

10. EMT couplings and connectors shall be made up ______.

    (a) of metal
    (b) in accordance with industry standards
    (c) tight
    (d) to be readily accessible

Article 362—Electrical Nonmetallic Tubing (ENT)

1. Article ______ covers the use, installation, and construction specifications for electrical nonmetallic tubing (ENT) and associated fittings.

    (a) 358
    (b) 362
    (c) 366
    (d) 392

2. Where a building is supplied with a(an) ______ automatic fire protective system, ENT shall be permitted to be used within floors and ceilings, exposed or concealed, in buildings exceeding three floors above grade.

    (a) listed
    (b) identified
    (c) approved
    (d) NFPA 72

3. ENT shall be permitted to be used above suspended ceilings in buildings exceeding ______ floor above grade where the building is protected throughout by an approved automatic fire protective system.

    (a) one
    (b) two
    (c) three
    (d) four

4. ENT and fittings can be ______, provided fittings identified for this purpose are used.

    (a) encased in poured concrete floors, ceilings, walls, and slabs
    (b) embedded in a concrete slab on grade where the tubing is placed on sand or approved screenings
    (c) installed in wet locations as permitted in 362.10
    (d) any of these

5. ENT is not permitted in hazardous (classified) locations, unless permitted in other articles of the *Code*.

    (a) True
    (b) False

6. ENT shall is permitted for direct earth burial.

    (a) True
    (b) False

7. ENT shall not be used where exposed to the direct rays of the sun, unless identified as ______.

    (a) high-temperature rated
    (b) sunlight resistant
    (c) Schedule 80
    (d) suitable for the application

8. Cut ends of ENT shall be trimmed inside and ______ to remove rough edges.

    (a) outside
    (b) tapered
    (c) filed
    (d) beveled

9. ENT shall be installed as a ______ system in accordance with 300.18 and shall be securely ______ by an approved means and supported in accordance with 362.30(A) and (B).

    (a) complete
    (b) underground
    (c) overhead
    (d) none of these

10. Cable ties used to securely fasten ENT shall be ______ for the application and for securing and supporting.

    (a) identified
    (b) labeled
    (c) listed
    (d) identified and listed

11. Unbroken lengths of electric nonmetallic tubing shall not be required to be secured where fished between access points for ______ work in finished buildings or structures and securing is impractical.

    (a) concealed
    (b) exposed
    (c) hazardous
    (d) completed

12. Electrical nonmetallic tubing may extend a maximum of ______ from a fixture terminal connection without support for tap connections to lighting fixtures.

    (a) 3 ft
    (b) 5 ft
    (c) 10 ft
    (d) 2 ft

13. Where ENT enters a box, fitting, or other enclosure, a bushing or ______ shall be provided to protect the wire from abrasion unless the box, fitting, or enclosure design provides equivalent protection.

    (a) adapter
    (b) coupling
    (c) connector
    (d) insulator

Article 376—Metal Wireways

1. Metal wireways shall not be permitted for ______.

    (a) exposed work
    (b) hazardous (classified) locations
    (c) wet locations
    (d) severe corrosive environments

2. Wireways shall be supported where run horizontally at each end and at intervals not to exceed ______.

    (a) 5 ft
    (b) 6 ft
    (c) 7 ft
    (d) 8 ft

3. Splices and taps are permitted within metal wireways provided they are accessible and shall not fill the wireway to more than ______ of its area at that point.

    (a) 35 percent
    (b) 40 percent
    (c) 55 percent
    (d) 75 percent

4. Power distribution blocks installed in metal wireways on the line side of the service equipment shall be marked ______ for use on the line side of service equipment or equivalent.

    (a) suitable
    (b) acceptable
    (c) allowed
    (d) approved

5. Power distribution blocks in metal wireways shall not have ______ live parts exposed within a(an) ______.

    (a) energized
    (b) concealed
    (c) insulated
    (d) uninsulated

Article 380—Multioutlet Assemblies

1. A multioutlet assembly can be installed in ______ locations.

    (a) dry
    (b) damp
    (c) damp and wet
    (d) dry and damp

2. A multioutlet assembly shall not be installed ______.

    (a) in hoistways
    (b) where subject to severe physical damage
    (c) where subject to corrosive vapors
    (d) all of these

3. Metal multioutlet assemblies can extend through (not run within) dry partitions if arrangements are made for removing the cap or cover on all ______ portions and no outlet is located within the partitions.

    (a) exposed
    (b) concealed
    (c) uninsulated
    (d) none of these

Article 386—Surface Metal Raceways

1. Article 386 covers the use, installation, and construction specifications for surface ______ and associated fittings.

    (a) nonmetallic raceways
    (b) metal raceways
    (c) metal wireways
    (d) enclosures

2. Unbroken lengths of surface metal raceways can be run through dry ______.

   (a) walls
   (b) partitions
   (c) floors
   (d) all of these

3. Surface metal raceways shall not be used ______.

   (a) where subject to severe physical damage
   (b) where subject to corrosive vapors
   (c) in hoistways
   (d) all of these

4. The voltage between conductors in a surface metal raceway shall not exceed ______ unless the metal has a thickness of not less than 0.040 in. nominal.

   (a) 150V
   (b) 300V
   (c) 600V
   (d) 1,000V

5. Surface metal raceways and associated fittings shall be supported ______.

   (a) in accordance with the manufacturer's installation instructions
   (b) at intervals appropriate for the building design
   (c) at intervals not exceeding 4 ft
   (d) at intervals not exceeding 8 ft

6. Splices and taps in surface metal raceways without removable covers shall be made only in ______.

   (a) boxes
   (b) raceways
   (c) conduit bodies
   (d) none of these

Article 392—Cable Trays

1. Cable tray systems, including ladder, ventilated trough, ventilated channel, solid bottom, and other similar structures are covered within Article ______.

   (a) 358
   (b) 362
   (c) 366
   (d) 392

2. Cable trays can be used as a support system for ______.

   (a) service conductors, feeders, and branch circuits
   (b) communications circuits
   (c) control and signaling circuits
   (d) all of these

3. Cable tray systems shall not be used ______.

   (a) in hoistways
   (b) where subject to severe physical damage
   (c) in hazardous (classified) locations
   (d) in hoistways or where subject to severe physical damage

4. Cable tray systems shall be permitted to have mechanically discontinuous ______ between cable tray runs or between cable tray runs and equipment.

   (a) portions
   (b) segments
   (c) pieces
   (d) any of these

5. Each run of cable tray shall be ______ before the installation of cables.

   (a) tested for 25 ohms of resistance
   (b) insulated
   (c) completed
   (d) all of these

6. Cable trays shall be ______ except as permitted by 392.18(D).

   (a) exposed
   (b) accessible
   (c) readily accessible
   (d) exposed and accessible

7. In industrial facilities where conditions of maintenance and supervision ensure that only qualified persons will service the installation, cable tray systems can be used to support ______.

   (a) raceways
   (b) cables
   (c) boxes and conduit bodies
   (d) all of these

8. Cable trays shall be supported at ______ in accordance with the installation instructions.

   (a) intervals
   (b) portions
   (c) segments
   (d) any of these

EQUIPMENT FOR GENERAL USE

Introduction to Chapter 4—Equipment for General Use

With the first three chapters of the *NEC* behind you, this fourth one is necessary for building a solid foundation in general equipment installations. Some examples of general equipment include but are not limited to luminaires, heaters, motors, air-conditioning units, generators, and transformers. The articles in Chapter 4 help you apply the first three chapters to installations involving general equipment. You must understand the first four chapters of the *Code* to properly apply these requirements to Chapters 5, 6, and 7, and at times to Chapter 8.

Chapter 4 is arranged in the following manner:

▶ **Article 404—Switches.** The requirements of Article 404 apply to switches of all types. These include snap (toggle) switches, dimmer switches, fan switches, knife switches, circuit breakers, and automatic switches such as time clocks, timers, and switches and circuit breakers used for disconnects.

▶ **Article 406—Receptacles and Attachment Plugs (Caps).** This article covers the rating, type, and installation of receptacles and attachment plugs. It also covers flanged surface inlets.

▶ **Article 408—Switchboards and Panelboards.** Article 408 covers specific requirements for switchboards, panelboards, and distribution boards that supply lighting and power circuits.

▶ **Article 410—Luminaires and Lamps.** This article contains the requirements for luminaires, lampholders, and lamps. Because of the many types and applications of luminaires, manufacturer's instructions are very important and helpful for proper installation.

▶ **Article 422—Appliances.** This article covers electric appliances used in any occupancy.

SWITCHES

Introduction to Article 404—Switches

Article 404 covers all types of switches, switching devices, and circuit breakers such as snap (toggle) switches, dimmer switches, fan switches, disconnect switches, circuit breakers, and automatic switches such as those used for time clocks and timers. Some topics covered in this material include:

- ▶ Switch connection types
- ▶ Damp and wet locations
- ▶ Indicating
- ▶ Accessibility

Part I. Installation

404.1 Scope

The requirements of Article 404 apply to all types of switches, switching devices, and circuit breakers. ▶Figure 404–1

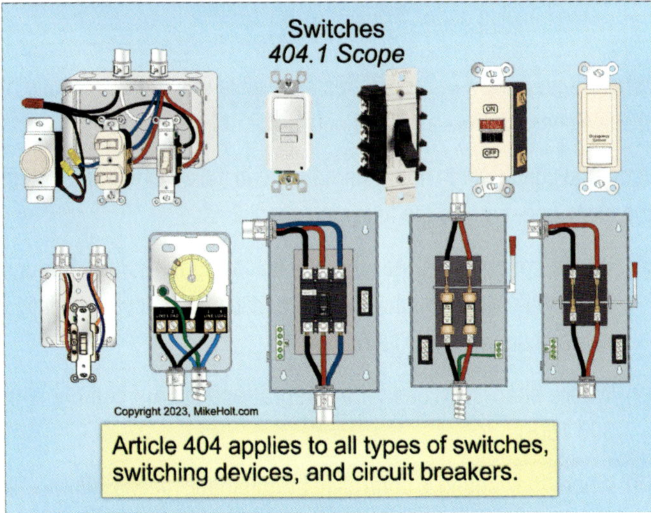

▶Figure 404–1

Article 404 does not cover wireless control equipment to which circuit conductors are not connected. ▶Figure 404–2

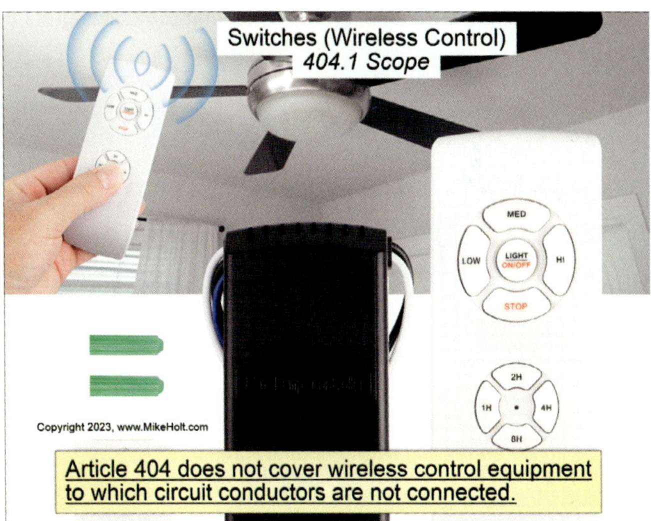

▶Figure 404–2

Note: See 210.70 for additional information related to branch circuits that include switches or listed wall-mounted control devices.

404.2 Switch Connections

(A) Three-Way and Four-Way Switches. Wiring for 3-way and 4-way switching must be done so only the phase conductors are switched. ▶Figure 404–3

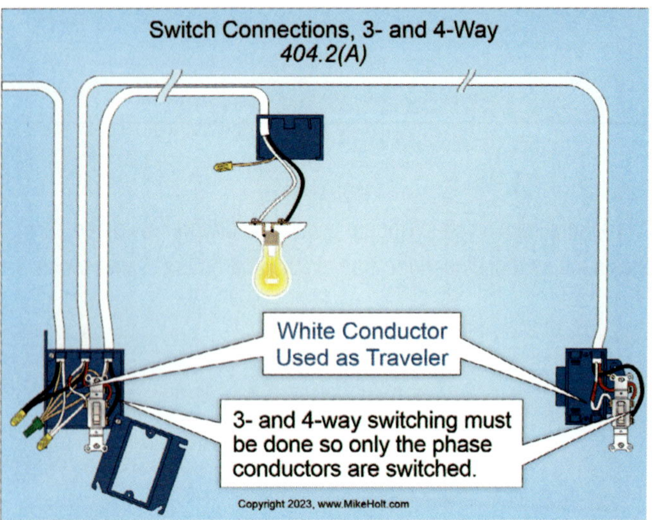

▶Figure 404–3

(C) Switches Controlling Lighting Loads. Switches controlling line-to-neutral lighting loads must have a neutral conductor installed at all switches serving bathroom areas, hallways, stairways, and habitable rooms or occupiable spaces as defined in the building code. ▶Figure 404–4

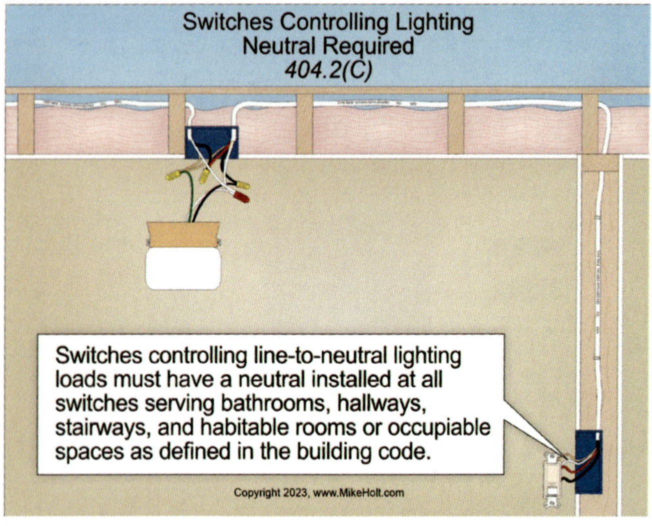

▶Figure 404–4

According to Article 100, "Habitable Room" is a room in a building for living, sleeping, eating, or cooking. Bathrooms, toilet rooms, closets, hallways, storage or utility spaces, and similar areas are excluded. ▶Figure 404–5

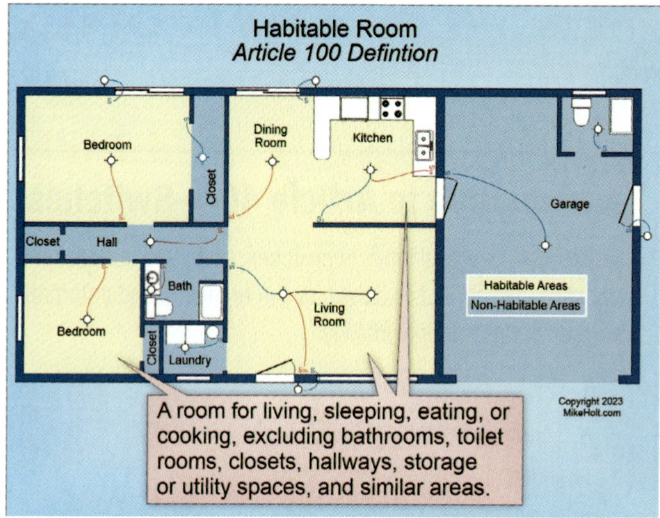

▶Figure 404–5

▶ According to the building code, an occupiable space is a room or enclosed space designed for human occupancy in which individuals congregate for amusement, educational or similar purposes or in which occupants are engaged at labor. An occupiable space is equipped with means of egress and light and ventilation facilities meeting the requirements of the building code.

Where 3-way and 4-way switches are visible in a room, only one of the switches requires a neutral conductor. ▶Figure 404–6

A neutral conductor is not required to be installed at lighting switch locations under any of the following conditions:

(1) Where conductors enter the box enclosing the switch through a raceway with enough cross-sectional area to accommodate a neutral conductor. ▶Figure 404–7

(2) Where snap switches with integral enclosures comply with 300.15(E).

(3) Where the lighting is controlled by automatic means.

(4) Where switches control receptacles. ▶Figure 404–8

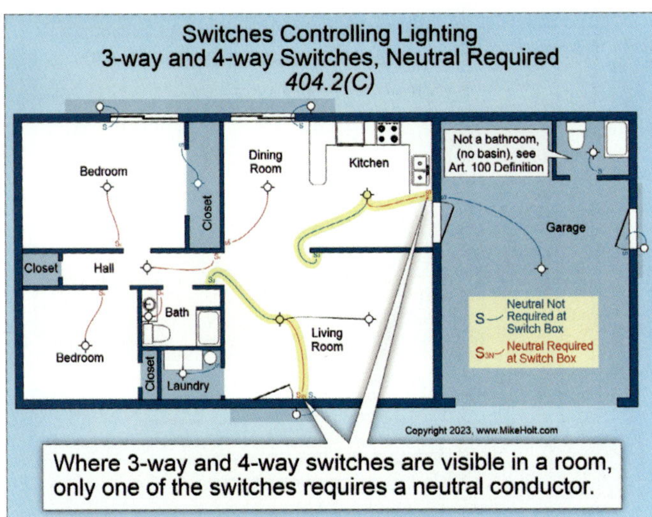

Where 3-way and 4-way switches are visible in a room, only one of the switches requires a neutral conductor.

▶Figure 404–6

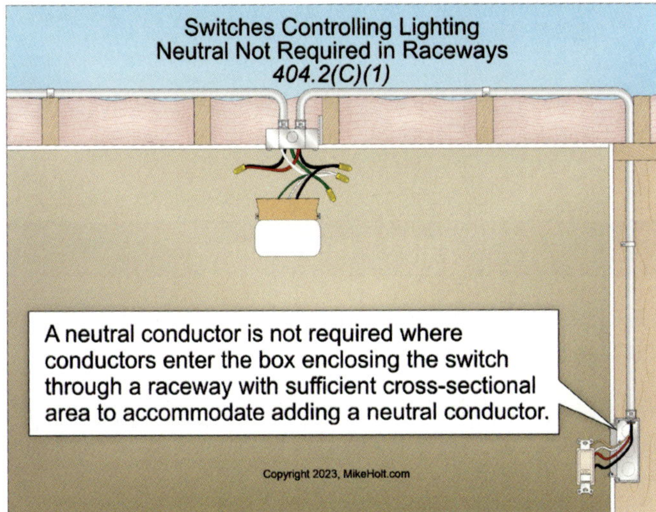

A neutral conductor is not required where conductors enter the box enclosing the switch through a raceway with sufficient cross-sectional area to accommodate adding a neutral conductor.

▶Figure 404–7

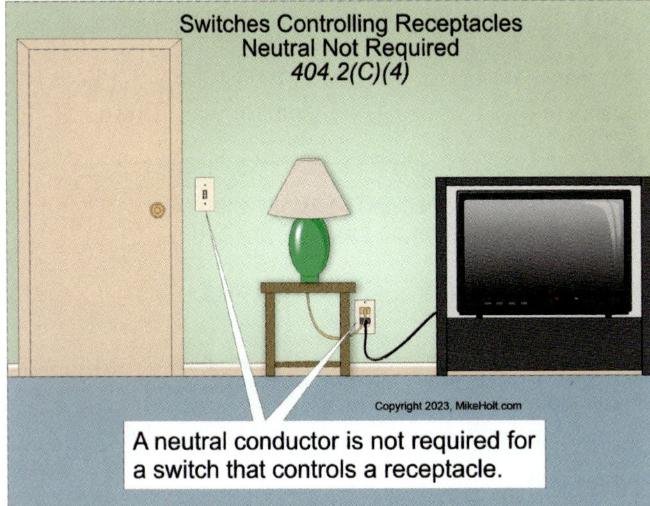

A neutral conductor is not required for a switch that controls a receptacle.

▶Figure 404–8

If not already present, a neutral conductor must be installed for any replacement switch that requires line-to-neutral voltage [404.22] to operate the electronics of the switch in the standby mode. ▶Figure 404–9

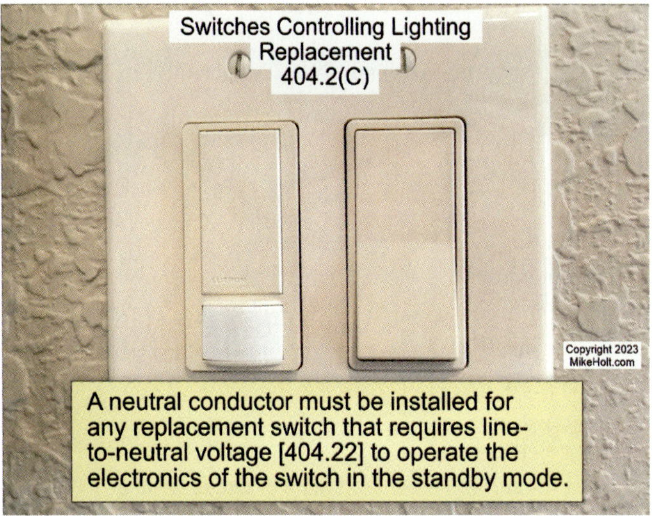

A neutral conductor must be installed for any replacement switch that requires line-to-neutral voltage [404.22] to operate the electronics of the switch in the standby mode.

▶Figure 404–9

Ex: A neutral conductor is not required for replacement switches installed in locations wired prior to the adoption of 404.2(C) where the neutral conductor cannot be extended without removing finish materials. The number of electronic lighting control switches without a neutral conductor on a branch circuit is not permitted to exceed five, and the number of switches connected to any feeder is not permitted to exceed 25.

Note: The purpose of the neutral conductor at a switch is to complete a circuit path for electronic lighting control devices that require a neutral conductor. ▶Figure 404–10

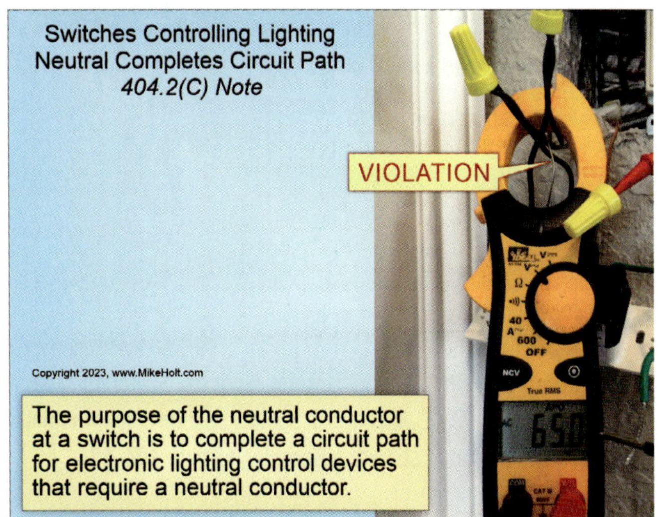

The purpose of the neutral conductor at a switch is to complete a circuit path for electronic lighting control devices that require a neutral conductor.

▶Figure 404–10

404.4 Damp or Wet Locations

(A) Surface-Mounted Switches or Circuit Breakers. Surface-mounted switches or circuit breakers in damp or wet locations must be installed in a weatherproof enclosure. ▶Figure 404–11

▶Figure 404–11

(B) Flush-Mounted Switches or Circuit Breakers. Flush-mounted switches or circuit breakers in damp or wet locations must have a weatherproof cover. ▶Figure 404–12

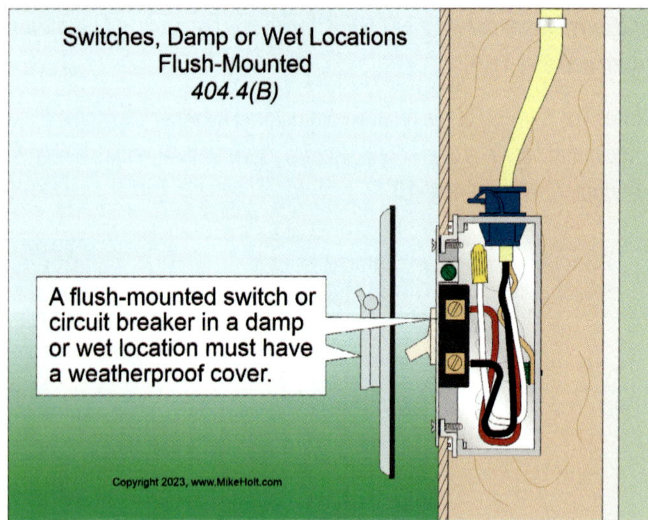

▶Figure 404–12

(C) Switches Within Tub and Shower Spaces. Switches are not permitted to be installed within tub or shower spaces unless installed as part of a listed tub or shower assembly. ▶Figure 404–13

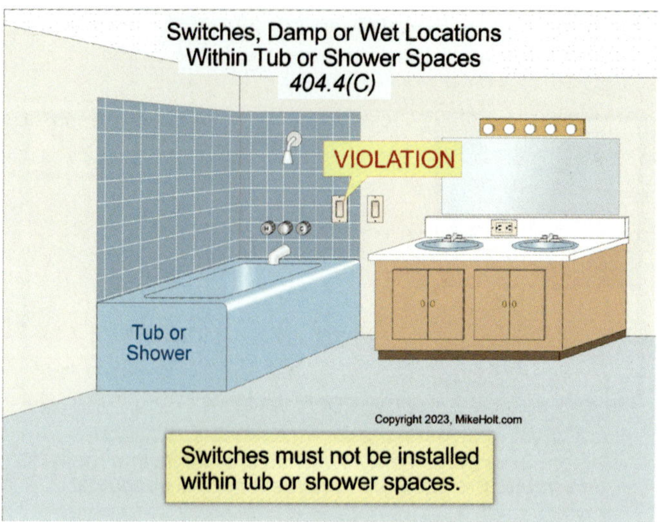

▶Figure 404–13

▶ The *Code* does not specify how far outside a tub or shower space a switch must be.

404.7 Indicating

Switches must be marked to indicate if the switch is in the "on" or "off" position.

When a switch or circuit breaker is operated vertically, the "up" position of the circuit breaker handle must be the "on" position. ▶Figure 404–14

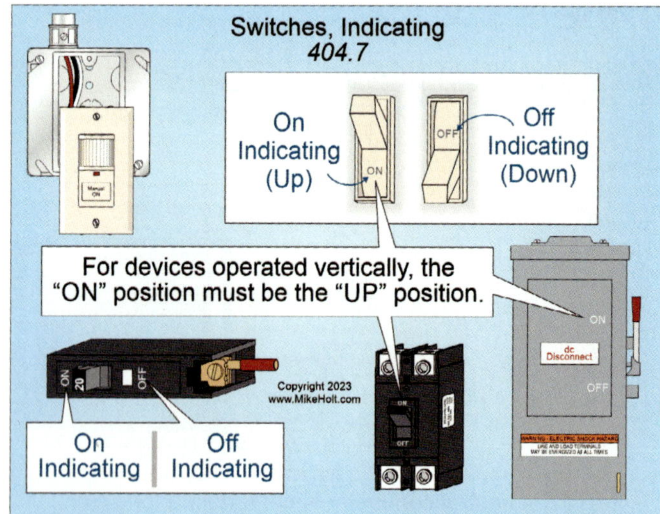

▶Figure 404–14

Ex 1: 3-way and 4-way switches, are not required to be marked "on" or "off."

(C) Connection of Switches. Single-throw knife switches must be connected so their blades are de-energized when the switch is in the "open" position.

Author's Comment:

▸ In accordance with "*UL 98 Standard for Enclosed and Dead-Front Switches*" section 6.7.1.11, a switch of the knife-blade type must be so arranged that the blades will be de-energized when the switch is open.

404.8 Accessibility

(A) Location. Switches and the switch handle of circuit breakers must be capable of being operated from a readily accessible location.

Maximum Height. The center of the grip of the operating handle of a switch or circuit breaker when in its highest position is not permitted to be more than 6 ft 7 in. above the floor or working platform except as follows: ▸**Figure 404–15**

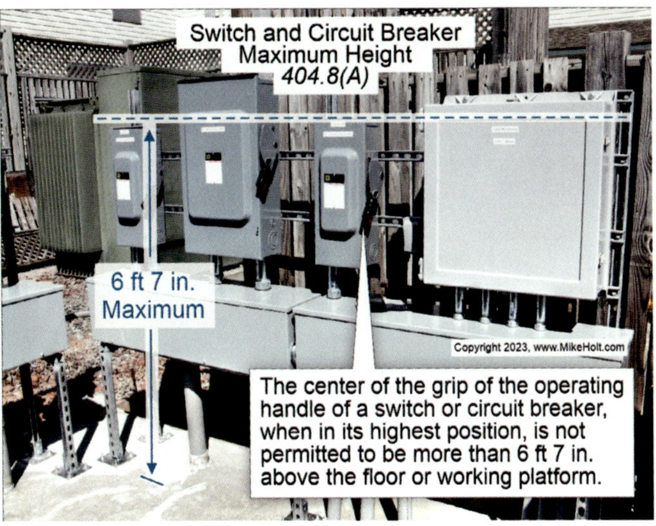

▸Figure 404–15

Author's Comment:

▸ There are no requirements for a minimum height above the floor or working platform for switches or circuit breakers. ▸**Figure 404–16**

▸Figure 404–16

(1) On busways, fusible switches and circuit breakers can be located at the same level as the busway where suitable means is provided to operate the handle of the device from the floor. ▸**Figure 404–17**

▸Figure 404–17

(2) Switches and circuit breakers can be mounted above 6 ft 7 in. if they are next to motors, appliances, or other equipment they supply. ▸**Figure 404–18**

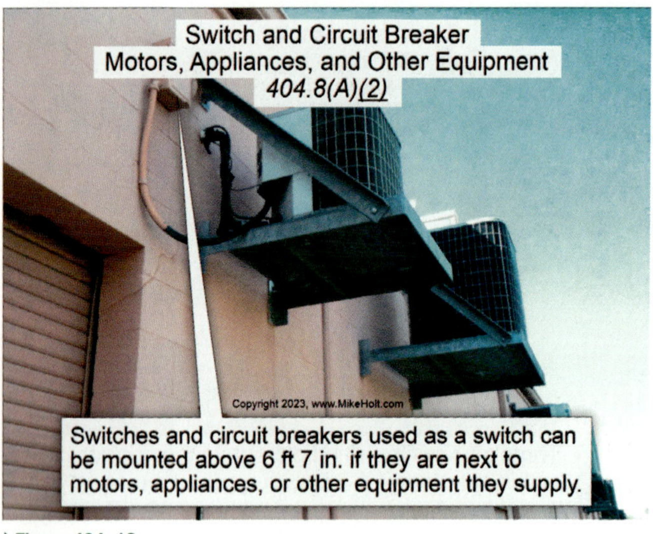

▶Figure 404–18

RECEPTACLES, ATTACHMENT PLUGS, AND FLANGED INLETS

Introduction to Article 406—Receptacles, Attachment Plugs, and Flanged Inlets

This article covers the rating, type, and installation of receptacles, attachment plugs, and flanged inlets. There are many types of receptacles such as self-grounding, isolated ground, tamper resistant, weather resistant, GFCIs and AFCIs, energy controlled, work surface and countertop assemblies, USBs, surge protectors, and so on. Some topics covered in this material include:

▶ Mounting

▶ Damp or wet locations

▶ Equipment grounding conductor terminals

▶ Tamper-resistant receptacles

According to Article 100, "Receptacle" is a contact device installed at an outlet for the connection of an attachment plug or equipment designed to mate with the contact device. ▶Figure 406–1

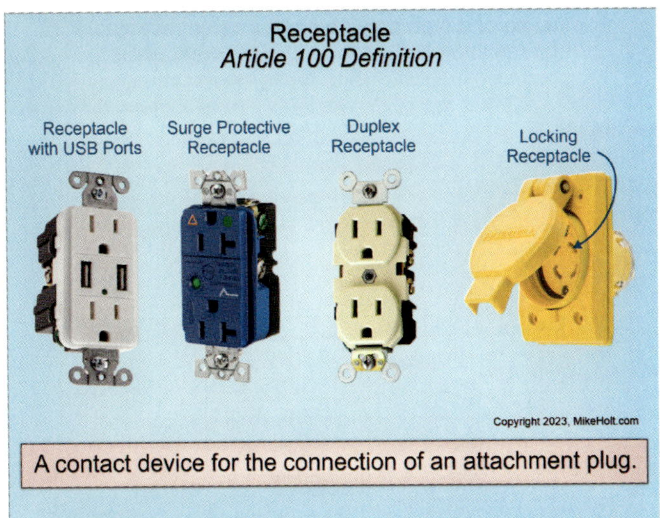

▶Figure 406–1

A single receptacle contains one contact device on the same yoke. A multiple receptacle has more than one contact device on the same yoke. ▶Figure 406–2

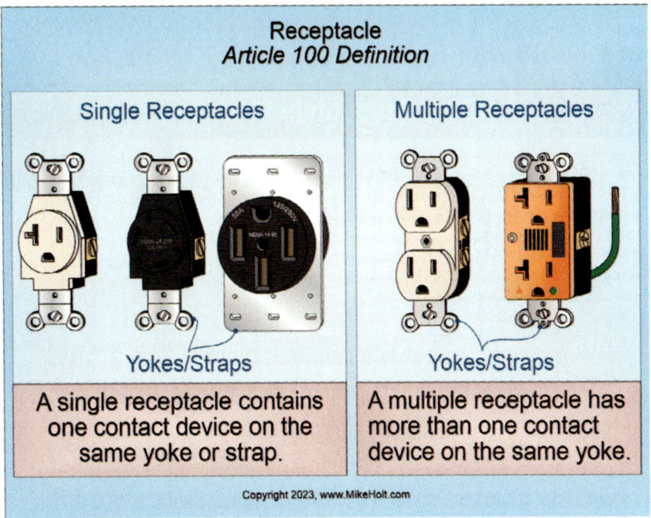

▶Figure 406–2

Author's Comment:

▶ A yoke is the metal mounting structure for such items as receptacles, switches, switches with pilot lights, and switch/receptacles to name a few.

Note: A duplex receptacle is an example of a multiple receptacle with two receptacles on the same yoke.

406.1 Scope

Article 406 covers the rating, type, and installation of receptacles, attachment plugs, and flanged inlets. ▶Figure 406–3

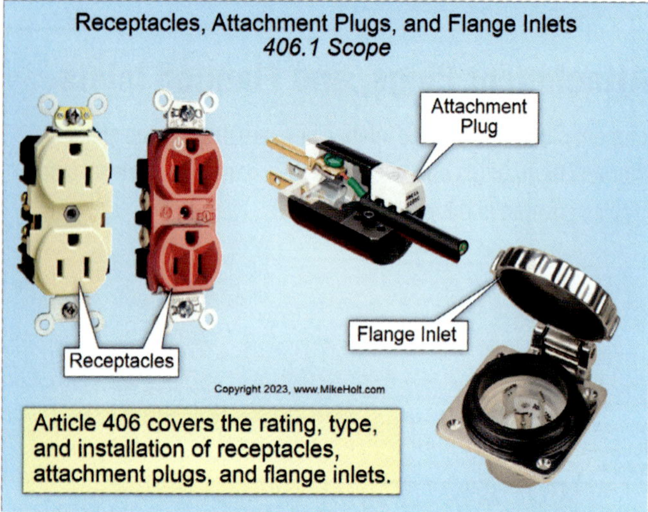

▶Figure 406–3

406.5 Receptacle Mounting

Receptacles must be installed in outlet boxes that are securely fastened in place in accordance with 314.23.

Author's Comment:

▶ Boxes containing a hub can be supported from a flexible cord connected to fittings that prevent tension from being transmitted to joints or terminals [400.14 and 314.23(H)(1)].

Screws used for attaching a receptacle to a box must be a type provided with a listed receptacle or machine screws having 32 threads per in. ▶Figure 406–4 and ▶Figure 406–5

(A) Boxes Set Back. Receptacles in outlet boxes that are set back from the finished surface must have the receptacle held rigidly to the finished surface. ▶Figure 406–6

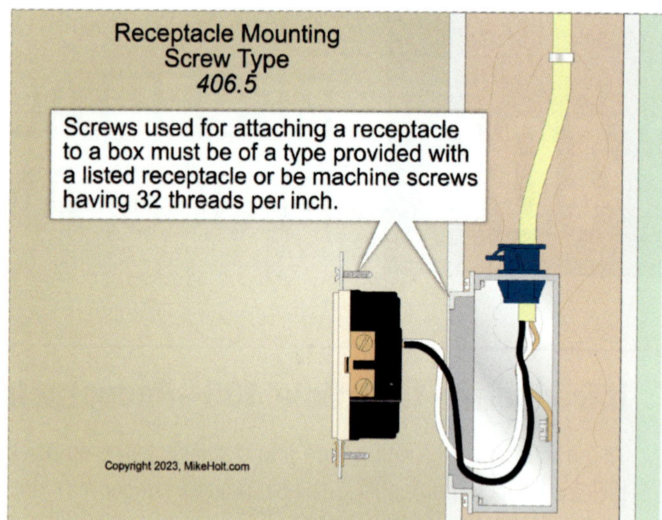

▶Figure 406–4

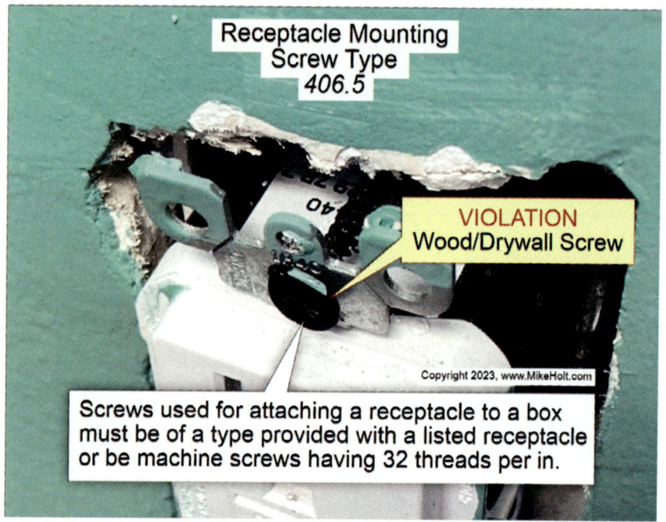

▶Figure 406–5

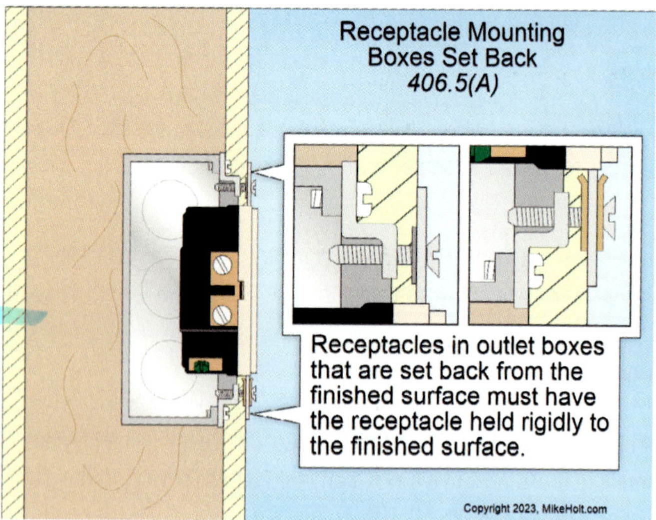

▶Figure 406–6

▸ In walls or ceilings of noncombustible material (such as drywall) outlet boxes are not permitted to be set back more than ¼ in. from the finished surface. In walls or ceilings of combustible material, outlet boxes must be flush with the finished surface [314.20]. There must not be any gaps of more than ⅛ in. at the edge of the outlet box [314.21].

(B) Boxes Flush with Surface. Receptacles in outlet boxes that are flush with the finished surface must have the receptacle held rigidly to the outlet box or raised cover. ▸**Figure 406–7**

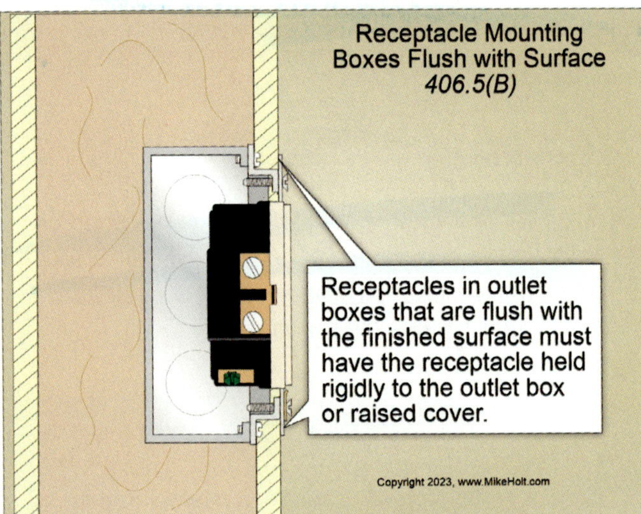

▸Figure 406–7

(C) Receptacles Mounted on Covers. Receptacles supported by a cover must be held rigidly to the cover with at least two screws. ▸**Figure 406–8**

(D) Position of Receptacle Faces. Receptacles must be flush with (or project from) the faceplates.

(E) Receptacles in Countertops. Receptacle assemblies installed in countertop surfaces must be listed for countertop applications. ▸**Figure 406–9**

(F) Receptacles in Work Surfaces. Receptacle assemblies listed for work surfaces or countertops can be installed in a work surface.

(G) Receptacle Orientation.

(1) Countertop and Work Surfaces. Receptacles are not permitted to be installed in a face-up position in or on countertop surfaces or work surfaces unless listed for countertop surface or work surface applications. ▸**Figure 406–10**

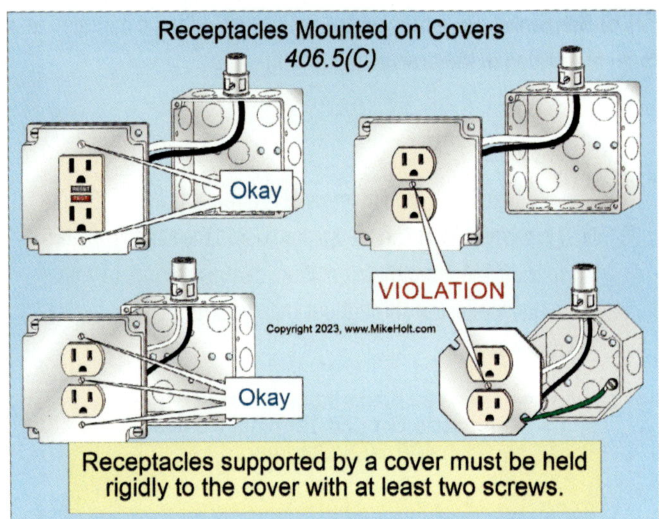

▸Figure 406–8

▸Figure 406–9

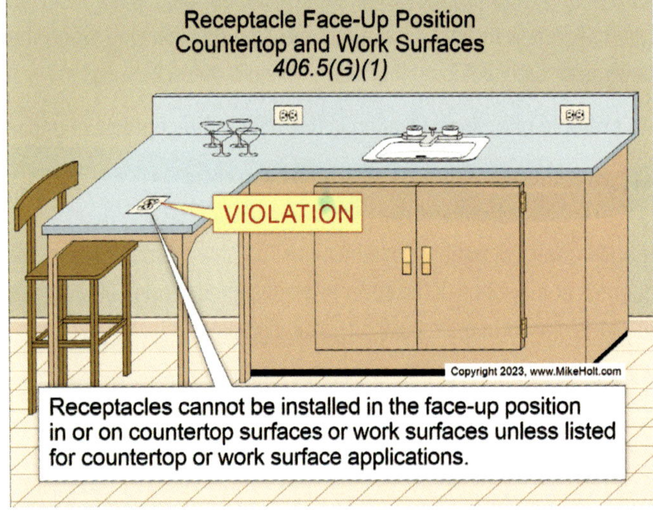

▸Figure 406–10

(2) Under Sinks. Receptacles are not permitted to be installed in a face-up position in the area below a sink.

Author's Comment:

▸ The position of the ground terminal of a receptacle is not specified in the *NEC* so it can be up, down, or to the side. Proposals to specify the mounting position of the ground terminal have been rejected throughout many *Code* revision cycles. ▸Figure 406–11

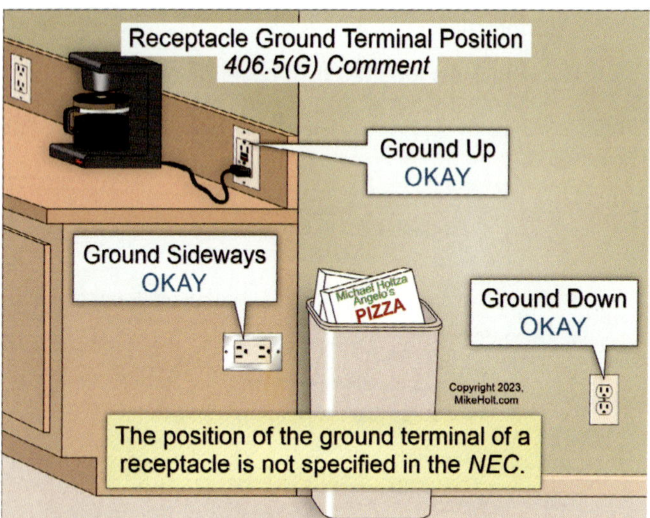

▸Figure 406–11

406.9 Receptacles in Damp or Wet Locations

(A) Damp Locations. Receptacles installed in a damp location must be the weather-resistant (WR) type. It must be installed in an enclosure that is weatherproof when an attachment plug is not inserted (damp location rated) or the attachment plug is inserted when the cover is closed (wet location rated). ▸Figure 406–12

An example of a damp location is one where a receptacle is under roofed open porches, canopies, or marquees, and not subjected to beating rain or water runoff.

Hinged covers of outlet box hoods must be able to open at least 90 degrees or fully open (if the cover is not designed to open 90 degrees from the closed to open position) after installation.

▸Figure 406–12

Author's Comment:

▸ The main difference between the cover for a 15A or 20A receptacle in a damp location [406.9(A)] or wet location [406.9(B)] is whether it is weather resistant when the attachment plug is inserted. ▸Figure 406–13

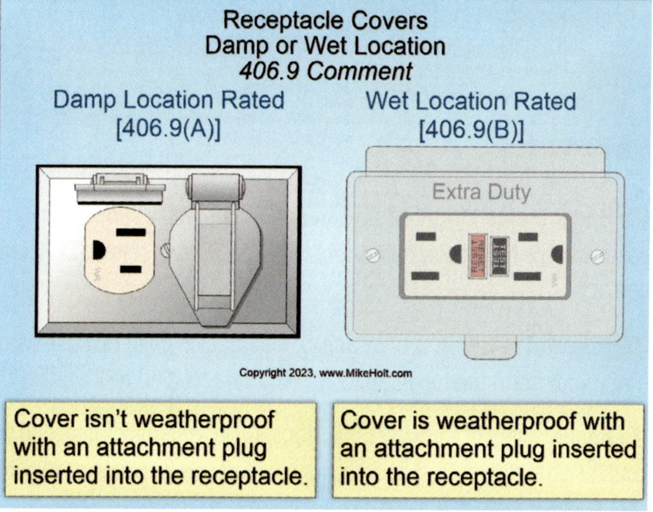

▸Figure 406–13

(B) Wet Locations.

(1) 15A and 20A Receptacles. 15A and 20A receptacles installed in a wet location must be within an enclosure that is weatherproof when an attachment plug is inserted using an outlet box hood identified as "extra duty." ▸Figure 406–14

▶Figure 406–14

Hinged covers of outlet box hoods must be able to open at least 90 degrees or fully open (if the cover is not designed to open 90 degrees from the closed to open position) after installation. ▶Figure 406–15

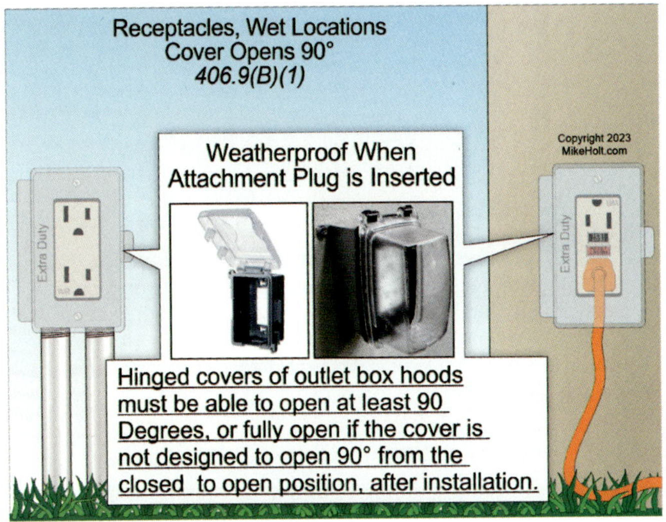

▶Figure 406–15

Nonlocking-type 15A and 20A receptacles in a wet location must be listed as weather-resistant (WR) type. ▶Figure 406–16

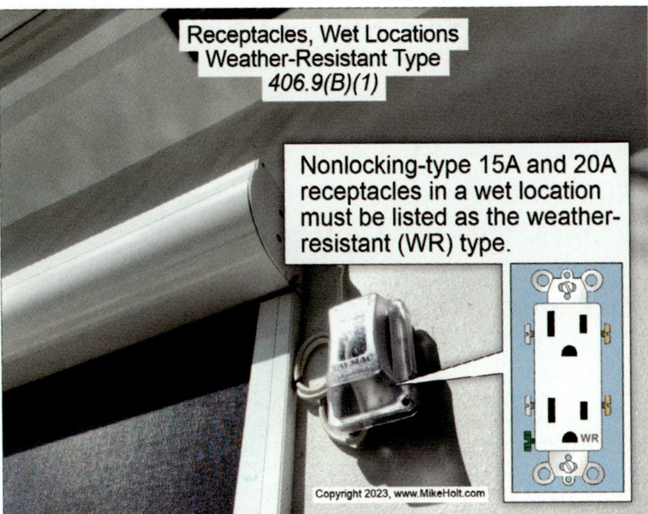

▶Figure 406–16

Author's Comment:

▸ Exposed plastic surface material of weather-resistant receptacles must have UV resistance to ensure deterioration from sunlight does not take place or is minimal. In testing, receptacles are subjected to temperatures cycling from very cold to very warm conditions and then subjected to additional dielectric testing. The rapid transition from the cold to warm temperatures changes the relative humidity and moisture content on the device, and the dielectric test ensures this will not create a breakdown of the insulation properties.

▸ A wet location is an area subject to saturation with water and unprotected locations exposed to weather [Article 100].

(2) Other Receptacles. Receptacles rated 30A or more installed in a wet location must be listed as the weather-resistant type and comply with (a) or (b).

(a) Unattended While in Use. A receptacle where the load is not attended while in use must be in an enclosure that is weatherproof when an attachment plug is inserted.

(b) Attended While in Use. A receptacle that will only be used while someone is nearby, such as one used with portable tools, can use an enclosure that is weatherproof when the cover is closed.

(C) Bathtub and Shower Space. Receptacles are not permitted inside a tub or shower or within 3 ft horizontally from any outside edge of a bathtub or shower stall. This includes the space measured vertically from the floor to 8 ft vertically above the top of the bathtub rim or shower stall threshold. ▶Figure 406–17

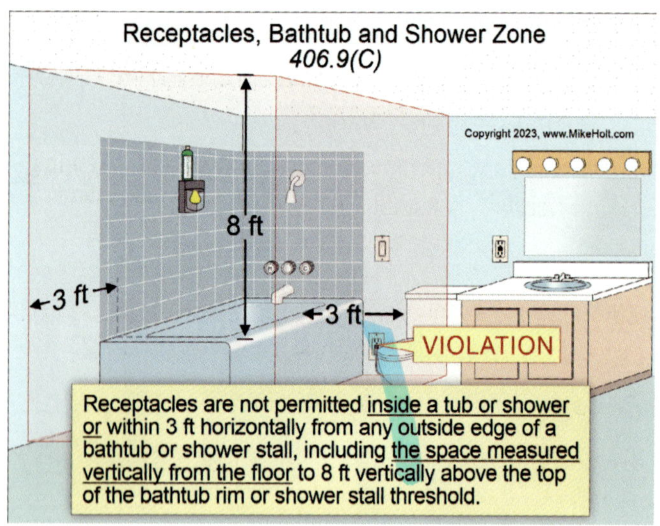

▶Figure 406–17

Ex 1: Receptacles for hydromassage bathtubs installed in accordance with 680.73 are permitted to be installed in the prohibited receptacle zone. ▶Figure 406–18

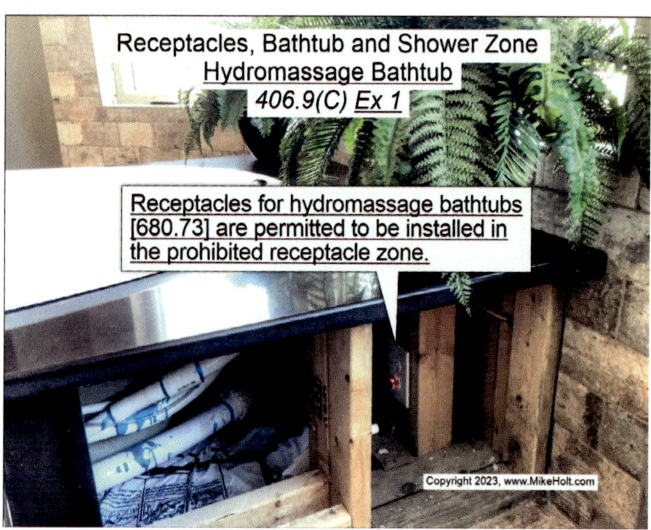

▶Figure 406–18

Ex 2: In dwelling unit bathrooms with less than the required zone, the bathroom sink receptacle, required by 210.52(D), is permitted to be located on the furthest wall opposite the bathtub rim or shower stall threshold. ▶Figure 406–19

Ex 4: In dwelling unit bathrooms, a single receptacle for an electronic toilet or electronic bidet seat is permitted in the prohibited receptacle zone if the receptacle is not in the space between the toilet and the bathtub or shower. ▶Figure 406–20

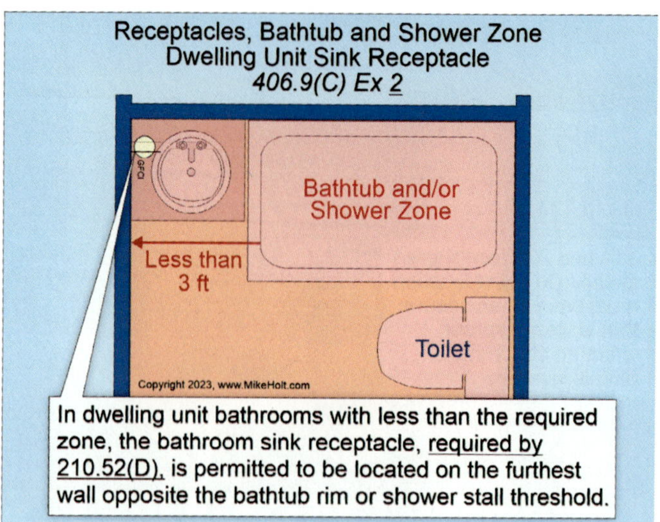

▶Figure 406–19

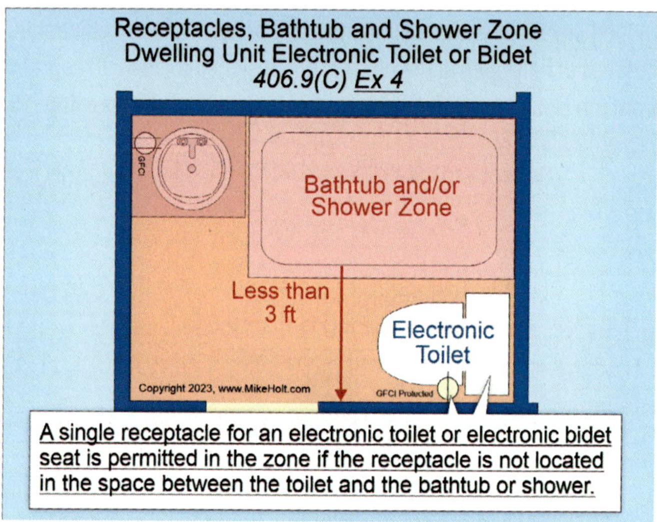

▶Figure 406–20

406.11 Connecting Receptacle Grounding Terminal to Equipment Grounding Conductor

The grounding terminal of receptacles must be connected to an equipment grounding conductor in accordance with 250.146.

406.12 Tamper-Resistant Receptacles

Nonlocking-type 15A and 20A receptacles in the following areas must be tamper resistant "TR":

Author's Comment:

▸ Inserting an object into one slot of a tamper-resistant receptacle does not open the internal shutter mechanism. Simultaneous pressure applied to the polarized slots is required to insert the plug. ▸Figure 406–21

▸Figure 406–21

(1) In dwelling units, boathouses, mobile homes, and manufactured homes, including their attached or detached garages and accessory buildings, and common areas of multifamily dwellings.

(2) In hotel and motel guest rooms and guest suites, and their common areas.

(3) In childcare facilities.

Author's Comment:

▸ A childcare facility is a building or portions of a building used for educational, supervision, or personal care services for five or more children seven years in age or less [Article 100].

(4) In preschools and education facilities.

Author's Comment:

▸ This applies to all educational facilities including high schools, colleges, vocational schools, universities, and so forth.

(5) Within clinics, medical and dental offices, outpatient facilities, and the following spaces:

a. Business offices accessible to the general public.

b. Lobbies and waiting spaces.

c. Spaces of nursing homes and limited care facilities used exclusively as patient sleeping rooms.

(6) Places of awaiting transportation, gymnasiums, skating rinks, fitness centers, and auditoriums.

(7) Dormitory units.

(8) Residential care/assisted living facilities, social and substance abuse rehabilitation facilities, and group homes.

(9) Foster care facilities, nursing homes, and psychiatric hospitals.

(10) Areas and common areas of agricultural buildings accessible to the general public.

Note 3: Areas of agricultural buildings frequently converted to hospitality areas include petting zoos, stables, and buildings used for recreation or educational purposes.

Ex to (1) through (10): Receptacles in the following locations are not required to be tamper resistant:

(1) Receptacles more than 5½ ft above the floor. ▸Figure 406–22

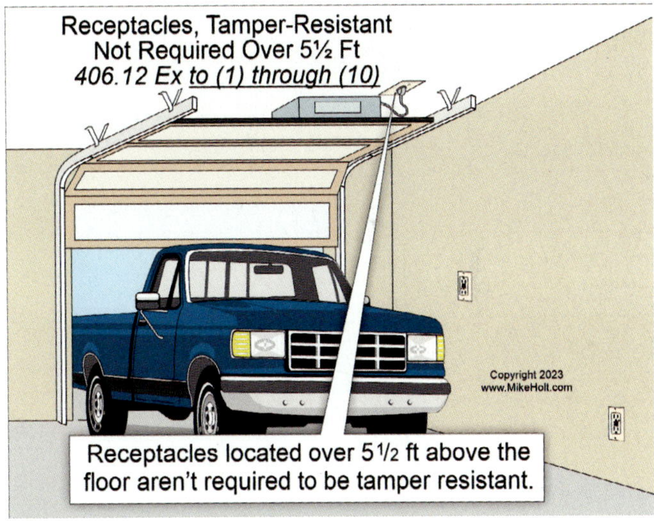

▸Figure 406–22

(2) Receptacles that are part of a luminaire or appliance.

(3) A receptacle within dedicated space for an appliance that in normal use is not easily moved.

(4) Nongrounding receptacles installed as permitted in 406.4(D)(2)(a).

ARTICLE 408

SWITCHBOARDS AND PANELBOARDS

Introduction to Article 408—Switchboards and Panelboards

Article 408 covers the specific requirements for switchboards and panelboards that control power and lighting circuits. Since these rules address the equipment at the heart of the premises electrical system, take some time to become familiar with them. Some topics covered in this material include:

- ▶ Circuit identification
- ▶ Unused openings
- ▶ Damp or wet locations
- ▶ Enclosures
- ▶ Orientation

Author's Comment:

- ▶ The slang term in the electrical field for a panelboard is "the guts." The requirements for panelboards are contained in Article 408.

Part I. General

408.1 Scope

Article 408 covers the requirements for switchboards and panelboards that control power and lighting circuits. ▶Figure 408–1

408.4 Circuit Directory and Description

(A) Circuit Descriptions. Circuits and circuit modifications must be provided with a legible and permanent description on a circuit directory.

(1) Switchboard. The circuit description must be located at each circuit breaker in a switchboard.

(2) Panelboard. The circuit description must be located on the face, inside, or in an approved location adjacent to the panel door. ▶Figure 408–2

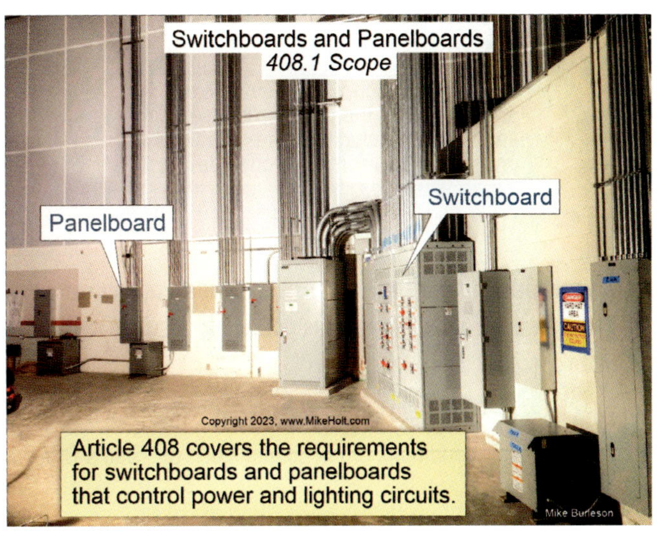

▶Figure 408–1

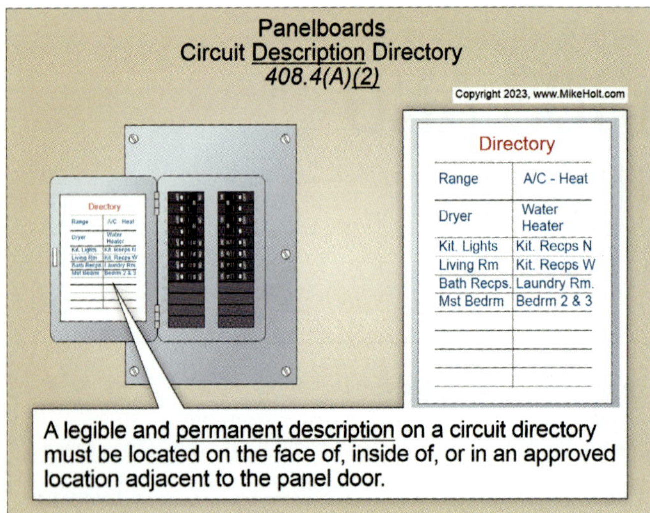

Panelboards
Circuit Description Directory
408.4(A)(2)

Copyright 2023, www.MikeHolt.com

A legible and permanent description on a circuit directory must be located on the face of, inside of, or in an approved location adjacent to the panel door.

▶Figure 408–2

(3) Purpose of Circuit Description. The circuit description must be clear and specific to the purpose or use of each circuit, including spare positions for unused overcurrent protective devices. ▶Figure 408–3

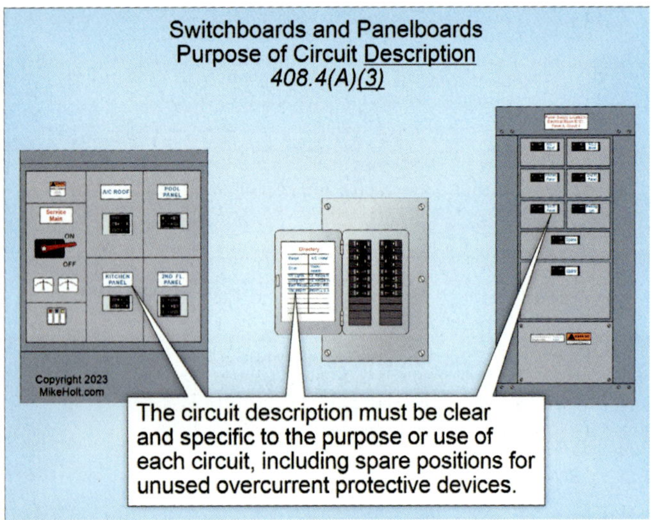

Switchboards and Panelboards
Purpose of Circuit Description
408.4(A)(3)

Copyright 2023
MikeHolt.com

The circuit description must be clear and specific to the purpose or use of each circuit, including spare positions for unused overcurrent protective devices.

▶Figure 408–3

(4) Circuit Description Details. The circuit description must have a degree of detail and clarity that is unlikely to result in confusion between circuits.

(5) Transient Conditions. The circuit description must not be dependent on transient conditions of occupancy such as "Dad's Office." ▶Figure 408–4

(6) Abbreviations and Symbols. The circuit description must be clear in explaining abbreviations and symbols when used. ▶Figure 408–5

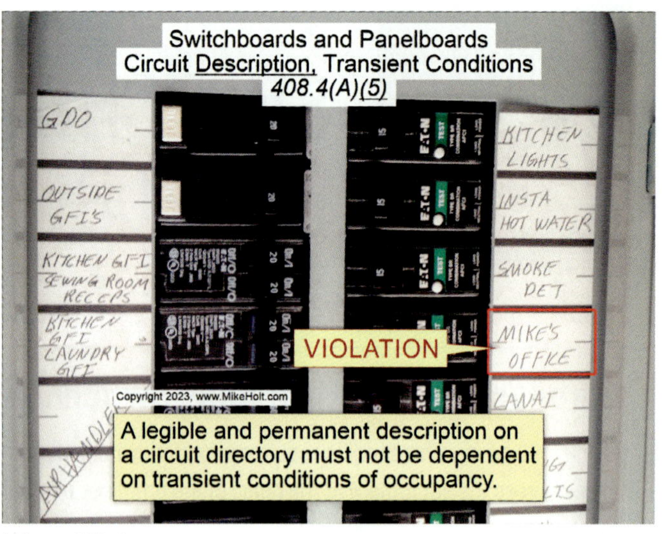

Switchboards and Panelboards
Circuit Description, Transient Conditions
408.4(A)(5)

Copyright 2023, www.MikeHolt.com

A legible and permanent description on a circuit directory must not be dependent on transient conditions of occupancy.

▶Figure 408–4

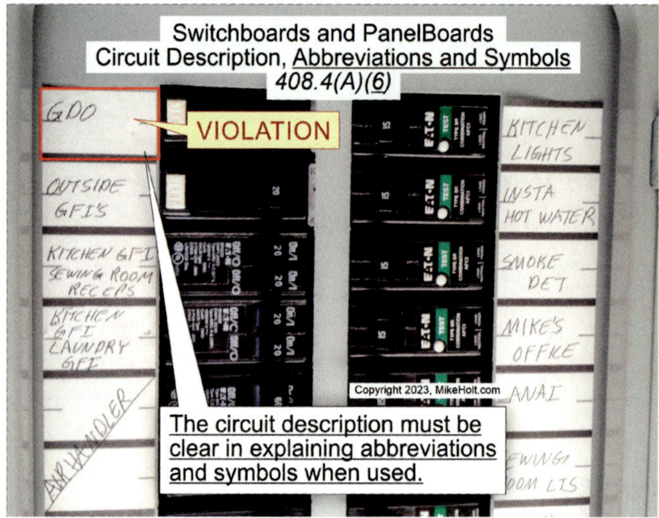

Switchboards and PanelBoards
Circuit Description, Abbreviations and Symbols
408.4(A)(6)

Copyright 2023, MikeHolt.com

The circuit description must be clear in explaining abbreviations and symbols when used.

▶Figure 408–5

(B) Description of Source of Supply. Switchboards and panelboards supplied by a feeder, in other than one- family or two-family dwelling units, must be marked as follows:

(1) With the identification and physical location where the power supply originates. ▶Figure 408–6

(2) With a permanent label that withstands the environment involved in accordance with 110.22(A).

(3) A method that is not handwritten must be used.

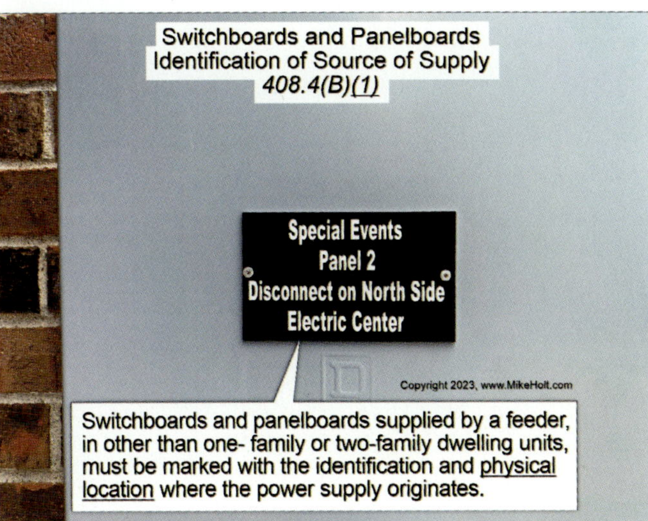

▶Figure 408–6

408.7 Unused Openings

Unused openings for circuit breakers must be closed using identified closures (or other approved means) which provide protection substantially equivalent to the wall of the enclosure. ▶**Figure 408–7**

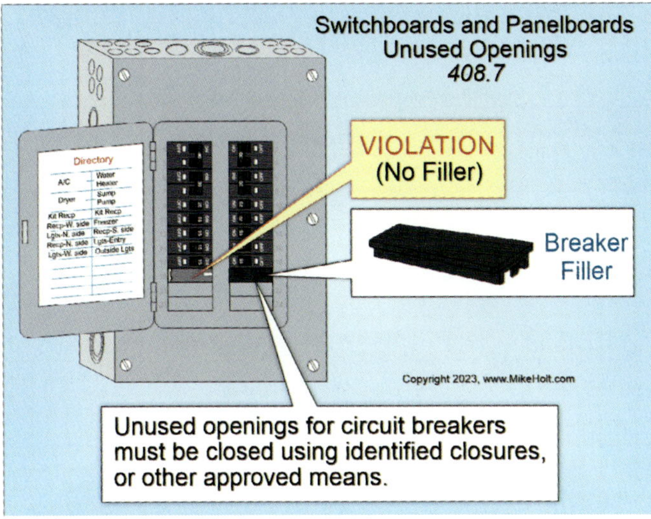

▶Figure 408–7

Part III. Panelboards

408.37 Panelboards in Damp or Wet Locations

Cabinets for panelboards installed in damp or wet locations must be weatherproof in accordance with 312.2.

408.38 Enclosure

Panelboards must be mounted in cabinets, cutout boxes, or identified enclosures and must have dead-front covers.

408.43 Panelboard Orientation

Panelboards are not permitted to be installed in the face-up or face-down position. ▶**Figure 408–8**

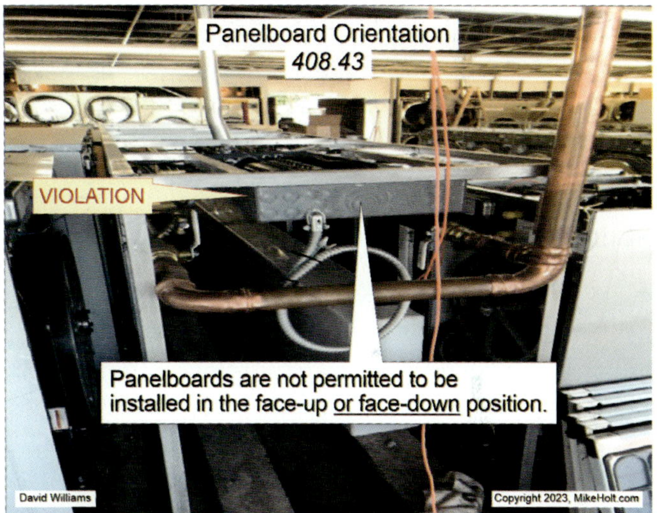

▶Figure 408–8

LUMINAIRES

Introduction to Article 410—Luminaires

This article covers luminaires, lampholders, lamps, decorative lighting products, lighting accessories for temporary seasonal and holiday use, portable flexible lighting products, and the wiring and equipment of such products and lighting installations. Article 410 is massive. It contains 84 sections divided into 17 parts. Several of these parts and their corresponding sections are not within the scope of this material. Some of the topics that are covered here include:

- ▶ Scope
- ▶ Wet and damp locations
- ▶ Luminaires in clothes closets

According to Article 100, "Luminaire" is a complete lighting unit consisting of a light source with parts designed to position the light source and connect it to the power supply. It may also include parts to protect and distribute the light. ▶Figure 410–1

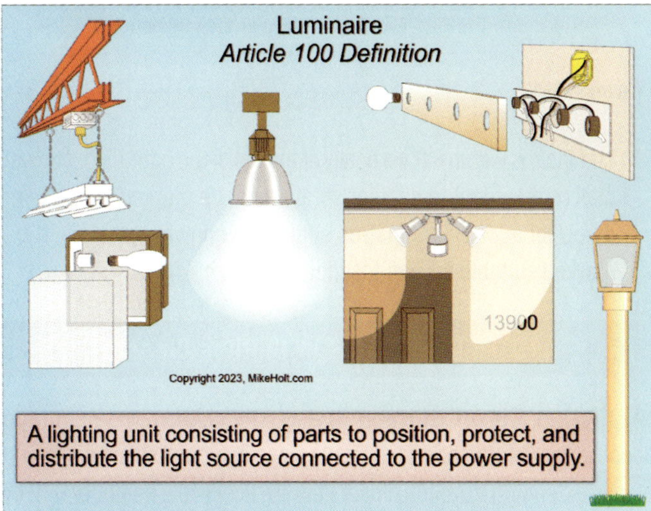

▶Figure 410–1

Part I. General

410.1 Scope

Article 410 covers luminaires, lampholders, lamps, decorative lighting products, lighting accessories for temporary seasonal and holiday use, portable flexible lighting products, and the wiring and equipment of such products and lighting installations. ▶Figure 410–2

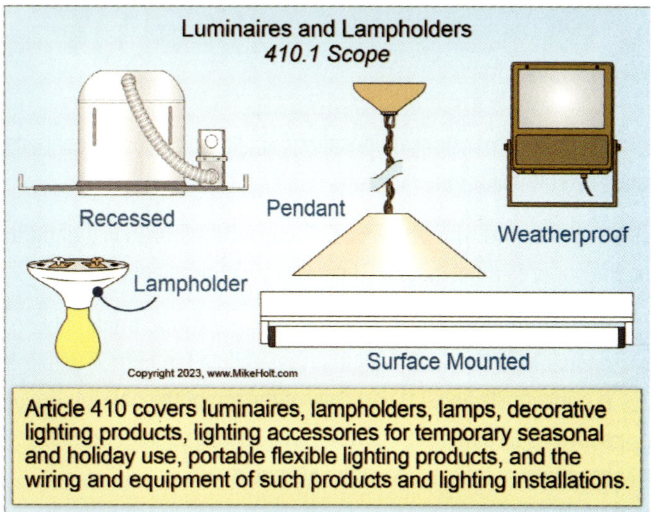

▶Figure 410–2

Author's Comment:

▸ Because of the many types and applications of luminaires, manufacturers' instructions are very important and helpful for proper installation. UL produces a pamphlet called the *Luminaire Marking Guide*, which provides information for properly installing common types of incandescent, fluorescent, and high-intensity discharge (HID) luminaires.

Part II. Luminaire Locations

410.10 Luminaires in Specific Locations

(A) Wet or Damp Locations. Luminaires installed in wet locations must be marked as suitable for wet locations. Luminaires installed in damp locations must be marked as suitable for wet locations or suitable for damp locations. ▸**Figure 410–3** and ▸**Figure 410–4**

▸Figure 410–3

(B) Corrosive Locations. Luminaires installed in corrosive locations must be suitable for the location.

(D) Bathtub and Shower Areas. A luminaire installed in a bathtub or shower area must meet all the following requirements:

(1) No part of chain or cord-suspended luminaires, track lighting, pendants, or luminaire (light kit) on paddle fan can be within 3 ft horizontally and 8 ft vertically of the top of the bathtub rim or shower stall threshold. This zone is all-encompassing and includes spaces over tubs or showers. ▸Figure 410–5

▸Figure 410–4

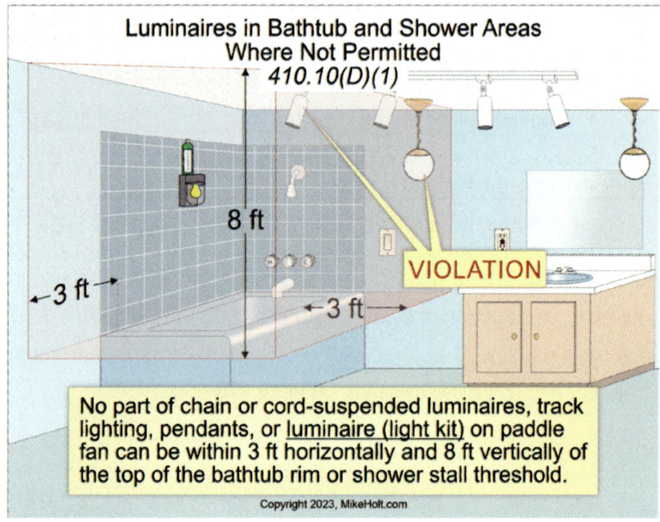

▸Figure 410–5

(2) Luminaires within 8 ft vertically of the top of the bathtub or shower stall (not subject to shower spray) must be marked suitable for damp locations. Luminaires subject to shower spray must be marked suitable for wet locations. ▸Figure 410–6

410.16 Luminaires in Clothes Closets

(A) Clothes Closet Storage Space. The clothes closet storage space is the volume bounded by the sides and back closet walls and planes extending from the closet floor vertically to a height of 6 ft, or to the highest clothes-hanging rod, and parallel to the walls at a horizontal distance of 24 in. from the sides and back of the closet walls, respectively.

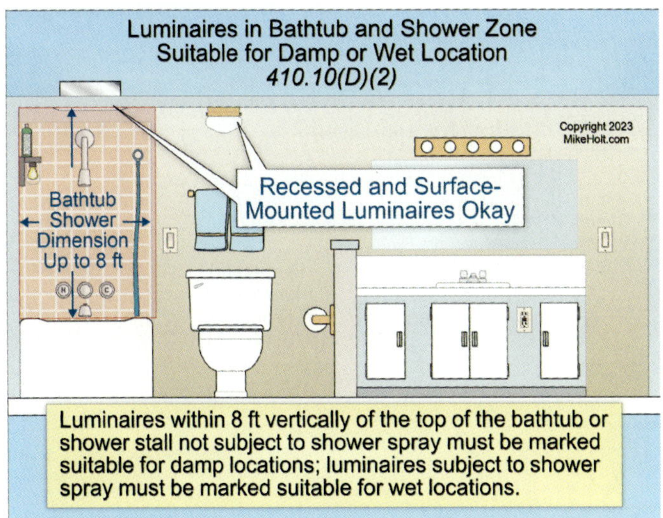

▶Figure 410–6

The volume extends vertically to the closet ceiling parallel to the walls at a horizontal distance of 12 in. or the width of the shelf, whichever is greater.

For a closet that permits access to both sides of a hanging rod, the clothes closet storage space includes the volume below the highest rod extending 12 in. on either side of the rod on a plane horizontal to the floor extending the entire length of the rod. ▶Figure 410–7

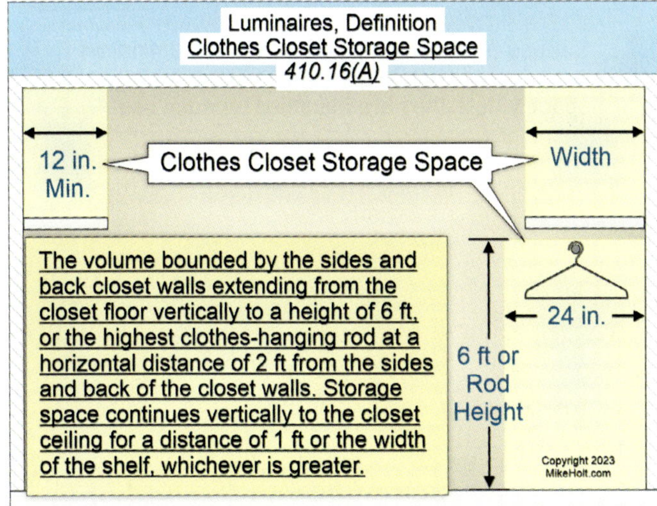

▶Figure 410–7

According to Article 100, "Clothes Closet Storage Space" is the area within a clothes closet where combustible materials can be kept. ▶Figure 410–8

(B) Luminaire Types Permitted. Only the following types of luminaires are permitted in the clothes closet storage space:

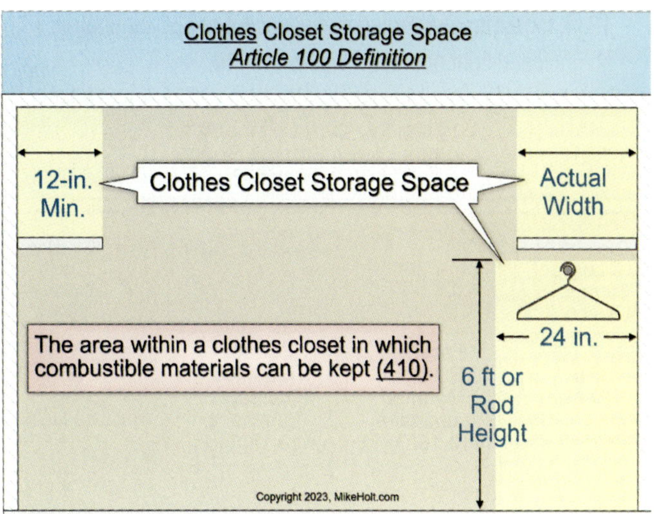

▶Figure 410–8

(1) Surface or recessed incandescent or LED luminaires with an enclosed light source.

(2) Surface or recessed fluorescent luminaires.

(3) Surface-mounted fluorescent or LED luminaires identified for use within the clothes closet storage space.

(C) Luminaire Types Not Permitted. Incandescent luminaires with open or partially enclosed lamps and pendant luminaires or lampholders are not permitted to be installed in the clothes closet storage space. ▶Figure 410–9

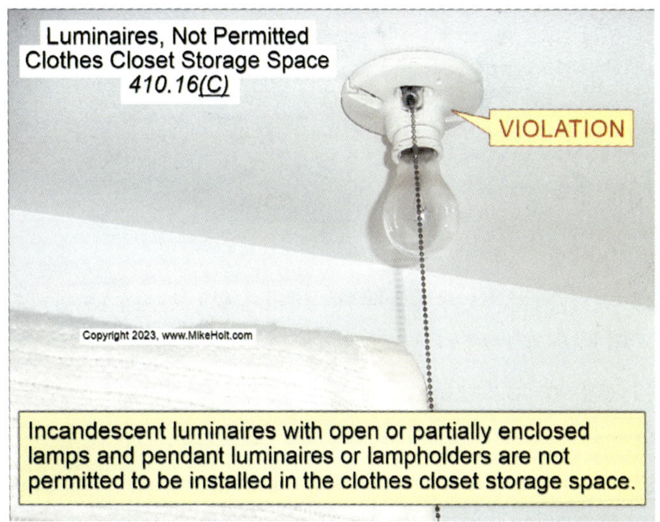

▶Figure 410–9

(D) Location of Luminaires. Luminaires must maintain a minimum clearance from the clothes closet storage space as follows:

(1) 12 in. for surface-mounted incandescent or LED luminaires with an enclosed light source. ▶**Figure 410–10**

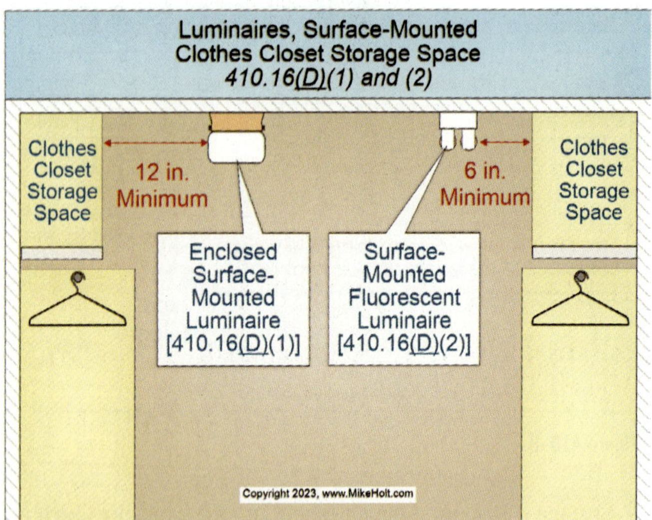

▶Figure 410–10

(2) 6 in. for surface-mounted fluorescent luminaires.

(3) 6 in. for recessed incandescent or LED luminaires with an enclosed light source. ▶**Figure 410–11**

(4) 6 in. for recessed fluorescent luminaires.

Ex: Surface-mounted fluorescent or LED luminaires are permitted within the clothes closet storage space if identified for this use. ▶**Figure 410–12**

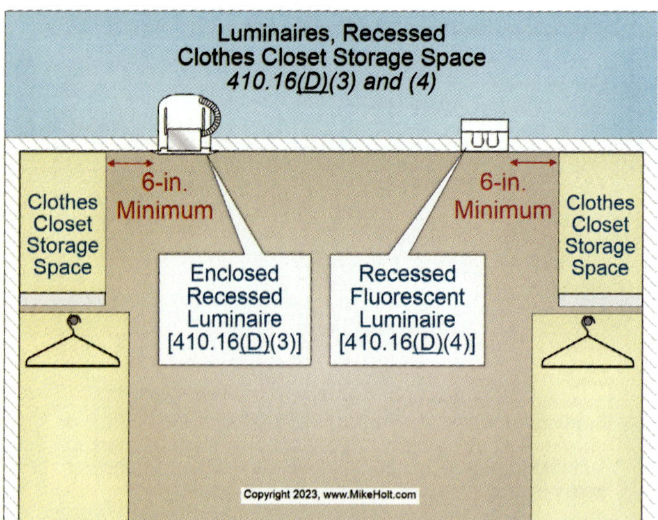

▶Figure 410–11

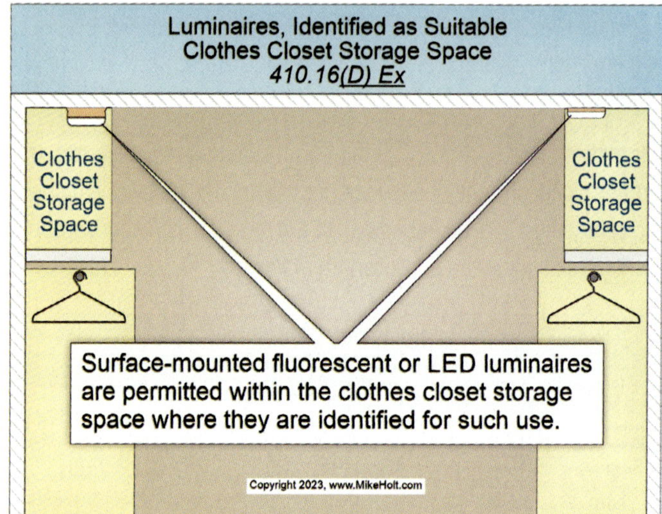

▶Figure 410–12

APPLIANCES

Introduction to Article 422—Appliances

This article covers electric appliances that are fastened in place, permanently connected, or cord-and-plug-connected in any occupancy. Some topics covered in this material include:

▸ Cord- and-plug connected appliances.

Part I. General

422.1 Scope

The scope of Article 422 includes appliances in any occupancy. ▸Figure 422–1

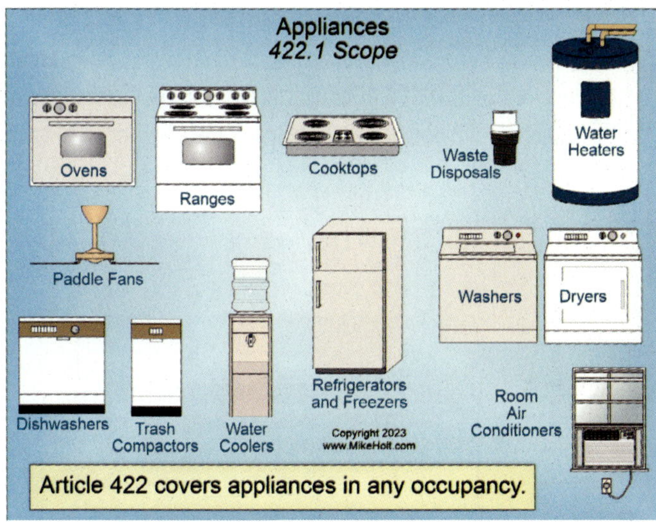

▸Figure 422–1

According to Article 100, "Appliance" is electrical equipment, other than industrial equipment, built in standardized sizes. Examples of appliances are ranges, ovens, cooktops, refrigerators, drinking water coolers, and beverage dispensers.

Part II. Branch-Circuit Requirements

422.16 Flexible Cords

(A) General. Flexible cords are permitted to be used to:

(1) Connect appliances to facilitate their frequent interchange or to prevent the transmission of noise or vibration [400.10(A)(6) and 400.10(A)(7)].

(2) Facilitate the removal or disconnection of appliances, where the fastening means and mechanical connections are specifically designed to permit ready removal for maintenance or repair and the appliance is intended or identified for flexible cord connection [400.10(A)(8)].

> **Author's Comment:**
>
> ▸ Flexible cords are not permitted for the connection of water heaters, furnaces, and other appliances fastened in place unless they are specifically identified to be used with a flexible cord. ▸**Figure 422–2**

(3) All cord-and-plug-connected electrically heated appliances that produce temperatures exceeding 121°C (250°F) on surfaces where the cord is likely to be in contact must be provided with one of the types of heater cords listed in Table 400.4.

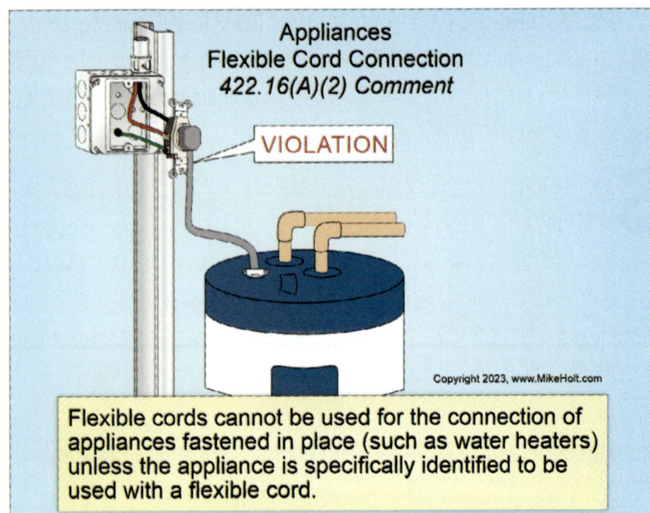

▶Figure 422–2

(B) Specific Appliances.

(1) In-Sink Waste Disposal. A flexible cord is permitted for an in-sink waste disposal if: ▶Figure 422–3

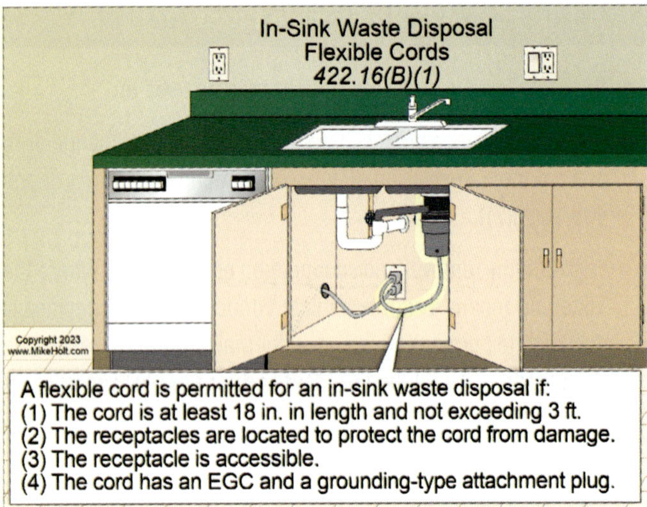

▶Figure 422–3

(1) The flexible cord is at least 18 in. long and does not exceed 3 ft in length.

(2) The receptacles are located so the flexible cord is protected from damage.

(3) The receptacle is accessible.

(4) The flexible cord has an equipment grounding conductor and terminated with a grounding-type attachment plug.

Ex: A listed appliance distinctly marked to identify it as protected by a system of double insulation is not required to be terminated with a grounding-type attachment plug.

(2) Built-In Dishwashers and Trash Compactors. A flexible cord is permitted for a dishwasher or trash compactor if:

(1) For a trash compactor, the flexible cord cannot be less than 3 ft long or exceed 4 ft in length, measured from the rear plane of the appliance. ▶Figure 422–4

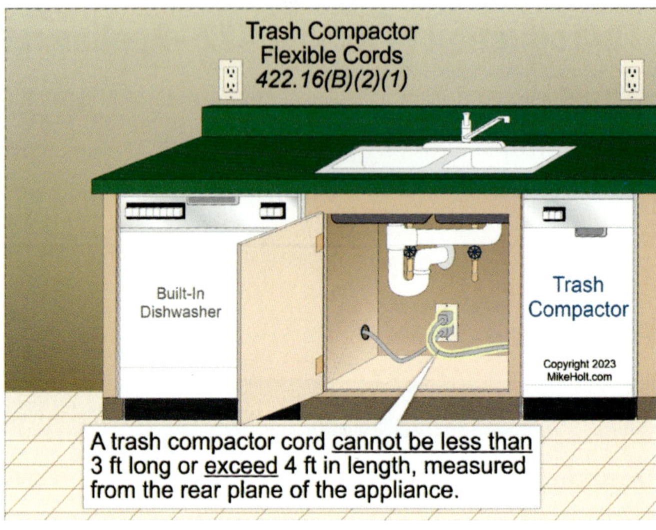

▶Figure 422–4

(2) For a dishwasher, the length of the flexible cord cannot be less than 3 ft long or exceed 6 ft 6 in. in length, measured from the face of the attachment plug to the rear plane of the appliance. ▶Figure 422–5

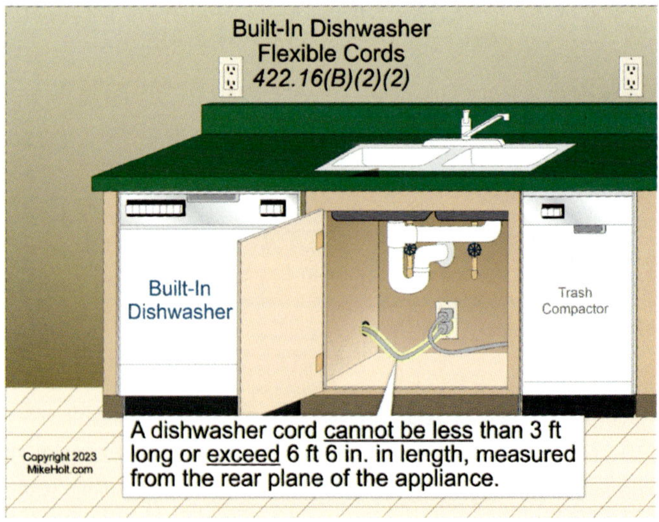

▶Figure 422–5

(3) The receptacles are located so the flexible cord is protected from damage.

(4) The receptacle for a trash compactor must be in the space occupied by the trash compactor or be in the space adjacent to the trash compactor. If a flexible cord passes through an opening, the cord must be protected against damage by a bushing, grommet, smoothed edged, or other approved means.

(5) The receptacle for the dishwasher is in the space adjacent to the dishwasher. If the flexible cord passes through an opening, it must be protected against damage by a bushing, grommet, smoothed edged, or other approved means. ▶Figure 422–6

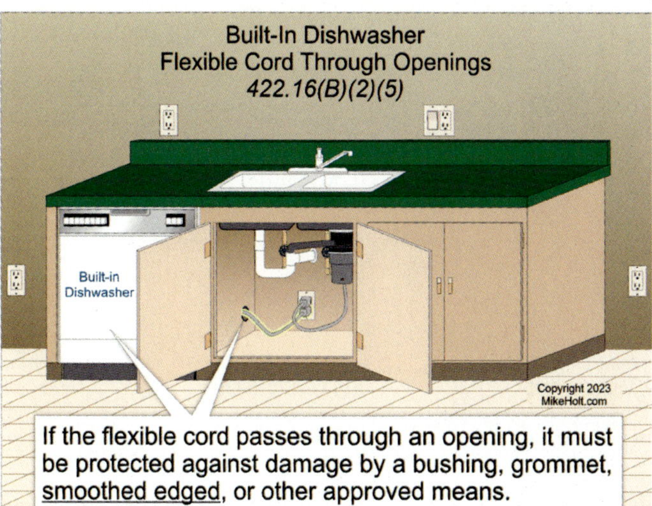

▶Figure 422–6

(6) The receptacle is accessible.

(7) The flexible cord has an equipment grounding conductor and terminated with a grounding-type attachment plug.

Ex: A listed appliance distinctly marked to identify it as protected by a system of double insulation is not required to be terminated with a grounding-type attachment plug.

> ### Author's Comment:
>
> ▸ The receptacle for the dishwasher is not permitted to be of the GFCI Type, because it is not in a readily-accessible spot as required by 210.8.

(3) Wall-Mounted Ovens and Counter-Mounted Cooking Units. Wall-mounted ovens and counter-mounted cooking units can be cord-and-plug-connected with a flexible cord identified as suitable for the purpose in the instructions of the appliance's manufacturer.

(4) Range Hoods and Microwave Oven/Range Hood Combinations. Range hoods and over-the-range microwave ovens with integral range hoods are permitted to be cord-and-plug-connected with a flexible cord. The cord must be identified as suitable for use on range hoods in the instructions of the appliance's manufacturer where all the following conditions are met: ▶Figure 422–7

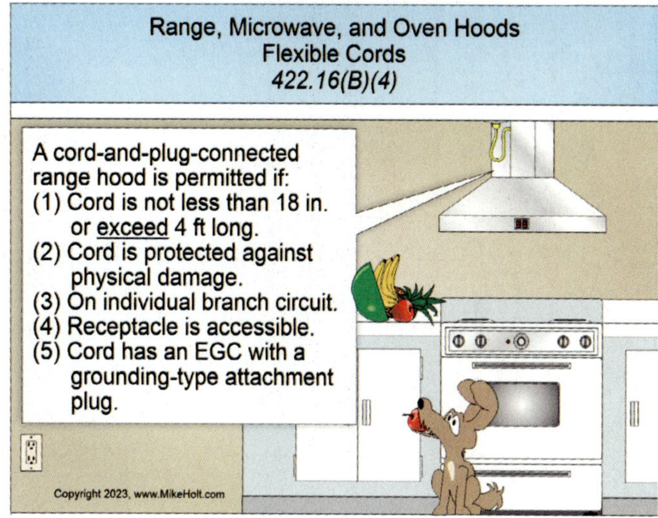

▶Figure 422–7

(1) The length of the cord is not less than 18 in. long and does not exceed 4 ft in length.

(2) Receptacles are located to protect against physical damage to the flexible cord.

(3) The receptacle is supplied by an individual branch circuit.

(4) The receptacle is accessible.

(5) The flexible cord has an equipment grounding conductor and terminated with a grounding-type attachment plug.

Ex: A listed appliance distinctly marked to identify it as protected by a system of double insulation is not required to be terminated with a grounding-type attachment plug.

REVIEW QUESTIONS

Please use the 2023 *Code* book to answer the following questions.

Article 404—Switches

1. Article 404 covers all _______ used as switches operating at 1,000V and below, unless specifically referenced elsewhere in this *Code* for higher voltages.

   (a) switches
   (b) switching devices
   (c) circuit breakers
   (d) all of these

2. Three-way and four-way switches shall be wired so that all switching is done only in the _______ circuit conductor.

   (a) ungrounded
   (b) grounded
   (c) equipment grounded
   (d) neutral

3. The grounded circuit conductor for the controlled lighting circuit shall be installed at the location where switches control lighting loads that are supplied by a grounded general-purpose branch circuit serving _______.

   (a) habitable rooms or occupiable spaces
   (b) attics
   (c) crawlspaces
   (d) all of these

4. Switches controlling line-to-neutral lighting loads shall not be required to have a grounded conductor provided at the switch location where a switch controls a _______.

   (a) ceiling fan
   (b) bathroom exhaust fan
   (c) lighting load consisting of all fluorescent fixtures with integral disconnects for the ballasts
   (d) receptacle load

5. Surface-mounted switches or circuit breakers in a damp or wet location shall be enclosed in a _______ enclosure or cabinet that complies with 312.2.

   (a) weatherproof
   (b) rainproof
   (c) watertight
   (d) raintight

6. Switches shall not be installed within tub or shower spaces unless installed as part of a _______ tub or shower assembly.

   (a) listed
   (b) identified
   (c) marked
   (d) any of these

7. _______ shall indicate whether they are in the open (off) or closed (on) position.

   (a) General-use switches
   (b) Motor-circuit switches
   (c) Circuit breakers
   (d) all of these

8. All switches and circuit breakers used as switches shall be located so that they can be operated from a readily ______ place.

    (a) accessible
    (b) visible
    (c) operable
    (d) open

9. Switches and circuit breakers installed adjacent to motors, appliances, or other equipment that they supply shall be permitted to be located ______ than 6 ft 7 in. and to be accessible by portable means.

    (a) lower
    (b) higher
    (c) no further
    (d) none of these

Article 406—Receptacles, Attachment Plugs, and Flanged Inlets

1. Article ______ covers the rating, type, and installation of receptacles, cord connectors, and attachment plugs (cord caps).

    (a) 400
    (b) 404
    (c) 406
    (d) 408

2. Receptacles mounted in boxes set back from the finished surface shall be installed such that the mounting ______ of the receptacle is(are) held rigidly at the finished surface.

    (a) screws
    (b) yoke or strap
    (c) cover plate
    (d) grounding clip

3. Receptacles mounted in boxes flush with the finished surface or projecting beyond it shall be installed so that the mounting yoke or strap of the receptacle is held rigidly against the ______.

    (a) box or box cover
    (b) faceplate
    (c) finished surface
    (d) bonding connection

4. Receptacles mounted to and supported by a cover shall be secured by more than ______ screw(s) unless listed and identified for securing by a single screw.

    (a) one
    (b) two
    (c) three
    (d) four

5. After installation, receptacle faces shall be flush with or project from faceplates of insulating material and shall project a minimum of ______ from metal faceplates.

    (a) 0.015 in.
    (b) 0.020 in.
    (c) 0.125 in.
    (d) 0.250 in.

6. Receptacle assemblies for installation in countertop surfaces shall be ______ for countertop applications.

    (a) identified
    (b) labeled
    (c) listed
    (d) approved

7. Receptacle assemblies and ______ receptacle assemblies listed for work surface or countertop applications shall be permitted to be installed in work surfaces.

    (a) AFCI
    (b) GFCI
    (c) current-limiting
    (d) all of these

8. Receptacles in or on countertop surfaces or work surfaces shall not be installed ______, unless listed for countertop or work surface applications.

    (a) in the sides of cabinets
    (b) in a face-up position
    (c) on GFCI circuits
    (d) on the kitchen small-appliance circuit

9. An outdoor receptacle in a location protected from the weather shall be installed in an enclosure that is weatherproof when the receptacle is ______.

    (a) covered
    (b) enclosed
    (c) protected
    (d) recessed in the finished surface

10. A receptacle is considered to be in a location protected from the weather when located under roofed open porches, canopies, marquees, and the like, where it will not be subjected to ______.

    (a) spray from a hose
    (b) a direct lightning hit
    (c) beating rain or water runoff
    (d) falling or wind-blown debris

11. Where required for receptacles in damp or wet locations, ______ covers of outlet box hoods shall be able to open at least 90 degrees, or fully open if the cover is not designed to open 90 degrees from the closed to open position, after installation.

    (a) flush
    (b) hinged
    (c) surface mounted
    (d) any of these

12. Receptacles of ______, 125V and 250V installed in a wet location shall have an enclosure that is weatherproof whether or not the attachment plug cap is inserted.

    (a) 15A and 20A
    (b) 30A and less
    (c) up to 50A
    (d) up to 100A

13. Where 15A and 20A receptacles are installed in a wet location, the outlet box ______ shall be listed and identified as extra-duty use.

    (a) sleeve
    (b) hood
    (c) threaded entry
    (d) mounting

14. All 15A and 20A, 125V and 250V nonlocking-type receptacles shall be listed and so identified as the ______ type.

    (a) weatherproof
    (b) weather-resistant
    (c) raintight
    (d) waterproof

15. A 30A, 208V receptacle installed in a wet location shall be listed weather-resistant type, and where the product intended to be plugged into it is not attended while in use, shall have an enclosure that is ______ with the attachment plug cap inserted or removed.

    (a) weatherproof
    (b) rainproof
    (c) raintight
    (d) any of these

16. Receptacles shall not be installed within a zone measured ______ horizontally from any outside edge of the bathtub or shower stall, including the space outside the bathtub or shower stall space below the zone, and 8 ft vertically above the top of the bathtub rim or shower stall threshold.

    (a) 3 ft
    (b) 4 ft
    (c) 5 ft
    (d) 6 ft

17. Receptacles shall not be installed inside of the tub or shower or within a zone measured 3 ft horizontally from any outside edge of the bathtub or shower stall. Receptacles installed where a hydromassage bathtub is ______ with the supply receptacle accessible only through a service access opening shall be permitted.

    (a) rated 20A or less
    (b) rated 30A or less
    (c) cord-and plug-connected
    (d) less than 125V

18. In bathrooms with less than the required zone, the receptacle required by 210.52(D) can be installed ______ the bathtub rim or shower stall threshold on the farthest wall within the room.

    (a) opposite
    (b) vertically in
    (c) horizontally in
    (d) any of these

19. In a dwelling unit, a ______ receptacle shall be permitted for an electronic toilet or an electronic bidet seat. The receptacle shall be readily accessible and cannot be located in the space between the toilet and the bathtub or shower.

    (a) duplex
    (b) single
    (c) quad
    (d) any of these

20. All nonlocking type 125V and 250V, 15A and 20A receptacles installed in ______ shall be listed as tamper resistant.

    (a) dwelling units
    (b) boathouses
    (c) mobile homes
    (d) all of these

21. Where tamper-resistant receptacles are required, receptacles located more than ______ above the floor shall not be required to be tamper resistant.

    (a) 4 ft
    (b) 5 ft
    (c) 5½ ft
    (d) 6 ft 7 in.

22. Nonlocking-type 15A and 20A, 125V and 250V receptacles in a dwelling unit shall be listed as tamper resistant except ______.

    (a) receptacles located more than 8½ ft above the floor
    (b) receptacles that are part of an appliance
    (c) receptacles that are part of a luminaire
    (d) receptacles that are part of a luminaire or appliance

23. Nonlocking-type 125V and 250V, 15A and 20A receptacles installed in ______ shall be listed as tamper resistant.

    (a) guest rooms and guest suites of hotels and motels
    (b) childcare facilities
    (c) preschools and elementary education facilities
    (d) all of these

24. Nongrounding 15A and 20A, 125V and 250V receptacles used for replacements as permitted in 406.4(D)(2)(a) shall not be required to be listed as tamper resistant.

    (a) True
    (b) False

25. All 15A and 20A, 125V and 250V nonlocking-type receptacles within clinics, medical and dental offices, and outpatient facilities in ______ shall be listed as tamper resistant.

    (a) business offices accessible to the general public spaces
    (b) lobbies, and waiting spaces
    (c) spaces of nursing homes and limited care facilities covered in 517.10(B)(2)
    (d) all of these

26. Nonlocking-type 125V and 250V, 15A and 20A receptacles installed in ______ shall be listed as tamper resistant.

    (a) places of awaiting transportation
    (b) gymnasiums, skating rinks, and auditoriums
    (c) dormitory units
    (d) all of these

27. Nonlocking-type 125V and 250V, 15A and 20A receptacles installed in ______ shall be listed as tamper resistant.

    (a) residential care/assisted living facilities
    (b) social and substance abuse rehabilitation facilities
    (c) group homes
    (d) all of these

28. Nonlocking-type 125V and 250V, 15A and 20A receptacles installed in ______ shall be listed as tamper resistant.

    (a) foster care facilities
    (b) nursing homes
    (c) psychiatric hospitals
    (d) all of these

29. Nonlocking-type 125V and 250V, 15A and 20A ______ installed in areas of agricultural buildings accessible to the general public and any common areas, shall be listed as tamper resistant.

    (a) receptacles
    (b) switches
    (c) overcurrent devices
    (d) none of these

30. Nonlocking-type 125V and 250V, 15A and 20A receptacles installed in areas of agricultural buildings converted to hospitality areas shall be listed as tamper resistant. These areas can include ______.

    (a) petting zoos
    (b) stables
    (c) buildings used for recreation or educational purposes
    (d) any of these

Article 408—Switchboards and Panelboards

1. Article 408 covers ______.

    (a) switchboards
    (b) switchgear
    (c) panelboards
    (d) all of these

2. Every panelboard circuit and circuit ______ shall be provided with a legible and permanent description.

    (a) location
    (b) installation
    (c) manufacturer
    (d) modification

3. Every panelboard circuit and circuit modification shall be provided with a legible and permanent description that is clear, evident, and specific to the purpose or use of each circuit including ______ positions with an unused overcurrent device.

    (a) spare
    (b) random
    (c) blank
    (d) special

4. Every panelboard circuit and circuit modification shall be provided with a legible and permanent description that is not dependent on ______ conditions of occupancy.

    (a) special
    (b) transient
    (c) random
    (d) any of these

5. Every panelboard circuit and circuit modification shall be provided with a legible and permanent description that is described with a degree of detail and clarity that is unlikely to result in confusion between circuits and is clear in explaining ______.

    (a) abbreviations and symbols
    (b) trademarks
    (c) listings
    (d) installer information and dates

6. All switchboards, switchgear, and panelboards supplied by a feeder(s) in ______ shall be permanently marked to indicate the identification and physical location where the power supply originates.

    (a) other than one- or two-family dwellings
    (b) all dwelling units
    (c) all nondwelling units
    (d) all dwelling units and all nondwelling units

7. The source of supply label required for switchboards, switchgear, and panelboards [408.4(B)] shall be permanently affixed, of sufficient durability to withstand the environment involved, and cannot be handwritten.

    (a) True
    (b) False

8. Unused openings for circuit breakers and switches in switchboards and panelboards shall be closed using ______, or other approved means that provide protection substantially equivalent to the wall of the enclosure.

    (a) duct seal and tape
    (b) identified closures
    (c) exothermic welding
    (d) sheet metal

9. Panelboards shall be mounted in cabinets, cutout boxes, or identified enclosures and where the available fault current is greater than ______, the panelboard and enclosure combination shall be evaluated for the application.

    (a) 5,000A
    (b) 10,000A
    (c) 12,500A
    (d) 22,500A

10. Panelboards ______ be installed in the face-up or face-down position.

    (a) shall not
    (b) are permitted to
    (c) listed for such purpose may
    (d) approved for such use may

Article 410—Luminaires

1. Article 410 covers luminaires, portable luminaires, lampholders, pendants, incandescent filament lamps, arc lamps, electric-discharge lamps, and ______, and the wiring and equipment forming part of such products and lighting installations.

    (a) decorative lighting products
    (b) lighting accessories for temporary seasonal and holiday use
    (c) portable flexible lighting products
    (d) all of these

2. Luminaires ______ suitable for wet locations shall be permitted to be used in a damp location.

    (a) marked
    (b) listed
    (c) identified
    (d) approved as

3. No parts of cord-connected luminaires, chain-, cable-, or cord-suspended luminaires, lighting track, pendants, or paddle fans with a light kit, shall be located within a zone measured 3 ft horizontally and ______ vertically from the top of the bathtub rim or shower stall threshold.

    (a) 4 ft
    (b) 6 ft
    (c) 8 ft
    (d) 12 ft

4. Luminaires located where subject to bathroom shower spray shall be marked suitable for ______ locations.

    (a) damp
    (b) wet
    (c) outdoor
    (d) wet or outdoor

5. Where luminaires are installed in a clothes closet, the clothes closet storage space shall be the volume bounded by the sides and back closet walls and planes extending from the closet floor vertically to a height of ______ or to the highest clothes' hanging rod.

    (a) 5½ ft
    (b) 6 ft
    (c) 6 ft 7 in.
    (d) 7 ft

6. A ______ type luminaire can be installed in a clothes closet storage space.

    (a) surface-mounted or recessed incandescent luminaire or LED luminaire with completely enclosed light source
    (b) surface-mounted or recessed fluorescent luminaire
    (c) surface-mounted fluorescent or LED luminaire identified as suitable for clothes closets
    (d) any of these

7. Incandescent luminaires with ______ enclosed lamps and pendant luminaires or lampholders shall not be permitted in clothes closet storage spaces.

    (a) open
    (b) partially
    (c) open or partially
    (d) any of these

8. Surface-mounted fluorescent or LED luminaires shall be permitted to be installed within the clothes closet storage space where ______ for this use.

    (a) identified
    (b) listed
    (c) approved
    (d) none of these

9. Surface-mounted fluorescent luminaires in clothes closet storage spaces are permitted on the wall above the door or on the ceiling, provided there is a minimum clearance of ______ from the storage space.

    (a) 3 in.
    (b) 6 in.
    (c) 8 in.
    (d) 12 in.

10. In clothes closet storage spaces, recessed incandescent or LED luminaires with a completely enclosed light source can be installed in the wall or the ceiling, provided there is a minimum clearance of ______ from the storage space.

    (a) 3 in.
    (b) 6 in.
    (c) 8 in.
    (d) 12 in.

Article 422—Appliances

1. Flexible cord for appliances is permitted to ______.

    (a) connect appliances to facilitate their frequent interchange
    (b) prevent the transmission of noise
    (c) facilitate the removal or disconnection of appliances that are fastened in place for maintenance or repair and the appliance is intended or identified for flexible cord connection
    (d) any of these

2. A waste disposer can be cord-and-plug-connected; the cord shall not be less than 18 in. or more than ______ in length.

   (a) 30 in.
   (b) 36 in.
   (c) 42 in.
   (d) 48 in.

3. Where a waste disposer is cord-and-plug-connected, the receptacles shall be ______ to protect against physical damage to the flexible cord.

   (a) located
   (b) shielded
   (c) guarded
   (d) any of these

4. The flexible cord for a(an) in-sink waste disposer shall have an equipment grounding conductor and terminate with a ______ attachment plug.

   (a) 3-wire
   (b) 4-wire
   (c) nongrounding-type
   (d) grounding-type

5. The length of the flexible cord for a trash compactor shall not be less than 3 ft or exceed ______ in length, measured from the face of the attachment plug to the plane of the rear of the appliance.

   (a) 2 ft
   (b) 4 ft
   (c) 6 ft
   (d) 8 ft

6. The length of the flexible cord for a built-in dishwasher shall not be less than 3 ft or exceed ______ in length, measured from the face of the attachment plug to the plane of the rear of the appliance.

   (a) 6½ ft
   (b) 7 ft
   (c) 7½ ft
   (d) 8 ft

7. Receptacles for built-in dishwashers and trash compactors shall be located so as to protect against physical damage to the ______.

   (a) flexible cord
   (b) cord cap
   (c) appliance
   (d) receptacle

8. Where a built-in trash compactor is to be cord-and-plug connected the receptacle shall be located ______ occupied by the appliance.

   (a) in the space
   (b) adjacent to the space
   (c) directly above the space
   (d) in the space or adjacent to the space

9. Where the flexible cord for a built-in trash compactor or dishwasher passes through an opening, it shall be protected against damage by a(an) ______.

   (a) bushing
   (b) grommet
   (c) approved means
   (d) any of these

10. Wall-mounted ovens and counter-mounted cooking units shall be permitted to be connected with a flexible cord identified as______ for the purpose.

    (a) listed
    (b) manufactured
    (c) suitable
    (d) sufficient

11. Range hoods shall be permitted to be cord-and-plug-connected with a flexible cord identified as suitable for use on range hoods in the installation instructions of the appliance manufacturer provided ______.

    (a) the length of the cord is not less than 18 in. and not over 4 ft
    (b) receptacles are located to protect against physical damage to the flexible cord
    (c) the receptacle is supplied by an individual branch circuit
    (d) all of these

FINAL EXAM A— STRAIGHT ORDER

Please use the 2023 *Code* book to answer the following questions.

1. Article _______ covers use and application, arrangement, and enforcement of the *National Electrical Code*.

   (a) 90
   (b) 110
   (c) 200
   (d) 300

2. The purpose of the *NEC* is for _______.

   (a) it to be used as a design manual
   (b) use as an instruction guide for untrained persons
   (c) the practical safeguarding of persons and property
   (d) interacting with inspectors

3. The *Code* does not cover installations under the exclusive control of an electric utility such as _______.

   (a) service drops or service laterals
   (b) electric utility office buildings
   (c) electric utility warehouses
   (d) electric utility garages

4. Chapters 1, 2, 3, and 4 of the *NEC* apply _______.

   (a) generally to all electrical installations
   (b) only to special occupancies and conditions
   (c) only to special equipment and material
   (d) all of these

5. Explanatory material, such as references to other standards, references to related sections of this *Code*, or information related to a *Code* rule, is included in this *Code* in the form of _______.

   (a) informational notes
   (b) footnotes
   (c) table notes
   (d) italicized text

6. Nonmandatory information relative to the use of the *NEC* is provided in informative annexes and are _______.

   (a) included for information purposes only
   (b) not enforceable requirements of the *Code*
   (c) enforceable as a requirement of the *Code*
   (d) included for information purposes only and are not enforceable requirements of the *Code*

7. The _______ is the neutral point.

   (a) common point on a wye-connection in a polyphase system
   (b) midpoint on a single-phase, 3-wire system
   (c) midpoint of a single-phase portion of a 3-phase delta system
   (d) any of these

8. ______ is, for grounded circuits, the voltage between the given conductor and that point or conductor of the circuit that is grounded; for ungrounded circuits, the greatest voltage between the given conductor and any other conductor of the circuit.

   (a) Line-to-line voltage
   (b) Voltage to ground
   (c) Phase-to-phase voltage
   (d) Neutral to ground voltage

9. Internal parts of electrical equipment, including busbars, wiring terminals, insulators, and other surfaces, shall not be damaged or contaminated by foreign materials such as ______, or corrosive residues.

   (a) paint, plaster
   (b) cleaners
   (c) abrasives
   (d) any of these

10. Pressure terminal or pressure splicing connectors and soldering lugs shall be ______ for the material of the conductor and shall be properly installed and used.

    (a) listed
    (b) approved
    (c) identified
    (d) all of these

11. ______, and access to and egress from working space, shall be provided and maintained about all electrical equipment to permit ready and safe operation and maintenance of such equipment.

    (a) Ventilation
    (b) Unrestricted movement
    (c) Circulation
    (d) Working space

12. Access to or egress from the required working space about electrical equipment is considered impeded if one or more simultaneously opened equipment doors restrict working space access to be less than ______ wide and 6½ ft high.

    (a) 24 in.
    (b) 28 in.
    (c) 30 in.
    (d) 36 in.

13. The minimum height of working spaces shall be clear and extend from the grade, floor, or platform to a height of ______ ft or the height of the equipment, whichever is greater.

    (a) 3 ft
    (b) 6 ft
    (c) 6½ ft
    (d) 7 ft

14. The grade, floor, or platform in the required working space about electrical equipment shall be as level and flat as ______ for the entire required depth and width of the working space.

    (a) practical
    (b) possible
    (c) required
    (d) none of these

15. An insulated grounded conductor ______ or smaller shall be identified by a continuous white or gray outer finish, or by three continuous white or gray stripes along its entire length on other than green insulation.

    (a) 8 AWG
    (b) 6 AWG
    (c) 4 AWG
    (d) 3 AWG

16. At the time of installation, grounded conductors ______ or larger can be identified by a distinctive white or gray marking at their terminations.

    (a) 10 AWG
    (b) 8 AWG
    (c) 6 AWG
    (d) 4 AWG

17. GFCI protection shall be provided for all 125V through 250V ______ in dwelling unit basements.

    (a) receptacles
    (b) switches
    (c) outlets
    (d) disconnects

18. In dwelling unit kitchens, GFCI protection shall be provided for 125V through 250V receptacles ______.

    (a) installed to serve the countertop surfaces
    (b) within 6 ft from the top inside edge of the bowl of the sink
    (c) installed to serve above or below the countertop surfaces
    (d) serving the kitchen

19. For dwellings, all outdoor outlets, other than those covered in 210.8(A) Ex 1, including outlets installed in ______, rated 50A or less, shall be provided with GFCI protection

    (a) garages that have floors located at or below grade level
    (b) accessory buildings
    (c) boathouses
    (d) all of these

20. All 120V, single-phase, 10A, 15A, and 20A branch circuits supplying outlets or devices installed in dwelling unit ______ shall be AFCI protected.

    (a) kitchens
    (b) garages
    (c) bathrooms
    (d) outdoor areas

21. In dwelling units, when determining the spacing of receptacle outlets, ______ on exterior walls shall not be considered wall space.

    (a) fixed panels
    (b) fixed glass
    (c) sliding panels
    (d) all of these

22. Floor receptacle outlets shall not be counted as part of the required number of receptacle outlets for dwelling unit wall spaces, unless they are located within ______ of the wall.

    (a) 6 in.
    (b) 12 in.
    (c) 18 in.
    (d) 24 in.

23. There shall be at least ______ receptacle(s) installed outdoors at a one-family dwelling and each unit of a two-family dwelling unit that is at grade level.

    (a) one
    (b) two
    (c) three
    (d) four

24. At least one receptacle outlet not more than ______ above a balcony, deck, or porch shall be installed at each balcony, deck, or porch that is attached to and accessible from a dwelling unit.

    (a) 2 ft
    (b) 3 ft
    (c) 6½ ft
    (d) 8 ft

25. At least one lighting outlet controlled by a listed wall-mounted control device shall be installed in dwelling unit hallways, stairways, and ______.

    (a) attached garages
    (b) detached garages with electric power
    (c) accessory buildings with electric power
    (d) all of these

26. For dwelling units, attached garages, detached garages with electric power, and accessory buildings with electric power, at least ______ exterior lighting outlet(s) controlled by a listed wall-mounted control device shall be installed to provide illumination on the exterior side of outdoor entrances or exits with grade-level access.

    (a) one
    (b) two
    (c) three
    (d) one or two

27. Rebar in multiple pieces used as a concrete-encased electrode shall be connected together by ______ tie wires or other effective means.

    (a) steel
    (b) plastic
    (c) aluminum
    (d) fiber glass

28. An electrode encased by at least 2 in. of concrete, located horizontally near the bottom or vertically and within that portion of a concrete foundation or footing that is in direct contact with the earth, is permitted as a grounding electrode when it consists of a bare copper conductor not smaller than ______.

    (a) 8 AWG
    (b) 6 AWG
    (c) 4 AWG
    (d) 1/0 AWG

29. ______ shall not be used as a grounding electrode(s).

    (a) Metal underground gas piping systems
    (b) Aluminum
    (c) Swimming pool structures and structural rebar
    (d) all of these

30. _______ electrodes shall be free from nonconductive coatings such as paint or enamel.

    (a) Rod
    (b) Pipe
    (c) Plate
    (d) all of these

31. Where a metal underground water pipe is used as a grounding electrode, the continuity of the grounding path or the bonding connection to interior piping shall not rely on _______ and similar equipment.

    (a) bonding jumpers
    (b) water meters or filtering devices
    (c) grounding clamps
    (d) all of these

32. If the supplemental electrode is a rod, pipe, or plate electrode, that portion of the bonding jumper that is the sole connection to the supplemental grounding electrode is not required to be larger than _______ copper.

    (a) 8 AWG
    (b) 6 AWG
    (c) 4 AWG
    (d) 1 AWG

33. All _______ that are spliced or terminated within the box shall be connected together. Connections and splices shall be made in accordance with 110.14(B) and 250.8 except that insulation shall not be required.

    (a) neutral conductors
    (b) equipment grounding conductors
    (c) phase conductors
    (d) switch-legs

34. The arrangement of grounding connections shall ensure that the disconnection or the removal of a luminaire, receptacle, or other device fed from the box does not interrupt the electrical continuity of the _______ conductor(s) providing an effective ground-fault current path.

    (a) grounded
    (b) ungrounded
    (c) equipment grounding
    (d) all of these

35. Where a cable or raceway-type wiring method is installed through bored holes in joists, rafters, or wood members, the holes shall be bored so that the edge of the hole is _______ the edges of the wood member.

    (a) not less than 1¼ in. from
    (b) immediately adjacent to
    (c) not less than ¹⁄₁₆ in. from
    (d) 90° away from

36. Cables laid in wood notches require protection against nails or screws by using a steel plate at least _______ thick, installed before the building finish is applied.

    (a) ¹⁄₁₆ in.
    (b) ⅛ in.
    (c) ¼ in.
    (d) ½ in.

37. Where raceways contain 4 AWG or larger insulated circuit conductors and these conductors enter a cabinet, a box, an enclosure, or a raceway the conductors shall be protected from abrasion during and after installation by an identified fitting providing a smoothly rounded _______ surface.

    (a) fiberglass
    (b) plastic
    (c) insulating
    (d) gray

38. Where raceways contain 4 AWG or larger insulated circuit conductors and these conductors enter a cabinet, a box, an enclosure, or a raceway the conductors shall be protected from abrasion during and after installation by _______.

    (a) an identified fitting that provides a smooth rounded insulating surface
    (b) a listed metal fitting that has smooth rounded edges
    (c) threaded hubs that provide a smooth rounded or flared entry
    (d) any of these

39. UF cable used with a 24V landscape lighting system can have a minimum cover of _______.

    (a) 6 in.
    (b) 12 in.
    (c) 18 in.
    (d) 24 in.

40. ______ shall be defined as the shortest distance measured between a point on the top surface of direct-buried cable and the top surface of finished grade.

    (a) Notched
    (b) Cover
    (c) Gap
    (d) Spacing

41. A(An) ______, with an integral bushed opening shall be used at the end of a conduit or other raceway that terminates underground where the conductors or cables emerge as a direct burial wiring method.

    (a) splice kit
    (b) connector
    (c) adapter
    (d) bushing or terminal fitting

42. All conductors of the same circuit shall be ______, unless otherwise specifically permitted in the *Code*.

    (a) bonded
    (b) grounded
    (c) the same size
    (d) in the same raceway or cable or be in close proximity in the same trench

43. Where independent support wires of a suspended ceiling assembly are used to support raceways, cable assemblies, or boxes above a ceiling, they shall be secured at ______ end(s).

    (a) one
    (b) both
    (c) the line and load
    (d) at the attachment to the structural member

44. Wiring located within the cavity of a fire-rated floor-ceiling or roof-ceiling assembly shall not be secured to, or supported by, the ceiling assembly, including the ceiling support ______.

    (a) wires
    (b) hangers
    (c) rods
    (d) none of these

45. The minimum size copper conductor permitted for voltage ratings up to 2,000V is ______.

    (a) 14 AWG
    (b) 12 AWG
    (c) 10 AWG
    (d) 8 AWG

46. Solid aluminum conductors of 8 AWG, 10 AWG, and 12 AWG shall be made of an AA-______ series electrical grade aluminum alloy conductor material.

    (a) 1,350
    (b) 2,000
    (c) 6,000
    (d) 8,000

47. The insulation of USE-2 cable is ______ resistant.

    (a) heat
    (b) moisture
    (c) sunlight
    (d) heat and moisture

48. Conductors that are intended for use as ungrounded conductors, whether used as a single conductor or in multiconductor cables, shall be finished to be clearly distinguishable from ______ conductors.

    (a) grounded
    (b) ungrounded
    (c) equipment grounding
    (d) grounded and equipment grounding

49. Where cable is used, each cable shall be ______ to the cabinet, cutout box, or meter socket enclosure.

    (a) secured
    (b) supported
    (c) strapped
    (d) stapled

50. Nonmetallic-sheathed cables can enter the top of surface-mounted cabinets, cutout boxes, and meter socket enclosures through nonflexible raceways not less than 18 in. and not more than ______ in length if all of the required conditions are met.

    (a) 3 ft
    (b) 10 ft
    (c) 25 ft
    (d) 100 ft

51. The number of 12 THWN-2 conductors permitted in a 4 × 4 × 1½ box is ______.

    (a) 7
    (b) 9
    (c) 11
    (d) 13

52. The total volume occupied by one 12/3 NM cable, one 12/2 NM cable, two internal cable clamps, and a single-pole switch is ______.

    (a) 2.00 cu in.
    (b) 4.50 cu in.
    (c) 14.50 cu in.
    (d) 20.25 cu in.

53. Where cable assemblies with nonmetallic sheaths are used, the sheath shall extend not less than ______ inside the box and beyond any cable clamp.

    (a) ¼ in.
    (b) ⅜ in.
    (c) ½ in.
    (d) ¾ in.

54. In installations within noncombustible walls or ceilings, the front edge of a box, plaster ring, extension ring, or listed extender employing a flush-type cover, shall be set back not more than ______ from the finished surface.

    (a) ⅛ in.
    (b) ¼ in.
    (c) ⅜ in.
    (d) ½ in.

55. Two intermediate metal or rigid metal conduits threaded wrenchtight into an enclosure can be used to support an outlet box containing devices or luminaires if each raceway is supported within ______ of the box.

    (a) 12 in.
    (b) 18 in.
    (c) 24 in.
    (d) 36 in.

56. A pendant box shall be supported from a multiconductor cord or cable in an approved manner that protects the conductors against strain. A connection to a box equipped with a hub shall be made with a(an) ______ cord grip attachment fitting marked for use with a threaded hub.

    (a) approved
    (b) listed
    (c) marked
    (d) identified

57. Armored cable shall not be installed ______.

    (a) in damp or wet locations
    (b) where subject to physical damage
    (c) where exposed to corrosive conditions
    (d) all of these

58. Exposed runs of AC cable can be installed on the underside of joists where supported at each joist and located so it is not subject to physical damage.

    (a) physical damage
    (b) severe damage
    (c) minor damage
    (d) any of these

59. MC cable is permitted for use in damp or wet locations where a corrosion-resistant jacket is provided over the metallic covering and ______.

    (a) the metallic covering is impervious to moisture.
    (b) a jacket resistant to moisture is provided under the metal covering.
    (c) the insulated conductors under the metallic covering are listed for use in wet locations.
    (d) any of these

60. MC cable shall not be used ______.

    (a) where subject to physical damage
    (b) direct buried in the earth or embedded in concrete unless identified for direct burial
    (c) exposed to cinder fills, strong chlorides, caustic alkalis, or vapors of chlorine or of hydrochloric acids
    (d) all of these

61. NM cable can be installed in multifamily dwellings and their detached garages permitted to be of Type(s) ______ construction.

    (a) III
    (b) IV
    (c) V
    (d) all of these

62. NM cable shall not be permitted to be installed ______ in dropped or suspended ceilings in other than one- and two-family and multifamily dwellings.

    (a) concealed
    (b) exposed
    (c) open
    (d) hidden

63. Flat NM cables shall not be stapled on edge.

    (a) True
    (b) False

64. Nonmetallic-sheathed cable shall be permitted to be unsupported where the cable is ______.

    (a) fished between access points through concealed spaces in finished buildings or structures
    (b) not more than 6 ft from the last point of cable support to the point of connection to a luminaire within an accessible ceiling in one-, two-, or multifamily dwellings
    (c) between framing members and exterior masonry walls
    (d) where installed in attics

65. Which of following statements about power and control tray cable is incorrect?

    (a) It may be used in a raceway.
    (b) It may be used for power, lighting, or control circuits.
    (c) It may be installed where it will be exposed to physical damage.
    (d) It may be used in cable trays in hazardous locations where the conditions of maintenance and supervision ensure that only qualified persons will service the installation.

66. ______ cable can be used for interior wiring as long as it complies with the installation requirements of Part II of Article 334, excluding 334.80.

    (a) SE
    (b) UF
    (c) MI
    (d) FCC

67. UF cable shall not be used in ______.

    (a) motion picture studios
    (b) storage battery rooms
    (c) hoistways
    (d) all of these

68. UF cable shall not be used ______.

    (a) in any hazardous (classified) location except as otherwise permitted in this *Code*
    (b) embedded in poured cement, concrete, or aggregate
    (c) where exposed to direct rays of the sun, unless identified as sunlight resistant
    (d) all of these

69. Trade size 1 IMC run straight with threaded couplings shall be supported at intervals not exceeding ______.

    (a) 8 ft
    (b) 10 ft
    (c) 12 ft
    (d) 15 ft

70. Horizontal runs of IMC supported by openings through framing members at intervals not exceeding ______ and securely fastened within 3 ft of terminations shall be permitted.

    (a) 5 ft
    (b) 8 ft
    (c) 10 ft
    (d) 15 ft

71. The total degrees of bends in a run of RMC shall not exceed ______ between pull points.

    (a) 120 degrees
    (b) 180 degrees
    (c) 270 degrees
    (d) 360 degrees

72. Cut ends of RMC shall be ______ or otherwise finished to remove rough edges.

    (a) threaded
    (b) reamed
    (c) painted
    (d) galvanized

73. Threadless couplings and connectors used with RMC in wet locations shall be ______.

    (a) listed for wet locations
    (b) listed for damp locations
    (c) nonabsorbent
    (d) weatherproof

74. Running threads shall not be used on RMC for connection at ______.

    (a) boxes
    (b) cabinets
    (c) couplings
    (d) meter sockets

75. Cable ties used to securely fasten flexible metal conduit shall be ______ for securement and support.

    (a) approved
    (b) labeled
    (c) listed
    (d) listed and identified

76. Flexible metal conduit shall not be required to be ______ where fished between access points through concealed spaces in finished buildings or structures and supporting is impracticable.

    (a) fastened
    (b) strapped
    (c) complete
    (d) secured and supported

77. LFMC shall not be required to be secured or supported where fished between access points through ______ spaces in finished buildings or structures and supporting is impractical.

    (a) concealed
    (b) exposed
    (c) hazardous (classified)
    (d) completed

78. For liquidtight flexible metal conduit, if flexibility is necessary after installation, unsecured lengths from the last point the raceway is securely fastened shall not exceed ______.

    (a) 3 ft for trade sizes ½ through 1¼
    (b) 4 ft for trade sizes 1½ through 2
    (c) 5 ft for trade sizes 2½ and larger
    (d) all of these

79. Field bends in PVC conduit shall be made only ______.

    (a) by hand forming the bend
    (b) with identified bending equipment
    (c) with a truck exhaust pipe
    (d) by use of an open flame torch

80. The total degrees of bends in a run of PVC shall not exceed ______ between pull points.

    (a) 120 degrees
    (b) 180 degrees
    (c) 270 degrees
    (d) 360 degrees

81. LFNC shall be permitted to be used exposed or concealed in locations subject to severe ______ influences or where subject to chemicals for which the materials are specifically approved.

    (a) corrosive
    (b) wet
    (c) dry
    (d) damp

82. Extreme cold can cause some types of liquidtight flexible nonmetallic conduit to become ______ and therefore more susceptible to damage from physical contact.

    (a) stiff
    (b) larger
    (c) weak
    (d) brittle

83. Galvanized steel and stainless steel EMT, elbows, couplings, and fittings can be installed in concrete, in direct contact with the earth, or in areas subject to severe corrosive influences where ______.

    (a) protected by corrosion protection
    (b) made of aluminum
    (c) made of stainless steel
    (d) listed for wet locations

84. When EMT is installed in wet locations, all supports, bolts, straps, and screws shall be ______.

    (a) made of aluminum
    (b) protected against corrosion
    (c) made of stainless steel
    (d) of nonmetallic materials only

85. ENT shall be permitted to be used above suspended ceilings in buildings exceeding ______ floor above grade where the building is protected throughout by an approved automatic fire protective system.

    (a) one
    (b) two
    (c) three
    (d) four

86. ENT and fittings can be ______, provided fittings identified for this purpose are used.

    (a) encased in poured concrete floors, ceilings, walls, and slabs
    (b) embedded in a concrete slab on grade where the tubing is placed on sand or approved screenings
    (c) installed in wet locations as permitted in 362.10
    (d) any of these

87. Where ENT enters a box, fitting, or other enclosure, a bushing or ______ shall be provided to protect the wire from abrasion unless the box, fitting, or enclosure design provides equivalent protection.

    (a) adapter
    (b) coupling
    (c) connector
    (d) insulator

88. Metal wireways shall not be permitted for ______.

    (a) exposed work
    (b) hazardous (classified) locations
    (c) wet locations
    (d) severe corrosive environments

89. Unbroken lengths of surface metal raceways can be run through dry ______.

    (a) walls
    (b) partitions
    (c) floors
    (d) all of these

90. Surface metal raceways shall not be used ______.

    (a) where subject to severe physical damage
    (b) where subject to corrosive vapors
    (c) in hoistways
    (d) all of these

91. Cable trays shall be ______ except as permitted by 392.18(D).

    (a) exposed
    (b) accessible
    (c) readily accessible
    (d) exposed and accessible

92. In industrial facilities where conditions of maintenance and supervision ensure that only qualified persons will service the installation, cable tray systems can be used to support ______.

    (a) raceways
    (b) cables
    (c) boxes and conduit bodies
    (d) all of these

93. All switches and circuit breakers used as switches shall be located so that they can be operated from a readily ______ place.

    (a) accessible
    (b) visible
    (c) operable
    (d) open

94. Switches and circuit breakers installed adjacent to motors, appliances, or other equipment that they supply shall be permitted to be located ______ than 6 ft 7 in. and to be accessible by portable means.

    (a) lower
    (b) higher
    (c) no further
    (d) none of these

95. An outdoor receptacle in a location protected from the weather shall be installed in an enclosure that is weatherproof when the receptacle is ______.

    (a) covered
    (b) enclosed
    (c) protected
    (d) recessed in the finished surface

96. In a dwelling unit, a ______ receptacle shall be permitted for an electronic toilet or an electronic bidet seat. The receptacle shall be readily accessible and cannot be located in the space between the toilet and the bathtub or shower.

    (a) duplex
    (b) single
    (c) quad
    (d) any of these

97. Nonlocking-type 15A and 20A, 125V and 250V receptacles in a dwelling unit shall be listed as tamper resistant except ______.

    (a) receptacles located more than 8½ ft above the floor
    (b) receptacles that are part of an appliance
    (c) receptacles that are part of a luminaire
    (d) receptacles that are part of a luminaire or appliance

98. Panelboards shall be mounted in cabinets, cutout boxes, or identified enclosures and where the available fault current is greater than _______, the panelboard and enclosure combination shall be evaluated for the application.

    (a) 5,000A
    (b) 10,000A
    (c) 12,500A
    (d) 22,500A

99. In clothes closet storage spaces, recessed incandescent or LED luminaires with a completely enclosed light source can be installed in the wall or the ceiling, provided there is a minimum clearance of _______ from the storage space.

    (a) 3 in.
    (b) 6 in.
    (c) 8 in.
    (d) 12 in.

100. Where the flexible cord for a built-in trash compactor or dishwasher passes through an opening, it shall be protected against damage by a(an) _______.

    (a) bushing
    (b) grommet
    (c) approved means
    (d) any of these

FINAL EXAM B— RANDOM ORDER

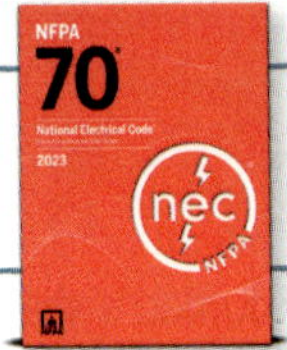

Please use the 2023 *Code* book to answer the following questions.

1. AC cable fittings shall not be permitted as a means of cable support.

   (a) True
   (b) False

2. Raceways may be used as a means of support where the raceway contains power-supply conductors for electrically controlled equipment and is used to _______ Class 2 or Class 3 circuit conductors or cables that are solely for the purpose of connection to the equipment control circuits.

   (a) support
   (b) secure
   (c) strap
   (d) none of these

3. The _______ ends of PVC conduit shall be trimmed inside and outside to remove the burrs and rough edges.

   (a) cut
   (b) new
   (c) old
   (d) blunt

4. Luminaires _______ suitable for wet locations shall be permitted to be used in a damp location.

   (a) marked
   (b) listed
   (c) identified
   (d) approved as

5. GFCI protection shall be provided for crawl space lighting outlets not exceeding _______.

   (a) 120V
   (b) 125V
   (c) 240V
   (d) 250V

6. NM cable shall be protected from physical damage by _______.

   (a) EMT
   (b) Schedule 80 PVC conduit
   (c) RMC
   (d) any of these

7. Underground raceways and cable assemblies entering a hand-hole enclosure shall extend into the enclosure, but they are not required to be _______.

   (a) bonded
   (b) insulated
   (c) mechanically connected to the enclosure
   (d) electrically connected to the enclosure

8. For one- and two-family dwellings, at least one receptacle outlet shall be installed in each _______.

   (a) separate unfinished portion of a basement
   (b) attached or detached garage with electric power
   (c) accessory building with electric power
   (d) all of these

9. All supports, bolts, straps, screws, and so forth, associated with the installation of RMC in wet locations shall be ______.

    (a) weatherproof
    (b) made of stainless steel
    (c) made of aluminum
    (d) protected against corrosion

10. PVC conduit shall be permitted to be ______.

    (a) encased in concrete
    (b) used for the support of luminaires
    (c) installed in movie theaters
    (d) none of these

11. Working space required by Section 110.26 shall not be used for ______.

    (a) storage
    (b) raceways
    (c) lighting
    (d) accessibility

12. PVC conduit is permitted in locations subject to severe corrosive influences and where subject to chemicals for which the materials are specifically ______.

    (a) approved
    (b) identified
    (c) listed
    (d) non-hazardous

13. A laundry receptacle outlet shall not be required in each dwelling unit of a multifamily building if laundry facilities are provided on the ______ for all building occupants.

    (a) premises
    (b) outside
    (c) inside
    (d) roof

14. Factory-installed receptacles mounted internally to bathroom ______ assemblies shall not require GFCI protection unless required by the installation instructions or listing.

    (a) surface-mounted luminaire
    (b) exhaust fan
    (c) electric baseboard heat
    (d) all of these

15. Nongrounding 15A and 20A, 125V and 250V receptacles used for replacements as permitted in 406.4(D)(2)(a) shall not be required to be listed as tamper resistant.

    (a) True
    (b) False

16. For the continuity of equipment grounding conductors and attachment in boxes, a connection used for ______ shall be made between the metal box and the equipment grounding conductor(s).

    (a) bonding
    (b) connections and splices
    (c) extending the length of the circuit
    (d) no other purpose

17. Rigid metal conduit that is directly buried outdoors shall have at least ______ of cover.

    (a) 6 in.
    (b) 12 in.
    (c) 18 in.
    (d) 24 in.

18. PVC-coated RMC shall be ______ in accordance with manufacturer's instructions to prevent damage to the exterior coating.

    (a) threaded
    (b) cut
    (c) bent
    (d) none of these

19. At least one lighting outlet controlled by a listed ______ shall be installed in every habitable room, kitchen, laundry area, and bathroom of a dwelling unit.

    (a) wall-mounted control device
    (b) switch
    (c) occupancy sensor
    (d) motion detector

20. Bends in LFNC shall be made so that the conduit will not be damaged and the internal diameter of the conduit will not be effectively reduced. Bends can be made ______.

    (a) manually without auxiliary equipment
    (b) with bending equipment identified for the purpose
    (c) with any kind of conduit bending tool that will work
    (d) by the use of an open flame torch

21. Power distribution blocks in metal wireways shall not have ______ live parts exposed within a(an) ______.

    (a) energized
    (b) concealed
    (c) insulated
    (d) uninsulated

22. Where conduit or tubing is used for the protection from physical damage of NM cable, it shall be provided with a bushing or adapter that provides protection from abrasion at the point the cable ______ the raceway.

    (a) enters and exits
    (b) leaves and comes into
    (c) begins and ends
    (d) none of these

23. Insulated conductors with letter designation of ______, are permitted in a wet location with a maximum operating temperature of 90°C.

    (a) USE
    (b) RHW
    (c) XHWN
    (d) THWN-2

24. All 15A and 20A, 125V and 250V nonlocking-type receptacles shall be listed and so identified as the ______ type.

    (a) weatherproof
    (b) weather-resistant
    (c) raintight
    (d) waterproof

25. All 125V through 250V receptacles installed in crawl spaces at or below grade level of dwelling units shall have ______ protection.

    (a) AFCI
    (b) GFCI
    (c) GFPE
    (d) none of these

26. Article ______ covers the installation and construction specifications of cabinets, cutout boxes, and meter socket enclosures.

    (a) 300
    (b) 310
    (c) 312
    (d) 314

27. Electrical hazards often occur because the initial ______ did not provide for increases in the use of electricity.

    (a) inspection
    (b) owner
    (c) wiring
    (d) builder

28. Where electrical equipment is installed under metal-corrugated sheet roof decking, the 1½-in. spacing is not required where metal-corrugated sheet roof decking is covered with a concrete slab with a minimum thickness of ______, measured from the top of the corrugated roofing.

    (a) ½ in.
    (b) 1 in.
    (c) 1½ in.
    (d) 2 in.

29. Splices and taps in surface metal raceways without removable covers shall be made only in ______.

    (a) boxes
    (b) raceways
    (c) conduit bodies
    (d) none of these

30. Article ______ covers the use, installation, and construction specifications for power and control tray cable, TC.

    (a) 326
    (b) 330
    (c) 334
    (d) 336

31. Compliance with the *Code* and proper maintenance result in an installation that is ______.

    (a) essentially free from hazard
    (b) not necessarily efficient or convenient
    (c) not necessarily adequate for good service or future expansion
    (d) all of these

32. The *Code* does not cover underground mine installations, or self-propelled mobile surface ______ machinery and its attendant electrical trailing cable.

    (a) paving
    (b) mining
    (c) harvesting
    (d) excavating

33. Bonded is defined as ______ to establish electrical continuity and conductivity.

    (a) isolated
    (b) guarded
    (c) connected
    (d) separated

34. Where AC cable is run across the top of a framing member(s) in an attic space not accessible by permanently installed stairs or ladders, guard strip protection shall only be required within ______ of the scuttle hole or attic entrance.

    (a) 3 ft
    (b) 4 ft
    (c) 5 ft
    (d) 6 ft

35. UF cable can be used in commercial garages.

    (a) True
    (b) False

36. Where raceways are installed in wet locations above grade, the interior of these raceways shall be considered a ______ location.

    (a) wet
    (b) dry
    (c) damp
    (d) corrosive

37. Working space is required for equipment operating at 1,000V, nominal, or less to ground and likely to require ______ while energized.

    (a) examination
    (b) adjustment
    (c) servicing or maintenance
    (d) all of these

38. A permitted wiring method for use in underground installations is ______.

    (a) SE cable
    (b) UF cable
    (c) THHN in PVC conduit
    (d) NM in a raceway

39. EMT couplings and connectors shall be made up ______.

    (a) of metal
    (b) in accordance with industry standards
    (c) tight
    (d) to be readily accessible

40. General requirements for the examination and approval, installation and use, access to and spaces about electrical conductors and equipment; enclosures intended for personnel entry; and tunnel installations are within the scope of ______.

    (a) Article 800
    (b) Article 300
    (c) Article 110
    (d) Annex J

41. Receptacles mounted in boxes flush with the finished surface or projecting beyond it shall be installed so that the mounting yoke or strap of the receptacle is held rigidly against the ______.

    (a) box or box cover
    (b) faceplate
    (c) finished surface
    (d) bonding connection

42. Underground ______ shall be installed so they are accessible without excavating sidewalks, paving, earth, or other substance that is to be used to establish the finished grade.

    (a) boxes and handhole enclosures
    (b) conduit bodies
    (c) handhole enclosures
    (d) none of these

43. The use, installation, and construction specifications for liquid-tight flexible metal conduit (LFMC) and associated fittings are covered within Article ______.

    (a) 300
    (b) 334
    (c) 350
    (d) 410

44. Article ______ covers the use, installation, and construction specifications for electrical nonmetallic tubing (ENT) and associated fittings.

    (a) 358
    (b) 362
    (c) 366
    (d) 392

45. USE cable is not permitted for ______ wiring.

    (a) underground
    (b) interior
    (c) aerial
    (d) aboveground installations

46. NM cable shall closely follow the _______ of the building finish or running boards when run exposed.

    (a) surface
    (b) edges
    (c) corners
    (d) none of these

47. Horizontal runs of RMC supported by openings through _______ at intervals not exceeding 10 ft and securely fastened within 3 ft of termination points shall be permitted.

    (a) walls
    (b) trusses
    (c) rafters
    (d) framing members

48. Grounding electrodes of bare or electrically conductive coated iron or steel plates shall be at least _______ thick.

    (a) ⅛ in.
    (b) ¼ in.
    (c) ½ in.
    (d) ¾ in.

49. NM cable on a wall of an unfinished basement installed in a listed raceway shall have a _______ installed at the point where the cable enters the raceway.

    (a) suitable insulating bushing or adapter
    (b) sealing fitting
    (c) bonding bushing
    (d) junction box

50. Where NM cable is run at angles with joists in unfinished basements and crawl spaces, it is permissible to secure cables not smaller than _______ conductors directly to the lower edges of the joist.

    (a) three, 6 AWG
    (b) four, 8 AWG
    (c) four, 10 AWG
    (d) two 6 AWG or three 8 AWG

51. Working space distances for enclosed live parts shall be measured from the _______ of equipment if the live parts are enclosed.

    (a) enclosure or opening
    (b) front or back
    (c) mounting pad
    (d) footprint

52. Kitchen wall countertop and work surface space receptacle outlets shall be installed so that no point along the wall line is more than _______ measured horizontally from a receptacle outlet in that space.

    (a) 10 in.
    (b) 12 in.
    (c) 16 in.
    (d) 24 in.

53. The interior of underground raceways shall be considered a _______ location.

    (a) wet
    (b) dry
    (c) damp
    (d) corrosive

54. Luminaires located where subject to bathroom shower spray shall be marked suitable for _______ locations.

    (a) damp
    (b) wet
    (c) outdoor
    (d) wet or outdoor

55. Metal underground systems or structures such as piping systems, underground tanks, and underground metal well casings that are not bonded to a metal _______ are permitted as grounding electrodes.

    (a) gas pipe
    (b) fire-sprinkler pipe
    (c) water pipe
    (d) none of these

56. Where a PVC conduit enters a box, fitting, or other enclosure, a _______ or adapter shall be provided to protect the wire from abrasion unless the box, fitting, or enclosure design provides equivalent protection.

    (a) bushing
    (b) connector
    (c) coupling
    (d) insulator

57. A system or circuit conductor that is intentionally grounded is called a(an) _______.

    (a) grounding conductor
    (b) unidentified conductor
    (c) grounded conductor
    (d) grounding electrode conductor

58. Three-way and four-way switches shall be wired so that all switching is done only in the _______ circuit conductor.

    (a) ungrounded
    (b) grounded
    (c) equipment grounded
    (d) neutral

59. Where more than two SE cables are installed in contact with thermal insulation, caulk, or sealing foam without maintaining spacing between cables, the ampacity of each conductor shall be _______ in accordance with Table 310.15(C)(1).

    (a) increased
    (b) adjusted
    (c) corrected
    (d) multiplied

60. A luminaire is a complete lighting unit consisting of a light source such as a lamp or lamps, together with the parts designed to position the _______ and connect it to the power supply.

    (a) lampholder
    (b) light source
    (c) fixture
    (d) bulb

61. At least one lighting outlet _______ shall be located at the point of entry to the attic, underfloor space, utility room, or basement where these spaces are used for storage or contain equipment requiring servicing.

    (a) that is unswitched
    (b) containing or controlled by a switch or listed wall-mounted control device
    (c) that is GFCI protected
    (d) that is shielded from damage

62. Where a building is supplied with a(an) _______ automatic fire protective system, ENT shall be permitted to be used within floors and ceilings, exposed or concealed, in buildings exceeding three floors above grade.

    (a) listed
    (b) identified
    (c) approved
    (d) NFPA 72

63. In order for a metal underground water pipe to be used as a grounding electrode, it shall be in direct contact with the earth for _______.

    (a) 5 ft
    (b) 10 ft or more
    (c) less than 10 ft
    (d) 20 ft or more

64. Except to detect alterations or damage, qualified electrical testing laboratory listed factory-installed _______ wiring of equipment does not need to be inspected for *NEC* compliance at the time of installation.

    (a) external
    (b) associated
    (c) internal
    (d) all of these

65. Where approved, RMC shall not be required to be securely fastened within _______ of the service head for above-the-roof termination of a mast.

    (a) 1 ft
    (b) 2 ft
    (c) 3 ft
    (d) 5 ft

66. _______ shall indicate whether they are in the open (off) or closed (on) position.

    (a) General-use switches
    (b) Motor-circuit switches
    (c) Circuit breakers
    (d) all of these

67. Securing or supporting of LFNC is not required where installed in lengths not exceeding _______ from the last point where the raceway is securely fastened for connections within an accessible ceiling to a luminaire(s) or other equipment.

    (a) 3 ft
    (b) 6 ft
    (c) 8 ft
    (d) 10 ft

68. When the *Code* uses _______, it indicates the actions are allowed but not required.

    (a) shall or shall not
    (b) shall not be permitted
    (c) shall be permitted
    (d) none of these

69. A receptacle is considered to be in a location protected from the weather when located under roofed open porches, canopies, marquees, and the like, where it will not be subjected to ______.

(a) spray from a hose
(b) a direct lightning hit
(c) beating rain or water runoff
(d) falling or wind-blown debris

70. Where RMC enters a box, fitting, or other enclosure, ______ shall be provided to protect the wire from abrasion, unless the design of the box, fitting, or enclosure affords equivalent protection.

(a) a bushing
(b) duct seal
(c) electrical tape
(d) seal fittings

71. Conductors for general wiring not specifically permitted elsewhere in this *Code* to be covered or bare shall ______.

(a) not be permitted
(b) be insulated
(c) be rated
(d) be listed

72. Where lighting outlets are installed for an interior stairway with ______ risers between floor levels, there shall be a listed wall-mounted control device at each floor level and at each landing level that includes a stairway entry to control the lighting outlets.

(a) three or more
(b) four or more
(c) six or more
(d) any number of

73. In the *NEC*, the word(s) ______ indicate a mandatory requirement.

(a) shall
(b) shall not
(c) shall be permitted
(d) shall or shall not

74. Expansion fittings for underground runs of direct buried PVC conduit emerging from the ground shall be provided above grade when required to compensate for ______.

(a) earth settling
(b) earth movement
(c) frost heave
(d) all of these

75. Where the opening to an outlet, junction, or switch point is less than 8 in. in any dimension, the length of free conductor of each conductor, spliced or unspliced, shall extend at least ______ outside the opening of the enclosure.

(a) 1 in.
(b) 3 in.
(c) 6 in.
(d) 12 in.

76. A waste disposer can be cord-and-plug-connected; the cord shall not be less than 18 in. or more than ______ in length.

(a) 30 in.
(b) 36 in.
(c) 42 in.
(d) 48 in.

77. Conductors in raceways shall be ______ between outlets, boxes, devices, and so forth.

(a) continuous
(b) installed
(c) copper
(d) in conduit

78. A multioutlet assembly can be installed in ______ locations.

(a) dry
(b) damp
(c) damp and wet
(d) dry and damp

79. All 125V through 250V receptacles installed in dwelling unit boathouses shall have ______ protection.

(a) GFCI
(b) AFCI
(c) GFPE
(d) SPGFCI

80. Cable tray systems shall not be used ______.

(a) in hoistways
(b) where subject to severe physical damage
(c) in hazardous (classified) locations
(d) in hoistways or where subject to severe physical damage

81. Liquidtight nonmetallic flexible conduit is not permitted to be used ______.

    (a) where subject to physical damage
    (b) where ambient and conductor temperatures exceed its listing
    (c) in lengths greater than 6 ft unless approved
    (d) all of these

82. Electrical metallic tubing that is directly buried under a two-family dwelling driveway shall have at least ______ of cover.

    (a) 6 in.
    (b) 12 in.
    (c) 18 in.
    (d) 24 in.

83. Receptacles installed for ______ and similar work surfaces as specified in 210.52(C) shall not be considered as the receptacle outlets required by 210.52(A).

    (a) countertops
    (b) tables
    (c) peninsulas
    (d) none of these

84. ENT shall not be used where exposed to the direct rays of the sun, unless identified as ______.

    (a) high-temperature rated
    (b) sunlight resistant
    (c) Schedule 80
    (d) suitable for the application

85. Article ______ covers the use, installation, and construction specifications for intermediate metal conduit (IMC) and associated fittings.

    (a) 342
    (b) 348
    (c) 352
    (d) 356

86. Handhole enclosures shall be designed and installed to withstand ______.

    (a) 600 lb of pressure
    (b) 3,000 lb of pressure
    (c) 6,000 lb of pressure
    (d) all loads likely to be imposed on them

87. Article ______ covers the use, installation, and construction specifications for electrical metallic tubing (EMT) and associated fittings.

    (a) 334
    (b) 350
    (c) 356
    (d) 358

88. Range hoods shall be permitted to be cord-and-plug-connected with a flexible cord identified as suitable for use on range hoods in the installation instructions of the appliance manufacturer provided ______.

    (a) the length of the cord is not less than 18 in. and not over 4 ft
    (b) receptacles are located to protect against physical damage to the flexible cord
    (c) the receptacle is supplied by an individual branch circuit
    (d) all of these

89. A PVC raceway covered in 2 in. of concrete is required to have a minimal buried depth of ______.

    (a) 6 in.
    (b) 12 in.
    (c) 18 in.
    (d) 24 in.

90. Stainless steel and aluminum fittings and enclosures shall be permitted to be used with galvanized steel RMC, and galvanized steel fittings and enclosures shall be permitted to be used with aluminum RMC where not subject to ______.

    (a) physical damage
    (b) severe corrosive influences
    (c) excessive moisture
    (d) all of these

91. A rod or pipe electrode shall be installed such that at least ______ of length is in contact with the soil.

    (a) 30 in.
    (b) 6 ft
    (c) 8 ft
    (d) 10 ft

92. The upper end of the rod electrode shall be _______ ground level unless the aboveground end and the grounding electrode conductor attachment are protected against physical damage as specified in 250.10.

    (a) no more than 1 in. above
    (b) no more than 2 in. above
    (c) no more than 3 in. above
    (d) flush with or below ground level

93. A _______ type luminaire can be installed in a clothes closet storage space.

    (a) surface-mounted or recessed incandescent luminaire or LED luminaire with completely enclosed light source
    (b) surface-mounted or recessed fluorescent luminaire
    (c) surface-mounted fluorescent or LED luminaire identified as suitable for clothes closets
    (d) any of these

94. All nonlocking type 125V and 250V, 15A and 20A receptacles installed in _______ shall be listed as tamper resistant.

    (a) dwelling units
    (b) boathouses
    (c) mobile homes
    (d) all of these

95. Unbroken lengths of electric nonmetallic tubing shall not be required to be secured where fished between access points for _______ work in finished buildings or structures and securing is impractical.

    (a) concealed
    (b) exposed
    (c) hazardous
    (d) completed

96. Where NM cables pass through cut or drilled slots or holes in metal members, the cable shall be protected by _______ which are installed in the opening prior to the installation of the cable and which securely cover all metal edges.

    (a) anti-short devices
    (b) sleeves
    (c) plates
    (d) listed bushings or grommets

97. The required working space for access to live parts of equipment operating at 300V to ground, where there are exposed live parts on one side and grounded parts on the other side, is _______.

    (a) 3 ft
    (b) 3½ ft
    (c) 4 ft
    (d) 4½ ft

98. The length of the flexible cord for a trash compactor shall not be less than 3 ft or exceed _______ in length, measured from the face of the attachment plug to the plane of the rear of the appliance.

    (a) 2 ft
    (b) 4 ft
    (c) 6 ft
    (d) 8 ft

99. One or more equipment grounding conductors brought into a nonmetallic outlet box shall be arranged to provide a connection to _______ in that box requiring connection to an equipment grounding conductor.

    (a) any fitting or device
    (b) a ground clip
    (c) a clamp(s)
    (d) the grounded conductor

100. All _______ PVC conduit fittings are suitable for connection to both Schedule 40 and Schedule 80 PVC conduit.

    (a) listed
    (b) marked
    (c) labeled
    (d) identified

ABOUT THE AUTHOR

Mike Holt

Mike Holt
Founder and President
Mike Holt Enterprises
Groveland, Florida

Mike Holt is an author, businessman, educator, speaker, publisher and *National Electrical Code* expert. He has written hundreds of electrical training books and articles, founded three successful businesses, and has taught thousands of electrical *Code* seminars across the U.S. and internationally. His dynamic presentation style, deep understanding of the trade, and ability to connect with students are some of the reasons that he is one of the most sought-after speakers in the industry.

His company, Mike Holt Enterprises, has been serving the electrical industry for almost 50 years, with a commitment to creating and publishing books, videos, online training, and curriculum support for electrical trainers, students, organizations, and electrical professionals. His devotion to the trade, coupled with the lessons he learned at the University of Miami's MBA program, have helped him build one of the largest electrical training and publishing companies in the United States.

Mike is committed to changing lives and helping people take their careers to the next level. He has always felt a responsibility to provide education beyond the scope of just passing an exam. He draws on his previous experience as an electrician, inspector, contractor and instructor, to guide him in developing powerful training solutions that electricians understand and enjoy. He is always mindful of how hard learning can be for students who are intimidated by school, by their feelings towards learning, or by the complexity of the *NEC*. He's mastered the art of simplifying and clarifying complicated technical concepts and his extensive use of illustrations helps students apply the content and relate the material to their work in the field. His ability to take the intimidation out of learning is reflected in the successful careers of his students.

Mike's commitment to pushing boundaries and setting high standards extends into his personal life as well. He's an eight-time Overall National Barefoot Waterski Champion. Mike has more than 20 gold medals, many national records, and has competed in three World Barefoot Tournaments. In 2015, at the tender age of 64, he started a new adventure—competitive mountain bike racing and at 65 began downhill mountain biking. Every day he continues to find ways to motivate himself, both mentally and physically.

Mike and his wife, Linda, reside in New Mexico and Florida, and are the parents of seven children and seven grandchildren. As his life has changed over the years, a few things have remained constant: his commitment to God, his love for his family, and doing what he can to change the lives of others through his products and seminars.

Special Acknowledgments

My Family. First, I want to thank God for my godly wife who's always by my side and for my children.

My Staff. A personal thank you goes to my team at Mike Holt Enterprises for all the work they do to help me with my mission of changing peoples' lives through education. They work tirelessly to ensure that, in addition to our products meeting and exceeding the educational needs of our customers, we stay committed to building life-long relationships throughout their electrical careers.

The National Fire Protection Association. A special thank you must be given to the staff at the National Fire Protection Association (NFPA), publishers of the *NEC*—in particular, Jeff Sargent for his assistance in answering my many *Code* questions over the years. Jeff, you're a "first class" guy, and I admire your dedication and commitment to helping others understand the *NEC*.

ABOUT THE ILLUSTRATOR

Mike Culbreath

Mike Culbreath
Graphic Illustrator
Alden, Michigan

Mike Culbreath has devoted his career to the electrical industry and worked his way up from apprentice electrician to master electrician. He started working in the electrical field doing residential and light commercial construction, and later did service work and custom electrical installations. While working as a journeyman electrician, he suffered a serious on-the-job knee injury. As part of his rehabilitation, Mike completed courses at Mike Holt Enterprises, and then passed the exam to receive his Master Electrician's license. In 1986, with a keen interest in continuing education for electricians, he joined the staff to update material and began illustrating Mike Holt's textbooks and magazine articles.

Mike started with simple hand-drawn diagrams and cut-and-paste graphics. Frustrated by the limitations of that style of illustrating, he took a company computer home to learn how to operate some basic computer graphics software. Realizing that computer graphics offered a lot of flexibility for creating illustrations, Mike took every computer graphics class and seminar he could to help develop his skills. He's worked as an illustrator and editor with the company for over 30 years and, as Mike Holt has proudly acknowledged, has helped to transform his words and visions into lifelike graphics.

Originally from South Florida, Mike now lives in northern lower Michigan where he enjoys hiking, kayaking, photography, gardening, and cooking; but his real passion is his horses. He also loves spending time with his children Dawn and Mac and his grandchildren Jonah, Kieley, and Scarlet.

ABOUT THE MIKE HOLT TEAM

There are many people who played a role in the production of this textbook. Their efforts are reflected in the quality and organization of the information contained in this textbook, and in its technical accuracy, completeness, and usability.

Technical Writing

Mario Valdes, Jr.
Technical Content Editor Mike Holt Enterprises,
Electrical Inspector, Electrical Plans Examiner,
Master Electrician
Mario@MikeHolt.com
Ocala, Florida

Mario Valdes is the Technical Content Editor and works directly with Mike to ensure that content is technically accurate, relatable, and valuable to all electrical professionals. He plays an important role in gathering research, analyzing data, and assisting Mike in the writing of the textbooks. He reworks content into different formats to improve the flow of information and to ensure expectations are being met in terms of message, tone, and quality. He edits illustrations and proofreads content to "fact-check" each sentence, title, and image structure. Mario enjoys working in collaboration with Mike and Brian to enhance the company's brand image, training products, and technical publications. He is a permanent member of the video teams, on which he has served since the 2017 *Code* cycle.

Mario is licensed as an Electrical Contractor, most recently having worked as an electrical inspector and plans examiner for an engineering firm in South Florida. Additionally, he was an Electrical Instructor for a technical college, teaching students pursuing an associate degree in electricity. He taught subjects such as ac/dc fundamentals, residential and commercial wiring, blueprint reading, and electrical estimating. He brings to the Mike Holt team a wealth of knowledge and devotion for the *NEC*.

He started his career at 16 years old in his father's electrical contracting company. Once he got his Florida State contractor's license, he ran the company as project manager and estimator. Mario's passion for the *NEC* prompted him to get his inspector and plans review certifications and embark on a new journey in electrical *Code* compliance. He's worked on complex projects such as hospitals, casinos, hotels and multi-family high rise buildings. Mario is very passionate about educating electrical professionals about electrical safety and the *National Electrical Code*.

Mario's a member of the IAEI, NFPA, and ICC, and enjoys participating in the meetings; he believes that by staying active in these organizations he'll be ahead of the game, with cutting-edge knowledge pertaining to safety codes.

When not immersed in the electrical world Mario enjoys fitness training. He resides in Pembroke Pines, Florida with his beautiful family, which includes his wife and his two sons. They enjoy family trip getaways to Disney World and other amusement parks.

Content Team

Daniel Brian House
Vice President of Digital and Technical Training
Mike Holt Enterprises, Instructor, Master
Electrician
Brian@MikeHolt.com
Ocala, Florida

Brian House is part of the content team that reviews our material to make sure it's ready for our customers. He also coordinates the team that constructs and reviews the textbooks and their supporting resources to ensure accuracy, clarity, and quality.

Brian is Vice President of Digital and Technical Training at Mike Holt Enterprises, and a Certified Mike Holt Instructor. He is a permanent member of the video teams, on which he has served since the 2011 *Code* cycle. Brian has worked in the trade since the 1990s in residential, commercial and industrial settings. He opened a contracting firm in 2003 that designed energy-efficient lighting retrofits, explored "green" biomass generators, and partnered with residential PV companies in addition to traditional electrical installation and service.

Brian leads the apprenticeship and digital product teams. They create cutting-edge training tools, and partner with in-house and apprenticeship training programs nationwide to help them reach the next level. He is also part of the content team that helps Mike bring his products to market, assisting in the editing of the textbooks, coordinating the content and illustrations, and assuring the technical accuracy and flow of the information.

Brian is high energy, with a passion for doing business the right way. He expresses his commitment to the industry and his love for its people in his teaching, working on books, and developing instructional programs and software tools.

Brian and his wife Carissa have shared the joy of their four children and many foster children during 25 years of marriage. When not mentoring youth at work or church, he can be found racing mountain bikes or SCUBA diving with his kids. He's passionate about helping others and regularly engages with the youth of his community to motivate them into exploring their future.

Editorial and Production

Toni Culbreath worked tirelessly to proofread and edit this publication. Her attention to detail and her dedication is irreplaceable. A very special thank you goes out to Toni (Mary Poppins) Culbreath for her many years of dedicated service.

Cathleen Kwas handled the design, layout, and typesetting of this book. Her desire to create the best possible product for our customers is greatly appreciated, and she constantly pushes the design envelope to make the product experience just a little bit better.

Vinny Perez and **Eddie Anacleto** have been a dynamic team. They have taken the best instructional graphics in the industry to the next level. Both Eddie and Vinny bring years of graphic art experience to the pages of this book and have been a huge help updating and improving the content, look, and style our graphics.

Dan Haruch is an integral part of the video recording process and spends much of his time making sure that the instructor resources created from this product are the best in the business. His dedication to the instructor and student experience is much appreciated.